THE BCOM SOLUTION

Every 4LTR Press solution includes:

Visually Engaging Textbook + **Online Study Tools** + **Tear-out Review Cards** + **Interactive eBook**

STUDENT RESOURCES:

- Interactive eBook
- Chapter Quizzes
- Assignments & Handouts
- Audio Chapter Summaries
- Cases
- Chapter Review Cards
- Flashcards (electronic & printable)
- Games: Crossword Puzzles & Quiz Bowl
- Glossary
- Learning Objectives
- PowerPoint® Notes
- Videos
- Grammar Tutorial
- Style Cards
- Templates
- Model Documents
- Language Review Quizzes

INSTRUCTOR RESOURCES:

- All Student Resources
- Engagement Tracker
- First Day of Class Instructions
- LMS Integration
- Custom Options through 4LTR+ Program
- Instructor's Manual
- Test Bank
- PowerPoint® Slides
- Instructor Prep Cards
- Videos

Students sign in at **www.cengagebrain.com**

Instructors sign in at **www.cengage.com/login**

"I like how it is presented and I like the concept, just looking at it makes me want to read it."

– **Chas Smith**, Student, *James Madison University*

Engagement Tracker launches, giving faculty a window into student usage of digital tools.

4LTR Press adds eBooks in response to a 10% uptick in digital learning preferences.

AUGUST 2010

1 out of every 3 (1,400) schools has adopted a 4LTR Press solution.

NOVEMBER 2010

750,000 students are IN.

Third party research confirms that 4LTR Press digital solutions improve retention and outcomes.

IN 2011

60 unique solutions across multiple course areas validates the 4LTR Press concept.

CourseMate

Students access the 4LTR Press website at 4x's the industry average.

IN 2011

2,000

APRIL 2011

1 out of every 2 (2,000) schools has a 4LTR Press adoption.

AUGUST 2011

Over 1 million students are IN.

We're always evolving. Join the 4LTR Press In-Crowd on Facebook at www.facebook.com/4ltrpress

2012 AND BEYOND

BCOM4

Carol M. Lehman
Debbie D. DuFrene

Vice President of Editorial, Business:
Jack W. Calhoun

Executive Editor, 4LTR Press: Neil Marquardt

Publisher: Erin Joyner

Acquisitions Editor: Jason Fremder

Product Development Manager, 4LTR Press:
Steve Joos

Associate Project Manager, 4LTR Press:
Pierce Denny

Managing Development Editor: Joanne Dauksewicz

Editorial Assistant: Megan Fischer

Senior Marketing Communications Manager:
Sarah Greber

Marketing Manager: Michelle Lockard

Marketing Coordinator: Leigh Smith

Director, Education Production: Barbara Fuller
Jacobsen

Content Project Manager: Emily Nesheim

Media Editor: John Rich

Manufacturing Planner: Ron Montgomery

Production Service: Integra

Senior Art Director: Stacy Shirley

Cover and Internal Designer: KeDesign,
Mason, OH

Cover Image Credits:
iStock Photo/© ROBERT ROBINSON
iStock Photo/© Joshua Hodge Photography
iStock Photo/© kristian sekulic
iStock Photo/© Yunus Arakon
iStock Photo/© Clerkenwell_Images
iStock Photo/© Ann Marie Kurtz
iStock Photo/© Carlos Gawronski

Objectives images: ©iStockphoto/Alexandr
Tovstenko

Rights Acquisition Director: Audrey Pettengill

Senior Rights Acquisition Specialist:
Deanna Ettinger

Photo Researcher: Susan Van Etten

For product information and technology assistance, contact us at
Cengage Learning Customer & Sales Support, 1-800-354-9706

For permission to use material from this text or product,
submit all requests online at **www.cengage.com/permissions**
Further permissions questions can be emailed to
permissionrequest@cengage.com

ExamView® is a registered trademark of eInstruction Corp. Windows is a registered trademark of the Microsoft Corporation used herein under license. Macintosh and Power Macintosh are registered trademarks of Apple Computer, Inc. used herein under license. © 2013 Cengage Learning. All Rights Reserved.

Cengage Learning WebTutor™ is a trademark of Cengage Learning.

Library of Congress Control Number: 2011940137

ISBN-13: 978-1-133-37247-9
ISBN-10: 1-133-37247-3
Package ISBN-13: 978-1-133-37243-1
Package ISBN-10: 1-133-37243-0

South-Western
5191 Natorp Boulevard
Mason, OH 45040
USA

Cengage Learning products are represented in Canada by Nelson Education, Ltd.

For your course and learning solutions, visit **www.cengage.com**
Purchase any of our products at your local college store or at our preferred online store **www.cengagebrain.com**

The editorial team at South-Western would like to extend a special thanks to Patricia Wyatt at Bossier Parish Community College for her outstanding contribution to revisions in BCOM 4.

Printed in the United States of America
1 2 3 4 5 6 7 15 14 13 12 11

Brief Contents

Contents

© iStockphoto.com/drflet

© Stockbyte/Getty Images

© iStockphoto.com/Valerie Loiseleux

© iStockphoto.com/Hamza Türkkol

© iStockphoto.com/Michal Rozanski

© iStockphoto.com/Pali Rao

© iStockphoto.com/Talaj

© First Light/Alamy

Résumé appearance is critical.

© iStockphoto.com/Jon Schulte

© iStockphoto.com/Albert Smirnov

© jitloac/Shutterstock

© iStockphoto.com/Andrew Rich

Establishing a Framework for Business Communication

Value of Communication

We communicate to satisfy needs in both our work and private lives. Each of us wants to be heard, appreciated, and wanted. We also want to accomplish tasks and achieve goals. A major value of communication is to help people feel good about themselves and about their organizations. Generally people communicate for three basic purposes: to inform, to persuade, and to entertain.

⊠ OBJECTIVE 1

Define communication and describe the value of communication in business.

What is communication? Communication is the process of exchanging information and meaning between or among individuals through a common system of symbols, signs, and behavior. Other words used to describe the communication process include *conversing, speaking, corresponding, writing,* and *listening.* Studies indicate that managers typically spend 60 to 80 percent of their time involved in communication. In your career activities, you will communicate in a wide variety of ways, including

- attending meetings and writing reports related to strategic plans and company policy.
- presenting information to large and small groups in face-to-face and virtual environments.
- explaining and clarifying management procedures and work assignments.
- coordinating the work of various employees, departments, and other work groups.
- evaluating and counseling employees.
- promoting the company's products/services and image.

OBJECTIVES

1 Define communication and describe the value of communication in business.

2 Explain the communication process model and the ultimate objective of the communication process.

3 Discuss how information flows in an organization.

4 Explain how legal and ethical constraints, diversity challenges, changing technology, and team environment act as strategic forces that influence the process of business communication.

The Communication Process

Effective business communication is essential to success in today's work environments. Recent surveys of executives document that abilities in writing and speaking are major determinants of career success in many fields.[1] Although essential to personal and professional success, effective business communication does not occur automatically. Your own experiences likely have taught you that a message is not interpreted correctly just because you transmitted it. An effective communicator anticipates possible breakdowns in the communication process—the unlimited ways the message can be misunderstood. This mind-set provides the concentration to design the initial message effectively and to be prepared to intervene at the appropriate time to ensure that the message received is on target.

☒ OBJECTIVE 2

Explain the communication process model and the ultimate objective of the communication process.

© Stephen Coburn/Shutterstock

Consider the communication process model presented in Figure 1-1. These seemingly simple steps actually represent a very complex process.

The Sender Encodes the Message

The sender carefully designs a message by selecting (1) words that clearly convey the message and (2) nonverbal signals (gestures, posture, facial expression, and so on) that reinforce the verbal message. The process of selecting and organizing the message is referred to as **encoding**. The sender's primary objective is to encode the message in such a way that the message received is the same (or as close as possible) as the message sent. Knowledge of the receiver's educational level, experience, viewpoints, and other information aids the sender in encoding the message. If information about the receiver is unavailable, the sender can use empathy for the receiver's position to gain fairly accurate insights to help in encoding the message.

The Sender Selects the Channel and Transmits the Message

encoding
the process of selecting and organizing a message
decoding
the process of interpreting a message

To increase the likelihood that the receiver will understand the message, the sender carefully selects an appropriate channel for transmitting the message.

Three typical communication channels are two-way, face-to-face; two-way, not face-to-face; and one-way, not face-to-face.

Selecting an inappropriate channel can cause the message to be misunderstood and can adversely affect human relations with the receiver. For example, for a complex subject, a sender might begin with a written document and follow up with a face-to-face, phone, or video conference discussion after the receiver has had an opportunity to study the document. Written documents are required when legal matters are involved and written records must be retained.

The Receiver Decodes the Message

The receiver is the destination of the message. The receiver's task is to interpret the sender's message, both verbal and nonverbal, with as little distortion as possible. The process of interpreting the message is referred to as **decoding**. Because words and nonverbal signals have different meanings to different people, countless problems can occur at this point in the communication process:

- The sender inadequately encodes the original message with words not present in the receiver's vocabulary, ambiguous or nonspecific ideas, or nonverbal signals that distract the receiver or contradict the verbal message.

- The receiver is intimidated by the position or authority of the sender, resulting in tension that prevents effective concentration on the message and failure to ask for needed clarification.

- The receiver prejudges the topic as too boring or difficult to understand and does not attempt to understand the message.

- The receiver is close-minded and unreceptive to new and different ideas.

With the infinite number of breakdowns possible at each stage of the communication process, it is indeed a miracle that effective communication ever occurs. The complexity of the communication process amplifies the importance of the next stage in the communication process—feedback to clarify misunderstandings.

Figure 1-1 The Communication Process Model

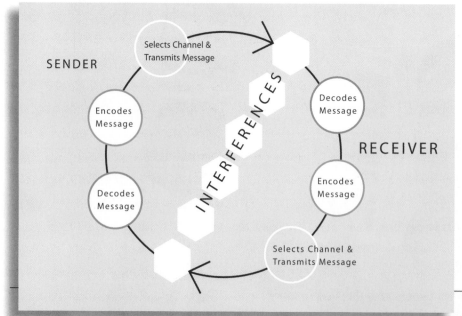

SENDER

Selects Channel & Transmits Message

Encodes Message

Decodes Message

INTERFERENCES

Decodes Message

RECEIVER

Encodes Message

Selects Channel & Transmits Message

© Cengage Learning 2010

The Receiver Encodes the Message to Clarify

When the receiver responds to the sender's message, the response is called **feedback**. The feedback might prompt the sender to modify or adjust the original message to make it clearer to the receiver. Feedback can be verbal or nonverbal. A remark such as "Could you clarify . . ." or a perplexed facial expression provides clear feedback to the sender that the receiver does not yet understand the message. Conversely, a confident "Yes, I understand," and a nod of the head likely signal understanding or encouragement.

Interferences Hinder the Process

Senders and receivers must learn to deal with the numerous factors that hinder the communication process. These factors are referred to as **interferences** or *barriers* to effective communication. Previous examples have illustrated some of the interferences that might occur at various stages of the communication process. For example,

- differences in educational level, experience, culture, and other characteristics of the sender and the receiver increase the complexity of encoding and decoding a message.
- physical interferences occurring in the channel include a noisy environment, interruptions, and uncomfortable surroundings.
- mental distractions, such as preoccupation with other matters and developing a response, rather than listening, create barriers to understanding.

You can surely compile a list of other barriers that affect your ability to communicate with friends, instructors, coworkers, supervisors, and others. By being aware of them, you can concentrate on removing these interferences.

Communicating within Organizations

☒ OBJECTIVE 3

Discuss how information flows in an organization.

To be successful, organizations must create an environment that energizes and encourages employees to accomplish tasks by promoting genuine openness and effective communication. **Organizational communication** is concerned with the movement of information within the company structure. Regardless of your career or level within an organization, your ability to communicate will affect not only the success of the organization but also your personal success and advancement within that organization.

Communication Flow in Organizations

Communication occurs in a variety of ways within an organization. Some communication flows are planned and structured; others are not. Some communication flows can be formally depicted, whereas some defy description.

Formal and Informal Channels

The flow of communication within an organization follows both formal and informal channels.

- **Formal communication channel.** This channel is typified by the formal organization chart, which is created by management to define individual and group relationships and to specify lines of responsibility. Essentially, the formal system is dictated by the technical, political, and economic environment of the organization. Within this system, people are required to behave in certain ways simply to get work done.
- **Informal communication channel.** This channel continuously develops as people interact within the formal system to accommodate their social and psychological needs. Because the informal channel undergoes continual changes and does not parallel the organizational chart, it cannot be depicted accurately by any graphic means.

When employees rely almost entirely on the formal communication system as a guide to behavior, the system might be identified as a *bureaucracy*. Procedures manuals, job descriptions, organization charts, and other written materials dictate the required behavior. Communication channels are followed strictly, and red tape is abundant. Procedures are generally followed exactly; terms such as *rules* and *policies* serve as sufficient reasons for actions. Even the most formal organizations, however, cannot function long before an

feedback
a receiver's response to a sender's message

interferences
also called barriers; *numerous factors that hinder the communication process*

organizational communication
the movement of information within the company structure

formal communication channel
a channel of communication typified by the formal organization chart; dictated by the technical, political, and economic environment of the organization

informal communication channel
a channel of communication that continuously develops as people interact within the formal system to accommodate their social and psychological needs

informal communication system emerges. As people operate within the organized system, they interact on a person-to-person basis and create an environment conducive to meeting their personal emotions, prejudices, likes, and dislikes.

In a workplace, employees are generally expected to satisfy a formal system of arriving at work on time, fulfilling their job duties, working well with others, and addressing their supervisor's requests. However, some employees may not openly accept these expectations and may arrive at work late and spend an undue amount of time "around the water cooler." If these informal practices become more widely spread, the purposes of the group may move from a focus on completing tasks to that of socializing with others. Obviously, the informal system benefits people because it meets their needs, but it also may affect the overall communication of the group in important ways.

The Grapevine as an Informal Communication System

The **grapevine**, often called the *rumor mill*, is perhaps the best-known component of the informal communication system. As people talk casually during breaks, text one another, or chat online, the focus usually shifts from topic to topic. One of the usual topics is work—job, company, supervisor, fellow employees. Even though the formal system includes definite communication channels, the grapevine tends to develop and operate within all organizations. Consider these points related to the accuracy and value of grapevine communication:

grapevine
the best-known component of the informal communication system

- As a communication channel, the grapevine has a reputation for being speedy but inaccurate. In the absence of alarms, the grapevine might be the most effective way to let occupants know that the building is on fire. It certainly beats sending an email.

- Although the grapevine often is thought of as a channel for inaccurate communication, in reality it is no more or less accurate than other channels. Even formal communication can become inaccurate and filtered as it passes from level to level in the organizational hierarchy.

- The inaccuracy of the grapevine has more to do with the message input than with the output. For example, the grapevine is noted as a carrier of rumors, primarily because it carries informal messages. If the input is a rumor, and nothing more, the output obviously will be inaccurate. But the output might be an accurate description of the original rumor.

- In a business office, news about promotions, personnel changes, company policy changes, and annual salary adjustments often is communicated through the grapevine long before being conveyed through formal channels. The process works similarly in colleges, where information about choice instructors typically is not officially published but is known by students through the grapevine. How best to prepare for examinations, instructor attitudes on attendance and homework, and even faculty personnel changes are messages that travel over the grapevine.

- A misconception about the grapevine is that the message passes from person to person until it finally reaches a person who can't pass it on—the end of the line. Actually, the grapevine works as a network

channel. Typically, one person tells two or three others, who each tell two or three others, who each tell two or three others, and so on. Thus, the message might spread to a huge number of people in a short time, especially now that the grapevine has gone hi-tech and social networking sites have become "gossip central."

- The grapevine has no single, consistent source. Messages might originate anywhere and follow various routes.

Due at least in part to widespread downsizing and corporate scandals during the last few years, employees in many organizations are demanding to be better informed. Some companies have implemented new formal ways, such as newsletters and intranets, as well as informal ways, including blogs and Twitter, for sharing information with their internal constituents. Company openness with employees about management decisions and financial issues means conveying more information through the formal system rather than risking its miscommunication through informal channels. The software company SAS has been on the list of the 100 Best Companies to Work For for 14 years. Its perks include on-site healthcare,

high quality childcare, summer camp for kids, car cleaning, a beauty salon, and more. Says one manager: "People stay at SAS in large part because they are . . . people don't leave SAS because they feel regarded—seen, attended to and cared for. I have stayed for that reason, and love what I do for that reason."[2]

An informal communication system will emerge from even the most carefully designed formal system. Managers who ignore this fact are attempting to manage blindfolded. Instead of denying or condemning the grapevine, the effective manager will learn to *use* the informal communication network. The grapevine, for instance, can be useful in counteracting rumors and false information.

Directions for Communication Flow

The direction in which communication flows in an organization can be downward, upward, or horizontal, as shown in Figure 1-2. Because these three terms are used frequently in communication discussions, they deserve clarification. Although the concept of flow seems simple, direction has meaning for those participating in the communication process.

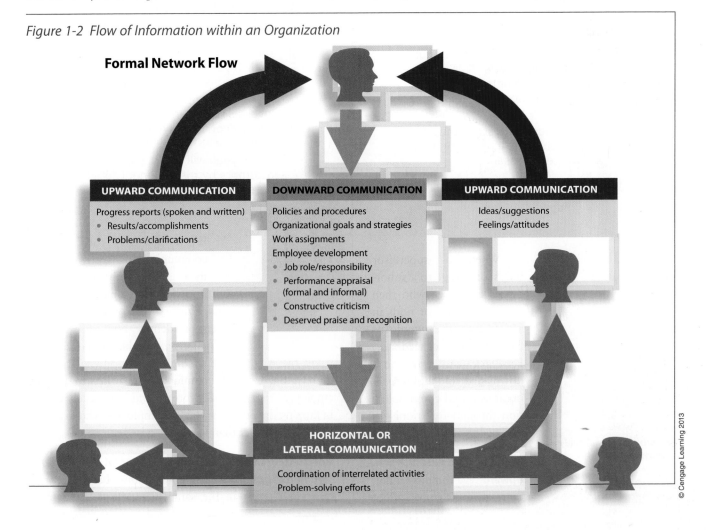

Figure 1-2 Flow of Information within an Organization

Formal Network Flow

UPWARD COMMUNICATION

Progress reports (spoken and written)
- Results/accomplishments
- Problems/clarifications

DOWNWARD COMMUNICATION

Policies and procedures
Organizational goals and strategies
Work assignments
Employee development
- Job role/responsibility
- Performance appraisal (formal and informal)
- Constructive criticism
- Deserved praise and recognition

UPWARD COMMUNICATION

Ideas/suggestions
Feelings/attitudes

HORIZONTAL OR LATERAL COMMUNICATION

Coordination of interrelated activities
Problem-solving efforts

Downward Communication. **Downward communication** flows from supervisor to employee, from policy makers to operating personnel, or from top to bottom on the organization chart. A simple policy statement from the top of the organization might grow into a formal plan for operation at lower levels. Teaching people how to perform their specific tasks is an element of downward communication. Another element is orientation to a company's rules, practices, procedures, history, and goals. Employees learn about the quality of their job performance through downward communication.

Downward communication normally involves both written and spoken methods and makes use of the following assumptions:

Downward Communication

- People at high levels in the organization usually have greater knowledge of the organization and its goals than do people at lower levels.
- Both spoken and written messages tend to become larger as they move downward through organizational levels. This expansion results from attempts to prevent distortion and is more noticeable in written messages.
- Spoken messages are subject to greater changes in meaning than are written messages.

© iStockphoto.com/Palli Rao

When a supervisor sends a message to a subordinate employee who then asks a question or nods in agreement, the employee has given signs of feedback. Feedback can flow both downward and upward in organizational communication through traditional as well as informal channels.

Upward Communication. **Upward communication** flows from the front lines of an organization to the top. When management requests information from lower organizational levels, the resulting information becomes feedback to that request. Employees talk to supervisors about themselves, their fellow employees, their work and methods of doing it, and their perceptions of the organization. These comments are feedback to the downward flow transmitted in both spoken and written form by group meetings, procedures or operations manuals, company news releases, the company intranet, and the grapevine.

Although necessary and valuable, upward communication involves risks. The following factors are important to consider when upward communication flow is involved:

Upward Communication

- Upward communication is primarily feedback to requests and actions of supervisors.
- Upward communication can be misleading because lower-level employees often tell their superiors what they think their superiors want to hear. Therefore, their messages might contradict their true observations and perceptions.
- Upward communication frequently involves risk to an employee and is dependent on trust in the supervisor.
- Employees will reject superficial attempts by management to obtain feedback.

© iStockphoto.com/Palli Rao

When effectively used, upward communication keeps management informed about the feelings of lower-level employees, taps the expertise of employees, helps management identify both difficult and potentially promotable employees, and paves the way for even more effective downward communication. Upward communication is key to keeping employees engaged and informed and is especially critical in tapping the power of younger employees who expect to collaborate rather than to be supervised.[3]

Horizontal Communication. **Horizontal**, or **lateral**, **communication** describes interactions between organizational units on the same hierarchical level. These

© iStockphoto.com/drfiet

interactions reveal one of the major shortcomings of organizational charts: They do not recognize the role of horizontal communication when they depict authority relationships by placing one box higher than another and define role functions by placing titles in those boxes. Yet management should realize that horizontal communication is the primary means of achieving coordination in a functional organizational structure. Units coordinate their activities to accomplish task goals just as adjacent workers in a production line coordinate their activities. So, for horizontal communication to be maximally effective, the people in any system or organization should be available to one another.

Many companies realize that the traditional hierarchy organized around functional units is inadequate for competing in increasingly competitive global markets. They value work teams that integrate work-flow processes rather than specialists in a single function or product. Such work teams break down communication barriers between isolated functional departments, and communication patterns take on varying forms to accommodate team activities.

Levels of Communication

Communication can involve sending messages to both large and small audiences. **Internal messages** are intended for recipients within the organization. **External messages** are directed to recipients outside the organization. When considering the intended audience, communication can be described as taking place on five levels: intrapersonal, interpersonal, group, organizational, and public. Figure 1-3 depicts the five audience levels. An effective communicator has a clearly defined purpose for each message and selected strategies for targeting his or her intended audience.

internal messages
messages intended for recipients within the organization

external messages
messages directed to recipients outside the organization

Figure 1-3 Levels of Communication

COMMUNICATION LEVELS	EXAMPLES
INTRAPERSONAL	
• Communication within oneself	Individual considers how others respond to his or her verbal and/or nonverbal communication.
• Not considered by some to be true communication as it does not involve a separate sender and receiver	
INTERPERSONAL	
• Communication between two people	Supervisor and subordinate, two coworkers
• Task goal to accomplish work confronting them	
• Maintenance goal to feel better about themselves and each other because of their interaction	
GROUP	
• Communication among more than two people	Work group, project team, department meeting
• Goal of achieving greater output than individual efforts could produce	
ORGANIZATIONAL	
• Groups combined in such a way that large tasks may be accomplished	Company, organization
• Goal of providing adequate structure for groups to achieve their purposes	
PUBLIC	
• The organization reaching out to its public to achieve its goals	Media advertisement, website communication, annual report
• Goal of reaching many with the same message	

Strategic Forces Influencing Business Communication

Communication does not take place in a vacuum, but rather is influenced by a number of forces at work in the environment. The effective communicator carefully considers each of these influences and structures communication responsively. Four critical forces influence the communication process and help to determine and define the nature of the communication that occurs, as shown in Figure 1-4. These forces are legal and ethical constraints, diversity challenges, changing technology, and team environment.

Strategic Force 1: Legal and Ethical Constraints

Legal and ethical constraints act as a strategic force on communication because they set boundaries in which communication rightfully occurs. International, federal, state, and local laws affect the way that various business activities are conducted. For instance, laws specify that certain information must be stated in messages that reply to credit applications and those dealing with the collection of outstanding debts. Furthermore, one's own ethical standards will often influence what he or she is willing to say in a message. For example, a system of ethics built on honesty might require that the message provide full disclosure rather than a shrouding of the truth. Legal responsibilities, then, are the starting point for appropriate business communication. One's ethical belief system, or personal sense of right and wrong behavior, provides further boundaries for professional activity.

The press is full of examples of unethical conduct in business and political communities, but unethical behavior is not relegated to the papers—it has far-reaching consequences. Those affected by decisions, the **stakeholders**, can include people inside and outside the organization. Employees and stockholders are obvious losers when a company fails. Competitors in the same industry also suffer, because their strategies are based on what they perceive about their competition. Beyond that, financial markets as a whole suffer due to erosion of public confidence.

Business leaders, government officials, and citizens frequently express concern about the apparent erosion of ethical values in society. Even for those who want to do the right thing, matters of ethics are seldom clear-cut decisions of right versus wrong, and they often contain ambiguous elements. In addition, the pressure appears to be felt most strongly by lower-level managers, often recent business school graduates who are the least experienced at doing their jobs.

The Foundation for Legal and Ethical Behavior

Although ethics is a common point of discussion, many find defining ethics challenging. Most people immediately associate ethics with standards and rules of conduct, morals, right and wrong, values, and honesty. Dr. Albert Schweitzer defined *ethics* as "the name we give to our concern for good behavior. We feel an obligation to consider not only our own personal well-being, but also that of others and of human society as a whole."[4] In

stakeholders
people inside and outside the organization who are affected by decisions

---

Figure 1-4 Strategic Factors Influencing Business Communication

LEGAL & ETHICAL CONSTRAINTS	DIVERSITY CHALLENGES	CHANGING TECHNOLOGY	TEAM ENVIRONMENT
• International Laws	• Cultural Differences	• Accuracy and Security Issues	• Trust
• Domestic Laws	• Language Barriers	• Telecommunications	• Team Roles
• Code of Ethics	• Gender Issues	• Software Applications	• Shared Goals and Expectations
• Stakeholder Interests	• Education Levels	• "High-touch" Issues	• Synergy
• Ethical Frameworks	• Age Factors	• Telecommuting	• Group Reward
• Personal Values	• Nonverbal Differences	• Databases	• Distributed Leadership

© Cengage Learning 2010

other words, **ethics** refers to the principles of right and wrong that guide you in making decisions that consider the impact of your actions on others as well as yourself.

Although the recorded accounts of legal and ethical misconduct would seem to indicate that businesses are dishonest and unscrupulous, keep in mind that millions of business transactions are made daily on the basis of honesty and concern for others. Why should a business make ethical decisions? What difference will it make? James E. Perrella, executive vice president of Ingersoll-Rand Company, gave a powerful reply to these questions:[5]

> *Many people, including many business leaders, would argue that such an application of ethics to business would adversely affect bottom-line performance. I say nay. . . . Good ethics, simply, is good business. Good ethics will attract investors. Good ethics will attract good employees. You can do what's right. Not because of conduct codes. Not because of rules or laws. But because you know what's right.*

Causes of Illegal and Unethical Behavior

Understanding the major causes of illegal and unethical behavior in the workplace will help you become sensitive to signals of escalating pressure to compromise your values. Unethical corporate behavior can have a number of causes:

- **Excessive emphasis on profits.** Business managers are often judged and paid on their ability to increase business profits. This emphasis on profits might send a message that the end justifies the means. According to former Federal Reserve Chairman Alan Greenspan, "infectious greed" ultimately pushed companies such as Enron, Global Crossing, and WorldCom into bankruptcy.[6]

- **Misplaced corporate loyalty.** A misplaced sense of corporate loyalty might cause an employee to do what seems to be in the best interest of the company, even if the act is illegal or unethical.

- **Obsession with personal advancement.** Employees who wish to outperform their peers or are working for the next promotion might feel that they cannot afford to fail. They might do whatever it takes to achieve the objectives assigned to them.

- **Expectation of not getting caught.** Thinking that the end justifies the means, employees often believe illegal or unethical activity will never be discovered. Unfortunately, a great deal of improper behavior

> **ethics**
> the principles of right and wrong that guide one in making decisions that consider the impact of one's actions on others as well as on the decision maker

Ethical Dilemmas . . .

Identifying ethical issues in typical workplace situations can be difficult, and coworkers and superiors might apply pressure for seemingly logical reasons. To illustrate, examine each of the following workplace situations for a possible ethical dilemma:

- In order to achieve profit expectations, a stockbroker hides the financial risk of an investment product from potential clients.

- To prevent an adverse effect on stock prices, corporate officers deliberately withhold information concerning a possible corporate takeover.

- To protect the organization, management decides not to publicize a design flaw in an automobile that could lead to possible injuries and even deaths to consumers because the announcement might result in legal actions.

- A supervisor takes advantage of his position and threatens an employee with dismissal if she does not acquiesce to his inappropriate requests and language use.

- Angry for an unfavorable performance appraisal of a colleague, an employee leaks confidential information to the colleague that creates distrust among others in the department and results in a lawsuit.

Your fundamental morals and values provide the foundation for making ethical decisions. However, as the previous examples imply, even seemingly minor concessions in day-to-day decisions can gradually weaken an individual's ethical foundation.

© StockLite/Shutterstock

escapes detection in the business world. Believing no one will ever find out, employees are tempted to lie, steal, and perform other illegal acts.

- **Unethical tone set by top management.** If top managers are not perceived as highly ethical, lower-level managers might be less ethical as a result. Employees have little incentive to act legally and ethically if their superiors do not set an example and encourage and reward such behavior. The saying "the speed of the leader is the speed of the pack" illustrates the importance of leading by example.

- **Uncertainty about whether an action is wrong.** Many times, company personnel are placed in situations in which the line between right and wrong is not clearly defined. When caught in this gray area, the perplexed employee asks, "How far is too far?"

- **Unwillingness to take a stand for what is right.** Often employees know what is right or wrong but are not willing to take the risk of challenging a wrong action. They might lack the confidence or skill needed to confront others with sensitive legal or ethical issues. They might remain silent and then justify their unwillingness to act.

Framework for Analyzing Ethical Dilemmas

Determining whether an action is ethical can be difficult. Learning to analyze a dilemma from both legal and ethical perspectives will help you find a solution that conforms to your own personal values. Figure 1-5 shows the four conclusions you might reach when considering the advisability of a particular behavior.

Dimension 1: Behavior that is illegal and unethical. When considering some actions, you will reach the conclusion that they are both illegal and unethical. The law specifically outlines the "black" area—those alternatives that are clearly wrong—and your employer will expect you to become an expert in the laws that affect your particular area. When you encounter an unfamiliar area, you must investigate any possible legal implica-

Figure 1-5 Four Dimensions of Business Behavior

DIMENSION 1 Behavior that is illegal and unethical	DIMENSION 2 Behavior that is illegal yet ethical
DIMENSION 3 Behavior that is legal yet unethical	DIMENSION 4 Behavior that is both legal and ethical

© Cengage Learning 2010

tions. Obviously, obeying the law is in the best interest of all concerned: you as an individual, your company, and society. Contractual agreements between two parties also offer guidance for legal decision making. Frequently, your own individual sense of right and wrong will also confirm that the illegal action is wrong for you personally. In such situations, decisions about appropriate behavior are obvious.

Dimension 2: Behavior that is illegal yet ethical. Occasionally, a businessperson will decide that even though a specific action is illegal, there is a justifiable reason to break the law. A case in point is a law passed in Vermont that makes it illegal for a pharmaceutical company to give any gift valued at more than $25 to doctors or their personnel.[7] Those supporting the law charge that the giving of freebies drives up medical costs by encouraging doctors to prescribe new, more expensive brand-name drugs. The law's opponents contend that the gifts do not influence doctors and are merely educational tools for new products. Although a pharmaceutical firm and its employees might see nothing wrong with providing gifts worth in excess of $25, they would be well advised to consider the penalty of $10,000 per violation before acting on their personal ethics. A better course of action would be to act within the law, possibly while lobbying for a change in the law.

Dimension 3: Behavior that is legal yet unethical. If you determine that a behavior is legal and complies with relevant contractual agreements and company policy, your next step is to

© Stockbyte/Getty Images

consult your company's or profession's *code of ethics.* This written document summarizes the company's or profession's *standards of ethical conduct.* Some companies refer to this document as a *credo.* If the behavior does not violate the code of ethics, then put it to the test of your own personal integrity. You may at times reject a legal action because it does not "feel right." Most Americans were appalled to learn that the marketing of sub-prime loans packaged as reputable securities has been blamed for causing the "Great Recession." Although they might have acted legally, their profiting at the expense of company employees, stockholders, and the public hardly seemed ethical. You might be faced with situations in which you reject a behavior that is legal because you would not be proud to have your family and community know that you engaged in it.

Dimension 4: Behavior that is both legal and ethical. Decisions in this dimension are easy to make. Such actions comply with the law, company policies, and your professional and personal codes of ethics.

The Pagano Model offers a straightforward method for determining whether a proposed action is advisable.[8] For this system to work, you must answer the following six questions honestly:

- Is the proposed action legal? (This is the core starting point.)

- What are the benefits and costs to the people involved?

- Would you want this action to be a universal standard, appropriate for everyone?

- Does the action pass the light-of-day test? That is, if your action appeared on television or others learned about it, would you be proud?

- Does the action pass the Golden Rule test? That is, would you want the same to happen to you?

- Does the action pass the ventilation test? Ask the opinion of a wise friend with no investment in the outcome. Does this friend believe the action is ethical?

Bernie Madoff was found guilty of securities fraud because he took investors' money and rather than investing it, he used it to pay off earlier investors. This Ponzie scheme cost victims more than $13 billion and resulted in Madoff's receiving a 150-year sentence in prison. "The message must be sent that Mr. Madoff's crimes were extraordinarily evil and that this kind of manipulation of the system is not just a bloodless crime that takes place on paper, but one instead that takes a staggering toll," U.S. District Judge Denny Chin said.[9]

Strategic Force 2: Diversity Challenges

Diversity in the workplace is another strategic force influencing communication. Differences between the sender and the receiver in areas such as culture, age, gender, and education require sensitivity on the part of both parties so that the intended message is the one that is received.

Understanding how to communicate effectively with people from other cultures has become more integral to the work environment as many U.S. companies are increasingly conducting business with international companies or becoming multinational. Candy manufacturer Jelly Belly learned a great deal about cultural differences when the company opened business operations in Thailand. In Thailand, many more employee amenities are required than U.S. employers are accustomed to providing. For example, a Thai employer is expected to provide transportation to and from work as well as free meals and a workout facility for its employees.[10]

When addressing cultural differences, successful communication must often span barriers of language and differing world views resulting from societal and religious beliefs and practices. When a person fails to consider these factors, communication suffers, and the result is often embarrassing and potentially costly. McDonald's is an example of a large U.S. company that has expanded its operations to include most major countries in the world. To be successful on an international scale, managers had to be aware of cultural differences and be willing to work to ensure that effective communication occurred despite these barriers.

Occasionally, however, a whopper of an intercultural communication faux pas occurs. That is what happened when McDonald's began its promotional campaign in Great Britain for the World Cup soccer championship. It seemed like a clever (and harmless) idea to reproduce the flags of the 24 nations participating in the event and print them on packaging—two million Happy Meal bags, to be exact. What marketing personnel failed to consider was that words from the Koran are printed on the Saudi flag. The idea that sacred words from Islam's holy book were mass printed to sell a product with the knowledge that the packages would be thrown into the trash angered and offended many Muslims, who immediately complained. McDonald's apologized for the gaffe and agreed to work with Saudis to find a solution to the problem.[11]

This example shows of how much "homework" is involved in maintaining good relations with customers or clients from other cultures. The potential barrier of language is obvious; however, successful managers know that much more is involved in communicating with everyone—across cultures, genders, ages, abilities, and other differences.

Communication Opportunities and Challenges in Diversity

As world markets continue to expand, U.S. employees at home and abroad will be doing business with more people from other countries. You might find yourself working abroad for a large American company, an international company with a plant in the United States, or a company with an ethnically diverse workforce. Regardless of the workplace, your **diversity skills**—that is, your ability to communicate effectively with both men and women of all ages, cultures, and minority groups—will affect your success in today's culturally diverse global economy.

Workplace diversity can lead to misunderstandings and miscommunications, but it also poses opportunities to improve both workers and organizations. Managers must be prepared to communicate effectively with workers of different nationalities, genders, races, ages, abilities, and other characteristics.

Managing a diverse workforce effectively will require you to communicate with *everyone* and to help all employees reach their fullest potential and contribute to the company's goals. To lessen miscommunication, which inevitably occurs, increasing numbers of companies have undertaken *diversity initiatives* and are providing diversity training seminars to help workers understand and appreciate gender and age differences and the cultures of coworkers.

For many U.S. corporations, such as Procter & Gamble, more than 70 percent of total sales in recent years has come from international operations.

© Feng lei sh/imaginechina via AP Images

Culture and Communication

Managers with the *desire* and the *skill* to conduct business in new international markets and to manage a diverse workforce effectively will confront problems created by cultural differences. The way messages are decoded and encoded is not just a function of the experiences, beliefs, and assumptions of the person sending or receiving those messages but also is shaped by the society in which he or she lives.

People learn patterns of behavior from their culture. The *culture* of a people is the product of their living experiences within their own society. Culture could be described as "the way of life" of a people and includes a vast array of behaviors and beliefs. These patterns affect how people perceive the world, what they value, and how they act. Differing patterns can also create barriers to communication.

Barriers to Intercultural Communication

Because cultures give different definitions of such basics of interaction as values and norms, people raised in two different cultures can clash in various ways.

- **Ethnocentrism.** Problems occur between people of different cultures primarily because people tend to assume that their own cultural norms are the right way to do things. They wrongly believe that the specific patterns of behavior desired in their own cultures are universally valued. This belief, known as **enthnocentrism**, is certainly natural; but learning about other cultures and developing sensitivity will help minimize ethnocentric reactions when dealing with other cultures.
- **Stereotypes.** We often form a mental picture of the main characteristics of another group, creating preformed ideas of what people in this group are

> "Your ability to communicate effectively with both men and women of all ages, cultures, and minority groups will affect your success in today's culturally diverse global economy."

diversity skills
the ability to communicate effectively with both men and women of all ages, cultures, and minority groups

ethnocentrism
the assumption that one's own cultural norms are the right way to do things

like. These pictures, called **stereotypes**, influence the way we interact with members of the other group. When we observe a behavior that conforms to the stereotype, the validity of the preconceived notion is reinforced. We often view the other person as a representative of a class of people rather than as an individual. People of all cultures have stereotypes about other cultural groups they have encountered. These stereotypes can interfere with communication when people interact on the basis of the imagined representative and not the real individual.

- **Interpretation of time.** The study of how a culture perceives time and its use is called **chronemics**. In the United States, we have a saying that "time is money." Canadians, like some northern Europeans who are also concerned about punctuality, make appointments, keep them, and complete them, and waste no time in the process. In some other cultures, time is the cheapest commodity and an inexhaustible resource; time represents a person's span on Earth, which is only part of eternity. To these cultures, engaging in long, casual conversations prior to serious discussions or negotiations is time well spent in establishing and nurturing relationships. On the other hand, the time-efficient American businessperson is likely to fret about wasting precious time.

- **Personal space requirements.** Space operates as a language just as time does. The study of cultural space requirements is known as **proxemics**. In all cultures, the distance between people functions in communication as "personal space" or "personal territory." In the United States, for example, for intimate conversations with close friends and relatives, individuals are willing to stay within about a foot and a half of each other; for casual conversations, up to two

or three feet; for job interviews and personal business, four to twelve feet; and for public occasions, more than twelve feet. However, in many cultures outside the United States, closer personal contact is accepted, or greater distance might be the norm.

- **Body language.** The study of body language is known as **kinesics**. Body language is not universal, but instead is learned from one's culture. Even the most basic gestures have varying cultural meanings—the familiar North American symbol for "okay" means zero in France, money in Japan, and an expression of vulgarity in Brazil. Similarly, eye contact, posture, and facial expressions carry different meanings throughout the world.

- **Translation limitations.** Words in one language do not always have an equivalent meaning in other languages, and the concepts the words describe are often different as well. Translators can be helpful, but keep in mind that a translator is working with a second language and must listen to one language, mentally cast the words into another language, and then speak them. This process is difficult and opens the possibility that the translator will fall victim to one or more cultural barriers.

Even if you cannot speak or write another language fluently, people from other cultures will appreciate simple efforts to learn a few common phrases.

Strategic Force 3: Changing Technology

Electronic tools have not eliminated the need for basic communication skills; they can, in fact, create new obstacles or barriers to communication that must be

Brazil, not okay

United States, okay

Other places, better check first

© Hemera Technologies/AbleStock.com Image/Jupiterimages

stereotypes
mental pictures that one group forms of the main characteristics of another group, creating preformed ideas of what people in this group are like

chronemics
the study of how a culture perceives time and its use

proxemics
the study of cultural space requirements

kinesics
the study of body language, which is not universal, but instead is learned from one's culture

overcome. These tools, however, also create opportunities that range from new kinds of communications to improved quality of the messages themselves. Electronic tools, such as the Internet, intranets, document production software, multimedia presentations, Web publishing tools, and email, can help people in various ways, such as by (1) collecting and analyzing data, (2) shaping messages to be clearer and more effective, and (3) communicating quickly and efficiently with others in geographically dispersed locations.

Using various communication technologies, individuals can often work in their homes or other remote locations and send and receive work from the company office electronically. **Telecommuting** (also referred to as *teleworking*) offers various advantages, including reduced travel time and increased work flexibility. Laptops and smartphones provide computing power and connectivity for professionals wherever they are.

While the public Internet is accessible to everyone and offers a wide array of information, private databases provide specialized and advanced information on specific topics. Databases

telecommuting

also called teleworking; *working at home or other remote locations and sending and receiving work from the company office electronically*

enable decision makers to obtain information quickly and accurately and offer these advantages:

- **Data organization**—the ability to organize large amounts of data.

- **Data integrity**—assurance that the data will be accurate and complete.

- **Data security**—assurance that the data are secure because access to a database is controlled through several built-in data security features.

Internal databases contain proprietary information that is pertinent to the particular business or organization and its employees. External databases (networks) allow users to access information from remote locations literally around the world and in an instant transfer that information to their own computers for further manipulation or storage. Information is available on general news, stocks, financial markets, sports, travel, weather, and a variety of publications.

Knowing how to "tunnel" through the vast amounts of irrelevant information available on the Internet to find what you want can be overwhelming. The experience can also be expensive in terms of human time spent and charges incurred for online time. Locating information from electronic sources requires that you

Legal and Ethical Implications of Technology

In addition to its many benefits, technology poses some challenges for the business communicator. For instance, technology raises issues of ownership, as in the case of difficulties that arise in protecting the copyright of documents transmitted over the Internet. Technology poses dilemmas over access, that is, who has the right to certain stored information pertaining to an individual or a company.

Technology threatens our individual privacy, our right to be left alone, free from surveillance or interference from other individuals or organizations. Common invasions of privacy caused by technology include

- monitoring your Internet use, infiltrating your information, and sending advertising based on your browsing history.

- monitoring the exact time employees spend on a specific task and between tasks and the exact number and length of breaks, and supervisors' or coworkers' reading of another employee's email and computer files.

- spreading of spyware and various computer "bugs" through the Internet.[12]

© iStockphoto.com/Nghe Tran

know the search procedures and methods for constructing an effective search strategy.

Effective use of various communication technologies helps ensure timely, targeted messages and responses and helps to build interpersonal relationships. This responsiveness leads to positive interactions with colleagues and strong customer commitment.

Strategic Force 4: Team Environment

As firms around the world face problems of decreasing productivity, faltering product quality, and worker dissatisfaction, work teams are seen as a way to help firms remain globally competitive. Decentralized decision making enables teams of people to communicate in a peer-to-peer fashion, rather than following traditional lines of authority, and new technologies give employees the ability to communicate easily and openly with one another and with those outside the firm.

Although worker involvement in the management process has long been the hallmark of Japanese business, many businesses in the United States and elsewhere are empowering self-directed work teams to accomplish various assignments.[13] The list of companies using self-directed work teams is diverse, including Hunt-Wesson, the Internal Revenue Service, the San Diego Zoo, Hewlett-Packard, Southwest Airlines, Toyota, Motorola, General Electric, and Corning.

Work Team Defined

The terms *team*, *work team*, *group*, *work group*, *cross-functional team*, and *self-directed team* are often used interchangeably.[14] Whatever the title, a **team** is a small number of people with complementary skills who work together for a common purpose. Team members set their own goals, in cooperation with management, and plan how to achieve those goals and how their work is to be accomplished. The central organizing element of a team is that it has a common purpose and measurable goals for which the team can be held accountable, independent of its individual members. Employees in a self-directed work team handle a wide array of functions and work with a minimum of direct supervision.[15]

A key element in team success is the concept of **synergy**, defined as a situation in which the whole is greater than the sum of the parts. Teams provide a depth of expertise that is unavailable at the individual level. Teams open lines of communication that then lead to increased interaction among employees and between employees and management. The result is that teams help compa-

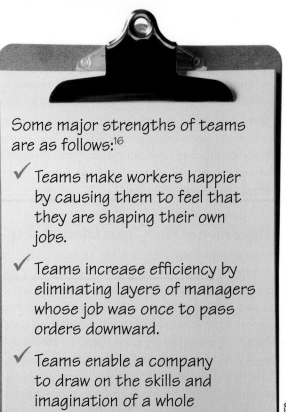

Some major strengths of teams are as follows:[16]

✓ Teams make workers happier by causing them to feel that they are shaping their own jobs.

✓ Teams increase efficiency by eliminating layers of managers whose job was once to pass orders downward.

✓ Teams enable a company to draw on the skills and imagination of a whole workforce.

© Image Source

nies reach their goals of delivering higher-quality products and services faster and with more cost effectiveness.

Communication Differences in Work Teams

In the past, most businesses were operated in a hierarchical fashion, with most decisions made at the top and communication following a top-down/bottom-up pattern. Communication patterns are different in successful team environments as compared with traditional organizational structures:

- Trust building is the primary factor that changes the organization's communication patterns.
- Open meetings are an important method for enhancing communication, as they educate employees about the business while building bridges of understanding and trust.
- Shared leadership, which involves more direct and effective communication between management and its internal customers, is common.
- Listening, problem solving, conflict resolution, negotiation, and consensus become important factors in group communication.

team
a small number of people with complementary skills who work together for a common purpose

synergy
a situation in which the whole is greater than the sum of the parts

- Information flows vertically up to management and down to workers, as well as horizontally among team members, other teams, and supervisors.

Communication is perhaps the single most important aspect of successful teamwork. Open lines of communication increase interaction between employees and management. All affected parties should be kept informed as projects progress.

Maximization of Work Team Effectiveness

Grouping employees into a team structure does not mean that they will automatically function as a team. A group must go through a developmental process to begin to function as a team. Members need training in such areas as problem solving, goal setting, and conflict resolution. Teams must be encouraged to establish the "three Rs"—roles, rules, and relationships.[17]

The self-directed work team can become the basic organizational building block to best ensure success in dynamic global competition. Skills for successful participation in team environments are somewhat different from those necessary for success in old-style organizations:

- Ability to give and take constructive criticism, listen actively, clearly impart one's views to others, and provide meaningful feedback.

- Skills in breaking down emotional barriers, such as insecurity or condescension.
- Ability to promote team functioning by removing process barriers, such as rigid policies and procedures.
- Understanding the feelings and needs of coworkers so members feel comfortable stating their opinions and discussing the strengths and weaknesses of the team.
- Skills in overcoming cultural barriers, such as stereotyped roles and responsibilities, that can separate workers from management.[18]
- Application of leadership skills that apply to a dynamic group setting and lead to team success. In dynamic team leadership, referred to as *distributed leadership*, the role of leader can alternate among members, and more than one leadership style can be active at any given time.[19]

Gender, cultural, and age differences among members of a team can present barriers to team communication. Knowing what behaviors can limit the group process is imperative to maximizing results. Team members might need awareness training to assist in recognizing behaviors that may hinder team performance and in overcoming barriers that can limit the effectiveness of their communication.

To improve group communication, time needs to be set aside to assess the quality of interaction. Questions to pose about the group process might include the following:

What are our common goals?

Is the group dealing with conflict in a positive way?

What in the group process is going well?

What about the group process could be improved?

What roles are members playing? For instance, is one person dominating while others contribute little or nothing?

© Rachel Epstein/PhotoEdit

USE THE TOOLS.

• Rip out the Review Cards in the back of your book to study.

Or Visit CourseMate to:

• Read, search, highlight, and take notes in the Interactive eBook
• Review Flashcards (Print or Online) to master key terms
• Test yourself with Auto-Graded Quizzes
• Bring concepts to life with Games, Videos, and Animations!

Go to CourseMate for **BCOM4** to begin using these tools.
Access at **www.cengagebrain.com**

Complete the Speak Up
survey in CourseMate at
www.cengagebrain.com

f Follow us at
www.facebook.com/4ltrpress

©iStockphoto.com/A-Digit | © Cengage Learning 2011

Focusing on Interpersonal and Group Communication

Behavioral Theories that Impact Communication

Interpersonal intelligence pertains to the ability to read, empathize, and understand others.[1] People with interpersonal intelligence are good with people and thrive in social interaction. Rather than being a quality that some are born with and others are not, interpersonal intelligence can be improved by broadening your understanding of human behavior and motivation and practicing certain behaviors when in interpersonal situations. Knowledge from the fields of sociology and psychology is helpful to understanding human needs and providing you with valuable insights about how to achieve effective communication in the workplace.

⊠ **OBJECTIVE 1**

Explain how behavioral theories about human needs, trust and disclosure, and motivation relate to business communication.

Recognizing Human Needs

Psychologist Abraham Maslow developed the concept of a hierarchy of needs through which people progress. In our society, most people have reasonably satisfied their two lower-level needs: (1) physiological needs (food and basic provision) and (2) security and safety needs (shelter and protection from the elements and physical danger). Beyond

interpersonal intelligence
the ability to read, empathize, and understand others

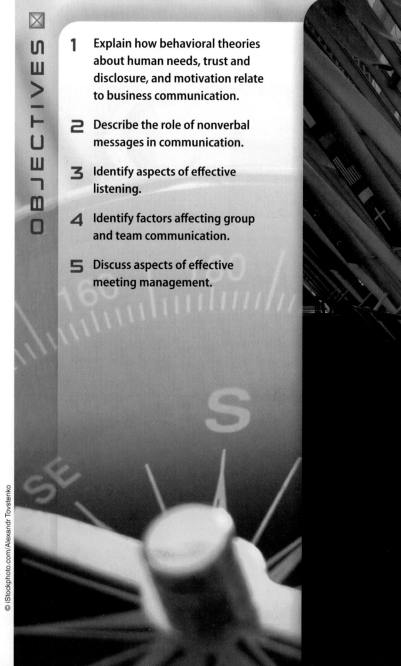

© iStockphoto.com/Alexandr Tovstenko

OBJECTIVES

1 Explain how behavioral theories about human needs, trust and disclosure, and motivation relate to business communication.

2 Describe the role of nonverbal messages in communication.

3 Identify aspects of effective listening.

4 Identify factors affecting group and team communication.

5 Discuss aspects of effective meeting management.

these two basic need levels, people progress to satisfy the three upper-level needs: (3) social needs for love, acceptance, and belonging; (4) ego or esteem needs to be heard, appreciated, and wanted; and (5) self-actualizing needs, including the need to achieve one's fullest potential through professional, philanthropic, political, educational, and artistic channels.

As people satisfy needs at one level, they move on to the next. The levels that have been satisfied still are present, but their importance diminishes. Effective communicators are able to identify and appeal to need levels in various individuals or groups. Advertising is designed to appeal to need levels. Luxury car and dream vacation ads appeal to ego needs, teeth whitening and anti-aging product messages appeal to social needs, and identity theft, health and fitness, and environmentally friendly commercials appeal to security and safety needs. Efforts to help employees satisfy their needs are essential, since a satisfied worker is generally more productive than a dissatisfied one. In communication activities, a sender's message is more likely to appeal to the receiver if the receiver's need is accurately identified.

© Orange Line Media/Shutterstock

Stroking

People engage in communication with others in the hope that the outcome might lead to mutual trust, mutual pleasure, and psychological well-being. The communication exchange is a means of sharing information about things, ideas, tasks, and selves.

Each communication interaction, whether casual or formal, provides an emotional **stroke** that can have either a positive or a negative effect on your feelings about yourself and others. Getting a pat on the back from the supervisor, receiving a congratulatory phone call or text message, and being listened to by another person are examples of everyday positive strokes. Negative strokes might include receiving a hurtful comment, being avoided or left out of conversation, and receiving a reprimand from a superior. By paying attention to the importance of strokes, managers can greatly improve communication and people's feelings about their work.

Exploring the Johari Window

As relationships develop, the people involved continue to learn about each other and themselves, as shown by the Johari Window in Figure 2-1. Area I, the free or open area, represents what we know about ourselves and what others know about us. Area II, the blind area, designates those things others know about us but that we don't know about ourselves; for example, you are the only person who can't see your physical self as it really is. Things we know about ourselves but that others don't know about us occupy the hidden or secret area III. Area IV includes the unknown: things we don't know about ourselves and others don't know about us, such as our ability to handle emergency situations if we've never been faced with them.

Each of the window areas can vary in size according to the degree to which we learn about ourselves and are willing to disclose things about ourselves to others. Reciprocal sharing occurs when people develop *trust* in each other. When a confidant demonstrates that he or she can be trusted, trust is reinforced and leads to an expansion of the open area of the Johari Window. Usually we are willing to tell people about various things that aren't truly personal. But we share personal thoughts, ambitions, and inner feelings only with selected others—those whom we have learned to trust. The relationships existing between supervisor and employee, doctor and patient, and lawyer and client are those of trust, but only in specific areas. In more intimate relationships with significant others, siblings, and parents, deeper, personal feelings are entrusted to each other.

The idea that trust and openness lead to better communication between two people also applies to groups. Managers engaged in *organizational development* (OD) are concerned with developing successful organizations by building effective small groups. They believe small group effectiveness evolves mostly from a high level of mutual trust among group members. The aim of OD is to open emotional as well as task-oriented communication. To accomplish this aim, groups often become involved in encounter sessions designed to enlarge the open areas of the Johari Window.[2]

stroke
emotional response one gets in a communication interaction that has either a positive or negative effect on feelings about oneself and others

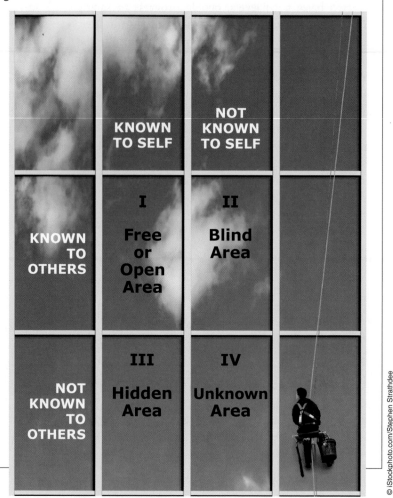

Figure 2-1 The Johari Window

KNOWN TO SELF / NOT KNOWN TO SELF

KNOWN TO OTHERS

I Free or Open Area

II Blind Area

NOT KNOWN TO OTHERS

III Hidden Area

IV Unknown Area

© iStockphoto.com/Stephen Strathdee

Contrasting Management Styles

Douglas McGregor, a management theorist, attempted to distinguish between the older, traditional view that workers are concerned only about satisfying lower-level needs and the more contemporary view that productivity can be enhanced by assisting workers in satisfying higher-level needs. Under the older view, management exercised strong control, emphasized the job to the exclusion of concern for the individual, and sought to motivate solely through external incentives—a job and a paycheck. McGregor labeled this management style Theory X. Under the contemporary style, Theory Y, management strives to balance control and individual freedom. By treating the individual as a mature person, management lessens the need for external motivation; treated as adults, people will act as adults.

The situational leadership model developed by Paul Hersey and Kenneth Blanchard does not prescribe a single leadership style, but advocates that what is appropriate in each case depends on the follower (subordinate) and the task to be performed. **Directive behavior** is characterized by the leader's giving detailed rules and instructions and monitoring closely that they are followed. The leader decides what is to be done and how. In contrast, **supportive behavior** is characterized by the leader's listening, communicating, recognizing, and encouraging. Different degrees of directive and supportive behavior can be desirable, given the situation.[3] Combining the ideas of Maslow and McGregor with those of Hersey and Blanchard leads to the conclusion that "the right job for the person" is a better philosophy than "the right person for the job."

The **Total Quality Management** movement focuses on creating a more responsible role for the worker in an organization. In a Total Quality Management environment, decision-making power is distributed to the people closest to the problem, who usually have the best information sources and solutions. Each employee, from the president to the custodian, is expected to solve problems, participate in team-building efforts, and expand the scope of his or her role in the organization. The goal of employee empowerment is to build a work environment in which all employees take pride in their work accomplishments and begin motivating themselves from within rather than through traditional extrinsic incentives.[4] Managers of many companies understand that empowering employees to initiate continuous improvements is critical for survival. Only companies producing quality products and services will survive in today's world market.

Nonverbal Communication

⊠ **OBJECTIVE 2**

Describe the role of nonverbal messages in communication.

Managers use verbal and nonverbal messages to communicate ideas to employees. *Verbal* means "through the use of words," either written or spoken. *Nonverbal* means "without the use of words." Although major attention in communication study is given to verbal messages, studies show that nonverbal elements can account for more than 90 percent of the total meaning of a message.[5] Nonverbal communication includes *metacommunication* and *kinesic messages*.

Metacommunication

A **metacommunication** is a message that, although *not* expressed in words, accompanies a message that *is* expressed in words. For example, "Don't be late for work" communicates caution; yet the sentence might imply (but not express in words) such additional ideas as "You are frequently late, and I'm warning you," or "I doubt your dependability." "Your solution is perfect" might also convey a metacommunication such as "You are efficient," or "I certainly like your work." Whether you are speaking or writing, you can be confident that those who receive your messages will be sensitive to the messages expressed in words and to the accompanying messages that are present but not expressed in words.

Kinesic Messages

People constantly send meaning through kinesic communication, an idea expressed through nonverbal behavior. In other words, receivers gain

directive behavior
characterized by leaders who give detailed rules and instructions and monitor closely that they are followed

supportive behavior
characterized by leaders who listen, communicate, recognize, and encourage their followers

Total Quality Management
focuses on creating a more responsible role for the worker in an organization by distributing decision-making power to the people closest to the problem, empowering employees to initiate continuous improvements

metacommunication
a nonverbal message that, although not expressed in words, accompanies a message that is expressed in words

additional meaning from what they see and hear—the visual and the vocal:

- **Visual kinesic communication**—gestures, winks, smiles, frowns, sighs, attire, grooming, and all kinds of body movements.
- **Vocal kinesic communication**—intonation, projection, and resonance of the voice.

Following are some examples of kinesic messages and the meanings they can convey.

Action	Possible Kinesic Message
A wink or light chuckle follows a statement.	"Don't believe what I just said."
A manager is habitually late for staff meetings and with email replies.	"My time is more important than yours. You can wait for me." Alternately, the action might be ordinary for a non-U.S.-born manager.
A group leader sits at a position other than at the head of the table.	"I want to demonstrate my equality with other members."
An employee wears clothing that reveals tattoos, which violates the company's dress code.	"Rules are for other people; I can do what I want." Alternately, "I do not understand the expectations."
A job applicant submits a résumé containing errors.	"My language skills are deficient." Alternately, "I didn't care to do my best."

Understanding Nonverbal Messages

Metacommunications and kinesic messages have characteristics that all communicators should take into account.

- **Nonverbal messages cannot be avoided.** Both written and spoken words convey ideas in addition to the ideas contained in the words used. All actions—and even the lack of action—have meaning to those who observe them.

> **visual kinesic communication**
> *gestures, winks, smiles, frowns, sighs, attire, grooming, and all kinds of body movements*
>
> **vocal kinesic communication**
> *intonation, projection, and resonance of the voice*

- **Nonverbal messages can have different meanings for different people.** If a team member smiles after making a statement, one member might conclude that the speaker was trying to be funny; another might conclude that the speaker was pleased about having made such a great contribution; another might see the smile as indicating friendliness.

- **Nonverbal messages vary between and within cultures.** Not only do nonverbal messages have different meanings from culture to culture, but men and women from the same culture typically exhibit different body language. As a rule, U.S. men make less body contact with other men than do women with women. Acceptable male body language might include a handshake or a pat on the back, while women are afforded more flexibility in making body contact with each other.

- **Nonverbal messages can be intentional or unintentional.** "You are right about that" can be intended to mean "I agree with you" or "You are right on *this* issue, but you have been wrong on all others discussed."

- **Nonverbal messages can contradict the accompanying verbal message and affect whether your message is understood or believed.** The adage "actions speak louder than words" reveals much about how people perceive messages. Picture a person who says, "I'm happy to be here," but looks at the floor, talks in a weak and halting voice, and clasps his hands timidly in front of his body. Because his verbal and nonverbal messages are contradictory, his audience might not trust his words. Similarly, consider the negative effect of a sloppy personal appearance by a job candidate.

- **Nonverbal messages can receive more attention than verbal messages.** If a supervisor repeatedly glances at his cell phone for text messages or rhythmically taps a pen while making a statement, the words might not register in the employee's mind. An error in basic grammar might receive more attention than the idea that is being transmitted.

- **Nonverbal messages provide clues about the sender's background and motives.** For example, excessive use of big words might suggest that a person reads widely or has an above-average education; it might also suggest a need for social recognition or insecurity about his or her social background.

- **Nonverbal messages are influenced by the circumstances surrounding the communication.** Assume that two men, Ganesh and Jacob, are friends at work. When they are together on the job, Ganesh sometimes puts his hand on Jacob's shoulder. To Jacob, the act could mean nothing

more than "We are close friends." But suppose Ganesh is a member of a committee that subsequently denies a promotion for Jacob. Afterward, the same act could mean "We are still friends," but it could also cause resentment. Because of the circumstances, the same act could now mean something such as "Watch the hand that pats; it can also stab."

- **Nonverbal messages can be beneficial or harmful.** Words or actions can be accompanied by nonverbal messages that help or hurt the sender's purpose. Metacommunications and kinesic communications can convey something such as "I am efficient in my business and considerate of others," or they can convey the opposite. They cannot be eliminated, but you can make them work for you instead of against you.

Listening as a Communication Skill

☒ OBJECTIVE 3

Identify aspects of effective listening.

Despite the fact that many professionals believe incorrectly that business communication is about presentation and not interaction, most managers spend a major part of their day listening and speaking with others. Listening to supervisors, employees, customers, and colleagues commonly consumes more of business employees' time than reading, writing, and speaking combined. Listening is an interpersonal skill as critical as the skill of speaking. CEO Brad Anderson of Best Buy explains that effective listening is central to the work culture of his young retail employees who have grown up in a digital age and expect a two-way conversation in a peer-to-peer fashion rather than a one-way lecture. Anderson emphasizes that being perceived as a poor listener would "shut him down as a CEO."[6]

Effective listening habits pay off in several ways:

- ☑ Good listeners are liked by others because they satisfy the basic human needs of being heard and being wanted.

- ☑ People who listen well are able to separate fact from fiction, cope effectively with false persuasion, and avoid having others use them for personal gain.

- ☑ Effective listening leads to sensitivity and tolerance toward key individuals who are critical to the organization's success, such as employees, customers, and suppliers.

- ☑ Effective listeners are engaged and constantly learning—gaining knowledge and skills that lead to increased creativity, job performance, advancement, and satisfaction.

- ☑ Job satisfaction increases when people know what is going on, when they are heard, and when they participate in the mutual trust that develops from good communication.

Listening depends on your abilities to receive and decode both verbal and nonverbal messages. The best-devised messages and sophisticated communication systems will not work unless people on the receiving end of spoken messages actually listen. Senders of spoken messages must assume their receivers can and will listen, just as senders of written messages must assume their receivers can and will read.

Listening for a Specific Purpose

Individuals satisfy a variety of purposes through listening: (1) interacting socially, (2) receiving information, (3) solving problems, and (4) sharing feelings with others. Each activity may call for a different style of listening or for a combination of styles.

- **Casual listening**. Listening for pleasure, recreation, amusement, and relaxation is casual listening. Some people listen to music all day long for relaxation and to mask unwanted sounds during daily routines, work periods, and daily commutes. Aspects of casual listening are as follows:
  - ○ It provides relaxing breaks from more serious tasks and supports our emotional health.
  - ○ It illustrates that people are selective listeners. You listen to what you want to hear. In a crowded room in which everyone seems to be talking, you can block out all the noise and engage in the conversation you are having with someone.
  - ○ It doesn't require much emotional or physical effort.

- **Listening for information**. Listening for information involves the search for data or material. In a lecture class, for example, the instructor usually has a strategy for guiding the class to desired goals. The instructor will probably stress several major points and use supporting evidence to prove or to reinforce them. When engaged in this type of listening, you could become so focused on recording every detail that you take copious notes with no organization. When listening for information:

casual listening
listening for pleasure, recreation, amusement, and relaxation

listening for information
listening that involves the search for data or material

○ Use an outlining process to help you capture main ideas and supporting subpoints in a logical way.

○ Watch the speaker as you listen to him or her, since most speakers exhibit a set of mannerisms composed of gestures and vocal inflections to indicate the degree of importance or seriousness that they attach to portions of their presentations.

- **Intensive listening.** When you listen to obtain information, solve problems, or persuade or dissuade (as in arguments), you are engaged in intensive listening. Intensive listening involves greater use of your analytical ability to proceed through problem-solving steps. When listening intensively:

○ Become a good summarizer.

○ Trace the development of the discussion and then move from there to your own analysis.

- **Empathetic listening.** *Empathy* occurs when a person attempts to share another's feelings or emotions. Counselors attempt to use empathetic listening in dealing with their clients, and good friends listen empathetically to each other. Empathy is a valuable trait developed by people skilled in interpersonal relations. When you take the time to listen to another, the courtesy is usually returned. When listening empathetically:

○ Avoid preoccupation with your own problems. Talking too much and giving strong nonverbal signals of disinterest destroy others' desire to talk.

○ Remember that total empathy can never be achieved simply because no two people are exactly alike. The more similar our experiences, however, the better the opportunity to put ourselves in the other person's shoes. Listening with empathy involves some genuine tact along with other good listening habits.

You might have to combine listening intensively and listening empathetically in some situations. Performance appraisal interviews, disciplinary conferences, and other sensitive discussions between supervisors and employees require listening intensively for accurate understanding of the message and listening for feelings, preconceived points of view, and background.

Bad Listening Habits

Most of us have developed bad listening habits in one or more of the following areas:

intensive listening
listening to obtain information, solve problems, or persuade or dissuade

empathetic listening
listening to others in an attempt to share their feelings or emotions

- **Faking attention.** Have you ever been introduced to someone only to realize 30 seconds later that you missed the name? We can look directly at a person, nod, smile, and *pretend* to be listening.

- **Allowing disruptions.** We welcome disruptions of almost any sort when we are engaged in somewhat difficult listening. The next time someone enters your classroom or meeting room, notice how almost everyone in the room turns away from the speaker and the topic to observe the latecomer.

- **Overlistening.** When we attempt to record many details in writing or in memory we can *overlisten* and miss the speaker's major points.

- **Stereotyping.** We make spontaneous judgments about others based on such issues as appearances, mannerisms, dress, and speech delivery. If a speaker doesn't meet our standards in these areas, we simply turn off our listening and assume the speaker can't have much to say.

- **Dismissing subjects as uninteresting.** People tend to use disinterest as a rationale for not listening. Unfortunately, the decision is usually made before the topic is ever introduced. A good way to lose an instructor's respect when you have to miss class is to ask, "Are we going to do anything important in class today?"

- **Failing to observe nonverbal aids.** To listen effectively, you must observe the speaker. Facial expressions and body motions always accompany speech and contribute much to messages.

Many bad listening habits develop simply because the speed of spoken messages is far slower than our ability to receive and process them. Normal speaking speeds

Overlistening

Allowing disruptions

Faking attention

are between 100 and 150 words a minute. The human ear can actually distinguish words in speech in excess of 500 words a minute, and many people read at speeds well beyond 500 words a minute. Finally, our minds process thoughts at thousands of words a minute.

Because individuals can't speak fast enough to challenge our ability to listen, listeners have a responsibility to make spoken communication effective. Good listening typically requires considerable mental and emotional effort.

Group Communication

Although much of your spoken communication in business will occur in one-to-one relationships, another frequent spoken communication activity will likely occur when you participate in groups, committees, and teams.

Failing to use nonverbal aids

Dismissing subject as uninteresting

© Image Source

Increasing Focus on Groups

Developments among U.S. businesses in recent years have shifted attention away from the employment of traditional organizational subunits as the only mechanisms for achieving organizational goals and toward the increased use of groups.

- **Flat organizational structures.** Many businesses today are downsizing and eliminating layers of management. Companies implementing Total Quality Management programs are reorganizing to distribute the decision-making power throughout the organization. The trend is to eliminate functional or departmental boundaries. Instead, work is reorganized in cross-disciplinary teams that perform broad core processes (e.g., product development and sales generation) and not narrow tasks (e.g., forecasting market demand for a particular product).

  In a flat organizational structure, communicating across the organization chart (among the cross-disciplinary teams) becomes more important than communicating up and down in a top-heavy hierarchy. An individual can take on an expanded **role** as important tasks are assumed. This role can involve power and authority that surpasses the individual's **status**, or formal position in the organizational chart. Much of the communication involves face-to-face meetings with team members rather than numerous, time-consuming "handoffs" as the product moves methodically from one department to another.

  The time needed to design a new card at Hallmark Cards decreased significantly when the company adopted a flat organizational structure. Team members representing the former functional areas (graphic artists, writers, marketers, and others) now work in a central area, communicating openly and frequently, solving problems and making decisions about the entire process as a card is being developed. For example, a writer struggling with a verse for a new card can solicit immediate input from the graphic artist working on the team rather than finalizing the verse and then "handing it off" to the art department.[7]

- **Heightened Focus on Cooperation.** Competition has been a characteristic way of life in U.S. companies. Organizations and individuals compete for a greater share of scarce resources, for a limited number of positions at the top of organizations, and for esteem in their professions. Such competition is a healthy sign of the human desire to succeed, and, in terms of economic behavior, competition is

role
tasks employees assume that can involve power and authority that surpasses their formal position on the organization chart

status
one's formal position in the organizational chart

Suggestions for Effective Listening

You can enhance the effectiveness of your face-to-face listening by following these suggestions:

- **Minimize environmental and mental distractions.** Take time to listen. Move to a quiet area where you are not distracted by noise or other conversation. Avoid becoming so preoccupied with what you will say next that you fail to listen.

- **Get in touch with the speaker.** Maintain an open mind while attempting to understand the speaker's background, prejudices, and points of view. Listen for emotionally charged words and watch for body language, gestures, facial expressions, and eye movements as clues to the speaker's underlying feelings.

- **Use your knowledge of speakers to your advantage.** Some people seem to run on and on with details before making the point. With this speaker, you must anticipate the major point but not pay much attention to details. Other speakers give conclusions first and perhaps omit support for them. In this case, you must ask questions to obtain further information.

- **Let the speaker know you are actively involved.** Show genuine interest by remaining physically and mentally involved; for example, avoid daydreaming, yawning, frequently breaking eye contact, looking at your cell phone or papers on your desk, or whispering.

- **Do not interrupt the speaker.** Try to understand the speaker's full meaning and wait patiently for an indication of when you should enter the conversation.

- **Ask reflective questions that assess understanding.** Simply restate in your own words what you think the other person has said. This paraphrasing will reinforce what you have heard and allow the speaker to correct any misunderstanding or add clarification.

- **Use probing prompts to direct the speaker.** Use probing statements or questions to help the speaker define the issue more concretely and specifically.

- **Use lag time wisely.** Listening carefully should be your primary focus; however, you can think ahead at times as well. Making written or mental notes allows you to provide useful feedback when the opportunity arises. If you cannot take notes during the conversation, record important points as soon as possible so you can summarize the speaker's key points.

Virtual Teams at IBM

About 40 percent of IBM's 400,000 employees are now virtual. Since 1995, when IBM first began encouraging its employees to telecommute, the company has been working on building a sense of personal connection among far-flung workers. "Humans are social animals. Without a real sense of community, most people just don't do their best work," says Dan Pelino, general manager of IBM's global healthcare and life sciences division. Responding to the need for community among virtual team members, the company added a social networking site called SocialBlue.[8]

fundamental to the private enterprise system. At the same time, when excessive competition replaces the cooperation necessary for success, communication can be diminished, if not eliminated.

Just as you want to look good in the eyes of your coworkers and supervisors, units within organizations want to look good to one another. This attitude can cause behavior to take the competitive form, a "win/lose" philosophy. When excessive competition has a negative influence on the performance of the organization, everyone loses.

Although competition is appropriate and desirable in many situations, many companies have taken steps through open communication and information and reward systems to reduce competition and to increase cooperation. Cooperation is more likely when the competitors (individuals or groups within an organization) have an understanding of and appreciation for others' importance and functions. This cooperative spirit is characterized as a "win/win" philosophy. One person's success is not achieved at the expense or exclusion of another. Groups identify a solution that everyone finds satisfactory and is committed to achieving. Reaching this mutual understanding requires a high degree of trust and effective interpersonal skills, particularly empathetic and intensive listening skills, and the willingness to communicate long enough to agree on an action plan acceptable to everyone.

Characteristics of Effective Groups

Groups form for synergistic effects. Through pooling their efforts, members can achieve more collectively than they could individually. At the same time, the social nature of groups contributes to the individual as well. While communication in small groups leads to decisions that are generally superior to individual decisions, the group process can motivate members, improve thinking, and assist attitude change.

As you consider the following factors of group communication, try to visualize their relationship to the groups to which you have belonged, such as in school, religious organizations, athletics, and social activities.

- **Common goals.** In effective groups, participants share a common goal, interest, or benefit. This focus on goals allows members to overcome individual differences of opinion and to negotiate acceptable solutions.

- **Role perception.** People who are invited to join groups have perceptions of how the group should operate and what it should achieve. In addition, each member has a self-concept that dictates how he or she will behave. Those known to be aggressive will attempt to be confrontational and forceful; those who like to be known as moderates will behave in moderate ways by settling arguments rather than initiating them. In successful groups, members play a variety of necessary roles and seek to eliminate nonproductive ones.

- **Longevity.** Groups formed for short-term tasks, such as arranging a dinner and program, will spend more time on the task than on maintenance. However, groups formed for long-term assignments, such as an accounting team auditing a major corporation, may devote much effort to

Although much research has been conducted in the area of group size, no optimal number of members has been identified. Groups of five to seven members are thought to be best for decision-making and problem-solving tasks. An odd number of members is often preferred because decisions are possible without tie votes.

© Dean Mitchell/Shutterstock

maintenance goals. Maintenance includes division of duties, scheduling, record keeping, reporting, and assessing progress.

- **Size.** The smaller the group, the more its members have the opportunity to communicate with each other. Large groups often inhibit communication because the opportunity to speak and interact is limited. However, when broad input is desired, large groups can be good if steps are taken to ensure that there is effective communication. Interestingly, large groups generally divide into smaller groups for maintenance purposes, even when the large group is task oriented.

- **Status.** Some group members will appear to have higher ranking than others. Consider a group in which the chief executive of the organization is a member. When the chief executive speaks, members agree. When members speak, they tend to direct their remarks to the one with high status—the chief executive. People are inclined to communicate with peers as their equals, but they tend to speak upward to their supervisor and downward to lower-level employees. In general, groups require balance in status and expertise.

- **Group norms.** A **norm** is a standard or average behavior. All groups possess norms. An instructor's behavior helps establish classroom norms. If some students are allowed to arrive late for class, others will begin to arrive late. If some are allowed to talk during lectures, the norm will be for students to talk. People conform to norms because conformity

norm
a standard or average behavior

is easy and nonconformity is difficult and uncomfortable. Conformity leads to acceptance by other group members and creates communication opportunities.

- **Leadership.** The performance of groups depends on several factors, but none is more important than leadership. Some hold the mistaken view that leaders are not necessary when an organization moves to a group concept. The role of leaders changes substantially, but they still have an important part to play. The ability of a group leader to work toward task goals while contributing to the development of group and individual goals is often critical to group success. Leadership activities may be shared among several participants, and leadership may also be rotated, formally or informally. As part of the group, the leader can affect the establishment of norms by determining who can speak and when, encouraging contribution, and providing motivation for effective group activity.[9]

Group Roles

Groups are made up of members who play a variety of roles, both positive and negative. Negative roles detract from the group's purposes and include those in the list below.

Negative Group Roles
- **Isolate**—one who is physically present but fails to participate
- **Dominator**—one who speaks too often and too long
- **Free rider**—one who does not do his or her fair share of the work
- **Detractor**—one who constantly criticizes and complains
- **Digresser**—one who deviates from the group's purpose
- **Airhead**—one who is never prepared
- **Socializer**—one who pursues only the social aspect of the group

© Radius Images/Jupiterimages

A list of positive group roles can be found on the following page.

Positive Group Roles
- **Facilitator** (also known as *gatekeeper*)—one who makes sure everyone gets to talk and be heard
- **Harmonizer**—one who keeps tensions low
- **Record keeper**—one who maintains records of events and activities and informs members
- **Reporter**—one who assumes responsibility for preparing materials for submission
- **Leader**—one who assumes a directive role

© Radius Images/Jupiterimages

In healthy groups, members may fulfill multiple roles, which rotate as the need arises. Negative roles are extinguished as the group communicates openly about its goals, strategies, and expectations. The opinions and viewpoints of all members are encouraged and expected.

From Groups to Teams

Some use the terms *group* and *team* interchangeably; others distinguish between them. The major distinction between a group and a team is in members' attitudes and level of commitment. A team is typified by a clear identity and a high level of commitment on the part of members. A variety of strategies has been used for organizing workers into teams:

- A **task force** is generally given a single goal and a limited time to achieve it.

- A **quality assurance team**, or *quality circle*, focuses on product or service quality, and projects can be either short- or long-term.

- A **cross-functional team** brings together employees from various departments to solve a variety of problems, such as productivity issues, contract estimations and planning, and multidepartment difficulties.

- A **product development team** concentrates on innovation and the development cycle of new products, and is usually cross-functional in nature. Consider the impact of team structures, as illustrated in the organizational chart in Figure 2-2 on the next page.

While chain of command is still at work in formal organizational relationships and responsibilities, team structures unite people from varying portions of the organization. Work teams are typically given the authority to act on their conclusions, although the level of authority varies, depending on the organization and the purpose of the team. Typically, the group supervisor retains some responsibilities, some decisions are made completely by the team, and the rest are made jointly.

Merely placing workers into a group does not make them a functional team. A group must go through a developmental process to begin to function as a team. The four stages of team development include:

1. **forming**—becoming acquainted with each other and the assigned task.

2. **storming**—dealing with conflicting personalities, goals, and ideas.

3. **norming**—developing strategies and activities that promote goal achievement.

4. **performing**—reaching the optimal performance level.

task force
a team of workers that is generally given a single goal and a limited time to achieve it

quality assurance team
a team that focuses on product or service quality; projects can be either short- or long-term

cross-functional team
a team that brings together employees from various departments to solve a variety of problems

product development team
usually cross–functional in nature; a group of employees who concentrate on innovation and the development cycle of new products

forming
stage one of team development in which team members become acquainted with each other and the assigned task

storming
stage two of team development in which team members deal with conflicting personalities, goals, and ideas

norming
stage three of team development in which team members develop strategies and activities that promote goal achievement

performing
stage four of team development in which team members reach the optimal performance level

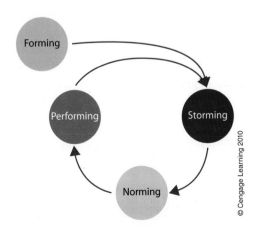

© Cengage Learning 2010

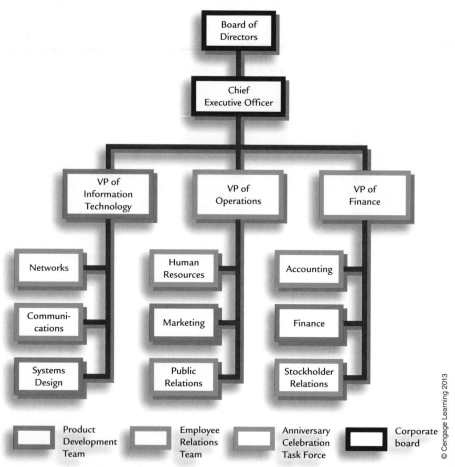

Figure 2-2 *Organizational Chart with Hierarchical and Team Structures*

© Cengage Learning 2013

For a variety of reasons, teams are often unable to advance through all four stages of development. Even long-term teams might never reach the optimal performing stage, settling instead for the acceptable performance of the norming stage.

Research into what makes workplace teams effective indicates that training is beneficial for participants in such areas as problem solving, goal setting, conflict resolution, risk taking, active listening, and recognizing the interests and achievements of others. Participants need to be able to satisfy one another's basic needs for belonging, personal recognition, and support. Team members at the performing stage of team development exhibit the following behaviors:[10]

- **Commitment.** They are focused on the mission, values, goals, and expectations of the team and the organization.

- **Cooperation.** They have a shared sense of purpose, mutual gain, and teamwork.

- **Communication.** They know that information must flow smoothly between top management and workers. Team members are willing to face confrontation and unpleasantness when necessary.

- **Contribution.** All members share their different backgrounds, skills, and abilities with the team.

Teams have existed for hundreds of years throughout many countries and cultures. Teams are more flexible than larger organizational groupings because they can be assembled, deployed, refocused, and disbanded more quickly, usually in ways that enhance rather than disrupt more permanent structures and processes. Organizational changes are often necessary, however, since support must be in place for performance evaluation, recognition, communication, and training systems. Strategies for bringing about needed change might include arranging site visits to similar organizations that already have teams, bringing in a successful team to speak to the organization, and bringing in consultants to discuss the team development process.

Meeting Management

☒ OBJECTIVE 5

Discuss aspects of effective meeting management.

Meetings are essential for communication in organizations. They present opportunities to acquire and disseminate valuable information, develop skills, and make favorable impressions on colleagues, supervisors, and subordinates. U.S. businesses spend more money on conducting meetings than does any other country in the world, and they also spend more time in meetings than do people of other countries.[11] International meetings are imperative for solid business reasons but are facing greater planning scrutiny because of tightening travel budgets and a recovering global economy.

Workers frequently have negative attitudes toward meetings because they perceive they are a waste of time. Studies support this opinion, revealing that as much as one-third of the time spent in meetings is unproductive. Negative attitudes toward meetings can be changed when meetings are conducted properly, giving attention to correct procedures and behavior. Successful meetings don't just happen; rather, they occur by design. Careful planning and attention to specific guidelines can help ensure the success of your meetings, whether they are conducted in a face-to-face format or electronically.

Face-to-Face Meetings

Face-to-face meetings continue to be the most-used meeting format in most organizations. They offer distinct advantages and are appropriate in the following situations:[12]

- ☑ When you need the richest nonverbal cues, including body, voice, proximity, and touch.
- ☑ When the issues are especially sensitive.
- ☑ When the participants don't know one another.
- ☑ When establishing group rapport and relationships is crucial.
- ☑ When the participants can be in the same place at the same time.

© Orla/Shutterstock

Face-to-face meetings can be enhanced with the use of various media tools such as flipcharts, handouts, and electronic slide decks. While face-to-face meetings provide a rich nonverbal context and direct human contact, they also have certain limitations. In addition to the obvious logistical issues of schedules and distance, face-to-face meetings may be dominated by overly vocal, quick-to-speak, and high-status members.

Electronic Meetings

Electronic meetings allow companies to reduce travel budgets, save professional time, and minimize the environmental impact caused by travel. A variety of technologies is available to facilitate electronic meetings. Participants may communicate with one another through telephones, computers, or video broadcast equipment using groupware or meeting management software applications. Electronic meetings offer certain advantages. They facilitate geographically dispersed groups, because they provide the choice of meeting at different places/same time, different places/different times, same place/same time, or same place/different times. Electronic meetings also speed up meeting follow-up activities because decisions and action items can be recorded electronically.

Electronic meetings also have certain limitations:[13]

- They cannot replace face-to-face contact, especially when group efforts are just beginning and when groups are trying to build group values, trust, and emotional ties.
- They can make it harder to reach consensus, because more ideas are generated and because it might be harder to interpret the strength of other members' commitment to their proposals.
- The success of same-time meetings is dependent on all participants having excellent keyboarding skills to engage in rapid-fire, in-depth discussion. This limitation might be overcome as the use of voice input systems becomes more prevalent.

Meetings of one 16-person department cost one company $1.6 million a year in lost productivity.[14]

Suggestions for Effective Meetings

Whether you engage in face-to-face or electronic meetings, observing the following guidelines can help to ensure that your meetings are productive:

- **Limit meeting length and frequency.** Any meeting held for longer than an hour or more frequently than once a month should be scrutinized. Ask yourself whether the meeting is necessary. Perhaps the purpose can be achieved in another way, such as email, instant messaging, or telephone.

agenda
a meeting outline that includes important information (e.g., date, beginning and ending times, place, topics to be discussed, and responsibilities of those involved)

brainstorming
the generation of many ideas from among team members

- **Make satisfactory arrangements.** Select a date and time convenient for the majority of expected participants. For face-to-face meetings, plan the meeting site with consideration for appropriate seating for attendees, media equipment, temperature and lighting, and necessary supplies. For electronic meetings, check hardware and software and connectivity components.

- **Distribute the agenda well in advance.** The **agenda** is a meeting outline that includes important information: date, beginning and ending times, place, topics to be discussed, and responsibilities of those involved. Having the agenda prior to the meeting allows participants to know what is expected of them. A sample agenda template is provided in Figure 2-3.

- **Encourage participation.** While it is certainly easier for one person to make decisions, the quality of the decision making is often improved by involving the team. Rational decision making may begin with **brainstorming**, the generation of many ideas from among team members. Brainstormed ideas can then be discussed and ranked, followed by some form of voting.

Figure 2-3   ~~SAMPLE~~   *Formal Generic Agenda for Meetings*

Agenda for [name of group] Meeting
Prepared on [date agenda created]
By [name of author of agenda]

Attendees: [those invited to attend, often in alphabetical order]
Date and time of meeting:
Location of meeting:
Subject: [major issues to be discussed or purpose of meeting]
Agenda items:

1. Call to order
2. Routine business [procedural or administrative matters]   (10–15 minutes)
   a. Approval of agenda for this meeting
   b. Reading and approval of minutes of last meeting
   c. Committee reports
3. Old business [unfinished matters from previous meeting]   (15–20 minutes)
   a. Discussion of issue(s) carried over from previous meeting
   b. Issue(s) arising from decision(s) made at previous meeting
4. New business   (20–25 minutes)
   a. Most important issue
   b. Next most important issue
   c. Other issues in decreasing order of importance
   d. Business from the floor not included on the agenda
      [only as time permits; otherwise, these issues should be
      addressed in the next meeting]
5. Adjournment

- **Maintain order.** An organized democratic process ensures that the will of the majority prevails, the minority is heard, and group goals are achieved as expeditiously as possible. Proper parliamentary procedure may be followed in formal meetings, as outlined in sources such as *Robert's Rules of Order* and *Jones' Parliamentary Procedure at a Glance*. For less formal meetings, the use of parliamentary procedure may not be necessary to ensure effective contribution by attendees.

- **Manage conflict.** In an autocratic organization, conflict might be avoided because employees are conditioned to be submissive. Such an environment, however, leads to smoldering resentment. On the other hand, conflict is a normal part of any team effort and can lead to creative discussion and superior outcomes. Maintaining focus on issues and not personalities helps ensure that conflict is productive rather than destructive.

- **Seek consensus.** While unanimous agreement on decisions is an optimal outcome, total agreement cannot always be achieved. **Consensus** represents the collective opinion of the group, or the informal rule that all team members can live with at least 70 percent of what is agreed upon.

- **Prepare thorough minutes.** Minutes provide a concise record of meeting actions, ensure the tracking and follow-up of issues from previous meetings, and assist in the implementation of previously reached decisions.

Meetings are an important management tool and are useful for idea exchange. They also provide opportunities for you, as a meeting participant, to communicate impressions of power and status. Knowing how to present yourself and your ideas and exhibiting knowledge about correct meeting management will assist you in your career advancement.

consensus
represents the collective opinion of the group, or the informal rule that all team members can live with at least 70 percent of what is agreed upon

Face-to-face meetings continue to be the most-used meeting format in many organizations.

Planning Spoken and Written Messages

In a report titled "Writing: A Ticket to Work . . . or a Ticket Out," the National Commission on Writing reported that two-thirds of salaried employees in large companies have some writing responsibilities, and getting hired and promoted in many industries requires strong writing abilities. While writing is important in most managerial-level jobs, the Commission also concluded that one-third of employees in corporate America write poorly. Knowing that effective communication is tied to the corporate bottom line and many employees can't write well, businesses are investing $3.1 billion annually to train employees to write.[1] Remedies are needed to prevent confusion, waste, errors, lost productivity, and a damaged corporate image—all caused by employees, customers, and clients muddling their way through unreadable messages.

As a capable communicator, you can immediately add value to your organization and set yourself apart from your peers who are struggling to articulate ideas in writing and in presentations. Communication that commands attention and can be understood easily is essential for survival during the information explosion we are experiencing today. On the job, you will be expected to process volumes of available information and shape useful messages that respond to the needs of customers or clients, coworkers and supervisors, and other key business partners. Additionally, increased use of electronic communication (email, texts, instant messages, blogs, videoconferences, etc.) will require you to be technologically savvy and capable of adapting the rules of good communication to the demands of emerging technology.

How can you learn to plan and prepare powerful business messages? The systematic analysis process as outlined in Figure 3-1 will help you develop messages that save you and your organization valuable time and

OBJECTIVES

1 Identify the purpose of the message and the appropriate channel.

2 Develop clear perceptions of the audience to enhance the impact of the communication and human relations.

3 Apply techniques for adapting messages to the audience, including strategies for communicating ethically and responsibly.

4 Recognize the importance of organizing a message before writing the first draft.

5 Select the appropriate message pattern (deductive or inductive) for developing messages to achieve the desired response.

Figure 3-1 Process for Planning and Preparing Spoken and Written Messages

STEP 1	STEP 2	STEP 3	STEP 4	STEP* 5	STEP* 6
Determine the purpose and select an appropriate channel	Envision the audience	Adapt the message to the audience's needs and concerns	Organize the message	Prepare the first draft	Revise and proofread for accuracy and desired impact

*You will focus on the planning process (Steps 1–4) in this chapter; you will learn to prepare the message in Chapter 4 (Steps 5–6).

© Cengage Learning 2010

"Communication that commands attention and can be understood easily is essential for survival during the information explosion we are experiencing today."

© Albert H. Teich/Shutterstock

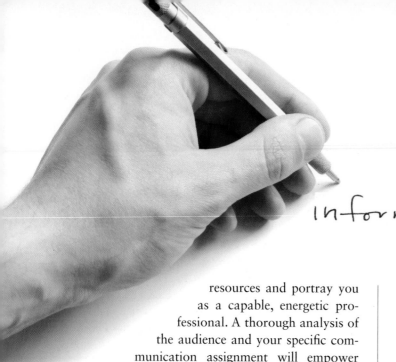

so forth. Some messages are intended to persuade—to influence or change the attitudes or actions of the receiver. These messages include promoting a product or service and seeking support for ideas and worthy causes presented to supervisors, employees, stockholders, customers or clients, and others. You will learn to prepare messages for each of these purposes.

Inform ?

Step 2: Envisioning the Audience

Perception is the part of the communication process that involves how we look at others and the world around us. It's a natural tendency to perceive situations from our own limited viewpoint. We use the context of the situation and our five senses to absorb and interpret the information bombarding us in unique ways.

Individual differences in perception account for the varied and sometimes conflicting reports given by eyewitnesses to the same accident. Our senses can be tricked when there is a difference in what we expect and what really is happening. For example, consider how your *perception* affects your ability to accurately or completely interpret an optical illusion.

Perception of reality is also limited by previous experiences and our attitudes toward the sender of the message. We support ideas that are in line with our own and decide whether to focus on the positive or the negative of a situation. We may simply refuse to hear a message that doesn't fit into our view of the world.

> ☒ OBJECTIVE 2
>
> **Develop clear perceptions of the audience to enhance the impact of the communication and human relations.**

resources and portray you as a capable, energetic professional. A thorough analysis of the audience and your specific communication assignment will empower you to write a first draft efficiently and to revise and proofread your message for accuracy, conciseness, and appropriate tone.

Step 1: Determining the Purpose and Channel

To speak or write effectively, you must think through what you are trying to say and understand it thoroughly before you begin. Ask yourself why you are preparing the message and what you hope to accomplish. Is the purpose to get information, to answer a question, to accept an offer, to deny a request, to seek support for a product or idea? Condense the answers into a brief sentence that outlines the purpose for writing or the central idea of your message. You will use the central idea to organize your message to achieve the results you desire.

> ☒ OBJECTIVE 1
>
> **Identify the purpose of the message and the appropriate channel.**

The major purpose of many business messages is to have the receiver understand logical information. Informative messages are used to convey the vast amounts of information needed to complete the day-to-day operations of the business—explain instructions to employees, announce meetings and procedures, acknowledge orders, accept contracts for services, and

persuade ?

© iStockphoto.com/Nicolas Loran / © iStockphoto.com/winterling / © Chapel Hill Photography

Much of the confusion in communication is caused by differences in the sender's and receiver's perceptions. For example, a manager's brief email requesting a status report on a task may come across as curt to the employees. Perceptions vary between individuals with similar backgrounds, and even more so when people from different cultures, generations, and genders communicate.

Overcoming perceptual barriers is difficult but essential if you are to craft messages that meet the needs and concerns of your audience. To help you envision the audience, first focus on relevant information you know about the receiver. The more familiar you are with the receiver, the easier this task will be. When communicating with an individual, you immediately recall a clear picture of the receiver—his or her physical appearance, background (education, occupation, religion, culture), values, opinions, preferences, and so on. Most importantly, your knowledge of the receiver's reaction in similar, previous experiences will aid you in anticipating how this receiver is likely to react in the current situation. Consider the following audience characteristics:

- **Age.** A message answering an elementary-school student's request for information from your company would not be worded the same as a message answering a similar request from an adult.

- **Economic level.** A solicitation for a business donation for a charity project written to a small business owner would likely differ from one written to a representative of a major corporation.

- **Educational/occupational background.** The technical jargon and acronyms used in a financial proposal sent to bank loan officers may be inappropriate in a proposal sent to a group of private investors.

- **Needs and concerns of the receiver.** Just as successful sales personnel begin by identifying the needs of the prospective buyer, an effective manager attempts to understand the receiver's frame of reference as a basis for organizing the message and developing the content.

- **Culture.** The vast cultural differences between people (e.g., language, expressions, customs, values, and religion) increase the complexity of the communication process. An email containing typical American expressions (e.g., "The frustration should cool down soon" and "the competition is backed to the wall") would likely confuse a manager from a different culture. Differences in values influence communication styles and message patterns. For example, Japanese readers value the beauty and flow of words and prefer an indirect writing approach, unlike Americans who prefer clarity and conciseness.[2]

- **Rapport.** A sensitive message prepared for a long-time client may differ significantly from a message prepared for a newly acquired client. Emails discussing expectations for completing an assignment may be briefer and more direct when sent to an employee with whom you share a strong business relationship built on mutual trust. The rapport created by previous dealings with the recipient aids understanding in a current situation.

- **Expectations.** Because accountants, lawyers, and other professionals are expected to meet high standards, a message from one of them containing errors in grammar or spelling would likely cause a receiver to question the credibility of the source.

You may find that envisioning an audience you know well is often such a conscious action that you may not even recognize that you are doing it. On the other hand, envisioning those you do not know well requires additional effort. In these cases, simply assume an empathetic attitude toward the receiver to assist you in identifying his or her frame of reference (knowledge, feelings, and emotions). In other words, project mentally how you believe you would feel or react in a similar situation and use that information to communicate understanding back to the person.

Consider the use (or lack) of empathy in the following workplace examples:

© Jupco Smokovski/Shutterstock

It can be difficult to see the world as others do.

Sample Message	Problem Analysis
Example 1: A U.S. manager's instructions to a new employee from an Asian culture:	• *The use of expressions peculiar to U.S. environment confuse and intimidate.*
I don't think we are even in the ball park here in terms of the cost estimate. If we can't get these numbers down, we will be out of the game in terms of what the competition might offer. We want to come up with a proposal that will knock this out of the park! Do you understand?	• *Open-ended question at the end disregards importance of saving face to a person of Asian culture. Cultural influences may prevent employee from asking questions that might indicate lack of understanding.*
Example 2: An excerpt from a message sent to Ms. Lee Thompson:	• *Misspelling receiver's name, misinterpreting gender, and showing disrespect for receiver.*
Mr. Thomson: The GPS system that you expressed interest in is now available as an option in our minivans. Our sales manager would be happy to provide a demonstration at your convinance. Please stop by on your next maintenance visit.	• *Omission of contact information reduces writer's credibility and shows lack of genuine concern for sender's needs.* • *Overlooking mechanical errors implies incompetence or carelessness.*

Taking the time and effort to obtain a strong mental picture of your audience through firsthand knowledge or your empathetic attitude *before* you write will enhance your message in the following ways:

1. **Establishes rapport and credibility needed to build long-lasting personal and business relationships.** Your receivers will appreciate your attempt to connect and understand their feelings. A likely outcome is mutual trust, which can greatly improve communication and people's feelings about you, your ideas, and themselves (as shown in the discussion of the Johari Window in Chapter 2).

2. **Permits you to address the receiver's needs and concerns.** Such knowledge allows you to select relevant content and to communicate in a suitable style.

3. **Simplifies the task of organizing your message.** From your knowledge of yourself and from your experiences with others, you can reasonably predict receivers' reactions to various types of messages. To illustrate, ask yourself these questions:

- Would I react favorably to a message saying my request is being granted or that a new client is genuinely pleased with a job I'd just completed?

- Would I experience a feeling of disappointment when I learn that my request has been refused or that my promised pay raise is being postponed?

- Would I need compelling arguments to convince me to purchase a new product or support a new company policy?

Now, reread the questions as though you were the message recipient. Because you know *your* answers, you can predict *others'* answers with some degree of accuracy. Such predictions are possible because of commonality in human behavior.

Your commitment to identifying the needs and concerns of your audience before you communicate is invaluable in today's workplace. Organizations must focus on providing quality customer service and developing work environments supportive of talented, diverse workers. Alienating valuable customers and talented employees as a result of poor audience analysis is not an option in today's competitive environment.

Step 3: Adapting the Message to the Audience

After you have envisioned your audience, you are ready to adapt your message to fit the specific needs of your audience. Adaptations include focusing on the receiver's point of view; communicating ethically and responsibly; building and protecting goodwill; using simple, contemporary language; writing concisely; and projecting a positive, tactful tone.

☒ **OBJECTIVE 3**

Apply techniques for adapting messages to the audience, including strategies for communicating ethically and responsibly.

Focus on the Receiver's Point of View

Ideas are more interesting and appealing if they are expressed from the receiver's viewpoint. Developing a "you attitude" rather than a "me attitude" involves thinking in terms of the other person's interests and trying to see a problem from the other's point of view. A letter, memo, email, or phone call reflecting a "you attitude" sends a direct signal of sincere concern for the receiver's needs and interest.

The use of the word *you* (appropriately used) conveys to receivers a feeling that messages are specifically for them. However, if the first-person pronoun *I* is used frequently, especially as the subject, the sender may impress others as being self-centered—always talking about self. Compare the following examples of sender-centered and receiver-centered statements:

"I"- or Sender-Centered	"You"- or Receiver-Centered
I want to let you know what a great job you have done as leader of the sales team.	Congratulations on landing the Revere account!
We will be changing the reporting deadline for sales soon.	You will find below the new schedule for the reporting of sales figures.

Compliments (words of deserved praise) are another effective way of increasing a receiver's receptiveness to ideas that follow. Give sincere compliments judiciously as they can do more harm than good if paid at the wrong time, in the wrong setting, in the presence of the wrong people, or for the wrong reasons. Likewise, avoid flattery (words of undeserved praise). Although the recipient may accept your flattery as a sincere compliment, it is more likely that the recipient will interpret your undeserved praise as an attempt to seek to gain favor or special attention. Suspicion of your motive makes effective communication less likely.

Communicate Ethically and Responsibly

The familiar directive "with power comes responsibility" applies especially to your use of communication skills. Because business communication affects the lives of many, you must accept responsibility for using it to uphold your own personal values and your company's standards of ethical conduct. Before speaking or writing, use the following guidelines to help you communicate ethically and responsibly.

- **Is the information stated as truthfully, honestly, and fairly as possible?** Good communicators recognize that ensuring a free flow of essential information is in the interest of the public and the organization. Merck, the manufacturer of the prescription pain reliever Vioxx, was sued by thousands of patients and patients' families for withholding information about known heart risks associated with taking the drug.[3] Similarly, failure to report the nature of his investment practices led to the arrest of the accountant of Bernard Madoff, the man who admittedly cheated thousands of investors out of billions of dollars in an illegal scheme. The SEC has accused Madoff's accountant, David Friehling, of lying to the American Institute of Certified Public Accountants rather than subject his audit work to peer review.[4] Your honor, honesty, and credibility will build strong,

How to Cultivate a "You Attitude"

To cultivate a "you attitude," concentrate on the following questions:

- Does the message address the receiver's major needs and concerns?
- Would the receiver feel this message is receiver-centered? Is the receiver kept clearly in the picture?
- Will the receiver perceive the ideas to be fair, logical, and ethical?
- Are ideas expressed clearly and concisely (to avoid lost time, money, and possible embarrassment caused when messages are misunderstood)?
- Does the message promote positive business relationships—even when the message is negative? For example, are *please, thank you,* and other courtesies used when appropriate? Are ideas stated tactfully and positively and in a manner that preserves the receiver's self-worth and cultivates future business?
- Is the message sent promptly and through the preferred channel to indicate courtesy?
- Does the message reflect the high standards of a business professional: accurate and appealing document design, quality printing, and absence of misspellings and grammatical errors?

long-lasting relationships and lead to the long-term success of your company. Sending complete, accurate, and timely information regardless of whether it supports your interests will help you build credibility.

- **Does the message embellish or exaggerate the facts?** Legal guidelines related to advertising provide clear guidance for avoiding *fraud*, the misrepresentation of products or services; however, overzealous sales representatives or imaginative writers can use language skillfully to create less-than-accurate perceptions in the minds of receivers. Businesses have learned the hard way that overstating the capabilities of a product or service (promising more than can be delivered) is not good for business in the long run. Researchers are at times tempted to overstate their findings to ensure continued funding or greater publicity. Eric T. Peohlman, a medical researcher, acknowledged that while at the University of Vermont he fabricated data in 17 applications for federal grants to make his work seem more promising. Under a plea agreement, he was barred for life from receiving federal funding and had to pay back $180,000, as well as asking scientific journals to retract and correct 10 articles he had authored.[5]

  While surveys indicate many job seekers believe companies expect résumé padding, companies repeatedly report that this perception is not true. Marilee Jones, dean of admissions at Massachusetts Institute of Technology, and David Edmonson, the former CEO of Radio Shack, resigned high-profile jobs for misstating their academic records. George O'Leary stepped down five days after been named head football coach at Notre Dame, admitting he lied about receiving a master's degree and playing college football.[6]

  Skill in communicating persuasively will be important throughout your profession. The techniques you will read about in this text, such as those related to writing a winning résumé and application message, will be helpful as you begin your career; however, these techniques should *not* be used if your motive is to exploit the receiver.

- **Are the ideas expressed clearly and understandably?** If a message is to be seen as honest, you must be reasonably confident that the receiver can understand it. Ethical communicators select words that convey the exact meaning intended and that are within the reader's vocabulary.

- **Is your viewpoint supported with objective facts?** Are facts accurately documented to allow the reader to judge the credibility of the source and to give credit where credit is due? Can opinions be clearly distinguished from facts? Have you evaluated honestly any real or perceived conflict of interest that could prevent you from preparing an unbiased message?

- **Are ideas stated with tact and consideration that preserves the receiver's self-worth?** The metaphor "An arrow, once it is shot, cannot be recalled" describes the irrevocable damage caused by cruel or unkind words.[7] Ego-destroying criticism, excessive anger, sarcasm, hurtful nicknames, betrayed secrets, rumors, and malicious gossip pose serious ethical problems in the workplace because they can ruin reputations, humiliate, and damage a person's self-worth. Serious legal issues arise when negative statements are false, constituting defamation. Written defamatory remarks are referred to as **libel**, and similar spoken remarks are referred to as **slander**. If you choose to make negative statements about a person, be sure the facts in question are supported. Additionally, you'll hone your abilities to convey negative information and to handle sensitive situations in a constructive, timely manner rather than ignoring them until they are out of control. For considerate, fair, and civilized use of words, follow this simple rule: Communicate with and about others with the same kindness and fairness that you wish others to use when communicating with and about you.

- **Are graphics carefully designed to avoid distorting facts and relationships?** Communicating ethically involves reporting data as clearly and accurately as possible. Misleading graphics result either from the developers' deliberate attempt to confuse the audience or from their lack of expertise in constructing ethical graphics.

Communication's Golden Rule

Communicate with and about others with the same kindness and fairness that you wish others to use when communicating with and about you.

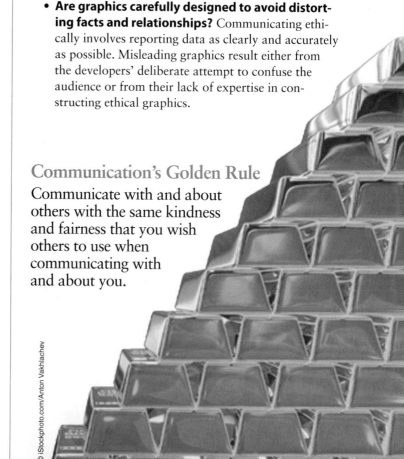
© iStockphoto.com/Anton Vakhlachev

Build and Protect Goodwill

Goodwill arises when a business is worth more than its tangible assets. Things such as a good name and reputation, a desirable location, a unique product, and excellent customer service can assure earnings, so the business has more value than simply its tangible assets. Businesses go to great lengths to build and protect goodwill and thus their futures. It is no surprise that effective communication is a key strategy.

Insensitive messages—whether directed to customers, employees, or business partners—can offend and alienate and will diminish a company's goodwill. Most of us don't intend to be insensitive but simply may not think carefully about the impact the tone of our words may have on others. **Tone** is the way a statement sounds and conveys the writer's or speaker's attitude toward the message and the receiver. To build and protect your company's goodwill, eliminate words that are overly euphemistic, condescending, demeaning, and biased.

Use Euphemisms Cautiously

A **euphemism** is a kind word substituted for one that may offend or suggest something unpleasant. For example, the idea of picking up neighborhood garbage does not sound especially inviting. Someone who does such work is often referred to as a *sanitation worker*. This term has a more pleasant connotation than *garbage collector*.

Choose the euphemistic terms rather than the negative terms shown in the following examples:

Negative Tone	Euphemistic Tone
aged or elderly	senior citizen
dying	fading away/near the end
used or secondhand	pre-owned
prison	correctional facility
disabled or handicapped	physically challenged/differently abled
patient management	care coordination/supportive services

Generally, you can recognize such expressions for what they are—unpleasant ideas presented with a little sugarcoating. Knowing the sender was simply trying to

CAUTION!
Euphemisms
Condescending Expressions
Demeaning Expressions
Connotative Tone

© iStockphoto.com/Aleksejs Jevsejenko

be polite and positive, receivers are more likely to react favorably. You should avoid, however, euphemisms that excessively sugarcoat and those that suggest subtle sarcasm. For example, to refer to a janitor as a *maintenance engineer* is to risk conveying a negative metacommunication, such as "This person does not hold a very respectable position, but I did the best I could to make it sound good." To the receiver (and to the janitor), just plain *janitor* would sound better.

You will also want to avoid **doublespeak**, also known as *doubletalk* or *corporate speak*. Such terms refer to euphemisms that deliberately mislead, hide, or evade the truth. This distortion of the truth is often found in military, political, and corporate language. A loss of credibility may result when a police officer refers to "nontraditional organized crime" rather than gang activity. Another example would be a politician who talks of an "enhanced interrogation technique" rather than "torture," or "collateral damage" or "friendly fire" rather than civilians killed accidentally by the military's own weapons. Companies use doublespeak when they make "workforce reductions" or offer workers a "career opportunity adjustment" or "voluntary termination." One company called the permanent shutdown of a steel plant an "indefinite idling" in an attempt to avoid paying severance or pension benefits to the displaced workers.[8]

Despite your training in writing, you may fall into the trap of mirroring the writing of people above you on the career ladder who prefer writing in doublespeak. They often choose doublespeak over clear, concise writing because of the misguided belief that doublespeak makes them sound informed and professional. Such vagueness protects them when they're unsure how their messages will be received and makes writing easy once they learn the code. Instead of falling into doublespeak, learn to develop clear, concise messages that clarify ideas and provide direction to recipients

goodwill
arises when a business is worth more than its tangible assets

tone
the way a statement sounds; it conveys the writer's or speaker's attitude toward the message and the receiver

euphemism
a kind word substituted for one that may offend or suggest something unpleasant

doublespeak
also called doubletalk *or* corporate speak; *euphemisms that deliberately mislead, hide, or evade the truth*

regardless of their culture while enhancing your credibility as an honest communicator. A CEO of a writing training company has another interesting angle on clear writing. He contends that "articulation of thought is an element of intelligence, and you can increase your intelligence through writing." Working to articulate ideas clearly and logically through writing makes people smarter![9] That is a motivating reason for perfecting writing (and speaking) skills in our professional and personal lives.

Avoid Condescending or Demeaning Expressions

Condescending words seem to imply that the communicator is temporarily coming down from a level of superiority to join the receiver on a level of inferiority; such words damage efforts to build and protect goodwill. Note how the reminders of inequality in the following examples hamper communication:

Ineffective Examples

My team always outshines others in the company, due, in part, to my experience as a leader.

You did not receive the promotion because John was a much better choice.

A demeaning expression (sometimes called a *dysphemism*) makes an idea seem negative or disrespectful. Avoid demeaning expressions because they divert attention from the real message to emotional issues that have little to do with the message. Many examples can be taken as contempt for an occupation or a specific job or position ("bean counters" for accountants, "ambulance chasers" for lawyers, "spin doctors" for politicians or public relations directors, and "shrinks" for psychiatrists). Like words that attack races or nationalities, words that ridicule occupations work against a communicator's purpose.

Many demeaning expressions are common across regions, ages, and perhaps even cultures. Some demeaning expressions belong to a particular company; for example, "turtles" was coined in one firm to mock first-year employees for their slow work pace. President Obama quickly recognized and apologized for his late-night talk show quip that equated his bowling skills to those of athletes with disabilities. Seeing the president's gaffe as a "teachable moment" for the country, Special Olympics Chairman Tim Shriver emphasized

denotative meaning
the literal meaning of a word that most people assign to it

connotative meaning
the literal meaning of a word plus an extra message that reveals the speaker's or writer's qualitative judgment

that "words hurt and words do matter and these words that in some respect can be seen as humiliating . . . do cause pain."[10] Effective communicators choose respectful expressions that build and protect goodwill.

Use Connotative Tone Cautiously

Human relations can suffer when connotative words are inadvertently or intentionally used instead of denotative words. The **denotative meaning** of a word is the literal meaning that most people assign to it. The **connotative meaning** is the literal meaning plus an extra message that reveals the speaker's or writer's qualitative judgment, as shown in this example:

Connotative Meaning with Negative Implication	Denotative Meaning (Preferred)
Please don't <u>hassle</u> the customer service representatives with too frequent questions.	Please don't <u>question</u> the customer service representatives too frequently.

The connotative meaning of "hassle" carries an additional message that the writer has a bias against asking questions. The connotation may needlessly introduce thoughts about whether asking questions is beneficial and distract the receiver from paying sufficient attention to the statements that follow. Connotations, like metacommunications discussed in Chapter 2, involve messages that are implied. In the preceding example, the connotation seems to be more harmful than helpful.

At times, however, connotations can be helpful, as seen in the following examples:

Connotative Meaning with Positive Meaning (Preferred)	Denotative Meaning
Our <u>corporate think tank</u> has developed an outstanding production process.	<u>Research and Development</u> has developed an outstanding production process.
Julia's likable personality <u>makes her a miracle worker</u> at contract negotiation.	Julia's likable personality is <u>beneficial</u> in contract negotiation.

In crafting business messages, rely mainly on denotative or connotative words that will be interpreted in a positive manner. To be sure that your connotative words are understood and will generate goodwill, consider your audience, the context, and the timing of the message.

- **Connotative words may be more easily misinterpreted than denotative words.** Because of differences in peoples' perceptions based on their life experiences, words that are perceived positively by one person may be perceived negatively by another. In some cases, receivers may simply not understand the connotative words. Damaged human relations occur when managers repeatedly convey connotative messages without considering whether employees can interpret the meanings as they are intended.

- **The appropriateness of connotations varies with the audience to which they are addressed and the context in which they appear.** For example, referring to a car as a "foreign job" or "sweet" might be received differently by teenagers than by senior citizens. Such expressions are less appropriate in a research report than in a blog or popular magazine.

Use Specific Language Appropriately

To help the receiver understand your message easily, select words that paint intense, colorful word pictures. Creating clear mental images adds energy and imagination to your message, thus increasing its overall impact.

General	Specific (Preferred)
The public outcry was huge.	More than 3 million emails were received from the public.
Please get back to me soon about your proposal changes.	Please supply me with the changes to the proposal by this Friday at noon.
Sara is a great manager.	Sara shines as a manager because of her ability to stay on task and yet make people feel supported.

Sometimes, using general statements can be useful in building and protecting goodwill. General words keep negative ideas from receiving more emphasis than they deserve. In addition, senders who don't have specific information or for some reason don't want to divulge it use general words.

General (Preferred)	Specific
Thank you for your explanation of the meeting with Julie.	Thank you for providing the details about the argument you had with Julie during last week's meeting.
I'm sorry to hear about your accident.	I'm sorry to hear about your awful car crash and the injuries to the occupants of the other vehicle.

Use Bias-Free Language

Being responsive to individual differences requires you to make a conscious effort to use bias-free (nondiscriminatory) language. Using language that does not exclude, stereotype, or offend others permits them to focus on your message rather than to question your sensitivity. Goodwill can be damaged when biased statements are made related to gender, race or ethnicity, religion, age, or disability. The following guidelines will help you avoid bias:

1. **Avoid referring to men and women in stereotyped roles and occupations.** The use of *he* to refer to anyone in a group was once standard and accepted; however, this usage is considered insensitive and, to some, offensive. Therefore, do not use the pronoun *he* when referring to a person in a group that may include women or the pronoun *she* to refer to a group that may include men; otherwise you may unintentionally communicate an insensitive message

AVOID

Bias

Cliches

Profanity

Outdated Expressions

that only women or only men can perform certain tasks or serve in certain professions. Follow these four approaches to avoid gender bias:

Guideline	Gender-Biased	Improved
Avoid using a pronoun	Each employee must complete <u>his</u> vacation request form.	Employees must complete a vacation request form.
Repeat the noun	Expect promptness from each employee. Ask him to . . .	Expect promptness from your <u>guide</u>. Ask the <u>guide</u> to . . .
Use a plural noun	Each employee should update and confirm his contact information.	Employees should update and confirm their contact information.
Use pronouns from both genders (when necessary, but not repeatedly)	Please page a doctor. He should respond . . .	Please page a doctor. <u>He or she</u> should respond . . .

2. **Use occupational titles that reflect genuine sensitivity to gender.** Note the gender-free titles that can be easily substituted to avoid bias:

Gender-Biased	Gender-Free
salesman	salesperson
chairman	chair

3. **Avoid designating an occupation by gender.** For example, omit "woman" in "A woman doctor has initiated this research." The doctor's profession, not the gender, is the point of the message. Similarly, avoid using the *-ess* ending to differentiate genders in an occupation:

Gender-Biased	Gender-Free
waiter or waitress	server
hostess	host

4. **Avoid using expressions that may be perceived to be gender-biased.** Avoid commonly used expressions in which "man" represents all humanity, such as "To go where no man has gone before," and stereotypical characteristics, such as "man hours," "man-made goods," and "work of four strong men." Note the improvements made in the following examples by eliminating the potentially offensive words.

Gender-Biased	Improved
Preparing the proposal was a <u>man-sized</u> task.	Preparing the proposal was an <u>enormous</u> task.
Luke is the best <u>man</u> for the job.	Luke is the best <u>person</u> for the job.

5. **Avoid racial or ethnic bias.** Include racial or ethnic identification only when relevant and avoid referring to these groups in stereotypical ways.

Racially or Ethnically Biased	Improved
The salespeople ran around like a bunch of wild <u>Indians</u>.	The salespeople were extremely busy on the floor today.
Please give your form to Shirley, the Asian woman.	Please give the form to Shirley, the woman at that desk.
The articulate <u>African American</u> engineer overseeing the product redesign plans suggested . . .	The engineer overseeing the product redesign plans suggested . . .

6. **Avoid age bias.** Include age only when relevant and avoid demeaning expressions related to age.

Age-Biased	Improved
John is <u>the older gentleman</u> who works downstairs.	John works downstairs in the office on the right.

7. **Avoid disability bias.** When communicating about people with disabilities, use people-first language. That is, refer to the person first and the disability second so that focus is appropriately placed on the person's ability rather than on the disability. Also avoid words with negative or judgmental connotations, such as *handicap*, *unfortunate*, *afflicted*, and *victim*. When describing people without disabilities, use the word *typical* rather than *normal*; otherwise you may

inadvertently imply that people with disabilities are abnormal. Consider these more sensitive revisions:

Insensitive	Sensitive (People-First)
<u>Blind</u> employees receive . . .	Employees <u>with vision impairments</u> receive . . .
The elevator is for the exclusive use of <u>handicapped</u> employees and should not be used by <u>normal</u> employees.	The elevator is for the exclusive use of employees <u>with disabilities</u>.

Use Contemporary Language

Business messages should reflect correct, standard English and contemporary language used in a professional business setting. Outdated expressions, dull clichés, and profanity reduce the effectiveness of a message and the credibility of a communicator.

Eliminate Outdated Expressions

Using outdated expressions will give your message a dull, stuffy, unnatural tone. Instead, substitute fresh, original expressions that reflect today's language patterns.

Outdated Expressions	Improvement
<u>As per your request,</u> the report has been submitted to the client.	<u>As you requested,</u> the report has been submitted to the client.
<u>Enclosed please find</u> a copy of my transcript.	The <u>enclosed</u> transcript should answer your questions.
<u>Very truly yours</u> (used as the complimentary close in a letter)	Sincerely

Curb Clichés

Clichés, or overused expressions, are common in our everyday conversations and in business messages. These handy verbal shortcuts are convenient, quick, easy to use, and often include simple metaphors and analogies that effectively communicate

the most basic idea or emotion or the most complex business concept. However, writers and speakers who routinely use stale clichés may be perceived as unoriginal, unimaginative, lazy, and perhaps even disrespectful. Less frequently used words capture the receiver's attention because they are original, fresh, and interesting.

Clichés present another serious problem. Consider the scenario of shoppers standing in line at a discount store with the cashier saying to each, "Thanks for shopping with us today; please come again." Because the last shopper has heard the words several times already, he or she may not consider the statement genuine. The cashier has used an expression that can be stated without thinking and possibly without meaning. A worn expression can convey messages such as "You are not special" or "For you, I won't bother to think; the phrases I use in talking with others are surely good enough for you." Original expressions convey sincerity and build strong human relations.

Cliché	Improvement
Pushed (or stretched) the envelope	Took a risk or considered a new option
Skin in the game	Committed to the project
Cover all the bases	Get agreement/input from everyone
That sucks!	That's unacceptable/ needs improvement

Eliminate Profanity

Increasing tolerance of profanity is an issue of concern to society as a whole and also for employers and employees as they communicate at work. You must consider the potential business liabilities and legal implications resulting from the use of profanity that may offend others or create a hostile work environment. Recognize that minimizing or eliminating profanity is another important way you must adapt your language for communicating effectively and fostering human relations in a professional setting.

Use Simple, Informal Words

Business writers prefer simple, informal words that are readily understood and less distracting

clichés
overused expressions that can cause their users to be perceived as unoriginal, unimaginative, lazy, and perhaps even disrespectful

than more difficult, formal words. If a receiver questions the sender's motive for using formal words, the impact of the message may be diminished. Likewise, the impact would be diminished if the receiver questioned a sender's use of simple, informal words. That distraction is unlikely, however, if the message contains good ideas that are well organized and well supported. Under these conditions, simple words enable a receiver to understand the message clearly and quickly.

To illustrate, consider the unnecessary complexity of a notice that appeared on a corporate bulletin board: "Employees impacted by the strike are encouraged to utilize the hotline number to arrange for alternative transportation to work. Should you encounter difficulties in arranging for alternative transportation to work, please contact your immediate supervisor." A simple, easy-to-read revision would be, "If you can't get to work, call the hotline or your supervisor."[11] For further illustration, note the added clarity of the following words:

Formal Words	Informal Words
terminate	end
procure	get
remunerate	pay
corroborate	support

Using words that have more than two or three syllables when they are appropriate is acceptable. However, you should avoid regular use of a long, infrequently used word when a simpler, more common word conveys the same idea. Professionals in some fields often use specialized terminology, referred to as **jargon**, when communicating with colleagues in the same field. In this case, the audience is likely to understand the words, and using the jargon saves time. However, when communicating with people outside the field, professionals should select simple, common words to convey messages. Using clear, jargon-free language that can be readily understood by non-native recipients and easily translated is especially important in international communication.

You should build your vocabulary so that you can use just the right word for expressing an idea and can understand what others have said. Just remember the purpose of business messages is not to advertise

jargon
specialized terminology that professionals in some fields use when communicating with colleagues in the same field

redundancy
a phrase in which one word unnecessarily repeats an idea contained in an accompanying word (e.g., "exactly identical")

a knowledge of infrequently used words but to transmit a clear and tactful message. For the informal communication practiced in business, use simple words instead of more complicated words that have the same meaning.

Communicate Concisely

Concise communication includes all relevant details in the fewest possible words. Abraham Lincoln's two-minute *Gettysburg Address* is a premier example of concise communication. Mark Twain alluded to the skill needed to write concisely when he said, "I would have written a shorter book if I had had time."

Some executives have reported that they read memos that are two paragraphs long but may only skim or discard longer ones. Yet it's clear that this survival technique can lead to a vital message being discarded or misread. Concise writing is essential for workers struggling to handle an avalanche of information that often is read on the run on a Blackberry or iPhone. Concise messages save time and money for both the sender and the receiver, as the receiver's attention is directed toward the important details and is not distracted by excessive words and details.

The following techniques will produce concise messages:

- **Eliminate redundancies.** A **redundancy** is a phrase in which one word unnecessarily repeats an idea contained in an accompanying word. "Absolutely necessary" and "negative misfortune" are redundant because both words have the same meaning; only "necessary" and "misfortune" are needed. A few of the many redundancies in business writing are shown in the following list. Be conscious of redundancies in your speech and writing patterns.

Redundancies to Avoid

Needless repetition:	advance forward, it goes without saying, best ever, cash money, important essentials, each and every, dollar amount, pick and choose, past experience
Unneeded modifiers:	new innovations, personal friend, actual experience, brief summary, complete stop, collaborate together, disappear from sight, honest truth, trickle down, month of May, personal opinion, red in color, severe crisis, currently available
Repeated acronyms:	ATM machine, PIN number, SAT tests, SIC code

Redundancy is not to be confused with repetition used for emphasis. In a sentence or paragraph, you may need to use a certain word again. When repetition serves a specific purpose, it is not an error. Redundancy serves no purpose and *is* an error.

- **Use active voice to reduce the number of words.** Passive voice typically adds unnecessary words, such as prepositional phrases. Compare the sentence length in each of these examples:

Passive Voice	Active Voice
The project plans will be revised by the chief engineer.	The chief engineer will revise the project plans.
The flex-time policy will be updated by human resources.	Human resources will update the flex-time policy.

- **Review the main purpose of your writing and identify relevant details needed for the receiver to understand and take necessary action.** More information is not necessarily better information. You may be so involved and perhaps so enthusiastic about your message that you believe the receiver needs to know everything that you know. Or perhaps you just need to devote more time to audience analysis and empathy.

- **Eliminate clichés that are often wordy and not necessary to understand the message.** For example, "Thank you for your letter," "I am writing to," "May I take this opportunity," "It has come to my attention," and "We wish to inform you" only delay the major purpose of the message.

- **Do not restate ideas that are sufficiently implied.** Notice how the following sentences are improved when ideas are implied. The revised sentences are concise, yet the meaning is not affected.

Wordy	Concise
She <u>reviewed her notes and studied</u> for the CPA exam.	She studied for the CPA exam.
The accountant <u>reviewed</u> the financial statements and <u>made revisions</u>.	The accountant revised the financial statements.

- **Shorten sentences by using suffixes or prefixes, making changes in word form, or substituting precise words for phrases.** In the follow-

ing examples, the expressions in the right column provide useful techniques for saving space and being concise. However, the examples in the left column are not grammatically incorrect. Sometimes their use provides just the right emphasis.

Wordy	Concise
He was an employee <u>who used his time efficiently.</u>	He was an <u>efficient</u> employee.
She reviewed the report <u>in a very rapid manner.</u>	She reviewed the report <u>rapidly.</u>
He believes the new policy guidelines <u>to be of little value.</u>	He believes the new policy guidelines are <u>valueless.</u>
Sales staff <u>with high energy levels</u> . . .	<u>Energetic</u> sales staff . . .
. . . arranged in <u>chronological order.</u>	. . . arranged <u>chronologically</u> . . .

- **Use a compound adjective.** By using the compound adjective, you can reduce the number of words required to express your ideas and thus save the reader a little time.

Wordy	Concise
The corporation values employees <u>who use their time efficiently.</u>	The corporation values <u>efficient</u> employees.
Fred Wyler, who <u>has the most seniority</u> in the organization, is . . .	Fred Wyler, the <u>most senior</u> employee, is . . .
The department <u>will hold a planning meeting all day</u> on February 24.	The <u>all-day planning meeting</u> will be held February 24.

Project a Positive, Tactful Tone

Being adept at communicating negative information will give you the confidence you need to handle sensitive situations in a positive, constructive manner. The following suggestions reduce the sting of an unpleasant thought:

- **State ideas using positive language.** Rely mainly on positive words—words that speak of what can be done instead of what cannot be done, of the pleasant instead of the unpleasant. In each of the following pairs, both sentences are sufficiently clear, but the positive words in the improved sentences make the message more diplomatic and promote positive human relations.

Negative Tone	Positive Tone
<u>Don't forget</u> to submit your time and expense report.	Remember to submit your time and expense report.
We <u>cannot</u> complete your order without your email address.	Please supply your email address so that we can complete your order.
You <u>forgot</u> to complete your time card for the week.	Please complete your time card so that your pay check can be processed on time.

- **Avoid using second person when stating negative ideas.** Use second person for presenting pleasant ideas; use third person for presenting unpleasant ideas. Note the following examples:

Pleasant Idea (second person preferred)

You delivered a compelling presentation.	*The person will appreciate the emphasis placed on his or her excellent performance.*

Unpleasant Idea (third person preferred)

The supply order was incorrectly filled out.	*"You filled out the supply order incorrectly" directs undiplomatic attention to the person who made the error.*

- **Use passive voice to convey negative ideas.** Presenting an unpleasant thought emphatically (as active verbs do) makes human relations difficult. Compare the tone of the following negative thoughts written in active and passive voices:

Active Voice	Passive Voice (Preferred for Negative Ideas)
Shawn did not complete the loan application correctly.	The loan application needed some revision.
Shelly missed the deadline for proposal submission by a week.	The proposal was submitted a week after deadline.

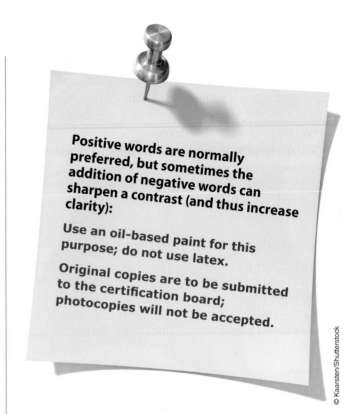

Positive words are normally preferred, but sometimes the addition of negative words can sharpen a contrast (and thus increase clarity):

Use an oil-based paint for this purpose; do not use latex.

Original copies are to be submitted to the certification board; photocopies will not be accepted.

Because the subject of each active sentence is the doer, the sentences are emphatic. Since the idea is negative, Melissa probably would appreciate being taken out of the picture. The passive voice sentences place more emphasis on the job than on who failed to complete it; they retain the essential ideas, but the ideas seem less irritating. For negative ideas, use passive voice.

Just as emphasis on negatives hinders human relations, emphasis on positives promotes human relations. Which sentence makes the positive idea more vivid?

Passive Voice	Active Voice (Preferred for Positive Ideas)
The proposal was submitted before the deadline.	Shelly submitted the proposal before the deadline.

Because "Shelly" is the subject of the active voice sentence, the receiver can easily envision the action. Pleasant thoughts deserve emphasis. For presenting positive ideas, use active voice.

- **Use the subjunctive mood.** Sometimes the tone of a message can be improved by switching to the subjunctive mood. **Subjunctive sentences** speak of a wish, necessity, doubt, or condition contrary to fact and use such conditional expressions as *I wish*, *as if*, *could*, *would*, and *might*. In the following examples, the sentence in the right column conveys a negative idea in positive language, which is more diplomatic than negative language.

Negative Tone	Subjunctive Mood Conveys Positive Tone
I <u>cannot</u> approve your request for a raise.	If money <u>were</u> available, I <u>would</u> approve your raise.
I <u>cannot</u> attend the planning meeting.	I <u>could</u> attend the planning meeting if the date <u>were</u> changed to next week.
I <u>don't believe</u> his statements about the product's efficiency.	I <u>wish</u> I <u>could</u> believe his statements about the product's efficiency.

Sentences in subjunctive mood often include a reason that makes the negative idea seem less objectionable and thus improves the tone. Tone is important, but clarity is even more important. The revised sentence in each of the preceding pairs sufficiently *implies* the unpleasant idea without stating it directly. If for any reason a writer or speaker suspects the implication is not sufficiently strong, a direct statement in negative terms is preferable.

- **Include a pleasant statement in the same sentence.** A pleasant idea is included in the following examples to improve the tone:

Negative Tone	Positive Tone
Your ability to meet deadlines is satisfactory.	While your ability to meet deadlines was satisfactory, <u>your work to motivate your team was excellent.</u>
Increased costs for fuel have negatively affected our bottom line.	Increased costs for fuel have negatively impacted our bottom line, but we hope changes in our electrical energy use <u>will help to offset</u> these increases.

To Recap

When adapting the message to the audience

☑ Focus on the receiver's point of view

☑ Communicate ethically and responsibly

☑ Build and protect goodwill

☑ Use contemporary language

☑ Use simple, informal words

☑ Communicate concisely

☑ Project a positive, tactful tone

subjunctive sentences *sentences that speak of a wish, necessity, doubt, or condition contrary to fact and employ such conditional expressions as I wish, as if, could, would, and might*

© Comstock Images/Jupiterimages

Step 4: Organizing the Message

After you have identified the specific ways you must adapt the message to your particular audience, you are ready to organize your message. In a discussion of communication, the word *organize* means "the act of dividing a topic into parts and arranging them in an appropriate sequence." Before undertaking this process, you must be convinced that the message is the right message—that it is complete, accurate, fair, reasonable, ethical, and logical. If it doesn't meet these standards, it should not be sent. Good organization and good writing or speaking cannot be expected to compensate for a bad decision.

If you organize and write simultaneously, the task seems hopelessly complicated. Writing is much easier if questions about the organization of the message are answered first: What is the purpose of the message, what is the receiver's likely reaction, and should the message begin with the main point? Once these decisions have been made, you can concentrate on expressing ideas effectively.

OBJECTIVE 4

Recognize the importance of organizing a message before writing the first draft.

Outline to Benefit the Sender and the Receiver

When a topic is divided into parts, some parts will be recognized as central ideas and the others as minor ideas (details). The process of identifying these ideas and arranging them in the right sequence is known as **outlining**. Outlining *before* communicating provides numerous benefits:

- **Encourages accuracy and brevity.** Outlining reduces the chance of leaving out an essential idea or including an unessential idea.

- **Permits concentration on one phase at a time.** Having focused separately on (a) the ideas that need to be included, (b) the distinction between major and minor ideas, and (c) the

outlining
the process of identifying central ideas and details and arranging them in the right sequence; should be completed prior to writing

sequence of ideas, total concentration can now be focused on the next challenge—expressing.

- **Saves time in structuring ideas.** With questions about which ideas to include and their proper sequence already answered, little time is lost in moving from one point to the next.

- **Provides a psychological lift.** The feeling of success gained in preparing the outline increases confidence that the next step—writing or speaking—will be successful, too.

- **Facilitates emphasis and de-emphasis.** Although each sentence makes its contribution to the message, some sentences need to stand out more vividly in the receiver's mind than others. An effective outline ensures that important points will appear in emphatic positions.

The preceding benefits derived from outlining are sender oriented. Because a message has been well outlined, receivers benefit, too:

- The message is more concise and accurate.
- Relationships between ideas are easier to distinguish and remember.
- Reactions to the message and its sender are more likely to be positive.

A receiver's reaction to a message is strongly influenced by the sequence in which ideas are presented. A beginning sentence or an ending sentence is in an emphatic position.

Sequence Ideas to Achieve Desired Goals

OBJECTIVE 5

Select the appropriate message pattern (deductive or inductive) for developing messages to achieve the desired response.

When planning your communication, you should strive for an outline that will serve you in much the same way a blueprint serves a builder or an itinerary serves a traveler. Organizing your message first will ensure that your ideas are presented clearly and logically and all vital components are included. To facilitate your determining an appropriate sequence for a business

© iStockphoto.com/drflet

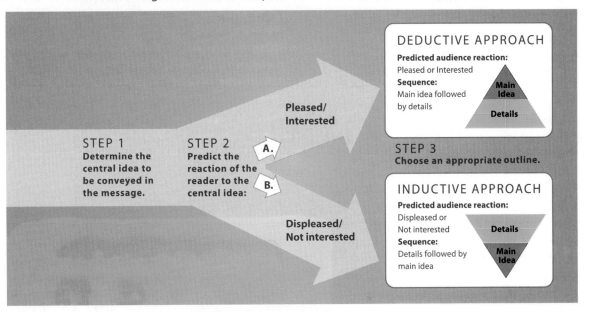

Figure 3-2 *Process of Selecting an Outline for a Spoken or Written Business Message*

DEDUCTIVE APPROACH

Predicted audience reaction:
Pleased or Interested
Sequence:
Main idea followed by details

Main Idea

Details

STEP 1
Determine the central idea to be conveyed in the message.

STEP 2
Predict the reaction of the reader to the central idea:

A.

B.

Pleased/ Interested

Displeased/ Not interested

STEP 3
Choose an appropriate outline.

INDUCTIVE APPROACH

Predicted audience reaction:
Displeased or Not interested
Sequence:
Details followed by main idea

Details

Main Idea

© Cengage Learning 2010

document or presentation, follow the three-step process illustrated in Figure 3-2. This process involves answering the following questions in this order:

1. **What is the central idea of the message?** Think about the *reason* you are writing or speaking—the first step in the communication process. What is your purpose—to extend a job offer, decline an invitation, or seek support for an innovative project? The purpose is the central idea of your message. You might think of it as a message condensed in one brief statement.

2. **What is the most likely receiver reaction to the message?** Ask, "If I were the one receiving the message I am preparing to send, what would *my* reaction be?" Because you would react with pleasure to good news and displeasure to bad news, you can reasonably assume a receiver's reaction would be similar. By considering anticipated receiver reaction, you build goodwill with the receiver. Almost every message will fit into one of four categories of anticipated receiver reaction, as shown in Figure 3-2: (1) pleasure, (2) displeasure, (3) interest but neither pleasure nor displeasure, or (4) no interest.

3. **In view of the predicted receiver reaction, should the central idea be listed first in the outline or should it be listed as one of the last items?** When a message begins with the major idea, the sequence of ideas is called **deductive**. When a message withholds the major idea until accompanying details and explanations have been presented, the sequence is called **inductive**.

Consider the receiver to determine whether to use the inductive or deductive sequence. If a receiver might be antagonized by the main idea in a deductive message, lead up to the main idea by making the message inductive. If a sender wants to encourage receiver involvement (to generate a little concern about where the details are leading), the inductive approach is recommended. Inductive organization can be especially effective if the main idea confirms the conclusion the receiver has drawn from the preceding details—a cause is worthy of support, a job applicant should be interviewed, a product/service should be selected, and so on. As you learn in later chapters about writing letters, memos, and email messages and about planning spoken communications, you will comprehend the benefits of using the appropriate outline for each receiver reaction:

deductive
a message in which the major idea precedes the details

inductive
a message in which the major idea follows the details

Deductive Order (main idea first)	Inductive Order (details first)
When the message will *please* the receiver	When the message will *displease* the receiver
When the message is *routine* (will not please nor displease)	When the receiver *might not be interested* (will need to be persuaded)

For determining the sequence of minor ideas that accompany the major idea, the following bases for idea sequence are common:

- **Time.** When writing a report or email message about a series of events or a process, paragraphs proceed from the first step through the last step.
- **Space.** If a report is about geographic areas, ideas can proceed from one area to the next until all areas have been discussed.
- **Familiarity.** If a topic is complicated, the presentation can begin with a known or easy-to-understand point and proceed to progressively more difficult points.

- **Importance.** In analytical reports in which major decision-making factors are presented, the factors can be presented in order of most important to least important, or vice versa.
- **Value.** If a presentation involves major factors with monetary values, paragraphs can proceed from those with greatest values to those with least values, or vice versa.

The same organizational patterns are recommended for written and spoken communication. These patterns are applicable in email messages, blogs, letters, memos, and reports.

Meeting Diverse Audiences' Needs

McDonald's Corp. is the world's most successful fast-food enterprise, and one of the reasons is its ability to market effectively to diverse audiences. In fact, it has won awards for its work with multicultural audiences from the Association of National Advertisers. One award was given to the franchise giant for its marketing to African-American audiences. In the spot, "Mom's Trust," a little girl asks her father, who takes her to McDonald's and buys her mother flowers, what makes him happy, and he replies, "Making my girls happy." The spot was a way of connecting with mothers and of including an African-American male, who is often omitted or ignored in advertising, said Priscilla Aviles Jamison, senior director, McDonald's U.S. marketing ethnic brands/creative. McDonald's has also successfully targeted Hispanic audiences with its television marketing campaigns, resulting in double-digit sales increases.[12]

© Susan Van Etten

© tatniz/Shutterstock

© Monkey Business Images/Shutterstock

4LTR Press solutions are designed for today's learners through the continuous feedback of students like you. Tell us what you think about **BCOM4** and help us improve the learning experience for future students.

YOUR FEEDBACK MATTERS.

Complete the Speak Up survey in CourseMate at www.cengagebrain.com

 Follow us at www.facebook.com/4ltrpress

Preparing Spoken and Written Messages

In Chapter 3, you learned about the importance of following a systematic process to develop business messages. The applications in Chapter 3 guided you in developing a clear, logical plan for your message that focuses on the needs of the receiver (Steps 1–4). Effectively capturing your ideas for various business communication situations involves skillful use of language and careful attention to accuracy and readability issues—the remaining two steps in this important process are shown in Figure 4-1.

Prepare the First Draft

Once you have determined whether the message should be presented deductively (main idea first) or inductively (explanation and details first) and have planned the logical sequence of minor points, you are ready to begin composing the message.

Normally, writing rapidly (with intent to rewrite certain portions, if necessary) is better than slow, deliberate writing (with intent to avoid any need for rewriting portions). The latter approach can be frustrating and can reduce the quality of the finished work. Time is wasted in thinking of one way to express an idea, discarding it either before or after it is written, waiting for new inspiration, and rereading preceding sentences.

⊠ OBJECTIVE 1

Apply techniques for developing effective sentences and unified and coherent paragraphs.

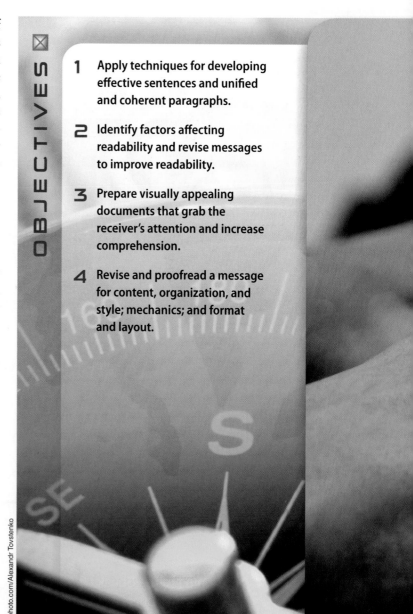

iStockphoto.com/Alexandr Tovstenko

O B J E C T I V E S

1   Apply techniques for developing effective sentences and unified and coherent paragraphs.

2   Identify factors affecting readability and revise messages to improve readability.

3   Prepare visually appealing documents that grab the receiver's attention and increase comprehension.

4   Revise and proofread a message for content, organization, and style; mechanics; and format and layout.

Figure 4-1 *Process for Planning and Preparing Spoken and Written Messages*

STEP 1	STEP 2	STEP 3	STEP 4	STEP* 5	STEP* 6
Determine the purpose and select an appropriate channel	Envision the audience	Adapt the message to the audience's needs and concerns	Organize the message	Prepare the first draft	Revise and proofread for accuracy and desired impact

*You focused on the planning process (Steps 1–4) in Chapter 3; you will learn to prepare the message (Steps 5–6) in this chapter.

© Cengage Learning 2010

Concentrating on getting your ideas down as quickly as you can is an efficient approach to writing. During this process, remember that you are preparing a draft and not the final copy. If you are composing at the computer, you can quickly and easily revise your draft throughout the composition process. This seamless approach to writing allows you to continue to improve your working draft until the moment you are ready to submit the final copy. Numerous electronic writing tools are available, and technology will continue to unfold to enhance the writing process.

Craft Powerful Sentences

Well-developed sentences help the receiver understand the message clearly and react favorably to the writer or speaker. In this section, you will learn about predominant use of active voice and emphasis of important points, which affect the clarity and human relations of your message.

Rely on Active Voice

Business communicators normally use active voice more heavily than passive voice because active voice conveys ideas more vividly. In sentences in which the subject is the *doer* of action, the verbs are called *active*. In sentences in which the subject is the *receiver* of action, the verbs are called *passive*. Review the differences in the impact of **passive voice** and **active voice**:

Using active voice makes the subject the actor.

© iStockphoto.com/Blaz Erzetic

Passive Voice	Active Voice
<u>Press releases are sent</u> to national media outlets on a daily basis from our corporate communication office.	<u>Our corporate communication office sends</u> press releases to national media outlets on a daily basis.

The active sentence invites the receiver to see the communication office as actively engaged with the media, while the passive sentence draws attention to the press releases. Using active voice makes the subject the actor, which makes the idea easier to understand. Sentences written using passive voice give receivers a less distinct picture. In the passive sentence, the receiver becomes aware that something was done to the press releases, but it does not reveal who did it.

Even when a passive sentence contains additional words to reveal the doer, the imagery is less distinct than it would be if the sentence were active: *Press releases created by the corporate communications staff are sent daily to national media outlets.* "Press releases" gets the most attention because it is the subject. The sentence seems to let a receiver know the *result* of action before revealing the doer; therefore, the sentence is less emphatic.

Although active voice conveys ideas more vividly, passive voice is useful for the following purposes:

- Concealing the doer. ("The reports have been compiled.")
- Placing more emphasis on *what* was done and who or what it was *done to* than on who *did* it. ("The reports have been compiled by our sales representatives.")
- Subordinating an unpleasant thought or avoiding finger-pointing. ("The Shipping Department has not been notified of this delay" rather than "You have not notified the Shipping Department of this delay.")

Emphasize Important Ideas

A landscape artist wants some features in a picture to stand out boldly and others to get little attention. A musician sounds some notes loudly and others softly. Likewise, a writer or speaker wants some ideas to be *emphasized* and others to be *de-emphasized*. Normally, pleasant and important ideas should be emphasized; unpleasant and insignificant ideas should be de-emphasized. Emphasis techniques include sentence structure, repetition, words that label, position, and space and format.

passive voice
when the subject of a sentence is the receiver of an action

active voice
when the subject of a sentence is the doer of an action

Sentence Structure For emphasis, place an idea in a simple sentence. The simple sentence in the following example has one independent clause. Because no other idea competes with it for attention, this idea is emphasized.

Simple Sentence Is More Emphatic	Compound Sentence Is Less Emphatic
Lisa works with customers daily.	Lisa works with customers daily, but she would prefer focusing on administrative duties.

For emphasis, place an idea in an independent clause; for de-emphasis, place an idea in a dependent clause. In the following compound sentence, the idea of taking a job is in an independent clause. Because an independent clause makes sense if the rest of the sentence is omitted, an independent clause is more emphatic than a dependent clause. In the complex sentence, the idea of taking a job is in a dependent clause. By itself, the clause would not make complete sense. Compared with the independent clause that follows ("Nicole really preferred . . ."), the idea in the dependent clause is de-emphasized.

Compound Sentence Is More Emphatic	Complex Sentence Is Less Emphatic
Lisa works with customers daily, but she would prefer focusing on administrative duties.	Although she works with customers on a daily basis, Lisa would prefer focusing on administrative duties.

Repetition To emphasize a word, let it appear more than once in a sentence. For example, a clever advertisement by OfficeMax used the word *stuff* repeatedly to describe generically several types of office-supply needs ranging from paper clips to color copies, and then ended succinctly with "OfficeMax . . .for your office stuff." Likewise, in the following example, "reception" receives more emphasis when the word is repeated.

Less Emphatic	More Emphatic
Her promotion was well received because of . . .	Her promotion was well received; this reception is attributed to . . .

Words that Label For emphasis or de-emphasis, use words that label ideas as significant or insignificant.

Note the labeling words used in the following examples to emphasize or de-emphasize an idea:

But most important of all . . .
A less significant aspect was . . .

Position To emphasize a word or an idea, position it first or last in a sentence, clause, paragraph, or presentation. Note the additional emphasis placed on the words *positive reception* and *disappointment* in the examples in the right column because these words appear as the *first* or the *last* words in their clauses.

Less Emphatic	More Emphatic
Her hard work contributed to the <u>positive reception</u> for her promotion; otherwise, <u>disappointment</u> may have been the result.	A <u>positive reception</u> resulted from her hard work; <u>disappointment</u> may have resulted without it.
Her promotion was <u>well received</u> because of her hard work; without that, <u>disappointment</u> may have been the result.	Her promotion was <u>well received</u>; without her hard work, it may have been a <u>disappointment</u>.

In paragraphs, the first and last words are in particularly emphatic positions. An idea that deserves emphasis can be placed in either position, but an idea that does not deserve emphasis can be placed in the middle of a long paragraph. The word *I*, which is frequently overused in messages, is especially noticeable if it appears as the first word. *I* is more noticeable if it appears as the first word in *every* paragraph. Avoid using the word *However* as the first word in a paragraph if the preceding paragraph is neutral or positive. These words imply that the next idea will be negative. Unless the purpose is to place emphasis on negatives, such words as *denied*, *rejected*, and *disappointed*, should not appear as the last words in a paragraph.

Likewise, the central idea of a written or spoken report appears in the introduction (the beginning) and the conclusion (the end). Good transition sentences synthesize ideas at the end of each major division.

Space and Format The various divisions of a report or spoken presentation are not expected to be of equal length, but an extraordinary amount of space devoted to a topic attaches special significance to that topic. Similarly, a topic that receives an especially small amount of space is de-emphasized. The manner in which information is physically arranged affects the emphasis it receives and consequently the overall impact of the message.

Develop Coherent Paragraphs

Well-constructed sentences are combined into paragraphs that discuss a portion of the topic being discussed. To write effective paragraphs, you must learn to (a) develop deductive or inductive paragraphs consistently, (b) link ideas to achieve coherence, (c) keep paragraphs unified, and (d) vary sentence and paragraph length.

Position the Topic Sentence Appropriately

Typically, paragraphs contain one sentence that identifies the portion of the topic being discussed and presents the central idea. That sentence is commonly called a **topic sentence**. For example, consider operating instructions prepared for company-owned GPS navigation systems. The overall topic is how to get satisfactory performance from the device. One portion of that topic is setup; another portion (paragraph) discusses operation; and so forth. Within each paragraph, one sentence serves a special function. Sentences that list the steps can appear as one paragraph, perhaps with steps numbered as follows:

To set up the system, take the following steps:

1. *Connect . . .*
2. *Go to menu settings to . . .*

In this illustration, the paragraphs are **deductive**; that is, the topic sentence *precedes* details. When topic sentences *follow* details, the paragraphs are **inductive**. As discussed previously, the receiver's likely reaction to the main idea (pleased, displeased, interested, not interested) aids in selecting the appropriate sequence.

When the subject matter is complicated and the details are numerous, paragraphs sometimes begin with a main idea, follow with details, and end with a summarizing sentence. But the main idea might not be in the first sentence; the idea could need a preliminary statement. Receivers appreciate consistency in the placement of topic sentences. Once they catch on to the writer or speaker's pattern, they know where to look for main ideas.

These suggestions seldom apply to the first and last sentences of letters, memos, and email messages. Such sentences frequently appear as single-sentence paragraphs. But for reports and long paragraphs of letters, strive for paragraphs that are consistently deductive or inductive. Regardless of which is selected, topic sentences are clearly linked with details that precede or follow.

Link Ideas to Achieve Coherence

Careful writers use coherence techniques to keep receivers from experiencing abrupt changes in thought. Although the word **coherence** is used sometimes to mean "clarity" or "understandability," it is used throughout this text to mean "cohesion." If writing or speaking is coherent, the sentences stick together; each sentence is in some way linked to the preceding sentences. Avoid abrupt changes in thought, and link each sentence to a preceding sentence.

The following techniques for linking sentences are common:

1. **Repeat a word that was used in the preceding sentence.** The second sentence in the following example is an obvious continuation of the idea presented in the preceding sentence.

    . . . to take responsibility for the decision. This responsibility can be shared . . .

topic sentence
a sentence that identifies the portion of the topic being discussed and presents the central idea of the paragraph

deductive paragraph
a paragraph in which the topic sentence precedes the details

inductive paragraph
a paragraph in which the topic sentence follows the details

coherence
cohesion, so that each sentence in some way is linked to the preceding sentences

© Inspirestock/Jupiterimages

2. **Use a pronoun that represents a noun used in the preceding sentence.** Because "it" means "responsibility," the second sentence below is linked directly with the first.

   . . . to take this responsibility. It can be shared . . .

3. **Use connecting words.** Examples include *however, therefore, yet, nevertheless, consequently, also,* and *in addition.* "However" implies "We're continuing with the same topic, just moving into a different phase." Remember, though, that good techniques can be overused. Unnecessary connectors are space consuming and distracting. Usually they can be spotted (and crossed out) in proofreading.

   . . . to take this responsibility. However, few are willing to . . .

Just as sentences within a paragraph must link, paragraphs within a document must also link. Unless a writer or speaker is careful, the move from one major topic to the next will seem abrupt. A good transition sentence can bridge the gap between the two topics by summing up the preceding topic and leading a receiver to expect the next topic:

Cost factors, then, seemed prohibitive until efficiency factors were investigated.

This sentence could serve as a transition between the "Cost" and "Efficiency" division headings. Because a transition sentence comes at the end of one segment and before the next, it emphasizes the central idea of the preceding segment and confirms the relationship of the two segments. While transition sentences are helpful if properly used, they can be overused. For most reports, transition sentences before major headings are sufficient. Normally, transition sentences before subheadings are unnecessary.

Keep Paragraphs Unified

Receivers expect the first paragraph of a message to introduce a topic, additional paragraphs to discuss it, and a final paragraph to tie all of the paragraphs together. The middle paragraphs should be arranged in a systematic sequence, and the end must be linked easily to some word or idea presented in the beginning. The effect of a message that is *not* unified is like that of an incomplete circle or a picture with one element obviously missing.

- A unified email message, letter, memo, or report covers its topic adequately but does not include extraneous material. The document should have a beginning sentence appropriate for the expected receiver reaction, paragraphs that present the bulk of the message, and an ending sentence that is an appropriate closing for the message presented.

- A unified report or presentation begins with an introduction that identifies the topic, reveals the thesis, and previews upcoming points. The introduction often includes some background, sources of information, and the method of treating data. Between the beginning and the ending, a unified report should have paragraphs arranged in a systematic sequence. A summary or conclusion brings all major points together.

Vary Sentence and Paragraph Length

Sentences of short or average length are easy to read and preferred for communicating clearly. However, keeping *all* sentences short is undesirable because the message might sound monotonous, unrealistic, or elementary. A two-word sentence is acceptable; so is a 60-word sentence—if it is clear. Just as sentences should vary in length, they should also vary in structure. Some complex or compound sentences should be included with simple sentences.

Variety is just as desirable in paragraph length as it is in sentence length. A paragraph can be from one line in length to a dozen lines or more. However, just as with sentence length, average paragraph length also should be kept short, as appropriate to the document type:

- Paragraphs in letters, memos, and email messages are typically shorter than paragraphs in business reports.

- First and last paragraphs are normally short (one to four lines), and other paragraphs are normally no longer than *six lines*. A short first paragraph is more inviting to read than a long first paragraph, and a short last paragraph enables a writer to emphasize parting thoughts.

- The space between paragraphs is a welcome resting spot. Long paragraphs are difficult to read and make a message appear uninviting. Paragraph length will vary depending on the complexity of the subject matter. However, as a general rule paragraphs should be no longer than *eight to ten lines*. This length usually allows enough space to include a topic sentence and three or four supporting statements. If the topic cannot be discussed in this space, divide the topic into additional paragraphs.

To observe the effect large sections of unbroken text have on the overall appeal of a document, examine the memos in Figure 4-2 on the next page. Without question, the memo with the short, easy-to-read paragraphs is more inviting to read than the memo with one bulky paragraph.

© Cengage Learning 2010

Figure 4-2 Contrast the Readability and Appeal of Bulky (left) versus Broken (right) Text

New Message	
To:	All employees
From:	Mary Kendall Welch, HR Manager
Subject:	Training Available through Podcasts

Everyone,

Can you image the convenience of upgrading your management skills as you make the daily commute to your office? It's possible with podcast training set to begin next week that includes an intriguing segment on leadership communication. All required training seminars, previously available via streaming video over the company intranet, are now available to be downloaded to your iPod. To encourage you to take advantage of this innovative learning method, you can purchase the latest generation iPod for $100—a substantial discount to the retail price. Simply order directly from the vendor's website and input LC413 for the discount code. Call technology support should you need assistance in downloading your first podcast. When you're not advancing your management skills to the next level, use your iPod to enjoy your favorite tunes and movies.

New Message	
To:	All employees
From:	Mary Kendall Welch, HR Manager
Subject:	Training Available through Podcasts

Everyone,

Can you imagine the convenience of upgrading your management skills as you make the daily commute to your office? It's possible with podcast training set to begin next week that includes an intriguing segment on leadership communication.

All required training seminars, previously available via streaming video over the company intranet, are now available to be downloaded to your iPod. To encourage you to take advantage of this innovative learning method, you can purchase the latest generation iPod for $100—a substantial discount to the retail price. Simply order directly from the vendor's website and input LC413 for the discount code.

Call technology support should you need assistance in downloading your first podcast. When you're not advancing your management skills to the next level, use your iPod to enjoy your favorite tunes and movies.

Although variety is a desirable quality, it should not be achieved at the expense of consistency. Using *I* in one part of a message and then without explanation switching to *we* is inadvisable. Using the past tense in one sentence and the present tense in another sentence creates variety at the expense of consistency—unless the shift is required to indicate actual changes in time. Unnecessary changes from active to passive voice and from third to first person are also discouraged.

Revise and Proofread

The speed and convenience of today's electronic communication have caused many communicators to confuse informality with sloppiness. Sloppy messages contain misspellings, grammatical errors, unappealing and incorrect formats, and confusing content—all of which create a negative impression of the writer and the company and affect the receiver's ability to understand the message. Some experts believe the increased use of email is leading to bosses becoming ruder. To combat against the harsh tone that often sets in when managers must respond to 300 to 500 emails weekly, Unilever is providing writing training and urging staff to think before they press the send button.[1]

As the sender, you are responsible for evaluating the effectiveness of each message you prepare. You must not use informality as an excuse to be sloppy. Instead, take one consultant's advice: "You can still be informal and not be sloppy. You can be informal and correct."[2] Take a good hard look at the messages you prepare. Commit to adjusting your message to the audience, designing appealing documents that are easily read, and following a systematic proofreading process to ensure error-free messages. This effort could save you from being embarrassed or jeopardizing your credibility.

☒ OBJECTIVE 2

Identify factors affecting readability and revise messages to improve readability.

Improve Readability

Although sentences are arranged in a logical sequence and are written coherently, the

To further support your writing, consider using Bullfighter, a computer program that helps business writers reduce jargon, corporate speak, and wordiness. Developed by the authors of Why Business People Speak Like Idiots, this free download is available at http://fightthebull.com and works as a convenient add-in to Microsoft Word and PowerPoint.

be understood. Despite simple language and short sentences, the message can be distorted by imprecise words, biased language, jargon, and translations that ignore cultural interpretations, to name just a few. The value of calculating a readability measure lies in the feedback you gain about average length of sentences and the difficulty of the words. Revise and recalculate the readability index and continue revising until you feel the reading level is appropriate for the intended audience.

receiver might find reading the sentences difficult. Several programs have been developed to measure the reading difficulty of your writing. Electronic tools aid you in making computations and identifying changes that will improve readability.

Understand Readability Measures

The grammar and style checker feature of leading word processing software calculates readability measures to aid you in writing for quick and easy reading and listening. The Fog index, a popular readability index developed by Robert Gunning, and the Flesch-Kincaid Grade Level calculator available in Microsoft Word consider the length of sentences and the difficulty of words to produce the approximate grade level at which a person must read in order to understand the material. For example, a grade level of 10 indicates a person needs to be able to read at the tenth-grade level to understand the material. Fortunately, you don't have to calculate readability manually, but understanding the manual calculation of the Fog index will illustrate clearly how sentence length and difficulty of words affect readability calculations and guide you in adapting messages.

Trying to write at the exact grade level of the receiver is not advised. You may not know the exact grade level, and even those who have earned advanced degrees appreciate writing they can read and understand quickly and easily. Also, writing a passage with a readability index appropriate for the audience does not guarantee the message will

The grammar and style feature in word processing programs also locates grammatical errors, including misspellings and common usage errors, such as the use of fragments, run-on sentences, subject-verb disagreement, passive voice, double words, and split infinitives. Because it can only guess at the structure of a sentence and then apply a rigid set of rules, a grammar and style checker, like spell-check, must be used cautiously. It is not a reliable substitute for a human editor who has an effective writing style and is familiar with the rules the software displays. Allow the software to flag misspellings and writing errors as you write, accept or reject the suggested changes based on your knowledge of effective writing, and use the readability measures to adjust your writing levels appropriately as shown in Figure 4-3 on the next page.

Apply Visual Enhancements to Improve Readability

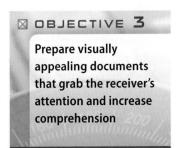

OBJECTIVE 3

Prepare visually appealing documents that grab the receiver's attention and increase comprehension

The vast amount of information created in today's competitive global market poses a challenge to you as a business writer. You must learn to create visually appealing documents that entice a receiver to read

Figure 4-3 *Improving Readability through Cautious Use of a Grammar and Style Checker*

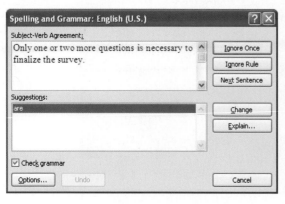

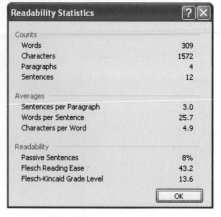

rather than discard your message. Additionally, an effective design will enable you to highlight important information for maximum attention and to transition a receiver smoothly through sections of a long, complex document. These design techniques can be applied easily using word processing software. However, add visual enhancements only when they aid in comprehension. Overuse will cause your document to appear cluttered and will defeat your purpose of creating an appealing, easy-to-read document.

Enumerations

To emphasize units in a series, place a number, letter, or bullet before each element. Words preceded by numbers, bullets, or letters attract the receiver's special attention and are easier to locate when the page is reviewed.

Original	Highlighted
To complete the process, please read the agreement, sign the form, and fax it to the coordinator.	To complete the process, please 1. Read the agreement 2. Sign the form 3. Fax it to the coordinator

Enumerated or Bulleted Lists

Writers often want to save space; however, cluttered text is unappealing and difficult to read. *Chunking*—a desktop publishing term—is an answer to the problem. Chunking involves breaking down information into easily digestible pieces. It's the communication equivalent of Butterfinger® BBs rather than the whole candy bar. The added white space divides the information into blocks, makes the page look more organized, and increases retention by 50 percent.[3]

Enumerated or bulleted lists can be used to chunk and add even greater visual impact to items in a series. Items appear on separate lines with numerals, letters, or various types of bullets (•, ◊, □, ✓, and so on) at the beginning. Multiple-line items often are separated by a blank line. This design creates more white space, which isolates the items from other text, and demands attention. Bullets are typically preferred over numerals unless the sequence of the items in the series is critical (e.g., steps in a procedure that must be completed in the correct order). In the following excerpt from a long analytical report, the four supporting reasons for a conclusion are highlighted in a bulleted list:

Original	Highlighted
Although there are some disadvantages that should not be overlooked, virtual teams provide many benefits, including cost savings from reduced travel, convenient access to team members, time savings and greater productivity, and the potential for greater creativity and better solutions.	Although there are some disadvantages that should not be overlooked, virtual teams provide many benefits, including • cost savings from reduced travel • convenient access to team members • time savings and greater productivity • potential for greater creativity and better solutions

Headings

Headings are signposts that direct the receiver from one section of the document to another. Studies have shown that readers find documents with headings easier to grasp and that they are more motivated to pay attention to the text, even in a short document such as a half-page warranty.[4] You'll find that organizing the content of various types of documents with logical, well-written headings will make the documents more readable and appealing. Follow these general guidelines for writing effective headings:

- Compose brief headings that make a connection with the receiver, giving clear cues as to the usefulness of the information (e.g., "How Do I Apply?"). Consider using questions rather than noun phrases to let readers know they are reading the information they need (i.e., choose "Who Is Eligible to Apply?" rather than "Eligible Loan Participants").[5] Consider talking headings that reveal the conclusions reached in the following discussion rather than general topic headings. For example, "Costs Are Prohibitive" is more emphatic than "Cost Factors."

- Strive for parallel structure of readings within a section. For example, mixing descriptive phrases with questions requires additional mental effort and distracts readers who expect parallel writing.

- Follow a hierarchy, with major headings receiving more attention than minor headings or paragraph headings. To draw more attention to a major heading, center it and use a heavier, larger typestyle or brighter text color.

Tables and Graphs

Tables and graphs are used to simplify and clarify information and to add variety to long sections of dense text. The clearly labeled rows and columns in a table organize large amounts of specific numeric data and facilitate analysis. Graphics such as pie, line, and bar charts visually depict relationships within the data; they provide quick estimates rather than specific information.

Lines and Borders

Horizontal and vertical lines can be added to partition text or to focus attention on a specific line(s). For example, a thin line followed by a thick line effectively separates the identification and qualifications sections of a résumé. Placing a border around a paragraph or section of text sets that information apart; adding shading inside the box adds greater impact. For example, a pull-quote format might spotlight a testimonial from a satisfied customer in a sales letter, important dates to remember in a memorandum, or a section of a document that must be completed and returned.

Relevant Images

A variety of interesting shapes can be used to highlight information and add appeal. Examples include creating a rectangular callout box highlighting a key idea with an arrow pointing to a specific number in a table, surrounding a title with a shaded oval for added impact, and using built-in designs to illustrate a process, cycle, hierarchy, or other relationship. Clip art or photos can also be added to reinforce an idea and add visual appeal. The following example from the Plain Language website shows how visual communication can convey important safety information more effectively than words can.

Before

This is a multipurpose passenger vehicle which will handle and maneuver differently from an ordinary passenger car, in driving conditions which may occur on streets and highways and off road. As with other vehicles of this type, if you make sharp turns or abrupt maneuvers, the vehicle may roll over or may go out of control and crash. You should read driving guidelines and instructions in the Owner's Manual, and WEAR YOUR SEAT BELTS AT ALL TIMES.

After

⚠ WARNING: HIGHER ROLLOVER RISK

Avoid Abrupt Maneuvers and Excessive Speed.

Always Buckle Up.

See Owner's Manual For Further Information.

Battling to manage an avalanche of information, the recipients of your messages will appreciate your extra effort to create an easy-to-read, appealing document. These fundamental techniques will be invaluable as you enhance printed documents such as letters, memos, reports, agendas, handouts, and minutes for meetings.

Use Systematic Procedures for Revising and Proofreading

⊠ **OBJECTIVE 4**

Revise and proofread a message for content, organization, and style; mechanics; and format and layout.

Errors in writing and mechanics may seem isolated, but the truth is, proofreading *is* important. You don't have to look far to see silly typos or obvious instances of writers relying only on the computer spell-check. The classifieds in a small-town newspaper advertised "fully fascinated and spade damnation puppies." The advertisement was for fully vaccinated and spayed Dalmatian puppies. These errors clearly illustrate how spell-check can fail, but goofs such as this one are not limited to small-town newspapers.

It was not a spelling error but a simple transposition in a telephone number that created an unbelievably embarrassing situation for a telecommunications giant. AT&T customers calling to redeem points earned in a True Rewards program were connected to pay-by-the-minute erotic phone entertainment.[6] Mistakes ranging from printing ordinary typos to running entirely erroneous ads forced newspapers to refund $10.6 million to dissatisfied advertisers and to print $10.5 million in free, make-good ads.[7] The University of California at San Diego inadvertently sent an acceptance email message to all 28,000 students it had rejected, raising their hopes only to dash them when the mistake was discovered and corrected.[8] Each of these actual mistakes illustrates that inattention to proofreading can be potentially embarrassing and incredibly expensive.

Following systematic revision procedures will help you produce error-free documents that reflect positively on the company and you. Using the procedures that follow, you will see that effective proofreading must be done several times, each time for a specific purpose.

Follow these simple procedures to produce a finished product that is free of errors in content, organization, and style; mechanics; and format and layout:

1. **Use spell-check to locate simple keying errors and repeated words.** When the software cannot guess the correct spelling based on your incor-rect attempt, you will need to consult a dictionary, other printed source, or online reference such as the Merriam-Webster online language center at http://m-w.com.

2. **Proofread the document onscreen, concentrating first on errors in content, organization, and style.** To locate errors, ask the following questions:

   - **Content.** Is the information complete? Have I included all the details the receiver needs to understand the message and to take necessary action? Is the information accurate? Have I checked the accuracy of any calculations, dates, names, addresses, and numbers? Have words been omitted?

   - **Organization.** Is the main idea presented appropriately, based on the receiver's likely reaction (deductive or inductive organization)? Are supporting ideas presented in a logical order?

   - **Style.** Is the message clear? Will the receiver interpret the information correctly? Is the message concise and written at an appropriate level for the receiver? Does the message reflect a considerate, caring attitude and focus primarily on the receiver's needs? Does the message treat the receiver honestly and ethically?

3. **Proofread a second time concentrating on mechanical errors.** You are searching for potentially damaging errors that spell-check cannot detect. These problem areas include:

   - **Grammar, capitalization, punctuation, number usage, and abbreviations.** Review the grammatical principles presented in the appendix if necessary.

   - **Word substitutions.** Check the proper use of words such as *your* and *you* and words that sound alike (*there*, *they're*, or *their*; *affect* or *effect*).

   - **Parts of the document other than the body.** Proofread the entire document. Errors often appear in the opening and closing sections of documents because writers typically begin proofreading at the first paragraph.

4. **Display the document in print preview mode and edit for format and layout.** Follow these steps to be certain the document adheres to appropriate business formats and is visually appealing:

   - Format according to a conventional format. Compare your document to the conventional business formats shown on your Style and Formatting cards and make any revisions. Are all standard parts of the document included

and presented in an acceptable format? Are all necessary special parts (e.g., attention line, enclosure) included? Does the message begin on the correct line? Should the right margin be justified or jagged?

- Be sure numbered items are in the correct order. Inserting and deleting text might have changed the order of these items.

- Evaluate the visual impact of the document. Could you increase the readability of long, uninterrupted blocks of text by using enumerated or indented lists, headings, or graphic borders or lines? Would adding images or varying print styles add visual appeal? View web documents on several different browsers to assure readability and appeal.

- Be certain the document is signed or initialed (depending on the document). Ensure that email messages are addressed to the appropriate person(s).

5. **Print a draft copy and proofread a third time if the document is nonroutine and complex.** Read from *right to left* to reduce your reading speed, allowing you to concentrate deliberately on each word. If a document is extremely important, you might consider reading the document aloud, spelling names and noting capitalization and punctuation, while another person verifies the copy.

6. **Print written documents on high-quality paper.**

The message in Figure 4-4 on the next page has been revised for (1) content, organization, and style; (2) mechanics; and (3) format and layout. Study the revisions made using the track-changes feature in word processing software. The commentary makes it easy to see how revising this draft improved the document's quality.

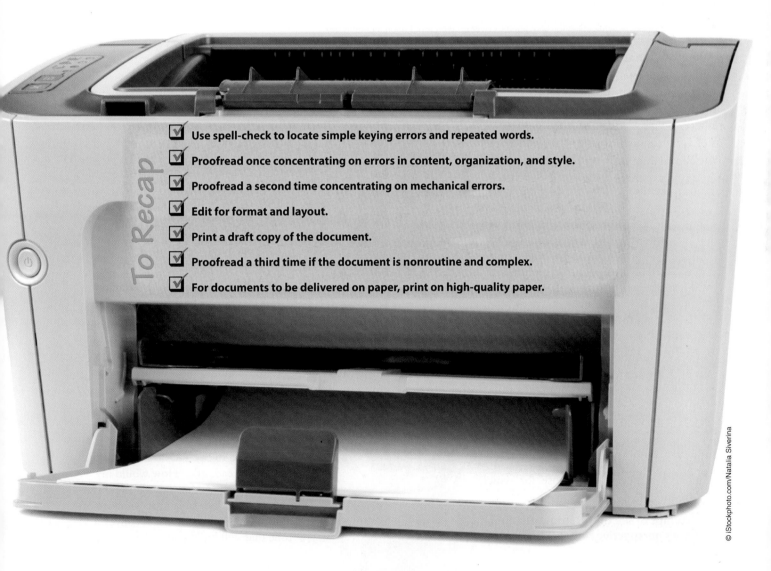

To Recap

- ☑ Use spell-check to locate simple keying errors and repeated words.
- ☑ Proofread once concentrating on errors in content, organization, and style.
- ☑ Proofread a second time concentrating on mechanical errors.
- ☑ Edit for format and layout.
- ☑ Print a draft copy of the document.
- ☑ Proofread a third time if the document is nonroutine and complex.
- ☑ For documents to be delivered on paper, print on high-quality paper.

Figure 4-4 Rough Draft of a Letter (excerpt)

September 8, 2012
Fax Transmission

Francis Fordham, President
Happy Cupcakes
2054 State Street
Boise, ~~Idaho~~ ID 83301

Dear Mr. Fordham:

Congratulations on the recent opening of your innovative cupcake bakery and wine bar! We are excited to learn of your interest in the Lexor commercial oven line _and believe you will find a model that meets your exact needs._

Available with radiant, direct fired convection and hybrid radiant/convection heating, Lexor ovens are highly energy efficient owing to both heating system design and their low surface area to volume ratio. Fully automated, they incorporate a user-friendly touch-screen interface, plus full-length viewing doors for visual inspection of the bake at every level and easy access for cleaning and maintenance.

Lexor ovens provide enormous advantages over conventional oven technologies, including

- Improved product quality and consistency. The ultra-compact design is based on a transport technology where pans are conveyed horizontally through the oven via a vertical 'S' configuration.

- Reduced footprint. Typically one-tenth the footprint of an equivalent tunnel oven, Lexor ovens offer a crucial advantage in environments where production floor space is at a premium ~~and.~~

- Superior flexibility. Lexor ovens offer superior flexibility, allowing product changes by simply changing pans, and ~~ancillary~~ _additional_ tooling.

Ms. Fordham, we are eager to schedule your visit to our nearby showroom to introduce our product line. At your convenience, please review the enclosed brochures and I will call you next week to schedule an appointment.

Annotations:
- Adds mailing notation.
- Uses two-letter state abbreviation.
- Corrects spelling of name.
- Adds smooth transition to next paragraph.
- Bullet list for emphasis and conciseness.
- Eliminates unnecessary comma.
- Replace with simple word for clarity.

Errors Undetectable by Spell-Check
Verify spelling of receiver's name, "Fordham."

Correct proofreading error.

Check correctness of word substitutions: "to" for "too" and "your" for "you."

Cultivate a Frame of Mind for Effective Revising and Proofreading

The following suggestions will guide your efforts to develop business documents that achieve the purpose for which they are intended.

- **Attempt to see things from your audience's perspective rather than from your**

own. Being empathetic with your audience isn't as simple as it seems, particularly when dealing with today's diverse workforce. Erase the mind-set, "I know what *I* need to say and how *I* want to say it." Instead, ask, "How would my audience react to this message? Is this message worded so that my audience can easily understand it? Does it convey a tone that will build goodwill?"

- **Revise your documents until you cannot see any additional ways to improve them.** Resist the temptation to think of your first draft as your last draft. Instead, look for ways to improve and be willing to incorporate valid suggestions once you have completed a draft. Experienced writers believe that there is no such thing as good writing, but there is such a thing as good rewriting. Author Dorothy Parker, who wrote for *Vanity Fair* and *Esquire*, once said, "I can't write five words but that I change seven."[9] Skilled speech writers might rewrite a script 15 or 20 times. Writers in public relations firms revise brochures and advertising copy until perhaps only a comma in the final draft is recognizable from the first draft. Even simple email messages require revision for clarity and mechanical errors, with extra passes needed depending on the number of recipients and the context of the message. Regardless of the message type, your careful revising will aid you in creating accurate, readable documents that produce results.

- **Be willing to allow others to make suggestions for improving your writing.** Because most of us consider our writing personal, we often feel reluctant to share it with others and can be easily offended if they suggest changes. This syndrome, called *writer's pride of ownership*, can prevent us from seeking needed assistance from experienced writers—a proven method of improving communication skills. On the job, especially in today's electronic workplace, your writing will be showcased to your supervisor, clients/customers, members of a collaborative writing team, and more. You have nothing to lose but much to gain by allowing others to critique your writing. This commitment is especially important considering the mistake hardest to detect is your own. However, you have the ultimate responsibility for your document; don't simply trust that someone else will catch and correct your errors.

The ability you've gained in following a systematic process for developing effective business messages will prove valuable as you direct your energies to developing effective messages as a member of a team. Refer to the "Check Your Communication" checklist on the Chapter 4 Review Card to review the guidelines for preparing and proofreading a rough draft.

Mea Culpa. Words are carefully analyzed and scrutinized when they are part of an apology. Pro golfer Tiger Woods found that to be true when he apologized publicly for extramarital affairs. In a press conference, Woods admitted to his wrongdoing and said, "For all that I have done, I am so sorry. I have a lot to atone for." Woods fared better than did Charlie Sheen, who went on a tirade after his television show, *Two and a Half Men*, was shut down. In that rant, he was accused of anti-Semitism when discussing the show's creator Chuck Lorre. Later, he apologized *sort of*, saying, "I'm sorry if I offended you. I didn't know you were so sensitive. . . . I didn't know you were gonna take your little ball and go home and punish everybody in the process."[10]

Communicating Electronically

Electronic Mail Communication

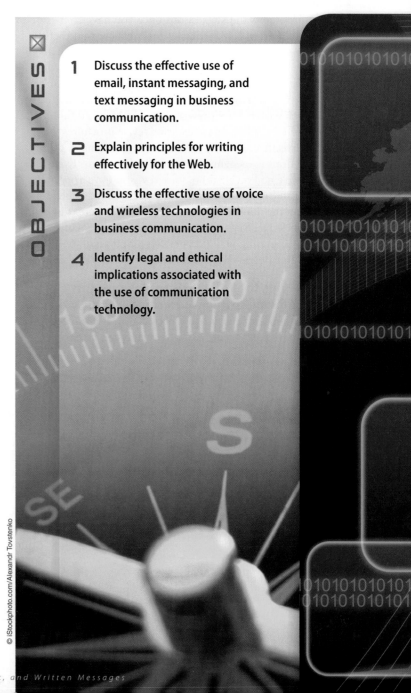

OBJECTIVES

1 Discuss the effective use of email, instant messaging, and text messaging in business communication.

2 Explain principles for writing effectively for the Web.

3 Discuss the effective use of voice and wireless technologies in business communication.

4 Identify legal and ethical implications associated with the use of communication technology.

A s you read in Chapter 1, the continuous evolution of technology has expanded communication options. Email, instant messaging, Web communications, and voice and wireless technologies are important tools for accomplishing company goals. A 2007 study indicated that email has overtaken the telephone in terms of the most common workplace communication tool.[1] The ability to use email communications effectively is essential to success in virtually every career.

☒ OBJECTIVE 1

Discuss the effective use of email, instant messaging, and text messaging in business communication.

Advantages of Email

Electronic mail, or email, offers numerous advantages. Its ready availability, convenience, and ease of use have resulted in its skyrocketing popularity. The advantages of email are numerous:

- **It facilitates the fast, convenient flow of information among users at various locations and time zones.** Mail service is often too slow for communicating timely information, and the telephone system is inconvenient and costly when communicating with people located in several locations and time zones. For these reasons, email is especially effective when sending a single message to several recipients and when needing to communicate 24 hours a day, 365 days a year.

- **It increases efficiency.** Email reduces "telephone tag" and unnecessary telephone interruptions caused when delivering messages that are unlikely to require a verbal response.
- **It reduces costs.** Sending email messages represents a substantial savings to companies in long-distance telephone costs and postal mail-outs.
- **It reduces paper waste.** Often an electronic message can be read and immediately discarded without the need for a printed copy.

Guidelines for Preparing Email Messages

Following these guidelines will enable you to use email efficiently and effectively when communicating with both valued coworkers and outside parties:

- **Send to single or multiple addressees.** The same message can be sent to one or many recipients simultaneously. Sending an email message to multiple recipients routinely involves keying the email address of each recipient into a distribution list and selecting the distribution list as the recipient.
- **Provide a useful subject line.** A descriptive subject line assists the receiver's understanding of the message and is helpful for future reference to it. Additionally, a well-written subject line in an email message will help the receiver sort through an overloaded mailbox and read messages in priority order. When writing a subject line, think of the five Ws—Who, What, When, Where, and Why—to give you some clues for wording. For instance, "Budget Committee Meeting on Thursday" is a more meaningful subject line than "Meeting."

© Twobee/Shutterstock

- **Restate the subject in the body of the message.** The body of the message should be a complete thought and should not rely on the subject line for elaboration. A good opening sentence might be a repetition of most of the subject line. Even if the reader skipped the subject line, the message would still be clear, logical, and complete.

- **Focus on a single topic directed toward the receiver's needs.** An email message is generally limited to one idea rather than addressing several issues. If you address more than one topic in a single email message, chances are the recipient will forget to respond to all points discussed. Discussing one topic allows you to write a descriptive subject line, and the receiver can file the single subject message in a separate mailbox if desired. If you must send a lengthy message, divide it into logical sections for easy comprehension.

- **Sequence your ideas based on anticipated reader reaction.** As you learned previously, ideas should be organized deductively when a message contains good news or neutral information; inductive organization is recommended when the message contains bad news or is intended to persuade. Email messages should be organized according to the sequence of ideas—for example, time order, order of importance, or geography. As a general rule, present the information in the order it is likely to be needed. For example, describe the nature and purpose of an upcoming meeting before giving the specifics (date, place, time).

netiquette
the buzzword for proper behavior on the Internet

- **Make careful use of jargon, technical words, and shortened terms.** The use of jargon and technical terms is more common in email messages than in business letters. Such shortcuts save time with audiences who will understand the intent. In practicing empathy, however, consider whether the receiver will likely understand the terms used.

- **Use graphic highlighting to add emphasis.** Enumerated or bulleted lists, tables, graphs, pictures, or other images can be either integrated into the content of the email or attached as supporting material.

- **Revise your email before sending.** Even the average email requires at least one pass to ensure that the intended message is clear, concise, and error-free. The number of passes increases depending on the number of people receiving the email and the complexity of the message. Revising for brevity and conciseness is a primary goal for messages that are often read on the run and on mobile devices. Keep to one screen, eliminate redundancies, and tighten wording. Avoid off-topic material that detracts from the email's single subject, as well as clever or amusing statements that are funny only to the writer.[2] Direct, concise messages sometimes sound impersonal and curt if not revised for goodwill. Question whether a phone call would be more appropriate for the message; a businesslike, yet conversational tone might sound less aggressive or demanding. Revise emails to achieve a similar tone.[3] Use the email spell check and then proofread onscreen for content and grammatical errors.

Effective Use of Email

The email message in Figure 5-1 illustrates guidelines for using professional email. The recipient's financial advisor begins his email message to his client by suggesting the need for a change in her investment strategy. The paragraphs that follow include timely information and a specific request for action to be taken.

While email offers various advantages in speed and convenience, problems arise when it is managed inappropriately. Learning fundamental **netiquette**, the buzzword for proper behavior on the Internet, will assure your online success. The following guidelines will assist you in using email effectively:

- **Check mail promptly.** Generally, a response to email is expected within 24 hours. Ignoring messages from coworkers can erode efforts to create an open, honest, and cooperative work environment. On the other hand, responding every second could indicate that you are paying more attention to your email than your job.

- **Do not contribute to email overload.** To avoid clogging the system with unnecessary messages, follow these simple guidelines:
  - Be certain individuals need a copy of the email, and forward an email from another person only with the original writer's permission.

To Recap—Email Advantages

☑ Allows communication 24 hours a day, 365 days a year.

☑ Reduces telephone interruptions by delivering messages that are unlikely to require a verbal response.

☑ Saves companies the costs of long-distance telephone bills and postal mail-outs.

☑ Reduces the need to print messages.

© iStockphoto.com/George Peters

Figure 5-1 GOOD *Good Example of an Email Message*

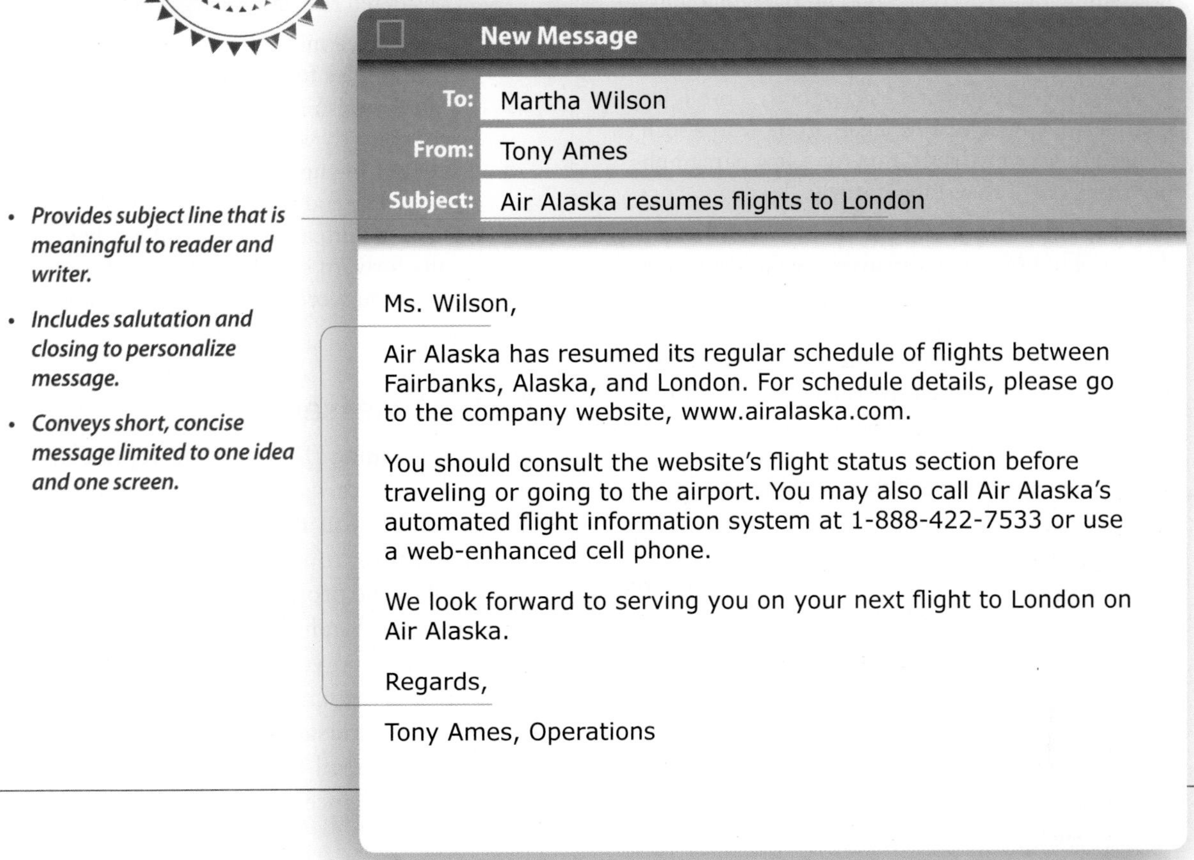

New Message

To:	Martha Wilson
From:	Tony Ames
Subject:	Air Alaska resumes flights to London

- *Provides subject line that is meaningful to reader and writer.*

- *Includes salutation and closing to personalize message.*

- *Conveys short, concise message limited to one idea and one screen.*

Ms. Wilson,

Air Alaska has resumed its regular schedule of flights between Fairbanks, Alaska, and London. For schedule details, please go to the company website, www.airalaska.com.

You should consult the website's flight status section before traveling or going to the airport. You may also call Air Alaska's automated flight information system at 1-888-422-7533 or use a web-enhanced cell phone.

We look forward to serving you on your next flight to London on Air Alaska.

Regards,

Tony Ames, Operations

© Cengage Learning 2013

- Never address an email requesting general action to more than one person if you want to receive an individual response. Sharing responsibility will lead to no one taking responsibility.

- Avoid sending formatted documents. Messages with varying fonts, special print features (e.g., bold, italics, etc.), and images take longer to download, require more storage space, and could be unreadable on some computers. In addition, enhancing routine email messages does not support the goals of competitive organizations, and employees and clients or customers might resent such frivolous use of time.

- Edit the original message when you reply to email if the entire body of the original message is not needed for context. Instead, you can cut and paste pertinent sections within a reply that you believe will help the recipient understand your reply. You can also key brief comments in all caps below the original section.

- Follow company policy for personal use of email. Obtain a private email account if you are job hunting or sending many private messages to friends and relatives.

- **Use email selectively.** Send short, direct messages for routine matters that need not be handled immediately (scheduling meetings, giving your supervisor quick updates, or addressing other uncomplicated issues).

- **Do not send messages when you are angry.** Email containing sensitive, highly emotional messages could be easily misinterpreted because of the absence of nonverbal communication (facial expressions, voice tone, and body language). Sending a *flame*, the online term used to describe a heated, sarcastic, sometimes abusive message or posting, might prompt a receiver to send a retaliatory response. Email messages written in anger and filled with emotion and sarcasm could result in embarrassment or even end up as evidence in litigation. Because of the potential damage to relationships and legal liability, read email messages carefully before sending them. Unless a response is urgent, store a heated message for an hour until you have cooled off and thought about the issue clearly and rationally. When you *must* respond immediately, you might acknowledge that your response is emotional and has not been thoroughly considered. Give this warning by using words such as "I need to vent my frustration for a few paragraphs" or "flame on—I'm writing in anger."[4]

- **Exercise caution against email viruses and hoaxes.** An ounce of prevention can avert the problems caused by deadly *viruses* that destroy data files or annoying messages that simply waste your time while they are executing. Install an *antivirus software program* that will scan your hard drive each time you start the computer or access external devices, and keep backups of important files. Be suspicious of email messages that contain attachments if they are from people you don't know. Email text is usually safe to open, but the attachment could contain an executable file that can affect your computer's operations. **Social networking sites** such as Facebook and MySpace are also common sources of viruses and spyware.

Additionally, be wary of *computer hoaxes*—email messages that incite panic, typically related to risks of computer viruses or deadly threats, and urge you to forward them to as many people as possible. Forwarding a hoax can be embarrassing and causes inefficiency by overloading email boxes and flooding computer security personnel with inquiries from alarmed recipients of your message. Investigate the possible hoax by visiting websites such as the following that post virus alerts and hoax information and provide tips for identifying a potential hoax:

- Urban legends: www.urbanlegends.com
- Snopes: www.snopes.com
- Truth or Fiction: www.truthorfiction.com

If a bogus message is forwarded to you, reply to the person politely that the message is a hoax. This action allows you to help stop the spread of the malicious message and will educate one more person about the evils of hoaxes.

- **Develop an effective system for handling email.** Some simple organization will allow you to make better use of your email capability:

  - Set up separate accounts for receiving messages that require your direct attention.
  - Keep your email inbox clean by reading an email and taking action immediately. Delete messages you are not using and those not likely to be considered relevant for legal purposes.
  - Move saved messages into a limited number of email folders for quick retrieval. The email search feature is also useful for identifying saved messages quickly. If you receive many messages, consider setting up your account to sort and prioritize messages, send form letters as replies to messages received with a particular subject line, automatically forward specified email, and sound an alarm when you receive a message from a particular person.

Instant Messaging

Instant messaging (IM), or chat, represents a blending of email with conversation. This real-time email technology allows you to maintain a list of people with whom you want to interact. You can send messages to any or all of the people on your list as long as the people are online. Sending a message opens up a window in which you and your contact can key messages that you both can see immediately. Figure 5-2 illustrates a sample IM conversation that occurred as a follow-up to a previous email from a legal services director to a software compliance officer.

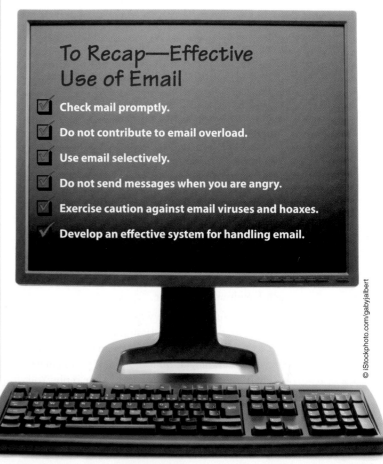

To Recap—Effective Use of Email

☑ **Check mail promptly.**

☑ **Do not contribute to email overload.**

☑ **Use email selectively.**

☑ **Do not send messages when you are angry.**

☑ **Exercise caution against email viruses and hoaxes.**

✓ **Develop an effective system for handling email.**

© iStockphoto.com/gabyjalbert

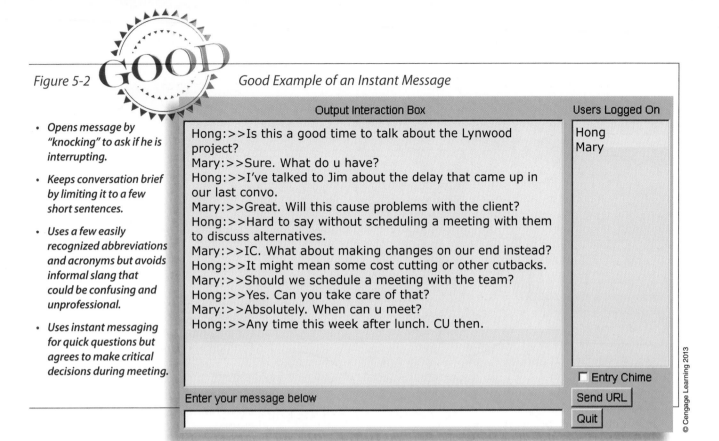

Figure 5-2 GOOD   *Good Example of an Instant Message*

- Opens message by "knocking" to ask if he is interrupting.

- Keeps conversation brief by limiting it to a few short sentences.

- Uses a few easily recognized abbreviations and acronyms but avoids informal slang that could be confusing and unprofessional.

- Uses instant messaging for quick questions but agrees to make critical decisions during meeting.

Output Interaction Box

Hong:>>Is this a good time to talk about the Lynwood project?
Mary:>>Sure. What do u have?
Hong:>>I've talked to Jim about the delay that came up in our last convo.
Mary:>>Great. Will this cause problems with the client?
Hong:>>Hard to say without scheduling a meeting with them to discuss alternatives.
Mary:>>IC. What about making changes on our end instead?
Hong:>>It might mean some cost cutting or other cutbacks.
Mary:>>Should we schedule a meeting with the team?
Hong:>>Yes. Can you take care of that?
Mary:>>Absolutely. When can u meet?
Hong:>>Any time this week after lunch. CU then.

Users Logged On

Hong
Mary

☐ Entry Chime

Enter your message below

Send URL

Quit

© Cengage Learning 2013

Business use of instant messaging has experienced phenomenal growth. Analysts estimate that in 90 percent of companies, some employees use IM, whether to close a sale, collaborate with a colleague, or just trade pleasantries with a colleague.[5] The best known IM programs are free and require no special hardware and little training. With some programs, users can exchange graphics and audio and video clips. Many of the guidelines that apply to the use of email for business purposes also apply to instant messaging. With IM, however, spelling and grammar matter less when trading messages at high speed. IM users often use shorthand for common words and phrases. IM and telephone communication also share common challenges: being sure that the sender is who he or she claims to be and that the conversation is free from eavesdropping.

Some managers worry that employees will spend too much work time using IM to chat with buddies inside and outside the company. They also emphasize that IM is not the right tool for every business purpose; employees should still rely on email when they need a record and use the telephone for a personal touch.

Text Messaging

Text messaging has grown in popularity as cell phones and other handheld devices with text capability have proliferated. Messages can be sent from one cell phone to another, a cell phone to a computer, or computer to computer. **Text messaging** on a cell phone or personal digital assistant is a refinement of computer instant messaging. The typical cell phone screen can accommodate no more than 160 characters, and because the keypad is far less versatile, text messaging puts an even greater premium on conciseness. An entire code book of acronyms and abbreviations has emerged, ranging from CWOT (complete waste of time) to DLTBBB (don't let the bed bugs bite). The use of emoticons has also advanced far beyond the traditional smiley face and includes drooling (:-) . . .) and secrecy (:X).

© iStockphoto.com/Alex Slobodkin

text messaging
messages that can be sent from one cell phone to another, a cell phone to a computer, or computer to computer; a refinement of computer instant messaging

Figure 5-3 Levels of Formality Required by Various Technologies

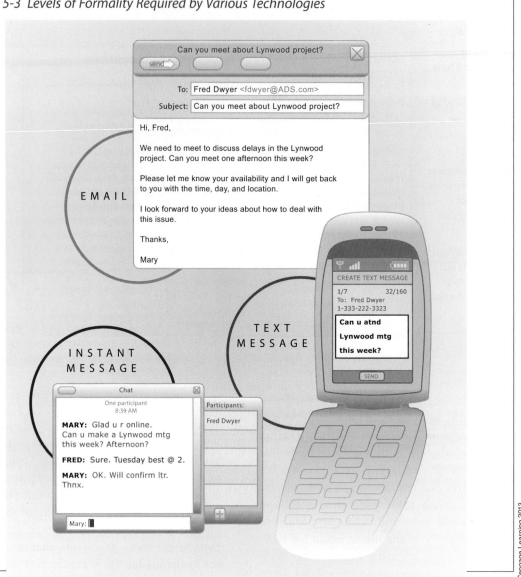

Inventive and young users frequently insert their own style, substituting "z" for "s," or "d" for "th." Shortened lingo or txt gets right to the point. For instance, a sender might send the following message that can be easily deciphered by most: "Pk u up @730." Cell phone programs are also available to assist in efficiency when texting. T9 (text on nine keys) and similar programs uses predictive text to finish words after the first few characters are keyed. T9 can be "trained" to recognize new vocabulary.[6]

Texting is a viable alternative to phone calls for those with hearing impairments. Economic and cultural factors have also driven the advancement of text messaging in some parts of the world where voice con-

versations are more expensive than texting and short conversations are considered impolite. Some of the most avid text messagers are clustered in Southeast Asia. The Chinese language is particularly well-suited to text messaging, because in Mandarin the names of the numbers are also close to the sounds of certain words.[7] Japanese commuters use their cell phones to text silently, as talking on the phones on the train would be impolite. In the United States, teenagers have popularized texting and carry the habit into places of work. Both abroad and at home, text messaging can be used as an avoidance mechanism that preserves the feeling of communication without the burden for actual intimacy or substance. Most text messages are superficial greetings and are often sent when the two parties are within speaking distance of each other. Like a wave or nod, they are meant to merely establish connection without getting specific.

While text messaging is generally a social communication tool, it does have some applications for business. Text messages can be sent or retrieved in situations when a ringing phone would be inappropriate, such as during meetings. With research showing that many more text messages are opened than are email messages, advertisers are using text messages to send their marketing messages.[8] Refer to Figure 5-3, which compares the completeness and relative formality of the email message to the informal nature of the instant message and the abbreviated style of the text message. Each medium requires its own appropriate writing style to maximize effectiveness and social expectations.

Electronic Messages and the Law

U.S. courts have established the right of companies to monitor the electronic mail of an employee because they own the facilities and intend them to be used for job-related communication only. On the other hand, employees typically expect that their email messages will be kept private. To protect themselves against liability imposed by the Electronic Communications Privacy Act (ECPA), employers simply provide a legitimate business reason for the monitoring (e.g., preventing computer crime, retrieving lost messages, and regulating employee morale) and obtain written consent to intercept email or at least notify employees. Employees who use the system after the notification may have given implied consent to the monitoring.[9]

The legal status of text messaging has been murkier. A 2008 court ruling made a distinction between electronic communications employers store on their servers and communication that is contracted out to third parties. Employers must have either a warrant or the employee's permission to view messages stored by someone other than the employer. Employers who intend to monitor electronic communications must be specific in their written employee policy statements that they intend to access text messages sent with company-issued devices.[10]

Remember that you are responsible for the content of any electronic message you send. Because electronic messages move so quickly between people and often become very informal and conversational, individuals might not realize (or might forget) their responsibility. If a person denies commitments made via an electronic message, someone involved can produce a copy of the message as verification.

Electronic communicators must abide by copyright laws. Be certain to give credit for quoted material and seek permission to use copyrighted text or graphics from printed or electronic sources. Unless you inform the reader that editing has occurred, do not alter a message you are forwarding or re-posting, and be sure to ask permission before forwarding it.

Federal and state bills related to employee privacy are frequently introduced for legislative consideration. Although litigation related to present privacy issues is underway, the development of law is lagging far behind technology; nevertheless, employers can expect changes in the laws as technology continues to develop. Electronic messages have often become the prosecutor's star witness, the corporate equivalent of DNA evidence, as it and other forms of electronic communication are subject to subpoena in litigation. Referring to this issue, former New York attorney general Eliot Spitzer had this to say: "Never write when you can talk. Never talk when you can nod. And never put anything in an email [that you don't want on the front page of the newspaper]."[11] Several perils of "evidence" mail that companies must address are illustrated in these cases:

"Never write when you can talk. Never talk when you can nod. And never put anything in an email [that you don't want on the front page of the newspaper]."

- Including inappropriate content in an email can humiliate and lead to indictment. Detroit Mayor Kwame Kilpatrick and his chief of staff were charged in a 12-count indictment including perjury and obstruction of justice when text messages exchanged between the two were revealed. The pair's secret love affair played out in the messages was also disclosed to a shocked public.[12] The press dubbed the resulting disastrous professional result as "death by Blackberry."

- Failing to preserve or destroying email messages in violation of securities rules is a sure path to destruction. Deleting Enron scandal-related messages led to Arthur Andersen's criminal conviction and eventually to Enron's implosion.

- Inability to locate emails and other relevant documents demanded by the courts is unacceptable and considered negligence by the courts. Penalties have included monetary fines, assessment of court costs or attorney's fees, and dismissal of the case in favor of the opposing side.[13]

On the other hand, evidence mail can protect a company from lawsuits. A company being sued by a female employee because a male executive had allegedly sexually abused her retrieved a trail of emails with lurid attachments sent by the female employee to the male executive named in the case.[14]

To avoid the legal perils of electronic communications, employees must be taught not to write loose, potentially rude, and overly casual messages; to avoid carelessly deleting messages; and to take the time to identify and organize relevant messages for quick retrieval.

intranet
Web platform for distributing information to employees at numerous locations; access limited to those with authorization

extranet
Web platform for distributing information to business partners such as vendors, suppliers, and customers; access limited to those with authorization

Web Page Communication

Although effective Web page development is a highly specialized activity, understanding the process will be useful to any business communicator. Organizations can use the Web not only to communicate with customers and clients but also to interact with business associates.

The World Wide Web is truly a universal communication medium, reaching a broad audience in diverse

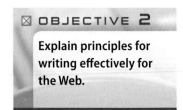

OBJECTIVE 2

Explain principles for writing effectively for the Web.

locations. The familiar Web platform can also be used for offering a company **intranet** to distribute various types of information to employees at numerous locations.

Business associates such as vendors, suppliers, and customers can utilize the Web to access a company's **extranet**. Both intranets and extranets restrict access to only authorized viewers; those viewers are provided passwords to access the sites. An organization can also establish a public website to extend its reach significantly and provide potential customers or clients with an always available resource for contact and product information.

Designing Web pages that are accessible by the millions of people with permanent or temporary disabilities, including visual impairments, is good for business.[15] Research by the 2004 Disability Rights Commission has found that the websites that were most accessible for users with disabilities were also easier for people without disabilities to operate, with some online tasks performed 35 percent faster on the more accessible sites.[16] U.S. businesses have legal requirements for online content to be available to everyone under equal opportunity and anti-discrimination laws. The National Federation of the Blind filed a class action suit against Target Corporation because the online store offered values that could not be accessed by screen reader software.[17] The Web Content Accessibility Guidelines provided by The World Wide Web Consortiums (W3C) at **www.w3.org** are helpful resources for assuring Web accessibility. The same group has also developed Mobile Web Accessibility Guidelines for making websites usable from mobile devices.

Writing for a Website

Many of the same standard rules for writing apply, whether writing for the Web or print. However, some important differences exist between readers of paper material and Web users:[18]

- Web users do not want to read. They skim, browse, and hop from one highlighted area to another trying to zero in on the word or phrase that relates to their search.

- English-speaking readers typically start scanning at the top left side of the main content area. Their attention moves from top to bottom and left to right. Given this pattern, placing frequently accessed items close to the top of the content area is important. Information should follow the pyramid style of writing common in newspaper writing: The main idea or conclusion

TIP SHEET:

The following tips will help you compose appropriate Web content:[19]

- **Be brief.** A good rule is to reduce the wording of any print document by 50 percent when you put it on the Web.

- **Keep it simple.** Use short words that allow for fast reading by people of various educational backgrounds. Use mixed case, since all caps are slower to read.

- **Consider appropriate jargon.** If all of your site users share a common professional language, use it. Otherwise, keep to concise yet effective word choices.

- **Use eye-catching headlines.** They catch interest, ask a question, present the unusual, or pose a conflict.

- **Break longer documents into smaller chunks.** Provide ways to easily move through the document and return to the beginning.

- **Use attention-getting devices judiciously.** Bold, font changes, color, and graphics do attract attention but can be overdone, causing important ideas to be lost.

- **Avoid placing critical information in graphic form only.** Many users are averse to slow-loading graphics and skip over them.

© Max Oppenheim/Digital Vision/Getty Images

is presented first, and subsequent sections and pages expand upon it.

- Users can more quickly scan items in columns rather than rows, especially if they are categorized, grouped, and have headings. You can have more lists on the Web than in a typical print document.

- Users refer infrequently to directions. It is unlikely they will read little notes, sidebars, and help files, so directions must appear in simple, numbered steps.

- In recognition of these Web user characteristics, writers should tailor their styles accordingly.

Effective Web writing involves moving beyond the paper mode into the Web mode of thinking. Understanding the distinctive expectations of Web readers will allow you to structure your ideas effectively and efficiently.

Writing Wikis

While a traditional website's content is usually controlled by the sponsoring individual or agency, a wiki is a collaborative website that hosts the collective work of many authors. Similar to a blog in structure and logic, a wiki allows anyone to edit, delete, or modify content, even the work of previous authors. While allowing everyday users to create and edit a Website encourages cooperative use of electronic information, the content posted at such sites should not be considered authoritative. When wiki writing, avoid the first-person blogging style and conform to the tone and flow of the existing article. Wikis are not typically the place for personal opinion and analysis. Instead, present factual information in clear, concise, and neutral language.[20]

Many businesses make use of wikis to encourage free flow of ideas within the organization. Content in a wiki can be updated in real time, without any real administrative effort, and without the need for deliberate distribution. Contributors simply visit and update a common Website. Wikis facilitate the exchange of information within and between teams. They allow maintenance of a series of unique documents with evolving content. Placing a document in a wiki does not necessarily make it editable by everyone with access to the wiki. For example, the marketing department can make a PowerPoint slide deck available to the sales team or the company at large without letting them change or overwrite it. Most companies implement their wikis behind a firewall to limit participation to their internal user base.[21]

Writing for Weblogs

In contrast to a wiki, a **weblog, or blog**, is a type of online journal typically authored by an individual and does not allow

weblog (or blog)
a type of online journal typically authored by an individual that does not allow visitors to change the original material posted, but to only add comments

An effective corporate blog begins with a clear goal, such as winning business or building customer loyalty.

© iStockphoto.com/Matthew Dixon

visitors to change the original posted material, but to only add comments. Some of the millions of blogs now populating the Web are online scrapbooks for pasting links, information, and quotes. Some resemble personal diaries, often illustrated with digital snapshots; others serve as digital soapboxes, providing a platform for airing opinions and commentary about the world at large or on a special topic of interest. Users (known as bloggers) add entries (referred to as posts) using a simple online form in their browsers, while the weblog publishing software takes care of formatting the page layout and creating archive pages.[22]

Blogs differ from websites in that blogs are dynamic, with rapidly changing content that does not require authorization to post. The creator of the message does not have to be familiar with special coding and uploads a message simply by clicking the "Publish" button.[23] Blogging allows average citizens to become publishers. Bloggers, however, should write each post with the realization that it is publicly available.

Blog formats have been adapted for business uses, including commercial publishing, marketing, and as a knowledge management tool. Blogs can store knowledge in searchable archives for future use. This function can be helpful, for example, for service teams as they search past communications to troubleshoot current problems. Many companies, such as Microsoft, Sun Microsystems, and General Motors, encourage blogging among employees.[24] An effective corporate blog begins with a clear goal, such as winning business or

building customer loyalty, and then provides relevant, frequently updated information for the target audience to return to regularly. Like other effective Web communications, blogs must be promoted creatively to attract avid readers.[25] Companies such as Dell and Southwest Airlines employ "communities and conversation teams" or a "social media team" who track comments posted on sites such Twitter, YouTube, Flickr, and Facebook, verify facts, and respond quickly to any customer complaint appearing in cyberspace. In addition to being an early warning system, these online conversations are sources of feedback on customer needs and pain points that lead to innovation in products and services.[26]

Internal blogs can be established that are not published to anyone outside the company. They present similar legal issues to those surrounding email and instant messaging. One of the most important considerations is whether posts are truly anonymous. The potential for anonymous speech creates an atmosphere that can encourage irresponsible behavior, such as harassment, defamation, and gossip. To reduce this problem, IT professionals can configure internal blogs so that all users can be identified, at least by the company.[27]

Voice and Wireless Communication

Not so long ago, voice communication referred strictly to communication over phone lines, and using the telephone effectively is still an important skill in any profession. Although the traditional telephone still plays an important role in business activity, voice communication extends to voice mail systems and cell phone usage. Both voice and data can be transmitted now using wireless communication systems.

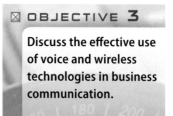

☒ OBJECTIVE 3

Discuss the effective use of voice and wireless technologies in business communication.

Voice Mail Communication

Voice mail technology allows flexibility in staying in touch without the aid of a computer and reduces telephone tag. Just as email communication can be enhanced by adhering to some basic principles, voice mail communication can be more effective by following recommended guidelines:[28]

- Update your greeting often to reflect your schedule and leave special announcements.
- Leave your email address, fax number, or mailing address on your greeting if this information might be helpful to your callers.
- Encourage callers to leave detailed messages. If you need certain standard information from callers, use your greeting to prompt them for it. Such information often eliminates the need to call back.
- Instruct callers on how to review their message or be transferred to an operator.
- Check your voice mail regularly, and return all voice messages within 24 hours.

When leaving a message, you can improve your communication by following these tips:[29]

- Speak slowly and clearly, and repeat your name and phone number at the beginning and end of the message.
- Spell your name for the recipient, who might need the correct spelling.
- Leave a detailed message, not just your name and number, to avoid prolonged phone tag.
- Keep your message brief, typically 60 seconds or less.
- Ensure that your message will be understandable. Don't call from places with distracting background noise or an inadequate signal connection.

The sound of your voice makes a lasting impression on the many people who listen to your greeting or the messages you leave. To ensure that the impression you leave is a professional one, review your voice greeting before you save it. Rerecord to eliminate verbal viruses ("um," "uh," stumbles), flat or monotone voice, and garbled or rushed messages that are difficult to understand. Consider scripting the message to avoid long, rambling messages. As you are recording, stand, smile, and visualize the person receiving the message; you'll hear the added energy, enthusiasm, and warmth in your voice.[30]

Remember that the voice mail message you leave should be seen as permanent. In some systems the digital files are backed up and stored for possible retrieval by managers or other company personnel. A voice mail message can also be used as evidence in a lawsuit or other legal proceeding.[31]

Cell Phone Communication

Mobile telephones, once a rarity, are now a standard accessory for many people throughout the world. In the United States, cell phones are as commonplace as landline phones, and the number continues to rise.

The increasing functionality and ease of use of cell phones have outstripped the development of rules for proper cell phone etiquette. According to a recent poll, almost 7 out of 10 Americans say they observe poor cell phone etiquette at least once every day.[32] Cell phone abuse in the workplace causes much annoyance and intrusion that leads to ineffectiveness and can endanger employee safety. Your attention to a few commonsense guidelines will help ensure that you are not seen as a rude phone user.[33]

- **Observe wireless-free quiet zones.** This obviously includes theaters, performances, and religious services,

but can also include meetings, restaurants, hospitals, and other public places. Exercise judgment about silencing your ringer, switching to vibrate mode, or turning off your phone. To increase the effectiveness of meetings, cell phone policies in some businesses ask that employees leave their cell phones at their desks; vibrating mode is acceptable for an anticipated emergency. To encourage proper cell phone etiquette, one business requires managers to deposit a designated amount of money in a jar should their cell phones ring during a meeting; monies collected are donated to a charity.

- **Respect others in crowded places.** Speak in low conversational tones, and consider the content of your conversation.

- **Think safety.** Some states and municipalities have banned the use of cell phones while driving. Others allow the use of hands-free devices only. Even if not illegal, cell phone usage increases the risk of accident by distracting the driver. Some companies are implementing cell phone policies that prohibit operators of company-owned vehicles from using cell phones or other communication devices while driving in order to minimize risks to their employees and liability resulting from accidents.

Cell phone users should remember that the technology is not secure. Perhaps you have overheard another party's phone conversation when using your cell phone. The radio frequencies that transmit the voice signals can be picked up by other equipment. For this reason, information that is confidential or sensitive should be shared using an alternate communication channel.

Wireless Communication and the Future

With the many communication innovations that have occurred in the last 20 years, one can only wonder what the next 20 years will hold. Whatever the breakthroughs, wireless technology will figure strongly in the changes. Wireless communication has freed us from the necessity of being literally plugged in while enabling us to communicate voice and high-speed data transmission virtually any time, anywhere.

Wireless technology drives many of the significant changes that are affecting today's businesses. Smartphones offer advanced capabilities beyond a typical mobile phone, with PC-like functionality. Applications include email access, data processing, and entertainment. Other functionality might include an additional interface such as a miniature QWERTY keyboard, touch screen or D-pad, built-in camera, contact management, navigation hardware and software, media software for playing music, browsing and viewing capability for photos and video

clips, and Internet browsers. Phone data can be synchronized with a computer and other communication devices for easy information access and manipulation. The future promises increased use of smartphones, especially touchscreens, by both consumers and professionals as well as the development of many innovative phone apps (shorthand for phone applications) that customize smartphone capabilities to fit users' needs. Security will continue to be a challenging consideration as workers use their phones to hold and transmit confidential information.[34]

The impact of wireless communication will be even more significant as voice-to-text and text-to-voice technology continues to develop. Voice input and output technology offers the ability to communicate through a computer system without a keyboard. Although such technology has been around for more than two decades, newer systems have more powerful processors, are smaller in size, and better tolerate variances in speakers' accents and inflections without sacrificing speed and accuracy.

Wireless capability will increase the timeliness of key business decisions, resulting in greater revenues and profitability. However, being able to make decisions quickly does not ensure that they will be the right decisions. As in the past, workers will need to have correct and timely information for making decisions. An additional challenge for the wireless era will be balancing electronic communication capabilities with the need for human interaction.

Appropriate Use of Technology

Technology offers numerous advantages, but a technological channel is not always the communication method of choice. Before sending a message, be certain the selected channel of communication is appropriate by considering

© iStockphoto.com/Alexander Samoilov

☒ **OBJECTIVE 4**

Identify legal and ethical implications associated with the use of communication technology.

the message's purpose, confidentiality issues, and human relations factors.

Determine the Purpose of the Message

If a message is straightforward and informative, chances are a technological option might be appropriate. Although the use of instantaneous and efficient communication methods is quite compelling, keep in mind that written communication, printed or online, cannot replace the personal interaction so essential in today's team-based work environments. Employees floors apart or in different offices or time zones benefit from email and Web communications, but two people sitting side by side or on the same floor shouldn't have to communicate solely by electronic means.

A second question when selecting among communication options is whether a permanent record of the message is needed or if a more temporary form such as a phone call or instant message would suffice.

Determine Whether the Information Is Personal or Confidential

As a general guideline, keep personal correspondence off-line if you don't want it to come back and haunt you. The content of an email message could have embarrassing consequences since such documents often become a part of public records and wireless communications might be unexpectedly intercepted. Your company technically "owns" your electronic communications and thus can monitor them to determine legitimate business use or potential abuse. Undeliverable email messages are delivered to a mail administrator, and many networks routinely store backups of all email messages that pass through them.

Even deleted messages can be "resurrected" with little effort, as several public figures discovered when investigators retrieved archived email as evidence in court cases. For sensitive situations, a face-to-face encounter is often preferred.

Decide Whether Positive Human Relations Are Sacrificed

Be wary of using an electronic communication tool as an avoidance mechanism. Remember, too, that some people do not regularly check their email or voice mail, and some have unreliable systems that are slow or prone to lose messages. Some news will be received better in person than through an electronic format that might be interpreted as cold and impersonal.

Additionally, some people, especially those of certain cultures, prefer a personal meeting even if you perceive that an electronic exchange of information would be a more efficient use of everyone's time. Choose the communication channel carefully to fit both your purpose and the preference of the receiver.

So you want to use your iPhone for work?

As people pack increasingly sophisticated smartphones in their personal life, they're clamoring to use those gadgets in the workplace as well. And many of their bosses are loosening up. This arrangement can bring benefits for both sides, but there are a lot of potential pitfalls, too, particularly in the area of security. So companies have adopted a variety of strategies to cope with this issue. For example, Kimberly-Clark Corp. has a hard-line solution: If a phone is lost or stolen, or an employee leaves, the company erases the device remotely. Another approach has been implemented by Nationwide Mutual Insurance Co., which uses software to carve out or wall off a part of an employee's device strictly for corporate use.[35]

© Pius Lee/Shutterstock

Delivering Good- and Neutral-News Messages

Deductive Organizational Pattern

You read in Chapter 4 that you can organize business messages either *deductively* or *inductively* depending on your prediction of the receiver's reaction to your main idea. Learning to organize business messages according to the appropriate outline will improve your chances of preparing a document that elicits the response or action you desire.

⊠ OBJECTIVE 1

Describe the deductive outline for good and neutral news and its adaptations for specific situations and for international audiences.

In this chapter, you will learn to compose messages that convey ideas that a receiver likely will find either *pleasing* or *neutral*. Messages that convey pleasant information are referred to as **good-news messages**. Messages that are of interest to the receiver but are not likely to generate an emotional reaction are referred to as **neutral-news messages**. The strategies discussed for structuring good-news and neutral-news messages generally can be applied to North American audiences. Because message expectations and social conventions differ from culture to culture, the effective writer will adapt as necessary when writing for various audiences. People in organizations use a number of channels to communicate with internal and

good-news messages
messages that convey pleasant information

neutral-news messages
messages that are of interest to the reader but are not likely to generate an emotional reaction

© iStockphoto.com/Alexandr Tovstenko

external audiences. When sending a message that is positive or neutral, you have numerous choices, as shown in Figure 6-1 on the next page. Depending on the message, recipient, and constraints of time and location, the best channel might be spoken or electronic. In addition to the electronic and verbal tools presented in Chapter 5 (email, instant messaging, Web communications, and phone), companies also use written documents such as memorandums and letters to communicate information.

The principles for preparing memorandums (commonly referred to as *memos*) are similar to those you've already applied when composing email messages, as both are channels for sharing information of a somewhat informal nature. Memos provide a tangible means of sharing information with people inside an organization. Letters are more formal, because they are used to convey information to external audiences such as customers, clients, business partners, or suppliers. Regardless of whether the audience is an internal or external one, communication should be carefully structured to achieve the desired purpose.

Good-news or neutral-news messages follow a **deductive** or **direct sequence**—the message begins with the main idea.

deductive (or direct) sequence
when the message begins with the main idea followed by supporting details

© LWA/Larry Williams/Blend Images/Corbis

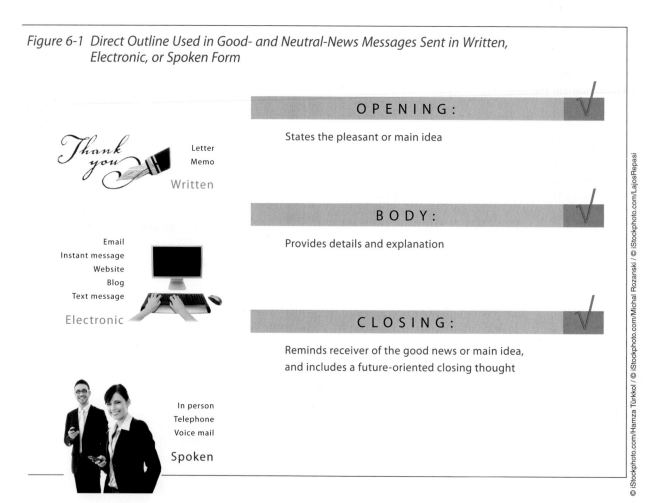

Figure 6-1 *Direct Outline Used in Good- and Neutral-News Messages Sent in Written, Electronic, or Spoken Form*

Written
Letter
Memo

Electronic
Email
Instant message
Website
Blog
Text message

Spoken
In person
Telephone
Voice mail

OPENING:
States the pleasant or main idea

BODY:
Provides details and explanation

CLOSING:
Reminds receiver of the good news or main idea, and includes a future-oriented closing thought

To present good news and neutral information deductively, begin with the major idea, followed by supporting details as depicted in Figure 6-1. In both outlines, the third point (closing thought) might be omitted without seriously impairing effectiveness; however, including it unifies the message and avoids abruptness.

The deductive pattern has several advantages:

- The first sentence is easy to write. After it is written, the details follow easily.

- The first sentence gets the attention it deserves in this emphatic position.

- Encountering good news in the first sentence puts receivers in a pleasant frame of mind, and they are receptive to the details that follow.

- The arrangement might save receivers some time. Once they understand the important idea, they can move rapidly through the supporting details.

As you study sample deductive messages in this chapter, note the *poor example* notations that clearly mark the examples of ineffective writing. Detailed comments highlight important writing strategies that have been applied or violated. While gaining experience in developing effective messages, you will also learn to recognize standard business formats. Fully formatted messages are shown as printed documents (letters on company letterhead or paper memos) or as electronic formats (email messages or online input screens).

Good-News Messages

Messages delivering good news are organized using a direct approach as illustrated in Figure 6-1. For illustration, you'll study examples of messages that convey positive news as well as thank-you and appreciation messages that generate goodwill.

⊠ OBJECTIVE 2

Prepare messages that convey good news, including thank-you and appreciation messages.

Positive News

The memo sent to all employees in Figure 6-2 begins directly with the

Figure 6-2  **Good Example of a Good-News Message**

INTEROFFICE MEMORANDUM

TO: All Employees
FROM: Gloria Martinello, Human Resources Manager   *GM*
DATE: May 15, 2011
SUBJECT: Casual Dress Policy Takes Effect July 1

A casual dress policy has been approved for First National Bank and will be effective July 1. As most of us agree, casual attire in the banking industry generally means "dressy casual," since virtually all of us interact with our clientele regularly throughout the day.

To maintain our traditional professional image while enjoying more relaxed attire, please follow these guidelines:

Men	**Women**
Sport or polo shirt, with collars	Pant suit
Khakis or corduroys	Sweater or blouse with pants or skirt
Loafers with socks	Loafers with socks
	Low heels with hosiery

Tennis shoes, open-toed shoes, sandals, jogging suits, shorts, jeans, sweatpants, and sweatshirts are inappropriate. Formal business attire should be worn when meeting with clients outside the office.

Please visit the HR website for the complete casual attire policy and illustrations of appropriate casual attire. If you have questions as you begin making changes in your wardrobe, please call me at ext. 59.

- Starts with main idea—announcement of new policy.

- Provides clear explanation to ensure policy is understood. Formats as table for quick, easy reference to specific details.

- Continues with additional discussion of policy.

- Encourages readers to ask questions or view additional information on company intranet.

Format Pointers
Uses template with standard memo headings for efficient production.

Includes writer's initials after printed name and title.

© Comstock Images/Jupiterimages

> **To express thanks for a gift**
> Thank you for the gift of the miniature rose plant in recognition of my recent promotion. The rose will find a welcome home in my newly planted rose garden. Thanks for your kindness and for this thoughtful gift.

> **To extend thanks for hospitality**
> Thank you for opening up your home for my recent employment interview. I enjoyed meeting your father and some of my potential colleagues. The gracious tea service you provided made a potentially stressful situation into a pleasurable conversation. Thanks again for your generosity.

main idea: the approval of a business casual dress policy. The discussion that follows includes a brief review of the policy and ends positively by encouraging employees to seek additional information from the company website or contact the writer.

Thank-You and Appreciation Messages

Empathetic managers take advantage of occasions to write goodwill messages that build strong, lasting relationships with employees, clients, customers, and various other groups. People are usually not reluctant to say, "Thank you," "What a great performance," "You have certainly helped me," and so on. Despite good intentions, however, often people don't get around to sending thank-you and appreciation messages. Because of their rarity, written appreciation messages are especially meaningful—even treasured.

Thank-You Messages

After receiving a gift, being a guest, attending an interview, or benefiting in various other ways, a thoughtful person will take the time to send a written thank-you message. A simple handwritten or electronically sent note is sufficient for some social situations. However, when written from a professional office to respond to a business situation, the message might be printed on company letterhead. Your message should be written deductively and reflect your sincere feelings of gratitude. The thank-you messages shown above (a) identify the circumstances for which the writer is grateful and (b) provide specific reasons the action is appreciated.

Appreciation Messages

You will write appreciation messages to recognize, reward, and encourage the receiver; however, you will also gain happiness from commending a deserving person. Such positive thinking can be a favorable influence on your own attitude and performance. In appropriate situations, you might wish to address an appreciation message to an individual's supervisor and send a copy of the document to the individual to share the positive comments. In any case, an appreciation message should be sent to commend deserving people and not for possible self-gain.

For full potential value, follow these guidelines for appreciation messages:

- **Send in a timely manner.** Sending an appreciation message within a few days of the circumstance will emphasize your genuineness. The receiver might question the sincerity of appreciation messages that are sent long overdue.

- **Avoid exaggerated language that is hardly believable.** You might believe the exaggerated statements to be true, but the recipient might find them unbelievable and insincere. Strong language with unsupported statements raises questions about your motive for the message.

- **Make specific comments about outstanding qualities or performance.** Compared to Figure 6-3, the following message might have minimal value to a speaker who has worked hard and has not been paid. Although the sender cared enough to say thank you, the message could have been given to any speaker, even if the sender had slept through the entire speech. Similarly, a note merely closed with "sincerely" does not necessarily make the ideas seem sincere. Including specific remarks about understanding and applying the speaker's main points makes the message meaningful and sincere.

Figure 6-3

GOOD *Good Example of an Appreciation Message*

New Message

To: Ren Nagano <rnagano@ch.com>

From: Nolan Sherrod <nsherrod@gemco.com>

Subject: Appreciation for Outstanding Work

Ren,

Completing the ropes course at Camp Horizon was a memorable and life-changing experience for every member of our office staff.

Your facilitators were masterful in allowing our teams to take risks while ensuring their safety. The course provided a diverse series of activities that enabled each staff member to participate, regardless of his or her physical limitations. Identifying the real leaders in our office was extremely interesting.

In the words of one colleague, "The ropes course has shown me I can do more than I have come to expect of myself." Thank you for helping us see our potential.

Best wishes,

Nolan Sherrod
Human Resources Director
Gemco, Inc.
901-555-1616, Fax 901-555-1302
nsherrod@gemco.com

• *Extends appreciation for company's provision of quality opportunities for team growth.*

• *Provides specific example without exaggerating or using overly strong language or insincere statements.*

• *Assures reader of tangible benefits gained.*

Format Pointers
Uses short lines, mixed case; omits special formatting such as emoticons and email abbreviations for improved readability.

© Cengage Learning 2013

Original: Your speech to Women in Business was very much appreciated. You are an excellent speaker, and you have good ideas. Thank you.

Improved: This past week I have found myself applying the principles you discussed last week at your presentation to Women in Business.

I have long had difficulty speaking in public, but your suggestion to identify the reason for my fear and to write down why the fear was unfounded lifted a weight I have been carrying for years. Thank you for the suggestions that have put me on the path to becoming a more confident public speaker.

The appreciation message in Figure 6-3 sent from a manager to the facilitator of a ropes course that employees recently completed conveys a warmer, more sincere compliment than a generic, exaggerated message. The net effects of this message are positive: The sender feels good for having passed on a deserved compliment and the facilitator is encouraged by the client's satisfaction with her team development program.

An apology is written much like an appreciation message. A sincere written apology is needed to preserve relationships when regrettable situations occur. However difficult to prepare, a well-written apology will usually be received favorably.

© iStockphoto.com/Sergei Korotkov

Routine Claims

A **claim** is a request for an adjustment. When business communicators ask for something to which they think they are entitled (such as a refund, replacement, exchange, or payment for damages), the message is called a *claim message*.

⊠ **OBJECTIVE 3**

Write messages presenting routine claims and requests and favorable responses to them.

claim
a request for an adjustment

routine claims
messages that assume that a claim will be granted quickly and willingly, without persuasion

persuasive claims
messages that assume a claim will be granted only after explanations and persuasive arguments have been presented

adjustment messages
messages that are fair responses by businesses to legitimate requests in claim messages by customers

Claim Message

Requests for adjustments can be divided into two groups: **routine claims** and **persuasive claims**. Persuasive claims, which are discussed in Chapter 8, assume that a request will be granted only after explanations and persuasive arguments have been presented. Routine claims (possibly because of guarantees, warranties, or other contractual conditions) assume that a request will be granted quickly and willingly, without persuasion. Because you expect routine claims to be granted willingly, a forceful, accusatory tone is inappropriate.

When the claim is routine, the direct approach shown in Figure 6-1 is appropriate. Let's consider the situation referred to in Figures 6-4 and 6-5. Surely, the computer sales company intended the laptop to be fully functioning. Because the damage—a broken fan—appears to be obvious, the computer sales company can be expected to correct the problem without persuasion. Thus, the purchasing manager can ask for an adjustment before providing an explanation, as shown in Figure 6-5. Beginning with the request for an adjustment gives it the emphasis it deserves. Note, however, that the message in Figure 6-4 is written inappropriately using an indirect approach—the details are presented before the main idea, and the tone is unnecessarily forceful.

Favorable Response to a Claim Message

Businesses *want* their customers to communicate when merchandise or service is not satisfactory. They want to learn of ways in which goods and services can be improved, and they want their customers to receive value for the money they spend. With considerable confidence, they can assume that writers of claim messages think their claims are valid. By responding fairly to legitimate requests in **adjustment messages**, businesses can gain a reputation for standing behind their goods and services. A loyal customer is likely to become even more loyal after a business has demonstrated its integrity.

Figure 6-4 **BAD** *Poor Example of a Routine Claim*

Mr. Bowls,

Our company recently purchased 24 laptop computers from your company for use by our sales personnel. We have been very pleased with their performance. Unfortunately, one of the laptops is no longer functioning because of a broken fan.

This has created a problem for one of our most productive sales team members, Maria Rodriguez, who is unable to submit customer orders electronically without her computer.

You should receive the damaged laptop tomorrow via overnight freight. Please replace or repair it and return it to us as soon as possible.

- *Introduction does not state the purpose of the message. Instead, it provides unneeded background.*

- *Paragraph provides more unnecessary background information.*

- *The routine request comes at the end of the message rather than at the beginning.*

© Cengage Learning 2013

New Message

To:	Tom Bowls <tbowls@computersolutions.com>
From:	Jennifer Reagan <jreagan@lauder.com>
Subject:	Laptop Repair or Replacement Needed

Mr. Bowls,

Please repair or send us a replacement for the laptop computer listed on the attached sales agreement. It has a faulty cooling fan.

You should receive the computer tomorrow via overnight freight.

The computer was purchased six months ago under our agreement with your company to provide our salespeople with laptops. The computers are covered by a 12-month warranty for faulty parts replacement. I spoke with your sales manager, Tom Wilkins, this morning and he instructed me to contact you for extradited service.

Our salesperson Maria Rodriguez eagerly awaits the return of her laptop. Our salespeople are highly dependent on their computers because they spend so much time on the road.

Thanks,

Jennifer Reagan
Purchasing Manager

Limits message to single idea expressed in meaningful subject line.

Emphasizes main idea (request for adjustment) by placing it in first sentence.

Provides explanation.

Ends on positive note, reminding reader of immediate need.

Format Pointers
Composes short, concise message that fits on one screen.

Includes salutation and closing to personalize message.

Ordinarily, a response to a written message is also a written message. Sometimes people communicate to confirm ideas they have already discussed on the phone. When the response to a claim is favorable, present ideas in the direct sequence. Although the word *grant* is acceptable when talking about claims, its use in adjustment messages is discouraged. An expression such as "Your claim is being granted" unnecessarily implies that you are in a position of power.

Because the subject of an adjustment is related to the goods or services provided, the message can include a brief sales idea. With only a little extra space, the message can include resale or sales promotional material. **Resale** refers to a discussion of goods or services already bought. It reminds customers and clients that they made a good choice in selecting a company with which to do business, or it reminds them of the good qualities of their purchase. **Sales promotional material** refers to statements made about related merchandise or service. For example,

a message about a company's recently purchased office furniture might also mention available office equipment. Mentioning the office equipment is using sales promotional material. Subtle sales messages that are included in adjustments have a good chance of being read, whereas direct sales messages might not be read at all.

Consider the ineffective response in Figure 6-6 on the next page to Jennifer Reagan's claim letter and the message it sends about the company's commitment. Now notice the deductive outline and the explanation in the revision in Figure 6-7 on the next page. Because the writer knows that Jennifer will be pleased the laptop has been repaired and shipped, the good news appears in the first sentence. The details and closing sentence follow naturally and show a desire to correct the problem.

resale
a discussion of goods or services already bought
sales promotional material
statements made about related merchandise or service

Figure 6-6   *Poor Example of a Positive Response to a Routine Claim*

Thank you for your letter of July 10. It has been referred to me for reply.

We have received the laptop of which you wrote and have taken a look at the cooling fan. We don't know the cause of the fan failure but will repair it and return it to you soon.

We apologize for any inconvenience.

- *This introduction states the obvious and does not address reader concerns.*

- *Paragraph is too descriptive of the writer's experience and should focus more narrowly on the reader's concerns.*

- *Ending is too generic to effectively promote goodwill.*

© Cengage Learning 2013

Figure 6-7   **GOOD**   *Good Example of a Positive Response to a Routine Claim*

	New Message
To:	Jennifer Reagan <jreagan@lauder.com>
From:	Tom Bowls <tbowls@computersolutions.com>
Subject:	Repaired Laptop Delivered Tomorrow

Ms. Reagan,

The repaired laptop has been shipped to you via overnight freight. You should receive it tomorrow.

The cooling fan has been replaced and we have conducted a systems test to ensure that all of the computer components are in working order.

We pride ourselves on our timely service response. Please do not hesitate to contact us with any concerns regarding your laptop order or their performance.

Sincerely,

Thomas Bowls
Manager, Customer Service

- *Begins with good news (main idea) with assurance of desired action.*

- *Presents explanation and assurance of a process for quality control.*

- *Attempts to regain possible lost goodwill by offering personalized assistance.*

© Cengage Learning 2013

Figure 6-8  *Poor Example of a Routine Request*

Subject: Need information

I have been searching for a relaxing location for my organization's national conference to be held in late March of next year. From looking at your website, it appears that Long Beach meets almost all our criteria. However, I am uncertain as to whether your hotel can accommodate our needs.

We expect that we may have as many as 600 attendees and perhaps half may need hotel accommodations. In addition, we expect as many as 100 technology companies to purchase booths to showcase their products. Does your hotel have facilities to meet these needs?

I look forward to receiving your reply as quickly as possible.

- • *The subject line could be more informational.*
- • *The introduction could more clearly state the purpose of the message.*
- • *The writer's needs could be stated more clearly and systematically.*
- • *The generic close fails to build goodwill or a sense of urgency.*

© Cengage Learning 2013

Routine Requests

Like claims, requests are divided into two groups: **routine requests** and **persuasive requests**. Persuasive requests, which are discussed in Chapter 8, assume that action will be taken after persuasive arguments are presented. Routine requests and favorable responses to them follow the deductive sequence.

Routine Request

Requests for information about people, prices, products, and services are common. Because these requests from customers and clients are door openers for future business, businesses accept them optimistically. At the same time, they arrive at an opinion about the sender based on the quality of the message. Follow the points in the deductive outline for preparing effective requests you are confident will be fulfilled.

The message in Figure 6-8 does not follow the deductive outline that is appropriate for a routine request. The request is too vague and the sales manager receiving the message is not provided with enough useful information.

Note that the revision in Figure 6-9 on the next page starts with a direct request for specific information. Then as much detail as necessary is presented to enable the receiver to answer specifically. The revision ends confidently with appreciation for the action requested. The email message is short, but because it conveys enough information and has a tone of politeness, it is effective.

Favorable Response to a Routine Request

The message in Figure 6-10 on page 95 responds favorably but with little enthusiasm to an online request for detailed information related to conference accommodations at a Pacific Coast hotel. With a little planning and consideration for the executive planning a major event, the message in Figure 6-11 on page 96 could have been written just as quickly. Note the specific answers to the manager's questions prepared in the convenient Q&A format and the helpful, sincere tone.

Positive Response to a Favor Request

Occasionally, as a business professional, you will be asked for special favors. You might receive invitations to speak at

© iStockphoto.com/Paul Wilkinson

routine requests
messages that assume that a request will be granted quickly and willingly, without persuasion

persuasive requests
messages that assume that a requested action will be taken after persuasive arguments are presented

Figure 6-9   *Good Example of a Routine Request*

GOOD

New Message

To: Dean Sutter <dsutter@lbluxurysuites.com>

From: Lizbeth Token <ltoken@nta.org>

Subject: Information Needed for Planning Large Conference in Long Beach

---

Mr. Sutter,

The helpful information on your website describing the panoramic views of the ocean and unique shopping and restaurant possibilities offered on Pine Avenue suggests that Long Beach could be an ideal location for our three-day annual technology conference. To assist us in selecting the site for this event scheduled for late March 2012, please provide the following information:

- Does your hotel contain a conference center with space for 100 sales booths and three smaller rooms for concurrent sales presentations and press announcements?

- Can the conference hotel provide a block of 300 rooms, preferably at conference rate? If not, are there other suitable hotels nearby?

- Does the hotel have the capacity to feed 600 attendees during the three-day event at its in-house cafes and restaurants? If not, could you please provide a list of other nearby establishments that might meet the needs of attendees for breakfast, lunch, and dinner?

- Could your concierge staff provide a list of attractions and other venues that attendees might visit during the conference dates?

The information you provide could likely confirm our expectation that the Long Beach Luxury Suites can meet our conference needs. At that point you will be contacted to assist us in making necessary reservations. Should you wish to talk to me directly, please call (307) 213-6770.

Thanks,

Lizbeth Token, Director
National Technology Association
307-213-6770, Fax: 307-213-6775
ltoken@nta.org

• *States request clearly.*

• *Asks specific questions with necessary explanation; uses list for emphasis.*

• *Expresses appreciation and alludes to benefits for quick action.*

• *Opens door for personal dialogue by providing telephone number.*

Format Pointers
Provides salutation appropriate for company.

Includes a complete signature block below writer's name for complete reference.

© Cengage Learning 2013

© iStockphoto.com/enviromantic

Figure 6-10  *Poor Example of a Positive Response to a Routine Request*

RE: Information Needed

Ms. Token,

I read your request and hopefully my hurried response will provide you the information you need.

Long Beach Luxury Suites can serve your needs with a 10,000-square foot conference center and accommodations for more than 700 guests. We also have three restaurants in the hotel as well as a coffee kiosk in the lobby. We are near Pine Avenue and Belmont Shore as well as many area attractions, such as the Long Beach Aquarium, Disneyland, and Knotts Berry Farm.

We are happy you're considering Long Beach and Long Beach Luxury Suites for your annual conference. Please contact either me or my staff to make the necessary reservations.

- *The subject line could be more informational.*

- *The introduction could be more positive and speak more narrowly to the reader's concerns.*

- *This discussion could be more specific and presented in an easier-to-read format.*

- *The close could be more effective at building goodwill and demonstrating a sincere interest in meeting the organization's needs.*

© Cengage Learning 2013

various civic or education events, spearhead fund-raising and other service projects, or offer your expertise in other ways. If you say "Yes," you might as well say it enthusiastically. Sending an unplanned, stereotyped acceptance suggests that the contribution will be similar.

If you find yourself responding to invitations frequently, you can draft a form message that you'll revise for each invitation you receive. Go to www.cengagebrain.com to view a TV production manager's gracious acceptance of an invitation to emcee an awards program for a civic group. This well-written acceptance illustrates how form messages can be effectively individualized to enable businesses to communicate quickly and efficiently.

Form Messages for Routine Responses

Form messages are a fast and efficient way of transmitting frequently recurring messages to which receiver reaction is likely favorable or neutral. Inputting the customer's name, address, and other variables (information that differs for each receiver) personalizes each message to meet the needs of its receiver. Companies might use form paragraphs that have been saved as

template documents. When composing a document, select the appropriate paragraph according to your receiver's request. After assembling the selected files on the computer screen, input the particular information for the situation (e.g., name and address) and print a copy of the personalized message on letterhead to send to the receiver.

Form letters have earned a negative connotation because of their tendency to be impersonal. Many people simply refuse to read such letters for that reason. Personalizing a form letter can circumvent this problem.

Routine Messages about Orders and Credit

Routine messages, such as customer order acknowledgments, are written deductively. Normally, credit information is requested and transmitted electronically from the national credit reporting agencies to companies requesting

© iStockphoto.com/drfiet

Figure 6-11  *Good Example of a Positive Response to a Routine Request*

New Message

To:	Lizbeth Token <ltoken@nta.org>
From:	Dean Sutter <dsutter@lbluxurysuites.com>
Subject:	Assistance for Planning Exciting Conference in Long Beach

Ms. Token,

Long Beach and the Long Beach Luxury Suites are the ideal location for the National Technology Association's annual conference. My staff and I can assist you with all your lodging, conference, and entertainment reservations.

Q: Does your hotel contain a conference center with space for 100 sales booths and three smaller rooms for sales presentations/press announcements?

A: Long Beach Luxury Suites Conference Center can easily meet your needs. We have a 10,000-square-foot conference space as well as 10 smaller meeting rooms.

Q: Can the hotel provide a block of 300 rooms at conference rate?

A: Yes, the Long Beach Luxury Suites has 700 boutique-style rooms that are available for conferences of 200 people or more at a 15 percent rate reduction.

Q: Does the hotel have the capacity to feed 600 attendees during the three-day event at its in-house cafes and restaurants?

A: Long Beach Luxury Suites provides a unique dining experience in its three restaurants: The Car-hop Diner, the Bahamas Grill, and the Blue Crab Bistro. A coffee bar is conveniently located in our lobby. Just outside our door on Pine Avenue, more than a dozen restaurants are within easy walking distance.

Q: Could your concierge staff provide a list of attractions and other venues that attendees might visit during the conference?

A: Long Beach Luxury Suites is within walking distance of the Cabrillo Marina where a variety of sea cruises are available. Nearby is Long Beach Aquarium with more than 3,000 species of marine animals. A short bus or taxi ride takes visitors to the Long Beach Art Museum or shopping at Belmont Shores. Of course, other nearby attractions include Disneyland, Knotts Berry Farm, and Universal Studios.

Please call my direct line (509) 569-6768 for more advice on organizing an exciting event on the shores of the beautiful Pacific Ocean.

Thanks,

Dean Sutter, Sales Manager
Long Beach Luxury Suites

Revises subject line after clicking "reply" to communicate enthusiasm for providing exceptional personalized service.

Shows sincere interest in request and person.

Highlights specific answers to recipient's questions using an articulate, concise writing style.

Encourages direct call and provides more useful information that communicates genuine interest in person and event.

Format Pointer
Uses Q&A format to enhance readability of response to series of detailed questions.

© Image Farm/Jupiterimages

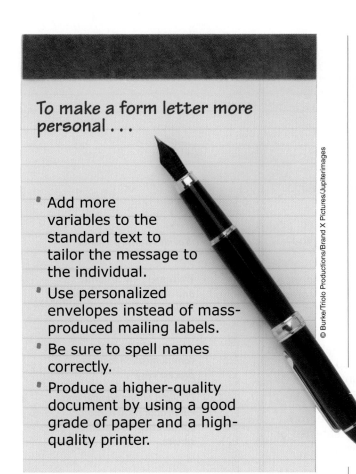

To make a form letter more personal . . .

- Add more variables to the standard text to tailor the message to the individual.
- Use personalized envelopes instead of mass-produced mailing labels.
- Be sure to spell names correctly.
- Produce a higher-quality document by using a good grade of paper and a high-quality printer.

© Burke/Triolo Productions/Brand X Pictures/Jupiterimages

Write messages acknowledging customer orders, providing credit information, and extending credit.

Acknowledging Customer Orders

When customers place orders for merchandise, they expect to get exactly what they ordered as quickly as possible. Most orders can be acknowledged by shipping the order; no message is necessary. For an initial order and for an order that cannot be filled quickly and precisely, companies typically send an **acknowledgment message**, a document that indicates the order has been received and is being processed. Typically, acknowledgment messages are preprinted letters or copies of the sales order. An immediate email message acknowledges an order placed online and confirms the expected date of shipment as shown in

Figure 6-12 on the next page. Individualized letters are not cost effective and will not reach the customer in a timely manner. Although the form message is impersonal, customers appreciate the order acknowledgment and information as to when the order will arrive.

Nonroutine orders, such as initial orders, custom orders, and delayed orders, require individualized acknowledgment messages. When well-written, these messages not only acknowledge the order but also create customer goodwill and encourage the customer to place additional orders.

Providing Credit Information

Replies to requests for credit information are usually simple—just fill in the blanks and return the document. If the request does not include a form, follow a deductive plan in writing the reply: the major idea first, followed by supporting details.

When providing credit information, you have an ethical and legal obligation to yourself, the credit references. However, when companies choose to request information directly from other businesses, individual credit requests and responses must be written.

acknowledgment message
a document that indicates an order has been received and is being processed

Tweeting the Customer Well

Email links, chat rooms, and bulletin boards on corporate websites foster dialogue that leads to strong relationships. Today, an increasing number of business people are participating in social exchange networking and blogging services, such as Twitter (**www.twitter.com**), to provide updates to customers.

"Tweet" postings must be brief; messages cannot exceed 140 characters.[1] Such forced brevity might be one reason for the service's popularity. If customers are invited to talk, companies must be prepared to respond with timely, effective—even if brief—messages.

© iStockphoto.com/Valerie Loiseleux

Figure 6-12 **GOOD** *Good Example of an Online Order Confirmation*

To:	Dillon McCrea <dmcrea@pmail.com>
From:	Maggie Fielding <mfielding@firstline.com>
Subject:	Firstline welcomes Dillon as valued customer

Dillon,

Welcome to Firstline Insurance! I'm excited to see that you have enrolled as a new customer.

You will be contacted soon by your personal customer service representative, Lucille Burns. Lucille has been with the company for ten years and is well versed in our product line and receives top rankings in customer service.

Lucille will make sure that you have the right financial products that suit you and your family's needs. She will keep in touch regarding your family's changing needs and will inform you about beneficial changes to your financial planning.

I have complete confidence in the care you will receive from Lucille, but if for any reason you aren't completely satisfied or have other concerns, please let me know right away.

You can reach me at 213-561-8300, extension 201, or you can email me at mfielding@firstline.com.

Thank you for trusting in us for your insurance needs.

Best regards,

Maggie Fielding
Customer Service Manager
Firstline Insurance Corp.

P.S. Be sure to watch your mailbox for our Welcome to Firstline package sent to new customers. You will receive coupons for discounts at several retail and restaurant outlets in your area as a sign of our appreciation for your business.

- *Provides warm, personal subject line.*
- *Welcomes new customer and acknowledges receipt of online order.*
- *Assures quality service by encouraging open communication to make process easy.*
- *Provides phone number and email address to reinforce commitment to customer service.*

© Cengage Learning 2013

credit applicant, and the business from which credit is requested. You must be able to document any statement you make to defend yourself against a defamation charge. Thus, good advice is to stick with facts; omit any opinions. "I'm sure he will pay promptly" is an opinion that should be omitted, but include the documentable fact that "His payments are always prompt." Can you safely say a customer is a good credit risk when all you know is that he/she had a good credit record when he/she purchased from you?

Extending Credit

A timely response is preferable for any business document, but it is especially important when communicating about credit. The Equal Credit Opportunity Act (ECOA) requires that a credit applicant be notified of the credit decision within 30 days of receipt of the request or application. The party granting the credit must also disclose the terms of the credit agreement, such as the address for sending or making payments, due dates for payments, and the interest rate charged.

When extending credit, follow these guidelines as you write deductively:

1. **Open by extending credit and acknowledging shipment of an order.** Because of its importance, the credit aspect is emphasized more than the acknowledgment of the order. In other cases (in which the order is for cash or the credit terms are already clearly understood), the primary purpose of writing might be to acknowledge an order.

2. **Indicate the basis for the decision to extend credit and explain the credit terms.** Indicating that you are extending credit on the basis of an applicant's prompt-paying habits with present creditors might encourage this new customer to continue these habits with you.

3. **Present credit policies.** Explain policies (e.g., credit terms, authorized discounts, payment dates). Include any legally required disclosure documents.

4. **Communicate a genuine desire to build a strong business relationship.** Include resale, sales promotional material, and comments that remind the customer of the benefits of doing business with you and encourage additional orders.

The letter in Figure 6-13 was written to a retailer; however, the same principles apply when writing to a consumer. Each message should be addressed in terms of individual interests. Dealers are concerned about markup, marketability, and display; consumers are concerned about price, appearance, and durability. Individual

Figure 6-13 *Good Example of Letter Extending Credit*

World Reflections
985 Hunter Avenue
Boston, MA 02194-0965
614-555-6790

January 24, 2012

Frances Ford
Purchasing Department
Pots and Pantries, Inc.
123 Colville Avenue
Spokane, WA 89001

Dear Ms. Ford:

Welcome to the most unique designs in glassware available in the U.S. Our expert buyers tour every region of the world to find the most innovative creations in kitchen and dining glassware.

Because of your current favorable credit rating, we are pleased to provide you with a $15,000 credit line subject to our standard 2/10, n/30 terms. By paying your invoice within ten days, you can save 2 percent on your glassware purchases.

You can use our convenient online ordering system to search our extensive line of glassware products and to place your orders. If you need additional assistance, please call our 24-hour service line, where you will be assisted by our number one-rated customer service personnel.

The most innovative glassware designs are now available to you and your customers, so please take some time to familiarize yourself with our extensive line.

Sincerely,

Luther Crosby

Luther Crosby
Credit Manager

- *Acknowledges customer's electronic access to product and implies credit extension.*

- *Recognizes dealer for earning credit privilege and gives reason for credit extension.*

- *Includes credit terms and encourages taking advantage of discount.*

- *Presents resaler a reminder of product benefits and encourages future business.*

- *Includes sales promotion; assumes satisfaction with initial order and looks confidently for future business.*

Legal and Ethical Considerations
Provides answer to request for credit within required time frame (30 days from receipt of request) and mentions terms of credit that will be provided, as required by law.

Uses letter channel rather than email to communicate a contractual message.

consumers might require a more detailed explanation of credit terms.

Companies receive so many requests for credit that the costs of individualized letters are prohibitive; therefore, most favorable replies to credit requests are form letters. To personalize the letter, however, the writer should merge the customer's name, address, amount of loan, and terms into the computer file containing the form letter information. Typically, form messages read something like this:

> **Dear [TITLE] [LAST NAME]:**
> Global Chocolatiers is pleased to extend credit privileges to you. Initially, you may purchase up to [CREDIT LIMIT] worth of merchandise. Our credit terms are [TERMS]. We welcome you as a credit customer at Global Chocolatiers and look forward to serving your needs for fine chocolates imported from around the world.

Although such form messages are effective for informing the customer that credit is being extended, they do little to build goodwill and promote future sales. Managers can personalize form messages that recipients do not perceive as canned responses.

Procedural Messages

Memos or email messages are the most frequently used methods of communicating standard operating procedures and other instructions, changes related to personnel or the organization, and other internal matters for which a written record is needed.

OBJECTIVE 5

Prepare procedural messages that ensure clear and consistent application.

Instructions to employees must be conveyed clearly and accurately to facilitate the day-to-day operations of business and to prevent negative feelings that occur when mistakes are made and work must be redone. Managers must take special care in writing standard operating procedures to ensure that all employees complete the procedures accurately and consistently.

Before writing instructions, walk through each step to understand it and to locate potential trouble spots. Then attempt to determine how much employees already know about the process and to anticipate any questions or problems. Then, as you write instructions that require more than a few simple steps, follow these guidelines:

1. **Begin each step with an action statement to create a vivid picture of the employee completing the task.** Using an action verb and the understood subject *you* is more vivid than a sentence written in the passive voice. For example, a loan officer attempting to learn new procedures for evaluating new venture loans can more easily understand "*identify* assets available to collateralize the loan" than "assets available to collateralize the loan should be identified."

2. **Itemize each step on a separate line to add emphasis and to simplify reading.** Number each step to indicate that the procedures should be completed in a particular order. If the order of steps is not important, use bullets rather than numbers.

3. **Consider preparing a flow chart depicting the procedures.** The cost and effort involved in creating a sophisticated flow chart might be merited for extremely important and complex procedures. For example, take a look at the flow chart in Figure 10-8, which simplifies the steps involved in processing a telephone order in an effort to minimize errors.

4. **Complete the procedure by following your instructions step-by-step.** Correct any errors you locate.

5. **Ask a colleague or employee to walk through the procedures.** This walk-through will allow you to identify ambiguous statements, omissions of relevant information, and other sources of potential problems.

Consider the seemingly simple task of requesting vacation leave. The human resource manager might respond, "No need for written instructions; just request vacation leave any way you wish." Ambiguous verbal instructions (reported in haste) could lead to confusion about vacation schedules and bad feelings about the efficiency of the process. The clear, consistent procedure in Figure 6-14 was prepared after the manager anticipated employee issues in requesting vacation leave. The policy is sent as an email attachment and posted to the company intranet for easy reference.

Figure 6-14 Good Example of a Procedural Email with an Attachment

New Message

To:	All Employees
From:	Milton Bergman <mbergman@procorp.com>
Subject:	New Procedure for Requesting Vacation Leave

Attachment: Vacation_Leave_Request_Procedures.docx
— • Includes attached file of document requiring involved formatting.

Hi, all,

With the recent and dramatic growth in the company, the challenge of processing employee requests for vacation leave has become a concern. To solve this issue, we have instituted an online process for requesting vacation leave, beginning March 31.
— • Introduces main idea.
— • Explains new procedures outlined in attached file.

To request vacation leave, please follow the procedure outlined in the attached file. (This file can also be found on the company intranet under "Human Resources." You can complete these procedures at any computer, including your home machine.

Thanks,

Milton Bergman
Human Resource Manager

Procedures for Requesting Vacation Leave
— • Provides descriptive title that clearly identifies procedures.

1. Access http://www.procorp.com/hr and click the Forms link.
— • Enumerates to direct attention to each step and emphasize need for sequence.

2. Scroll down the list that appears and click on Vacation Leave Request.
— • Begins each item with action verb to help employees visualize completing procedures.

3. Provide the information requested in the form. Be certain to complete the required items denoted with asterisks.

4. Check your email for the response to your request, which typically will arrive within 48 hours.

5. Make sure that you notify your manager of your approved leave time so that he or she may plan accordingly.
— • Includes date of last revision to ensure currentness.

If you have questions, please contact a human resource coordinator by emailing hrinfo@procorp.com. A coordinator will contact you within 24 hours.

Dated 02/22/2012

Delivering Bad-News Messages

Choosing an Appropriate Channel and Organizational Pattern

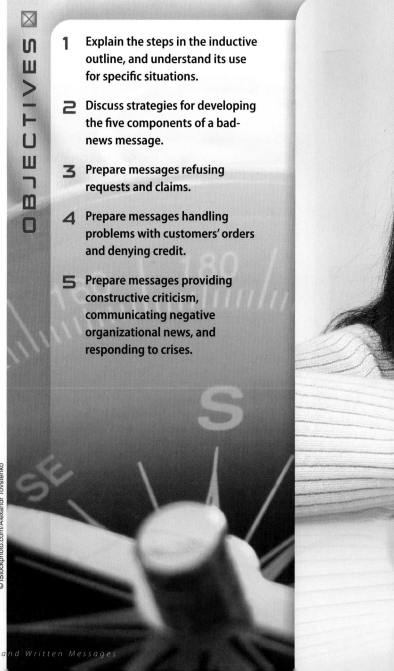

An organization's ability to handle difficult situations with tact and empathy powerfully influences the perceptions of employees, local citizens, and the public at large. As a skilled communicator, you will attempt to deliver bad news in such a way that the recipient supports the decision and is willing to continue a positive relationship. To accomplish these goals, allow empathy for the receiver to direct your choice of an appropriate channel and an outline for presenting a logical discussion of the facts and the unpleasant idea. Use tactful and effective language to aid you in developing a clear, yet sensitive, message.

⊠ **OBJECTIVE 1**

Explain the steps in the inductive outline, and understand its use for specific situations.

OBJECTIVES

1 Explain the steps in the inductive outline, and understand its use for specific situations.

2 Discuss strategies for developing the five components of a bad-news message.

3 Prepare messages refusing requests and claims.

4 Prepare messages handling problems with customers' orders and denying credit.

5 Prepare messages providing constructive criticism, communicating negative organizational news, and responding to crises.

Channel Choice and Commitment to Tact

Personal delivery has been the preferred medium for delivering bad news because it signals the importance of the news and shows empathy for the recipient. Face-to-face delivery also provides the benefit of nonverbal communication and immediate feedback, which minimizes the misinterpretation of these highly sensitive

© iStockphoto.com/Alexandr Tovstenko

messages. Personal delivery, however, carries a level of discomfort and the potential for escalation of emotion. A voice on the telephone triggers the same discomfort as a face-to-face meeting, and the increased difficulty of interpreting the intensity of nonverbal cues over the telephone only adds to the natural discomfort associated with delivering negative information.

You must be cautious when you deliver bad news electronically, whether by email or electronic postings. While you might feel more comfortable avoiding the discomfort of facing the recipient, the impersonal nature of the computer might lead to careless writing that is tactless and unempathetic, and perhaps even defama-

tory. Stay focused and follow the same communication strategies you would apply if you were speaking face to face or writing a more formal message. Regardless of the medium, your objective is to help the receiver understand and accept your message, and this requires empathy and tact.

"You're fired" became a familiar phrase immortalized by Donald Trump on the hit show *The Apprentice*. Though such bluntness might work on television, it is rarely recommended in actual work situations. Tactlessness can have serious effects when your personal response fails to soothe negative feelings and ensure a harmonious relationship with a customer, client, or

© Dynamic Graphics Group/Jupiterimages

employee. You might find it difficult to show tact when you doubt the legitimacy of a request or simply don't have the time to prepare an effective bad-news message. When this conflict exists, you must remember that your message delivered on behalf of the company is a direct reflection on the company's image.

Use of the Inductive Approach to Build Goodwill

Just as good news is accompanied by details, bad news is accompanied by supporting reasons and explanations. If the bad news is presented in the first sentence, the reaction is likely to be negative: "They never gave me a fair chance"; "That's unfair"; "This just can't be." Having made a value judgment on reading the first sentence, receivers are naturally reluctant to change their minds before the last sentence—even though the intervening sentences present a valid basis for doing so. Once disappointed by the idea contained in the first sentence, receivers are tempted to concentrate on *refuting* (instead of *understanding*) supporting details.

From the communicator's point of view, details that support a refusal are very important. If the supporting details are understood and believed, the message might be readily accepted and good business relationships preserved. Because the reasons behind the bad news are so important, the communicator needs to organize the message in such a way as to emphasize the reasons.

The chances of getting the receiver to understand the reasons are much better *before* the bad news is presented than *after* the bad news is presented. If the bad news precedes the reasons, the message might be discarded before this important portion is even read, or the disappointment experienced when reading the bad news might interfere with the receiver's ability to comprehend or accept the supporting explanation.

The five-step outline shown in Figure 7-1 simplifies the process of organizing bad-news messages. These five steps are applied in messages illustrated in this chapter.

Although the outline has five points, a bad-news message may or may not have five paragraphs. More than one paragraph might be necessary for conveying supporting reasons. In the illustrations in this chapter, note that the first and final paragraphs are seldom lon-

---

Figure 7-1 Inductive Outline Used in Bad-News Messages Sent in Written, Electronic, or Spoken Form

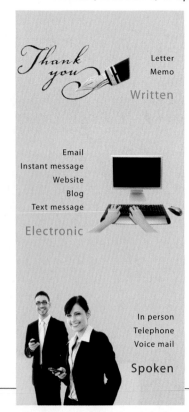

Thank you

Letter
Memo

Written

Email
Instant message
Website
Blog
Text message

Electronic

In person
Telephone
Voice mail

Spoken

OPENING: ✓

Begins with neutral idea that leads to refusal or bad news

BODY: ✓

1. Presents facts, analysis, and reasons for refusal or bad news

2. States bad news using positive tone and de-emphasis techniques

3. Includes counterproposal or "silver lining" idea when possible or appropriate

CLOSING: ✓

Closes with ideas that shift focus away from refusal or bad news and indicates continuing relationship with receiver

ger than two sentences. In fact, one-sentence paragraphs at the message's beginning look inviting to read.

The inductive sequence of ideas has the following advantages:

- Sufficient identification of the subject of the message without first turning off the receiver.
- Presentation of the reasons *before* the refusal, where they are more likely to be understood and will receive appropriate attention.
- Avoidance of a negative reaction. By the time the reasons are read, they seem sensible, and the refusal is foreseen. Because it is expected, the statement of refusal does not come as a shock.
- De-emphasis of the refusal by closing on a neutral or pleasant note. By showing a willingness to cooperate in some way, the sender conveys a desire to be helpful.

You might speculate that receivers might become impatient when a message is inductive. Concise, well-written explanations are not likely to make a receiver impatient. They relate to the receiver's problem, present information not already known, and help the receiver understand. However, if a receiver becomes impatient while reading a well-written explanation, that impatience is less damaging to understanding than would be the anger or disgust that often results from encountering bad news in the first sentence.

Exceptions to the Inductive Approach

Normally, the writer's purpose is to convey a clear message and retain the recipient's goodwill; thus, the inductive outline is appropriate. In the rare circumstances in which a choice must be made between clarity and goodwill, clarity is the better choice. When the deductive approach will serve a communicator's purpose better, it should be used. For example, if you submit a clear and tactful refusal and the receiver submits a second request, a deductive presentation might be justified in the second refusal. Apparently, the refusal needs the emphasis provided by a deductive outline.

Placing a refusal in the first sentence can be justified when one or more of the following circumstances exists:

- The message is the second response to a repeated request.
- A very small, insignificant matter is involved.
- The request is obviously ridiculous, immoral, unethical, illegal, or dangerous.
- The sender's intent is to "shake" the receiver.
- The sender–recipient relationship is so close and longstanding that satisfactory human relations can be taken for granted.
- The sender *wants* to demonstrate authority.

In most situations, the preceding circumstances do not exist. When they do, a sender's goals might be accomplished by stating bad news in the first sentence.

Developing a Bad-News Message

Developing a bad-news message following the inductive outline is challenging. The following suggestions will aid you in writing the (1) introductory paragraph, (2) explanation, (3) bad-news statement, (4) counterproposal or silver lining idea, and (5) closing paragraph.

Writing the Introductory Paragraph

The introductory paragraph in the bad-news message should accomplish the following objectives: (1) provide a buffer to cushion the bad news that will follow, (2) let the receiver know what the message is about without stating the obvious, and (3) serve as a transition into the discussion of reasons without revealing the bad news or leading the receiver to expect good news. If these objectives can be accomplished in one sentence, that sentence can be the first paragraph.

© iStockphoto.com/Albert Smirnov

Avoid the following weaknesses when writing the introductory paragraph:

- **Empty acknowledgments of the obvious.** *"I am writing in response to your letter requesting . . ."* or *"Your message of the 14th has been given to me for reply"* wastes space to present points of no value. Beginning with *I* signals the message might be writer-centered.

- **Tipping off the bad news too early.** *"Although the refund requested in your letter of May 1 cannot be approved, . . ."* might cause an immediate emotional reaction resulting in the message being discarded or interfering with understanding the explanations that follow.

  The neutral statement *"Your request for an adjustment has been considered. However, . . ."* does not reveal whether the answer is "Yes" or "No," but the use of "however" signals that the answer is "No" before the reasons are presented. Such a beginning has about the same effect as an outright "No."

- **Starting too positively so as to build false hopes.** Empathetic statements such as *"I can understand how you felt when you were asked to pay an extra $54"* might lead the receiver to expect good news. When a preceding statement has implied that an affirmative decision will follow, a negative decision is all the more disappointing.

Study the following examples that use transition statements to achieve a coherent opening:

Your employment application package has been reviewed by Human Resources.	Reveals the topic as a reply to a recipient's employment application.
Human Resources personnel . . .	Uses "Human Resources personnel" to transition from first to second paragraph.
Following your request for permission to submit a proposal to continue subsidizing employees' access to exercise facilities, we reviewed recent records of attendance.	Reveals subject of message as reply to employee's request.
In the past two years, attendance . . . *Last year, two incidents . . .*	Uses "recent" and "attendance" to tie second paragraph to first.

Here are several ideas that can be incorporated into effective beginning paragraphs:

- **Compliment.** A message denying a customer's request could begin by recognizing the customer's promptness in making payments.

- **Point of agreement.** A sentence that reveals agreement with a statement made in the message could get the message off to a positive discussion of other points.

- **Good news.** When a message contains a request that must be refused and another that is being answered favorably, beginning with the favorable answer can be effective.

- **Resale.** A claim refusal could begin with some favorable statement about the product.

- **Review.** Refusal of a current request could be introduced by referring to the initial transaction or by reviewing certain circumstances that preceded the transaction.

- **Gratitude.** In spite of the unjustified request, the receiver might have done or said something for which you are grateful. An expression of gratitude could be used as a positive beginning.

Presenting the Facts, Analysis, and Reasons

The reasons section of the bad-news message is extremely important because people who are refused want to know why. When people say "No," they usually do so because they think "No" is the better answer for all concerned. They can see how recipients will ultimately benefit from the refusal. If a message is based on a sound decision, and if it has been well written, recipients will understand and accept the reasons and the forthcoming refusal statement as valid.

To accomplish this goal, begin with a well-written first paragraph that transitions the receiver smoothly into the reasons section. Then, develop the reasons section following these guidelines:

- **Provide a smooth transition from the opening paragraph to the explanation.** The buffer should help set the stage for a logical movement into the discussion of the reasons.

- **Include a concise discussion of one or more reasons that are logical to the receiver.** Read the section aloud to identify flaws in logic or the need for additional explanation.

- **Show receiver benefit and/or consideration.** Emphasize how the receiver will benefit from the decision. Avoid insincere, empty statements such as "To improve our service to you, . . ."

- **Avoid using "company policy" as the reason.**
Disclose the reason behind the policy, which likely will include benefits to the receiver. For example, a customer is more likely to understand and accept a 15 percent restocking fee if the policy is not presented as the "reason" for the refusal.

The principles for developing the reasons section are illustrated in Figure 7-2, a letter written by an accounting firm refusing to accept a financial audit engagement.

Writing the Bad-News Statement

A paragraph that presents the reasoning behind a refusal at least partially conveys the refusal before it is stated directly or indirectly. Yet one sentence needs to convey (directly or by implication) the conclusion to which the preceding details have been leading. A refusal (bad news) needs to be clear; however, you can subordinate the refusal so that the reasons get the deserved emphasis. The following techniques will help you achieve this goal.

- **Position the bad-news statement strategically.**
Using the inductive outline positions the bad-news statement in a less important position—sandwiched between an opening buffer statement and a positive closing. Additionally, the refusal statement should be included in the same paragraph as the reasons, since placing it in a paragraph by itself would give too much emphasis to the bad news. When the preceding explanation is tactful and relevant, resentment over the bad news is minimized. Positioning the bad-news statement in the dependent clause of a complex sentence will also cushion the bad news. This technique places the bad news in a less visible, less emphatic position. In the sentence, *"Although the company's current financial condition prevents us from providing raises this year, we hope to make up for the freeze when conditions improve."* the emphasis is directed toward a promise of raises at another time.

- **Use passive voice, general terms, and abstract nouns.** Review the *emphasis techniques* that you studied in Chapter 3 as you consider methods for presenting bad news with human relations in mind.

- **Use positive language to accentuate the positive.** Simply focus on the good instead of the bad, the pleasant instead of the unpleasant, or what can be done instead of what cannot be done. Compared with a negative idea presented in negative terms, a negative idea presented in positive terms is more likely to be

---

Figure 7-2 Developing the Components of a Bad-News Message

Access to effective legal representation is a key component of our country's democracy, providing every citizen with adequate representation in the court system. For this reason, it is imperative that you have access to the best attorney possible in your upcoming proceedings.

To eliminate the appearance of a conflict of interest or bias, it is important to contract with an attorney who has no financial ties to the defendant. Our attorney, Conley Wilkes, was a significant contributor to your re-election campaign. Because of this indirect financial interest, we recommend that you seek another firm to defend you in your upcoming court action.

For other legal matters of a personal or civil nature, such as the preparation of a will, legal consultations, etc., we are available to provide service. Our attorneys are ready to provide you professional assistance. Please call me at 310-508-3100 to discuss these services.

- Begins with statement with which both can agree. Sets stage for reasons by presenting importance of quality attorney.

- Reveals subject of message and transitions into reasons.

- Supports refusal with logical reasoning.

- States refusal positively and clearly using complex sentence and positive language.

- Includes counterproposal as alternative.

- Closes with focus on continuing business relationship.

© Cengage Learning 2010

accepted. When you are tempted to use the following terms, search instead for words or ideas that sound more positive:

Words that evoke negative feelings

complaint	incompetent	misled	regrettable
error	inexcusable	mistake	unfortunate
failure	lied	neglect	wrong

Words that evoke positive feelings

accurate	concise	enthusiasm	productive
approval	durable	generous	recommendation
assist	energetic	gratitude	respect

- **Imply the refusal when the receiver can understand the message without a definite statement of the bad news.** By *implying* the "No" answer, the response has the following positive characteristics: (1) it uses positive language, (2) it conveys reasons or at least a positive attitude, and (3) it seems more respectful. For example, during the noon hour one employee says to another, "Will you go with me to see this afternoon's baseball game?" "No, I won't" communicates a negative response, but it seems unnecessarily direct and harsh. The same message (invitation is rejected) can be clearly stated in an *indirect* way (by implication) by saying "I must get my work done," or even, "I'm a football fan." Note the positive tone of the following implied refusals:

Implied Refusal	**Underlying Message**
I wish I could.	• Other responsibilities prohibit, but recipient would like to accept.
Had you selected our newest insurance product, you could have reduced your monthly rates by 10 percent or more.	• States a condition under which answer would have been "Yes" instead of "No." Note use of subjunctive words "had" and "could."
By accepting the new terms, Conduit Energy would have doubled its contracting costs.	• States the obviously unacceptable results of complying with request.

Offering a Counterproposal or "Silver Lining" Idea

counterproposal
in a bad-news message, an alternative to the action requested that follows the negative news and can assist in preserving future relationships with the receiver

Following negative news with an alternative action, referred to as a **counterproposal**, will assist in preserving a relationship with the receiver. Because it states what you *can* do, including

a counterproposal might eliminate the need to state the refusal directly. The counterproposal can follow a refusal stated in a tactful, sensitive manner. When global Internet services and media company AOL was faced with laying off 2,000 workers, the silver lining offered was a generous severance package and aid in transitioning to other job opportunities.[1]

While the counterproposal might represent a tangible benefit, at times it is more intangible in nature. For instance, in a letter that informs a job applicant that he or she was not selected to fill the position, the counterproposal might be an offer to reconsider the applicant's résumé when other appropriate positions become available. Any counterproposal must, of course, be reasonable. For instance, when informing a customer of an inability to meet a promised delivery deadline, an unreasonable counterproposal would be to offer the merchandise at no charge. A reasonable counterproposal might be to include some additional items at no charge or to offer a discount certificate good on the customer's next order.

When no reasonable counterproposal is apparent, the sender might be able to offer a "silver lining" thought that turns the discussion back into the positive direction. For instance, a statement to tenants announcing an increase in rent might be followed by a description of improved lighting that will be installed in the parking lot of the apartment complex. When offering a counterproposal or silver lining statement, care must be taken to ensure that the idea does not seem superficial or minimize the recipient's situation.

Closing Positively

After presenting valid reasons and a tactful refusal followed with a counterproposal or silver lining statement, a closing paragraph should demonstrate empathy without further reference to the bad news. A pleasant closing paragraph should close with an empathetic tone and achieve the following goals:

- **De-emphasize the unpleasant part of the message.** End on a positive note that takes the emphasis away from the bad news previously presented. A statement of refusal (or bad news) in the last

When no reasonable counterproposal is apparent, the sender might be able to offer a "silver lining" thought that turns the discussion back into the positive direction.

© iStockphoto.com/Jon Schulte

sentence or paragraph would place too much emphasis on it. Preferably, *reasons* (instead of bad news) should remain uppermost in the receiver's mind. Placing bad news last would make the ending seem cold and abrupt.

- **Add a unifying quality to the message.** Make your final sentence an *appropriate* closing that brings a unifying quality to the whole message. Repetition of a word or reference to some positive idea that appears early in the message serves this purpose well. Avoid restatement of the refusal or direct reference to it. This paragraph is usually shorter than the preceding explanatory paragraphs, often one or two sentences.

- **Include a positive, forward-looking idea.** This idea might include a reference to some pleasant aspect of the preceding discussion or a future aspect of the business relationship, resale or sales promotion, or an offer to help in some way. Consider the following closures that apply these suggestions:

Reference to some pleasant aspect of the preceding discussion:

"Your decision to refinance your mortgage last year was a wise choice." Home mortgage and other provisions had been mentioned in the early part of a letter to a client who was refused a double-indemnity settlement.

Use of resale or sales promotional material:

"Selecting our new hybrid Breeze with its 50-miles-per-gallon fuel usage was a wise decision with today's gas prices." A reminder that the hybrid has superior gas mileage will assist in regaining

goodwill after a customer's request for free repair has been refused.

An expression of willingness to assist in some other *way:*

Specifically, you might offer an alternative solution to the receiver's problem or useful information that could not be presented logically with the bad news. *"Our representative will show you some samples during next week's sales call."* The samples are being proposed as a possible solution to the receiver's problem.

Avoid including the following types of statements in the closing paragraph:

- **Trite statements that might seem shallow and superficial.** The well-worn statement, "Thank you for your interest," is often used thoughtlessly. It might seem shallow and superficial. "When we can be of further help, please do not hesitate to call or write" is also well worn and negative. *Further help* might seem especially inappropriate to someone who has just read a denial.

- **Statements that could undermine the validity of your refusal.** The statement "We trust this explanation is satisfactory" or "We hope you will understand our position" could be taken as a confession of doubt about the validity of the decision. Use of *position* seems to heighten controversy; positions are expected to be defended. Saying "We are sorry to disappoint you" risks a negative reply: "If it made you feel so bad, why did you do it?" It can also be interpreted as an apology for the action taken. If a decision merits an apology, its validity might be questionable.

- **Statements that encourage future controversy.** Statements such as "If you have questions, please do not hesitate to let us know" could also be perceived as doubt and possibly communicate a willingness to change the decision. If the decision is firm, including this type of closing could result in your having to communicate the negative message a second time.

Note the closing paragraph in Figure 7-2 is a positive, forward-looking statement that includes sales promotion of other services the accounting firm can offer.

© iStockphoto.com/Mike Brittain

Study the techniques used to cushion this bad-news statement:

Although the Denley Road property was selected as the building site, proximity to the railroad was considered a plus for the Nicholson property.

- States what was done rather than what was not done.
- Includes a positive idea ("proximity to the railroad") to accentuate a positive aspect and cushion the bad news.
- Uses passive voice ("property was selected") to depersonalize the message.
- Places the bad news in the dependent clause of a complex sentence ("although the Denley Road property was selected"). The positive idea in the independent clause ("proximity to the railroad") will receive more attention.

Refusing a Request

It's a good idea to use the inductive approach (reasons before refusal) for refusing requests for a favor, an action, or even a donation. Present clear, understandable reasons in a way that minimizes the receiver's disappointment.

You can examine a company's refusal to provide an executive to work for a community organization in Figure 7-3. This *response* to prior correspondence uses the same principles of sequence and style that are recommended for messages that *initiate* communication about unpleasant topics.

☒ **OBJECTIVE 3**

Prepare messages refusing requests and claims.

Figure 7-3  *Good Example of a Refusal for a Favor*

2700 Ridgeway • Cambridge, MA 02139-2700
• Phone 617 555-8700 • 617 555-7961

HILSTROM INDUSTRIES

March 18, 2011

Mr. Jon Koch, President
Naperville Historical Society
375 Devon Building
Richmond, VA 23261-9835

Dear Jon:

You are to be commended for your commitment to restoring Naperville's historical downtown shopping district. In this age of megamalls and Internet shopping, the culture of a traditional main street lined with home-owned and operated shops needs to be preserved.

The success of this project depends on a good project director. The organizational, leadership, and public relations activities you described demand an individual with upper-level managerial experience. During the last year, Hilstrom has decentralized its organization, reducing the number of upper-level managers to the minimal level needed. Although our current personnel shortage prevents us from lending you an executive, we do want to support your worthy project.

Kevin Denny in our senior executive corps has a keen interest in historical preservation, having served on the board of a similar organization while living in Vermont. If you can benefit from his services, call him at 555-8700, extension 65.

Sincerely,

Russ Cooper
Director

- *Introduces subject without revealing whether answer will be "Yes" or "No."*

- *Gives reasons that will seem logical to reader.*

- *Subordinates refusal by placing it in dependent clause of complex sentence. Alludes to help in another form.*

- *Closes positively with counterproposal. Conveys genuineness by summarizing executive's responsibilities and providing telephone number.*

Format Pointer
Signs first name only because writer knows receiver well.

Figure 7-4 *Poor Example of a Refusal to an Employee's Request*

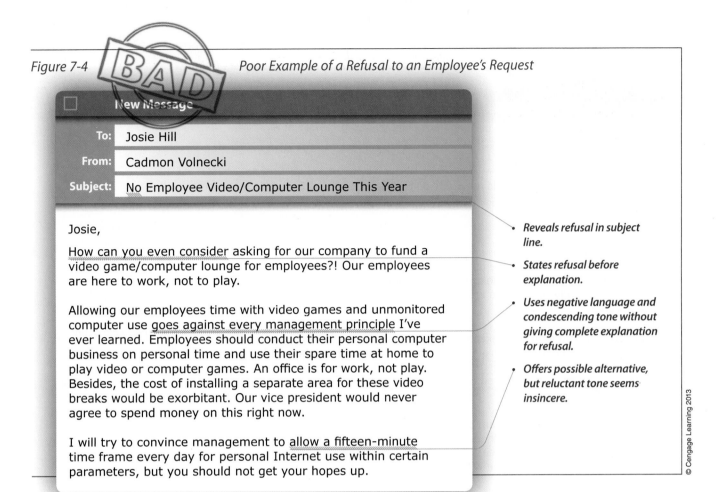

To: Josie Hill
From: Cadmon Volnecki
Subject: No Employee Video/Computer Lounge This Year

Josie,

How can you even consider asking for our company to fund a video game/computer lounge for employees?! Our employees are here to work, not to play.

Allowing our employees time with video games and unmonitored computer use goes against every management principle I've ever learned. Employees should conduct their personal computer business on personal time and use their spare time at home to play video or computer games. An office is for work, not play. Besides, the cost of installing a separate area for these video breaks would be exorbitant. Our vice president would never agree to spend money on this right now.

I will try to convince management to allow a fifteen-minute time frame every day for personal Internet use within certain parameters, but you should not get your hopes up.

- Reveals refusal in subject line.
- States refusal before explanation.
- Uses negative language and condescending tone without giving complete explanation for refusal.
- Offers possible alternative, but reluctant tone seems insincere.

© Cengage Learning 2013

The same principles apply whether the communication is a spoken message, letter, memo, or email message.

Companies have learned that building employee relationships is just as important as developing customer goodwill. Refusing employees' requests requires sensitivity and complete, honest explanations, qualities not included in the bad email in Figure 7-4. The manager's hasty and vague response to a valued employee's request to create an employee video lounge uses a direct, blunt approach. In the revision illustrated in Figure 7-5 on the next page, the manager takes the time to prepare a response that reflects detailed explanation supporting the refusal and genuine respect for the employee.

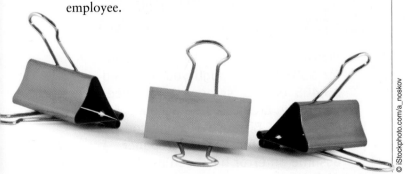

© iStockphoto.com/a_noskov

Denying a Claim

Companies face a challenging task of refusing claims from customers while maintaining goodwill and building customer loyalty. Claim refusals are necessary when a warranty does not apply or has expired or a customer has misused the product. Companies must also write refusals when customers ask for something that a company simply can't do. For example, many retailers charge customers a $25–$40 fee on returned checks. A retailer who receives a customer's request to waive the charge must refuse because the claim is inconsistent with the retailer's policies and objectives.

The inductive approach is helpful in communicating this disappointing news to customers. Presenting the explanation for the refusal first leads customers through the reasoning behind the decision and helps them *understand* the

⊠ OBJECTIVE 4

Prepare messages handling problems with customers' orders and denying credit.

Figure 7-5

GOOD — *Good Example of a Refusal to an Employee's Request*

New Message

To:	Todd Turnbill
From:	Diego Juarez
Subject:	Request for Employee Exercise Facility

Todd,

Because we want you to work at the highest level possible, your suggestion to construct an employee exercise facility on site has been carefully considered. Taking a break from work to exercise is an excellent way to energize employees and to ensure a healthy workforce.

Constructing an employee exercise facility on site would be a time-consuming and expensive project because of architectural, labor, and building material costs. Construction of the 1,000-square-foot facility and fitting it with the required exercise equipment would cost nearly $200,000.

In response to your idea, I am checking with existing exercise facilities located near our offices to see if we might arrange a reduced membership fee for employees. The company might also be able to subsidize a portion of the fee with the savings in reduced sick time you mentioned.

Todd, I will get back to you as soon as I have gathered information about the costs of membership at local facilities.

Regards,

Diego Juarez
Human Resources Manager
Software Solutions
Redmond, WA 90349
509-823-4211, Fax 509-823-4200
djuarez@softwaresolutions.com

- *Cushions bad news with sincere compliment for suggestion.*
- *Transitions to reasons and provides complete explanation for refusal.*
- *Restates reason to justify refusal.*
- *Includes logical alternative and closes with positive look toward future expansion.*

Format Pointers
Sends message by email—medium preferred by recipient.

Includes .sig file to identify writer and provide contact information.

© Cengage Learning 2013

---

claim is unjustified by the time the refusal is presented. Tone is especially important when denying claims. Present the reasons objectively and positively without casting blame or judgment on the customer for the problem. Avoid lecturing a customer on the actions he or she should have taken to have avoided the problem. Finally, close the message with resale or sales promotional material that indicates you expect future business. Although disappointed with your decision, customers continue doing business with companies who make fair, objective decisions and communicate the reasons for those decisions in a positive, respectful manner.

Assume a manufacturer of LED screens receives the following email from a customer.

New Message

To:	Craig Turner [cturner@electronicsplus.com]
From:	Jon Frakes [jfrakes@tvoptions.com]
Subject:	Refund Error

Please issue a credit to my account for $535.24. Although you accepted $3,405 of LED screens I returned, you only credited my account for $2,869.76. Because I could find no explanation for the discrepancy, I assume an error has been made.

Figure 7-6   *Poor Example of a Claim Denial*

Your message questioning your statement has been received. I am sorry, but we cannot adjust your account as you requested. Clearly, the statement is correct.

Each of the order forms you have completed states that returns are subject to a 15 percent restocking charge. Surely you saw this information printed in **bold** print on the order forms, and our telephone operators also explain our return policy thoroughly when customers place orders. I am sure you can appreciate the cost and effort we incur to restock merchandise after the holiday season is over.

Thank you for doing business with us. If you have any further questions, please do not hesitate to call or message us.

- *The introduction might be more positive by acknowledging customer's wise decision to buy product.*

- *A more tactful explanation of the reason for the refusal might prepare the reader for an implied refusal at the end of the paragraph.*

- *The conclusion does not build goodwill because it is too generic.*

© Cengage Learning 2013

The company's return policy allows customers to return unsold merchandise at the end of the holiday season, subject to a 15 percent restocking charge. The return policy is printed clearly on the inside cover of its catalog and in bold print at the bottom of both the printed and Internet order forms. Telephone operators explain the restocking charge to customers placing orders via the company's toll-free number.

The customer's inquiry shows a lack of understanding of the return policy. Although a frustrated company representative might question why the customer can't read the return policy, the response must be more tactful than that illustrated in Figure 7-6. The revision in Figure 7-7 on the next page reveals the subject of the message in the first sentence and leads into a discussion of the reasons. Reasons for the restocking fee, including benefits to the customer, precede the refusal. The tone is positive and respectful. The refusal statement uses several de-emphasis techniques to cushion its impact, and the final sentence turns the discussion away from the refusal with reference to future business with the customer.

Denying Credit

Once you have evaluated a request for credit and have decided "No" is the better answer, your primary writing challenge is to refuse credit so tactfully that you keep the business relationship on a cash basis. When requests for credit are accompanied with an order, your credit refusals might serve as order acknowledgments. Of course, every business message is directly or indirectly a sales message. Prospective customers will be disappointed when they cannot buy on a credit basis. However, if you keep them sold on your goods and services, they might prefer to buy from you on a cash basis instead of seeking credit privileges elsewhere.

When the credit investigation shows that applicants are poor credit risks, too many credit writers no longer regard them as possible customers. They write to them in a cold, matter-of-fact manner. They do not consider that such applicants might still be interested in doing business on a cash basis and might qualify for credit later.

In credit denials, as in other types of refusals, the major portion of the message should be an explanation for the denial. You cannot expect your receiver to agree that your "No" answer is the right answer unless you give the reasons behind it.

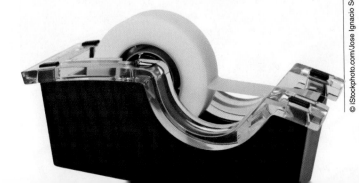

© iStockphoto.com/Jose Ignacio Soto

Figure 7-7 **GOOD** *Good Example of a Claim Denial*

NEWPORT LEISURE INDUSTRIES

860 MONMOUTH STREET
NEWPORT, KY 41071-6218

TELEPHONE: 800-555-6000
FAX: 800-555-0583

June 14, 2011

Snowcap Limited
Attention Lindsey Tucker
1905 Southhaven Street
Santa Fe, NM 87501-7313

Ladies and Gentlemen:

Restocking of Returned Merchandise

The HighFly skis you stocked this past season are skillfully crafted and made from the most innovative materials available. Maintaining a wide selection of quality skiing products is an excellent strategy for developing customer loyalty and maximizing your sales.

Our refund policies provide you the opportunity to keep a fully stocked inventory at the lowest possible cost. You receive full refunds for merchandise returned within 10 days of receipt. For unsold merchandise returned after the primary selling season, a modest 15 percent restocking fee is charged to cover our costs of holding this merchandise until next season. The credit applied to your account for $2,069.75 covers merchandise you returned at the end of February.

While relaxing from another great skiing season, take a look at our new HighFly skis and other items available in the enclosed catalog for the 2012 season. You can save 10 percent by ordering premium ski products before May 10.

Sincerely,

Galen Fondren

Galen Fondren
Credit Manager

Enclosure: Catalog

Legal and Ethical Consideration
Avoids corrective language that might insult, belittle, or offend.

- Uses subject line that identifies subject without revealing refusal.

- Uses resale to cushion bad news and lead into explanation.

- Presents clear explanation of reasons behind policy with emphasis on ways reader benefits.

- Implies refusal by stating amount credited to account.

- Shifts emphasis away from refusal by presenting silver lining sales promotion for next season's merchandise.

- Specifies enclosure to emphasize importance of exact items.

© Cengage Learning 2013

© Jurgen Ziewe/Shutterstock

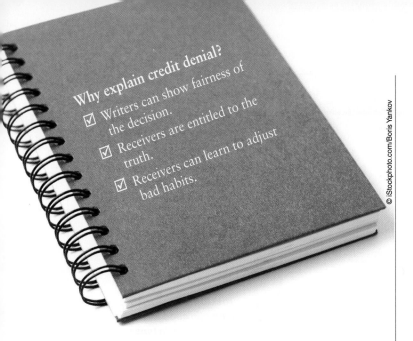

Why explain credit denial?
☑ Writers can show fairness of the decision.
☑ Receivers are entitled to the truth.
☑ Receivers can learn to adjust bad habits.

Delivering Constructive Criticism

A person who has had a bad experience as a result of another person's conduct might be reluctant to write or speak about that experience. However, because one person took the time to communicate, many could benefit. Although not always easy or pleasant, communicating about negatives can be thought of as a social responsibility. For example, a person who returns from a long stay at a major hotel might, upon returning home, write a letter or email message to the management commending certain employees. If the stay had not been pleasant and weaknesses in hotel operation had been detected, a tactful message pointing out the negatives would probably be appreciated. Future guests could benefit from the effort of that one person.

⊠ **OBJECTIVE 5**

Prepare messages providing constructive criticism, communicating negative organizational news, and responding to crises.

Before communicating about the problem, an individual should recognize the following risks: being stereotyped as a complainer, being associated with negative thoughts and perceived in negative terms, and appearing to challenge management's decisions concerning hotel operations. Yet such risks might be worth taking because of the benefits:

- The communicator gets a feeling of having exercised a responsibility.
- Management learns of changes that need to be made.
- The hotel staff about whom the message is written modifies techniques and is thus more successful.
- Other guests will have more enjoyable stays in the hotel.

In the decision to communicate about negatives, the primary consideration is intent. If the intent is to hurt or to get even, the message should not be sent. Including false information would be *unethical* and *illegal*. To avoid litigation charges and to respond ethically, include only specific facts you can verify and avoid evaluative words that present opinions about the person's character or ability. For example,

Both writers and readers benefit from the explanation of the reasons behind the denial. For writers, the explanation helps to establish fair-mindedness; it shows that the decision was not arbitrary. For receivers, the explanation not only presents the truth to which they are entitled, it also has guidance value. From it they learn to adjust habits and, as a result, qualify for credit purchases later.

Because of the legal implications involved in denying credit, legal counsel should review your credit denial messages to ensure that they comply with laws related to fair credit practices. For example, the Equal Credit Opportunity Act (ECOA) requires that the credit applicant be notified of the credit decision within 30 calendar days following application. Applicants who are denied credit must be informed of the reasons for the refusal. If the decision was based on information obtained from a consumer reporting agency (as opposed to financial statements or other information provided by the applicant), the credit denial must include the name, address, and telephone number of the agency. It must also remind applicants that the **Fair Credit Reporting Act** provides them the right to know the nature of the information in their credit file. In addition, credit denials must include a standard statement that the ECOA prohibits creditors from discriminating against credit applicants on the basis of a number of protected characteristics (race, color, religion, national origin, sex, marital status, and age).

To avoid litigation, some companies choose to omit the explanation from the credit denial letter and invite the applicant to call or come in to discuss the reasons. Alternately, they might suggest that the receiver obtain further information from the credit reporting agency whose name, address, and telephone number are provided.

Fair Credit Reporting Act
federal law that provides consumers the right to know the nature of the information in their credit file and gives them other protections when they apply for and are denied credit

Figure 7-8 **BAD** *Poor Example of a Constructive Criticism*

Samuel Frandsen, an accounting auditor in your firm, is not working out well on our audit. He is constantly accepting cellphone calls, even while in meetings with our employees. The constant distraction of his phone conversation, sometimes highly personal, has our employees complaining that he is preoccupied with non-business matters. He has even asked our employees to repeat conversations that he missed while on his cellphone.

Although extensive knowledge of auditing procedures is important, Frandsen's lack of respect for others far outweighs his professional expertise. I seriously hope Frandsen is able to take steps to correct the situation.

- A more positive or neutral introduction would help to better maintain goodwill.

- This information should be placed in a second paragraph that describes specific behaviors to maintain neutrality.

- The close would better maintain goodwill if it were more positive in tone and content.

© Cengage Learning 2013

instead of presenting facts, the message in Figure 7-8 judges the staff member sent to perform an accounting audit at a client's office. Overall, the message is short, general, and negative. By comparison, the revision in Figure 7-9 has positive intent, is factual, uses positive language, and leaves judgment to the recipient.

Communicating Negative Organizational News

Being able to initiate messages that convey bad news is as important as responding "No" to messages from customers/clients and others outside the company. Employees and the public are seeking, and expecting, *honest* answers from management about situations adversely affecting the company—slumping profits, massive layoffs, bankruptcy, a variety of major changes in the organization, and negative publicity that affects the overall health of the business and retirement plans, to name a few.

Managers who can communicate negative information in a sensitive, honest, and timely way can calm fears and doubts and build positive employee and public relations. Effective managers recognize that employee morale as well as public goodwill, is fragile—easily damaged and difficult to repair. If handled well, these bad-news messages related to the organization can be opportunities to treat employees, customers, and the general public with respect, thus building unity and trust.

Strong internal communication is a key to involving employees in corporate strategies and building an important sense of community. Transparency can have a positive effect on an organization's culture. According to a recent workplace survey, open, honest communication between corporate leaders and employees can lead to a more productive and ethical workplace. According to Deloitte Chairman Sharon Allen, motivating communication patterns are "increasingly critical to retaining talent and preserving the health of today's organizations.[2]

Obviously, business and competitive reasons prevent a company from always being completely transparent with its staff, but every attempt should be made to do so when possible. The best companies use a variety of communication tools that promote an open exchange of honest, candid communication and welcome input from employees. Newsletters, email updates, town hall or focus meetings, videoconferencing, phone calls, and discussion boards drive home relevant messages and allow employees to pose questions to management. This quality two-way communication involves employees in corporate strategies; employees who are aware of company goals and potential problems feel connected and accountable. Informed employees are also better prepared for bad news when it must be shared.

Breaking Bad News

Assuming this long-term commitment to keep employees informed, the following suggestions provide guidance in breaking bad news to employees and the public:[3]

© Image Ideas/Jupiterimages

Figure 7-9

GOOD

Good Example of a Constructive Criticism

⊘SI
Office Systems Incorporated
2500 lincoln Green Road/Austin,
TX 78710-2500 / Phone: 512-555-9000 / Fax: 512-555-6573.

March 24, 2012

Charlise Smit
Cutter, Delay, and Smit Associates
3504 Elm Street
Cincinnati, OH 50340

Dear Ms. Smit:

Your auditing team has been working with us on site for about 10 days with excellent results. Early in the audit, Samuel Frandsen, one of your auditors, identified several key problems with our accounting procedures that we will address.

While working with our staff, Samuel's attention is constantly diverted from conversations by his receipt of cellphone calls. Although he rarely stops the meeting, the constant distraction of his conversation—sometimes personal in nature—has caused some of our employees to comment that he is preoccupied with non-business matters. Our managers cited several occasions when Samuel had to ask them to repeat a conversation that occurred while he was on the phone.

Samuel is obviously quite good at his job; his expertise in accounting procedures explains why he is a member of your respected team. Please convey my concerns to Samuel confidentially so that the rest of his time in our office will go smoothly for him and for us.

Sincerely

Daniel Sykes
Chief Financial Officer

- Introduces discussion of audit work underway.

- *Conveys fair-mindedness and establishes credibility by acknowledging good as well as bad points.*

- *Presents verifiable statements without labeling them in negative, judgmental terms.*

- *Ends on pleasant note that seeks to add credibility to preceding negatives.*

Legal and Ethical Considerations
Conveys positive intent to help— not to hurt or get even.

Avoids potential litigation charges by including specific, verifiable facts and avoiding evaluative, judgmental statements.

Uses "confidential" as safeguard; information is intended for professional use only, not designed to hurt or to be thought of as gossip.

Format Pointer
Uses letter channel rather than email to communicate a sensitive message.

© Cengage Learning 2013

- **Convey the bad news as soon as possible.** Timeliness will minimize damage caused by rumors and will give employees the concern and respect they deserve. Nestlé Purina and others in the pet food industry acted early and effectively to recall potentially deadly pet food tainted with wheat gluten from China and to assure pet owners that steps were in place to ensure healthy ingredients.[4]

- **Give a complete, rational explanation of the problem.** Be candid about what is happening, why, and its effect on employees, customers, and the public. Provide enough detail to establish your credibility and provide context so your audience can understand the situation. Stressing positive aspects will provide needed balance and avoid sugarcoating or minimizing the severity of the news to the point that the message is misunderstood. Bridgestone,

makers of Firestone tires, was criticized for botching its recovery efforts from claims of accidents being caused by faulty tires when it initially attempted to blame Ford for the problems instead of taking responsibility and seeking corrective actions.[5]

- **Show empathy.** There is really no good way to break bad news, such as the announcement of layoffs or closures, to employees. The economic downturn and job insecurity has resulted in increased stress for many employees, which raises the potential for workplace aggression. However, methods that reflect respect and proper timing reduce the likelihood of an emotional boil over.[6]

- **Respond to the feelings.** Allow people adequate time to react to the bad news. Listen attentively for understanding and then address the concerns, issues, and potential problems presented.

- **Follow up.** Let people know what will happen next—what is expected of employees or customers, and what the company will do and when. Plan to repeat your explanations and assurances that you are available to respond to concerns in several communications that extend over a given time.

Consider the company president who emailed employees about a relocation of the company's manufacturing facility (Figure 7-10). The president should not be surprised to learn that employees are resisting the relocation; some perceive the company to be an enemy uprooting families from their homes simply for financial gain. In his revision (Figure 7-11), the president anticipates the employees' natural resistance to this stunning announcement and crafts a sensitive message.

A printed memo is a more effective channel for communicating this sensitive and official information than the efficient, yet informal, email message. The revision indicates that the company's internal communications (newsletters and intranet) have been used to prepare the employees for this negative announcement. Thus, the official memo is no surprise; nor is the company's commitment to listen to the employees' concerns and to provide up-to-date information as it develops.

Responding to Crisis Situations

Crises can occur in any organization, disrupting business activity and posing significant political, legal, financial, or governmental impacts. Crisis situations can result from various events, including accidents, weather-related disasters, equipment failures, procedural errors, and deliberate maliciousness. When crises occur, the communication that is offered can either help ease situations or worsen them. Rather than waiting for a crisis to occur, an organization should examine its state of preparedness and have a carefully considered plan of action that includes the following steps:

- Anticipate potential crises in terms of areas of vulnerability and what could happen.

- Establish emergency procedures, including an alternate command center and chain of command. Ensure that more than one employee is media trained and able to respond appropriately if needed.

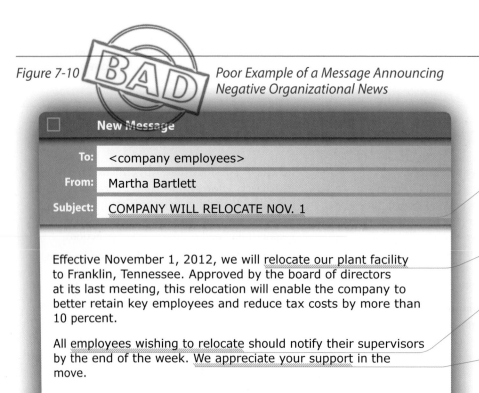

Figure 7-10 BAD — *Poor Example of a Message Announcing Negative Organizational News*

New Message

To: <company employees>

From: Martha Bartlett

Subject: COMPANY WILL RELOCATE NOV. 1

Effective November 1, 2012, we will relocate our plant facility to Franklin, Tennessee. Approved by the board of directors at its last meeting, this relocation will enable the company to better retain key employees and reduce tax costs by more than 10 percent.

All employees wishing to relocate should notify their supervisors by the end of the week. We appreciate your support in the move.

- *Bad news should not be announced in subject line. Better to provide reasons for change first.*

- *Introduction should serve as a buffer to naturally lead reader to "bad news."*

- *Additional paragraphs should be added to provide an explanation for the move.*

- *The close should let people know what will happen next and what the company will do.*

INTEROFFICE MEMORANDUM

TO: All Employees
FROM: Martha Bartlett, President
DATE: June 4, 2012
SUBJECT: Proposed Plan for Managing Future Growth

Our company has weathered the recent recession by taking advantage of international business opportunities in Asia. Our location in Southern California has provided us a well-educated and skilled workforce to produce the innovation needed in today's automobile market.

However, the rise in cost-of-living due to high taxes, comparatively high housing costs, and relatively higher costs for food and utilities has made it more difficult to retain top employees. The cost-of-living in Southern California is 15 percent higher than many other parts of the country. The school system in Los Angeles is one of the poorest in the country in terms of graduation rates from high school. Similarly, L.A. ranks at the top of the list in terms of time spent commuting on overcrowded freeways.

Housing prices, although dramatically lower than they were several years ago, are still well above the national average, particularly in safe neighborhoods with good schools. All of these issues make it much more difficult to retain skilled employees who have the option to move to other parts of the country without these challenges. In fact, three of our top engineers have left in the past year, citing the high cost of living and poor school system as their reasons.

While relocating could provide a long-term economic benefit to the company in terms of tax savings, moving out of Los Angeles could enhance the quality of life for all of us. Consequently, we have been working with state and local governments in other parts of the country to find an area with lower cost-of-living, good neighborhoods and schools, and a skilled labor force. This search has led us to identify Franklin, Tennessee, a thriving suburb located approximately 18 miles south of Nashville, as our new plant location.

Your supervisor will explain the logistics of the relocation at your next team meeting. In the meantime, please visit the Franklin link on the company intranet to read more about what Tennessee can offer us and our families. Check back for updates on the FAQ page designed to provide responses to your concerns. Now let us work together for a smooth transition to Franklin.

- Uses subject line to introduce topic but does not reveal bad news.

- Uses buffer to introduce topic familiar to employees through previous communication and leads into reasons.

- Provides rational explanation including benefits.

- Presents bad news while reminding receiver of benefits.

- Follows up assuring continued exchange of timely information through discussions and Web pages.

- Ends with positive appeal for unity.

Legal and Ethical Consideration
Uses memo channel rather than email for conveying sensitive message.

© Cengage Learning 2013

- Identify who will need to be contacted and plan for multiple means of disseminating information. Cell phones and text messaging have proven themselves valuable when other contact means might not work, but keep in mind that telecommunication circuits can be overloaded in mass disaster situations, necessitating multiple means for sharing news.

- Ensure current contact information is available for employees, media, and other pertinent parties.

- Maintain an up-to-date fact sheet about the company, its products/services, locations, and operations.

While crises can seldom be predicted, an organization can position itself to respond to them appropriately when they do occur. Having a well-prepared plan of action for dealing with emergencies can make the difference in an organization's survival and collapse.

In responding to a crisis, the message conveyed is extremely important in reassuring employees and business partners and in shaping public opinion. These guidelines can help ensure an effective message:

- Determine what your message is and prepare a checklist of what it should contain before writing.
- Keep the message simple, and arrange it in logical sections.
- Include verbiage that demonstrates your concern, compassion, and control.
- Prepare separate messages for internal and external audiences, including the appropriate level of detail.

Home   About   Staff   Capabilities   M.O.   News   Clients   Cases   Testimonials   Contact

DBMediaStrategies Inc.   2011

Crisis Communications

Media Training

Strategic Communications

Media Management

Public Relations

Speech, Editorial, Presentation Writing

"Sooner or later comes a crisis in our affairs and how we meet it determines our future happiness and success."

What is DBMediaStrategies?

DBMediaStrategies Inc. helps businesses, individuals and institutions navigate through the media thicket and devises communications strategies for their messages to be received, understood and tailored for specific audiences.

WHY CHOOSE?

Every 4LTR Press solution comes complete with a visually engaging textbook in addition to an interactive eBook. Go to CourseMate for **BCOM4** to begin using the eBook. Access at **www.cengagebrain.com**

Delivering Persuasive Messages

Persuasion Strategies

Business people regularly seek to persuade others. **Persuasion** is the ability to influence others to accept your point of view. It is not an attempt to trap someone into taking action favorable to the communicator. Instead, it is an honest, organized presentation of information on which a person can choose to act. Professionals in all fields benefit from well-prepared communications that persuade others to accept their ideas or buy their products, services, or ideas.

⊠ **OBJECTIVE 1**

Develop effective outlines and appeals for messages that persuade.

How do you learn to persuade others through spoken and written communication? Have you ever made a persuasive request, written employment documents or an essay for college entry or a scholarship, or given a campaign speech? If so, you already have experience with this type of communication. While the persuasive concepts discussed in this chapter are directed primarily at written communication, they can also be applied in many spoken communication situations.

For persuasion to be effective, you must understand your product, service, or idea; know your audience; anticipate the arguments that might come from the audience; and have a rational and logical response to those arguments. Remember, persuasion need not be a hard sell; it can simply be a way of getting a client or your supervisor to say yes.

persuasion
the ability of a sender to influence others to accept his or her point of view

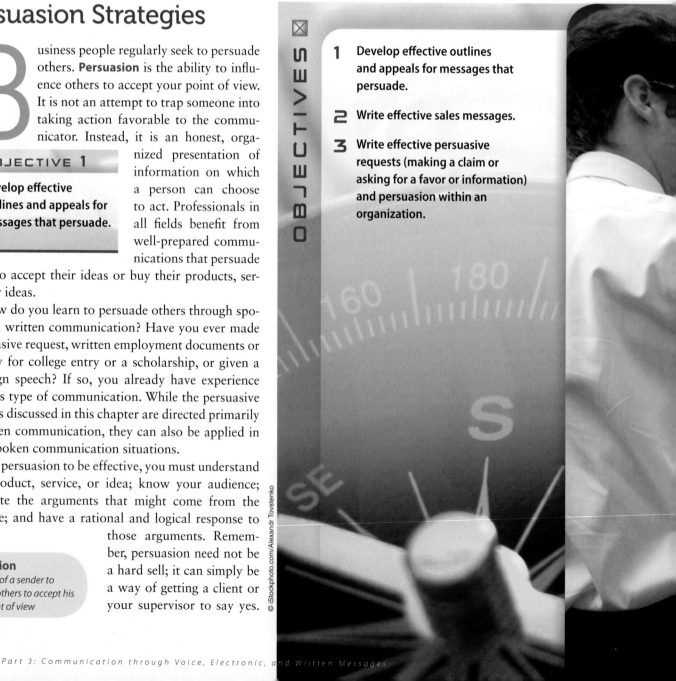

⊠ **OBJECTIVES**

1 Develop effective outlines and appeals for messages that persuade.

2 Write effective sales messages.

3 Write effective persuasive requests (making a claim or asking for a favor or information) and persuasion within an organization.

© iStockphoto.com/Alexandr Tovstenko

Although much of this chapter concentrates on selling products and services, similar principles apply to selling an idea, your organization, and your own abilities.

Plan Before You Write

Success in writing is directly related to success in preliminary thinking. If the right questions have been asked and answered, the composing will be easier and the message will be more persuasive. Specifically, you need information about (1) your product, service, or idea; (2) your audience; and (3) the desired action.

Know the Product, Service, or Idea

You cannot be satisfied with knowing the product, service, or idea in a general way; you need details. Get your information by (1) reading available literature; (2) using the product and watching others use it; (3) comparing the product, service, or idea with others; (4) conducting tests and experiments; and (5) soliciting reports from users.

Before you write, you need concrete answers to such questions as these:

- What will the product, service, or idea do for the receiver(s)?

© Marcin Balcerzak/Shutterstock

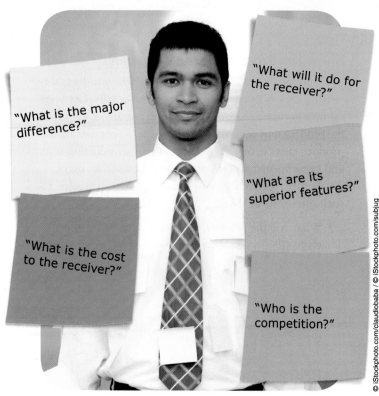

"What is the major difference?"

"What will it do for the receiver?"

"What are its superior features?"

"What is the cost to the receiver?"

"Who is the competition?"

- What are its superior features (e.g., design and workmanship or receiver benefit)?
- How is the product or service different from its competition? How is the proposed idea superior to other viable alternatives?
- What is the cost to the receiver?

Similar questions must be answered about other viable alternatives or competing products. Of particular importance is the question, "What is the major difference?" People are inclined to choose an item (or alternative) that has some distinct advantage. For example, some people might choose a particular car model because of its style and available options; still others might choose the model because of its safety record.

Know the Receiver

Who are the people to whom the persuasive message is directed? What are their wants and needs? Is a persuasive message to be written and addressed to an individual or to a group? If it is addressed to a group, what characteristics do the members have in common? What are their common goals, their occupational levels, and their educational status? To what extent have their needs and wants been satisfied? How might cultural differences affect your message?

AIDA

the four basic steps of the persuasive process, including gaining attention, generating interest, creating desire, and motivating action

Recall the discussion of Maslow's need hierarchy in Chapter 2. Some people might respond favorably to appeals to physiological, security, and safety needs (to save time and money, to be comfortable, to be healthy, or to avoid danger). People with such needs would be impressed with a discussion of the benefits of convenience, durability, efficiency, or serviceability. Others might respond favorably to appeals to their social, ego, and self-actualizing needs (to be loved, entertained, remembered, popular, praised, appreciated, or respected). Consider the varying appeals used in a memo to employees and to supervisors seeking support of teleworking. The memo to employees would appeal to the need for greater flexibility and reduced stress. Appeals directed at supervisors would focus on increased productivity and morale, reduced costs for office space, and compliance with the Clean Air Act, a federal law requiring companies to reduce air pollution and traffic congestion.

Identify the Desired Action

What do you want the receiver to do? Complete an online order and make a payment? Receive a demonstration version for trial? Return a card requesting a representative to call? Email for more information? Approve a request? Accept a significant change in service, style, and procedures? Whatever the desired action, you need to have a clear definition of it before composing your message.

Use the Inductive Approach

Over 100 years ago, Sherwin Cody summarized the persuasive process into four basic steps called **AIDA**.[1] The steps have been varied somewhat and have had different labels, but the fundamentals remain relatively unchanged. The persuasive approach illustrated in Figure 8-1 is inductive. The main idea, which is the request for action, appears in the *last* paragraph after presenting the details—convincing reasons for the receiver to comply with the request.

Each step is essential, but the steps do not necessarily require equal amounts of space. Good persuasive messages do not require separate sentences and paragraphs for each phase of the outline. The message *could* gain the receiver's attention and interest in the same sentence, and creating desire *could* require many paragraphs.

Apply Sound Writing Principles

The principles of unity, coherence, and emphasis are just as important in persuasive messages as in other

Figure 8-1 Inductive Outline Used in Persuasive Messages Sent in Written, Electronic, or Spoken Form

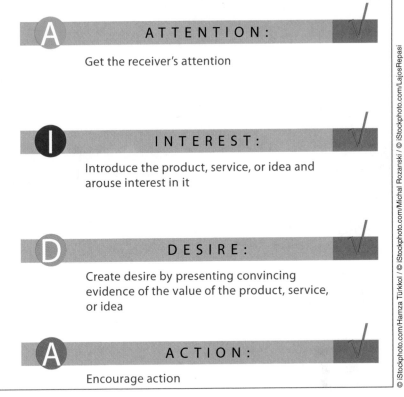

ATTENTION:
Get the receiver's attention

INTEREST:
Introduce the product, service, or idea and arouse interest in it

DESIRE:
Create desire by presenting convincing evidence of the value of the product, service, or idea

ACTION:
Encourage action

messages. In addition, the following principles seem to be especially helpful in preparing persuasive messages:

- **Keep paragraphs short.** The spaces between paragraphs show the dividing place between ideas, improve appearance, and provide convenient resting places for the eyes. Hold the first and last paragraph to three or fewer lines; a one-line paragraph (even a very short line) is acceptable. You can even use paragraphs less than one sentence long by putting four or five words on the first line and completing the sentence in a new paragraph. Be careful to include key attention-getting words that either introduce the product, service, or idea or lead to its introduction.

- **Use concrete nouns and active verbs.** Concrete nouns and active verbs help receivers see the product, service, or idea and its benefits more vividly than do abstract nouns and passive verbs.

- **Use specific language.** General words won't mean much unless they are well supported with specifics. Specific language is space consuming (saying that something is "great" requires fewer words than telling what makes it so); therefore, persuasive messages are usually longer than other messages. Still, persuasive messages need to be concise; they should say what needs to be said without wasting words.

- **Let receivers have the spotlight.** If receivers are made the subject of some of the sentences, if they can visualize themselves with the product in their hands, or if they can get the feel of using it for enjoyment or to solve problems, the chances of creating a desire are increased.

- **Stress a central selling point or appeal.** A thorough analysis ordinarily will reveal some feature that is unique or some benefit that is not provided by other viable alternatives—the **central selling point**. This point of difference can be developed into a theme that is woven throughout the entire message. Or, instead of using a point of difference as a central selling point, a writer could choose to stress a major satisfaction to be gained from using the item or doing as asked. A central selling point (*theme*) should be introduced early and reinforced throughout the remainder of the message.

central selling point
the primary appeal on which a persuasive message focuses

© iStockphoto.com/Mykola Velychko

Sales Messages

The four-point persuasive outline is appropriate for an *unsolicited sales message*—a letter, memo, or email message written to someone who has not requested it. A *solicited sales message* has been requested by a potential buyer or supporter; that is, the message is prepared to answer this interested person's questions.

A person requesting sales information has given some attention to the product, service, or idea already; therefore, an attention-getting sentence is hardly essential. However, such a sentence is needed when the receiver is not known to have expressed an interest previously. The very first sentence, then, is deliberately designed to make a receiver put aside other thoughts and concentrate on the rest of the message.

Gain Attention

Various techniques have been successful in convincing receivers to consider an unsolicited sales message. Regardless of the technique used, the attention-getter should achieve several important objectives: introduce a relationship, focus on a central selling feature, and use an original approach.

Some commonly used attention-getting devices include:

→ **A personal experience:** When a doctor gives you instructions, how often have you thought, "I wish you had time to explain" or "I wish I knew more about medical matters"?

→ **A solution to a problem (outstanding feature/benefit):** Imagine creating a customized multimedia presentation that. . . .

→ **A startling announcement:** More teens die as a result of suicide each month than die in auto accidents in the same time period.

→ **A what-if opening:** What if I told you there is a savings plan that will enable you to retire three years earlier?

→ **A question:** Why should you invest in a company that has lost money for six straight years?

→ **A story:** Here's a typical day in the life of a manager who uses a Blackberry.

→ **A proverb or quote from a famous person:** Vince Lombardi, one of the most successful coaches in the history of football, once said, "If winning isn't everything, why do they keep score?" At Winning Edge, we specialize in making you the winner you were born to be.

→ **A split sentence:** Sandy beaches, turquoise water, and warm breezes . . . it's all awaiting you on your Mesa cruise.

→ **An analogy:** Like a good neighbor, State Farm is there.

Other attention-getters include a gift, an offer, a bargain, or a comment on an enclosed product sample.

Introduce a Relationship between the Receiver and the Product, Service, or Idea

Remaining sentences grow naturally from this beginning sentence. If receivers do not see the relationship between the first sentence and the sales appeal, they could react negatively to the whole message—they might think they have been tricked into reading it. For example, consider the following poor attention-getter:

 Would you like to be the chief executive officer of one of America's largest companies? As CEO of Graham Enterprises, you can launch new products, invest in third world countries, or arrange billion dollar buyouts. Graham Enterprises is one of several companies at your command in the new computer software game developed by Creative Diversions Software.

© Tatiana Popova/iStockphoto.com

The beginning sentence of the preceding ineffective example is emphatic because it is a short question. However, it suggests the message will be about obtaining a top management position, which it is not. All three sentences combined suggest high pressure. The computer software game has relevant virtues, and one of them could have been emphasized by placing it in the first sentence.

Focus on a Central Selling Feature

Almost every product, service, or idea will in some respects be superior to its competition. If not, such factors as favorable price, fast delivery, or superior service can be used as the primary appeal. This central selling point must be emphasized, and one of the most effective ways to emphasize a point is by position in the message. An outstanding feature mentioned in the middle of a message might go unnoticed, but it will stand out if mentioned in the first sentence. Note how the following opening sentence introduces the central selling feature and leads naturally into the sentences that follow:

One of Soviet Georgia's senior citizens thought Dannon was an excellent yogurt. She ought to know. She's been eating yogurt for 137 years.

Dannon Yogurt is a part of a healthy nutrition plan that can add years to your life, too. It's high in important nutrients including calcium, protein, vitamin B12, potassium, phosphorus, and riboflavin, as well as being a great way to reduce fat and calories from your meals.

Use an Original Approach

To get the reader's attention and interest, you must offer something new and fresh. Thus, choose an anecdote likely unfamiliar to your receiver or use a unique combination of words to describe how a product, service, or idea can solve the receiver's problem:

The nine-year-old boy rushes to the store's toy department, unaware that his parents are far behind him in housewares. Surrounded by the latest action figures, electronic games, and cartoon DVDs, he hardly knows where to start in his search for the perfect gifts to include on his holiday wish list. For the next hour, his parents indulge his enthusiasm as he tries out every displayed product.

In many ways, Adobe Photoshop Elements is like that toy department. The new Photoshop offers a plethora of powerful, useful features that will hold your attention for hours on end.

Generate ⓘnterest by Introducing the Product, Service, or Idea

A persuasive message is certainly off to a good start if the first sentences cause the receiver to think, "Here's a solution to one of my problems," "Here's something I need," or "Here's something I want." You can lead the receiver to such a thought by introducing the product, service, or idea in the very first sentence. If you do, you can succeed in both getting attention and creating interest in one sentence. An effective introduction of the product, service, or idea is cohesive and action centered, and continues to stress a central selling point.

Be Cohesive

If the attention-getter does not introduce the product, service, or idea, it should lead naturally to the introduction. Note the abrupt change in thought and the unrelatedness of the attention-getter to the second paragraph in the following example:

Employees appreciate a company that provides a safe work environment.

The Adcock Human Resources Association has been conducting a survey for the last six months. Their primary aim is to improve the safety of office work environments.

The last words of the first sentence, "safe work environment," are related to "safety of office work environments"—the last words of the last sentence. No word or phrase in the first sentence connects the words of the second sentence, which creates an abrupt, confusing change in thought. In the following revision, the second sentence is tied to the first by the word "that's." "Safety" in the second sentence refers to "protection" in the third. The LogicTech low-radiation monitor is introduced as a means of providing a safe work environment. Additionally, notice that the attention-getter leads smoothly to the discussion of the survey results.

Employees appreciate a company that provides a safe work environment.

That's one thing the Tucker Human Resources Association learned from its six-month survey of the safety of the office work environment. For added protection from radiation emissions, more companies are purchasing LogicTech's low-radiation computer monitors. . .

Be Action Oriented

To introduce your offering in an interesting way, you must place the product, service, or idea in your receivers' hands and talk about using it or benefiting from accepting your idea. They will get a clearer picture when reading about something happening than when reading a product description. Also, the picture becomes all the more vivid when the receiver is in the spotlight. In a sense, you do not sell products, services, or ideas; instead, you sell the pleasure people derive from their use. Logically, then, you have to focus more on that use than about the offering itself. If you put receivers to work using your product, service, or idea to solve problems, they will be the subject of most of your sentences.

Some product description is necessary and natural. In the following example, the writer focuses on the product and creates an uninteresting, still picture:

Careful shaping creates a rear stay assembly that is able to deflect vertically, absorbing road shock while staying extremely rigid for confident cornering.

In a sense, you do not sell products, services, or ideas; instead, you sell the pleasure people derive from their use.

In the revision, a person is the subject of the message and is enjoying the benefits of the road bike.

You will channel your inner "Lance Armstrong" when you mount the Cannondale Synapse road bike. You will corner confidently due to its rear stay assembly, which has been shaped to deflect enormous amounts of road shock. Your confidence will grow with the ability to sit more upright, the result of a taller head tube and a longer wheelbase. No wonder Synapse won Bicycling magazine's "Best Plush Bike" award and Top Velo's "Cyclosportif Bike of the Year."[2]

Stress a Central Selling Point

If the attention-getter does not introduce a distinctive feature, it should lead to it. Note below how the attention-getter introduces the distinctive selling feature (light weight) and how the following sentences keep the receivers' eyes focused on that feature:

Once you pick up the iPad 2, it'll be hard to put down. That's the idea behind the all-new design. It's 33 percent thinner and up to 15 percent lighter, so it feels even more comfortable in your hands. And it makes surfing the web, checking email, watching movies, and reading books so natural, you might forget there's incredible technology under your fingers.

Two powerful cores in one A5 chip mean iPad can do twice the work at once. You'll notice the difference when you're surfing the web, watching movies, making FaceTime video calls, gaming, and going from app to app. Multitasking is smoother, apps load faster, and everything just works better.[3]

By stressing one main point, you do not limit the message to that point. For example, while light weight is being stressed, other features are also mentioned.

Create **D**esire by Providing Convincing Evidence

After you have made an interesting introduction to your product, service, or idea, present enough supporting evidence to satisfy your receivers' needs. Keep one or two main features uppermost in the receivers' minds, and include evidence that supports these features. For example, using fuel economy as an outstanding selling feature of hybrid cars while presenting abundant evidence about performance would be inconsistent.

Present and Interpret Factual Evidence

Few people will believe general statements without having supporting factual evidence. Saying a certain method is efficient is not enough. You must say how it is efficient and present some data to illustrate this. Saying a piece of furniture is durable is not enough. Durability exists in varying degrees. You must present information that shows what makes it durable and also define how durable. Durability can be established, for example, by presenting information about the manufacturing process, the quality of the raw materials, or the skill of the workers:

If you're looking for plush comfort, then look no further than Ashley's DuraPella® upholstery collection. DuraPella® is a high-tech fabric that is a breakthrough in comfort and durability. DuraPella® consists of 100% MicroDenier Polyester Suede, which gives you the subtle look and elegant feel of suede, yet is durable and stain-resistant . . . the best of both worlds! Everyday spills like coffee, wine, and even ballpoint pen are cleaned easily and effectively with a mixture of low pH balance liquid soap and water. You can enjoy luxury in everyday living with DuraPella®.

Presenting research evidence (hard facts and figures) to support your statements is another way to increase your chances of convincing your audience. Presenting results of a research study takes space but makes the message much more convincing than general remarks about superior durability and appearance.

Evidence must not only *be* authentic; it must *sound* authentic, too. Talking about pages treated with special protectants to retard aging and machine-sewn construction suggests the sender is well informed, which increases receiver confidence. Facts and figures are even more impressive if they reflect comparative advantage, as illustrated in the following example:

With thousands of new viruses created every day, relying on traditional security updates isn't enough anymore. Unlike the competition, exclusive McAfee Active Protection™ technology instantly analyzes and blocks new and emerging threats in milliseconds so there's virtually no gap in your protection. McAfee is 99.9 percent effective in detecting Malware, the best rating among competitors.[4]

Naturally, your receivers will be less familiar with the product, service, or idea and its uses than you will be. Not only do you have an obligation to give information, you should interpret it if necessary and point out how the information will benefit the receiver. Notice how the following example clearly interprets *why* induction is superior to electric or gas cooktops. The interpretation makes the evidence understandable and thus convincing.

Cold Statement Without Interpretation	Specific, Interpreted Fact
Cooking with an induction cooktop is the latest in technology for a restaurant environment or for just the average household.	Induction cooking is an entirely new way of cooking. Forget about red-hot electric coils or open gas flames. An induction cooktop converts your cookware into the heating element by using a magnetic field to energize the atoms in the cookware. Your food cooks faster, using less energy, while providing you with instantaneous temperature control.

The previous example uses a valuable interpretative technique—the comparison. You can often make a point more convincing by comparing something unfamiliar with something familiar. Most people are familiar with electric coils and gas flames, so they can now visualize how the cookware becomes the heating element. Comparison can also be used to interpret prices. Advertisers frequently compare the cost of sponsoring a child in a third-world country to the price of a fast-food lunch. An insurance representative might write this sentence: *The monthly premium for $300,000 of term life insurance is $18, the mere cost of two movie tickets.*

Do not go overboard and bore or frustrate your receivers with an abundance of facts or technical data. Never make your receivers feel ignorant by trying to impress them with facts and figures they might not understand.

Be Objective

Use language people will believe. Specific, concrete language makes your message sound authentic. Excessive superlatives, exaggerations, flowery statements, unsupported claims, and incomplete comparisons all make your message sound like high-pressure sales talk. Just one such sentence can destroy confidence in the whole message. Examine the statements in the following paragraphs to see whether they give convincing evidence. Would they make a receiver want to buy? Or do they merely remind the receiver of someone's desire to sell?

This antibiotic is the best on the market today. It represents the very latest in biochemical research.

Effective persuasion has enabled Habitat for Humanity to raise in excess of $1 billion annually to support its goal—to provide safe, decent, affordable housing to low-income families.

Identifying the best-selling antibiotic requires gathering information about all antibiotics marketed and then choosing the one with superior characteristics. You know the sender is likely to have a bias in favor of the particular drug being sold. However, you do not know whether the sender actually spent time researching other antibiotics or whether he or she would know how to evaluate this information. You certainly do not know whether the sender knows enough about biochemical research to say truthfully what the very best and latest is.

Similarly, avoid preposterous statements (*Gardeners are turning handsprings in their excitement over our new weed killer!*) or subjective claims (*Stretch out on one of our memory foam mattresses. It's like floating on a gentle dream cloud on a warm, sunny afternoon. Ah, what soothing relaxation!*). Even though some people might be persuaded by such writing, many will see it as absurd.

Note the incomplete comparison in the following example: *SunBlock provides you better protection from the sun's dangerous ultraviolet rays.* Is SunBlock being compared with *all* other sunscreens, *most* other sunscreens, *one* unnamed brand, or others? Unless an additional sentence identifies the other elements in the comparison, you do not know. Too often, the writer of such a sentence hopes the receiver will assume the comparison is with *all* others. Written with that intent, the incomplete comparison is *unethical*. Likewise, statements of certainty are often inaccurate or misleading.

Include Testimonials, Guarantees, and Enclosures

One way to convince prospective customers that they will like your product, service, or idea is to give them concrete evidence that other people like it. Tell what others have said (with permission, of course) about the usefulness of your offering. Guarantees and free trials convey both negative and positive connotations. By revealing willingness to refund money or exchange an unsatisfactory unit, a writer confesses a negative: The purchase could be regretted or refused.

However, the positive connotations are stronger than the negatives: The seller has a definite plan for ensuring that buyers get value for money spent. In addition, the seller conveys willingness for the buyer to check a product, service, or idea personally and compare it with others. The seller also implies confidence that a free trial will result in a purchase and that the product will meet standards set in the guarantee. A long or complex guarantee can be included in an enclosure or attachment.

A message should persuade the receiver to read an enclosure, attachment, or file link that includes more detailed information. Thus, refer to the added material late in the message after the major portion of the evidence has been given. An enclosure or link is best referred to in a sentence that is not a cliché ("Enclosed you will find," or "We have enclosed a brochure") and says something else:

> The enclosed annual report will help you understand the types of information provided to small- and medium-sized companies by Lincoln Business Data, Inc.

> Click here to view the huge assortment of clearance-priced items and other end-of-season specials.

Subordinate the Price

Logically, price should be introduced late in the message—after most of the advantages have been discussed. Use the following techniques to overcome people's natural resistance to price:

- **Introduce price only after creating a desire for the product, service, or idea and its virtues.** Let receivers see the relationship of features and benefits to the price.

- **Use figures to illustrate that the price is reasonable or that the receiver can save money.** Example: Purigard saves the average pool owner about $50 in chemicals each month; thus, the $200 unit pays for itself in a single swim season.
- **State price in terms of small units.** Thirty dollars a month seems like less than $360 a year.
- **Invite comparison of like products, services, or ideas with similar features.**
- **Consider mentioning price in a complex or compound sentence that relates or summarizes the virtues of the product, service, or idea.** Example: For just $8 a month, NetFlix brings you dozens of newly released movies and TV shows, all conveniently downloaded to your current game system.

Motivate Ⓐction

For proper clarity and emphasis, the last paragraph should be relatively short. Yet it must accomplish four important tasks: specify the specific action wanted, present it as easy to take, encourage quick action, and ask confidently.

Make the Action Clear and Simple to Complete

Define the desired action in specific terms that are easy to complete. For example, you might ask the receiver to complete an order blank and return it with payment, place a phone call, or order online. General instructions such as "Let us hear from you," "Take action on the matter," and "Make a response" are ineffective. Make action simple to encourage receivers to act immediately. Instead of asking receivers to fill in their names and addresses on order forms or return cards and envelopes, do that work for them. Otherwise, they might see the task as difficult or time consuming and decide to procrastinate.

Restate the Reward for Taking Action (Central Selling Point)

The central selling point should be introduced early in the message, interwoven throughout the evidence section, and included in the last paragraph as an emphatic, final reminder of the reason for taking action.

Provide an Incentive for Quick Action

If the receiver waits to take action on your proposal, the persuasive evidence will be harder to remember, and the receiver will be less likely to act. Therefore, you prefer the receiver to act quickly. Reference to the central selling point (assuming it has been well received) helps to stimulate action. Commonly used appeals for getting

quick action are to encourage customers to buy while prices are in effect, while supplies last, when a rebate is being offered, when it is a particular holiday, or when they will receive benefits.

Ask Confidently for Action

If you have a good product, service, or idea and have presented evidence effectively, you have a right to feel confident. Demonstrate your confidence when requesting action: "To save time in organizing appointments and tasks, complete and return. . . ." Avoid statements suggesting lack of confidence, such as "If you want to save time in organizing appointments and tasks, complete and return. . . . ," "If you agree. . . . ," and "I hope you will. . . ."

Observe how the following closing paragraph accomplishes the four important tasks of an effective sales message:

☑ refers to the central selling point,

☑ makes a specific action easy,

☑ provides an incentive for quick action, and

☑ asks confidently for action.

Simply dial 1-800-555-8341. Then input the five-digit number printed in the top right corner of the attached card. Your name and address will be entered automatically into our system, a speedy way to get your productivity software to you within five working days along with a bill for payment. When you order by August 12, you will also receive a free subscription to Time Resource Magazine. *TMC's new productivity software is as easy to use as it is to order!*

Figures 8-2 (on the next page) and 8-3 (on page 133) illustrate poor and good *unsolicited sales messages* for a service. Figure 8-4 on page 134 presents an unsolicited sales message promoting a product. The same principles apply in writing a *solicited sales message*, with one exception: Because the solicited sales message is a response to a request for information, an attention-getter is not essential. Typically, sales messages are longer than messages that present routine information or convey good news. Specific details (essential in prompting action) require space.

More and more organizations are using email as a means to persuade existing and potential customers to buy their products. While email marketing is a relatively new field, marketers are learning how to use email effectively with various audiences.

Figure 8-2  *Poor Example of a Sales Message Promoting a Service*

Dear Ms. Fox:

We have all the capabilities of a full-service agency, like advertising, media buying, public relations, digital, brand strategy, and planning. But we also offer unique services that can truly bring brand engagement to life.

We believe social media is a sweeping fire that influences and shapes how we live, work, learn, and play. Powered by people, social media evolves rapidly and often. From millennials to matures, hundreds of millions of consumers take part in some form of social media — are you part of the conversation?

Let our team help you communicate your message — whether it's driving sales, bringing together people for important causes, or reputation management. There couldn't be a more critical time to harness the power of online conversations to instantly affect your brand.

Our billing hours are in line with the industry. At just $300 per hour, our team of consultants can help you to maximize your marketing strategies to attract and retain valuable customers.

If you contact us before May 15, you will also receive a free assessment of your current marketing program from our proprietary MarketLab analysis tool. Please call me at 509-788-1302 to make an appointment with a consultant today.

Introduction might better engage the reader by addressing his or her needs in a more personal way.

The language is a bit overblown and vague in terms of concrete actions or results. This approach may damage the writer's credibility in the area of trust.

This paragraph adds little in terms of concrete actions or results.

The cost of the consultant might put off the reader before he or she has a chance to be persuaded by concrete results or actions.

The close might be considered too direct for a "cold-call" message.

© Cengage Learning 2013

To gain desired attention from customers, email messages must be carefully timed to arrive when they will gain the most attention. Over-messaging can be annoying, while under-messaging can cause the company to miss potential sales. The subject line is of utmost importance, as it must catch the attention of the reader and create a desire to learn more.

Persuasive Requests

The preceding discussion of sales messages assumed the product, service, or cause was sufficiently worthy to reward the receiver for taking action. The discussion of persuasive requests assumes requests are reasonable—that compliance is justified when the request is for an adjustment and that compliance will (in some way) be rewarded when the request is for a favor.

⊠ **OBJECTIVE 3**

Write effective persuasive requests (making a claim or asking for a favor or information) and persuasion within an organization.

Common types of persuasive requests are claim requests and messages that ask for special favors and information. Although their purpose is to get favorable action, the messages invite action only after attempting to create a desire to take action and providing a logical argument to overcome any anticipated resistance.

Making a Claim

Claim messages are often routine because the basis for the claim is a guarantee or some other assurance that an adjustment will be made without need of persuasion. However, when an immediate remedy is doubtful, persuasion is necessary. In a typical large business, customer service representatives handle claims.

Figure 8-3  Good Example of a Sales Message Promoting a Service

SOUTHER AND ASSOCIATES
Full-service Brand Engagement
4208 Olympic Boulevard
Portland, OR 92001
503-655-2304

April 1, 2012

Louisa Fox, Marketing Manager
Learner Consumer Products Group
2304 Pike Market Street
Seattle, WA 90322

Dear Ms. Fox:

Are you looking for help developing your organization's social media platform? . . . improve your retail marketing? . . . plan your external communication program? . . . enhance your mass advertising strategy? Then you need the services of the full-service brand engagement firm Souther and Associates to develop an integrated media plan that ensures your company's continued success.

Uses a series of phrases rather than complete sentences to gain attention. Introduces needs familiar to a marketing director.

With Souther and Associates full-service capabilities, you will receive support in all of the following areas:

Presents "everything-in-one-place" service as solution to problem and reinforces central selling point.

• Social media. Leverage the millions of conversations taking place through the use of social media by taking advantage of our four-step approach, which tracks conversations and dialogue; extracts insights from consumer conversations; interacts with key influences, brand advocates, and detractors; and measures consumer sentiment, advocacy, and engagement.

Uses easy-to-read bulleted list to present evidence that reflects understanding receiver's desired needs.

• Retail marketing. Engage consumers away from the noise and competing advertising, and reach them on an intimate, meaningful, and locally relevant level that will help you to drive trial, traffic, and sales.

Keeps focus on receiver by use of second person, active-voice sentences.

• Communication planning. Build preference for your brand by translating emotional insights into high impact brand strategy and innovation. Our experts bypass consumers' rational thinking with tools and techniques that are reactive and observational. Then, we integrate these emotional insights with your brand's functional benefits to create the foundation for lasting behavior change.

• Influence marketing. Mass advertising still plays an important role in branding, but these days, credibility is especially important, and who is more credible than a trusted professional? We identify professionals to give your products that powerful endorsement.

States specific action with reward. Makes action easy and provides incentive for quick response.

Visit www.souther.com today and check out the list of consulting services we provide and read real-life stories from past clients about how we increased brand awareness for them. If you contact us before May 15, you will also receive a free assessment of your current marketing program from our proprietary MarketLab analysis tool. Our team is ready to assist you in improving the impact of your marketing programs today. Please call me at 509-788-1302 to make an appointment with a consultant.

Sincerely,

Frank Forester

Frank Forester
Engagement Director

Enclosure

Figure 8-4 GOOD *Good Example of a Sales Message Promoting a Product*

New Message

To:	Trudy Jansen <tjansen@hotmail.com>
From:	Janet Freeman <jfreeman@southcountryspa.com>
Subject:	Remove Years from Your Face

Trudy,

What would you say if we told you that we could help you erase 10 years from your face, without surgery? . . . without any down time? . . . without the cost? Women across the country are waking up to renewed complexions with the help of our Facial Regeneration System.

You are invited to attend a free demonstration of the product at South Country Spa on September 4 at 7 p.m. You will see how easy it is to use the system and will see a visual presentation of before-and-after results. Clinician Susan Twigg will be on hand to answer your questions. Wine, cheese, and fruit will also be served.

Take a moment to visit our website at www.facialregeneration.com to view a video demonstration of the system and to hear testimonials from satisfied users. At the same time, please click on the "Spa Evening" link to RSVP your attendance at the South Country Spa event on September 4. Your invitation acceptance will automatically enter you in a drawing for free spa services at the center.

Would you like to join hundreds of women who have used the Facial Regeneration System to erase the years from their face? Register for the Spa Evening today or schedule a personal consultation to determine the benefits you might receive from facial rejuvenation. Learn for yourself whether the Facial Regeneration System could do for you what it has already done for so many.

Best regards,

Janice Freeman
Spa Manager and Owner

- *Sends customized email message to customers who may be interested in product.*

- *Gains attention by introducing familiar annoyances; presents improved skin appearance as central selling point.*

- *Introduces product as potential solution to reader's skin concerns.*

- *Builds interest by offering an invitation to see the product demonstrated.*

- *Requests specific action and associates it with central selling point.*

Legal and Ethical Consideration
Abides by requirements under the Federal Trade Commission Act regarding false and deceptive advertising.

© Cengage Learning 2013

Often, any reasonable claim will be adjusted to the customer's satisfaction. Therefore, venting strong displeasure in the claim message will likely alienate the claims adjuster—the one person whose cooperation is needed. Remember, adjusters might have had little or nothing to do with the manufacture and sale of the product or direct delivery of the service. They did not create the need for the claim.

Companies should welcome claims. Only a small percentage of claims are from unethical individuals; the great bulk is from people who believe they have a legitimate complaint. Research indicates that only four percent of customers complain, so for every complaint received, many more customers have been dissatisfied. Complaints help companies identify problem areas and correct them. Another advantage that companies derive from the claim process is that when complaints are handled appropriately, complainers can become very loyal customers.[5] Thus, the way a complaint is handled determines, to a large extent, the goodwill toward the company.

Like sales messages, persuasive claims should use an inductive sequence. Unlike routine claim messages, persuasive claims do not begin by asking for an adjustment.

Two major changes would improve the poor example in Figure 8-5: (1) writing inductively (to reduce the chance of a negative reaction in the first sentence), and (2) stressing an appeal throughout the message (to emphasize an incentive for taking favorable action). In a persuasive claim, an appeal serves the same purpose that a central selling feature does in a sales message. Both serve as a theme; both remind the receiver of a benefit gained from doing as asked. Note the application of these techniques in the revision in Figure 8-6 on the next page.

Knowledge of effective claim writing should never be used as a means of taking advantage of someone. Hiding an unjustifiable claim under a cloak of untrue statements is difficult and strictly unethical. Adjusters typically are fair-minded people who will give the benefit of the doubt, but they will not satisfy an unhappy customer simply to avoid a problem.

Asking a Favor

Occasionally, everyone has to ask someone else for a special favor—action for which there is little reward, time, or inclination. For example, suppose a professional association wants to host its annual fund-raiser dinner at an exclusive country club. The program chair of the association must write the club's general manager requesting permission to use the facility. Will a deductive message be successful?

When a deductive approach is used in a persuasive situation, chances of getting cooperation are minimal. For example, what might be a probable reaction to the following beginning sentence? *Please send me, without charge, your $450 interactive video training game on workplace safety.*

If the first sentence gets a negative reaction, a decision to refuse might be made instantly. Having thought "No," the receiver might not read the rest of the message or might hold stubbornly to that decision in spite of a well-written persuasive argument that follows the opening sentence. Note that the letter in Figure 8-7 on the next page asks the favor before presenting any

Figure 8-5   *Poor Example of a Persuasive Claim*

We just reviewed the initial design for the StreetWare print advertisement and find it totally unacceptable. It must be redone to our specifications.

We made it clear that our target market is young, hip, urban consumers, who are of diverse ethnic and racial backgrounds. Instead, the ad you sent contains photographs of only African American men.

Call us immediately to discuss the changes that you need to make to meet our requirements.

• *Introduction is too direct. May damage goodwill.*

• *The tone is too negative to be persuasive and fails to provide a clear and persuasive reason for requested change.*

• *Close is too demanding to maintain goodwill.*

Figure 8-6

Streetware Inc.
2304 42th Street, Hoboken, NJ 12001, 203-662-4400

August 26, 2012

Donald Williams
Advertising Director
A-Team Marketing Inc.
234 27th Avenue
New York, NY 03201

Dear Donald:

When StreetWare negotiated with your firm to produce our first print advertisement, we were impressed with your previous ad campaigns and proven record of success. Especially provocative was your ad campaign for HipHop Stylin', with its obvious appeal to young, hip, urban consumers, our target market.

In our meeting with your creative team, we focused on the techniques used in the HipHop Stylin' campaign and specifically asked to see images of urban youth of varying ethnicities and genders, wearing our shoes. After viewing the initial design for the advertisement, we were disappointed with the lack of diversity in the choice of people pictured in the ad. Since urban communities are often composed of individuals from many ethnicities and races, we are concerned that the ad may not directly appeal to many in our potential market.

With the A-Team's reputation for creative ad campaigns, we are confident that the advertisement can be reshot to meet our expectations. We are happy to meet with you again if you would like more specific feedback as to our requested changes. Please call me at 203-662-4434 if a meeting would be helpful in this regard.

Sincerely,

Bill Lewis

Bill "Big Dog" Lewis
Marketing Manager

- *Seeks attention by giving sincere compliment that reveals subject of message.*

- *Continues central appeal—commitment to creative production—while providing needed details.*

- *Presents reasoning that leads to request and subtle reminder of central appeal.*

- *Connects specific request with firm's commitment to develop a creative production.*

Legal and Ethical Consideration
Uses letter rather than less formal email format to add formality to contractual agreement.

© Cengage Learning 2013

Figure 8-7

There are no organic vegetables available in your store. We live in a community where there is a large group of people who are concerned about the safety of their food. Have you considered providing organic vegetables in your produce section?

You've probably already considered this, but I would be very interested in having this option when shopping.

- *Does not use an inductive approach to set a more positive tone.*

- *Fails to provide good reasons to comply with the request.*

- *Close does little to build goodwill or encourage compliance.*

Figure 8-8 Good Example of a Persuasive Request (asking a favor)

Lula Turner
Route 1, Stowe Mountain Road,
Stowe, Vermont 34006, 307-677-1301

November 22, 2012

George Bacon
General Manager
EastTown Food Center
345 Center Avenue
Stowe, Vermont 34006

Dear Mr. Bacon:

As a regular customer of EastTown Food Center, I have appreciated your efforts to meet the needs of residents of the local community. The recent addition of an Asian food section to the store to address demographic changes in the community has been greatly appreciated.

Another helpful change would be to add some organic produce options to your vegetable section. Many of us in the community are concerned about the quality and safety of our food and would take advantage of such an option.

As you probably know, there are many fine growers of organic vegetables in the area. This collaboration between you and the local growers might benefit you both in increased sales revenue and goodwill in the community.

Sincerely,

Lula Turner

Lula Turner

- • *Begins with sincere compliment that sets stage for request that follows.*

- • *Explains rationale for request with discussion of benefits to store and its customers.*

- • *Connects specific action to rewards for taking action.*

© Cengage Learning 2013

benefit for doing so. The letter illustrated in Figure 8-8 above uses an inductive approach and applies the principles discussed earlier. As this message shows, if the preceding paragraphs adequately emphasize a receiver's reward for complying, the final paragraph need not shout loudly for action.

Requesting Information

Requests for information are common in business. Information for research reports frequently is obtained by questionnaire, and the reliability of results is strongly influenced by the percentage of return. If a message inviting respondents to complete a questionnaire is written carelessly, the number of responses might be insufficient.

The most serious weakness is asking for action too quickly and providing no incentive for action. Sometimes the reward for taking action is small and indirect, but the message needs to make these benefits evident.

Persuading within an Organization

The majority of memos are of a routine nature and essential for the day-to-day operation of the business, for example, giving instructions for performing work assignments, scheduling meetings, providing project progress reports, and so on. In many organizations, such matters are handled through the use of email rather than paper memos. These routine messages, as well as messages conveying good news, are written deductively. However, some circumstances require that a supervisor write a persuasive message that motivates employees to accept a change in their jobs that might have a negative effect on the employees or generate resistance (e.g., a job transfer, change in work procedures, software upgrade, etc.).

For example, Steak and Ale restaurant faced the challenge of communicating to its employees a significant change in service and style, which included new uniforms. Rather than coercing or demanding that employees accept the change, a letter from Bob Mandes, president of Steak and Ale, emphasized reasons the changes were being made (benefits to guests, the company, and the employees) and the employee's important role in implementing the changes. Using a lighthearted, entertaining approach, the message and accompanying magazine provided (a) a visual model of the fresh, crisp, and professional look the company expected with the uniform change and (b) helpful information on ways to achieve this look. Note the "you" orientation in the "style flashes" interwoven throughout the magazine excerpt that follows:

Out of control hair is the biggest turnoff to Guests in restaurants—they don't want it wandering into their food. So pull your hair back and pull in a better tip.

If you wear a lot of jewelry, Guests may think you don't need as large a tip.

Your smile is the most important part of your appearance and it's the first signal to Guests that their Steak and Ale experience will be a memorable one. Your smile tells Guests, "I'm happy you're here!" But hey, don't take our word for it. Check out the recent study by Boston College which found that smiling suggests an awareness of the needs of others. Maybe that's the reason behind the phrase "winning smile."[6]

The detailed language leaves no doubt in an employee's mind as to what management considers clean, crisp, and professional. However, by continually emphasizing the benefits employees gain from the change, management garners support for the high standards being imposed.

Similarly, employees must often make persuasive requests of their supervisors. For example, they might recommend a change in procedure, acquisition of equipment or software, or attendance at a professional development program. They might justify a promotion or job reclassification or recommendation for policy changes, and so on. Persuasive memos and email messages are longer than most routine messages because of the extra space needed for developing an appeal and providing convincing evidence.

When preparing to write the memo in Figure 8-9, the human resources manager recognizes that productivity concerns could affect the president's reaction to his proposal to pilot-test substituting "e-breaks" for traditional coffee breaks. Anticipating resistance, the manager writes inductively and builds a logical, compelling argument for her proposal.

Deductive sequence (main idea first) works well for routine messages and good-news messages.

Inductive sequence (details first) works well if the reader needs to be persuaded.

© iStockphoto.com/Ju-Lee

Figure 8-9 GOOD *Good Example of a Persuasive Memo*

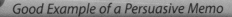

To: John Seneca
From: Laura Tillman
Date: February 3, 2012
Subject: Exercise Incentive Program

During our leadership meeting last month, HR Director Christian Wills noted a significant uptick in employee sick-day requests over the past year. A discussion followed about the cost of sick-days to the company. As you recall, I offered to do some research on how other firms of our size have responded to this issue.

My research has found that on-site exercise programs have resulted in notable decreases in sick-pay requests. Obviously, we don't have space for such a program, but an alternative would be to provide an incentive for employees to exercise at the Pumped! workout facility located just a block from our offices.

In my research I found that a number of organizations offer employees incentives for their active involvement in exercise programs. These incentives include free movie tickets, dinners, coffee mugs, T-shirts, etc. I am proposing that we provide such incentives by using the savings we should achieve through decreased sick time.

I have approached the management of Pumped! and it is willing to offer our employees a discounted membership if we can guarantee a 50 percent sign-up rate. With our goals of decreasing sick-leave requests, would you allow me to test the exercise incentive program in the sales department during March? Employees participating in the program would be asked to sign up for the program and to turn in a stamped sheet from Pumped!, indicating the number of times they have used the facility during the month. At the end of the pilot program, I will compile a report of the results, thereby allowing us to consider whether to expand the program to all departments.

- *Opens with reference to meeting discussion and company goal.*
- *Builds interest by mentioning benefits of the program.*
- *Presents a solution to the identified problem.*
- *Alludes to benefits and closes with specific action to be taken.*
- *Reduces potential resistance by tracking use and reporting results.*

Understanding the Report Process and Research Methods

Characteristics of Reports

"Hi, Teresa. This is Ken in the legal department. Do you know whether the contract for the new shipping service will be ready today? Management wants me to review it so we can move on it by Monday."

"Hi, Ken. The new contractor signed it an hour ago. The agreement is exactly like the previous contract with the current supplier, so it shouldn't take long to review. It should be in your office any moment now. Felicity is bringing it up."

This brief exchange illustrates a simple reporting task. A question has been posed; the answer given (along with supporting information) satisfies the reporting requirement. Although Teresa might never have studied report preparation, she did an excellent job; so Ken in turn can report to his supervisor. Teresa's spoken report is a simple illustration of the four main characteristics of reports:

⊠ **OBJECTIVE 1**

Identify the characteristics of a report and the various classifications of business reports.

- **Reports typically travel upward in an organization because they usually are requested by a higher authority.** In most cases, people would not generate reports unless requested to do so.

- **Reports are logically organized.** In Teresa's case, she answered Ken's question first and then supported the answer with evidence to justify it. Through your study of message organization, you learned the

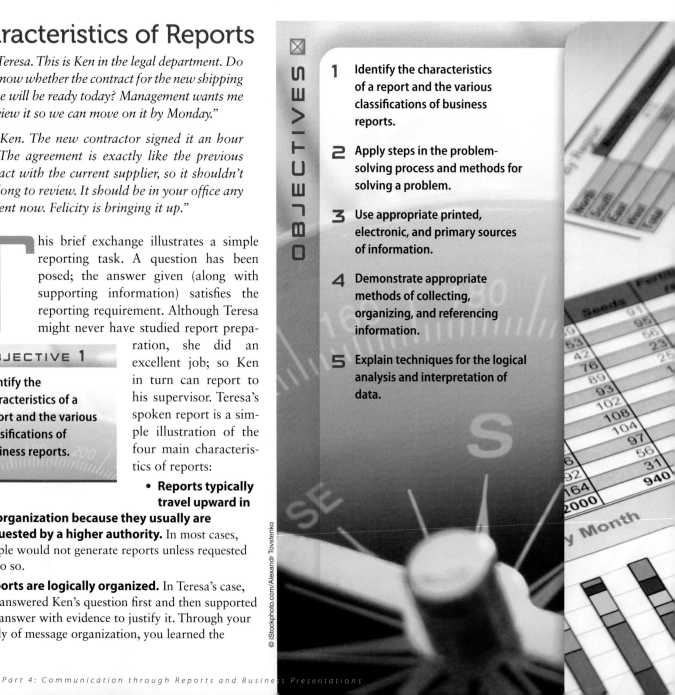

⊠ **OBJECTIVES**

1 Identify the characteristics of a report and the various classifications of business reports.

2 Apply steps in the problem-solving process and methods for solving a problem.

3 Use appropriate printed, electronic, and primary sources of information.

4 Demonstrate appropriate methods of collecting, organizing, and referencing information.

5 Explain techniques for the logical analysis and interpretation of data.

difference between deductive and inductive organization. Emily's report was deductively organized. If Emily had given the supporting evidence first and followed that with the answer that she would meet the deadline, the organization of her reply would have been inductive and would still have been logical.

- **Reports are objective.** Because reports contribute to decision making and problem solving, they should be as objective as possible; when nonobjective (subjective) material is included, the report writer should make that known.

- **Reports are generally prepared for a limited audience.** This characteristic is particularly true of

reports traveling within an organization and means that reports, like letters, memos, and emails, should be prepared with the receivers' needs in mind.

Types of Reports

Based on the four characteristics, a workable definition of a *report* is an orderly, objective message used to convey information from one organizational area to another or from one organization to another to assist in decision making or problem solving. Reports have been classified in numerous ways by management and by report-preparation authorities. The form, direction,

© Natiliap/Shutterstock

functional use, and content of the report are used as bases for classification. However, a single report might fit several classifications. The following brief review of classification illustrates the scope of reporting and establishes a basis for studying reports.

formal report *carefully structured report that is logically organized and objective, contains much detail, and is written in a style that tends to eliminate such elements as personal pronouns*

informal report *usually a short message written in natural or personal language*

informational report *a report that carries objective information from one area of an organization to another*

analytical report *a report that presents suggested solutions to problems*

vertical report *a report that can be upward- or downward–directed*

lateral report *a report that travels between units on the same organizational level*

internal report *a report that travels within an organization, such as a production or sales report*

external report *a report prepared for distribution outside an organization*

periodic report *a report that is issued on regularly scheduled dates*

functional report *a report that serves a specified purpose within a company*

- **Formal or informal reports.** The formal/informal classification is particularly helpful because it applies to all reports. A **formal report** is carefully structured; it is logically organized and objective, contains much detail, and is written in a style that tends to eliminate such elements as personal pronouns. An **informal report** is usually a short message written in natural or personal language. An internal memo generally can be described as an informal report. All reports can be placed on a continuum of formality, as shown in Figure 9-1. The distinction among the degrees of formality of various reports is explained more fully in Chapter 11.

- **Short or long reports.** Reports can be classified generally as short or long. A one-page memo is obviously short, and a report of 20 pages is obviously long. What about in-between

lengths? One important distinction generally holds true: As it becomes longer, a report takes on more characteristics of formal reports. Thus, the classifications of formal/informal and short/long are closely related.

- **Informational or analytical reports.** An **informational report** carries objective information from one area of an organization to another. An **analytical report** presents suggested solutions to problems. Company annual reports, monthly financial statements, reports of sales volume, and reports of employee or personnel absenteeism and turnover are informational reports. Reports of scientific research, real estate appraisal reports, and feasibility reports by consulting firms are analytical reports.

- **Vertical or lateral reports.** The vertical/lateral classification refers to the directions in which reports travel. Although most reports travel upward in organizations, many travel downward. Both represent vertical reports and are often referred to as *upward-directed* and *downward-directed* reports. The main function of **vertical reports** is to contribute to management *control*, as shown in Figure 9-2. **Lateral reports**, on the other hand, assist in *coordination* in the organization. A report traveling between units on the same organizational level, as between the production department and the finance department, is lateral.

- **Internal or external reports.** An **internal report**, such as a production or sales report, travels within an organization. An **external report**, such as a company's annual report to stockholders, is prepared for distribution outside an organization.

- **Periodic reports.** **Periodic reports** are issued on regularly scheduled dates. They are generally directed upward and serve management control purposes. Daily, weekly, monthly, quarterly, semiannual, and annual time periods are typical for periodic reports. Preprinted forms and computer-generated data contribute to uniformity of periodic reports.

- **Functional reports.** A **functional report** serves a specified purpose within a company. The functional

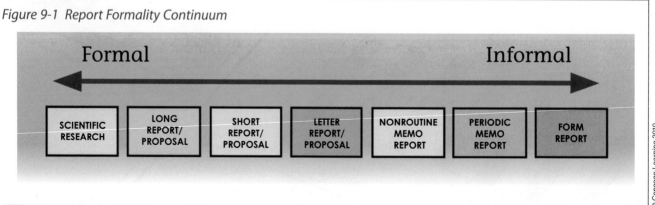

Figure 9-1 Report Formality Continuum

Formal ← → Informal

| SCIENTIFIC RESEARCH | LONG REPORT/ PROPOSAL | SHORT REPORT/ PROPOSAL | LETTER REPORT/ PROPOSAL | NONROUTINE MEMO REPORT | PERIODIC MEMO REPORT | FORM REPORT |

© Cengage Learning 2010

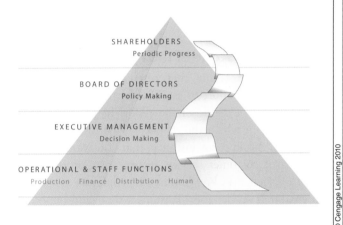

Figure 9-2 The General Upward Flow of Reports

SHAREHOLDERS
Periodic Progress

BOARD OF DIRECTORS
Policy Making

EXECUTIVE MANAGEMENT
Decision Making

OPERATIONAL & STAFF FUNCTIONS
Production   Finance   Distribution   Human

© Cengage Learning 2010

classification includes accounting reports, marketing reports, financial reports, personnel reports, and a variety of other reports that take their functional designation from their ultimate use. For example, a justification of the need for additional personnel or for new equipment is described as a *justification report* in the functional classification.

Proposals

A **proposal** is a written description of how one organization can meet the needs of another; for example, by providing products or services or solving problems. Businesses issue *calls for bids* that present the specifications for major purchases of goods and certain services. Most governmental and non-profit agencies issue *requests for proposals*, or RFPs. Potential suppliers prepare proposal reports telling how they can meet that need. Those preparing the proposal create a convincing document that will lead to obtaining a contract.

In our information-intensive society, proposal preparation is a major activity for many firms. In fact, some companies hire consultants or designate employees to specialize in proposal writing. Chapter 11 presents proposal preparation in considerable detail.

As you review these report classifications, you will very likely decide—correctly—that almost all reports could be included in these categories. A report may be formal or informal, short or long, informational or analytical, vertically or laterally directed, internal or external, periodic or nonperiodic, functionally labeled, a proposal, or some other combination of these classifications. These report categories are in common use and provide necessary terminology for the study and production of reports.

Basis for Reports: The Problem-Solving Process

The upward flow of reports provides management with data that someone might use to make a decision. The purpose is to use the data to solve a problem. Some problems are recurring and call for a steady flow of information; other problems might be unique and call for information on a one-time basis. A problem is the basis for a report. The following steps are used for finding a solution:

1. Recognize and define the problem.
2. Select a method of solution.
3. Collect and organize the data and document the sources.
4. Arrive at an answer.

Only after all four steps have been completed is a report written for presentation. Reports represent an attempt to communicate how a problem was solved. These problem-solving steps are completed *before* the report is written in final form.

Recognizing and Defining the Problem

Problem-solving research cannot begin until the researchers define the problem. Frequently, those requesting a report will attempt to provide a suitable definition. Nevertheless, researchers should attempt to state the problem clearly and precisely to ensure they are on the right track.

© iStockphoto.com/Pali Rao

Step 1 in the problem-solving process

proposal
a written description of how one organization can meet the needs of another

Using Problem Statements, Statements of Purpose, and Hypotheses

The **problem statement**, or statement of the problem, is the particular problem that is to be solved by the research. The **statement of purpose** is the goal of the study and includes the aims or objectives the researcher hopes to accomplish. Research studies often have both a problem statement and a statement of purpose. For example, a real estate appraiser accepts a client's request to appraise a building to determine its market value. The problem is to arrive at a fair market value for the property. The purpose of the appraisal, however, might be to establish a value for a mortgage loan, to determine the feasibility of adding to the structure, or to assess the financial possibility of demolishing the structure and erecting something else. Thus, the purpose might have much to do with determining what elements to consider in arriving at an answer. In other words, unless you know *why* something is wanted, you might have difficulty knowing *what* is wanted. Once you arrive at the answers to the *what* and *why* questions, you will be on your way to solving the problem.

A **hypothesis** is a statement to be proved or disproved through research. For example, a study of skilled manufacturing employees under varying conditions might be made to determine whether production would increase if each employee were part of a team, as opposed to being a single unit in a production line. For this problem, the hypothesis could be formulated in this way:

> **Hypothesis:** Productivity will increase when skilled manufacturing employees function as members of production teams rather than as single units in a production line.

Because the hypothesis tends to be stated in a way that favors one possibility or is prejudiced toward a particular answer, many researchers prefer to state hypotheses in the null form. The *null hypothesis* states that no relationship or difference will be found in the factors being studied, which tends to remove the element of prejudice toward a certain answer. The null hypothesis for the previous example could be written as follows:

> **Null hypothesis:** No significant difference will be found in productivity between workers organized as teams and workers as individual production line units.

problem statement
the particular problem that is to be solved by the research

statement of purpose
the goal of the study; includes the aims or objectives the researcher hopes to accomplish

hypothesis
a statement to be proved or disproved through research

Using the problem/purpose approach, the hypothesis approach, or both is a choice of the researcher. In many ways, the purpose of a study is determined by the intended use of its results.

Limiting the Scope of the Problem

A major shortcoming that often occurs in research planning is the failure to establish or to recognize desirable limits. The *scope* of the report helps to establish boundaries in which the report will be researched and prepared. Assume, for instance, that you want to study salaries of customer service agents. Imagine the enormity of such a task. Millions of people are employed in customer service jobs. Perhaps a thousand or so different types of jobs fall into this classification. Use the *what, why, when, where,* and *who* questions to reduce such a problem to reasonable proportions.

Here are the limits you might set as the human resources manager of an online travel booking company, such as Expedia:

What: A study of salaries of online customer service agents

Why: To determine whether salaries in our firm are competitive and consistent

When: Current

Where: United States

Who: Customer service agents in online travel booking sites

Now you can phrase the problem this way:

Statement of purpose: *The purpose of this study is to survey salaries of customer service agents of online travel booking sites working in the United States to determine whether our salaries are competitive and consistent.*

Note that this process of reducing the problem to a workable size has also established some firm limits to the research. You have limited the problem to current salaries, the particular area, and a certain type of business. Note, too, how important the *why* was in helping to establish the limits. Limiting the problem is "zeroing in on the problem."

In some reports, it is desirable to differentiate between the boundaries that were placed on the project outside the control of the researcher(s) and those that were chosen by the researcher(s). Boundaries imposed outside the control of the researchers are called *limitations*; they might include the assignment of the topic, allotted budget, and time for completion of the report. These boundaries affect what and how the topic can be researched. Boundaries chosen by the researcher(s) to make the project more manageable are called *delimitations*; they might include the sources and methods chosen for research.

Defining Terms Clearly

Words often have more than one meaning, and technical or special-use words might occur in the report that are not widely used or understood. Such terms would require a definition for the reader's understanding of the information presented. In the previously used example concerning the study of customer service staff salaries, a comparison of one travel booking site's salaries with those paid by others would be meaningful only if the information gathered from other sites relates to identical jobs. A job description defining the duties performed by a booking agent, for example, would help ensure that all firms would be talking about the same job tasks regardless of the job title. In addition, the term *salary* requires definition. Is it hourly, weekly, monthly, or yearly? Are benefits included?

Documenting Procedures

The procedures or steps a writer takes in preparing a report are often recorded as a part of the written report. This **procedures** section, or **methodology**, adds credibility to the research process and also enables subsequent researchers to repeat, or replicate, the study in another setting or at a later time. Reports that study the same factors in different time frames are called **longitudinal studies**.

The procedures section of a report records the major steps taken in the research, and possibly the reasons for their inclusion. It might, for instance, tell the types of printed and electronic sources that were consulted and the groups of people interviewed and how they were selected. Steps in the procedures section are typically listed in chronological order, so that the reader has an overall understanding of the timetable that existed for the project.

Selecting a Method of Solution

After defining the problem, the researcher will plan how to arrive at a solution. The research methods you use to collect necessary information can be secondary, primary, or both.

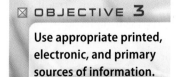

OBJECTIVE 3

Use appropriate printed, electronic, and primary sources of information.

Secondary Research

Secondary research provides information that has already been created by others. Researchers save time and effort by not duplicating research that has already been undertaken. They can access this information easily through the aid of electronic databases and bibliographic indexes. Suppose that a marketing manager has been asked to investigate the feasibility of implementing a strategic information system. The manager knows other companies are using this technology. By engaging in secondary research, the manager can determine the boundaries of knowledge before proceeding into the unknown.

Certain truths have been established and treated as principles reported in textbooks and other publications. However, because knowledge is constantly expanding, the researcher knows that new information is available. The job, then, is to canvass the literature of the field and attempt to redefine the boundaries of knowledge.

Secondary research accomplishes the following objectives:

- Establishes a point of departure for further research
- Avoids needless duplication of costly research efforts
- Reveals areas of needed research
- Makes a real contribution to a body of knowledge

Secondary research can be gathered by means of traditional printed sources or by using electronic tools.

Printed Sources. Major categories of printed sources are books, periodicals, and government documents. Books are typically cataloged in libraries by call number, with larger libraries using the

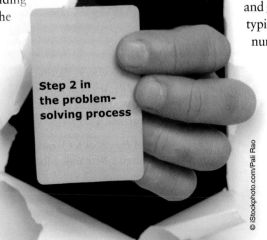

Step 2 in the problem-solving process

© iStockphoto.com/Pali Rao

procedures (or methodology)
the steps a writer takes in preparing a report; often recorded as a part of the written report

longitudinal studies
reports that study the same factors in different time frames

secondary research
provides information that has already been reported by others

Library of Congress classification system. Traditional card catalogs in libraries have been replaced by online catalogs, which allow the user to locate desired books by author, title, subject, or key word. A wide assortment of reference books is typically available for use within libraries; these include dictionaries, encyclopedias, yearbooks, and almanacs. Some of these volumes contain general information on a wide array of topics, while others are designed for a specific field of study.

Periodicals, referred to as *serials* by librarians, include various types of publications that are released on a regular, periodic basis. Newspapers, magazines, and journals are all types of periodicals. Newspapers, which are usually published daily, are a good initial source for investigation, since they give condensed coverage of timely topics. Magazines might be published weekly, monthly, bimonthly, or in some other interval. They are typically written for a general readership, providing expanded coverage in an easy-to-read format. Journals, on the other hand, are written for more specialized audiences, are peer reviewed, and are more research oriented and thus more credible. Journal articles share the results of research studies and provide data that support their findings. They also provide bibliographies or citation lists that can be used to locate related materials. Articles on specific topics can be located using both printed and online indexes. A partial list of these sources is shown in Figure 9-3.

Electronic Sources. The availability of computer-assisted data searches has simplified the time-consuming task of searching through indexes, card catalogs, and other sources. Weekly and monthly updates keep electronic databases current, and they are easy to use. Databases such as LexisNexis Academic Universe have full-text retrieval capability, meaning you can retrieve the entire article for reviewing and printing. Other databases offer only some articles in full text, with citations or abstracts provided for others. Note the list of electronic databases for business users listed in Figure 9-3.

The Internet and its subset, the World Wide Web, have made thousands of reference sources available in a matter of seconds. However, the vastness of this resource can be overwhelming to the novice researcher.

Figure 9-3 Useful Reference Sources

Printed Indexes

Business Periodicals Index
Education Index
The New York Times Index
Readers' Guide to Periodical Literature
Social Science and Humanities Index
The Wall Street Journal Index

Electronic Databases

ABI/INFORM
Academic Search Elite
Business & Company Resource Center
Business Dateline
Business Source Premier
DIALOG Information Services
ERIC
First Search
FSI Online
General BusinessFile
LexisNexis Academic Universe
Periodical Abstracts
ProQuest
Westlaw

Biography

Who's Who in America
Similar directories for specific geographic areas, industries, and professions

General Facts and Statistics

Statistical Abstract of the United States
Bureau of the Census publications
Dictionaries (general and discipline specific)
Encyclopedia (*Americana* or *Britannica*)
Fortune Directories of U.S. Corporations
World Atlas
LexisNexis Statistics
Almanacs

Report Style and Format

American Psychological Association. (2010).
    Publication Manual of the American Psychological Association (6th ed.). Washington, DC: Author.
    [www.apastyle.org]

Gibaldi, J. (2003). *MLA Handbook for Writers of Research Papers* (6th ed.). New York: Modern Language Association.
    [www.mla.org/style_faq]

© iStockphoto.com/Helder Almeida

TELL US MORE ABOUT YOURSELF

Social bookmarking websites, such as Flickr, Digg, and del.icio.us provide users with a place to share favorite Web pages and files. The sites track the links users access, and businesses can use this information to target markets and reveal potential markets.

The following tips will help to make your Internet search more productive:

- **Choose your search engine or database appropriately.** A *search engine* is a cataloged database of websites that allows you to search specific topics. Several popular search engines exist, including Yahoo!, AltaVista, HotBot, and Excite. Megasearch engines such as Google and Bing, which index billions of web pages, search through a number of other engines to produce "hits."[1] (A *hit* is a located website that contains the word or words specified in the search.) You want to obtain a sufficient number of hits, but not thousands. Although the variety of these larger engines is greater, they pose more difficulty in narrowing a search.

Electronic databases provide access to articles from newspapers, magazines, journals, and other types of publications. The database provider might charge a subscription fee or a document delivery fee to access articles. These types of databases are not accessible by a search engine and are often described as the *hidden Internet*. Many libraries provide access to these databases. Some databases are suited for topic searches of general interest; others are geared toward specialized fields. A topic search will produce a listing of references and article abstracts, or even full-text articles in some cases. Databases available through your library might include Business Source Premier (an offering of EBSCO), Academic Search Elite, LexisNexis Academic Universe, ABI Inform First Search, Business and Company Resource Center, General BusinessFile, and others.

- **Structure searches from broad to specific.** Use words for your topic that are descriptive and do not have multiple meanings. Once sites have been located for your general topic, you can use *Boolean logic* to narrow the selection. Boolean operands (*and, or, not*) serve to limit the identified sites. The following example shows how these delimiters can assist you in locating precisely what you want:
  - Using the key phrase *workplace productivity* will produce all sites that have either of the key words in the title or descriptors.
  - Placing "and" between key words will produce hits that have both words.
  - Keying *workplace productivity not United States* will eliminate hits that refer to the United States.

- **Use quotation marks when literal topics are desired.** Putting quotation marks around your topic words can drastically affect the number of hits. The quotation marks cause the search engine to look for the designated words as a phrase, thus producing only those sites that have the phrase present. Without the quotation marks, the search engine will treat the words individually and produce many more hits, most of which might not be useful. For instance, if you are looking for sites related to "international communication," placing quotation marks around the desired phrase would eliminate the sites that deal with international topics that are not communication oriented.

- **Look for Web pages that have collections of links to other related topics.** Clicking on these hyperlinks will allow you to maximize your time investment in the data gathering phase of your research.

- **Be adaptable to the various access format requirements.** Each search engine and database has its own particular format and instructions for use. The method for specifying and narrowing your search will vary.

Primary Research

After reviewing the secondary data, you might need to collect primary data to solve your problem. **Primary research** relies on firsthand data, such as responses from pertinent individuals or observations of people or phenomena related to your study. Recognized methods to obtain original information are observational studies, experimental research, and normative surveys.

Observational studies are those in which the researcher observes and statistically analyzes

primary research
data collected for the first time, usually for a specific purpose

observational studies
studies in which the researcher observes and statistically analyzes certain phenomena in order to assist in establishing new principles or discoveries

certain phenomena to assist in establishing new principles or discoveries. For example, market analysts observe buying habits of certain income groups to determine the most desirable markets. Internal auditors analyze expected patterns in expense reimbursement amounts to identify potential fraud activity. Developing an objective system for quantifying observations is necessary to collect valid data. For example, to gain insight on the effect of a comprehensive ethics program, a researcher might record the number of incidents of ethical misconduct reported or the number of calls made to an ethics help-line designed to provide advice about proper conduct. Observational studies typically involve no contact with the human subjects under study.

Experimental research typically involves the study of two or more samples that have exactly the same components before a variable is added to one of the samples. Any differences observed are viewed as due to the variable. Like scientists, businesses use experimental research to solve various problems. For example, a company conducts new employee training with all new hires. Two training methods are presently used: New hires in one regional office receive their training in a traditional classroom setting with other new employees, while employees at the other regional office take a web-based training class. Management wants to determine whether one method is superior to the other in terms of learning success. During the period of the study, learning differences in the two study groups are noted. Because the training method is assumed to be the only significant variable, any difference is attributed to its influence. Experimental research involves very careful recordkeeping and can require informed consent from participants who are subjected to experimental methods.

Normative survey research is undertaken to determine the status of something at a specific time. Survey instruments such as questionnaires, opinion surveys, checklists, and interviews are used to obtain information from participants. Election opinion polls represent one type of normative survey research. The term normative is used to qualify surveys because surveys reveal "norms" or "standards" existing at the time of the survey. A poll taken two months before an election might have little similarity to one taken the week preceding the election.

The sample will possess the same characteristics in the same proportions as the total population.

Surveys can help verify the accuracy of existing norms. The U.S. Census is conducted every decade to establish an actual population figure, and each person is supposedly counted. In effect, the census tests the accuracy of prediction techniques used to estimate population during the years between censuses. A survey of what employees consider a fair benefits package would be effective only for the date of the survey. People retire, move, and change their minds often; these human traits make survey research of opinions somewhat tentative. Yet surveys remain a valuable tool for gathering information on which to base decisions and policies.

Researchers normally cannot survey everyone, particularly if the population is large and the research budget is limited. **Sampling** is a survey technique that eliminates the need for questioning 100 percent of the population. Sampling is based on the principle that a sufficiently large number drawn at random from a population will be representative of the total population; that is, the sample will possess the same characteristics in the same proportions as the total population. For example, a company collecting market research data before introducing a new low-fat food product would survey a small number of people. The data are considered *representative* if the sample of people surveyed has the same percentage of ages, genders, purchasing power, and so on as the anticipated target market.

As a researcher, you must be cautious about drawing conclusions from a sample and generalizing them to a population that might not be represented by the sample. For example, early-morning shoppers might differ from afternoon or evening shoppers; young adults might differ from senior citizens; male shoppers might differ from female shoppers. A good researcher defines the population as distinctly as possible and uses a sampling technique to ensure that the sample is representative.

Whether a survey involves personal interviewing or the distribution of items such as checklists or questionnaires, some principles of procedure and planning are common to both methods. These principles assure the researcher that the data gathered will be both valid (i.e., it will measure what the researcher

experimental research
the study of two samples that have exactly the same components before a variable is added to one of the samples

normative survey research
research to determine the status of something at a specific time

sampling
a survey technique that eliminates the need for questioning 100 percent of the population

intended to measure) and reliable (i.e., it will measure data accurately).

- **Validity** refers to the degree to which the data measure what you intend to measure. It generally results from careful planning of the questionnaire or interview questions or items. Cautious wording, preliminary testing of items to detect misunderstandings, and some statistical techniques are helpful in determining whether the responses to the items are valid. A *pilot test* of the instrument is often conducted prior to the full-scale survey so that a smaller number of participants can test the instrument, which can then be revised prior to wide-scale administration.

- **Reliability** refers to the level of consistency or stability over time or over independent samples; that is, reliable data are reasonably accurate or repeatable. Reliability results from asking a large enough sample of people so that the researcher is reasonably confident the results would be the same even if more people were asked to respond or if a different sample were chosen from the same population. For example, if you were to ask 10 people to react to a questionnaire item, the results might vary considerably. If you were to add 90 more people to the sample, the results might tend to reach a point of stability, where more responses would not change the results. Reliability would then be reasonably established.

Responses to surveys conducted by mail often represent only a small percentage of the total mailings. In some cases, a return of three to five percent is considered adequate and is planned for by researchers. In other cases, such as employee surveys or questionnaires, a return of considerably more than half the mailings might be a planned result. Selecting an appropriate data collection method and developing a sound survey instrument are crucial elements of an effective research study.

Collecting and Organizing the Data

☒ OBJECTIVE 4

Demonstrate appropriate methods of collecting, organizing, and referencing information.

Step 3 in the problem-solving process

© iStockphoto.com/Pali Rao

Collecting the right data and ensuring that they are recorded

appropriately is paramount to the success of a business report. Various techniques can assist in this process when collecting both secondary and primary research.

Collecting Secondary Data

When beginning to collect secondary data, beware of collecting too much information—one of the major deterrents to good report writing. Although you want to be thorough, you do not want to collect and record such a large amount of information that you will hardly know where to begin your analysis.

The availability of computer-assisted data searches has simplified the time-consuming task of searching through indexes, card catalogs, and other sources. For example, suppose you select an online database such as Business Source Premier or an Internet search engine such as Google to research the role of microblogging in the workplace. By inputting the key terms *microblogging* and *Twitter* in an online database, you receive the screen output in Figure 9-4 on the next page. The screen output contains information that will facilitate your research.

First, you can quickly evaluate the relevance of references by reading each article's title and abstract, if available, to determine appropriateness to your topic. Retrieved full-text articles can be read and analyzed for useful information, saved, and printed for later use. Be sure to record a full bibliographic citation for each reference you obtain to avoid the need to relocate the online source or revisit the library to find it again.

After you have located relevant sources, you can take notes using various methods. When your aim is to *learn*, the following technique for taking notes is effective: (1) read an article rapidly and put it aside, (2) *from memory*, list main and supporting points, and (3) review the article to see whether all significant points have been included.

Rapid reading forces concentration, builds a strong understanding of the topic, and reveals relationships between ideas. Traditionally, researchers read the article and immediately wrote notes on cards. Currently, researchers typically prefer copying and pasting

validity
the degree to which the data measure what the researcher intends to measure

reliability
the level of consistency or stability over time or over independent samples

Figure 9-4 A Sample Computer Data Search Using an Online Database

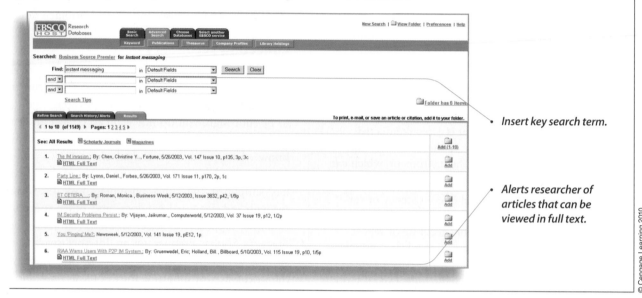

Insert key search term.

Alerts researcher of articles that can be viewed in full text.

relevant information into a word-processing file or high-lighting important points on a photocopy or printout of the article; then from the selected passages, they compose notes at the keyboard.

You can use two kinds of note-taking: direct quotation or paraphrase. The *direct quotation method* involves citing the exact words from a source. This method is useful when the exact words have specific impact or expert appeal. The *paraphrase method* involves summarizing information in your own words without changing the author's intended meaning. Put direct quotes in quotation marks, and indicate the page numbers, if available.

plagiarism

the presentation of someone else's ideas or words as your own

Collecting Data through Surveys

The method of distribution and the makeup of the questionnaire are critical factors in successful survey research.

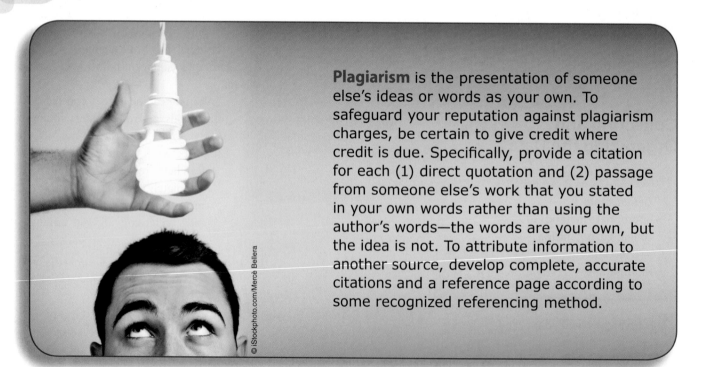

Plagiarism is the presentation of someone else's ideas or words as your own. To safeguard your reputation against plagiarism charges, be certain to give credit where credit is due. Specifically, provide a citation for each (1) direct quotation and (2) passage from someone else's work that you stated in your own words rather than using the author's words—the words are your own, but the idea is not. To attribute information to another source, develop complete, accurate citations and a reference page according to some recognized referencing method.

Selecting a Data Collection Method. Selecting an appropriate data collection method is crucial to effective research. Researchers must consider various factors when selecting an appropriate method for collecting data, as illustrated in Figure 9-5 on the next page.

Developing an Effective Survey Instrument. No matter which survey technique or combination of techniques is used, the way in which the survey instrument is designed and written has much to do with the validity and reliability of results, response rate, and quality of information received.

The construction of the survey instrument—usually a questionnaire or interview guide—is critical to obtaining reliable and valid data. Before developing items for a questionnaire or opinion survey, a researcher should visualize the ways responses will be compiled and included in a final report. Here are some suggestions for developing an effective questionnaire:

- **Provide brief, easy-to-follow directions.** Explain the purpose of the study in a cover letter or in a brief statement at the top of the questionnaire so that the respondents understand your intent. While a screening question might be needed to determine whether the respondent is qualified to answer a set of questions, minimize confusing "skip-and-jump" instructions such as the following:

  If you answered Yes to item 4, skip directly to item 7; if you answered No, explain your reason in items 5 and 6.

  Consider using electronic survey systems that advance respondents to the next question based on answers to screening questions.

- **Arrange the items in a logical sequence.** If possible, the sequence should proceed from easy to difficult items; simple, nonthreatening items involve respondents and encourage them to finish. You might group related items such as demographic questions or those that use the same response options (multiple choice, rating scales, open-ended questions).

- **Create an appealing, easy-to-comprehend design.** Use typefaces, bold, underline, and italics to emphasize important ideas. Use text boxes and graphic lines to partition text so that the reader can identify and move through sections quickly.

- **Use short items that ask for a single answer to one idea.** Include only the questions needed to meet the objectives of your study, since long questionnaires affect the return rate negatively.

- **Design questions that are easy to answer and to tabulate.** Participants might not take the time to answer numerous open-ended questions that require essay-style answers. When open-ended questions are included, provide enough space for respondents to answer adequately.

- **Strive to write clear questions that all respondents will interpret in the same way.** Avoid words with imprecise meanings (e.g., several, usually) and specialized terms and difficult words that respondents might not understand. Use accurate translations for each concept presented if other cultures are involved. Provide examples for items that might be difficult to understand.

- **Ask for information that can be recalled readily.** Asking for "old" information might not result in sound data.

- **Provide all possible answer choices on multiple-choice items.** Add an "undecided" or "other" category so that respondents are not forced to choose a nonapplicable response.

- **Ask for factual information whenever possible.** Opinions might be needed in certain studies, but opinions might change daily. As a general rule, the smaller the sample, the less reliable are any conclusions based on opinions.

- **Decide on an optimal number of choices to place on a ranking scale.** Ranking scales, also called Likert scales, allow participants to indicate their opinion on a numbered continuum. When deciding the numbers to place on the scale, consider the tendency of some groups to choose the noncommittal midpoint in a scale with an odd number of response choices (for instance, choosing 3 on a scale from 1 to 5).

- **Avoid questions that might be threatening or awkward to the respondent.** For sensitive issues, such as age and income, allow respondents to select among ranges if possible. Ensure that ranges do not overlap, and provide for all possible selections.

- **Consider the advisability of prompting a forced answer.** A forced answer question can be used to determine which single factor is most critical to a respondent, as shown in the following examples:

  Of all the problems listed, which is the single most critical problem for you personally?

  Should city taxes be levied to fund a city recreational complex?

  ❏ Yes   ❏ No

  When using forced choice items, avoid "leading questions" that cause people to answer in a way that is not their true opinion or situation. The following item is an example of such a question:

  Have you stopped confronting employees who disagree with your management decisions?

  ❏ Yes   ❏ No

Figure 9-5 Selecting an Appropriate Data Collection Method

METHOD	ADVANTAGES	LIMITATIONS
Mailed surveys 	• Are relatively inexpensive to administer • Can reach a wide number of people who complete the survey at their convenience • Allow anonymity, which may produce more honest responses • Remove difference-in-status barriers	• Can be expensive if follow-up mailings are required • Yield a low response rate • Are not useful for obtaining detailed information
Telephone surveys 	• Provide inexpensive and rapid data collection • Allow personal contact between interviewer and respondent for clarification or follow-up questions	• Must be relatively short to minimize perceived intrusion and to increase typical small return rate • May exclude respondents with unlisted numbers and those without telephones
Personal interviews 	• Are useful to obtain in-depth answers and explore sensitive topics • Allow personal contact between interviewer and respondent for clarification and follow-up questions	• Are time-consuming and resource intensive • Require proper interviewer • Vary in value, depending on quality and consistency of interviewer
Email polling 	• Is inexpensive • Provides for easy response • Yields quick results that can be updated electronically as responses are received	• Is limited to respondents with computer access

- **Include a postage-paid envelope with a mailed questionnaire.** A higher response rate results when this courtesy is provided. Include your return information at the bottom of the questionnaire in the event the envelope is misplaced.

Various types of items can be used in questionnaire design, depending on your purpose and the characteristics of your participants. Figure 9-6 on the next page illustrates the principles of effective questionnaire design.

A final step in questionnaire design is to test the instrument by asking others to complete and critique the questionnaire. For surveys of major importance, researchers typically conduct a pilot study, administering the questionnaire to a small group of the population involved. This process allows them to correct problems in clarity and design, and typically leads to better response and quality of answers. A pilot study might uncover factors affecting your results, which you can address in the final research design and before conducting the actual survey.

Researchers must select from among the several formats available the one best suited to the situation. Criteria for selecting one alternative over the others might include the following: Which format leaves the least chance for misinterpretation? Which format provides information in the way it can best be used? Can it be tabulated easily? Can it be cross-referenced to other items in the survey instrument?

Avoiding Data-Gathering Errors

If acceptable data-gathering techniques have been used, data will measure what they are intended to measure (have validity) and will measure it accurately (have reliability). Hopefully, a carefully designed research process will yield useful data for analysis.

Documenting Sources of Information

A crucial part of ethical, honest research writing is documenting or referencing sources fairly and accurately. Although time consuming and tedious, careful attention to documentation marks you as a respected, highly professional researcher.

An important first step is to pledge that you will not, for any reason, present someone else's ideas as your own. Then, develop a systematic checklist for avoiding plagiarism. Carelessly forgetting to enclose someone else's words within quotation marks or failing to paraphrase another's words can cause others to question your ethical conduct. When you feel that the tedious work required to document sources fairly and accurately is not worth the time invested, remind yourself of the following reasons for documentation:

- **Citations give credit where it is due—to the one who created the material.** People who document demonstrate high standards of ethical conduct and responsibility in scholarship. Those exhibiting this professional behavior will gain the well-deserved trust and respect of peers and superiors.

- **Documentation protects writers against plagiarism charges.** Plagiarism occurs when someone steals material from another and claims it as his or her own writing. Besides suffering embarrassment, the plagiarist might be assessed fines, penalties, or professional sanctions.

- **Documentation supports your statements.** If recognized authorities have said the same thing, your work takes on credibility; you have put yourself in good company.

- **Documentation can aid future researchers pursuing similar material.** Documentation must be complete and accurate so that the researcher can locate the source.

Many style guides are available to advise writers how to organize, document, and produce reports and manuscripts. Figure 9-3 includes two of the most popular authoritative style manuals. The *Publication Manual of the American Psychological Association* has become the most-used guide in the social and "soft" sciences and in many scholarly journals. The *MLA Handbook for Writers of Research Papers* is another authoritative source used in the humanities.

Some common errors at the data gathering stage:

- ☒ Using samples that are too small
- ☒ Using samples that are not representative
- ☒ Using poorly constructed data-gathering instruments
- ☒ Using information from biased sources
- ☒ Failing to gather enough information to cover all important aspects of a problem
- ☒ Gathering too much information

© Image Source

Figure 9-6 Example of an Effective Questionnaire

1. **Rank the following job factors in order of their importance to you. Add other factors important to you in the space provided.**

		1	2	3	4	5	6	7
a.	Wages	○	○	○	○	○	○	○
b.	Health and retirement benefits	○	○	○	○	○	○	○
c.	Job security	○	○	○	○	○	○	○
d.	Ability to maintain balance between work and family life	○	○	○	○	○	○	○
e.	Creativity and challenge of work assignment	○	○	○	○	○	○	○
f.	Perceived prestige of work	○	○	○	○	○	○	○
g.		○	○	○	○	○	○	○
h.		○	○	○	○	○	○	○

- Uses variety of items to elicit different types of responses.
- Uses clear, concise language to minimize confusion.
- Provides clear instructions for answering each item.

2. **Which of the following is the single job satisfaction factor that you feel needs more attention in our company? (Please select only one.)**

- ○ Wages
- ○ Health and retirement benefits
- ○ Job security
- ○ Ability to maintain balance between work and family life
- ○ Creativity and challenge of work assignment
- ○ Perceived prestige of work
- ○ Other (specify) [▼]

- Provides additional lines to allow for individual opinions.

3. **How would you rate your overall job satisfaction?**

Very unsatisfied 1	Unsatisfied 2	Somewhat unsatisfied 3	Somewhat satisfied 4	Satisfied 5	Very satisfied 6
○	○	○	○	○	○

- Provides even number of rating choices to eliminate "fence" responses.

4. **How would you rate your overall job satisfaction 12 months ago?**

Very unsatisfied 1	Unsatisfied 2	Somewhat unsatisfied 3	Somewhat satisfied 4	Satisfied 5	Very satisfied 6
○	○	○	○	○	○

- Asks for easily recalled information.

5. **Indicate your age group:**

- ○ 20–29
- ○ 30–39
- ○ 40–49
- ○ 50–59
- ○ 60–69
- ○ 70 years and over

- Provides nonoverlapping categories of response and open-ended final category.

6. **Indicate your time with the company:**

- ○ Less than 1 year
- ○ 1–3 years
- ○ 4–6 years
- ○ 7–10 years
- ○ Over 10 years

7. **What could the company do to enhance your satisfaction as a company employee?**

[   ]

Thanks for your participation. Click to submit your questionnaire.

[Submit]

Format Pointers

Provides adequate space for answering open-ended item.

Keeps length as short as possible while meeting survey objectives.

Includes instructions for submitting completed questionnaire.

© Pali Rao/iStockphoto.com

Follow these general suggestions for preparing accurate documentation:

- **Decide which authoritative style manual to follow for preparing in-text parenthetical citations or footnotes (endnotes) and the bibliography (references).** Some companies and most journals require writers to prepare reports or manuscripts following a particular style manual. Once you are certain you have selected the appropriate manual, follow it precisely as you prepare the documentation and produce the report.

- **Be consistent.** If you are carefully following a format, you shouldn't have a problem with consistency. For example, one style manual might require an author's initials in place of first name in a bibliography; another manual requires the full name. The placement of commas and periods and other information varies among manuals. Consult the manual, apply the rules methodically, and proofread carefully to ensure accuracy and consistency.

Citations. Two major types of citations are used to document a report: source notes and explanatory notes. Depending on the authoritative style manual used, these notes might be positioned in parentheses within the report, at the bottom of the page, or at the end of the report.

- **Source notes.** These citations acknowledge the contributions of others. They might refer readers to sources of quotations, paraphrased portions of someone else's words or ideas, and quantitative data used in the report. Source notes must include complete and accurate information so that the reader can locate the original source if desired.

- **Explanatory notes.** These citations are used for several purposes: (1) to comment on a source or to provide information that does not fit easily in the text, (2) to support a statistical table, or (3) to refer the reader to another section of the report. The following sample footnote describes the mathematics involved in preparing a table:

  The weighted opinion was derived by assigning responses from high to low as 5, 4, 3, 2, 1; totaling all respondents; and dividing by the number of respondents.

In this case, the asterisk (*) was used rather than a number to identify the explanatory footnote both in the text and in the citation. This method is often used when only one or two footnotes are included in the report. If two footnotes appear on the same page, two asterisks (**) or numbers or letters are used to distinguish the second from the first. An explanatory note that supports a graphic or a source note that provides the reference from which data were taken appears immediately below the graphic.

Referencing Methods. Various reference methods are available for the format and content of source notes: in-text parenthetical citations, footnotes, and endnotes. Note the major differences among the methods in the following discussion.

- **In-text parenthetical citations.** The *APA Publication Manual*, *MLA Handbook*, and some other documentation references eliminate the need for separate footnotes or endnotes. Instead, an in-text citation, which contains abbreviated information within parentheses, directs the reader to a list of sources at the end of a report. The list of sources at the end contains all publication information on every source cited. This list is arranged alphabetically by the author's last name or, if no author is provided, by the first word of the article title.

- **Footnote citation method.** Placing citations at the bottom of the page on which they are cited is the footnote citation. The reader can conveniently refer to the source if the documentation is positioned at the bottom of the page. Alternatively, a list of footnotes can be included in an endnotes page at the end of the document in the order they appeared. Footnotes and endnotes are not used in APA and MLA referencing, as these styles permit the use of in-text citations only.

- **References (APA) or Works Cited (MLA).** The APA and MLA styles use different terms to distinguish between these types of lists. This document is an alphabetized list of the sources used in preparing a report. Each entry contains the publication information necessary for locating the source. In addition, the bibliographic entries give evidence of the nature of sources the author consulted. The term *bibliography* (literally "description of books") is sometimes used to refer to this list. A researcher often uses sources that provide information but do not result in citations. To acknowledge that you might have consulted these works and to provide the reader with a comprehensive reading list, you might include them in the list of sources.

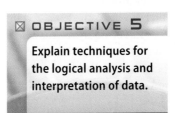

☒ **OBJECTIVE 5**

Explain techniques for the logical analysis and interpretation of data.

Arriving at an Answer

Even the most intelligent person cannot be expected to draw sound conclusions from faulty

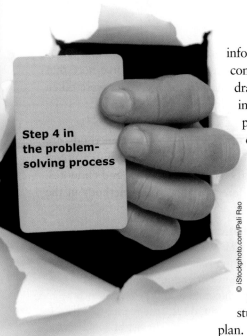

Step 4 in the problem-solving process

© iStockphoto.com/Pali Rao

information. Sound conclusions can be drawn only when information has been properly organized, collected, and interpreted.

Analyzing the Data

Follow a step-by-step approach to the solution of your research problem. Plan your study and follow the plan. Question every step for its contribution to the objective, and keep a record of actions. In a formal research study, the researcher is expected to make a complete report. Another qualified person should be able to make the same study, use the same steps, and arrive at the same conclusion.

Suppose you have conducted a survey and collected several hundred replies to a 30-item questionnaire. Appropriate statistical analysis must be applied to interpret survey results. Statistical analysis is a complex task, involving specialized understanding that is gained through appropriate training, but some of the common terms are identified here. *Tabulation* techniques should be used to reduce quantitative data such as numerous answers to questionnaire items. For instance, you might want to tabulate the number of males and females participating in the study, along with the appropriate percentages for each gender.

For many kinds of studies, *measures of central tendency* might help in describing distributions of quantitative data. The *range* assists the researcher in understanding the distribution of the scores. The *mean*, *median*, and *mode* are descriptions of the average value of the distribution.

Other statistical techniques may be used. For example, *correlation analysis* might be used to determine whether a relationship existed between how respondents answered one item and how they answered another. Were males, for example, more likely to have chosen a certain answer to another item on the survey than were females?

The report process is one of reducing the information collected to a size that can be handled conveniently in a written message, as shown in Figure 9-7. Visualize the report process as taking place in a huge funnel. At the top of the funnel, pour in all the original information. Then, through a process of compression within the funnel, take these steps:

1. Evaluate the information for its usefulness.
2. Reduce the useful information through organization of notes and data analysis.
3. Combine like information into understandable forms through the use of tables, charts, graphs, and summaries. (See Chapter 10.)
4. Report in written form the information that remains. (See Chapter 11.)

Interpreting the Data

Your ethical principles affect the validity of your interpretations. Through all steps in the research process, you must attempt to maintain the integrity of the research. Strive to remain objective, design and conduct an unbiased study, and resist any pressure to slant research to support a particular viewpoint.

Some common errors that seriously hinder the interpretation of data include the following:

- ☒ **Trying, consciously or unconsciously, to make results conform to a prediction or desire.** Seeing predictions come true might be pleasing, but objectivity is much more important. Facts should determine conclusions.

- ☒ **Hoping for spectacular results.** An attempt to astonish supervisors by preparing a report with revolutionary conclusions can have a negative effect on accuracy.

- ☒ **Attempting to compare when commonality is absent.** Results obtained from one study might not always apply to other situations. Similarly, research with a certain population might not be consistent when the same research is conducted with another population.

- ☒ **Assuming a cause–effect relationship when one does not exist.** A company president might have been in office one year, and sales might have doubled. However, sales might have doubled in spite of the president rather than because of the president.

- ☒ **Failing to consider important factors.** For example, learning that McDonald's was considering closing its restaurants in Kassel, Germany, a manager of an industrial supply company recommended that his firm reconsider its plans to expand its operation into Germany. The manager failed to recognize that the adverse impact of a new tax on disposable containers, not an unfavorable German economy or government, was the reason McDonald's was considering closing its restaurants.[2]

Figure 9-7 The Report Process

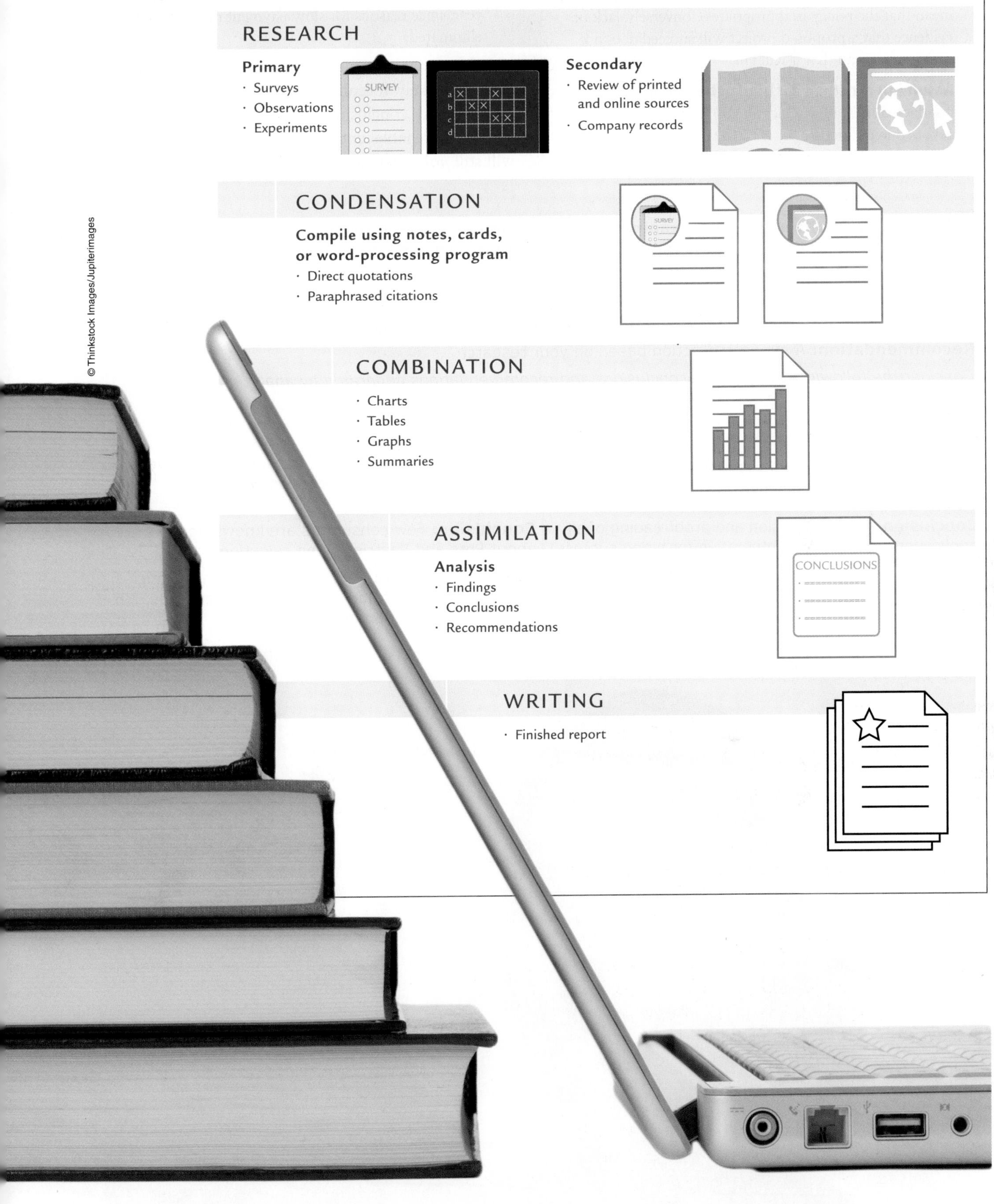

RESEARCH

Primary
· Surveys
· Observations
· Experiments

Secondary
· Review of printed and online sources
· Company records

CONDENSATION

Compile using notes, cards, or word-processing program
· Direct quotations
· Paraphrased citations

COMBINATION

· Charts
· Tables
· Graphs
· Summaries

ASSIMILATION

Analysis
· Findings
· Conclusions
· Recommendations

WRITING

· Finished report

☒ **Basing a conclusion on lack of evidence.** "We have had no complaints about our present policy" does not mean that the policy is appropriate. Conversely, lack of evidence that a proposed project will succeed does not necessarily mean that it will fail.

☒ **Assuming constancy of human behavior.** A survey conducted in March indicating 60 percent of the public favors one political party over the other might not have the same results if conducted in November. Because some people paid their bills late last year does not mean a company should refuse to sell to them next year, since reasons for slow payment might have been eliminated.

If you avoid common data-collection errors, you are more likely to collect valid and reliable data and reach sound conclusions. However, if you interpret valid and reliable data incorrectly, your conclusions will still *not* be sound.

Keep in mind the differences in meaning of some common research terms as you analyze your material and attempt to seek meaning from it. Most research reports include all three of the following items or sections.

Finding: A specific, measurable fact from a research study

Conclusion: Summation of major facts and evidence derived from findings

Recommendation: A suggested action based on your research

Consider the following examples of conclusions and recommendations generated by analyzing research findings:

Example 1

Finding: Fully 80 percent of responding recruiters said they would eliminate an applicant from consideration if errors were found in application materials.

Conclusion: Careful revision and proofreading of all application materials are imperative for hiring success.

Recommendation: Students should carefully proofread all application materials before submitting them to potential employers.

Example 2

Finding: Only 10 percent of consumers surveyed knew that Pots and Pantries sells kitchen and bathroom linens.

Conclusion: Few consumers are knowledgeable about Pots and Pantries' linen selection.

Recommendation: Pots and Pantries' marketing strategy should include new advertisements to highlight its selection of linens.

© Alex Aranda/Shutterstock

THE IN-CROWD

Share your 4LTR Press story on Facebook at www.facebook.com/4ltrpress for a chance to win.

To learn more about the In-Crowd opportunity 'like' us on Facebook.

Managing Data and Using Graphics

Communicating Quantitative Information

Before you can interpret quantitative data, the elements must be classified, summarized, and condensed into a manageable size. This condensed information is meaningful and can be used to answer your research questions. For example, assume that you have been given 400 completed questionnaires from a study of employee needs for financial planning. This large accumulation of data is overwhelming until you tabulate the responses for each questionnaire item by manually inputting or compiling responses received through an online survey or optically scanning the responses into a computer. Then, you can apply appropriate statistical analysis techniques to the tabulated data.

⊠ **OBJECTIVE 1**

Communicate quantitative information effectively.

The computer generates a report of the total responses for each possible answer to each item. For example, the tabulation of responses from each employee about his or her most important need in financial planning might appear like this:

Retirement Annuities	128
Traditional and Roth IRA	104
Mutual Funds	80
Internet Stock Trading	52
Effective Charitable Giving	36
	400

⊠ **OBJECTIVES**

1 Communicate quantitative information effectively.

2 Apply principles of effectiveness and ethical responsibilities in the construction of graphic aids.

3 Select and design appropriate and meaningful graphics.

4 Integrate graphics within documents.

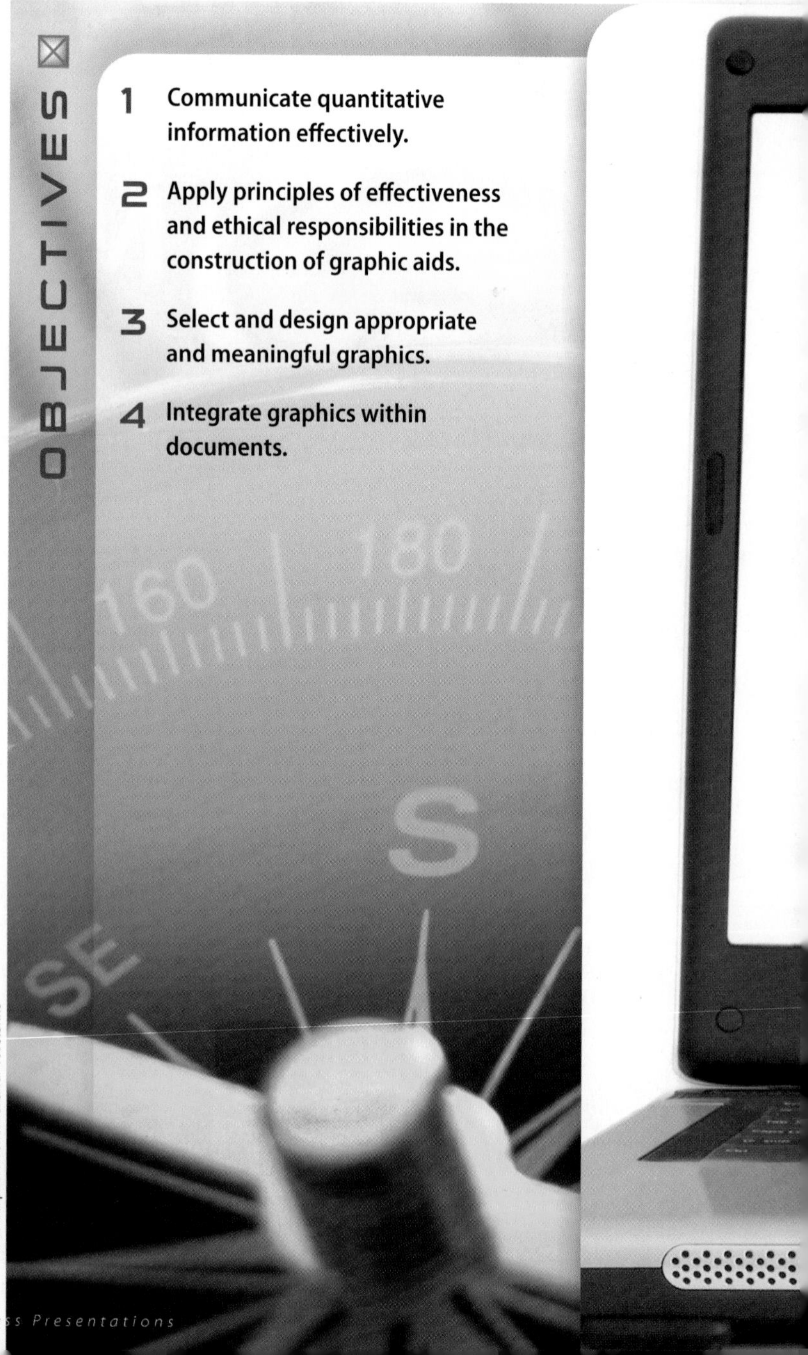

© iStockphoto.com/Alexandr Tovstenko

The breakdown reduces 400 responses to a manageable set of information. The tabulation shows only five items, each with a specific number of responses from the total of 400 questionnaires. Because people tend to make comparisons during analysis, the totals are helpful. People generally want to know proportions or ratios, and these are best presented as percentage parts of the total. Thus, the numbers converted to percentages are as follows:

Personal Development Need	Number	Percentage
Retirement Annuities	128	32
Traditional and Roth IRA	104	26
Mutual Funds	80	20
Internet Stock Trading	52	13
Effective Charitable Giving	36	9
	400	100

Now analyzing the data becomes relatively easy. Of the survey participants, 13 percent selected Internet stock trading, and only 9 percent selected effective charitable giving. Other observations, depending on how exactly you intend to interpret percentages, could be that a fifth of the employees selected mutual funds. Combining data in two categories allows you to summarize that slightly more than one half of the employees

© Bornshtein/Shutterstock

selected retirement annuities and individual retirement accounts.

When tabulating research results of people's opinions, likes, preferences, and other subjective items, rounding off statistics to fractions helps paint a clear picture for readers. In actuality, if the same group of people were asked this question again a day or two later, a few probably would have changed their minds. For example, an employee who had not indicated a desire for retirement planning may have learned of the benefits of a Roth IRA during a civic club meeting. The next day, the employee might indicate a desire for training in IRAs and retirement annuities.

Fractions, ratios, and percentages are examples of **common language**. In effect, common language reduces difficult figures to the "common denominators" of language and ideas. Although "104 of 400 prefer traditional and Roth IRAs" is somewhat easy to understand, "26 percent prefer . . ." is even easier, and "approximately one out of four indicate a preference for traditional and Roth IRAs" is even more understandable.

Common language also involves the use of indicators other than actual count or quantity. The Dow Jones Industrial Average provides a measure of stock market performance and is certainly easier to understand than the complete New York Stock Exchange figures. Similarly, oil is

common language
reduces difficult figures to the common denominators of language and ideas

counted in barrels rather than in the quart or gallon sizes purchased by consumers. Because of inflation, dollars are not accurate items to use as comparisons from one year to another in certain areas; for example, automobile manufacturers use "automobile units" to represent production changes in the industry. The important thing for the report writer to remember is that reports are communication media, and everything possible should be done to make sure communication occurs effectively.

Using Graphics

Imagine trying to put in composition style all the information available in a financial statement. Several hundred pages might be necessary to explain material that could otherwise be contained in three or four pages of balance sheets and income statements. Even then, the reader would no doubt be thoroughly confused! To protect readers from being overwhelmed or simply bored with data, report writers can design visually appealing graphics that are appropriate for the data being presented. Data reported in a table, graph, or picture will make your written analysis clearer to the reader.

☒ OBJECTIVE 2

Apply principles of effectiveness and ethical responsibilities in the construction of graphic aids.

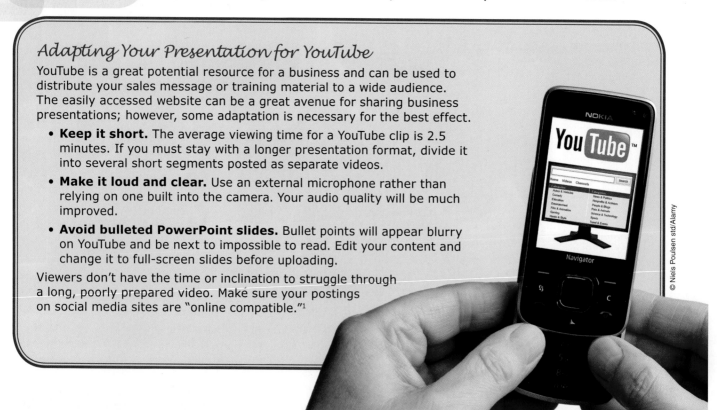

Adapting Your Presentation for YouTube

YouTube is a great potential resource for a business and can be used to distribute your sales message or training material to a wide audience. The easily accessed website can be a great avenue for sharing business presentations; however, some adaptation is necessary for the best effect.

- **Keep it short.** The average viewing time for a YouTube clip is 2.5 minutes. If you must stay with a longer presentation format, divide it into several short segments posted as separate videos.

- **Make it loud and clear.** Use an external microphone rather than relying on one built into the camera. Your audio quality will be much improved.

- **Avoid bulleted PowerPoint slides.** Bullet points will appear blurry on YouTube and be next to impossible to read. Edit your content and change it to full-screen slides before uploading.

Viewers don't have the time or inclination to struggle through a long, poorly prepared video. Make sure your postings on social media sites are "online compatible."[1]

© Niels Poulsen std/Alamy

The term **graphics** is used in this chapter to refer to all types of illustrations used in written and spoken reports. The most commonly used graphics are tables, bar charts, line charts, pie charts, pictograms, maps, flowcharts, diagrams, and photographs.

Effective and Ethical Use of Graphics

The use of graphics with a written discussion serves three purposes: to clarify, to simplify, or to reinforce data. As you read this chapter, ask yourself if the discussion would be effective if the accompanying graphic figures were not included. Use the following questions to help you determine whether using a graphic element is appropriate and effective in a written or spoken report.

- **Is a graphic needed to clarify, reinforce, or emphasize a particular idea?** Or can the material be covered adequately in words rather than in visual ways? To maintain a reasonable balance between words and graphics, save graphics for data that are difficult to communicate in words alone.

- **Does the graphic presentation contribute to the overall understanding of the idea under discussion?** Will the written or spoken text add meaning to the graphic display?

- **Is the graphic easily understood?** Does the graphic emphasize the key idea and spur the reader to think intelligently about this information? Follow these important design principles:

  o Avoid *chartjunk*. This term, coined by design expert Edward Tufte, describes decorative distractions that bury relevant data.[2] Extreme use of color, complicated symbols and art techniques, and unusual combinations of typefaces reduce the impact of the material presented.

  o Develop a consistent design for graphics. Arbitrary changes in the design of graphics (e.g., use of colors, typefaces, three-dimensional or flat designs) within a written or spoken report can be confusing as the receiver expects consistency in elements within a single report.

  o Write meaningful titles that reinforce the point you are making. For example, a receiver can interpret data faster when graphics use a talking title; that is, a title that interprets the data. Consider the usefulness of the following graphic titles for a physician browsing through a complex table at the hospital in the middle of the night:[3]

  Descriptive Title: *White-Cell Counts During April*

  Talking Title: *White-Cell Count Has Fallen throughout April*

The talking title saves the physician time in understanding the report and also ensures the accuracy of the physician's interpretation, proper diagnosis, and treatment of the patient. Similarly, poor business decisions can be averted if graphic titles reveal key information. You will learn more about the appropriate use of descriptive and talking headings as you study the preparation of informational and analytical reports in Chapter 11.

- **Is the graphic honest?** Visual data can be distorted easily, leading the reader to form incorrect opinions about the data.

- **Can a graphic used in a presentation be seen by the entire audience?** Electronic presentations, flip charts, whiteboards, and overhead transparencies are the visual means most often used to accompany presentations.

The key to preparing effective graphics is selecting an appropriate graphic for the data and developing a clean, simple design that allows the reader or audience to quickly extract the needed information and meaning.

> We remember more of what we both see *and* hear than of what we receive through only one sensory channel. When text and graphics are combined, retention goes up an average of 42 percent.[4]

Types of Graphic Aids

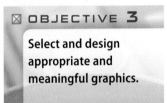

OBJECTIVE 3

Select and design appropriate and meaningful graphics.

Using powerful software programs, managers can perform data management functions discussed in this chapter to produce highly professional graphics. The information can be reproduced in a variety of ways for integrating into reports and for supporting highly effective presentations.

Selecting the graphic type that will depict data in the most effective manner is the first decision you must make. After identifying the idea you want your receiver to understand, you can choose to use a table, bar chart, line chart, pie chart, flowchart, organization chart,

graphics
all types of illustrations used in written and spoken reports

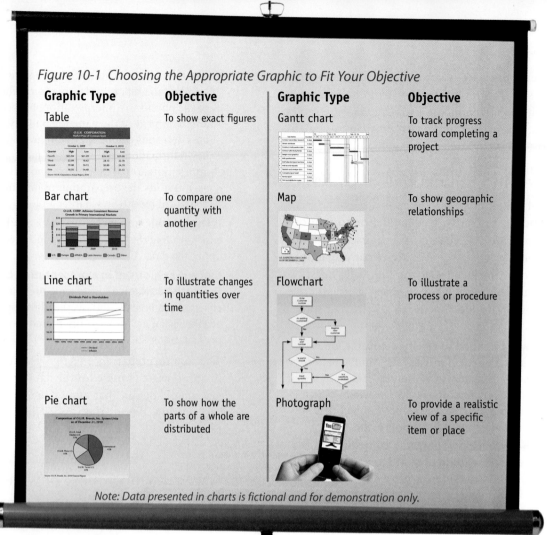

Figure 10-1 Choosing the Appropriate Graphic to Fit Your Objective

Graphic Type	Objective	Graphic Type	Objective
Table	To show exact figures	Gantt chart	To track progress toward completing a project
Bar chart	To compare one quantity with another	Map	To show geographic relationships
Line chart	To illustrate changes in quantities over time	Flowchart	To illustrate a process or procedure
Pie chart	To show how the parts of a whole are distributed	Photograph	To provide a realistic view of a specific item or place

Note: Data presented in charts is fictional and for demonstration only.

© C Squared Studios/Photodisc/Getty Images

photographs, models, and so on. Use Figure 10-1 to help you choose the graphic type that matches the objective you hope to achieve.

Figures 10-2 through 10-8 on the following pages illustrate a variety of graphics commonly used in reports. The figures show acceptable variations in graphic design, including placement of the caption (figure number and title), inclusion or exclusion of grid lines, proper labeling of the axes, proper referencing of the source of data, and other features. When designing graphics, adhere to the requirements in your company policy manual or the style manual you are instructed to follow. Then be certain that you design graphics for a particular document or presentation consistently. When preparing a graphic for a slide show or mounted chart, remove the figure number and include the title only.

Tables

A **table** presents data in columns and rows, which

aid in clarifying large quantities of data in a small space. Proper labeling techniques make the content clear. Guidelines for preparing an effective table follow and are illustrated in Figure 10-2:

- **Number tables and all other graphics consecutively throughout the report.** This practice enables you to refer to "Figure 1" rather than to "the following table" or "the figure on the following page."

- **Give each table a title that is complete enough to clarify what is included without forcing the reader to review the table.** Table titles can be quite long as they can contain sources of data, numbers included in the table, and the subject, as shown in Figure 10-2. Titles should be written in either all capitals or upper and lowercase letters. Titles that extend beyond one line should be arranged on the page so that they are balanced.

- **Label columns of data clearly enough to identify the items.** Usually, column headings are short and easily arranged. If, however, they happen to be lengthy, use some ingenuity in planning the arrangement.

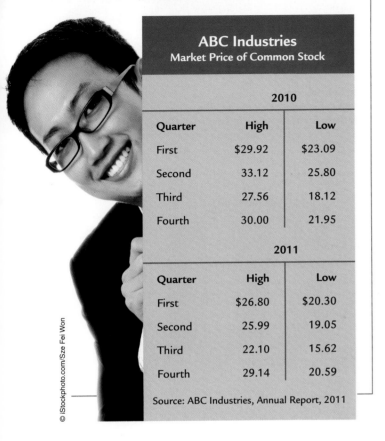

Figure 10-2 Effective Table Layout, Identifying Information, Labels, and Source

ABC Industries		
Market Price of Common Stock		
2010		
Quarter	High	Low
First	$29.92	$23.09
Second	33.12	25.80
Third	27.56	18.12
Fourth	30.00	21.95
2011		
Quarter	High	Low
First	$26.80	$20.30
Second	25.99	19.05
Third	22.10	15.62
Fourth	29.14	20.59

Source: ABC Industries, Annual Report, 2011

- **Indent the second line of a label for the rows (horizontal items) two or three spaces.** Labels that are subdivisions of more comprehensive labels should be indented, as should summary labels such as "total."

- **Place a superscript symbol beside an entry that requires additional explanation and include the explanatory note beneath the visual.**

- **Document the source of the data presented in a visual by adding a source note beneath the visual.** If more than one source was used to prepare a visual, use superscripts beside the various information references and provide the sources beneath the figure.

Bar Charts

A **bar chart** is an effective graphic for comparing quantities (see Figure 10-3 on the next page). The length of the bars, horizontal or vertical, indicates quantity. The vertical bars in Figure 10-3a (left) show changes in the number of subscribers to a popular mail movie-rental business. Because of the lengthy labels, horizontal bars are ideal for depicting the top objections to drinking water shown in Figure 10-3a (right). Variations of the simple bar chart make it useful for a variety of purposes:

- **Grouped bar charts** (also called *clustered bar charts*) are useful for comparing more than one quantity. Figure 10-3b shows changes in the average inflation-adjusted prices in three major housing markets.

- **Segmented bar charts** (also called *subdivided, stacked bar,* or *100 percent bar charts*) show how components contribute to a total figure. The segments in Figure 10-3c illustrate that sales outside of a company's three primary market areas (Japan, the United States, and Europe) are steadily becoming a large portion of the company's total sales.

- **Pictograms** use pictures or symbols to illustrate objects, concepts, or numerical values. A simple use of a pictogram is a picture of an envelope used to represent an email message. Pictograms are common in everyday life, such as on signs in public places or roads, whereas the term "icon" is specific to interfaces on computers or other electronic devices. An image of a house is used in Figure 10-3d to depict home sales in the United States over a twenty-year period.

- The **Gantt chart**, another variation of the bar chart, is useful for tracking progress toward completing a series of events over time. The Gantt chart in Figure 10-3e, prepared using Microsoft Project, plots the output on the *y*-axis (activities involved in planning and implementing a research study) and the time (days planned to complete the activity) on the *x*-axis. This version of the Gantt chart not only schedules the important activities

bar chart
a graphic used to compare quantities

grouped bar chart
a graphic used for comparing more than one quantity (set of data) at each point along the y–axis (vertical) or x–axis (horizontal); also called a clustered bar chart

segmented bar chart
a graphic used to show how different facts (components) contribute to a total figure; also called a subdivided, stacked bar, or 100 percent bar chart

pictogram
a graphic that uses pictures or symbols to illustrate objects, concepts, or numerical relationships

Gantt chart
a specific type of bar chart that is useful for tracking progress toward completing a series of events over time

Figure 10-3 Variety of Bar Chart Formats

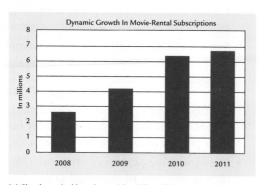

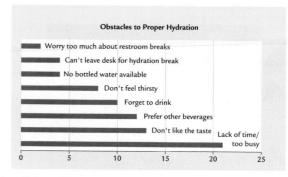

(a) Simple vertical bar chart with gridlines (left) and simple horizontal bar with data table and no gridlines (right)

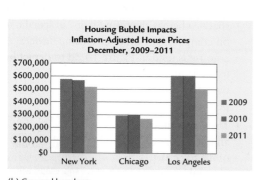

(b) Grouped bar chart

(c) Segmented bar chart

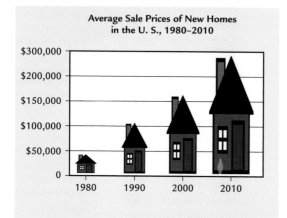

(d) Pictograms: Poor example (left) and good example (right)

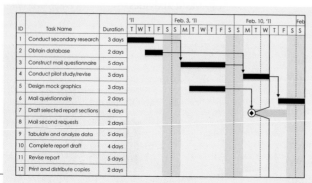

(e) Gantt chart

Note: Data presented in charts is fictional and for demonstration only.

© Cengage Learning 2013

required to complete this research but also plots the *actual* progress of each activity along with the *planned* progress. Simple Gantt charts can be created using a spreadsheet program such as Microsoft Excel.

In addition to the suggestions for developing tables, here are further suggestions related to constructing bar charts:

- **Avoid visual distortion that could exaggerate the data.** Begin the quantitative axis at zero, divide the bars into equal increments, and use bars of equal width.

- **Position chronologically or in some other logical order.**

- **Use color to convey meaning.** For example, use variations in color to distinguish among the bars when the bars represent different data. Avoid large surfaces of bright colors that may be tiring to the audience and detract from the data.

- **Avoid fancy formatting such as 3D that makes values more difficult to distinguish.**

- **Keep the labeling simple to reduce clutter and increase readability.** Exclude nonessential information such as data labels, gridlines, and explanatory notes if the meaning is understood. To determine labeling needs, consider the audience's use of the data. Omit actual amounts if a visual estimate is adequate for understanding the relationships presented in the chart. Include the data values above the bars or as a data table for an audience who expects specific data.

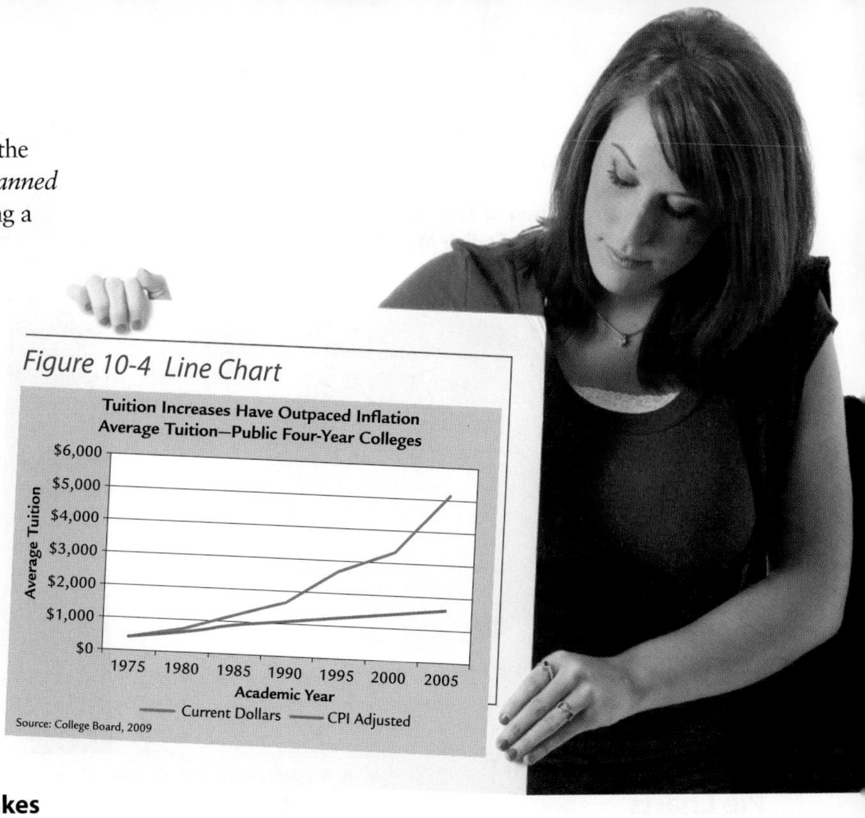

Line Charts

A **line chart** depicts changes in quantitative data over time and illustrates trends. The line chart shown in Figure 10-4 shows the degree to which college tuition increases have outpaced inflation. When constructing line charts, keep these general guidelines in mind:

- **Use the vertical axis for amount and the horizontal axis for time.**

- **Begin the vertical axis at zero.**

- **Divide the vertical and horizontal scales into equal increments.** The vertical or quantity increments, however, need not be the same as the horizontal or time increments so that the line or lines drawn will have reasonable slopes. Unrealistic scales might produce startling slopes that could mislead readers.

An **area chart**, also called a *cumulative line chart* or a *surface chart*, is similar to a segmented bar chart

Figure 10-4 Line Chart

Tuition Increases Have Outpaced Inflation
Average Tuition—Public Four-Year Colleges

[Line chart with vertical axis "Average Tuition" labeled $0, $1,000, $2,000, $3,000, $4,000, $5,000, $6,000 and horizontal axis "Academic Year" labeled 1975, 1980, 1985, 1990, 1995, 2000, 2005. Legend: Current Dollars, CPI Adjusted]

Source: College Board, 2009

because it shows how different factors contribute to a total. An area chart is especially useful when you want to illustrate changes in components over time. For example, the area chart in Figure 10-5 illustrates changes in the actions of visitors to a company's website. A company decision maker can easily recognize the growth in the number of hits and orders placed. The cumulative total of the number of hits, registrations, and orders is illustrated by the top line on the chart. The amount of each component can be estimated by visual assessment.

line chart
a graphic that depicts changes in quantitative data over time and illustrates trends

area chart
a graphic that shows how different factors contribute to a total; also referred to as a cumulative line chart or surface chart

Figure 10-5 Area Chart

Internet Site Visits Yielding More Orders
2007–2011

[Area chart with vertical axis "Number of Hits (000s)" labeled 0, 50, 100, 150, 200, 250, 300 and horizontal axis labeled 2007, 2008, 2009, 2010, 2011. Legend: Access only, Register only, Order]

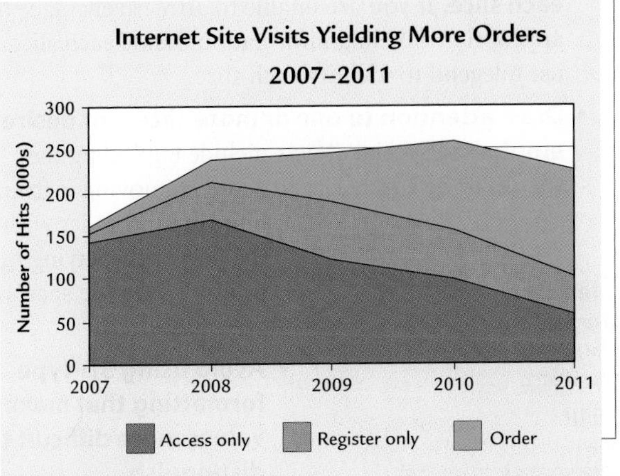

© Cengage Learning 2013

Figure 10-6 Pie Chart

**Proportion of Sales by Business Segment
Year Ending March 31, 2012**

- All Other 4%
- Financial Services 6%
- Brokerage Services 10%
- Insurance 14%
- Mortgage Services 67%

Source: ABC Industries, Annual Report, 2012

© Cengage Learning 2013

Pie Charts

Pie charts, like segmented charts and area charts, show how the parts of a whole are distributed. Pie charts are effective for showing percentages (parts of a whole), but they are ineffective in showing quantitative totals or comparisons. Bars are used for those purposes. The pie chart in Figure 10-6 shows the proportion of sales a corporation earned from its various business segments.

Here are some general guidelines for constructing pie charts:

- **Position the largest slice or the slice to be emphasized at the twelve o'clock position.** Working clockwise, place the other slices in descending order of size or some other logical order of presentation.

- **Label each slice and include information about the quantitative size (percentage, dollars, etc.) of each slice.** If you are unable to attractively place the appropriate labeling information beside each slice, use a legend to identify each slice.

- **Draw attention to one or more slices for desired emphasis.** Special effects include exploding the slice(s) to be emphasized (that is, removing it from immediate contact with the pie) or displaying or printing only the slice(s) to be emphasized.

- **Avoid using 3D-type formatting that makes values more difficult to distinguish.**

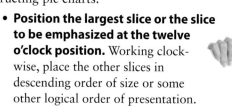
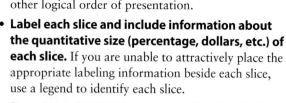

Your software may limit your ability to follow rules explicitly, and the nature of the data or the presentation may require slight deviations. For example, if you intend to explode the largest pie slice, placing it in the twelve o'clock position may not be desirable because the slice is likely to intrude into the space occupied by a title positioned above the graphic.

Maps

A **map** shows geographic relationships. This graphic type is especially useful when a receiver may not be familiar with the geography discussed in a report. The map shown in Figure 10-7 effectively presents the distribution of electoral votes by political party in the 2008 U.S. presidential election. The map gives the information visually and thus eliminates the difficulty of explaining the information in words. In addition to

Figure 10-7 Map Conveying Statistical Data

U.S. president race

GOP ★ McCain   Dems Obama   '08

Results as of 2 p.m. ET, Nov. 5

Electoral votes*
McCain 173
Obama 364
270 needed to win

*If Mo. and N.C. votes go as trending; one of Nebraska's electoral votes has not been awarded

Source: AP

© 2008 MCT

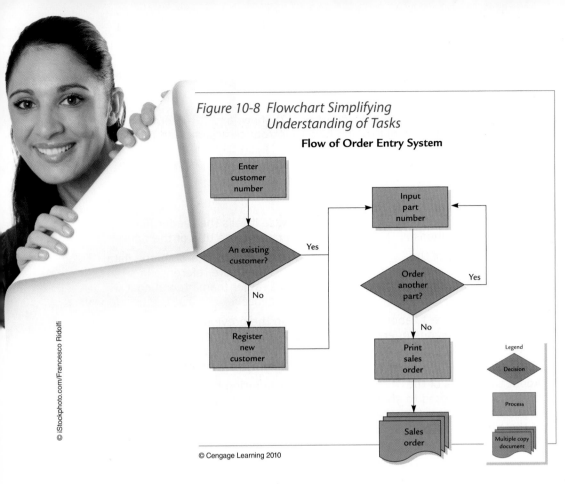

Figure 10-8 Flowchart Simplifying Understanding of Tasks

Flow of Order Entry System

Enter customer number

An existing customer? — Yes

No

Register new customer

Input part number

Order another part? — Yes

No

Print sales order

Sales order

Legend

Decision

Process

Multiple copy document

© Cengage Learning 2010

---

being less confusing, a map is more concise and interesting than a written message.

Flowcharts

A **flowchart** is a step-by-step diagram of a procedure or a graphic depiction of a system or organization. A variety of problems can be resolved by using flowcharts to support written analyses. For example, most companies have procedure manuals to instruct employees in certain work tasks. Including a flowchart with written instructions minimizes the chance of errors. The flowchart in Figure 10-8 illustrates the procedures for processing a telephone order in a series of simple steps. If this information had been presented only in a series of written steps, the customer service manager would have to rely not only on the input operators' reading ability but also on their willingness to study the written procedures.

Organization charts, discussed in Chapter 1, are widely used to provide a picture of the authority structure and relationships within an organization. They provide employees with an idea of what their organization looks like in terms of the flow of authority and responsibility. When businesses change (because of new employees or reorganization of units and responsibilities), organization charts must be revised. Revisions

to organizational charts are simple when prepared using word processing or graphics software.

Other Graphics

Other graphics, such as architectural plans, photographs, cartoons, blueprints, and lists of various kinds, may be included in reports. The availability of graphics and sophisticated drawing software facilitate inclusion of these more complex visuals in reports and spoken presentations. Photographs are used frequently in annual reports to help the general audience understand complex concepts and to make the documents more appealing to read. Frequently, you must include some graphic material in a report that would make the narrative discussion otherwise unwieldy. In this case, the material might be placed in an appendix and only referred to in the report.

flowchart
a step–by–step diagram of a procedure or a graphic depiction of a system or organization

Always mention a graphic in text immediately before it appears.

Introducing Graphics in Text

The pattern for incorporating graphics in text is (1) introduce, (2) show, and (3) interpret and analyze. The examples below show how not to and how to introduce graphic and tabular material.

		Example	Rationale
X	**Poor:**	Figure 1 shows preferences for shopping locations.	Poor because it tells the reader nothing more than would the title of the figure.
✔	**Acceptable:**	About two-thirds of the consumers preferred to shop in suburban areas rather than in the city. (See Figure 1.)	Acceptable because it interprets the data, but it places the figure reference in parentheses rather than integrating it into the sentence.
✔⁺	**Better:**	As shown in Figure 1, about two-thirds of the consumers preferred to shop in suburban areas rather than in the city.	Better than the previous examples but puts reference to the figure at the beginning, thus detracting from the interpretation of the data.
✔⁺⁺	**Best:**	About two-thirds of the consumers preferred to shop in suburban areas rather than in the city, as shown in Figure 1.	Best for introducing figures because it talks about the graphic and also includes introductory phrasing, but only after stressing the main point.

Including Graphics in Text

Text and graphics are partners in the communication process. If graphics appear before readers have been informed, they will begin to study the graphics and draw their own inferences and conclusions. For this reason, always introduce a graphic in the text immediately before the graphic appears. A graphic that follows an introduction and brief explanation will supplement what has been said in the report. Additional interpretation and needed analysis should follow the graphic.

⊠ OBJECTIVE **4**

Integrate graphics within documents.

Positioning Graphics in Text

Ideally, a graphic should be integrated within the text material immediately after its introduction. A graphic that will not fit on the page where it is introduced should appear at the top of the following page. The previous page is filled with text that would have ideally followed the graphic. In this chapter, figures are placed as closely as possible to their introductions in accordance with these suggestions. However, in some cases, several figures may be introduced on one page, making perfect placement difficult and sometimes impossible.

When interpreting and analyzing the graphic, avoid a mere restatement of what the graphic obviously shows. Instead, emphasize the main point you are making. Contrast the boring style of the following discussion of graphic data with the improved revision:

Obvious Restatement of Data:	When asked to identify the causes of ineffective meetings, 10 percent of employees blamed poor communication skills, 8 percent cited egocentric behavior by attendees, 7 percent attributed nonparticipation, and 6.5 percent said the discussion became sidetracked.	

Emphasis on Main Point:	The most cited reason for ineffective meetings is poor communication skills, while issues related to poor interpersonal communication skills were also blamed.	

Your analysis may include summary statements about the data, compare information in the figure to information obtained from other sources, or extend the shown data into reasonably supported speculative outcomes. Strive to transition naturally from the discussion of the graphic into the next point you wish to make.

Consistency Counts

Throughout the discussion of tables and graphs, the term *graphics* has been used to include all illustrations. Although your report may include tables, graphs, maps, and even photographs, you will find organizing easier and writing about the illustrations more effective if you label each item as a "Figure" followed by a number; then number the items consecutively.

Some report writers prefer to label tables consecutively as "Table 1," etc., and graphs and charts consecutively in another sequence as "Graph 1," etc. When this dual numbering system is used, readers of the report may become confused if they come upon a sentence that reads, "Evidence presented in Tables 3 and 4 and Graph 2 supports. . . ." Both writers and readers appreciate the single numbering system, which makes the sentence read, "Evidence presented in Figures 3, 4, and 5 supports. . . ."

Organizing and Preparing Reports and Proposals

Parts of a Formal Report

Reports serve a variety of purposes; the type of report you prepare depends on the subject matter, the purpose of the report, and the readers' needs. The differences between a formal report and an informal report lie in the format and possibly in the writing style. At the short, informal end of the report continuum described in Chapter 9, a report could look exactly like a brief memorandum. At the long, formal extreme of the continuum, the report might include most or all of the parts shown in Figure 11-1 on page 174.

⊠ **OBJECTIVE 1**

Identify the parts of a formal report and the contribution each part makes to the report's overall effectiveness.

A business report rarely contains all of the parts shown but may include any combination of them. The preliminary parts and addenda are organizational items that support the body of a report. The body contains the report of the research and covers the four steps in the research process. The organization of the body of a report leads to the construction of the contents page.

Because individuals usually write to affect or influence others favorably, they often add report parts as the number of pages increases. When a report exceeds one or two pages, you might add a cover or title page. When the body of a report exceeds four or five pages, you might even add a finishing touch by placing the report in a binder or binding it in a professional manner. Reports frequently take on the characteristics of the formal end of the continuum simply by reason of length. First, note how the preliminary parts and addenda items shown

OBJECTIVES ⊠

1 Identify the parts of a formal report and the contribution each part makes to the report's overall effectiveness.

2 Organize report findings.

3 Prepare effective formal reports using an acceptable format and writing style.

4 Prepare effective short reports in memorandum, email, and letter formats.

5 Prepare effective proposals for a variety of purposes.

© iStockphoto.com/Alexandr Tovstenko

in Figure 11-2 on page 175 increase in number as the report increases in length. Second, notice the order in which report parts appear in a complete report and the distribution of reports in print and electronic forms.

Memo and letter reports are often one page in length, but they can be expanded into several pages. As depicted, long reports may include some special pages that do not appear in short reports. The format you select—long or short, formal or informal—may help determine the supporting preliminary and addenda items to include.

To understand how each part of a formal report contributes to reader comprehension and ease of access to the information in the report, study the following explanations of each part shown in Figure 11-1. The three basic sections—preliminary parts, report text, and addenda—are combined to prepare a complete formal report.

Preliminary Parts of a Report

Preliminary parts are included to add formality to a report, emphasize report content, and aid the reader in locating

preliminary parts
report sections included to add formality to a report, emphasize report content, and aid the reader in locating information in the report quickly and in understanding the report more easily

© Dmitriy Shironosov/Shutterstock

Figure 11-1 Parts of a Formal Report: Preliminary Parts, Report Text, and Addenda

PRELIMINARY PARTS

Half-title page (Title Fly)	Title page	Authorization	Transmittal	Table of contents	Table of figures	Executive summary
Contains report title; adds formality.	Includes title, author, and date; adds formality.	Provides written authorization to complete report.	Presents report to reader and summarizes main points or analysis.	Provides overview of report and order in which information will be presented; contains headings and page numbers.	Includes number, title, and page number of tables and graphics.	Summarizes essential elements in report.

REPORT TEXT

Introduction	Body	Analysis
Orients reader to topic and previews major divisions.	Presents information collected.	Reviews main points presented in body and may include conclusions and recommendations.

ADDENDA

References	Appendix	Index
Includes alphabetical list of sources used in preparing report.	Contains supplementary information that supports report, but placing this information in report would make report bulky and unmanageable.	Includes alphabetical guide to subjects in report.

information in the report quickly and in understanding the report more easily. These parts might include a half-title page, title page, authorization, transmittal, table of contents, table of figures, and executive summary. The most frequently used preliminary parts are described here.

Title Page

The title page includes the title, author, date, and often the name of the person or organization who requested the report. A title page is often added when opting for a formal report format rather than a memorandum or letter arrangement.

The selected title should be descriptive and comprehensive; its words should reflect the content of the report. Avoid short, vague titles or excessively long titles. Instead, use concise wording to identify the topic adequately. For example, a title such as "Marketing Survey: Noncarbonated Beverages" leaves the reader confused when the title could have been "Noncarbonated Beverage Preferences of College Students in Boston." To give some clues for writing a descriptive title, think of the "Five Ws": *Who, What, When, Where,* and *Why*. Avoid such phrases as "A Study of . . .," "A Critical Analysis of . . .," or "A Review of . . . ."

Follow company procedures or a style manual to place the title attractively on the page. Arrange the title consistently on the half-title page, title page, and the first page of a report.

Table of Contents

The table of contents provides the reader with an analytical overview of the report and the order in which information is presented. Thus, this preliminary part aids the reader in understanding the report and in locating a specific section of it. The list includes the name and location (beginning page number) of every report part except those that precede the contents page. Include the list of figures and the transmittal, executive summary, report headings, references, appendices, and index. Placing spaced periods (leaders) between the report part and the page numbers helps lead the reader's eyes to the appropriate page number.

Word processing software simplifies the time-consuming, tedious task of preparing many of the preliminary and addenda report parts, including the table of contents. Because the software can generate these parts automatically, report writers can make last-minute changes to a report with updated preliminary and addenda parts.

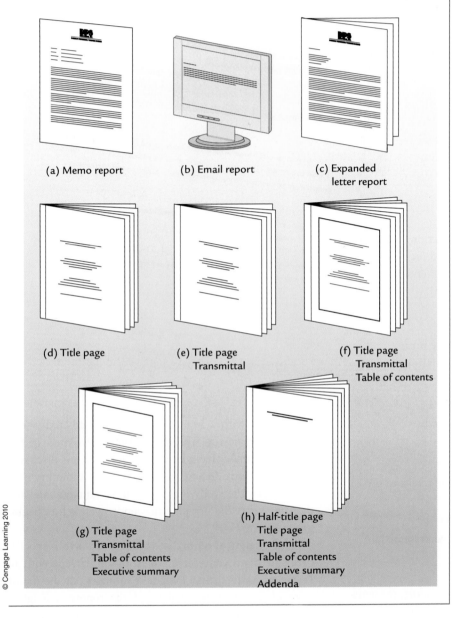

Figure 11-2 The Number of Assisting Parts Increases as the Length of a Report Increases

(a) Memo report

(b) Email report

(c) Expanded letter report

(d) Title page

(e) Title page
Transmittal

(f) Title page
Transmittal
Table of contents

(g) Title page
Transmittal
Table of contents
Executive summary

(h) Half-title page
Title page
Transmittal
Table of contents
Executive summary
Addenda

© Cengage Learning 2010

Executive Summary

The **executive summary** (also called the *abstract*, *overview*, or *précis*) summarizes the essential elements in an entire report. This overview simplifies the reader's understanding of a long report and is positioned before the first page of the report.

Typically, an executive summary is included to assist the reader in understanding a long, complex report. Because of the increased volume of information that managers must review, some managers require an executive summary regardless of the length and complexity of a report. The executive summary presents the report in miniature: the introduction, body, and summary as well as any conclusions and recommendations. Thus, an executive summary should (1) introduce briefly the report and preview the major divisions, (2) summarize the major sections of the report, and (3) summarize the report summary and any conclusions and recommendations. Pay special attention to topic sentences and to concluding sentences in paragraphs or within sections of reports. This technique helps you write concise executive summaries based on major ideas and reduces the use of supporting details and background information.

To assist them in staying up-to-date professionally, busy executives frequently request assistants to prepare executive summaries of articles they do not have time to read and conferences and meetings they cannot attend. Many practitioner journals include an executive summary (abstract) of each article. The executive summary provides the gist of the article and alerts the executive to articles that should be read in detail. The executive summary is prepared with the needs of specific executive readers in mind. For instance,

executive summary
short summary of the essential elements in an entire report; also called an abstract, overview, *or précis*

Table of Figures

To aid the reader in locating a specific graphic in a report with many graphics, the writer might include a list of figures separate from the contents. The list should include a reference to each figure that appears in the report, identified by both figure number and name, along with the page number on which the figure occurs. The contents and the figures can be combined on one page if both lists are brief. Word processing software can be used to automatically generate the list of figures.

a technically oriented executive may require more detail, whereas a strategist may require more analysis. An executive summary should "boil down" a report to its barest essentials without making the overview meaningless. Top executives should be able to glean enough information and understanding to feel confident making a decision.

Preliminary pages are numbered with small Roman numerals (i, ii, iii, and so on). Figure 11-1 provides more information about the purpose of each preliminary part.

Report Text

The report itself contains the introduction, body, summary, and any conclusions and recommendations. Report pages are numbered with Arabic numerals (1, 2, 3, and so on).

Introduction

The introduction orients the reader to the problem. It may include the following information:

- what the topic is
- why it is being reported on
- the scope and limitations of the research
- where the information came from
- an explanation of special terminology
- a preview of the major sections of the report to provide coherence and transitions:
  - how the topic is divided into parts
  - the order in which the parts will be presented

Body

The body, often called the heart of the report, presents the information collected and relates it to the problem. To increase readability and coherence, this section contains numerous headings to denote the various divisions within a report. Refer to the section titled "Organization of Formal Reports" in this chapter for an in-depth discussion of preparing the body.

Analysis

A good report ends with an analysis of what the reported information means or how it should be acted upon. An informational

analytical report
a type of report designed to solve a specific problem or answer research questions

report ends with a brief summary that adds unity to a report by reviewing the main points presented in the body. A summary includes only material that is discussed in a report. Introducing a new idea in the summary may suggest that the study was not completed adequately or that the writer did not plan the report well before beginning to write.

An **analytical report** is designed to solve a specific problem or answer research questions. It will end with an "analysis," which may include a summary of the major research findings, particularly if the report is lengthy. Reviewing the major findings prepares the reader for the conclusions, which are inferences the writer draws from the findings. If required by the person/organization authorizing the report, recommendations follow the conclusions. Recommendations present the writer's opinion on a possible course of action based on the conclusions. Review the examples of findings, conclusions, and recommendations presented in Chapter 9.

For a long report, the writer may place the summary, the conclusions, and the recommendations in three separate sections or in one section referred to as "Analysis." For shorter reports, all three sections are often combined.

Sales Performance and Analysis

While the year has been a tough battle to reach our projected figures, we've made great progress in every area. These figures are the result of a combination of factors, hard work, dedication, perseverance, great management, fantastic employees and determination.

Overall, there has been an increase in sales and performance of 90%. The breakdown for each department is outlined in each specific section. These figures are on par with out expected earnings and outlook.

Corporate Communications and strategy have increased well beyond expected gains. These figures are also the result of expectional planning and implementation.

Please see the Corporate Communications section on page 24 for full details.

Page 16

© iStockphoto.com/Spiffy J

Report Addenda

The **addenda** to a report may include materials used in the research that are not appropriate to be included in the report itself. The three basic addenda parts are the references, appendices, and index. Addenda parts continue with the same page numbering system used in the body of the report.

References

The references (also called *works cited* or *bibliography*) section is an alphabetical listing of the sources used in preparing the report. Because the writer may be influenced by any information consulted, some reference manuals require all sources consulted to be included in the reference list. When the reference list includes sources not cited in the report, it is referred to as a *bibliography* or a list of *works consulted*. If a report includes endnotes rather than in-text parenthetical citations (author and date within the text), the endnotes precede the references. Using word processing software to create footnotes and endnotes reduces much of the effort of preparing accurate documentation.

Appendix

An appendix contains supplementary information that supports the report but is not appropriate for inclusion in the report itself. This information may include questionnaires and accompanying transmittal letters, summary tabulations, verbatim comments from respondents, complex mathematical computations and formulas, legal documents, and a variety of items the writer presents to support the body of the report and the quality of the research. Placing supplementary material in an appendix helps prevent the report body from becoming excessively long.

If the report contains more than one appendix, label each with a capital letter and a title. For example, the two appendices (or appendixes) in a report could be identified as follows:

> Appendix A: Cover Letter Accompanying
> Customer Satisfaction Survey
>
> Appendix B: Customer Satisfaction Survey

Each item included in the appendix must be mentioned in the report. A reference within the report to the two appendices mentioned in the previous example might appear as follows:

> The cover message (Appendix A) and the customer satisfaction survey (Appendix B) were distributed by email to 1,156 firms on February 15, 2011.

Index

The index is an alphabetical guide to the subject matter in a report. The subject and each page number on which the subject appears are listed. Word-processing software can generate the index automatically. Each time a new draft is prepared, a new index with revised terms and correct page numbers can be generated quickly and easily.

addenda
may include all materials used in the research but not appropriate to be included in the report itself

© Feng Yu/Shutterstock

Organization of Formal Reports

OBJECTIVE 2

Organize report findings.

The authors of certain types of publications known as tabloids typically have no valid documentation to support their claims, so they make up their own support. Hopefully, absolutely no one believes them. The purpose of such publications is to entertain, not to inform. The writer of a bona fide report, however, must do a much more convincing and thorough job of reporting.

Writing Convincing and Effective Reports

As discussed in Chapter 9, reports often require you to conduct research to find quotes, statistics, or ideas from others to back up the ideas presented. This support from outside sources serves to bolster the research as well as your credibility. Doing research and taking notes, however, are only parts of the process of putting together a well-documented, acceptable report. Careful organization and formatting ensure that the reader will understand and comprehend the information presented. While many companies have their own style manuals that give examples of acceptable formats for reports, this section presents some general organization guidelines.

Outlining and Sequencing

The content outline serves as a framework on which to build the report. In the development of the outline, the writer identifies the major and minor points that are to be covered and organizes them into a logical sequence. Outlining is an essential prerequisite to writing the report. The outline is a planning document and is thus subject to modification as the writer develops the report.

Developing an outline requires the writer to think about the information to be presented and how it can best be organized for the clear understanding of the reader. Assume, for instance, you must select the type of Internet service for employees to use in a new start-up company. You are deciding between installing Ethernet cabling or a wireless system. You must choose the Internet system that will best serve portable computing needs of a small company and present your reasons and recommendations in a **justification report**.

You gather all available information from suppliers

justification report
a report that outlines comparative information clearly to the reader; used commonly when comparing items for purchase

of the two Internet systems, research their use in companies of similar size, and compare the two against a variety of criteria. Your final selection is a wireless system. Why did you select it? What criteria served as decision guides? When you write the report, you will have to tell the reader—the one who will pay for the equipment—how the selection was made so that he or she is "sold" on your conclusion.

If you organize your report so that you tell the reader everything about the two systems—wireless vs. Ethernet—each in a separate section, the reader may have trouble making comparisons. Your content outline might look like this:

> I. Introduction
>   A. The Problemv
>   B. The Method Used
> II. Wireless Internet
> III. Ethernet
> IV. Conclusion

Note that this outline devotes two Roman numeral sections to the findings, one to the introduction that presents the problem and the method, and one to the conclusion. This division is appropriate because the most space must be devoted to the findings. However, the reader may have difficulty comparing the Internet service because the information is in two different places. Would discussing the differences in Internet service in the same section of the report be better? Would prices be compared more easily if they were all in the same section? Most reports should be divided into sections that reflect the criteria used rather than into sections devoted to the alternatives compared.

If you selected your service based on cost, service/warranties, expandability, and availability of applications, these criteria (rather than the Internet systems themselves) might serve as divisions of the findings. Then your content outline would appear this way:

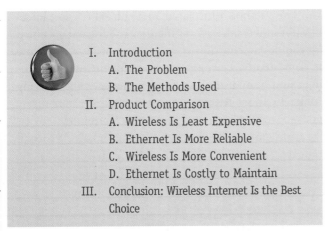

I. Introduction
   A. The Problem
   B. The Methods Used
II. Product Comparison
   A. Wireless Is Least Expensive
   B. Ethernet Is More Reliable
   C. Wireless Is More Convenient
   D. Ethernet Is Costly to Maintain
III. Conclusion: Wireless Internet Is the Best Choice

The outline now has three major sections, with the product comparison consisting of four subsections. When the report is prepared in this way, the features of each Internet system (the evaluation criteria) are compared in the same section, and the reader is led logically to the conclusion.

Note the headings used in Sections II and III. These are called *talking headings* because they talk about the content of the section and even give a conclusion about the section. Adding page numbers after each outline item will convert the outline into a contents page. Interestingly, the headings justify the selection of wireless Internet. As a result, a knowledgeable reader who has confidence in the researcher might be satisfied by reading only the content headings.

In addition to organizing findings for analytical reports by criteria, report writers can also use other organizational plans. When a report is informational and not analytical, you should use the most logical organization. A report on sales might be divided by geographic sales region, by product groups sold, by price range, or by time periods. A report on the development of a product might use chronological order. By visualizing the whole report first, you can then divide it into its major components and perhaps divide the major components into their parts.

A final caution: Beware of overdividing the sections. Too many divisions might make the report appear disorganized and choppy. On the other hand, too few divisions might cloud understanding for the reader.

When developing content outlines, some report writers believe that readers expect the beginning of the body to be an introduction, so they begin the outline with the first heading related to findings. In our example, then, Section I would be "Product Comparison." Additionally, when they reach the contents page, readers may eliminate the Roman numeral or other outline symbols.

The research process consists of inductively arranged steps as shown in Figure 11-3: (1) Problem, (2) Method, (3) Findings, and (4) Conclusion. Note how the four steps of research have been developed through headings in the Roman numeral outline and in a contents page for a report. When the report is organized in the same order, its users must read through the body to learn about the conclusions—generally the most important part of the report to users. To make the reader's job easier, report writers may organize the report deductively, with the conclusions at the beginning. This sequence is usually achieved by placing a synopsis or summary at the beginning:

Figure 11-3 The Basic Outline Expands into a Contents Page

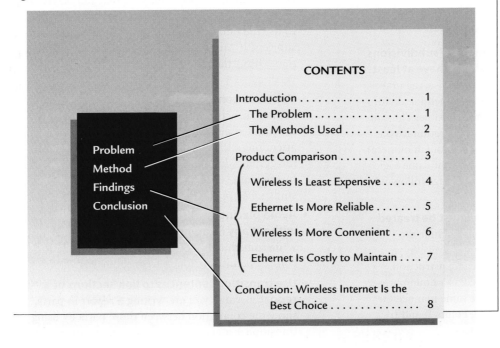

CONTENTS

Introduction 1
   The Problem 1
   The Methods Used 2

Product Comparison 3

   Wireless Is Least Expensive 4

   Ethernet Is More Reliable 5

   Wireless Is More Convenient 6

   Ethernet Is Costly to Maintain 7

Conclusion: Wireless Internet Is the
   Best Choice 8

Problem
Method
Findings
Conclusion

```
REPORT TITLE IN DEDUCTIVE SEQUENCE
REVEALS THE CONCLUSION

    I.   Conclusion Reported in the Synopsis
    II.  Body of the Report
         A.  Problem
         B.  Method
         C.  Findings
    III. Conclusion
```

This arrangement permits the reader to get the primary message early and then to look for support in the body of the report. The deductive arrangement contributes to the repetitious nature of reports, but it also facilitates understanding.

Using Headings Effectively

Headings are signposts informing readers about what text is ahead. Headings take their positions from their relative importance in a complete outline. For example, in a Roman numeral outline, "I" is a first-level heading, "A" is a second-level heading, and "1" is a third-level heading:

```
    I.   First-Level Heading
         A.  Second-Level Heading
         B.  Second-Level Heading
              1.  Third-Level Heading
              2.  Third-Level Heading
    II.  First-Level Heading
```

Two important points about the use of headings also relate to outlines:

- **Because second-level headings are subdivisions of first-level headings, you should have at least two subdivisions (A and B).** Otherwise, the first-level heading cannot be divided—something divides into at least two parts or it is not divisible. Thus, in an outline, you must have a "B" subsection if you have an "A" subsection following a Roman numeral, or you should have no subsections. The same logic applies to the use of third-level headings following second-level headings.

- **All headings of the same level must be treated consistently.** Consistent elements include the physical position on the page, appearance (type style, underline), and grammatical construction. For instance, if Point A is worded as a noun phrase, Point B should be worded in the same manner. Or if Point I is a complete sentence, Points II and III should also be worded as sentences.

The method illustrated in Figure 11-3 is typical but not universal. Always identify the format specified by the documentation style you are using and follow it consistently. Develop fourth- and fifth-level headings simply by using boldface, underline, and varying fonts. In short reports, however, organization rarely goes beyond third-level headings; thoughtful organization can limit excessive heading levels in formal reports.

Choosing a Writing Style for Formal Reports

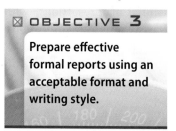

OBJECTIVE 3

Prepare effective formal reports using an acceptable format and writing style.

As you might expect, the writing style of long, formal reports is more formal than that used in many other routine business documents. The following suggestions should be applied when writing a formal report:

- **Avoid first-person pronouns as a rule.** In formal reports, the use of *I* is generally unacceptable. Because of the objective nature of research, the fewer personal references you use the better. However, in some organizations the first person is acceptable. Certainly, writing is easier when you can use yourself as the subject of sentences.

- **Use active voice.** "Authorization was received from the IRS" might not be as effective as "The IRS granted authorization." Subjects that can be visualized are advantageous, but you should also attempt to use the things most important to the report as subjects. If "authorization" were more important than "IRS," the writer should stay with the first version.

- **Use tense consistently.** Because you are writing about past actions, much of your report writing is in the past tense. However, when you call the reader's attention to the content of a graphic, remember that the graphic *shows* in the present tense; and use the future-tense verb if you want to mention that the study *will convince* the reader.

- **Avoid placing two headings consecutively without any intervening text.** For example, always write something following a first-level heading and before the initial second-level heading.

- **Use transition sentences to link sections of a report.** Because you are writing a report in parts, show the connection between those parts by using transition sentences. "Although several advantages accrue from its use, the incentive plan also presents problems" may be a sentence written at the end of a section stressing advantages and before a section stressing problems.

- **Use a variety of coherence techniques.** Just as transition sentences bind portions of a report together, certain coherence techniques bind sentences together: repeating a word, using a pronoun, or using a conjunction. If such devices are used, each sentence seems to be joined smoothly to the next. The following words and phrases keep you from making abrupt changes in thought:

Time Connectors	Contrast Connectors
at the same time	although
finally	despite
further	however
initially	in contrast
next	nevertheless
since	on the contrary
then	on the other hand
while	yet

Similarity Connectors	Cause-and-Effect Connectors
for instance/example	alternately
in the same way	because
just as	but
likewise	consequently
similarly	hence
thus	therefore

Other ways to improve transition include the following:

- **Use tabulations and enumerations.** When you have a series of items, bullet them or give each a number and list them consecutively. This list of writing suggestions is easier to understand because it contains bulleted items.

- **Define terms carefully.** When terms are not widely understood or have specific meanings in the study, define them. Definitions should be written in the term-family-differentiation sequence: "A dictionary (*term*) is a reference book (*family*) that contains a list of all words in a language (*point of*

difference)." "A sophomore is a college student in the second year."

- **Check for variety.** In your first-draft stage, most of your attention should be directed toward presenting the right ideas and support. When reviewing the rough draft, you may discover certain portions with a monotonous sameness in sentence length or construction. Changes and improvements in writing style at this stage are easy and well worth the effort.

Enhancing Credibility

Readers are more likely to accept your research as valid and reliable if you have designed the research effectively and collected, interpreted, and presented the data in an objective, unbiased manner. The following writing suggestions will enhance your credibility as a researcher:

- **Avoid emotional terms.** "The increase was fantastic" doesn't convince anyone. However, "The increase was 88 percent—more than double that of the previous year" does convince.

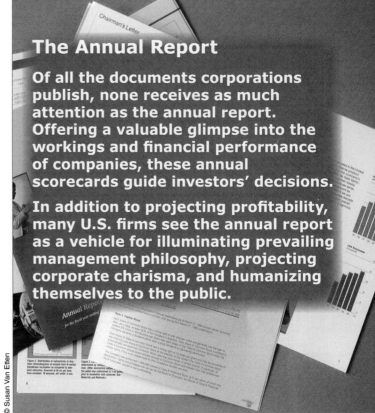

The Annual Report

Of all the documents corporations publish, none receives as much attention as the annual report. Offering a valuable glimpse into the workings and financial performance of companies, these annual scorecards guide investors' decisions.

In addition to projecting profitability, many U.S. firms see the annual report as a vehicle for illuminating prevailing management philosophy, projecting corporate charisma, and humanizing themselves to the public.

© Susan Van Etten

- **Identify assumptions.** Assumptions are things or conditions taken for granted. However, when you make an assumption, state that clearly. Statements such as "Assuming all other factors remain the same . . ." inform the reader of important assumptions.
- **Label opinions.** Facts are preferred over opinion, but sometimes the opinion of a recognized professional is the closest thing to fact. "In the opinion of legal counsel, . . ." lends conviction to the statement that follows and lends credence to the integrity of the writer.
- **Use documentation.** Citations and references (works cited) are evidence of the writer's scholarship and honesty. These methods acknowledge the use of secondary material in the research.

Short Reports

Short reports incorporate many of the same organizational strategies as long reports. However, most **short reports** include only the minimum supporting materials to achieve effective communication. Short reports focus on the body—problem, method, findings, and conclusion. In addition, short reports might incorporate any of the following features:

⊠ **OBJECTIVE 4**

Prepare effective short reports in memorandum, email, and letter formats.

- personal writing style using first or second person
- contractions when they contribute to a natural style
- graphics to reinforce the written text
- headings and subheadings to partition portions of the body and to reflect organization
- memorandum, email, and letter formats when appropriate

short reports
reports that include only the minimum supporting materials to achieve effective communication

form reports
reports that meet the demand for numerous, repetitive reports; include college registration forms, applications for credit, airline tickets, and bank checks

Memorandum, Email, and Letter Reports

Short reports are often written in memorandum, email, or letter format. The memorandum report is directed to an organizational insider, as are most email reports. The letter report is directed to a reader outside the organization. Short reports to internal and external readers are illustrated in Figures 11-4 on the next page and 11-5 on page 184. The commentary in the right column will help you understand how effective writing principles are applied.

The memo report in Figure 11-4 communicates the sales activity of an appliance department during one month of the fiscal period. The periodic report is formatted as a memorandum because it is prepared for personnel within the company and is a brief, informal report. An outside consultant presents an audit of a company's communication program in the short report in Figure 11-5. A concise, professional email will serve as a transmittal for this one-page report sent to the client as an email attachment.

The report in Figure 11-6 on pages 185–188 is written deductively. Implementation of cross-cultural teams is described in an expanded letter report written by a consultant to a client (external audience). The consultant briefly describes the procedures used to analyze the problem, presents the findings in a logical sequence, and provides specific recommendations.

Form Reports

Form reports meet the demand for numerous, repetitive reports. College registration forms, applications for credit, airline tickets, and bank checks are examples of simple form reports. Form reports have the following benefits:

- When designed properly, form reports increase clerical accuracy by providing designated places for specific items.
- Forms save time by telling the preparer where to put each item and by preprinting common elements to eliminate the need for narrative writing.
- In addition to their advantages of accuracy and saving time, forms make tabulation of data relatively simple. The value of the form is uniformity.

Most form reports, such as a bank teller's cash sheet, are informational. At the end of the teller's work period, cash is counted and totals are entered in

Figure 11-4 Short, Periodic Report in Memorandum Format

SALT LAKE (HOME AND OFFICE)
3480 State Street, Salt Lake City, UT 84009,
801-667-2403, FAX 901-667-2400

TO: Sandra Linkletter, President
FROM: Donald Worthy, Sales Manager
DATE: April 1, 2012
SUBJECT: Monthly Sales Report, Appliance Department

Sales for the month remained at about the same level as previous months this year at $23,819. Sales figures for the month by item are as follows:

Item	Quantity Sold	Total Revenue from Sales ($)
Washers	12	5,102
Dryers	11	6,543
Stoves	8	4,276
Refrigerators	10	5,899
Dish Washers	6	1,989

This month, we continued to publish a circular, which was distributed each Thursday in the *News Tribune*. The cost of that circular is $2,400 per month. That was our only cost of advertising and marketing. Please see the attached file for a complete breakdown of the departments' costs and sales for the month.

We continue to employ two full-time salespeople on the floor and two part-time salespersons to cover the weekend shift. Current staffing levels are sufficient for the current sales volume, but if the home construction sector improves, we expect appliance sales to increase along with that improvement. If this occurs, we will need to hire an additional full-time and part-time sales person to return to our 2008 employment numbers.

We are continuing to look at ways that we might increase our marketing presence in the local community. One suggestion offered by Dale, one of our full-time sales persons, is to have a weekly promotion that runs as a banner on our web page. We could institute this opportunity storewide and have banners for the other departments running randomly with ours throughout the week. The cost of such a promotional program storewide needs to be calculated; perhaps this is something that we might put on our agenda for next week's managers' meetings.

Attachment

- *Includes headings to serve formal report functions of transmittal and title page.*

- *Uses deductive approach to present periodic report requested by management on monthly basis.*

- *Uses table to highlight standard information; allows for easy update when preparing subsequent report.*

- *Includes suggestion for improving storewide marketing and sales.*

- *Attaches information page that would be appendix item in a formal report.*

Format Pointer
Uses memorandum format for brief periodic report prepared for personnel within company.

designated blanks. Cash reports from all tellers are then totaled to arrive at period totals and perhaps to be verified by computer records.

In addition to their informational purpose, form reports assist in analytical work. A residential appraisal report assists real estate appraisers in analyzing real property. With this information, the appraiser is able to determine the market value of a specific piece of property.

Many form reports are computer generated. For example, an automated hospital admission process

Figure 11-5 Audit Report in Short Report Format

Communication Audit of Franklin Associates' External Communication Program

The communication audit of Franklin Associates' external communication program has been completed. The procedures we used and our findings are summarized below.

PROCEDURES

Specific procedures involved were to

1. Identify the organization's purposes and strategic objectives.
2. Identify the major audiences or stakeholders of the organization.
3. Establish the appropriate channels or media for communicating corporate messages based on the outcome of the initial steps in the process.

FINDINGS

Findings from each of these three steps can be found below.

- Franklin Associates is a consultant to the oil and gas industry. It is a well-established business with a 100-year history. Its branding is well-recognized, but in recent years, it has been surpassed by several new entrants who have marketed themselves as innovative and using the latest technologies. This has created a challenge for Franklin Associates in terms of its external branding.
- Franklin's major external stakeholders include its clients, the media, investors, government agencies, competitors, and the public. In terms of its clients, Franklin has focused its marketing efforts on the largest oil and gas producers. Because there are so few, this has created some competitive challenges for Franklin.
- Franklin's most common methods for communicating its corporate message include press releases; a company web site; and personal communications with its clients through use of written, oral and electronic media.

CONCLUSIONS AND RECOMMENDATIONS

The following recommendations are made:

1. Continue advertising and service promotion at current levels but with some changes that help you to better reach mid-sized clients and increase your market share.
2. Update the design for your company logo and roll out a campaign that introduces this new image to current and prospective customers.
3. Develop a plan for shaping public opinion on issues important to Franklin Associates. As a consultant for the oil industry, it is important to show that your organization is interested in addressing global climate issues.

Thank you for the opportunity to assist you in reviewing your external communication program. We are also available to help you in completing the final step in the audit process: Create, refine, and test new messages with the appropriate stakeholders. If you are interested in continuing our consulting relationship in order to develop an implementation plan, please call me at 415-640-9001 to be of assistance to you with your software compliance needs.

Introduces overall topic and leads into procedures and findings.

Uses side heading to denote beginning of body.

Uses numbered list to add emphasis to important information.

Uses bulleted list to add emphasis to important information.

Uses side heading to denote beginning of recommendation section.

Uses enumerations to emphasize recommendations.

Format Pointers
Uses short format for report prepared by outside consultant.

Uses email channel to transmit formatted document as attachment for quick, convenient delivery.

Summarizes ideas succinctly in one-page report for easy reading.

© Cengage Learning 2013

Figure 11-6 Short Report in Expanded Letter Format, Page 1

GMS GLOBAL MANAGEMENT STRATEGIES
8702 Willow Street, Roanoke, VA 23056 412-554-7706, FAX 412-544-7700

Management Consulting and Corporate Training

August 24, 2012

Camille LaBry, President
Global Financial Advisors, Inc.
6602 Elmhurst Avenue
Chicago, IL 40032

Dear Ms. LaBry:

RECOMMENDATIONS FOR GLOBAL LEADERSHIP TRAINING PROGRAM

Thank you for allowing us to assist you in outlining a plan for developing a global leadership training program for Global Financial Advisors, Inc. As you know, the need to proactively train managers to work in diverse teams has increased as organizations become more global in reach and operations.

Procedures

In preparing this report, a variety of resources were consulted, including paper and online resources. Additionally, meetings of 12 globally diverse teams within your organization were videotaped and the meetings were transcribed and coded for analysis to determine whether communication behaviors differed when U.S. members were a minority or majority in the team. This data was collected to determine how to best integrate your managers, many of whom are from the U.S. This data as well as results from surveys to determine team member satisfaction, along with published research, led to the recommendations in this report.

Findings

Research revealed useful information concerning the unique challenges faced by leaders of globally diverse teams.

Challenges Faced by Globally Diverse Teams

Previous research on globally diverse teams noted the challenges that such teams face in the workplace. Along with the benefits that a diverse workplace provides, more cultural diversity in a team leads to the higher likelihood of conflict (Oetzel et al., 2005). Studies have demonstrated that the composition of a team determines its success and may prevent the group from reaching its performance potential (Earley & Gibson, 2002; Earley & Mosakoski, 2000; Jehn, Northcraft, & Neale, 1999; Ravlin, Thomas, & Ilsev, 2000). Studies on culturally diverse teams demonstrate that moderately heterogeneous groups experience significant communication problems, relational conflict, and low team identity that have a dysfunctional impact on team effectiveness (Jehn, Chadwick, & Thatcher, 1997). As a rule, heterogeneous teams report reduced satisfaction with the team, which, in turn, negatively affects team performance (Earley & Mosakoski, 2000; Jehn, Northcraft, & Neale, 1999; Ravlin, Thomas, & Ilsev, 2000).

(continued on next page)

Letterhead and letter address function as title page and transmittal.

Uses deductive approach to present main idea to president.

Provides research methods and sources to add credibility.

Uses centered heading to denote major division of body.

Uses transition sentence to move reader smoothly to minor section.

Uses side heading to denote minor section.

Format Pointer
Uses subject line to introduce topic of letter report.

© Cengage Learning 2013

Figure 11-6 Short Report in Expanded Letter Format, Page 2

Ms. Camille LaBry
Page 2
August 24, 2012

Results from Studies of Your Globally Diverse Teams

Based on our analysis of our videotapes of your meetings, we found that differences in participation and contribution rates became more pronounced as those of other cultures became a minority when mixed with members from the U.S. In teams where the majority of members are from the U.S., those from other cultures fall behind in almost all areas used to measure participation and contribution. They produce fewer turns and words (contribution), while they are performing significantly fewer communication behaviors considered to be attempts at participating.

Our survey results indicated that this change in participation and contribution may also affect the team member's satisfaction with the team. The results of our attitudinal survey indicate that group members who were the majority in the group, regardless of cultural background, had a high degree of satisfaction in both areas of inquiry:

- Their satisfaction with the group decision-making process (98%)
- Their perceived sense of inclusion and value in the process (95%)

Recommendations for Globally Diverse Teams

Neyer and Harzing (2008) found that experiences in cross-cultural interactions do serve to improve one's agilities to adapt in such situations. One advantage gained through experience is the overcoming of cultural stereotypes that often stand in the way of effective communication. Cross-cultural experience also leads to the establishment of norms that support interaction among individuals and to the development of mutual consideration for people (Neyer & Harzing, 2008).

Some individuals are better suited than are others for membership in globally diverse teams due to their temperament and experiences. Qualities that are important to successful membership in globally diverse teams include the following (Adler & Gundersen, 2008; Hurn & Jenkins, 2000):

- Flexibility and adaptability
- Strong interpersonal skills
- Ability to think both globally and locally
- Linguistic skills
- Listening (interpretive) skills
- Initiative
- Enthusiasm
- Consensus-building skills
- Patience and empathy
- Nonjudgmental attitude

(continued on next page)

Uses side heading and transition sentence to move reader smoothly to minor section.

Provides APA citations for direct quotes and paraphrased information.

Uses bullets to highlight qualities important to globally diverse teams.

© Cengage Learning 2013

Figure 11-6 Short Report in Expanded Letter Format, Page 3

Ms. Camille LaBry
Page 3
August 24, 2012

A primary goal of globally diverse teams should be to increase understanding of differences between cultures so that normal business activity can occur. Some suggestions for building harmony include the following:

- Provide cross-cultural training to increase ability to identify and cope with potential conflicts (Dunkel & Meierewert, 2004).
- Select a skillful leader who can perceive and facilitate handling of potential cultural misunderstandings (Hurn & Jenkins, 2000).
- Strive for transparency in all stages of activity, which aids in the development of trust.
- Set clear, specific agenda with no surprises that could be seen as hidden agendas (Hurn & Jenkins, 2000).
- Encourage the use of questions to solicit input and check for understanding.

Success in globally diverse teams is largely dependent on the formation of a group culture that supersedes the individual cultural norms of the various members.

Summary

In the global business environment, the success of many organizations depends on the effective functioning of globally diverse teams. Obviously, teams cannot pay constant attention to cross-cultural differences. However, teams whose members recognize, respect, and respond to cultural expectations for behavior enhance their prospects for achieving high levels of performance. Education about other cultures and experience in cross-cultural exchange will serve to strengthen team members' ability to interact effectively in globally diverse teams.

Thank you for the opportunity to provide this information concerning globally diverse team development. Please let us know how we can assist you further with this project or with other related matters.

Sincerely,

Landon Miles
Landon Miles, Consultant

Enclosure: Reading list

(continued on next page)

Uses bulleted list to highlight strategies for development of globally diverse teams.

Combines summary with recommendation as is typical in short reports.

Closes with courteous offer to provide additional service.

Includes enclosure notation to alert reader to enclosed reading list.

Format Pointer
Includes complimentary close and signature to comply with letter format.

Figure 11-6 Short Report in Expanded Letter Format, Page 4

Ms. Camille LaBry
Page 4
August 24, 2012

Reading List

Adler, N. J., & Gundersen, A. (2008). *International dimensions of organizational behavior*. Boston: Kent.

Dunkel, A., & Meierewert, S. (2004). Cultural standards and their impact on teamwork: An empirical analysis of Austrian, German, Hungarian and Spanish culture differences. *Journal for East European Management Studies, 9*, 147–174.

Earley, C. P., & Gibson, C. B. (2002). *Multinational work teams: A new perspective*. Mahwah, NJ: Lawrence Erlbaum Associates, Publishers.

Earley, C. P., & Mosakoski, E. (2000). Creating hybrid team cultures: An empirical test of transnational team functioning. *Academy of Management Journal, 43*, 26–49.

Hurn, B. F., & Jenkins, M. (2000). International peer group development. *Industrial and Commercial Training, 32*(4), 128–131.

Jehn, K. A., Northcraft, G. B., & Neale, M. A. (1999). Why differences make a difference: A field study of diversity, conflict, and performance in workgroups. *Administrative Science Quarterly, 44*(4), 741–163.

Neyer, A., & Harzine, A. (2008). The impact of culture on interactions: Five lessons learned from the European Commission. *European Management Journal, 26*(5), 325–334. doi:10.1016/j.emj.2008.05.005

Oetzel, J. G. (1998). Explaining individual communication processes in homogeneous and heterogeneous groups through individualism-collectivism and self-construal. *Human Communication Research, 25*(2), 202–224.

Ravlin, E. C., Thomas, D. C., & Ilsev, A. (2000). Beliefs about values, status, and legitimacy in multicultural groups: Influences on intra-group conflict. In P. C. Earley & H. Singh (Eds.), *Innovations in international and cross-cultural management* (pp. 58–83). Thousand Oaks, CA: Sage.

Format Pointers

Uses Readings List instead of References as the title to comply with employing company preference.

Includes alphabetical listing of all cited sources using APA 6th edition referencing style to comply with employing company preference.

Includes digital object identifier (DOI) for electronic resources when available.

expedites the repetitive patient reports that must be created. The admission clerk inputs the patient information using the carefully designed input screen. If the patient has been admitted previously, the patient's name, address, and telephone number are displayed automatically for the clerk to verify. When the clerk inputs the patient's date of birth, the computer calculates the patient's age, eliminating the need to ask a potentially sensitive question and ensuring accuracy when patients cannot remember their ages. All data are stored in a computer file and retrieved as needed to generate numerous reports required during a patient's stay, such as the admissions summary sheet, admissions report, pharmacy profile, and even the addressograph used to stamp each page of the patient's record and the identification arm band.

Using the computer to prepare each report in the previous example leads to higher efficiency levels and minimizes errors because recurring data are entered only once. Preparing error-free form reports is a critical public relations tool because even minor clerical errors may cause patients or customers to question the organization's ability to deliver quality service. The "Check Your Communication" section on the Chapter 11 Review Card provides a comprehensive checklist for use in preparing effective reports.

The federal tax return is one of America's least-liked form reports.

© iStockphoto.com/Rudyanto Wijaya

Proposals

Managers prepare **internal proposals** to justify or recommend purchases or changes in the company; for instance, installing a new computer system, introducing telecommuting or other flexible work schedules, or reorganizing the company into work groups. An **external proposal**, as described in Chapter 9, is a written description of how one organization can meet the needs of another by, for example, providing products or services. Written to generate business, external proposals are a critical part of the successful operation of many companies.

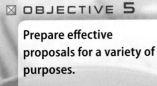

⊠ **OBJECTIVE 5**

Prepare effective proposals for a variety of purposes.

Proposals may be solicited or unsolicited. **Solicited proposals** are invited and initiated when a potential customer or client submits exact specifications or needs in a bid request or a request for proposal, commonly referred to as an *RFP*. Governmental agencies such as the Department of Education solicit proposals and place orders and contracts based on the most desirable proposal. The bid request or RFP describes a problem to be solved and invites respondents to describe their proposed solutions.

An **unsolicited proposal** is prepared by an individual or firm who sees a problem to be solved and submits a solution. For example, a business consultant is a regular customer of a family-owned retail store. On numerous occasions she has attempted to purchase an item that was out of stock. Recognizing that stock shortages decrease sales and profits, she prepares a proposal to assist the business in designing a computerized perpetual inventory with an automatic reordering system. For the business to accept the proposal, the consultant must convince the business that the resulting increase in sales and profits will more than offset the cost of the computer system and the consulting fee.

Proposal Structure

A proposal includes (1) details about the manner in which the problem will be solved and (2) the price to be charged or costs to be incurred. Often the proposal is a lengthy report designed to "sell" the prospective buyer on the ability of the bidder to perform. However, a simple price quotation also constitutes a proposal in response to a request for a price quotation.

The format of a proposal depends on the length of the proposal and the intended audience:

Format	Proposal Length and Intended Audience
Memo or email report	Short; remains within the organization
Letter report	Short; travels outside the organization
Formal report	Long; remains within the organization or travels outside the organization

Most work resulting from proposals is covered by a working agreement or contract to avoid discrepancies in the intents of the parties. In some cases, for example, users of outside consultants insist that each consultant be covered by a sizable general personal liability insurance policy that also insures the company. Many large firms and governmental organizations use highly structured procedures to ensure understanding of contract terms.

The following general parts, or variations of them, might appear as headings in a proposal: (1) Problem or Purpose, (2) Scope, (3) Methods or Procedures, (4) Materials and Equipment, (5) Qualifications, (6) Follow-Up and/or Evaluation, (7) Budget or Costs, (8) Summary, and (9) Addenda. In addition to these parts, a proposal might include preliminary report parts such as the title page, transmittal message, and contents, as well as addenda parts such as references, appendix, and index.

Problem and/or Purpose

Problem and purpose are often used as interchangeable terms in reports. Here is the introductory purpose statement, called "Project Description," in a proposal by a firm to contribute to an educational project:

Project Description: The University of Southern California's Continuing Education Program is developing a unique online leadership communication program aimed at busy professionals. The program will highlight how communication constructs organizational culture and will demonstrate how leaders can create positive change through communication practices. Change management programs are often unsuccessful, but this new approach has been proven to increase the success of organizational change efforts.

Note how the heading "Project Description" has been used in place of "Purpose." In the following opening statement, "Problem" is used as the heading:

Problem: Costs of maintaining and upgrading information technology (IT) systems has increased year after year. In order to identify ways of decreasing IT costs, this report will examine the benefits of contracting for IT services rather than staffing the function internally.

The purpose of the proposal may be listed as a separate heading (in addition to "Problem") when the proposal intends to include objectives of a measurable nature. When you list objectives such as "To reduce overall expenses for maintenance by 10 percent," attempt to list measurable and attainable objectives and list only enough to accomplish the purpose of selling your proposal. Many proposals are rejected simply because writers promise more than they can actually deliver.

Scope

When determining the scope of your proposal, you can place limits on what you propose to do or on what the material or equipment you sell can accomplish. The term *scope* need not necessarily be the only heading for this section. "Areas Served," "Limitations to the Study," and "Where (*specify topic*) Can Be Used" are examples of headings that describe the scope of a proposal. Here is a "Scope" section from a consulting firm's proposal to conduct a salary survey:

What the Study Will Cover: To assist Home Health Industries in formulating its salary and benefits program for all employees, HR Consulting will include an analysis of compensation (salary and benefits) for no fewer than five of Home Health's competitors in the same geographic region. In addition to salaries, the study will also include insurance, incentives, deferred compensation, medical, and retirement plans. Additionally, HR Consulting will make recommendations for Home Health's compensation program.

Another statement of scope might be as follows:

Scope: This report will examine the past 10 years of production, marketing, and sales data for the automobile industry worldwide and will extrapolate from that data any significant trends that we might use to base future production planning and plant location.

Methods and/or Procedures

The method(s) used to solve the problem or to conduct the business of the proposal should be spelled out in detail. In this section, simply think through all the steps necessary to meet the terms of the proposal and write them in sequence. When feasible, you should include a time schedule for implementation of the project.

Materials and Equipment

For large proposals, such as construction or research and development, indicate the nature and quantities of materials and equipment to be used. In some cases, several departments will contribute to this section. When materials and equipment constitute a major portion of the total cost, include prices. Much litigation arises when clients are charged for "cost overruns." When contracts are made on the basis of "cost plus XX percent," the major costs of materials, equipment, and labor/personnel must be thoroughly described and documented.

Qualifications

Assuming your proposal is acceptable in terms of services to be performed or products to be supplied, your proposal must convince the potential buyer that you have the expertise to deliver what you have described and that you are a credible individual or company. Therefore, devote a section to presenting the specific qualifications and special expertise of the personnel involved in the proposal. You may include past records of the bidder and the recommendations of its past customers, and the proposed cost. Note how the brief biography of the principal member in the following excerpt from a proposal contributes to the credibility of the proposer:

> *Principals: Miranda Scopes has an M.B.A. from Wharton and has worked as marketing director at Century Properties for five years. Before working at Century, she was marketing director at Crysalus Real Estate. Ronald Bowman has been director of sales at Century for nine years. Before joining Century, he worked at ElmTree Properties.*

In another related section, the proposal might mention other work performed:

> *Major Clients: St. Luke's Hospital, Hailey, ID; Twin Falls Regional Hospital, Twin Falls, ID: Spokane General Hospital, Spokane, ID; Little Hospital of Mary, San Pedro, CA: Sparks-Reno Regional Medical Center, Sparks, NV; Torrance Hospital, Torrance, CA. Personal references available on request.*

Follow-Up and/or Evaluation

Although your entire proposal is devoted to convincing the reader of its merit, clients are frequently concerned about what will happen when the proposed work or service is completed. Will you return to make certain your work is satisfactory? Can you adjust your method of research as times change?

If you propose to conduct a study, do not promise more than you can deliver. Not all funded research proves to be successful. If you propose to prepare a study in your firm's area of expertise, you may be more confident. A public accounting firm's proposal to audit a company's records need not be modest. The accountant follows certain audit functions that are prescribed by the profession. However, a proposal that involves

providing psychological services probably warrants a thoughtful follow-up program to evaluate the service.

Budget or Costs

The budget or cost of the program should be detailed when materials, equipment, outside help, consultants, salaries, and travel are to be included. A simple proposal for service by one person might consist of a statement such as "15 hours at $200/hour, totaling $3,000, plus mileage and expenses estimated at $550." Present the budget or costs section after the main body of the proposal.

Summary

You might conclude the proposal with a summary. This summary may also be used as the initial section of the proposal if deductive sequence is desired.

Addenda

When supporting material is necessary to the proposal but would make it too bulky or detract from it, include the material as addenda items. A bibliography and an appendix are examples of addenda items. References used should appear in the bibliography or as footnotes. Maps, questionnaires, letters of recommendation, and similar materials are suitable appendix items.

A short, informal proposal that includes several of the parts previously discussed is shown in Figure 11-7 on the next two pages. This proposal consists of three major divisions: "Purpose," "Proposed Course of Instruction," and "Cost." The "Proposed Course of Instruction" section is divided into five minor divisions to facilitate understanding. Wanting to increase the chances of securing the contract, the writer made sure the proposal was highly professional and had the impact needed to get the reader's attention. To add to the overall effectiveness of the proposal, the writer incorporated appealing, but not distracting, page design features. Printing the proposal with a laser printer using fonts of varying sizes and styles resulted in a professional appearance and an appealing document. The reader's positive impression of the high standards exhibited in this targeted proposal is likely to influence his or her confidence in the writer's ability to present the proposed seminar.

Proposal Preparation

Writers have much flexibility in preparing proposals. When they find a particular pattern that seems to be successful, they no doubt will adopt it as their basic plan. The ultimate test of a proposal is its effectiveness in achieving its purpose. The task is to assemble the

Figure 11-7 Short Proposal, Page 1

**PROPOSAL FOR STAFF DEVELOPMENT SEMINAR:
PROMOTING EFFECTIVE GLOBALLY DIVERSE TEAMS**

for Global Financial Advisors, Inc.

by Landon Miles, Communications Consultant

August 24, 2012

Purpose

Because of its global diversification strategy, Global Financial Advisors, Inc. has more than 24 globally diverse teams in its 10 international locations. The proposed training course is designed to help participants understand how to communicate more effectively while working as part of a globally diverse team.

Proposed Course of Instruction

The training course will be delivered by Angela Powers, an engaging associate with 10 years of experience providing cross-cultural training in a corporate environment. Because behavior in globally diverse teams is a reflection of one's personality, communication practices, and cultural understanding, the program will actively involve participants and facilitate personal application of the new strategy.

Teaching/Learning Methods

This activity-oriented training program will involve response to videos, role playing, and case discussion. The trainer will act as a facilitator to assist each participant in assessing communication behaviors and expectations and planning effective strategies for improving overall effectiveness while working as a member of a globally diverse team.

Program Content

The following topics constitute the content core of the program:

- Challenges faced by globally diverse teams
- Differences and similarities in cultural values, beliefs, and practices
- Issues globally diverse teams face in the stages of team development
- Strategies for effective communication within globally diverse teams

Learning Materials

The following materials will be provided to facilitate learning:

- Copies of current published articles on the importance and function of globally diverse teams
- Consultant-development workbook for each participant

(continued on next page)

- *Describes problem and presents proposed plan as solution to problem.*

- *Uses headings to aid reader in understanding proposal's organization. Boldface font adds emphasis.*

- *Divides "Proposed Course of Instruction" into five minor divisions for easier comprehension. Describes course content, instructional method, and design in detail.*

- *Uses bulleted lists to highlight course components and learning materials.*

Format Pointer
Incorporates page design features to enhance appeal and readability (e.g., headings styles including color; crisp, open fonts and wide linespacing for easy onscreen reading or print copy; bulleted lists; and appealing table).

Figure 11-7 Short Proposal, Page 2

Global Financial Advisors, Inc.   August 24, 2012   Page 2

Length of Course

As requested by management, this course will consist of three two-hour sessions; each session will be held on a selected day of the week for three consecutive weeks.

Number of Participants

The seminar will serve all 102 Global Financial Advisors' employees who are working in globally diverse teams.

Cost

All teaching-learning materials will be provided by the consulting firm and include workbooks, videos, and video camera and recorder. Exact cost figures are as follows:

Workbooks and other materials for 102 participants	$1,200.00
Equipment lease fees	300.00
Professional fees (6 hours' instruction @ $250/hour)	1,500.00
Travel/meals	775.00
Total	$3,775.00

Includes informational header to identify second page and client.

Itemizes costs so reader understands exactly how figure was calculated. Disclosing detailed breakdown gives reader confidence that cost is accurate.

parts of a proposal in a way that persuades the reader to accept it.

As with most report writing, first prepare the pieces of information that you will assemble later as the "whole" report. Determine the parts to include, select one part that will be easy to prepare, prepare that part, and then go on to another. When you have completed the parts, you can arrange them in whatever order you like, incorporate the transitional items necessary to create coherence, and then put the proposal in finished form. Allow adequate time after completing the research and writing for proofreading and editing. Figures should be checked carefully for accuracy, since underreporting costs can lead to a financial loss if the proposal is accepted, and overreported costs may lead to refusal of the proposal. If you fail to allow sufficient time for proposal completion, you may miss the required deadline for proposal submission.

If you become part of a collaborative writing team producing a proposal of major size, you will probably be responsible for writing only a small portion of the total proposal. For example, a proposal team of 16 executives, managers, and engineers might be required to prepare an 87-page proposal presenting a supplier's plan to supply parts to a military aircraft manufacturer.

After the group brainstorms and plans the proposal, a project director delegates responsibility for the research and origination of particular sections of the proposal. Finally, one person compiles all the sections, creates many of the preliminary and addenda parts, and produces and distributes the final product.

Check figures carefully. Underreporting costs can lead to financial loss, and overreporting costs might lead to refusal of the proposal.

© Kurhan/Shutterstock

Designing and Delivering Business Presentations

Planning an Effective Business Presentation

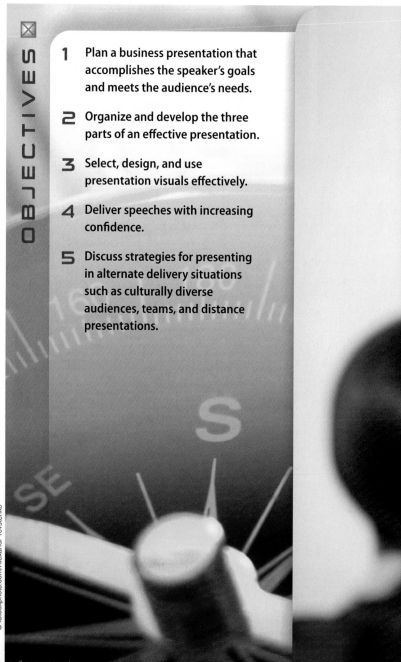

The simplicity of writing email and talking on the phone has deterred many workers from learning to communicate in front of people with authority and authenticity.[1] Being a skilled business communicator requires skill in both writing and speaking. A business presentation is an important means of exchanging information for decision making and policy development, relating the benefits of the services offered, and sharing our goals, values, and vision. Because multiple people receive the message at the same time and are able to provide immediate feedback for clarification, presentations can significantly reduce message distortion and misunderstanding.

> ☒ **OBJECTIVE 1**
>
> **Plan a business presentation that accomplishes the speaker's goals and meets the audience's needs.**

Many of the presentations you give will be formal, with sufficient time allowed for planning and developing elaborate visual support. You might present information and recommendations to external audiences such as customers and clients whom you've never met or to an internal audience made up of coworkers and managers you know well. You can also expect to present some less formal presentations, often referred to as **oral briefings**. An oral briefing might entail a short

> **oral briefings**
> *informal presentations prepared and presented with little time for planning and developing*

© iStockphoto.com/Alexandr Tovstenko

update on a current project requested during a meeting without advance notice or a brief explanation in the hallway when your supervisor walks past. Sales representatives give oral briefings daily as they present short, informal pitches for new products and services.

Regardless of the formality of the presentation, the time given to prepare, the nature of the audience (friends or strangers), or the media used (live, distant, Web, or DVD delivery on demand) your success depends on your ability to think on your feet and speak confidently as you address audience needs. Understanding the purpose you hope to achieve through your presen-

tation and conceptualizing your audience will enable you to organize the content in a way the audience can understand *and* accept.

Identify Your Purpose

Determining what you want to accomplish during a presentation is a fundamental principle of planning an effective presentation. Some speech coaches recommend completing the following vital sentence to lay the foundation for a successful presentation: "At the end of my presentation, the audience will _____." In his book

© jeka/Shutterstock

Bye-Bye, PowerPoint Slides?

Technology advancements have revolutionized business presentations. Internet-based programming languages, such as Java, make it possible to offer splashy graphics, animation, and real-time data updates on websites, cell phones, and other media players.

© Cobalt88/Shutterstock

Do's and Taboos of Public Speaking, Axtell provides two excellent mechanisms for condensing your presentation into a brief, achievable purpose that will direct you in identifying and supporting the major points:[2]

- Ask yourself, "What is my message?" Then, develop a phrase, a single thought, or a conclusion you want the audience to take with them from the presentation. This elementary statement will likely be the final sentence in your presentation—the basic message you want the audience to remember.

- Imagine a member of your audience has been asked to summarize your message. Ideally, you want to hear them describe your central purpose.

Know Your Audience

A common mistake for many presenters is to presume they know the audience without attempting to find out about them. If you expect to get results, you must commit the time to know your audience and focus your presentation on them—from planning your speech to practicing its delivery.

As a general rule, audiences *do* want to be in tune with a speaker. Yet people listen to speeches about things of interest to them. "What's in it for me?" is the question most listeners ask. A speech about global warming to a farm group should address the farmers' problems, for example, and not focus on theories of global warming. Additionally, different strategies are needed for audiences who think and make decisions differently. For instance, different strategies are needed for making a successful presentation to sell software to a group of

lawyers than to a group of doctors. Lawyers typically think quickly and are argumentative and decisive while doctors are often cautious, skeptical, and don't make quick purchasing decisions.[3]

To deliver a presentation that focuses on the wants and expectations of an audience, you must determine who they are, what motivates them, how they think, and how they make decisions. Helpful information you can obtain about most audiences includes ages, genders, occupations, educational levels, attitudes, values, broad and specific interests, and needs. In addition, you should also consider certain things about the occasion and location. Patriotic speeches to a group of military veterans will differ from speeches to a group of new recruits, just as Fourth of July speeches will differ from Veterans Day speeches. Seek answers to the following questions when you discuss your speaking engagement with someone representing the group or audience:

© iStockphoto.com/Maria Toutoudaki

1. *Who* is the audience and *who* requested the presentation? General characteristics of the audience should be considered, as well as the extent of their knowledge and experience with the topic, attitude toward the topic and you as a credible speaker, anticipated response to the use of electronic media, and required or volunteer attendance.

2. *Why* is this topic important to the audience? What will the audience do with the information presented?

3. *What* environmental factors affect the presentation?
   ○ How many will be in the audience?
   ○ Will I be the only speaker? If not, where does my presentation fit in the program? What time of day?
   ○ How much time will I be permitted? Minimum? Maximum?
   ○ What are the seating arrangements? How far will the audience be from the speaker? Will a microphone or other equipment be available?

Answers to these questions reveal whether the speaking environment will be intimate or remote, whether the audience is likely to be receptive and alert or nonreceptive and tired, and whether you will need to use additional motivational or persuasive techniques.

Organizing the Content

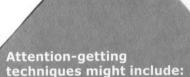

OBJECTIVE 2

Organize and develop the three parts of an effective presentation.

With an understanding of the purpose of your business presentation—why you are giving it and what you hope to achieve—and a conception of the size, interest, and background of the audience, you are prepared to outline your presentation and identify appropriate content. First introduced by famous speech trainer Dale Carnegie and still recommended by speech experts today, the simple but effective presentation format includes an introduction, a body, and a closing. In the introduction, tell the audience what you are going to tell them; in the body, tell them; and in the closing, tell them what you told them.

Although this design might sound repetitive, it works quite well. The audience processes information verbally and cannot slow the speaker down when information is complex. Thus, repetition aids the listener in processing the information that supports the speaker's purpose.

Introduction

What you say at the beginning sets the stage for your entire presentation and initiates your rapport with the audience. However, inexperienced speakers often settle for unoriginal and overused introductions, such as "My name is . . . , and my topic is . . ." or "It is a pleasure . . . ," or negative statements, such as apologies for lack of preparation, boring delivery, or late arrival, that reduce the audience's desire to listen. An effective introduction accomplishes the following goals:

- **Captures attention and involves the audience.** Choose an attention-getter that is relevant to the subject and appropriate for the situation.

© iStockphoto.com/Pali Rao

Attention-getting techniques might include:

- a shocking statement or startling statistic.
- a quotation by an expert or well-known person.
- a rhetorical or open-ended question that generates discussion from the audience.
- an appropriate joke or humor.
- a demonstration or dramatic presentation aid.
- an anecdote or timely story from a business periodical.
- a personal reference, compliment to the audience, or a reference to the occasion of the presentation.

© iStockphoto.com/Ju-Lee

To involve the audience directly, ask for a show of hands in response to a direct question, allow the audience time to think about the answer to a rhetorical question, or explain why the information is important and how it will benefit the listeners. Consider the following examples.

An alcohol awareness speech to young people might begin with a true story:

"My daughter was a straight 'A' student who had just been accepted by Harvard. But her dream of becoming a lawyer ended the night she drove her car into a tree after a party with friends and suffered serious brain trauma."

A report presenting plan for restructuring could introduce the subject and set the stage for the findings (inductive sequence) or the recommendation (deductive sequence):

Inductive: "When the company experienced a dramatic downturn in stock values, a management team immediately began to put together a plan to cut costs and improve productivity."

Deductive: "By reducing levels of management and cutting red tape, we can decrease costs and improve productivity, ensuring future growth of our company."

- **Establishes rapport.** Initiate rapport with the listeners; convince them that you are concerned that they benefit from the presentation and that you are qualified to speak on the topic. You might share a personal story that relates to the topic but reveals something about yourself, or discuss your background or a specific experience with the topic being discussed.

- **Presents the purpose statement and previews the points that will be developed.** To maintain the interest you have captured, present your purpose statement directly so that the audience is certain to hear it. Use original statements and avoid clichés such as "My topic today is . . ." or "I'd like to talk with you about . . ." Next, preview the major points you will discuss in the order you will discuss them. For example, you might say, "First, I'll discuss . . . , then . . . , and finally . . . ."

"Communication skills are consistently identified as the key to management and organizational success. Our business communication program will provide your management team the benefits of improved employee morale, greater efficiency, and a reduced error rate."

Revealing the presentation plan will help the audience understand how the parts of the body are tied together to support the purpose statement, thus increasing their understanding. For a long, complex presentation, you might display a presentation visual that lists the points in the order they will be covered. As you begin each major point, display a slide that contains that point and perhaps a related image. These section slides partition your presentation just as headings do in a written report, and thus move the listener more easily from one major point to the next.

© iStockphoto.com/Chris Hepburn

Body

In a typical presentation of 20 to 30 minutes, limit your presentation to only a few major points (typically three to five) to combat time constraints and your audience's ability to concentrate and absorb. Making every statement in a presentation into a major point—something to be remembered—is impossible, unless the presentation lasts only two or three minutes.

Once you have selected your major points, locate your supporting material. You can use several techniques to ensure the audience understands your point and to reinforce it:

- **Provide support in a form that is easy to understand.** Three techniques will assist you in accomplishing this goal:

  1 **Use simple vocabulary and short sentences that the listener can understand easily and that sound conversational and interesting.** Spoken communication is more difficult to process than written communication; therefore, complex, varied vocabulary and long sentences often included in written documents are not effective in a presentation.

  2 **Avoid jargon or technical terms that the listeners might not understand.** Instead, use plain English that the audience can easily comprehend. Make your speech more interesting and memorable by using word pictures to make your points. Matt Hughes, a speech consultant, provides this example: "If your message is a warning of difficulties ahead, you might say: 'We're climbing a hill that's getting steeper, and there are rocks and potholes in the road.'"[4]

  3 **Use a familiar frame of reference.** Drawing analogies between new ideas and familiar ones is another technique for generating understanding. For example, noting that the U.S. blog-reading audience is already one-half the size of the newspaper-reading population helps clarify an abstract or complex concept. Saying that "infodumping" is the verbal equivalent of email spam explains well the expected consequences of overloading an audience with too many details.[5]

- **Provide relevant statistics.** Provide statistics or other quantitative measures to lend authority and credibility to your points. A word of warning: Do not overwhelm your audience with excessive statistics. Instead, round off numbers and use broad terms or word pictures that the listener can remember. Instead of "68.2 percent" say "more than two-thirds"; instead of "112 percent rise in production" say "our output more than doubled."

- **Use quotes from prominent people.** Comments made by other authorities are helpful in establishing credibility.

- **Use interesting anecdotes.** Audiences like and remember anecdotes or interesting stories that tie into the presentation and make strong emotional connections. In her book *Whoever Tells the Best Story Wins*, Annette Simmons stresses that when telling stories, the storyteller allows the audience to feel his or her presence and reveals a trace of humanity, which is vital for developing understanding, influence, and strong relationships with his or her audience. She encourages leaders to craft personal stories into specific, intentional messages that communicate values, vision, and important lessons.[6] While communicating their values, leaders communicate the values they expect from employees. As with jokes, be sure you can get straight to the point of a story.

- **Use jokes and humor appropriately.** A joke or humor can create a special bond between you and the audience, ease your approach to sensitive subjects, disarm a nonreceptive audience, or make your message easier to understand and remember. Plan your joke carefully so that you can (1) get the point across as quickly as possible, (2) deliver it in a conversational manner with interesting inflections and effective body movements, and (3) deliver the punch line effectively. If you cannot tell a joke well, use humor instead—amusing things that happened to you or someone you know, one-liners, or humorous quotations that relate to your presentation. Refrain from any humor that reflects negatively on race, color, religion, gender, age, culture, or other personal areas of sensitivity.

  > "A funny thing happened on my way here . . ."

- **Use presentation visuals.** Presentation visuals, such as handouts, whiteboards, flip charts, transparencies, electronic presentations, and demonstrations, enhance the effectiveness of the presentation. Develop presentation visuals that will enable your audience to see, hear, and even experience your presentation.

- **Encourage audience involvement.** Skilled presenters involve their audiences through techniques such as asking reflective questioning, role playing, directing audience-centered activities, and incorporating current events or periodicals that tie directly to the message. One communications coach's advice for getting an audience "to sit up and listen" is to make the presentation contemporary by working Twitter, texting, video, and other technologies into the speech.[7]

Closing

The closing provides unity to your presentation by "telling the audience what you have already told them." The conclusion should be "your best line, your most dramatic point, your most profound thought, your most memorable bit of information, or your best anecdote."[8] Because listeners tend to remember what they hear last, use these final words strategically. Develop a closing that supports and refocuses the audience's attention on your purpose statement.

- **Commit the time and energy needed to develop a creative, memorable conclusion.** An audience is not impressed with endings such as "That's all I have" or "That's it." Useful concluding techniques include summarizing the main points that have been made in the presentation and using anecdotes, humor, and illustrations. When closing an analytical presentation, state your conclusion and support it with the highlights from your supporting evidence: "In summary, you should select our communication training program because it offers. . . ." In a persuasive presentation, the closing is often an urgent plea for the members of the audience to take some action or to look on the subject from a new point of view.

- **Tie the closing to the introduction to strengthen the unity of the presentation.** For example, you might answer the rhetorical question you asked in the opening, refer to and build on an anecdote included in the introduction, and so on. A unifying close to an alcohol awareness presentation might be "So, please ensure that you or a friend will not experience my daughter's disappointment, or worse, by drinking responsibly and designating a sober driver, if you party and travel."

- **Use transition words that clearly indicate you are moving from the body to the closing.** Attempt to develop original words rather than rely on standard statements such as "In closing," or "In conclusion."

- **Practice your closing until you can deliver it without stumbling.** Use your voice and gestures to communicate this important idea clearly, emphatically, and sincerely rather than fade out at the end as inexperienced speakers often do.

- **Smile and stand back to accept the audience's applause.** A solid closing does not require a "thank you"; instead wait confidently for the audience's spontaneous applause to thank you for a worthwhile presentation. Appear eager to begin a question-and-answer period or walk with assurance to your seat.

Designing Compelling Presentation Visuals

Speakers who use presentation visuals are considered better prepared and more interesting, and achieve their goals more often than speakers who do not use visuals. Presentation visuals support and clarify a speaker's ideas and help the audience visualize the message. A speaker using presentation visuals reaches the receiver with double impact—through the eyes and the ears—and achieves the results quoted in an ancient Chinese proverb: "Tell me, I'll forget. Show me, I'll remember. But involve me and I'll understand." Research studies confirm that using visuals enhances a presentation.

☒ **OBJECTIVE 3**

Select, design, and use presentation visuals effectively.

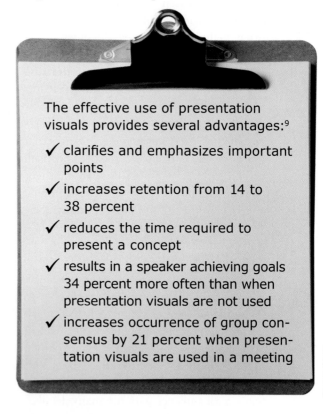

The effective use of presentation visuals provides several advantages:[9]

✓ clarifies and emphasizes important points

✓ increases retention from 14 to 38 percent

✓ reduces the time required to present a concept

✓ results in a speaker achieving goals 34 percent more often than when presentation visuals are not used

✓ increases occurrence of group consensus by 21 percent when presentation visuals are used in a meeting

© Image Source

Types of Presentation Visuals

A speaker must select the appropriate medium or combination of media to accomplish the purpose and to meet the needs of a specific audience. The most common presentation visuals are discussed in Figure 12-1.

Figure 12-1 Selecting an Appropriate Presentation Visual   201

VISUAL	ADVANTAGES	LIMITATIONS
HANDOUTS	• Provide detailed information that audience can examine closely • Extend a presentation by providing resources for later use • Reduce the need for note taking and aid in audience retention	• Can divert audience's attention from the speaker • Can be expensive
 **BOARDS AND FLIP CHARTS**	• Facilitate interaction • Are easy to use • Are inexpensive if traditional units are used	• Require turning speaker's back to audience • Are cumbersome to transport and can be messy and not professional looking • Provide no hard copy and must be developed on-site if traditional units are used
 **OVERHEAD TRANSPARENCIES**	• Are simple to prepare and use • Allow versatile use; can be prepared beforehand or while speaking • Are inexpensive and readily available	• Are not easily updated and are awkward to use • Require special acetate sheets and markers unless using a document camera • Pose potential for equipment failure
ELECTRONIC PRESENTATIONS	• Meet audience expectations of visual standards • Enhance professionalism and credibility of the speaker • Provide special effects to enhance retention, appeal, flexibility, and reuse	• Can lead to poor delivery if misused • Can be expensive and time-consuming • Can require highly developed skills • Pose technology failure and transportability challenges
  **35MM SLIDES**	• Are highly professional • Depict real people and places • Show color and detail dramatically	• Require a darkened room • Create a formal environment not conducive to group interaction • Lack flexibility in presentation sequence
MODELS OR PHYSICAL OBJECTS	• Are useful to demonstrate an idea • Show dimensions • Can feel more immediate and provide clearer example than images	• Can compete with the speaker for attention • If model, can be expensive and time-consuming to build

Design of Presentation Visuals

Computer technology has raised the standards for presentation visuals; however, inexperienced designers often use too many visuals and make them overly complex and difficult to understand. Not only are live audiences subjected to "PowerPoint poisoning," but "docu-points" are often sent when a different type of communication is called for. An "electability" PowerPoint slideshow sent by the 2008 Hillary Clinton Campaign to all House Democrats contained nine slides, 275 words, one table, three bar charts, and two pie charts. Such "docu-points" are usually less effective than a concise, well-designed handout or summary report.[10]

Your goal is to create an appealing, easy-to-read design that supports your main points without overwhelming the audience. Presentation visuals should possess the same degree of professionalism as your delivery and personal appearance. You can create dynamic and useful presentation visuals, including slides, handouts, and notes pages, by following these simple guidelines:

- **Limit the number of visual aids used in a single presentation.** While audiences value being able to "see" your points, they also welcome the variety provided by listening and the break from concentrating on visuals. Design compelling visuals that direct the audience's attention to major points and clarify or illustrate complex information. Use precise, vivid language that will involve the audience and enrich your message and delivery style.

- **Limit slide content to key ideas presented in as few words as possible.** Well-organized, crisp slide content enhances the audience's ability to grasp the speaker's meaning and find immediate value in the information. Good content also leads to an extemporaneous delivery rather than a speaker's monotonous reading of scripted slides. Short text lines are also easier for the eye to follow and open up the slide with appealing white space.

- **Develop only one major idea using targeted keywords the audience can scan quickly, understand, and remember.** Full sentences can be used for a direct quotation; otherwise, less is more. William Earnest, author of *Save Our Slides*, offers a cure for verbalitis: "PowerPoint is not a word processor"—it is a visual medium in which fewer words are always more.[11]

  - Keep type sizes large enough to read when projected and to discourage crowding slides with text. Strive for these font sizes: slide titles, 44 points; main bullets, 32 points; sub-bullets, 24 points. Do not use text smaller than 18 points as it is unreadable when projected.

  - Limit slide titles and headings to four words and follow the 7 × 7 rule, which limits text to 7 lines per slide and 7 words per line. Eliminate articles (*a*, *an*, *the*), understood pronouns/possessives (*we, you, your*), simple verbs and infinitive beginnings (*are, to*), and repetitive phrasing.[12]

  - Develop powerful bulleted lists that are easy to follow and remember. For easy recall, limit the list to three to five main bullets, but absolutely no more than seven. To eliminate confusion and rereading, use bulleted lists that are grammatically parallel. One item appearing out of place weakens the emphasis given to each item and can distract audience attention from the message. Be certain each major point relates to the key concept presented in the slide title and each subpoint relates to its major point. Unless sequence is important, use bullets as they add less clutter and are easier to follow than numbers.

- **Choose an effective template and powerful images to reinforce ideas, illustrate complex ideas, and enliven boring content.** Images and shapes are more visually appealing and memorable than words, and they enable audiences to grasp information more easily. Today's audiences expect media-rich, dynamic visuals, not a speaker's dense crutch notes displayed on screen. Although photographs and clip art available in your presentation software gallery are acceptable, avoid images that are overused, outdated, grainy, and convey an unprofessional tone. Instead search for or create high-quality, professional images that convey the desired message and can project onscreen without distortion.

- **Choose an effective color scheme.** The colors you choose and the way you combine them determine the overall effectiveness of your presentation and add a personal touch to your work. Follow these simple rules to plan a non-distracting, complementary color scheme that has unity with the template graphics:

  - **Limit colors to no more than three colors on a slide to avoid an overwhelming feel.**

  - **Begin by selecting a background color that conveys the appropriate formality and tone.** Choose cool colors (blue and green) in muted shades for formal presentations; choose warm colors (red, orange, and yellow) or brighter shades of cool colors for a less formal and perhaps trendy look. Think carefully about whether your color selection has a natural association with your topic or organization. For example, a presentation on environmentally friendly policies might incorporate colors naturally associated with nature and cleanliness (earth tones, white and blue); a presentation to Coca-Cola likely would be designed around the company colors of red and white.

- **Choose complementary foreground (text) colors that have high contrast to the background to ensure readability.** To ensure high contrast, choose either dark text on a light background or light text on a dark background. For example, the often-used color scheme of yellow slide title text and white bulleted list with a blue background is a good choice because the colors are complementary and have high contrast. Choose a slightly brighter color for the slide title that distinguishes it from the color chosen for the bullet list.

Black text against a white background has the greatest contrast. A blue background with yellow text contrasts well, but a light blue background with white text would be difficult to read because of low contrast. Evaluate the readability of the following contrast variations.

High-contrast options:	Dark text on a light background	Light text on dark background

Poor contrast options:	White text on a light blue background	Bright text on a bright background

Because the lower resolution of projectors can wash out colors and make them less vibrant than what is seen on a printed page or computer screen, choose options with very high—not minimally high—contrast. Project your presentation ahead of time in the room where you are to present so you can assess the color scheme. You can also double check for readability and typographical errors at the same time.

- **Choose the accent colors that complement the color scheme.** Accent colors are used in small doses to draw attention to key elements: bullet markers; bars/slices in graphs, backgrounds (fills) of shapes and lines, selected text; or drawings that are color coded for emphasis. Avoid red and green when differentiating important points as almost 10 percent of the population is color impaired and cannot distinguish between red and green. The red and green bars in a graph would be seen as one large area.

- **Choose an appealing font that can be read onscreen easily.** Avoid delicate, decorative, or condensed choices that are difficult to read when projected. The clean, simple lines of a sans serif font, such as Calibri, Tahoma, or Verdana, are ideal for projecting on a large screen, newspaper headline, sign, or billboard. A *sans serif font* has no short cross-strokes, known as *serifs*, which provide extra detail that helps guide the eye on print media. Examples of serif fonts are Cambria, Times New Roman and Garamond.

- **Follow these keyboarding rules for easy reading.** Use capital letters sparingly as they are difficult to read from a distance. Capitalize the first letter of important words in slide titles (initial caps) and the first letter of the first word and proper nouns in a bulleted list (sentence case). Omit hard-to-see punctuation at the end of bulleted lists and elsewhere, and avoid abbreviations and hyphenations that might cause confusion.

- **Reflect legal and ethical responsibility in the design of presentation visuals.** Like the graphics you developed in Chapter 10, presentation visuals should be uncluttered, easily understood, and depict information honestly.

- **Proofread the visual carefully following the same systematic procedures used for printed letters and reports and electronic communication.** Misspellings in visuals are embarrassing and diminish your credibility. Double check to be certain that names of people, companies, and products are spelled correctly.

Figure 12-2 on the next page offers a review of slide design guidelines. The poor example (left) includes many common slide design errors that are corrected in the good example (right).

Design Tips for Audience Handouts and Notes Pages

Audience handouts should add value for individual audience members; otherwise, the information can better be conveyed in a projected format for group benefit. An effective handout can help audience members remember your message, serve as a reference for later consideration or action, and encourage involvement when space is provided for note taking or response. You can prepare useful presenter notes on small index cards or on pages generated by electronic presentation software.

Figure 12-2 Designing Compelling Slides: Poor (left) and Good (right) Examples

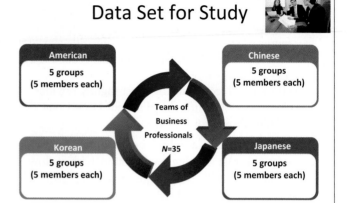

Data set for study of culturally diverse teams and communication practices

- First Sample: Five homogeneous groups—five persons each—of Americans
- Second Sample: Five homogeneous groups—five persons each—of Koreans
- Third Sample: Five homogeneous groups—five persons each—of Chinese
- Fourth Sample: Five homogeneous groups—five persons each—of Japanese

© Neustockimages/iStockphoto.com

Data Set for Study

American
5 groups
(5 members each)

Chinese
5 groups
(5 members each)

Teams of Business Professionals
N=35

Korean
5 groups
(5 members each)

Japanese
5 groups
(5 members each)

The revised slide
- Includes short descriptive title that captures major idea of slide.
- Limits slide content to meet the 7 x 7 criteria.
- Recognizes the difference between a written communication channel and a visual one through enhanced use of visual elements and reduction of text.
- Takes advantage of SmartArt feature of Microsoft PowerPoint to increase visual appeal while reducing time needed for custom design creation.
- Uses a simple but appealing template with high-quality, relevant image that is large enough for audience to see and has not been overused.
- Uses high-contrast background and sans serif fonts to assure legibility. Color choices are complementary and convey a professional tone.
- Uses initial caps in slide title, capitalizes the first word in bulleted list, and omits period at end of bulleted items.
- Proofreads carefully to avoid misspellings that damage credibility.

Refining Your Delivery

Afer you have organized your message, you must identify the appropriate delivery method, refine your vocal qualities, and practice your delivery.

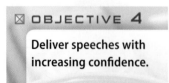

⊠ OBJECTIVE 4

Deliver speeches with increasing confidence.

Delivery Method

Four presentation methods can be used: memorized, scripted, impromptu, and extemporaneous. Impromptu and extemporaneous styles are generally more useful for business presentations.

Memorized presentations are written out ahead of time, memorized, and recited verbatim. Memorization has the greatest limitations of the speech styles. Speakers are almost totally unable to react to feedback, and the speaker who forgets a point and develops a mental block might lose the entire speech. Memorized speeches tend to sound monotonous, restrict natural body gestures and motions, and lack conviction. For short religious or fraternal rites, however, the memorized presentation is often impressive.

Manuscript, or *scripted*, **presentations** involve writing the speech word for word and reading it to the audience. For complex material and technical conference presentations, manuscript presentations ensure content coverage. Additionally, this style protects speakers against being misquoted (when accuracy is absolutely critical) and fits into exact time

memorized presentation
a presentation in which a speaker writes out a speech, commits it to memory, and recites it verbatim

manuscript presentation
a presentation in which a speaker writes out the entire speech and reads it to the audience; also called a scripted presentation

constraints, as in television or radio presentations. Speeches are sometimes read when time does not permit adequate preparation or when several different presentations are given in one day (e.g., the speaking demands of the President of the United States and other top-level executives). Manuscript presentations limit speaker–audience rapport, particularly when speakers keep their eyes and heads buried in their manuscripts. Teleprompters that project the manuscript out of view of the audience allow the speaker to appear to be speaking extemporaneously.

Impromptu presentations are frightening to many people because the speaker is called on without prior notice. Experienced speakers can easily analyze the request, organize supporting points from memory, and present a simple, logical response. In many cases, businesspeople can anticipate a request and be prepared to discuss a particular idea when requested (e.g., status report on an area of control at a team meeting). Because professionals are expected to present ideas and data spontaneously on demand, businesspeople must develop the ability to deliver impromptu presentations.

Extemporaneous presentations are planned, prepared, and rehearsed but not written in detail. Brief notes prompt the speaker on the next point, but the words are chosen spontaneously as the speaker interacts with the audience and identifies this audience's specific needs. Extemporaneous presentations include natural body gestures, sound conversational, and can be delivered with conviction because the speaker is speaking "with" the listeners and not "to" them. The audience appreciates a warm, genuine communicator and will forgive an occasional stumble or groping for a word that occurs with an extemporaneous presentation.

Vocal Qualities

The sound of your voice is a powerful instrument used to deliver your message and to project your professional image. To maximize your vocal strengths, focus on three important qualities of speech: phonation, articulation, and pronunciation.

Phonation involves both the production and the variation of the speaker's vocal tone. You project your voice and convey feelings—even thoughts—by varying your vocal tones. Important factors of phonation are pitch, volume, and rate. These factors permit us to recognize other people's voices over the phone.

- **Pitch.** The highness or lowness of the voice is called pitch. Pleasant voices have medium or low pitch; however, a varied pitch pattern is desirable. The pitch of the voice rises and falls to reflect emotions;

for example, fear and anger are reflected in a higher pitch; sadness, in a lower pitch. Lower pitches for both men and women are perceived as sounding more authoritative; higher pitches indicate less confidence and suggest pleading or whining. Techniques discussed later in this section can help you lower the pitch of your voice.

- **Volume.** The loudness of tones is referred to as volume. Generally, good voices are easily heard by everyone in the audience but are not too loud. Use variety to hold the audience's attention, emphasize words or ideas, and create a desired atmosphere (energetic, excited tone versus dull, boring one).

- **Rate.** The speed at which words are spoken is called rate. Never speak so quickly that the audience cannot understand your message or so slowly that they are distracted or irritated. Vary the rate with the demands of the situation. For example, speak at a slower rate when presenting a complex concept or emphasizing an important idea. Pause to add emphasis to a key point or to transition to another major section of the presentation. Speak at a faster rate when presenting less important information or when reviewing.

An inherent problem related to speaking rate is verbal fillers—also called nonwords. Verbal fillers, such as *uhhh, ahhh, ummm,* and *errr,* are irritating to the audience and destroy your effectiveness. Many speakers fill space with their own verbal fillers; these include *you know, I mean, basically, like I said, okay,* and *as a matter of fact.* Because of the conversational style of impromptu and extemporaneous presentations, a speaker will naturally struggle for a word or idea from time to time. Become aware of verbal fillers you frequently use by critiquing a recording of yourself and then focus on replacing fillers with a three- to five-second pause. This brief gap between thoughts gives you an opportunity to think about what you want to say next and time for your audience to absorb your idea. Presenting an idea (sound bite) and then pausing briefly is an effective way to influence your audience positively. The listener will not notice the slight delay, and the absence of meaningless words will make you

impromptu presentation
a presentation in which a speaker is called on without prior notice

extemporaneous presentation
a presentation in which a speaker plans, prepares, and rehearses but does not write everything down; brief notes prompt the speaker, but the exact words are chosen spontaneously as the speaker interacts with the audience and identifies its specific needs

phonation
the production and variation of a speaker's vocal tone

appear more confident and polished. Also avoid annoying speech habits, such as clearing your throat or coughing, that shift the audience's attention from the speech to the speaker.

The following activities will help you achieve good vocal qualities:

- **Breathe properly and relax.** Nervousness affects normal breathing patterns and is reflected in vocal tone and pitch. The better prepared you are, the better your phonation will be. Although relaxing might seem difficult to practice before a speech, a few deep breaths, just as swimmers take before diving, can help.

- **Listen to yourself.** A recording of your voice reveals much about pitch, intensity, and duration. Most people are amazed to find their voices are not quite what they had expected. "I never dreamed I sounded that bad" is a common reaction. Nasal twangs usually result from a failure to speak from the diaphragm, which involves taking in and letting out air through the larynx, where the vocal cords operate. High pitch can occur from the same cause, or it can be a product of speaking too fast or experiencing stage fright.

- **Develop flexibility.** A good speaking voice is somewhat musical, with words and sounds similar to notes in a musical scale. Read each of the following sentences aloud and emphasize the *italicized* word in each. Even though the sentences are identical, emphasizing different words changes the meaning.

© First Light/Alamy

I am happy you are here.	*Maybe I'm the only happy one.*
I *am* happy you are here.	*I really am.*
I am *happy* you are here.	*Happy best describes my feeling.*
I am happy *you* are here.	*Yes, you especially.*
I am happy you *are* here.	*You may not be happy, but I am.*
I am happy you are *here.*	*Here and not somewhere else.*

Articulation involves smooth, fluent, and pleasant speech. It results from the way in which a speaker produces and joins sounds. Faulty articulation is often caused by not carefully forming individual sounds. Common examples include:

- dropping word endings—saying *workin'* for *working*
- running words together—saying *kinda* for *kind of*, *gonna* for *going to*
- imprecise enunciation—saying *dis* for *this*, *wid* for *with*, *dem* for *them*, *pin* for *pen*, or *pitcher* for *picture*

These examples should not be confused with *dialect*, which people informally call an *accent*. A dialect is a variation in pronunciation, usually of vowels, from one part of the country to another. Actually, everyone speaks a dialect; speech experts can often identify, even pinpoint, the section of the country from where a speaker comes. In the United States, common dialects are New England, New York, Southern, Texan, Mid-Western, and so forth. Within each of these, minor dialects often arise regionally or from immigrant influence. The simple fact is that when people interact, they influence each other even down to speech sounds. Many prominent speakers have developed a rather universal dialect, known as Standard American Speech or American Broadcast English, that seems to be effective no matter who the audience is. This model for professional language is widely used by newscasters and announcers and is easily understood by those who speak English as a second language because they likely listened to this speech pattern on television as they learned the language.

You can improve the clarity of your voice, reduce strain and voice distortion, and increase your expressiveness by following these guidelines:

- **Stand up straight with your shoulders back and breathe from your diaphragm rather than your chest.** If you are breathing correctly, you can then use your mouth and teeth to form sounds precisely. For example, vowels are always sounded with the mouth open and the tongue clear of the palate.

Consonants are responsible primarily for the distinctness of speech and are formed by an interference with or stoppage of outgoing breath.

- **Focus on completing the endings of all words, not running words together, and enunciating words correctly.** To identify recurring enunciation errors, listen to a recording and seek feedback from others.

- **Obtain formal training to improve your speech.** Pursue a self-study program by purchasing recordings that help you reduce your dialect and move more closely to a universal dialect. You can also enroll in a diction course to improve your speech patterns or arrange for private lessons from a voice coach.

Pronunciation involves using principles of phonetics to create accurate sounds, rhythm, stress, and intonation. People might articulate perfectly but still mispronounce words. A dictionary provides the best source to review pronunciation. Two pronunciations are often given for a word, the first one being the desired pronunciation and the second an acceptable variation. An American adopting a pronunciation commonly used in England, such as *shedule* for *schedule* or *a-gane* for *again*, could be seen negatively. In some cases, leeway exists in pronunciation. The first choice for pronouncing *data* is to pronounce the first *a* long, as in *date*; but common usage is fast making pronunciation of the short *a* sound, as in *cat*, acceptable. Likewise, the preferred pronunciation of *often* is with a silent *t*. Good speakers use proper pronunciation and refer to the dictionary frequently in both pronunciation and vocabulary development.

When your voice qualities combine to make your messages pleasingly receptive, your primary concerns revolve around developing an effective delivery style.

Delivery Style

Speaking effectively is both an art and a skill. Careful planning and practice are essential for increasing speaking effectiveness.

Before the Presentation

Follow these guidelines when preparing for your presentation:

- **Prepare thoroughly.** You can expect a degree of nervousness as you anticipate speaking before a group. This natural tension is constructive because it increases your concentration and your energy and enhances your performance. Even Kara DioGuardi, a fourth judge added to the 2009 *American Idol* season, admitted being nervous as she adjusted to giving short, meaningful advice in front of 30 million people on the most-watched TV show in the nation.[13]

  Being well prepared is the surest way to control speech anxiety. Develop an outline for your presentation that supports your purpose and addresses the needs of your audience, and take advantage of every opportunity to gain speaking experience.

- **Prepare effective presentation support tools.** Follow the guidelines presented in the preceding section to select and design visuals, handouts, and notes pages appropriate for your audience and purpose. Additionally, develop a contingency plan in the event of technical difficulties with computer equipment, such as hard copies of the slides or a backup computer pre-loaded and ready. Arrive early so you can troubleshoot unexpected technological glitches. Despite your degree of planning, however, technical problems might occur during your presentation.

pronunciation
using principles of phonetics to create accurate sounds, rhythm, stress, and intonation

© Yuri Arcurs/Shutterstock

"Never, never, never give a speech on a subject you don't believe in. You'll fail. On the other hand, if you prepare properly, know your material, and *believe* in it . . . your audience will not only hear but *feel* your message."
John Davis, a successful speech coach[14]

Remain calm and correct them as quickly and professionally as you can. Take heart in the fact that Bill Gates' computer once crashed when he introduced a new version of Windows!

- **Practice, but do not rehearse.** Your goal is to become familiar with the key phrases on your note cards so that you can deliver the presentation naturally as if you are talking with the audience—not reciting the presentation or acting out a role. Avoid overpracticing, which can make your presentation sound mechanical and limit your ability to respond to the audience.

- **Practice the entire presentation.** This practice will allow you to identify (1) flaws in organization or unity, (2) long, complex sentences or ineffective expressions, and (3) "verbal potholes." Verbal potholes include word combinations that could cause you to stumble, words you have trouble pronouncing ("irrelevant" or "statistics"), and words that accentuate your dialect ("get" can sound like "git" regardless of the intention of a Southern speaker).

- **Spend additional time practicing the introduction and conclusion.** You will want to deliver these important parts with finesse while making a confident connection with the audience. A good closing leaves the audience in a good mood and can help overcome some possible weaknesses during the speech. Depending on the techniques used, consider memorizing significant brief statements to ensure their accuracy and impact (e.g., direct quotation, exact statistic, etc.).

- **Practice displaying presentation visuals so that your delivery appears effortless and seamless.** Your goal is to make the technology virtually transparent, positioned in the background to support *you* as the primary focus of the presentation. First, be sure you know basic commands for advancing through your presentation without displaying distracting menus. Develop skill in returning to a specific slide in the event of a computer glitch or an audience question.

- **Seek feedback on your performance to help you** to polish your delivery and improve organization. Critique your own performance by practicing in front of a mirror and evaluating a recording of your presentation. If possible, present to a small audience ahead of time for feedback and to minimize anxiety when presenting to the real audience.

- **Request a lectern to hold your notes and to steady a shaky hand, at least until you gain some confidence and experience.** Keep in mind, though, that weaning yourself from the lectern will eliminate a physical barrier between you and the audience. Without the lectern, you will speak more naturally. If you are using a microphone, ask for a portable microphone so that you can move freely.

- **Request a proper introduction if the audience knows little about you.** An effective introduction will establish your credibility as a speaker on the subject and will make the audience eager to hear you. You can prepare your own introduction as professional speakers do, or you can provide concise, targeted information that answers these three questions: (1) Why is the subject relevant? (2) Who is the speaker? and (3) What credentials qualify the speaker to talk about the subject? Talk with the person introducing you to verify any information, especially the pronunciation of your name, and to review the format of the presentation (time limit, question-and-answer period, etc.). Be certain to thank the person who made the introduction as you begin your presentation. "Thank you for your kind introduction, Ms. Garcia" is adequate. Then, follow with your own introduction to your presentation topic.

- **Dress appropriately to create a strong professional image and to bolster your self-confidence.** An audience's initial impression of your personal appearance, your clothing and grooming, affects their ability to accept you as a credible speaker. Because first impressions are difficult to overcome, take time to groom yourself immaculately and to select clothing that is appropriate for the speaking occasion and consistent with the audience's expectations.

- **Arrive early to become familiar with the setup of the room and to check the equipment.** Check the location of your chair, the

© iStockphoto.com/DSGpro

lectern, the projection screen, light switches, and electrical outlets. Check the microphone and Internet connection and ensure that all equipment is in the appropriate place and working properly. Project your electronic presentation so you can adjust the color scheme to ensure maximum readability. Finally, identify the technician who will be responsible for resolving any technical problems that might occur during the presentation.

During the Presentation

The following are things you can do during your presentation to increase your effectiveness as a speaker:

- **Communicate confidence, warmth, and enthusiasm for the presentation and the time spent with the audience.** "Your listeners won't care how much you know until they know how much you care," is pertinent advice.[15]

  ○ **Exhibit a confident appearance with alert posture.** Stand tall with your shoulders back and your stomach tucked in. Stand in the "ready position"—no slouching, hunching over the lectern, or rocking. Keep weight forward with knees slightly flexed so you are ready to move easily rather than rooted rigidly in one spot, hiding behind the lectern.

  ○ **Smile genuinely throughout the presentation.** Pause as you take your place behind the lectern, and smile before you speak the first word. Smile as you finish your presentation and wait for the applause.

  ○ **Maintain steady eye contact with the audience in random places throughout the room.** Stay with one person approximately three to five seconds—long enough to finish a complete thought or sentence to convince the listener you are communicating individually with him or her. If the audience is large, select a few friendly faces and concentrate on speaking to them rather than to a sea of nondescript faces.

  ○ **Refine gestures to portray a relaxed, approachable appearance.** Vary hand motions to emphasize important points; otherwise, let hands fall naturally to your side. Practice using only one hand to make points unless you specifically need two hands, such as when drawing a figure or showing dimensions or location. Eliminate any nervous gestures that can distract the audience (e.g., clenching your hands in front of or behind your body, steepling your hands, placing your hands in your pockets, jingling keys or change, or playing with a ring or pen).

  ○ **Move from behind the lectern and toward the audience to reduce the barrier created**

between you and the audience. You can stand to one side and casually present a relaxed pose beside the lectern. However, avoid methodically walking without a purpose.

- **Exercise strong vocal qualities.** Review the guidelines provided for using your voice to project confidence and credibility.

- **Watch your audience.** They will tell you how you are doing and whether you should shorten your speech. Be attentive to negative feedback in the form of talking, coughing, moving chairs, and other signs of discomfort.

- **Use your visuals effectively.** Many speakers will go to a great deal of effort to prepare good presentation visuals—and then not use them effectively. Inexperienced speakers often ignore the visual altogether or fall into the habit of simply nodding their heads toward the visual. Neither of these techniques is adequate for involving the audience with the visual. In fact, if the material is complex, the speaker is likely to lose the audience completely.

  ○ **Step to one side of the visual so the audience can see it.** Use a pointer if necessary. Direct your remarks to the audience, so that you can maintain eye contact and resist the temptation to look over your shoulder or turn your back to read the information from the screen behind you.

  ○ **Paraphrase the visual rather than reading it line for line.** To increase the quality of your delivery, develop a workable method of recording what you plan to say about each graphic.

- **Handle questions from the audience during the presentation.** Questions often disrupt carefully laid plans. At the same time, questions provide feedback, clarify points, and ensure understanding. When people ask questions that will be answered later in the presentation, say, "I believe the next slide will clarify that point; if not, we will come back to it." If the question can be answered quickly, you should do so while indicating that it will also be covered more later.

  Anticipate and prepare for questions that might be raised. You can generate presentation visuals pertaining to certain anticipated questions and display them only if the question is posed. An audience will appreciate your thorough and complete explanation and your ability to adjust your presentation to their needs—this strategy is much more professional than stumbling through an explanation or delaying the answer until the information is available. Speakers giving electronic presentations have ready access to enormous amounts of information that can be displayed instantly for audience discussion. Hyperlinks created within a presentation file will move a speaker instantaneously to a specific slide, another file, or an embedded music or video file.

- **Keep within the time limit.** Be prepared to complete the presentation within the allotted time. In many organizations, speakers have one or more rehearsals before delivering reports to a group such as a board of directors. These rehearsals, or dry runs, are made before other executives, and are critiqued, timed, revised, and rehearsed again. Presentation software makes rehearsing your timing as simple as clicking a button and advancing through the slides as you practice. By evaluating the total presentation time and the time spent on each slide, you can modify the presentation and rehearse it again until the presentation fits the time slot.

After the Presentation

How you handle the time following a presentation is as important as preparing for the presentation itself:

- **Be prepared for a question-and-answer period.** Encourage the audience to ask questions, recognizing an opportunity to ensure that your presentation meets audience needs. Paraphrasing the question allows you time to reflect on what was asked, ensures that everyone heard the question, and assures the questioner that he or she was understood. You can ask the questioner if your answer was adequate. Be courteous even to hostile questioners so you will maintain the respect of your audience. Stay in control of the time by announcing that you have time for one or two more questions, and then invite individual questions when the presentation is over.

- **Distribute handouts.** Distribute the handout when it is needed, rather than at the beginning of the presentation. Otherwise, the audience might read the handout while you are explaining background information needed to understand the written ideas. If you expect the audience to take notes directly on the handout or if the audience will need to refer to the handout immediately, distribute the handout at the beginning of the presentation or before it begins. To keep control of the audience's attention, be sure listeners know when they should be looking at the handout or listening to you. If the handout is intended as resource material only, post the handout to a web page or place it on a table at the back of the room and at the front for those who come by to talk with you after the presentation.

Adapting to Alternate Delivery Situations

As you've learned, presenting a dynamic presentation that focuses on the audience's needs and expectations is the fundamental principle in presenting effectively. Along with the solid foundation you've set for spoken communication, you'll also need to adapt your presentation style to the ever-changing business environment and the special needs of culturally diverse audiences. Delivering team presentations and presenting in distance formats are other common situations you'll need to master.

Culturally Diverse Audiences

When speaking to a culturally diverse audience, you will want to be as natural as possible, while adjusting your message for important cultural variations. Using empathy, you can effectively focus on the listener as an individual rather than a stereotype of a specific culture. Be open and willing to learn, and you will reap the benefits of communicating effectively with people who possess a variety of strengths and creative abilities. Additionally, follow these suggestions for presenting to people from outside your own culture:

- **Speak simply.** Use simple English and short sentences. Avoid acronyms and expressions that can be confusing to nonnative English speakers—namely slang, jargon, figurative expressions, and sports analogies.

- **Avoid words that trigger negative emotional responses such as anger, fear, or suspicion.** Such "red flag" words vary among cultures; thus, try to anticipate audience reaction and choose your words carefully.

- **Enunciate each word precisely and speak somewhat slowly.** Clear, articulate speech is especially important when the audience is not familiar with various dialects and vocabulary. Avoid the temptation to speak in a loud voice, a habit considered rude in any culture and especially annoying to the Japanese, who perceive the normal tone of North Americans as too loud.

- **Be extremely cautious in the use of humor and jokes.** Cultures that prefer more formality might think you are not serious about your purpose or find your humor and jokes inappropriate. Asians, for instance, do not appreciate jokes about family members and the elderly.

- **Learn the culture's preferences for a direct or indirect presentation.** While North Americans tend to prefer directness, with the main idea presented first, people from many cultures, such as Japanese, Latin American, and Arabic, consider a straightforward approach tactless and rude.

- **Adapt to subtle differences in nonverbal communication.** The direct eye contact expected by most North Americans is not typical of Asian listeners who often keep their eyes lowered and avoid eye contact to show respect. Arab audiences might stare into your eyes in an attempt to "see into the window of the soul." Cultures also vary on personal space and degree of physical contact (slap on the back or arm around the other as signs of friendship).

- **Adapt your dress and presentation style to fit the formality of the culture.** Some cultures prefer a higher degree of formality than the casual style of North Americans. To accommodate, dress conservatively; strive to connect with the audience in a formal, reserved manner; and use highly professional visuals rather than jotting ideas on a flip chart.

- **Seek feedback to determine whether the audience is understanding your message.** Observe listeners carefully for signs of misunderstanding, restating ideas as necessary. Consider allowing time for questions after short segments of your presentation. Avoid asking "Is that clear?" or "Do you understand?" as these statements might elicit a "Yes" answer if the person perceives saying "No" to be a sign of incompetence.

Potential frustrations can also occur when presentations or meetings bring together North Americans, who see "time as money," with people of cultures who are not time conscious and who believe that personal relationships are the basis of business dealings (e.g., Asian, Latin American). When communicating with cultures that are not time driven, be patient with what you might consider time-consuming formalities and courtesies and lengthy decision-making styles when you would rather get right down to business or move to the next point. Recognize that the presentation might not begin on time or stay on a precise schedule. Allow additional time at the beginning of the presentation to establish rapport and credibility with the audience, and perhaps provide brief discussion periods devoted to building relationships during the presentation.

Be patient and attentive during long periods of silence; in many cultures people are inclined to stay silent unless they have something significant to say or if they are considering (not necessarily rejecting) an idea. In fact, some Japanese have asked how North Americans can think and talk at the same time. Understanding patterns of silence can help you feel more comfortable during these seemingly endless moments and less compelled to fill the gaps with unnecessary words or to make concessions before the other side has a chance to reply.

Other significant points of difference between cultures are the varying rules of business etiquette. Should you use the traditional American handshake or some other symbol of greeting? Is using the person's given name acceptable? What formal titles should be used with a surname? Can you introduce yourself, or must you have someone else who knows the other person introduce you? Are business cards critical, and what rules should you follow when presenting a business

© STR/epa/Corbis

card? Should you have business cards that are printed in two languages?

Gift-giving can be another confusing issue. When you believe a gift should be presented to your event host, investigate the appropriateness of gift giving, types of gifts considered appropriate or absolutely inappropriate, and colors of wrapping to be avoided in the speaker's culture. Liquor, for example, is an inappropriate gift in Arab countries.

Gaining competence in matters of etiquette will enable you to make a positive initial impression and concentrate on the presentation rather than agonizing over an awkward, embarrassing slip in protocol. Your audience will appreciate your willingness to learn and value their customs. Being sensitive to cultural issues and persistent in learning specific differences in customs and practices can minimize confusion and unnecessary embarrassment.

Team Presentations

Because much of the work in business today is done in teams, many presentations are planned and delivered by teams of presenters. Well-conducted team presentations give an organization an opportunity to showcase its brightest talent while capitalizing on each person's unique presentation skills. Email, collaborative software, and other technologies make it easy to develop, edit, review, and deliver impressive team presentations.

The potential payoff of many team presentations is quite high—perhaps a $200,000 contract or a million-dollar account. Yet, according to experts, team presentations fail primarily because presenters don't devote enough time and resources to develop and rehearse them.[16] Resist the sure-to-fail strategy of "winging" a team presentation rather than taking the time to do it correctly. Instead, adapt the skills you already possess in planning and delivering an individual presentation to ensure a successful team presentation. Follow these guidelines as you plan and prepare your team presentation:

- **Select a winning team.** Begin by choosing a leader who is well liked and respected by the team, is knowledgeable of the project, is well organized, and will follow through. Likewise, the leader should be committed to leading the team in the development of a cohesive strategy for the presentation as well as the delegation of specific responsibilities to individual

A member of a winning team will have:
☞ Complementary strengths/style
☞ Ability to meet expectations
☞ Willingness to support team strategy
☞ Willingness to commit to schedule

© iStockphoto.com/Andresr

members. Frank Carillo, president of Executive Communications Group, warns team presenters that a frequent problem with "divvying up" work into pieces is that the "pieces don't fit together well when they come back."[17]

The core team members, along with management, should choose a balanced mix of individuals who each has something important to contribute to the team. Use these questions to guide team selection: What are this member's complementary strengths and style (e.g., technical expertise, personality traits, and presentation skills)? Can this member meet the expectations of the audience (e.g., a numbers person, technical person, person with an existing relationship with the audience)? Is this member willing to support the team strategy and commit to the schedule?[18]

- **Agree on the purpose and schedule.** The team as a whole should plan the presentation using the same process used for an individual presentation. Agreeing on the purpose to be achieved and selecting content that focuses on a specific audience will prevent the challenges caused by an individual's submitting off-target material. The quality of the presentation deteriorates when material must be redone hurriedly in the final days before the deadline or when unacceptable material is included just because the team worked so hard on it. Mapping out a complete presentation strategy can also minimize bickering among team members because of uneven workloads or unfavorable work assignments.

The team will also need to agree on a standard design for presentation visuals to ensure consistency in the visuals prepared by individual presenters. Assign a person to merge the various files, to edit for consistency in design elements and the use of jargon and specialized terminology, and to proofread carefully for grammatical accuracy.

Developing a rehearsal schedule ensures adequate time for preparation and practice. Many experts recommend five practice sessions to produce team presentations that are delivered with a unified look. Planning time in the schedule to present before a review team is especially useful for obtaining feedback on team continuity and adjustments needed to balance major discrepancies in the delivery styles of individual presenters.

- **Practice ahead of time.** The team must be well prepared, which will require several rehearsals. Each member must know what others will say to avoid repetition and to fit the time slot. The team must also work out logistical details such as where people will stand, who will run the slides, and when handouts will be distributed. A great deal of the rehearsal time for a team presentation should be spent planning and rehearsing appropriate verbal and physical transitions between team members. The transitions serve to introduce each part of the presentation and make the whole presentation cohesive. This continuity makes the team look polished and conveys team commitment.

Follow these suggestions for delivering seamless, impressive team presentations:

- **Decide who will open and conclude the presentation.** The team member who knows the audience and has established rapport is a logical choice for these two critical sections of a presentation. If no one knows the audience, select the member with the strongest presentation skills and personality traits for connecting well with strangers. This person will introduce all team members and give a brief description of the roles they will play in the presentation.

- **Build natural bridges between segments of the presentation and presenters.** A lead presenter must build a bridge from the points that have been made that will launch the following presenter smoothly into what he or she will discuss. If a lead presenter forgets to make the connection to the next section clear, the next person must summarize what's

been said and then preview his or her section. These transitions might seem repetitive to a team that has been working extensively with the material; however, audiences require clear guideposts through longer team presentations. Also, courtesies such as maintaining eye contact, thanking the previous speaker, and clearing the presentation area for the next speaker communicate an important message that the presenters are in sync and work well together.

- **Deliver as a team.** You must present a unified look and communicate to the audience that you care about the team. Spend your time on the "sideline" paying close attention to the current presenter, monitoring the audience for feedback, and being ready to assist the presenter with equipment malfunctions, handouts, and so on. Avoid side conversations and reading notes, yawning, or coughing. To keep an audience engaged in a team presentation, Frank Carillo recommends that team members not presenting should focus on the presenter at least two-thirds of the time. "It may be the 27th time you've heard it, but for that audience it's the first time. Keep it fresh for the listeners."[19]

- **Field questions as a team.** Decide in advance who will field questions to avoid awkward stares and silence that erode the audience's confidence in your team. Normally, the person presenting a section is the logical person to field questions about that section. You can refer questions to team members who are more knowledgeable, but avoid pleading looks for someone else to rescue you. Rather, check visually to see if the person wants to respond and ask if he or she would like to add information. Tactfully contradict other presenters *only* when the presenter makes a mistake that will cause misunderstanding or confusion. While you should be ready to help presenters having difficulty, resist the urge to tack on your response to a presenter's response when the question has already been answered adequately.

Distance Presentations

Videoconferencing has been used for some time for large, high-exposure activities, such as quarterly executive staff presentations, companywide addresses, new product launches, and crisis management. The technology's lower cost, improved quality, and increased ease of use have opened videoconferencing to many settings.

Substantial cost savings from reduced travel is a compelling reason for companies to use videoconferencing. Threats of terrorism and contagious disease provide more reasons for companies to restrict business travel and look for alternative delivery methods. In addition, important communication benefits, such as the following, can be achieved with videoconferencing:[20]

Become proficient in delivering and participating through distance technology.

- improving employee productivity by calling impromptu videoconferences to clear up issues
- involving more people in key decisions rather than limiting important discussions to those who are allowed to travel
- involving expertise critical to the mission, regardless of geographic boundaries
- creating a consistent corporate culture rather than depending on memos to describe company policy
- improving employees' quality of life by reducing travel time that often cuts into personal time (e.g., Saturday night layovers for a reasonable airfare)

Internet conferencing, or *webcasting*, allows a company to conduct a presentation in real time over the Internet simultaneously with a conference telephone call. Because it runs on each participant's Internet browser, a presentation can reach hundreds of locations at once. While listening to the call, participants can go to a designated website and view slides or a PowerPoint presentation that is displayed in sync with the speaker's statements being heard on the phone. Participants key comments and questions in chat boxes or press a keypad system to respond to an audience poll, thus giving valuable feedback without interrupting the speaker.

Companies deliver live Web presentations on issues ranging from internal briefings on new developments and organizational and procedural changes to product strategy and training presentations. Ernst & Young uses Web presentations to announce organizational changes and has found it to be an effective alternative to memos and emails that weren't always remembered or understood. People most affected by an organizational change are able to interact with leaders announcing the change.

Follow these guidelines for adapting your presentation skills to videoconferences and Web presentations:

- **Determine whether a distance delivery method is appropriate for the presentation.** Is the presentation purpose suited to the technology? Can costs in time, money, and human energy be justified? Are key people willing and able to participate? For example, a videoconference for a formal presentation such as an important speech by the CEO to a number of locations justifies the major expense and brings attention to the importance of the message. Distance delivery formats are inappropriate for presentations that cover highly sensitive or confidential issues, for persuasive or problem-solving meetings where no relationship has been established among the participants, and whenever participants are unfamiliar with and perhaps unsupportive of the technology.

- **Establish rapport with the participants prior to the distance presentation.** If possible, meet with or phone participants beforehand to get to know them and gain insights about their attitudes. This rapport will enhance your ability to interpret subtle nonverbal cues and to cultivate the relationship further through the distance format. Emailing or faxing a short questionnaire or posting presentation slides with a request for questions is an excellent way to establish a connection with participants and to ensure that the presentation is tailored to audience needs. Some enterprising distance presenters engage participants in email discussions before the presentation and then use this dialogue to develop positive interaction during the presentation.

- **Become proficient in delivering and participating through distance technology.** Begin by becoming familiar with the equipment and the surroundings.

internet conferencing
a method of real–time conferencing that allows a company to conduct a presentation in real time over the Internet simultaneously with a conference telephone call; also called webcasting

Although technical support staff might be available to manage equipment and transmission tasks, your goal is to concentrate on the contribution you are to make and not your intimidation with the delivery method.

○ **Concentrate on projecting positive nonverbal messages.** Keep a natural, friendly expression; relax and smile. Avoid the tendency to stare into the camera. Instead, look naturally at the entire audience as you would in a live presentation. Speak clearly with as much energy as you can. If a lag occurs between the video and audio transmission, adjust your timing to avoid interrupting other speakers. Use gestures to reinforce points, but avoid fast or excessive motion that will appear blurry. Avoid side conversations, coughing, and clearing your throat, which could trigger voice-activated microphones. Pay close attention to other presenters to guard against easy distraction in a distance environment and to capture subtle nonverbal cues. You will need to judge the vocal tone of the person asking a question because you might not see faces.

○ **Adjust camera settings to enhance communication.** Generally, adjust the camera so that all participants can be seen, but zoom in more closely on participants when you wish to clearly observe nonverbal language. Project a wide-angle shot of yourself during rapport-building comments at the presentation's beginning and zoom in to signal the start of the agenda or to emphasize an important point during the presentation. Some systems accommodate a split screen, but others allow participants to view either you or your presentation visuals only. You will want to switch the camera

between a view of you and your visuals, depending on what is needed at the time.

• **Develop high-quality graphics appropriate for the particular distance format.** Even more than in a live presentation, you will need graphics to engage and maintain participants' attention. Graphics are a welcome variation to the "talking head"—you—displayed on the screen for long periods. Some companies provide assistance from a webmaster or graphics support staff in preparing slide shows specifically for distance presentations. Also, e-conferencing companies will develop and post presentation slides and host live Web presentations including managing email messages and audience polling. Regardless of the support you receive, you should understand basic guidelines for preparing effective visuals for videoconferencing and Web presentations.

○ **Videoconferences.** Readability of text will be a critical issue when displaying visuals during a videoconference because text becomes fuzzy when transmitted through compressed video. Select large, sturdy fonts and choose a color scheme that provides high contrast between the background and the text. Stay with a tested color scheme such as dark blue background, yellow title text, and white bulleted list text to ensure readability. Projecting your visuals ahead of time so you can adjust the color scheme, font selections, and other design elements is an especially good idea.

○ **Web presentations.** In addition to considering overall appeal, clarity, and readability, Web presentations must be designed for minimal load time and compatibility with various computers. For your first presentation, consider using a Web template in your electronic presentations software and experiment with the appropriateness of other designs as you gain experience.

Stand-alone presentations designed specifically for Web delivery require unique design strategies to compensate for the absence of a speaker.[21]

- Consider posting text-based explanations in the notes view area or adding vocal narration.

- Develop interactive slide formats that allow viewers to navigate to the most useful information in your presentation. For example, design an agenda slide that includes hyperlinks to the first slide in each section of the presentation.

- Select simple, high-quality graphics that convey ideas effectively.

- Plan limited animation that focuses audience attention on specific ideas on the slide.

- Consider adding video if bandwidth is not an issue.

Preparing Résumés and Application Messages

Preparing for the Job Search

OBJECTIVES

1 Prepare for employment by considering relevant information about yourself as it relates to job requirements.

2 Identify career opportunities using traditional and electronic methods.

3 Prepare an organized, persuasive résumé that is adapted for print and electronic postings.

4 Utilize employment tools other than the résumé that can enhance employability.

5 Write an application message that effectively introduces an accompanying print (designed) or electronic résumé.

Managing your career begins with recognizing that securing a new job is less important than assessing the impact of that job on your life. Work isn't something that happens from 8 A.M. to 5 P.M., with life happening after 5 P.M. Life and work are interconnected, and true satisfaction comes from being able to fully express yourself in what you do. This means merging who you are—your values, emotions, capabilities, and desires—with the activities you perform on the job.[1]

> ⊠ **OBJECTIVE 1**
>
> Prepare for employment by considering relevant information about yourself as it relates to job requirements.

An ideal job provides satisfaction at all of Maslow's need levels, from basic economic to self-actualizing needs. The right job for you will not be drudgery; the work itself will be satisfying and give you a sense of well-being. Synchronizing your work with your core beliefs and talents leads to enthusiasm and fulfillment. You will probably work 10,000 days of your life, not including time spent commuting and on other related activities. Why spend all this time doing something unfulfilling when you could just as easily spend it doing what you enjoy?

Your **résumé** is a vital communication tool that

résumé
a vital communication tool that provides a basis for judgment about a person's capabilities on the job

© iStockphoto.com/Alexandr Tovstenko

provides a basis for judgment about your capabilities on the job. In preparing this document, your major tasks will be gathering essential information about yourself and the job using traditional and electronic resources, planning and organizing the résumé to showcase your key qualifications, and adapting the résumé for various types of delivery. You will need to supplement your résumé with examples of your accomplishments and abilities. Finally, you'll prepare persuasive application messages appropriate for the delivery of your résumé.

Gathering Essential Information

The job search begins with research—collecting, compiling, and analyzing information—in order to assess your marketability. The research phase of the job search involves the steps shown in Figure 13-1 on the next page and are summarized as follows:

1. **Gather relevant information for decision making.** Complete a self-assessment to identify your own job-related qualifications, and an analysis of the career field that interests you and of a specific job in that

© jeka/Shutterstock

Figure 13-1 *Process of Applying for a Job*

STEP 1	STEP 2	STEP 3	STEP 4	STEP 5
Conduct research and analysis of self, career, and job	Identify a job listing using traditional and electronic sources	Prepare targeted résumé and application message in required formats	Consider supplementing the résumé: Portfolio (print or electronic) or video recording	Interview with companies

RÉSUMÉ PRESENTATION AND DELIVERY OPTIONS

Print (Designed)
- Mail to company accompanied by application letter
- Mail as follow-up to electronic submission

Scannable
- Print résumé formatted for computer scanning

Electronic Postings
- Email to network contacts, career and corporate sites, and career service centers
- Online form
- Electronic portfolio at personal website
- Beamer to PDA or cell phone

© Cengage Learning 2013

field. Follow up with an interview of a career person in your field to acquire additional information.

2. **Prepare a company/job profile.** Compile the information you gathered into a format that allows you to compare your qualifications with the company and job requirements. This organized information will help you determine a possible match between you and the potential job.

3. **Identify unique selling points and specific support.** Determine several key qualifications and accomplishments that enhance your marketability. These are the key selling points you'll target in your résumé and later in a job interview.

Identifying Potential Career Opportunities

Plan to begin your job search for prospective employers months in advance. Waiting too long to begin and then hurrying through the job search process could affect your ability to land a satisfying job.

Before you begin, take the time to develop an organized strategy for your search efforts. You might download a template such as Microsoft's job search log (**http://office.microsoft.com/en-us/templates/results.aspx?qu=job%20search%20log**) or invest in software such as Winway Résumé and Résumé Maker Deluxe to simplify the task of tracking your contacts. You'll need a record of the name, address, email address, and telephone number of each potential employer. Later, record the date of each job contact you make and receive (along with what you learned from the contact), the name of the contact person, the date you sent a résumé, and so on.

Your search for potential career opportunities likely will involve traditional and electronic job search sources.

Using Traditional Sources

Traditional means of locating a job include printed sources, networks, career services centers, employers' offices, employment agencies and contractors, and professional organizations.

Printed Sources. Numerous printed sources are useful in identifying firms in need of employees. Responses to advertised positions in the employment sections of newspapers should be made as quickly as possible after the ad is circulated. If your résumé is received early and is impressive, you could get a favorable response before other applications are received. If an ad requests that responses be sent to a box number without giving a name, be cautious. The employer could be legitimate but does not want present employees to know about the ad or does not want applicants to phone or drop by. However, you have a right to be suspicious of someone who wants to remain obscure while learning everything you reveal in your résumé. Print job listings can also be found in company newsletters, industry directories, and trade and professional publications, which often are available on the Internet.

Networks. The majority of job openings are never advertised. Therefore, developing a network of contacts is often the most valuable source of information about jobs. Your network could include current and past employers, guest speakers in your classes or at student organization meetings, business contacts you met while interning or participating in shadowing or over-the-shoulder experiences, and so on. Let these individuals know the type of job you are seeking and ask their advice for finding employment in today's competitive market.

Career Services Centers. You will want to register with your college's career services center at least three semesters before you graduate. Typically, the center has a website and a browsing room loaded with career information and job announcement bulletins. Career counseling is available at most career services centers including workshops on résumé writing, interviewing, etiquette, mock interviews, "mocktail" parties for learning to mingle in pre-interview social events, and more. Through the center, you can learn about job fairs at which you can meet prospective employers and schedule on-campus, phone, and video interviews with company recruiters.

Most career services centers use electronic tracking systems. Rather than submitting printed résumés, students input their résumés into a computer file following the specific requirements of the tracking system used by the college or university. A search of the résumé database generates an interview roster of the top applicants for a campus recruiter's needs. Some centers assist students in preparing electronic portfolios to supplement their résumés.

Employers' Offices. Employers who have not advertised their employment needs might respond favorably to a phone or personal inquiry. The receptionist might be able to provide useful information, direct you to someone with whom you can talk, or set up an appointment.

Employment Agencies and Contractors. City, county, state, and federal employment agencies provide free or inexpensive services. Some agencies offer online listings or phone recordings so that applicants can get information about job opportunities and procedures for using their services. The fee charged by private agencies is paid by either the employee or the employer and usually is based on the first month's salary and due within a few months. Some agencies specialize in finding high-level executives or specialists for major firms. Employment contractors specialize in providing temporary employees and might be able to place you in a position on a temporary basis until you find a full-time job.

Professional Organizations. Officers of professional organizations, through their contacts with members, can be good sources of information about job opportunities. Much job information is exchanged at meetings of professional associations. In addition to job listings in journals or organization websites, interviews are sometimes conducted at conference locations.

In addition to the professional growth that comes from membership in professional organizations, active participation is a good way to learn about jobs. Guest speakers share valuable information about the industry and its career and job opportunities. Employers are often favorably impressed when membership and experiences gained are included on the résumé and discussed during an interview. They are even more impressed if the applicant has been an officer in the organization, as it indicates leadership, community commitment, and willingness to serve without tangible reward, social acceptance, or high level of aspiration. By joining and actively participating in professional, social, and honorary organizations, you increase your opportunities to develop rapport with peers and professors and gain an edge over less-involved applicants.

Using Electronic Job Searches

An increasing number of companies and job hunters are using the Internet to assist in various stages of the job search process. Convenience, speed, and accessibility are all reasons for the popularity of electronic job searches among human resources managers. The cost of electronic recruiting is lower than traditional methods, and applicants and employers can respond more quickly. Job seekers can use the Internet to complement rather than replace the traditional methods previously discussed.

Locating Career Guidance Information. According to one career consultant, "Most people in the old days could go into an organization [during a job interview] and not really know about it and hope for the best. Now, people can understand the organization before they even apply."[2] The Internet places at your fingertips a wealth of information that will prepare you for the job interview if you use it as a research tool. Suggestions follow for effectively using the career guidance information you can locate on the Internet:

- **Visit career sites for information related to various phases of the job search.** You'll find a wide range of timely discussions at career sites: planning a job search, finding a job you love, researching employers, working a career fair, crafting winning résumés and cover letters, negotiating a salary, and so on.

- **Visit corporate websites to learn about companies.** You can locate information online for targeting your résumé appropriately and to prepare for the job interview. Read mission statements or descriptions of services to see how the organization describes itself, and review the annual report and strategic plan to learn about the financial condition and predicted growth rates. Search for "What's New" or "News" sections promoting new developments, as well as career opportunities and job postings. Evaluating the development and professional nature of the website will give you

an impression of the organization. Supplement this information with independent sources to confirm the company's stability and status, as negative news likely will not be posted on the website.

- **Identify specific skills companies are seeking.** Study the job descriptions provided on corporate home pages and job sites to identify the skills required for the job and the latest industry buzzwords. Use this information to target your résumé to a specific job listing and to generate keywords for an electronic résumé.

- **Network electronically with prospective employers.** It's easy to network online by attending electronic job fairs, chatting with career counselors, participating in news groups and listservs applicable to your field, and corresponding by email with contacts in companies. The value of these electronic networking experiences is to learn about an industry and career, seek valued opinions, and uncover potential job opportunities. By applying effective communication strategies for an online community, you can make a good impression, create rapport with employment contacts online, and polish your interviewing skills.

Identifying Job Listings. You can use the Internet to locate job opportunities in several ways:

- Look in the employment section of companies' corporate websites to see if they are advertising job openings.

- Search the electronic databases of job openings of third-party services.

- Access online job classifieds from daily and trade newspapers. CareerBuilder (**www.careerbuilder.com**) offers the classifieds of a number of major newspapers.

- Subscribe to a newsgroup through UseNext (**http://office.microsoft.com/en-us/templates/results.aspx?qu=job%20search%20log**) that gives you access to jobs by geographic location and specific job categories.

- Subscribe to services such as America Online (**http://office.microsoft.com/en-us/templates/results.aspx?qu=job%20search%20log**) that provide job search sites and services by keying "Career."

Online and printed sources will help you learn to search particular databases. The following general suggestions will help you get started:

- Input words and phrases that describe your skills rather than job titles because job titles vary by company.

- Use specific phrases such as "entry-level job" or "job in advertising" rather than "job search."

- Start with a wider job description term, such as "pharmaceutical sales jobs," then narrow down to the specific subject, geographic region, state, and so forth.

- Don't limit yourself to one search engine; try several and bookmark interesting sites.
- Stay focused on your goal and don't get distracted as you go.

Searching for useful career sites among the hundreds available can be quite time consuming. CareerBuilder, JobCentral, and Monster.com are major career sites offering a wide array of information and services.

Planning a Targeted Résumé

In order to match your interests and qualifications with available jobs, you'll need an effective résumé. To win a job interview in today's tight market where job seekers outnumber positions, you need more than a general résumé that documents your education and work history. The powerful wording of a **targeted résumé** reflects the requirements of a specific job listing that you have identified through traditional and electronic job search methods.

⊠ OBJECTIVE 2

Identify career opportunities using traditional and electronic methods.

An employer typically scans résumés quickly looking for reasons to reject the applicant, schedule an interview, or place in a stack for rereading. This initial scan and a second brief look for those who make the cut give little time to explain why you are the best person for the job. To grab an employer's attention, you must selectively choose *what to say*, *how to say it*, and *how to arrange it* on the page so that it can be read quickly but thoroughly. A concise, informative, easy-to-read summary of your relevant qualifications will demonstrate that you possess the straightforward communication skills demanded in today's information-intensive society.

The goal of the résumé is to get an interview, so ask yourself this question: "Does including this information increase my chances of getting an interview?" If the answer is "Yes," include the information; if the answer is "No," omit the information and use the space to develop your qualifications. When selecting information to be included, you must also be cautious of the temptation to inflate your résumé to increase your chances of being hired.

Another name for "résumé" is *"curriculum vitae"* or "CV," which is Latin for "course of one's life."

Standard Parts of a Résumé

A winning résumé contains standard parts that are adapted to highlight key qualifications for a specific job. The sample résumés and in-depth explanation of each standard part provided in Figures 13-2 to 13-5 (see pages 229–235) will prepare you for creating a résumé that describes your qualifications best.

Identification

Your objective is to provide information that will allow the interviewer to reach you. Include your name, current address, phone number, and email address. Provide a clear, benign email address that reflects a positive impression (e.g., no "mustangsally"). You should also include your website address to provide access to more detailed information.

To ensure that the interviewer can quickly locate the identification information, center it on the page or use graphic design elements to call attention to your name. You should include a permanent address (parent's or other relative's address) if you are interviewing when classes are not in session. Leave a clear, straightforward greeting on your phone that portrays you as a person serious about securing a job. Eliminate music, clever sayings, or background noise.

Job and/or Career Objective

Following the "Identification" section, state your job/career objective—the job you want. Interviewers can see quickly whether the job you seek matches the one they have to offer. A good job/career objective must be specific enough to be meaningful yet general enough to apply to

targeted résumé
a résumé that reflects the requirements of a specific job listing

a variety of jobs. The following example illustrates a general objective that has been revised to describe a specific job:

General Objective	Specific Objective
A challenging position that offers an opportunity for growth.	Entry into financial assets training program with advancement to portfolio management.
A position with a stable financial institution that provides an opportunity for development and career advancement.	Position with an innovative marketing team with a special interest in new brand development.

Some experts argue that a statement of your job or career objective can limit your job opportunities; your objective should be obvious from your qualifications. In general, however, making your objective clear at the beginning assures the interviewer that you have a definite career goal.

Career Summary

To survive the interviewer's 40-second scan, you must provide a compelling reason for a more thorough review of your résumé. Craft a persuasive introductory statement that quickly synthesizes your most transferable skills, accomplishments, and attributes and place it in a section labeled "Summary" or "Professional Profile."

In this synopsis of your key qualifications, communicate why you should be hired. Your answer should evolve naturally from the career objective and focus on your ability to meet the needs of the company you have identified from your extensive research. Combining the career objective with the career statement is an acceptable strategy as noted in the following examples:

Separate Objective and Career Summary

Objective Obtain an entry-level human resources position in an international company with an opportunity to specialize in global management strategies.
Career Summary Dual degrees in human resource management and international business, including study abroad in Asia; internship experience with three multinational corporations; self-motivated; achievement oriented.

Combined Objective with Career Summary

Professional Profile Position in corporate communications with advancement potential. Internship experience with two leading public relations firms, creating press materials and web site content. Strong written and oral communication skills.

Linked Objective and Career Summary

Profile Position as sales representative in which demonstrated commission selling and hard work bring rewards.
Accomplishments:
- Three years' straight commission sales
- Average of $35,000–$55,000 a year in commissioned earnings
- Consistent success in development and growth of territories

A high-impact career summary, once considered optional, has become a standard section of résumés in today's fast-paced information age. Develop your résumé to skillfully target the requirements of a specific position; then compose a career summary sure to interest any interviewer who instantly sees an applicant with exactly the skills needed.

Qualifications

The "Qualifications" section varies depending on the information identified in the analysis of self, career, and job. This information is used to divide your qualifications into appropriate parts, label them appropriately, and arrange them in the best sequence. Usually, qualifications stem from your education and work experience (words that appear as headings in the résumé). Order these categories according to which you perceive as more impressive to the employer, with the more impressive category appearing first. For example, education is usually the chief qualification of a recent college graduate. However, a sales representative with related work experience might list experience first, particularly if the educational background is inadequate for the job sought.

Education. Beginning with the most recent, list the degree, major, school, and graduation date. Include a blank line between schools for easy reading. The interviewer will probably want to know first whether you have the appropriate degree, then the institution, and then other details. Recent or near college graduates should omit high school activities because that information is "old news." However, include high school activities if they provide a pertinent dimension to your qualifications. For example, having attended high school abroad is a definite advantage to an applicant seeking employment in an international firm. In addition, high school accomplishments could be relevant for freshmen or sophomores seeking cooperative education assignments, scholarships, or part-time jobs. Of course, this information will be replaced with college activities when the résumé is revised for subsequent jobs or other uses.

Include overall and major grade-point averages if they are B or better—but be prepared to discuss any omissions during an interview. Some recruiters recommend that every candidate include his or her grade-point average, since an omission might lead the reader to assume the worst. Honors and achievements that relate directly to education can be incorporated in this section or included in a separate section. Listing scholarships, appearance on academic lists, and initiation into honor societies is common; but consider also including business-relevant skills you've developed including client projects, team building, and field experiences. If honors and achievements are included in the "Education" section, be sure to include plenty of white space or use bullets to highlight these points (see Figure 13-2 on page 229 and Figure 13-4 on page 231).

The "Education" section could also include a list of special skills and abilities such as foreign language and computer competency. A list of courses typically required in your field is unnecessary and occupies valuable space. However, you should include any courses, workshops, or educational experiences that are not usual requirements, such as internships, cooperative education semesters, "shadowing," and study abroad.

Work Experience. The "Work Experience" section provides information about your employment history. For each job held, list the job title, company name, dates of employment, primary responsibilities, and key accomplishments. The jobs can be listed in reverse chronological order (beginning with the most recent) or in order of job relatedness. Begin with the job that most obviously relates to the job being sought if you have gaps in your work history, if the job you are seeking is very different from the job you currently hold, or if you are just entering the job market and have little, if any, related work experience.

Arrange the order and format of information about each job (dates, job title, company, description, and accomplishments) so that the most important information is emphasized—but format all job information consistently. If you have held numerous jobs in a short time, embed dates of employment within the text rather than surround them with white space. Give related job experience added emphasis by listing it first or surrounding it with white space.

Employers are interested in how you can contribute to their bottom line, so a winning strategy involves concentrating on accomplishments and achievements. Begin with the job title and company name that provides basic information about your duties, and then craft powerful descriptions of the quality and scope of your performance. These bullet points will provide deeper insight into your capability, ambition, and personality and set you apart from other applicants who take the easy route of providing only a work history.

Return to the in-depth analysis you completed at the beginning of the job search process to recall insights as to how you can add immediate value to this company. Consider the following questions to spur your recognition of marketable skills from your education, work, and community experiences.[3]

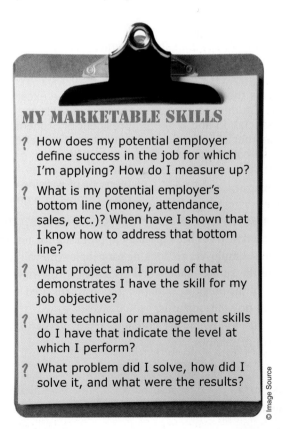

MY MARKETABLE SKILLS

? How does my potential employer define success in the job for which I'm applying? How do I measure up?

? What is my potential employer's bottom line (money, attendance, sales, etc.)? When have I shown that I know how to address that bottom line?

? What project am I proud of that demonstrates I have the skill for my job objective?

? What technical or management skills do I have that indicate the level at which I perform?

? What problem did I solve, how did I solve it, and what were the results?

© Image Source

Because interviewers spend such a short time reading résumés, the style must be direct and simple. Therefore, a résumé should use crisp phrases to help employers see the value of the applicant's education and experiences. To save space and to emphasize what you have accomplished, use these stylistic techniques:

1. Omit pronouns referring to yourself (*I, me, my*).

2. Use subject-understood sentences.

3. Begin sentences with action verbs as shown in the following examples:

Instead of	Use
I had responsibility for developing sales materials.	Developed sales materials, including brochures and web site promotions.
My duties included meeting with potential clients to review financial products.	Met with potential clients and used interpersonal communication skills to sell wide range of financial products.
I was the treasurer of my fraternity and managed a charitable fund-raising event.	Managed a $200,000-plus budget and organized a charitable fund-raising event that garnered $15,000, a 25 percent increase over previous year.
I worked in retail sales, selling fashions and accessories.	Named salesperson of the year for sales of more than $50,000.
I was the president of the Student Marketing Association and a member of a winning case-competition team.	Demonstrated excellent leadership skills as president of Student Marketing Association and collaborative teamwork skills as member of winning case-competition group.

Action verbs are especially appropriate for résumés, because employers are looking for people who will work. Note the subject-understood sentences in the right column of the previous example: Action words used as first words provide emphasis.

The following list contains action verbs that are useful in résumés:

achieved	drafted	participated
analyzed	increased	planned
assisted	initiated	recruited
compiled	managed	streamlined
developed	organized	wrote

To avoid a tone of egotism, do not use too many adjectives or adverbs that seem overly strong. Plan to do some careful editing after writing your first draft.

Honors and Activities. Make a trial list of any other information that qualifies you for the job. Divide the list into appropriate divisions and then select an appropriate label. Your heading might be "Honors and Activities." You might include a section for "Activities," "Leadership Activities," or "Memberships," depending on the items listed. You might also include a separate section on "Military Service," "Civic Activities," "Volunteer Work," or "Interests." If you have only a few items under each category, use a more general term and combine the lists. If your list is lengthy, divide it into more than one category as interviewers prefer "bite-size" pieces that are easy to read and remember.

Resist the urge to include everything you have ever done; keep in mind that every item you add distracts from other information. Consider summarizing information that is relevant but does not merit several separate lines—for example, "Involved in art, drama, and choral groups." To decide whether to include certain information, ask these questions: How closely related is it to the job being sought? Does it provide job-related information that has not been presented elsewhere?

Personal Information

Because a résumé should contain primarily information that is relevant to an applicant's experience and qualifications, you must be selective when including personal information that is not related to the job you are seeking. The space could be used more effectively to include more about your qualifications or to add more white space. Personal information is commonly placed at the end of the résumé just above the "References" section because it is less important than qualifications (education, experience, and activities).

Under the 1964 Civil Rights Act (and subsequent amendments) and the Americans with Disabilities Act (ADA), employers cannot make hiring decisions based on gender, age, marital status, religion, national origin, or disability. Employers prefer not to receive information about these protected areas because questions could be raised about whether the information was used in the hiring decision.

Follow these guidelines related to personal information:

- **Do not include personal information that could lead to discriminatory hiring.** Exclude height, weight, color of hair and eyes, and a personal photograph on the résumé.

Living Online?

Your Facebook or MySpace profile, photos, and "innermost" thoughts create a shadow résumé that may hurt your employment opportunities far into the future. A recent employer survey indicated that 44 percent of employers use social networking sites to examine the profiles of job candidates, and 39 percent have looked up the profile of a current employee.[4]

- **Reveal ethnic background (and other personal information) only if it is job related.** For example, certain businesses might be actively seeking employees in certain ethnic groups because the ethnic background is a legitimate part of the job description. For such a business, ethnic information is useful and appreciated.

- **Include personal information (other than information covered by employment legislation) that will strengthen your résumé.** Select information that is related to the job you are seeking or that portrays you as a well-rounded, happy individual off the job. Include interests, hobbies, favorite sports, and willingness to relocate. You can also include the following topics if you have not covered them elsewhere in the résumé: spoken and written communication skills, computer competency, foreign language or computer skills, military service, community service, scholastic honors, job-related hobbies, and professional association memberships.

- **Consider whether personal information might be controversial.** For example, listing a sport that an interviewer might perceive to be overly time consuming or dangerous would be questionable. An applicant seeking a position with a religious or political organization could benefit from revealing a related affiliation.

References

Providing potential employers a list of references (people who have agreed to supply information about you when requested) complements your employment credentials. Listing names, addresses, phone numbers, and email addresses of people who can provide information about you adds credibility to the résumé. Employers, former employers, and college instructors are good possibilities. Friends, relatives, and neighbors are not (because of their perceived bias in your favor). Some career experts recommend including a peer to document your ability to work as a member of a team, an important job skill in today's team-oriented environment.[5] According to Bob Daugherty, who heads U.S. recruiting for PricewaterhouseCoopers, the best references are people who work for the organization you are looking to join.[6] You'll gain these employee referrals through strong relationships developed through proactive and professional networking through traditional and electronic means. Update your reference list often to be certain that your choices remain relevant and credible (e.g., none are deceased or dismissed for embezzlement).

References can be handled on the résumé in several ways. As the closing section of your résumé, you can provide a list of references, include a brief statement that references are available on request or from a career services center, or omit any statement regarding references assuming that references are not needed until after an interview. You can list references directly on the résumé if you have limited qualifications to include, if you know a company interviews applicants *after* references are contacted, or when you believe the names of your references will be recognizable in your career field. You could include a statement such as "For references. . ." or "For additional information . . ." and give the address of the career services center of your college or university, the job bank posting your credentials, or the URL of your electronic portfolio.

Withholding references until they are requested prevents unnecessary or untimely requests going to your present employer. This action also conveys genuine courtesy to the references. Even the most enthusiastic references could become apathetic if required to provide recommendations to endless interviewers. For this same reason, be sure to communicate with references regularly if your job search continues longer than expected. Suggestions for communicating with references are discussed in Chapter 14.

When preparing a separate list of references to be given after a successful interview, place the word *References* and your name in a visible position as shown in Figure 13-3 on page 230. Balance the list (name, address, phone number, and relationship of reference to applicant) attractively on the page and use the same paper used for printing the résumé. Whether it is handed to the interviewer personally or mailed, the references page professionally complements your résumé. Confident that you have a good message, you are now ready to put it in writing—to construct a résumé that will impress an employer favorably.

Types of Résumés

The general organization of all résumés is fairly standard: identification (name, address, phone number, and email address), job objective, qualifications, personal information, and references. The primary organizational challenge is in dividing the qualifications section into parts, choosing labels for them, and arranging them in the best sequence. When you review your self-, career, and job analyses data and career/job profile, you will recognize that your qualifications stem mainly from your education and your experience. Your task is to decide how to present these two categories of qualifications. Résumés usually are organized in one of three ways: reverse chronological order (most recent activity listed first), functional order (most important activity listed first), or a chrono-functional, which combines the chronological and functional orders as the name implies. To determine which organizational plan to use, draft your résumé in each.

Chronological Résumé

The **chronological résumé** is the traditional organi-

Résumé appearance is critical.

© iStockphoto.com/Jon Schulte

zational format for résumés. Two headings normally appear in the portion that presents qualifications: "Education" and "Experience." Which one should appear first? Decide which one you think is more impressive to the employer, and put that one first. Within each section, the most recent information is presented first. Reverse chronological order is easier to use and is more common than functional order; however, it is not always more effective.

The chronological résumé is an especially effective format for applicants who have progressed up a clearly defined career ladder and want to move up another rung. Because the format emphasizes dates and job titles, the chronological résumé is less effective for applicants who have gaps in their work histories, are seeking jobs different from the job currently held, or are just entering the job market with little or no experience.[7]

If you choose the chronological format, look at the two headings from the employer's point of view, and reverse their positions if doing so is to your advantage. In the "Experience" section, jobs are listed in reverse-chronological order. Assuming you have progressed typically, your latest job is likely to be more closely related to the job being sought than the first job held. Placing the latest or current job first will give it the emphasis it deserves. Include beginning and ending dates for each job.

Functional Résumé

In a **functional résumé**, points of primary interest to employers—transferable skills—appear in major

---

chronological résumé
the traditional organizational format for résumés with headings that spotlight an applicant's education and experience

functional résumé
the organizational format for résumés that highlights an applicant's transferable skills

headings. These headings highlight what an applicant can *do* for the employer—functions that the applicant can perform well. Under each heading, an applicant could draw from educational and/or work-related experience to provide supporting evidence.

A functional résumé requires a complete analysis of self, career, and the job sought. Suppose, for example, that a person seeking a job as an assistant hospital administrator wants to emphasize qualifications by placing them in major headings. From the hospital's advertisement of the job and from accumulated job appraisal information, an applicant sees this job as both an administrative and a public-relations job. The job requires skill in communicating and knowledge of accounting and finance. Thus, headings in the "Qualifications" section of the résumé could be "Administration," "Public Relations," "Communication," and "Budgeting." Under "Public Relations," for example, an applicant could reveal that a public relations course was taken at State University, from which a degree is to be conferred in May, and that a sales job at ABC Store provided abundant opportunity to apply principles learned. With other headings receiving similar treatment, the qualifications portion reveals the significant aspects of education and experience.

Order of importance is the best sequence for functional headings. If you have prepared an accurate self- and job analysis, the selected headings will highlight points of special interest to the employer. Glancing at headings only, an employer can see that you understand the job's requirements and have the qualities needed for success.

Having done the thinking required for preparing a functional résumé, you are well prepared for a question that is commonly asked in interviews: "What can you do for us?" The answer is revealed in your major headings. They emphasize the functions you can perform and the special qualifications you have to offer.

If you consider yourself well qualified, a functional résumé is worth considering. If your education or experience is scant, a functional résumé could be best for you. Using "Education" and "Experience" as headings (as in a chronological résumé) works against your purpose if you have little to report under the headings; the format would emphasize the absence of education or experience.

Chrono-Functional Résumé

The **chrono-functional résumé** combines features of chronological and functional résumés. This format can give quick assurance that educational and experience requirements are met and still use other headings that emphasize qualifications.

Preparing Résumés for Print and Electronic Delivery

Format requirements for résumés have changed significantly in recent years. Whether presented on paper or electronically, the arrangement of a résumé is just as important as the content. If the arrangement is unattractive, unappealing, or in poor taste, the message might never be read. Errors in keyboarding, spelling, and punctuation could be taken as evidence of a poor academic background, lack of respect for the employer, or carelessness. Recognize that résumés serve as your introduction to employers and indicate the quality of work you'll produce.

⊠ **OBJECTIVE 3**

Prepare an organized, persuasive résumé that is adapted for print and electronic postings.

As in preparing other difficult documents, prepare a rough draft as quickly as you can and then revise as many times as needed to prepare an effective résumé that sells you. After you are confident with the résumé, ask at least two other people to check it for you. Carefully select people who are knowledgeable about résumé preparation and the job you are seeking and can suggest ways to present your qualifications more effectively. After you have incorporated those changes, ask a skillful proofreader to review the document.

To accommodate employers' preferences for the presentation and delivery of résumés, you'll need three versions of your résumé as shown in Figure 13-1: a designed résumé printed on paper, a scannable résumé to be read by a computer, and a designed résumé accessible through email and websites.

Preparing a Print (Designed) Résumé

Your print (designed) résumé is considered your primary marketing document, and appearance is critical. To win out among hundreds of competing résumés, it must look professional and reflect current formatting and production standards while maintaining a distinctive conservative tone. Follow these guidelines for designing and producing a highly professional résumé:

chrono-functional résumé
a résumé that combines features of chronological and functional résumés

- **Develop an appealing résumé format that highlights your key qualifications and distinguishes your résumé.** Use the power of your word processing software for style enhancements rather than settle for overused, inflexible templates. Study the example résumés in this chapter and models from other sources for ideas for enhancing the style, readability, and overall impact of the document. Then create a custom design that best highlights your key qualifications.

- **Format information for quick, easy reading.** To format your résumé so that it can be read at a glance, follow these guidelines:

  o Use attention-getting headings to partition major divisions, and add graphic lines and borders to separate sections of text.

  o Use an outline format when possible to list activities and events on separate lines, and include bullets to emphasize multiple points.

  o Use 10-point fonts or larger to avoid reader eye strain.

  o Use type styles and print attributes to emphasize key points. For example, to draw attention to the identification and headings, select a bold sans serif font (e.g., Calibri or Arial) slightly larger than the serif font (e.g., Cambria or Times New Roman) used for the remaining text. Capitalization, indention, and print enhancements (underline, italics, bold), are useful for adding emphasis. Limit the number of type styles and enhancements, however, so the page is clean and simple to read.

  o Include identification on each page of a multiple-page résumé. Place your name and a page number at the top of the second and successive pages with "Continued" at the bottom of the first page. The interviewer is reexposed to your name, and pages can be reassembled if separated.

- **Create an appealing output to produce top professional quality.**

  o Check for consistency throughout the résumé. Consistency in spacing, end punctuation, capitalization, appearance of headings, and sequencing of details within sections will communicate your eye for detail and commitment to high standards.

  o Balance the résumé attractively on the page with approximately equal margins. Allow generous white space so the résumé looks uncluttered and easy to read.

- **Consider adding a statement of your creativity and originality.** Be certain that your creativity will not be construed as gimmicky and distract from the content of the résumé. Demonstrating creativity is particularly useful for fields such as advertising, public relations, graphic design, and those requiring computer proficiency.

  o Select paper of a standard size (8 1/2" by 11"), neutral color (white, buff, or gray), and high quality (preferably 24-pound, 100-percent cotton fiber). Consider using a mailing envelope large enough to accommodate the résumé without folding. The unfolded documents on the reader's desk will get favorable attention and will scan correctly if posted to an electronic database.

  o Print with a laser printer that produces high-quality output. Position paper so the watermark is read across the sheet in the same direction as the printing.

Some employers insist that the "best" length for a résumé is one page, stating that long résumés are often ignored. However, general rules about length are more flexible. Most students and recent graduates can present all relevant résumé information on one page. However, as you gain experience, you might need two or more pages to format an informative, easy-to-read résumé. A résumé forced on one page will likely have narrow margins and large blocks of run-on text (multiple lines with no space to break them). This dense format is unappealing and complicates the interviewer's task of skimming quickly for key information.

The rule about length is simple: Be certain your résumé contains only relevant information presented as concisely as possible. A one-page résumé that includes irrelevant information is too long. A two-page résumé that omits relevant information is too short.

The résumés illustrated in Figures 13-2 and 13-4 (see page 231) demonstrate the organizational principles for the chronological and functional résumés. A references page is illustrated in Figure 13-3 on page 230. Study the various layouts to decide on one that will highlight your key qualifications most effectively.

Preparing Electronic Résumé Submissions

To this point you have focused on the preparation of a print résumé. However, in the digital age of instant information, you'll use various online methods to apply for a job and present your qualifications to prospective employers.

The easiest and most common method of putting your résumé online is through emailing a résumé to a job bank for posting or to a networking contact who asked you to send a résumé. Many job banks, corporate sites, and career services centers require you to respond to specific openings by completing an online form or

Figure 13-2  *Chronological Résumé*

Tina Freeman
159 Figueroa St.
Mesa, AZ 85009
801-755-4918
tfree@gmail.com

OBJECTIVE Challenging position in commercial lending with advancement opportunities.

CAREER SUMMARY Honors student with degree emphasis in finance; three years of experience in banking; internship in commercial lending department; strong communication skills; achievement oriented

EDUCATION Bachelor of Business Administration, finance emphasis
Central Arizona State University, expected graduation, May 2012
GPA 3.9 on a 4.0 scale

RELATED EXPERIENCE Teller (part-time), Mesa Bank and Loan, Mesa, AZ, 2009 to present
- Provide customer service support to small business and individual customers, answering questions about their accounts and banking products and services.
- Maintained a balanced cash drawer of $3,000 daily.
- Attended quarterly training seminars on banking products and services

Intern, **Commercial Lending Department**, FarWest Bank, Phoenix, AZ, summer, 2011
- Prepared application documents for small commercial loans.
- Met with clients to introduce them to loan product options.
- Communicated with clients about the status of the loan process.

VOLUNTEER WORK Phoenix Regional Food Bank, Phoenix, AZ 2008 to present
Coordinate delivery of bulk shipments to five local distribution centers

LANGUAGES Native fluency in English
Conversational Spanish

SKILLS Proficient in Microsoft Office Suite

HONORS AND ACTIVITIES Dean's List (3.6 GPA or higher)
Beta Gamma Sigma (business honor society, upper 10% of senior class)
Student Investment Club

- Includes email address that reflects professional image.

- Reveals position sought and powerful summary of qualifications.

- Positions education as top qualification for recent graduate. Includes high GPA.

- Edges out competition by expanding on related experience and work achievements.

- Emphasizes activities that reflect service attitude, high level of responsibility, and people-orientation.

- Uses separate sections to emphasize proficiencies listed in job requirements.

- Lists academic recognitions and highlights relevant skills.

- Omits references to use space for additional qualifications; references furnished when requested.

Format Pointers
Places name at top center for easy viewing (top right is also acceptable). Uses bold font to distinguish identification section and headings from remaining text.

Uses two-column format for easy location of specific sections.

Creates visual appeal through custom format rather than commonly used template, short readable sections focusing on targeted qualifications, and streamlined bulleted lists.

Diversity Considerations
Follows standard format and rules for résumés for application with U.S. company. Specific formats vary for specific countries and federal government.

© Cengage Learning 2013

"The best references are people who work for the organization you are looking to join."

—Bob Daugherty,
U.S. Recruiting,
PricewaterhouseCoopers

Figure 13-3 GOOD *References Page*

Tina Freeman
159 Figueroa St.
Mesa, AZ 85009
801-755-4918
tfree@gmail.com

REFERENCES

John Oliver
Manager, Commercial Lending
FarWest Bank
P.O. Box 1555
Mesa, AZ 85009
801-555-9000
joliver@farwest.com
Relationship: Immediate supervisor during summer internship, 2011

Dr. Yolanda Rodriquez, Professor
Finance Department
Central Arizona State University
120 Gila Avenue, FIN 240
Mesa, AZ 85009
801-555-8956
yrodriqu@casu.edu
Relationship: Academic adviser and professor for finance courses

Leonard Hawes
Manager of Teller Services
Mesa Bank and Loan
345 Sonora Way
Mesa, AZ 85009
801-555-3209
lhawes@mesabank.com
Relationship: Immediate supervisor, 2009 to present

Include professor and immediate supervisors as references, but excludes friends, relatives, or clergy to avoid potential bias.

Includes for each reference full contact information, including email address if available, and relationship to job applicant.

Format Pointers
Prepares reference page at same time as résumé and makes available immediately after successful interview. Paper (color, texture, and size) and print type match résumé.

Balances references attractively.

© iStockphoto.com/micropic

© Cengage Learning 2013

Figure 13-4  Functional Résumé

Todd Smithers
432 Elm Street
Elk, NV 87009
705-855-4491
tsmith@gmail.com

OBJECTIVE   Position in sales with advancement to marketing and promotion.

CAREER
SUMMARY
- Degree in business administration with three years of part-time experience in sales.
- Develop web site promotion strategies for small-business clients.
- Strong communication skills, particularly in the area of sales and customer service.

RELEVANT
SKILLS

MARKETING AND PROMOTIONS
- Worked as part of a team charged with developing web site promotion strategies for a broad range of clients.
- Designed promotional flyers for video game retailer and distributed to local business community and potential individual customers.
- Worked as part of a team tasked with creating a marketing program for a small business in Marketing Fundamentals course.

TECHNOLOGY SKILLS
- Well-versed in use of Microsoft Office Suite, InDesign, and DreamWeaver.
- Experienced in use of gaming programs and technology.
- Designed and created web sites for clients at a public relations and marketing firm.

COMMUNICATION
- Provided customer service to game enthusiasts by answering questions about gaming products and their functionality.
- Worked with diverse group of students providing coaching as a volunteer math tutor for Sparks Elementary School.
- Collaborated successfully with diverse groups as part of course requirements for business administration degree.

EMPLOYMENT
HISTORY
Marketing intern, Askhaver and Associates, Summer 2011
Sales associate, Gaming & More, 2010 to present (part-time)

EDUCATION   B.S., Business Administration, Central Nevada College, Expected graduation May 2012

REFERENCES   Tim Harris, Partner, Askhaver and Associates, 214 Desert Dr., Reno, NV 89040, 852-203-5678.
Sam Perkins, Manager, Gaming & More, 4506 Central Ave., Reno, NV 89040, 852-334-2121.
Dr. Fred Ware, Advisor, Business Administration, Central Nevada College, P.O. Box 2340, Reno, NV 89040, 852-334-7073.

Includes clear objective and descriptive summary statements to grab attention and invite close reading.

Arranges qualifications into sections that emphasize applicant's relevant skills and accomplishments. Uses headings that show applicant knows what skills are needed to succeed in sales.

Uses employers' names and dates to match skills with work history.

Limits education and work history to quick overview of basic qualifications and accommodates employers' preference for chronological format.

Lists references for employer convenience and to strengthen résumé.

Format Pointers
Places name at top center where it can be easily seen.

Uses bold font to distinguish identification section and headings from remaining text.

Creates visual appeal with easy-to-read columnar format and balanced page arrangement.

pasting your résumé into a designated section of the form. Frequently, you can input information directly on the website or download the form to be submitted by email, fax, or mail. You might also choose to post your résumé on your personal website as part of an electronic portfolio that showcases evidence of your qualifications. You could also develop a **beamer**, or *beamable résumé*, a quick version of your résumé designed in a format suitable for broadcasting on smartphones. Recruiting professionals predict that millions of these electronic résumés will be exchanged silently at conferences, business meetings, and power lunches, similar to exchanging business cards.[8]

Electronic submissions are quick and easy but present new challenges and many opportunities to jeopardize your employment chances and compromise your privacy. Just consider recent struggles you might have faced in dealing with viruses and unwelcomed emails, attempting to access nonworking links, and more. Before sending your résumé into cyberspace, follow these suggestions to ensure that your electronic submission is both professional and technically effective:

- **Choose postings for your résumé with purpose.**
  Online résumé postings are not confidential. Once your résumé is online, anyone can read it, including your current employer. You might also begin to receive junk mail and cold calls from companies who see your résumé online; even more seriously, you could become a victim of identity theft. To protect your privacy online, limit personal information disclosed in the résumé and post only to sites with password protection allowing you to approve the release of your résumé to specific employers. Dating your electronic résumé will also prevent embarrassment should your employer find an old version of your résumé, which could occur as result of exchange of résumés between career sites and delays in updating postings.

  Protect your references' privacy by omitting their names when posting online. Withholding this information will prevent unwelcomed calls by recruiters and other inappropriate contacts and threats to privacy. Because technology allows broadcast of your résumé to all available positions on a career site, read postings carefully and apply only to those that match your qualifications. This action improves the efficiency of the job selection process for the company and the applicant and depicts fair, ethical behavior.

beamer
a quick version of a résumé designed in a format suitable for broadcasting on smartphones; also called a beamable résumé

inline résumé
a résumé included in the body of an email message

text résumé
a plain text (unformatted) version of a résumé

- **Don't hurry.** The speed, convenience, and informality of filling in online boxes or composing an email cover letter for an attached résumé can lead to sloppiness that reflects negatively on your abilities and attitude. Make sure every aspect of your electronic submission is top-notch just as you would for a print résumé. Provide all information exactly as requested, write concise, clear statements relevant to the job sought, and proofread carefully for grammatical and spelling errors. If you direct an employer to an electronic portfolio, devote necessary time to make it attractive, informative, and technically sound. Double-check your files to ensure they can be opened and retain an appealing format. Finally, read the posting carefully to learn how long your résumé will remain active, how to update it, and how to delete it from the site.

- **Include your résumé in the format requested by the employer or job bank.** You could be instructed to send the résumé as an attachment to the message or include it in the body of an email message, known as an **inline résumé**. The inline résumé is becoming the preferred choice as fear of computer viruses and daily email overload prevent employers from opening attachments.

  Unless instructed to send your attachment in a specific format such as Word, save your résumé and cover letter in one file beginning with the cover letter as an ASCII or Rich Text Format file with line length limited to 65 characters and spacing. This plain text version, referred to as a **text résumé**, removes formatting and lacks the appeal of your designed résumé; however, you can be confident that an employer can open the file and won't have to spend time "cleaning up" your résumé if it doesn't transmit correctly. For this reason, you'll also paste the text version of your résumé below your email message when sending an inline résumé.

  As an added safeguard, send yourself and a couple of friends a copy of the résumé and see how it looks on different computers before sending it out to an employer. If you wish, follow up with a print résumé and cover letter on high-quality paper.

- **Include a keyword summary after the identification section.** You'll want to grab the employer's attention by placing the keywords on the first screen (within the first 24 lines of text). Providing this relevant information will motivate the employer to keep scrolling down to see how the keywords are supported rather than click to the next résumé.

- **Email a cover message to accompany an online résumé.** Some companies consider this cover email message to be prescreening for a job interview. Write a formal, grammatically correct message just as you would if you were sending an application letter in the mail.

Some print résumés become electronic files when they are scanned by the employer into an electronic database where they can be read and sorted by a computer. Companies of all sizes are using **electronic applicant-tracking systems** to increase efficiency of processing the volume of résumés received in a competitive market. Such systems store scanned résumés in an electronic database where they can be sorted by keywords with a resulting ranking of applicants. The system can also automatically prepare letters of rejection and interview offers and store the résumés of hired applicants for future promotion consideration.

When seeking a job with a company that scans résumés into an electronic database, you will need to submit a **scannable résumé** as well as a print résumé that will be read by a person. If you are unsure whether a company scans résumés, call and ask. If still in doubt, take the safe route and submit your résumé in both formats.

Formatting a Scannable Résumé

To ensure that the scanner can read your résumé accurately and clearly, you must prepare a plain résumé with no special formatting. Follow these guidelines to prepare an electronic résumé that can be scanned accurately:

- **Use popular, nondecorative typefaces.** Typefaces such as Cambria and Times New Roman are clear and distinct and will not lose clarity in scanning.

- **Use 10- to 14-point font.** Computers cannot read small, tight print well. With a larger font, your résumé may extend to two pages, but page length is not an issue because a computer is reading the résumé.

- **Do not include italics, underlining, open bullets, or graphic lines and boxes.** Use boldface or all capitals for emphasis. Italicized letters that touch and underlining that runs into the text result in a garbled scanned image. Design elements, such as graphic lines, shading, and shadowing effects can confuse equipment. Use solid bullets (•) because an open bullet (○) could be read as an "o".

- **Use ample white space.** Use at least one-inch margins. Leave plenty of white space between the sections of a résumé so the computer recognizes the partitions.

- **Print on one side of white, standard-size paper with sharp laser print.** Colored and textured paper

scans poorly, and the scanner can pick up dirty specks on a photocopy.

- **Use a traditional résumé format.** Complex layouts that simulate catalogs or newspaper columns can confuse scanners.

- **Do not fold or staple your résumé.** If you must fold it, do not do so on a line of text.

Making a Scannable Résumé Searchable

You have two concerns in preparing a scannable résumé. You want to (1) be certain information is presented in a manner the computer can read, and (2) maximize the number of "hits" your résumé receives in a computerized résumé search. Follow these guidelines for making your print résumé searchable:

- **Position your name as the first readable item on the page.** Follow with your address, phone number, fax number, and email below your name on separate lines.

- **Add powerful keywords in a separate section called "Keywords" or "Keyword Summary" that follows the identification.** To identify key words, ask yourself what words best describe your qualifications. Make maximum use of industry jargon and standard, easily recognizable abbreviations (e.g., B.A., M.S.) in the keyword summary and the body of the résumé, as these buzzwords will likely be matches with the computer's keywords.

- **Format the keyword summary to maximize hits.** Capitalize the first letter of each word and separate each keyword with a period. Position keywords describing your most important qualifications first and move to the least important ones. Order is important because some systems stop scanning after the first 80 keywords. The usual order is (a) job title, occupation, or career field, (b) education, and (c) essential skills for a specific position. Be certain to include keywords that describe interpersonal traits, such as *adaptable, flexible, sensitive, team player, willing to travel, ethical, industrious, innovative, open minded,* and *detail oriented.*

- **Support your keywords with specific facts in the body of the résumé.** Use synonyms of your keywords in the body in the event the computer does not recognize the keyword (e.g., use *M.B.A.*

electronic applicant-tracking systems
systems that increase the efficiency of processing résumés by storing scanned résumés in an electronic database where they can be sorted by keywords with a resulting ranking of applicants

scannable résumé
a résumé formatted to ensure a scanner can accurately read and convert it into a digital format

in the keyword summary and *Master of Business Administration* in the body; use *presentation graphics software* in the keyword summary and a specific program in the body). One unfortunate applicant reported using "computer-assisted design" consistently throughout his résumé when the computer was searching for "CAD." Also, use a specific date of graduation in the education section. Some computer programs read two dates beside an institution to mean the applicant did not earn the degree (e.g., 2007–2011).

The scannable résumé Thomas Kincaid prepared when seeking an entry-level audit position in a public accounting firm appears in Figure 13-5. Note how he presents qualifications that correspond to the company/job profile posted at your companion website at **www.cengagebrain.com**. The scannable résumé is formatted for scanning into an electronic database to be matched with employer requirements.

Supplementing a Résumé

Some candidates feel their career accomplishments are not appropriately captured in a standard résumé. Two additional tools for communicating your qualifications and abilities are the portfolio and the employment video.

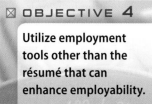

professional portfolio
a portfolio presented in digital format and distributed to prospective employers via a website, CD/DVD, or other media; also called an electronic portfolio or e-portfolio

multimedia résumé
a résumé created with presentation software such as Camtasia Studio and sent to prospective employers on CD/DVD or posted on the applicant's personal website

Professional Portfolios

The **professional portfolio** (also called the *electronic portfolio* or *e-portfolio* when presented in a digital format) can be used to illustrate past activities, projects, and accomplishments. It is a collection of artifacts that demonstrate your communication, people, and technical skills. Although portfolios were once thought of as only for writers, artists, or photographers, they are now seen as appropriate for other fields of work when the applicant wants to showcase abilities.

Many portfolios are now presented in digital format, making the portfolio easier to organize and distribute to prospective employers via a website or burned to a CD or other media. With the availability of user-friendly software, college campuses are offering e-portfolio systems that aid students in reflecting on their experiences and producing e-portfolios. Just as students currently are not asked if they have an email account, predictions are that soon they will also be expected to have "a Web space that represents their learning and their assessment."[9]

A clear understanding of your audience's needs and your qualifications will allow you to develop a logical organizational structure for your portfolio. Some possible items to include are:

- sample speeches with digitized audio or video clips of the delivery
- performance appraisals
- awards
- certificates of completion
- reports, proposals, or written documents prepared for classes or on the job
- brochures or programs describing workshops attended
- commendation messages, records, or surveys showing client or customer satisfaction with service

After selecting the items for inclusion in your portfolio, select the appropriate software or binder you will use to showcase your accomplishments. Once you're organized, you can add items that demonstrate you have the characteristics the employer is seeking. Maintain your portfolio even after you are hired because it can demonstrate your eligibility for promotion, salary increase, advanced training, or even justify why you should not be laid off.

For illustration purposes, take a look at Thomas Kincaid's electronic portfolio shown in Figure 13-6 on page 236 that was created using a Microsoft Web template and posted to his personal website.

Employment Videos

A video recording can be used to extend the impact of the printed résumé visually. A video can capture your stage presence and ability to speak effectively and add a human dimension to the written process. Current technology enables applicants to embed video segments into **multimedia résumés** created with presentation software such as Camtasia Studio and sent to prospective employers on CD or DVD or posted on the applicant's personal website.

Figure 13-5 GOOD *Scannable Résumé*

THOMAS KINCAID
742 Willow Tree Lane
Nashville, TN 54800
430-324-9044
tkincaid@netdoor.com
www.netdoor/tkincaid

Professional Profile

- First-year audit staff in an international accounting firm with an interest in forensic accounting
- Technical proficiency in ERP systems, ACL, database, and spreadsheet software
- Realistic forensic and audit experience through an internship with a regional CPA firm
- Superior leadership and team orientation developed through student organizations; strong written and spoken communication skills
- Fluency in Spanish

Keywords

Entry-level audit position. Master's and bachelor's degrees in accounting. Professional internship. Forensic accounting. Spanish fluency. Team player. Ethical. Adaptable. Willing to relocate. Word, Excel, Access, PowerPoint. ACL. ERP Systems. Web design.

Education

M.P.A., Accounting, Systems Emphasis, Sam Houston State University, May 2012, GPA 3.8
B.B.A., Accounting, Sam Houston State University, May 2010, GPA 3.6
- President's Scholar, 2008–2011
- Beta Alpha Psi (honorary organization for financial information students)

Technical Skills

- Proficient in database, spreadsheet, ERP systems, ACL, and web design
- Fluent Spanish; have traveled to Mexico

Related Employment

Professional Internship, Smith & Lewis, CPAs, Dallas, Texas, June–August, 2011
- Involved in audits of companies in the oil and gas and retail sectors
- Developed time management, team building, and communication skills while completing independent projects with diverse work teams
- Demonstrated ability to accept and respond to criticism, learn job tasks quickly, and perform duties with minimal supervision

Leadership Activities

Beta Alpha Psi, 2009–2012
- Served as local chapter president
- Received commendation from chapter advisor

An attractive and fully formatted hard copy version of this document is available upon request

Last revised 2/15/12

Positions name as first readable item.

Includes position sought and reason to hire in separate section.

Includes "Keyword Summary" section listing qualifications that match job description.

Supports keywords with specific facts.

Uses synonyms of keywords in body to ensure match with database.

Emphasizes willingness to provide professional, more impressive document.

Includes date of last revision to avoid confusion or embarrassment if résumé is accessed after hiring.

Format Pointers
Keeps résumé simple and readable by computer: ample white space especially between sections; easy-to-read font of 10 to 14 points; solid bullets; and no italics, underlining, or graphic lines or borders.

Mails cover letter and print résumé unfolded and unstapled in large envelope.

Figure 13-6 Electronic Portfolio Posted to an Applicant's Personal Website

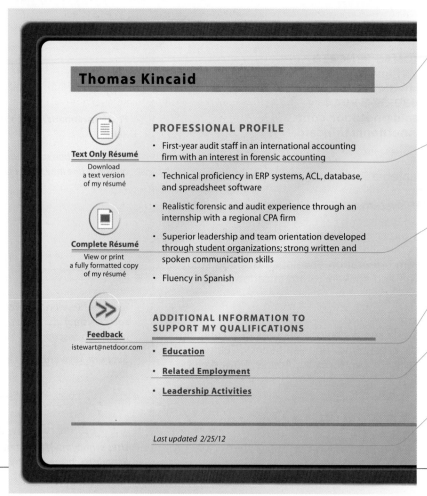

Thomas Kincaid

Text Only Résumé
Download
a text version
of my résumé

PROFESSIONAL PROFILE

• First-year audit staff in an international accounting firm with an interest in forensic accounting

• Technical proficiency in ERP systems, ACL, database, and spreadsheet software

Complete Résumé
View or print
a fully formatted copy
of my résumé

• Realistic forensic and audit experience through an internship with a regional CPA firm

• Superior leadership and team orientation developed through student organizations; strong written and spoken communication skills

• Fluency in Spanish

Feedback
istewart@netdoor.com

ADDITIONAL INFORMATION TO SUPPORT MY QUALIFICATIONS

• **Education**

• **Related Employment**

• **Leadership Activities**

Last updated 2/25/12

Callouts:
- *Begins with name and professional profile just as on résumé. Omits information that might encourage illegal discrimination.*
- *Includes link to ASCII or Rich Text Format (RTF) version that an employer can download to a database.*
- *Includes link to formatted résumé read by scrolling down and printed with one command.*
- *Provides email link to invite further communication.*
- *Includes links to information with section titles found in printed résumé.*
- *Includes latest revision date to avoid confusion or embarrassment if résumé is accessed after hiring.*

video résumé
a résumé created as a video for posting on the Web, on sites such as YouTube

Video résumés, which job-seekers post on sites such as YouTube, are the latest trend in developing creative job qualifications. You can learn some important lessons for your video project by taking a look at the abundance of good and bad examples already posted. If possible, solicit the help of someone with film experience and follow these simple suggestions for creating a visually enhanced résumé that is brief, showcases your key qualifications, and reflects your personality:[10]

• Keep your video simple with one stationary shot using a good camera and tripod. Avoid gimmicky effects and excessive panning that distract from the message.

• Use proper lighting, making sure that the employer can see your face. Avoid light behind you that casts shadows.

• Invest in a good quality microphone and speak clearly and at an appropriate pace for easy listening.

• Choose clothing appropriate for the job you are seeking. Video yourself wearing different clothing and watch the video to select the ideal choice. Avoid clothing that gaps and bunches when you sit, as well as bright colors and close patterns that tend to vibrate when filmed.

• Edit your video to eliminate dead air and other imperfections that detract from a professional image.

Employment videos are more commonly used to obtain employment in career fields for which verbal delivery or visual performance is a key element. These fields include broadcasting and the visual and performing arts. The following guidelines apply when preparing an employment video:

• Be sure the video makes a professional appearance and is complimentary to you. A "home movie" quality recording will be a liability instead of an asset to your application.

- Avoid long "talking head" segments. Include segments that reflect you in a variety of activities; shots that include samples of your work are also desirable.
- Remember that visual media (such as photographs and videos) encourage the potential employer to focus on your physical characteristics and attributes, which might lead to undesired stereotyping and discrimination.

Be sure to advertise the availability of your portfolio and employment video to maximize its exposure. List your URL address in the identification section of your résumé. In your application letter, motivate the prospective employer to view your portfolio or video by describing the types of information included. Talk enthusiastically about the detailed supplementary information available during your job interview and encourage the interviewer to view it when convenient. Note Thomas Kincaid's promotion of his e-portfolio when you read his application letter later in this chapter (see Figure 13-7 on the next page).

Composing Application Messages

☒ OBJECTIVE 5

Write an application message that effectively introduces an accompanying print (designed) or electronic résumé.

When employers invite you to send either a print or electronic résumé, they expect you to include an **application message** (also known as a *cover message*). A mailed paper résumé should be accompanied by an application letter. When a résumé is submitted electronically, the application "letter" can take the form of an email message. As you have learned, a résumé summarizes information related to the job's requirements and the applicant's qualifications. An application message complements a résumé by (1) introducing the applicant, (2) attracting interest to the résumé, and (3) interpreting the résumé in terms of employer benefits. When mailed, the application message is placed on top of the résumé so it can be read first by the employer.

Because it creates interest and points out employer benefits, the application message is persuasive and, thus, written inductively. It is designed to convince an employer that qualifications are adequate just as a sales message is designed to convince a buyer that a product will satisfy a need. Like sales messages, application messages can be either solicited or unsolicited. Job advertisements *solicit* applications. Unsolicited application messages have greater need for attention-getters; otherwise, solicited and unsolicited application messages are based on the same principles.

Unsolicited application messages are the same basic message (perhaps with slight modifications) sent to many prospective employers. By sending unsolicited messages, you increase your chances of locating potential openings and possibly alert employers to needs they had not previously identified for someone of your abilities. However, sending unsolicited messages has some disadvantages. Because the employer's specific needs are not known, the opening paragraph will likely be more general (less targeted to a specific position) than the opening paragraph in solicited messages. The process could also be time consuming.

Thomas Kincaid wrote the letter in Figure 13-7 to accompany a chronological résumé he prepared after completing the company/job profile of an entry-level auditor. The time Thomas devoted to analyzing the job, the company, and his qualifications was well spent.

Persuasive Organization

A persuasive message is designed to convince the reader to take action, which in this case is to read the résumé and invite you to an interview. Because an application message is persuasive, organize it as you would a sales message:

application message
a message placed on top of the résumé so it can be read first by the employer; also called a cover message

unsolicited application message
an unrequested message sent to many prospective employers and containing the same basic message

Sales Message	Application Message
Gets attention	Gets attention
Introduces product	Introduces qualifications
Presents evidence	Presents evidence
Encourages action	Encourages action
=	=
(sells a product, service, or idea)	(results in an interview)

Figure 13-7  *Example of an Application Letter*

THOMAS KINCAID
742 Willow Tree Lane
Nashville, TN 54800
430-324-9044
tkincaid@netdoor.com

February 18, 2012

Connie Cruthers, Partner
Samson & Cooke, CPAs
5400 Musicmaker Street
Nashville, TN 54909

Dear Ms. Cruthers:

Dr. Ellis, an accounting professor at Sam Houston State University, told me that Samson & Cooke has an auditing position available. A systems emphasis in my master's degree and related work experience qualify me for this auditing position.

Because of my interest in fraud investigation, I enhanced my credentials with an emphasis in forensic accounting. Courses in fraud examination and criminology have given me the skills to extract data from ERP systems and detect evidence of fraud using ACL, Excel, and Access. Unstructured, often ambiguous problems that require creative solutions are among my favorite assignments.

My internship at Smith & Lewis has prepared me for audit assignments in your firm by providing:

• Firsthand interaction with practicing auditors and clients, often working long, irregular hours.

• A proven ability to work effectively as a member of an audit team, building trust and credibility with clients and a diverse staff.

• Excellent performance ratings with commendations for superior technical proficiency and strong written and spoken communication skills.

Please review the enclosed résumé for additional information about my accounting education and related work experience. Work samples and further details are available in my electronic portfolio at www.netdoor/istewart. I look forward to talking with you about how my skills and experiences can benefit Samson & Cooke.

Sincerely,
Thomas Kincaid
Thomas Kincaid

Enclosure

Addresses letter to specific person using correct name and job title.

Identifies how applicant learned of position, specific position sought, and background.

Discusses how education relates to job requirements.

Uses bulleted list to highlight qualifications corresponding to job requirements.

Introduces résumé and website for additional information.

Encourages employer to take action without sounding pushy or apologetic.

Format Pointers
Formats as formal business letter since message is accompanying print résumé. Abbreviated email message including online résumé in ASCII or RTF format would be appropriate for electronic submission.

Uses same high-quality, standard size paper as for résumé in neutral color; includes writer's address and contact information.

Like a well-written sales message, a well-written application message uses a central selling feature as a theme. The central selling feature is introduced in the first or second paragraph and stressed in paragraphs that follow. Two to four paragraphs are normally sufficient for supporting evidence. Consider order of importance as a basis for their sequence, with the most significant aspects of your preparation coming first.

Gain the Receiver's Attention

To gain attention, begin the message by identifying the job sought and describing how your qualifications fit the job requirements. This information will provide instant confirmation that you are a qualified applicant for an open position. An employer who reads hundreds of application letters and résumés will appreciate this direct, concise approach.

For an announced job, you should indicate in the first paragraph how you learned of the position—for example, employee referral, customer referral, executive referral, newspaper advertising, or job fair. Your disclosure will confirm you are seeking an open job as well as facilitate evaluation of the company's recruiting practices. Note that the opening of the letter in Figure 13-7 indicates the applicant learned of the position through a referral from a professor.

An opening for an unsolicited message must be more persuasive: You must convince the interviewer to continue to read your qualifications even though a job might not exist. As in the opening of a solicited message, indicate the type of position sought and your qualifications but be more creative in gaining attention. The following paragraph uses the applicant's knowledge of recent company developments and an intense interest in the company's future to gain receiver attention.

> In the past five years, MedLabs has experienced phenomenal growth through various acquisitions, mergers, and market expansion. With this growth comes new opportunities, new customers, and the need for new team players to work in product line development. While following the growth of MedLabs, I have become determined to join this exciting team and am eager to show you that my educational background, leadership abilities, and internship experience qualify me for the job.

Provide Evidence of Qualifications

For graduates entering the world of full-time work for the first time, educational backgrounds are usually more impressive than work histories. They can benefit from interpreting their educational experiences as meaningful, job-related experiences. An applicant for a human resources position should do more than merely report having taken courses in organizational behavior.

> In my organizational behavior class, I could see specific application of principles encountered in my human relations and psychology classes. Questions about leadership and motivation seemed to recur throughout the course: What really motivates employees? Why are managers feared at many levels? How can those fears be overcome? How can egos be salvaged? The importance of the human element was a central focus of many courses and my research report, "The HR Manager as a Psychologist."

Your application message will not necessarily refer to information learned in a class. Recognizing that managers must be tactful (a point on which the person reading the message will surely agree), the applicant included some details of a class. That technique is a basic in persuasion: Do not just say a product or idea is good; say what makes it good. Do not just say that an educational or work experience was beneficial; say what made it so.

By making paragraphs long enough to include interpretation of experiences on the present or previous job, you show an employer that you are well prepared for your next job. For example, the following excerpt from an applicant whose only work experience was at a fast-food restaurant is short and general:

> I have been the shift leader at Submarines Plus for the past year and have supervised a crew of five on the evening shift. I received high performance evaluations for my work as a leader.

Added details and interpretation could make the value of the work experience more convincing:

> As shift leader at Submarines Plus, I have learned to listen to crew members' concerns and make them feel valued by acting on their suggestions. I have trained crew members in policies and procedures and must reinforce those procedures for existing employees. I am able to preserve a good working relationship with my crew even in sometimes difficult conversations.

The applicant has called attention to qualities that managers like to see in employees: willingness to listen, speed, accuracy, concern for clients or customers, a positive attitude, fairness, and tact. As a learning experience, the Submarines Plus job has taught or reinforced principles that the employer sees can be transferred to the job being sought.

In this section, you can discuss qualifications you have developed by participating in student organizations, student government, athletics, or community organizations. Be specific in describing gained skills that can be applied directly on the job—for example, organizational, leadership, spoken and written communication skills, and budgeting and financial management. You can also use your involvement as a channel for discussing important personal traits vital to the success of a business, such as interpersonal skills, motivation, imagination, responsibility, and team orientation.

> For the past year, I have served as treasurer for Alpha Chi Epsilon. In that duty, I have managed a $200,000 annual budget. By coordinating our yearly charitable fund-raising event, I have exercised leadership and organizational and communication skills.

Finally, end this section with an indirect reference to the résumé. If you refer to it in the first or second paragraph, readers might turn from the message at that point and look at the résumé. Avoid the obvious statement "Enclosed please find my résumé" or "A résumé is enclosed." Instead, refer indirectly to the résumé while restating your qualifications. The following sentence emphasizes that references can confirm applicant's qualifications:

> References listed on the enclosed résumé would be glad to comment on my marketing education and experience.

Encourage Action

Once you have presented your qualifications and referred to your enclosed résumé, the next move is to encourage the receiver to extend an invitation for an interview. The goal is to introduce the idea of action without apologizing for doing so and without being demanding or "pushy." If the final paragraph (action closing) of your message is preceded by impressive paragraphs, you need not press hard for a response. Just mentioning the idea of a future discussion is probably sufficient. If you have significant related experience that you have developed as a central selling feature, mentioning this experience in the action closing adds unity and stresses your strongest qualification one last time. Forceful statements about *when* and *how* to respond are unnecessary and irritating. Avoid these frequently made errors:

- **Setting a date.** "May I have an appointment with you on March 14?" The date you name could be inconvenient; or even if it is convenient for the employer, your forwardness in setting it could be resented.
- **Expressing doubt.** "If you agree," "I hope you will," and "Should you decide" use subjunctive words that indicate lack of confidence.

I hope you will . . .

I know how busy you are . . .

You may call me at 555-6543 . . .

When a date and time can be arranged, I would like to talk with you.

© iStockphoto.com/Andresr

- **Sounding apologetic.** "May I take some of your time" or "I know how busy you are" might seem considerate, but an apology is inappropriate when discussing ways you can contribute to a company.
- **Sounding overconfident.** "I will call you next week to set an appointment time that works for both of us." This statement is presumptuous and egotistical.
- **Giving permission to call.** "You may call me at 555-6543." By making the call sound like a privilege ("may call") you could alienate the reader. Implied meaning: You are very selective about the calls you take, but the employer does qualify.

The following sentences are possible closing sentences that refer to an invitation to interview. They are not intended as model sentences that should appear in your message. Because finding the right job is so important, you will be well rewarded for the time and thought you invest in original wording.

- **"When a date and time can be arranged, I would like to talk with you."** The statement does not indicate who will do the arranging, and the meeting place and the subject of the conversation are understood.
- **"I would appreciate an opportunity to discuss the loan officer's job with you."** The indirect reference to action is not forceful. However, if the applicant has impressive qualifications, the reader will want an interview and will not need to be pushed.
- **"I look forward to talking with you about how my skills and experiences can benefit Hannover Industries."** The statement asks for the interview and re-emphasizes the applicant's strong qualifications.

General Writing Guidelines

An excellent application message might be the most difficult message you ever attempt to write. It's natural to feel uncomfortable writing about yourself; however, your confidence will increase as you study the wealth of model documents available through your career services center and other sources. The writing principles you've been introduced to in this chapter should help you to write a thoughtful, original message that impresses the interviewer. Instead of standard verbiage included in dozens of models, your self-marketing connects *your* experiences to your future with a specific company and reflects *your* personality and values. The following writing techniques will help distinguish your application message from the competition:

- **Substitute fresh, original expressions that reflect contemporary language.** Overly casual expressions and overused statements will give your message a dull, unimaginative tone. Obvious ideas such as "This is an application," "I read your ad," and "I am writing to apply for," are sufficiently understood without making direct statements. With the application message *and* résumé in hand, a reader learns nothing from "I am enclosing my résumé for your review." Observe caution in choosing overused words such as *applicant, application, opening, position, vacancy,* and *interview*.

- **Avoid overuse of "I" and writer-focused statements.** Because the message is designed to sell your services, some use of "I" is natural and expected; but

© Goodluz/Shutterstock

restrict the number of times "I" is used, especially as the first word in a paragraph. Focus on providing specific evidence that you can meet the company's needs. The employer is not interested in reading about your need to earn more income, to be closer to your work, to have more pleasant surroundings, or to gain greater advancement opportunities.

- **Avoid unconvincing generalizations that could sound boastful.** Self-confidence is commendable, but overconfidence (or worse still, just plain bragging) is objectionable. Overly strong adjectives, self-judgmental terms, and unsupported generalizations damage your credibility. Instead of labeling your performance as "superior" or "excellent," or describing yourself as "an efficient, technically skilled team player" give supporting facts that show the interviewer you can deliver on what you're selling.

- **Tailor the message to the employer's need.** To impress the interviewer that your message is not a generic one sent to everyone, provide requested information and communicate an understanding of the particular company, job requirements, and field.

- **Provide requested information.** Job listings often request certain information: "Must provide own transportation and be willing to travel. Give educational background, work experience, and salary expected." Discuss these points in your application message. Preferably, the question of salary is left until the interview, allowing you to focus your message on your contributions to the company—not what you want from the company (money). Discussion of salary isn't meaningful until after a mutually successful interview; however, if an ad requests a statement about it, the message should address it. You may give a minimum figure or range, indicate willingness to accept a figure that is customary for work of that type, or indicate a preference for discussing salary at the interview.

- **Communicate knowledge of the company, job requirements, and language of the field.** Your statements about a company's rapid expansion or competitive advantage show you really are interested in the company, read widely, do more than you are required to do, and gather information before making decisions. However, phrase these statements carefully to avoid the perception of insincere flattery. For example, referring to the employer as "*the* leader in the field," "*the* best in the business," or "a great company" could appear as an attempt to get a favorable decision as a reward for making a complimentary statement. To reflect your understanding of the job requirements, use indirect statements that are informative and tactful. Direct statements such as "The requirements of this job are . . ." presents information the employer presumes you already know; "An auditor should be able to . . ." and "Sales personnel should avoid . . ." sound like a lecture and could be perceived as condescending.

Discussing experiences related to a specific job requirement or your preference for work that requires this skill reveals your understanding without a direct statement. Including terminology commonly used by the profession allows you to communicate clearly in terms the reader understands; it also saves space and implies your background in the field.

- **Focus on strengths and portray a positive attitude.** Concentrate on the positive aspects of your education or experience that have prepared you for the particular job. Apologizing for a shortcoming or admitting failure only weakens your case and raises questions about your self-esteem. Do not discuss your current employer's shortcomings. Regardless of how negatively you perceive your present employer, that perception has little to do with your prospective employer's needs. Also, if you speak negatively of your present employer, you could be perceived as someone who would do the same to the next employer.

Finishing Touches

The importance of professional formatting and careful proofreading of a print document is generally understood. However, proofing and formatting a "real" résumé and letter appears more important to some applicants than producing quality email submissions. Employers frequently voice concern with the sloppiness and unprofessional appearance and content of electronic submissions. To survive the skeptical eye of an interviewer scanning for ways to reject an applicant, allow yourself time to produce a professional-looking document regardless of the presentation or delivery option you've chosen. Include these steps in your finishing phase:

- Regardless of your delivery option, address your application letter or email message to the specific individual who is responsible for hiring for the position you are seeking rather than sending the document to the "Human Resources Department" or "To Whom It May Concern." If necessary, consult the company's annual report or website, or call the company to locate this information.
- Verify the correct spelling, job title, and address, and send a personalized message to the appropriate individual.
- Keep the message short and easy to read. A one-page letter is sufficient for most applications from students and graduates entering the job market.
- Apply visual enhancements learned previously to enhance the appeal and readability of the message and to draw attention to your strengths.
- Definitely keep the paragraphs short and consider listing your top four or five achievements or other important ideas in a bulleted list.

- Use paper that matches the résumé (color, weight, texture, and size). The watermark should be readable across the sheet in the same direction as the printing. Since you're using plain paper, include your street address and city, state, and zip code above the date or formatted as a letterhead at the top of the page.
- Include "Enclosure" below the signature block to alert the employer that a résumé is enclosed. The proper letter format is shown in the example in Figure 13-7.
- Get opinions from qualified individuals and make revisions where necessary.

When preparing an application message for email submission, career experts recommend formatting it as a business letter with the complete address of the company exactly as presented in a letter sent by mail and a formal closing such as "Sincerely." To help people reach you, include a full signature block with your mailing and email addresses, and phone number(s). The recipient can easily contact you without opening your attachments. While seemingly unnecessary, the email address is useful when a recipient forwards your email to someone else who might want to reply to you but cannot see your email address. Exclude quotes from your signature block that could be misunderstood or offensive. Add an enclosure notation drawing attention to your résumé attachment provided as requested by the employer, such as "Résumé attached as Word document."

To compete with the high volumes of junk mail, daily messages, and fear of computer viruses, you must provide a motive for an interviewer to open an unexpected message from an unknown person. Messages with missing or vague subject lines might be ignored or deleted immediately. To bring attention to your message, include the name of the person referring you to the position directly in the subject line or mention your email is a follow-up to a conversation, for example, "RE: Follow-up: Résumé for . . . ." If the message is unsolicited, describe the specific value you can add to the company, for example, "Résumé for Forensics Accountant with Extensive ACL Skills." Stay away from tricks such as marking an email "urgent" or adding "re" to pass your message off as a reply to an earlier message.

Check any instructions provided by the prospective employer and follow them precisely. Typically, however, you will want to send a complete letter and copy of your résumé by regular mail as a follow-up to the email submission. These suggestions are illustrated in Figure 13-8, a sample application letter an applicant sent after talking with a prospective employer at a career fair.

Figure 13-8 Example of Application Message Sent by Email

New Message

To: dhelmsley@nationalbank.com
From: tfree@gmail.com
Subject: Career Fair Follow-up: Résumé for Tina Freeman
Attachment: 📎 tina_freeman.doc

February 25, 2012

Doris Helmsley
Recruiter
National Bank and Trust
1240 27th Avenue
New York, NY 03140-1000

Dear Ms. Helmsley:

It was a pleasure meeting you at the career fair this morning. The opportunities offered in commercial lending identify your company as a leader in today's financial products marketplace.

My experience and knowledge of banking and commercial lending enable me to be a valuable asset to your company:

- Knowledge of banking and commercial lending practices, necessary documentation, and consumer laws.

- Demonstrated commitment to delivering excellent customer service to customers and clients.

- Hard-working and achievement oriented as demonstrated by part-time employment throughout college, volunteer work with the local food bank, and maintenance of a 3.9 GPA.

After you have reviewed the attached résumé that you requested for additional information about my education and related work experience, please message me so we can discuss my joining National Bank and Trust.

Sincerely,

Tina Freeman
159 Figueroa St.
Mesa, AZ 85009
801-755-4918
tfree@gmail.com

Résumé text included in email below and attached as MS Word attachment.

- Provides specific subject line that ensures message will be opened.

- Email program automatically shows attached file containing resume.

- Reveals how applicant learned of position and confirms knowledge of and interest in company.

- Condenses persuasive application message to one screen. Avoids tendency to send impersonal message stating résumé is attached.

- Introduces résumé and reminds interviewer that submission was requested.

- Encourages employer to take action without sounding pushy or apologetic.

- Includes email address in .sig file to simplify access to all contact information without opening attached résumé.

- Includes enclosure notation pointing out that résumé is sent as required by the company.

Format Pointers
Formats as formal business letter with complete address exactly as done when job credentials are sent by mail. Complete letter and printed copy of résumé will be sent as follow-up to email.

© Cengage Learning 2013

Interviewing for a Job and Preparing Employment Messages

Understanding Types of Employment Interviews

Most companies conduct various types of interviews before hiring a new employee. While the number and type of interviews vary among companies, applicants typically begin with a screening interview often completed by phone or videoconferencing, an in-depth interview, an on-site interview with multiple interviewers, and sometimes a stress interview. Depending on the goals of the interviewer, interviews follow a structured or an unstructured approach.

Structured Interviews

In a **structured interview** the interviewer follows a predetermined agenda, including a checklist of questions and statements designed to elicit necessary information and reactions from the interviewee. Because each applicant answers the same questions, the interviewer has comparable data to evaluate. A particular type of structured interview is the behavior-based interview, in which you are asked to give specific examples of occasions in which

structured interview
interview format generally used in the screening process in which the interviewer follows a predetermined agenda, including a checklist of items or a series of questions and statements designed to elicit the necessary information or interviewee reaction

© iStockphoto.com/Alexandr Tovstenko

you demonstrated particular behaviors or skills. The interviewer already knows what skills, knowledge, and qualities successful candidates must possess. The examples you provide will indicate whether you possess them.[1]

Many companies are finding computer-assisted interviews to be a reliable and effective way to conduct screening interviews. Applicants use a computer to provide answers to a list of carefully selected questions. A computer-generated report provides standard, reliable information about each applicant that enables an interviewer to decide whether to invite the applicant for a second interview. The report flags any contradictory responses (e.g., an applicant indicated he was terminated for absenteeism but later indicated that he thought his former employer would give him an outstanding recommendation), highlights any potential problem areas (e.g., an applicant responded that she would remain on the job less than a year), and generates a list of structured interview questions for the interviewer to ask (e.g., "Terrance, you said you feel your former employer

would rate you average. Why don't you feel it would be higher?").

Research has shown that applicants prefer computer interviews to human interviews and that they respond more honestly to a computer, feeling less need to give polite, socially acceptable responses. Because expert computer systems can overcome some of the inherent problems with traditional face-to-face interviews, the overall quality of the selection process improves. Typical interviewer errors include talking too much, forgetting to ask important questions, being reluctant to ask sensitive or tough questions, forming unjustified negative first impressions, obtaining unreliable and illegal information that makes an applicant feel judged, and using interview data ineffectively.[2] Regardless of whether the interview is face-to-face or computer assisted, you will need to provide objective, truthful evidence of your qualifications as they relate to specific job requirements.

Unstructured Interviews

An **unstructured interview** is a freewheeling exchange and can shift from one subject to another, depending on the interests of the participants. Some experienced interviewers are able to make a structured interview seem unstructured. The goal of many unstructured interviews is to explore unknown areas to determine the applicant's ability to speak comfortably about a wide range of topics.

Stress Interviews

A **stress interview** is designed to place the interviewee in an anxiety-producing situation so an evaluation can be made of the interviewee's performance under stress. In all cases, interviewees

© iStockphoto.com/Oleg Prikhodko

should attempt to assess the nature of the interview quickly and adjust behavior accordingly. Understanding that interviewers sometimes deliberately create anxiety to assess your ability to perform under stress should help you handle such interviews more effectively. As the following discussion of different interviewer styles reveals, you can perform much better when you understand the interviewer's purpose.

Series Interviews

As organizations have increased emphasis on the team approach to management and problem solving, selecting employees who best fit their cultures and styles has become especially important. Involving key people in the organization in the candidate selection process has led to new interview styles. In a series interview, the candidate meets individually with a number of different interviewers. Each interviewer will likely ask questions from a differing perspective; for instance, a line manager might ask questions related to the applicant's knowledge of specific job tasks while the vice president of operations might ask questions related to the applicant's career goals. Some questions will likely be asked more than once in the process. A popular trend in organizations that desire a broad range of input in the hiring decision but want to avoid the drawn-out nature of series interviews is to conduct group interviews.

Virtual Interviews

Technology is allowing much business activity, including job interviews, to be conducted virtually. Companies such as IBM, Microsoft, Nike, and Hallmark Cards save money and time by screening candidates through video interviews from remote locations. **Virtual interviews** help to widen the applicant pool and decrease the cost of travel (since they can be conducted regardless of geography) and fill the position more quickly. The consensus is that the video interview is excellent for screening applicants, but a face-to-face interview is appropriate whenever possible for the important final interview.

unstructured interview
a freewheeling exchange that may shift from one subject to another, depending on the interests of the participants
stress interview
interview format designed to place the interviewee in an anxiety-producing situation so an evaluation of the interviewee's performance under stress may be made
virtual interview
interview conducted using videoconferencing technology

AP Images/Ted S. Warren

Preparing for an Interview

College students frequently schedule on-campus interviews with representatives from various business organizations. Following the on-campus interviews, successful candidates often are invited for further interviews at the company location. The purpose of the second interview is to give executives and administrators other than the human resources interviewer an opportunity to appraise the candidate. Whether on campus or at the company location, interview methods and practices vary with the situation.

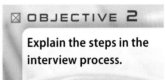

⊠ **OBJECTIVE 2**

Explain the steps in the interview process.

Pre-interview planning involves learning something about the company or organization, studying yourself, and making sure your appearance and mannerisms will not detract from the impression you hope to make.

Research the Company

Nothing can hurt a job candidate more than knowing little about the organization. No knowledge indicates insincerity, and the interviewer does not want to waste precious interview time providing candidates with information they should have considered long before. Preparation will also arm candidates with information needed to develop pertinent qualifications and point their stories to solve an employer's specific problems.

Companies that have publicly traded stock are required to publish annual reports that are available in school libraries or online. Be sure to read news items and blog posts and sign up to receive news alerts from the prospective company for current company information up until the day of the interview. Use social networking utilities such as LinkedIn and Hoovers.com to find profiles of company leaders and gain insights on the types of managers this company employs.

Employees of the company or other applicants who have interviewed might be of help to the interviewee. Employee reviews of selected companies, salaries, and sample interview questions are available online, and some universities share taped interviews with various company recruiters. Information about the company and the job sought pertinent in an interview includes the following:

Various companies have direct hookups with the career services centers of colleges and universities to interview students. These virtual interviews allow students to meet large companies whose representatives typically would not visit colleges with small applicant pools and to interview with companies whose representatives could not travel because of financial constraints or other reasons. Students simply sit in front of a camera, dial in, and interview with multiple interviewers; in some cases, several applicants are interviewed simultaneously. As you would imagine, some candidates who interview well in person can fail on camera or in a group conference call. Virtual interviewing is an excellent method for screening out candidates who are unable to communicate their competence, enthusiasm, and conviction in a technology-rich environment.

You should prepare for a virtual interview differently than you would for a traditional interview. First, suggest a preliminary telephone conversation with the interviewer to establish rapport. Arrive early and acquaint yourself with the equipment; know how to adjust the volume and other camera functions for optimal performance after the interview begins. Second, concentrate on projecting strong nonverbal skills: speak clearly but do not slow down; be certain you are centered in the frame; sit straight; look up, not down; and use gestures and an enthusiastic voice to communicate energy and reinforce points while avoiding excessive motion that will appear blurry. Third, realize voices can be out of step with the pictures if there is a lag between the video and audio transmissions. You will need to adjust to the timing (e.g., slow down voice) to avoid interrupting the interviewer.

Company Information

Be sure to research the following on the companies with which you interview:

- **Name.** Know, for example, that the publishing company Cengage Learning was so named to reflect the company's mission to be a "center of engagement" for its global customers.[3]
- **Status in the industry.** Know the company's share of the market, its *Fortune* 500 standing (if any), its sales, and its number of employees.
- **Latest stock market quote.** Be familiar with current market deviations and trends.
- **Recent news and developments.** Read current business periodicals, news, and blogs for special feature articles on the company, its new products, and its corporate leadership.
- **Scope of the company.** Is it local, national, or international?
- **Corporate officers.** Know the names of the chairperson, president, and chief executive officer.
- **Products and services.** Study the company's offerings, target markets, and innovative strategies.

Job Information

Be sure to know the following about the job you are seeking:

- **Job title.** Know the job titles of typical entry-level positions.
- **Job qualifications.** Understand the specific knowledge and skills desired.
- **Probable salary range.** Study salaries in comparable firms, as well as regional averages.
- **Career path of the job.** What opportunities for advancement are available?

Study Yourself

When you know something about the company, you will also know something about the kinds of jobs or training programs the company has to offer. Next, compare your qualifications to the company/job profile. This systematic comparison of your qualifications and job requirements helps you identify pertinent information (strengths or special abilities) to be included in your résumé. If you cannot see a relationship between you and the job or company, you might have difficulty demonstrating the interest or sincerity needed to sell yourself.

Plan Your Appearance

An employment interviewer once said she would not hire a job applicant who did not meet her *extremities* test: fingernails, shoes, and hair must be clean and well kept. This interviewer felt that if the candidate did not take care of those details, the candidate could not really be serious about, or fit into, her organization. Other important guidelines include avoiding heavy makeup and large, excessive jewelry. Select conservative clothes, and be certain clothing is clean, unwrinkled, and properly fitted. Additionally, avoid smoking, drinking, or wearing heavy fragrance.

You can locate a wealth of information on appropriate interview dress from numerous electronic and printed sources. Additionally, talk with professors in your field, professors of business etiquette and professional protocol, personnel at your career services center, and graduates who have recently acquired jobs in your field. Research the company dress code—real

or implied—ahead of time. If you *look* and *dress* like the people who already work for the company, the interviewer will be able to visualize you working there.

Plan Your Time and Materials

One of the worst things you can do is be late for an interview. If something should happen to prevent your arriving on time, phone an apology. Another mistake is to miss the interview entirely. Plan your time so that you will arrive early and can unwind and review mentally the things you plan to accomplish. Be sure to bring a professional briefcase or notebook that contains everything you will need during the interview. These items might include copies of your résumé, a list of references and/or recommendations, a professional-looking pen, paper for taking notes, highlights of what you know about the company, a list of questions you plan to ask, and previous correspondence with the company.

Practice

The job interview could be the most important face-to-face interaction you ever have. You will be selling yourself in competition with others. How you listen and how you talk are characteristics the interviewer will be able to measure. Your actions, your mannerisms, and your appearance will combine to give the total picture of how you are perceived. Added to the marketable skills you have acquired from your education, experience, and activities, your interview performance can give a skilled interviewer an excellent picture of you. Practicing for an interview will prepare you to handle the nervousness that is natural when interviewing. However, do not memorize answers, as it will sound rehearsed and insincere. Instead, think carefully about how your accomplishments match the job requirements and practice communicating these ideas smoothly, confidently, and professionally.

Prepare for standard interview questions and other interview issues following suggestions provided later in this chapter. Once you are satisfied you have identified your key selling points, have a friend ask you interview questions you have developed and surprise you with others. Participate in mock interviews with someone in your career services center or with a friend, alternating roles as interviewer and interviewee. Then follow each practice interview with a constructive critique of your performance.

Conducting a Successful Interview

The way you handle an interview will vary somewhat depending on your stage in the hiring process. Regardless of whether you are being screened by a campus recruiter in person, by phone or videoconference, or have progressed to an on-site visit, an interview will have three parts: the opening formalities, an information exchange, and the closing.

⊠ OBJECTIVE 3

Prepare effective answers to questions often asked in job interviews, including illegal interview questions.

The Opening Formalities

According to management consultant Dan Burns, most candidates don't realize that in the first 60 seconds, interviewers typically decide whether the candidate will

Interviewers typically decide about a candidate in the first 60 seconds. You must enter the door selling yourself!

© iStockphoto.com/Oleg Prikhodko

be moved to the top of the list or dropped from consideration. Burns emphasizes that skills missing during the interview are important because he assumes these same deficiencies will carry over during employment.[4] Clearly, since the impression created during the first few seconds of an interview often determines the outcome, you cannot afford to take time to warm up in an interview. You must enter the door selling yourself!

Common courtesies and confident body language can contribute to a favorable first impression in the early moments when you have not yet had an opportunity to talk about your qualifications:

- **Use the interviewer's name and pronounce it correctly.** Even if the interviewer calls you by your first name, always use the interviewer's surname unless specifically invited to do otherwise.

- **Apply a firm handshake.** Usually, the interviewer will initiate the handshake, although you may do so. In either case, apply a firm handshake. You do not want to leave the impression that you are weak or timid. At the same time, you do not want to overdo the firm grip and leave an impression of being overbearing.

- **Wait for the interviewer to ask you to be seated.** If you aren't invited to sit, choose a chair across from or beside the interviewer's desk.

- **Maintain appropriate eye contact, and use your body language to convey confidence.** Sit erect and lean forward slightly to express interest. For a professional image, avoid slouching, chewing gum, and fidgeting.

- **Be conscious of nonverbal messages.** If the interviewer's eyes are glazing over, end your answer, but expand it if they are bright and the head is nodding vigorously. If the interviewer is from a different culture, be conscious of subtle differences in nonverbal communication that could affect the interviewer's perception of you. For example, a North American interviewer who sees eye contact as a sign of trust might perceive an Asian female who keeps her eyes lowered as a sign of respect to be uninterested or not listening.[5] Women should also be aware of typical "feminine behavior" during the interview. For instance, women nod more often than men when an interviewer speaks. Women are also likely to smile more and have a rising intonation at the end of sentences; such behaviors can convey a subservient attitude.[6]

Following the introductions, many interviewers will begin the conversation with nonbusiness talk to help you relax and to set the stage for the information exchange portion of the interview. Other interviewers bypass these casual remarks and move directly into the interview.

The Information Exchange

Much of the information about you will appear on your résumé or application form and is already available to the interviewer. Thus, the interviewer most likely will seek to go beyond such facts as your education, work experience, and extracurricular activities. He or she will attempt to assess your general attitude toward work and the probability of your fitting successfully into the organization.

Presenting Your Qualifications

Your preparation pays off during the interview. Like a defense attorney ready to win a case, you are ready to present evidence that you should be hired. According to Joyce Kennedy and Thomas Morrow, leading career consultants, your case will have three major points: You must convince the interviewer that you (1) can do the job, (2) will do the job, and (3) will not stress out everyone else while doing the job.[7] That's an overwhelming task. Where do you begin? You learned during your study of persuasive writing that saying you're the best at what you do is not convincing. To convince an interviewer to allow you to continue to the next interview or to extend you a job offer, you must provide specific, concrete evidence that your qualifications match the job description and equip you to add immediate value to the company. Use the following guidelines to help you relate your skills and knowledge to the job:

- **List five or six key points that you want to emphasize.** You will probably want to present your education as a major asset. You should point out its relationship to the job sought. Even more important, the fact that you have succeeded in academics indicates that you have the ability and self-discipline to learn. Because most companies expect you to learn something on the job, your ability to learn and thus quickly become productive will be your greatest asset. Even lack of work experience can be an asset: You have acquired no bad work habits that you will have to unlearn.

  Additionally, be sure to provide evidence of your interpersonal skills. Communicate that you can get along with others and are sensitive to diversity.

  ○ What did you do in college that helped you get along with others?

  ○ Were you a member, an officer, or president of an organization? What did you accomplish? How did others perceive you? Were you a leader? How did your followers respond to your leadership style? To your commitment to ethical standards?

  ○ Can you organize projects, motivate people to complete important goals, and deal with difficult people?

The extracurricular activities listed on your résumé give an indication of these traits, but how you talk about them in your interview helps to demonstrate them. "I started as public relations vice president and was subsequently elected to higher office for four semesters, eventually becoming president" is a statement that proves your leadership qualities. If you can show your organization moved to greater heights, you will appear successful as well. You can also use questions about your extracurricular activities to show that you have broad, balanced interests rather than a single, time-consuming avocation that could lead to burnout and stress if carried to the job.

What are other skills that graduating students need to succeed in a cross-cultural, interdependent workforce? While academic performance is weighted more heavily for some types of jobs than others, the ability to juggle a complicated schedule is weighed heavily by many employers as an important job-success factor. Additionally, a UNESCO report of employer views revealed certain skills to be essential for workers in today's business climate as shown in Figure 14-1.[8]

Consider these general job-success traits and then use your knowledge of the job requirements and your own strengths to develop your "central selling features." These key points targeted to your audience are the central element of a winning argument: You are able and willing to become a contributing part of a high-performance team that will enhance the company's performance.

- **Be prepared to answer standard interview questions.** These questions are designed to show (a) why you want the job, (b) why you want to work for this organization, and (c) why the company should want you. Practice concise but fully developed answers that reflect your personality and your communication power. While one-word answers aren't adequate, long-winded answers can prevent interviewers from asking you other planned questions critical to making an informed decision.

- **Be prepared to answer behavioral questions.** These questions are designed to challenge you to provide evidence of your skills or the behaviors required to perform the job. Rather than asking applicants how they feel about certain things, interviewers are finding that asking potential employees for specific examples to illustrate their answers is a more objective way to evaluate applicants' skills.

  Behavioral questions include the following:

  ○ Describe a time when you worked well under pressure, worked effectively with others, organized a major project, motivated and led others, solved a difficult problem, or used persuasion to convince someone to accept your idea.

  ○ What was the most difficult problem you had to overcome in your last job (or an academic or

Figure 14-1 Skills Needed: Balance of Soft and Hard Skills

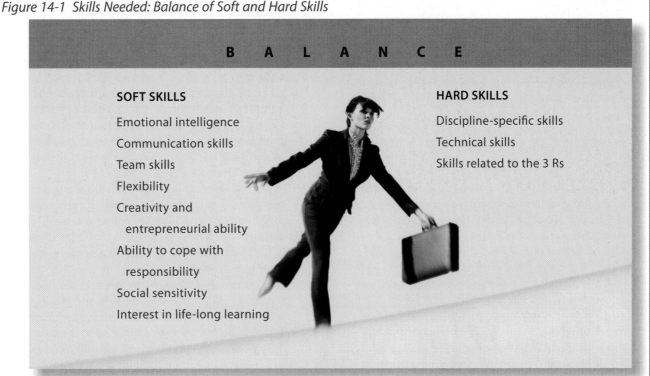

BALANCE

SOFT SKILLS

Emotional intelligence

Communication skills

Team skills

Flexibility

Creativity and
 entrepreneurial ability

Ability to cope with
 responsibility

Social sensitivity

Interest in life-long learning

HARD SKILLS

Discipline-specific skills

Technical skills

Skills related to the 3 Rs

© iStockphoto.com/Andrew Rich

extracurricular activity)? How did you cope with it? What lesson did you learn from the situation? Share a time you applied the lesson learned.

- Tell me about a time you had difficulty working with a supervisor or coworker (or professor or peer in a team in a class setting). How did you handle the situation?

- Describe something you have done that shows initiative and willingness to work or required you to think on your feet to solve a problem.

- How have your extracurricular activities, part-time work experience, or volunteer work prepared you for work in our company?

- Tell me about a time you hit a wall trying to push forward a great idea.

To prepare for answering behavioral questions, brainstorm to identify stories that illustrate how your qualifications fit the job requirements. These stories should show you applying the skills needed on the job. Career counselors recommend using the STAR method (Situation or Task/Action/Result) as a consistent format to help you present a complete answer to these open-ended questions. You first describe a situation or task you were involved in, the action you took, and finally the result of your effort.[9]

- **Be prepared to demonstrate logical thinking and creativity.** Many interviewers ask applicants to solve brain teasers and riddles, create art out of paper bags, and solve complex business problems. Some are asked to "do the job before we give it to you," for example, write a press release on the spot or field a tech-support call.[10] These techniques are used to gauge an applicant's ability to think quickly and creatively and observe an emotional response to an awkward situation. You cannot anticipate this type of interview question, but you can familiarize yourself with mind teasers that have been used. Most importantly, however, recognize the interviewer's purpose; relax, and do your best to showcase your logical reasoning, creativity, or your courage to even try.

- **Display a professional attitude.** First, communicate your sincere interest in the company; show that you are strongly interested in the company and not just taking an interview for practice. Reveal your knowledge of the company gained through reading published information, and refer to the people you have talked with about the working conditions, company achievements, and career paths.

Second, focus on the satisfaction gained from contributing to a company rather than the benefits you will receive. What's important in a job goes beyond financial reward. All applicants are interested in a paycheck; any job satisfies that need—some will pay more, some less. Recognize that the paycheck

© jitloac/Shutterstock

is a part of the job and should not be your primary concern. Intrinsic rewards such as personal job satisfaction, the feeling of accomplishment, and making a contribution to society are ideas to discuss in the interview. You should like what you are doing and find a challenging job that will satisfy these needs.

- **Be prepared to discuss salary and benefits.** For most entry-level positions, the beginning salary is fixed. However, if you have work experience, excellent scholarship records, or added maturity, you might be able to obtain a higher salary. The interviewer should initiate the salary topic. What you should know is the general range for candidates with your qualifications so that your response to a question about how much you would expect is reasonable.

If you have other job offers, you are in a position to compare salaries, jobs, and companies. In this case, you might suggest to the interviewer that you would expect a competitive salary and that you have been offered X dollars by another firm. If salary has not been mentioned, and you really want to know about it, simply ask courteously how much the salary would be for someone with your qualifications. In any case, if you really believe the job offers the nonmonetary benefits you seek, do not attempt to make salary a major issue.

Typically, an interviewer will introduce the subject of benefits without your asking about them. In some cases, a discussion of total salary and "perks" is reserved for a follow-up interview. If nothing has been said about certain benefits, you should take the liberty of asking, particularly when an item is especially important to you.

- **Be knowledgeable of interview questions and information on your social networking sites that might lead to discriminatory hiring practices.** The Equal Employment Opportunity Commission (EEOC) and Fair Employment Practices Guidelines make it clear that an employer cannot legally discriminate against a job applicant on the basis of race, color, gender, age, religion, national origin, or disability. Interviewers must restrict questions to an applicant's ability to perform specific job-related functions essential to the job sought. Generally, the following topics should not be introduced:

  - *National origin and religion.* "You have an unusual accent; where were you born?" "What religious holidays will require you to miss work?"

  - *Age.* "I see you attended Central High School; what year did you graduate?" "Could you provide a copy of your birth certificate?"

  - *Disabilities, health conditions, and physical characteristics not reasonably related to the job.* "Do you have a disability that would interfere with your ability to perform the job? "Have you ever been injured on the job?" "Have you ever been treated by a psychiatrist?" "How much alcohol do you consume each week?" "What prescription drugs are you currently taking?"

  - *Marital status, spouse's employment, or dependents.* "Are you married?" "Who is going to care for your children if you work for us?" "Do you plan to have children?" "Is your spouse employed?" Additionally, employers may not ask the names or relationships of people with whom you live.

  - *Arrests or criminal convictions that are not related to the job.* "Have you ever been arrested other than for traffic violations? If so, explain." Keep in mind that the arrest/conviction record of a person applying for a job as a law enforcement officer or a teacher could be highly relevant to the job, but the same information could be illegal for a person applying for a job as an engineer.

  Since interviewers may ask illegal questions because of lack of training or an accidental slip, you must decide how to respond. You can refuse to answer and state the question is improper, though you risk offending the interviewer. A second option is to answer the inappropriate question, knowing it is illegal and unrelated to job requirements. A third approach is to provide a low-key response such as "How does this question relate to how I will do my job?" or to answer the legitimate concern that likely prompted the question. For example, an interviewer who asks, "Do you plan to have children?" is probably concerned about how long you might remain on the job. An answer to this concern would be "I plan to pursue a career regardless of whether I decide to raise a family." If you can see no legitimate concern in a question, such as "Do you own your home, rent, or live with parents?" answer, "I'm not sure how that question relates to the job. Can you explain?"[11]

Asking Questions of the Interviewer

Both the interviewer and interviewee want to know as much as possible about each other before making a commitment to hire. A good way to determine whether the job is right for you is to ask pertinent questions.

Good questions show the interviewer that you have initiative and are interested in making a well-informed decision. Responses can provide insight to job requirements that you can then show you possess. Therefore, be sure not to say, "I don't have any questions." Focus on questions that help you gain information about the company and the job that you could not learn from published sources or persons other than the interviewer. Respect the interviewer's time by avoiding questions that indicate you are unprepared (for example, questions about the company's scope, products/services, job requirements, or new developments). Avoid questions about salary, required overtime, and benefits that imply you are interested more in money and the effort required than in the contribution you can make.

The Closing

The interviewer will provide cues indicating that the interview is completed by rising or making a comment about the next step to be taken. At that point, do not prolong the interview needlessly. Simply rise, accept the handshake, thank the interviewer for the opportunity to meet, and close by saying you look forward to hearing from the company. The tact with which you close the interview can be almost as important as the first impression you made. Be enthusiastic. If you really want the job, you must ask for it.

Your ability to speak confidently and intelligently about your abilities will help you secure a desirable job. Effective interviewing skills will be just as valuable once you begin work. You will be involved in interviews with your supervisor for various reasons: to seek advice or information about your work and working conditions, to receive informal feedback about your progress, to receive a deserved promotion, and to discuss other personnel matters. In addition, your supervisor will likely conduct a performance appraisal interview to evaluate your performance. This formal interview typically occurs annually on the anniversary of your start of employment.

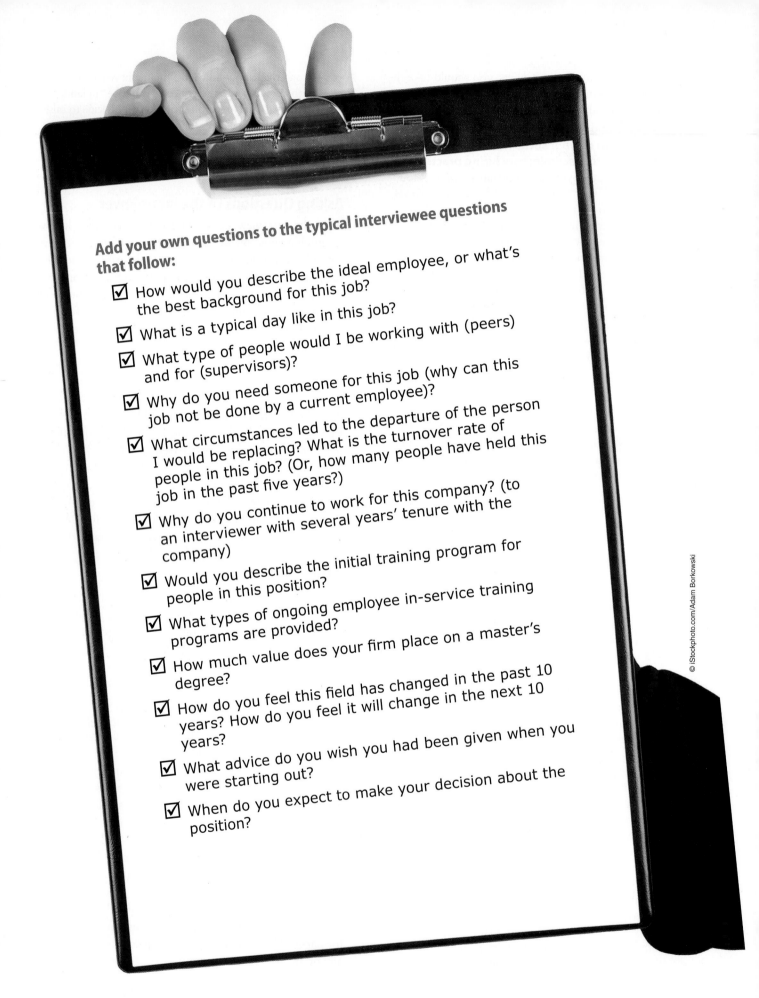

Add your own questions to the typical interviewee questions that follow:

☑ How would you describe the ideal employee, or what's the best background for this job?

☑ What is a typical day like in this job?

☑ What type of people would I be working with (peers) and for (supervisors)?

☑ Why do you need someone for this job (why can this job not be done by a current employee)?

☑ What circumstances led to the departure of the person I would be replacing? What is the turnover rate of people in this job? (Or, how many people have held this job in the past five years?)

☑ Why do you continue to work for this company? (to an interviewer with several years' tenure with the company)

☑ Would you describe the initial training program for people in this position?

☑ What types of ongoing employee in-service training programs are provided?

☑ How much value does your firm place on a master's degree?

☑ How do you feel this field has changed in the past 10 years? How do you feel it will change in the next 10 years?

☑ What advice do you wish you had been given when you were starting out?

☑ When do you expect to make your decision about the position?

Preparing Other Employment Messages

P reparing a winning résumé and application letter is an important first step in a job search. To expedite your job search, you will need to prepare other employment messages. For example, you might complete an application form, send a follow-up message to a company that does not respond to your résumé, send a thank-you message after an interview, accept a job offer, reject other job offers, and communicate with references. A career change will require a carefully written resignation letter.

Application Forms

Before going to work on a new job, you will almost certainly complete the employer's application and employment forms. Some application forms, especially for applicants who apply for jobs with a high level of responsibility, are very long. They can actually appear to be tests in which applicants give their answers to hypothetical questions and write defenses for their answers. Increasing numbers of companies are designing employment forms as mechanisms for acquiring information about a candidate that often is not included in the résumé. Application forms also ensure consistency in the information received from each candidate and can prevent decisions based on illegal topics which might be presented in a résumé.

Follow-Up Messages

When an application message and résumé do not elicit a response, a follow-up message might bring results. Sent a few weeks after the original message, it includes a reminder that an application for a certain job is on file, presents additional education or experience accumulated and its relationship to the job, and closes with a reference to desired action. In addition to conveying new information, follow-up messages indicate persistence (a quality that impresses some employers). Figure 14-2 shows a good example of a follow-up letter.

Figure 14-2  *Example of a Follow-Up Letter*

Dear Ms. Francis:

Recently, I applied for an accounting position with Tucker & Barns and now have additional qualifications to report.

The enclosed updated resume shows that I attended a financial accounting workshop sponsored by the National Accounting Association. The seminar was aimed at educating accountants in the new financial accounting laws recently passed by Congress. The seminar will enable me to ensure that all accounting practices of your clients comply with those laws.

Ms. Francis, I would welcome the opportunity to visit your office and talk more about the contributions I could make as an accountant with Tucker & Barns. Please write or call me at (340) 642-5003.

- States main idea and clearly identifies position being sought.

- Refers to enclosed résumé; summarizes additional qualifications.

- Assures employer that applicant is still interested in job.

Format Pointers
Format as formal business letter, but could have sent message electronically if previous communication with employer had been by email.

Print letter and envelope with laser printer on paper that matches résumé and application letter.

© Cengage Learning 2013

Thank-You Messages

What purposes are served in sending a thank-you message, even though you expressed thanks in person after the interview or a discussion with a special employer at a career fair? After a job interview, a written message of appreciation is a professional courtesy and enhances your image within the organization. To be effective, it must be sent promptly. For maximum impact, send a thank-you message the day of the interview or the following day. Even if during the interview you decided you do not want the job or you and the interviewer mutually agreed that the job is not for you, a thank-you message is appropriate. As a matter of fact, if you've made a positive impression, interviewers might forward your résumé to others who are seeking qualified applicants.

The medium you choose for sending this message depends on the intended audience. If the company you've interviewed with prefers a traditional style, send a letter in complete business format on high-quality paper that matches your résumé and application letter. If the company has communicated with you extensively by email, follow the pattern and send a professional email that can be read in a timely manner. Choosing to send an email rather than slower mail delivery can give you a competitive edge over other candidates whose mailed letters arrive several days later than yours.

RESIST THE URGE

TO VENT, RANT, OR TELL YOUR BOSS HOW TO RUN THE BUSINESS. IT'S NOT PROFESSIONAL IN A RESIGNATION LETTER.

© James Dawson/Image Farm/Jupiterimages

After an interview has gone well and you think a job offer is a possibility, include these ideas in the message of appreciation: express gratitude, identify the specific job applied for, refer to some point discussed in the interview (the strength of the interview), and close by making some reference to the expected call or message that conveys the employer's decision. The tone of this business message should remain professional regardless of the personal relationship you might have developed with the interviewer and the informality encouraged by email. The message could be read by many others once it is placed in your personnel file as you complete annual appraisals and compete for promotions. Specific points to cover are outlined in Figure 14-3.

The résumé, application letter, and thank-you message should be stored in a computer file and adapted for submission to other firms when needed. Develop a database for keeping a record of the dates on which documents and résumés were sent to certain firms and answers were received, names of people talked with, facts conveyed, and so on. When an interviewer calls, you can retrieve and view that company's record while you are talking with the interviewer.

Job-Acceptance Messages

A job offer may be extended either by phone or in writing. If a job offer is extended over the phone, request that the company send a written confirmation of the job offer. The confirmation should include the job title, salary, benefits, starting date, and anything else negotiated.

Often, companies require a written acceptance of a job offer. Note the deductive sequence of the message shown in Figure 14-4: acceptance, details, and closing (confirms the report-for-work date).

Job-Refusal Messages

Like other messages that convey unpleasant news, job-refusal messages are written inductively—with a beginning that reveals the nature of the subject, explanations that lead to a refusal, the refusal, and a pleasant ending. Of course, certain reasons (even though valid in your mind) are better left unsaid, such as questionable company goals or methods of operation, negative attitude of present employees, possible bankruptcy, unsatisfactory working conditions, and so on. The applicant who prefers not to be specific about the reason for turning down a job might write this explanation: *After thoughtfully considering job offers received this week, I have*

Figure 14-3

GOOD *Example of a Thank-You Message*

New Message

To: jchen@bhps.org

From: eswenson@gmail.com

Subject: Appreciation for Office Interview

Dear Ms. Chen:

Thank you for the opportunity to visit the Bird Habitat Preservation Society for an interview yesterday. I enjoyed meeting you and your staff and the opportunity to learn about the important programs sponsored by the BHPS.

Having lived in Bend for more than seven years, I often read reports about how the BHPS has influenced the development in the area. The office visit allowed me to learn more about the mission of the BHPS, from monitoring the number of birds in the area, educating residents, and promoting legislative initiatives, to writing state and federal grants to fund preservation activities.

After visiting your office on Friday, I am confident that my interest and previous experience working at the Wild Lands Conservation office in Bend will allow me to contribute immediately to the BHPS's important role as an environmental steward for the region. I would also gain valuable real-world experience needed to enhance my public policy degree at the university.

Ms. Chen, I am eager to receive an offer from the BHPS for the planning position. If you need additional information in the meantime, please contact me.

Thanks,

Elise Swenson

- States main idea of appreciation for interview and information gained.

- Includes specific points discussed during interview, increasing sincerity and recall of applicant.

- Assures employer of applicant's continued interest in position.

- Politely reminds employer that applicant is awaiting reply.

Format Pointer
Prepare as email message because previous communication with the company has been by email.

© Cengage Learning 2013

Figure 14-4 **GOOD** *Example of a Job-Acceptance Message*

I accept your employment offer as a programmer. Thank you for responding so quickly after our discussion on Friday.

As you requested, I have signed the agreement outlining the specific details of my employment. Your copy is enclosed, and I have kept a copy for my records.

If you should need to communicate with me before I report to work on June 1, please call me at 777-2323.

- States main idea of the job acceptance.

- Continues with any necessary details.

- Confirms beginning employment date.

© Cengage Learning 2013

decided to accept a job in the marketing department of an Internet applications firm.

You might want to be more specific about your reasons for refusal when you have a positive attitude toward the company or believe you will want to reapply at some later date. The letter excerpt in Figure 14-5 includes the reasons for refusal.

Resignation Messages

Resigning from a job requires effective communication skills. You might be allowed to give your notice in person or be required to write a formal resignation. Your supervisor will inform you of the company's policy. Regardless of whether the resignation is given orally or in writing, show empathy for your employer by giving enough time to allow the employer to find a replacement. Because your employer has had confidence in you, has benefited from your services, and will have to seek a replacement, your impending departure *is* bad news. As such, the message is written inductively. It calls attention to your job, gives your reasons for leaving it, conveys the resignation, and closes on a positive note. A written resignation is shown in Figure 14-6.

A resignation is not an appropriate instrument for telling managers how a business should be operated. Harshly worded statements could result in immediate termination or cause human relations problems during your remaining working days. If you can do so sincerely, recall positive experiences you had with the company. Doing so will leave a lasting record of your goodwill, making it likely that your supervisor will give you a good recommendation in the future.

Recommendation Requests

Companies seek information from references at various stages. Some prefer talking with references prior to an interview, and others, after a successful interview. Specific actions on your part will ensure that your references are treated with common courtesy and that references are prepared for the employer's call.

- **Remind the reference that he/she had previously agreed to supply information about you.** Identify the job for which you are applying, give a complete address to which the message is to be sent, and indicate a date by which the prospective employer needs the message. By sharing information about job requirements and reporting recent job-related experiences, you can assist the reference in writing an effective message. Indicate your gratitude, but do not apologize for making the request. The reference has already agreed to write on your behalf and will likely take pleasure in assisting a deserving person.

- **Alert the reference of imminent requests for information, especially if considerable time has elapsed since the applicant and reference have last seen each other.** Enclosing a recent résumé and providing any other pertinent information (for example, name change) will enable the reference to write a message that is specific and convincing. To ensure on-target job references, politely explain the types of information you perceive relevant to the job sought: specific job skills, work ethic, attitude and demeanor toward work, leadership style, and so on. If the job search becomes longer than anticipated, a follow-up message to references explaining the

Figure 14-5 GOOD *Example of a Job-Refusal Message*

I appreciate your spending time with me discussing the public relations job.

Your candid comparison of my background and opportunities in public relations and marketing was especially helpful. Having received job offers in both fields, I am now convinced that a career in marketing is more consistent with my aptitudes and goals. Today, I am accepting a job in the marketing department of Online App Development.

Thank you for your confidence demonstrated by the job offer. When I receive reports of Franklin's continued success, I will think of the dedicated people who work for the company.

• *Begins with neutral but related idea to buffer bad news.*

• *Presents reasons diplomatically that lead to refusal.*

• *Ends message on positive note that anticipates future association with company.*

Figure 14-6  Example of a Resignation Message

SUBJECT: PLEASURE OF SERVING APPLETREE RESTAURANT

My job as as a Manager for the last two years has been a rewarding experience. It has taught me much about the restaurant business, including staff management, menu development, and managing budgets.

Developing appealing menu options has been challenging. From the time I declared a major in management, I have wanted to manage to focus more on corporate strategy development and implementation. Now, that goal is becoming a reality, as I have accepted a job as the regional manager for the Steak and Ale franchise, beginning two weeks from today. If satisfactory with you, I would like February 15 to be my last day in my position here.

Thank you for the confidence you placed in me, your positive rapport with the staff, and your expressions of appreciation for my work. As I continue my career, I will always recall pleasant memories of my position at AppleTree.

- Begins with appreciative comments to buffer bad news.

- Presents reasons that lead to main idea, the resignation.

- States resignation, including additional details.

- Conveys genuine appreciation for experience gained and ends on cordial note.

© Cengage Learning 2013

delay and expressing gratitude for their efforts is appropriate.

- **Send a sincere, original thank-you message after a position has been accepted.** This thoughtful gesture will build a positive relationship with a

person who might continue to be important to your career. The message in Figure 14-7 is brief and avoids clichés and exaggerated expressions of praise but instead gives specific examples of the importance of the reference's recommendation.

Figure 14-7  Example of a Thank-You Message to a Reference

Thank you so much for the letter of recommendation you prepared for my application to CorpComm Associates. I learned today that I have been hired and will begin work next month.

Because the position is in public relations, I believe your comments about my performance in your communication classes carried a great deal of weight. Ms. Myer commented that she was impressed with the wealth of evidence and examples you provided to support your statements, unlike the general recommendations she frequently receives.

Dr. Worsham, I appreciate your helping me secure an excellent position in a highly competitive job market. Thanks for the recommendation and your outstanding instruction. I look forward to talking with you about how I am faring in the real world when I return to campus for fall homecoming.

- States main idea of appreciation for recommendation. Informs reference of success in locating job.

- Communicates sincere appreciation for assistance; uses specific examples and avoids exaggeration.

- Restates main idea and anticipates continued relationship; is original and sincere.

© Cengage Learning 2013

Grammar and Usage Appendix

Polishing your language skills will aid you in preparing error-free documents that reflect positively on you and your company. This text appendix is an abbreviated review that focuses on common problems frequently encountered by business writers and offers a quick "refreshing" of key skills.

Grammar

Sentence Structure

1. **Rely mainly on sentences that follow the normal subject-verb-complement sequence for clarity and easy reading.**

   <u>Jennifer</u> and <u>I</u> <u>withdrew</u> for two <u>reasons</u>.
      (subject)   (verb)   (complement)

Original	**Better**
There are two <u>reasons</u> for our withdrawal.	Two <u>reasons</u> for our withdrawal are . . . .
	<u>Jennifer</u> and <u>I</u> withdrew for two reasons.
<u>It</u> is necessary that we withdraw.	<u>We</u> must withdraw.
<u>Here</u> is a copy of my résumé.	The enclosed <u>résumé</u> outlines . . . .

   There, *it*, and *here* are *expletives*—filler words that have no real meaning in the sentence.

2. **Put pronouns, adverbs, phrases, and clauses near the words they modify.**

Incorrect	**Correct**
Angie put a new type of gel in her hair, <u>which</u> she had just purchased.	Angie put a new type of <u>gel</u>, <u>which</u> she had just purchased, in her hair.
He works <u>only</u> in the call center during peak periods.	He works in the call center <u>only</u> during peak periods.
The clerk stood near the fax machine <u>wearing a denim skirt</u>.	The clerk <u>wearing a denim skirt</u> stood near the fax machine.

3. **Do not separate subject and predicate unnecessarily.**

Incorrect	**Clear**
<u>She</u>, hoping to receive a bonus, <u>worked</u> rapidly.	Hoping to receive a bonus, <u>she</u> <u>worked</u> rapidly.

4. **Place an introductory phrase near the subject of the independent clause it modifies.** Otherwise, the phrase dangles. To correct the dangling phrase, change the subject of the independent clause, or make the phrase into a dependent clause by assigning it a subject.

Incorrect	**Correct**
<u>When</u> a young boy, <u>my mother</u> insisted I learn a second language. [Implies that the mother was once a young boy.]	<u>When I was a young boy</u>, my mother insisted I learn a second language.
<u>Working</u> at full speed every morning, <u>fatigue</u> overtakes me in the afternoon. [Implies that "fatigue" was working at full speed.]	<u>Working</u> at full speed every morning, <u>I</u> become tired in the afternoon.
	<u>Because I work</u> at full speed every morning, <u>fatigue</u> overtakes me in the afternoon.
<u>To function</u> properly, <u>you</u> must oil the machine every hour. [Implies that if "you" are "to function properly," the machine must be oiled hourly.]	<u>If the equipment</u> is to function properly, <u>you</u> must oil it every hour.
	<u>To function properly</u>, the <u>equipment</u> must be oiled every hour.

5. **Express related ideas in similar grammatical form (use parallel construction).**

Incorrect	Correct
The machine operator made three resolutions: (1) <u>to be punctual</u>, (2) <u>following instructions carefully</u>, and third, <u>the reduction of waste</u>.	The machine operator made three resolutions: <u>to be punctual</u>, <u>to follow instructions carefully</u>, and <u>to reduce waste</u>.
The human resources manager is concerned with the <u>selection</u> of the right worker, <u>providing</u> appropriate orientation and the <u>worker's progress</u>.	The human resources manager is concerned with <u>selecting</u> the right worker, <u>providing</u> appropriate orientation, and <u>evaluating</u> the worker's progress.

6. **Do not end a sentence with a needless preposition.**

Where is the new sushi bar to be <u>located</u> (not *located at*)?

The applicant did not tell us where he was <u>going</u> (not *going to*).

End a sentence with a preposition if for some reason the preposition needs emphasis.

I am not concerned with what he is paying <u>for</u>. I am concerned with what he is paying <u>with</u>.

The prospect has everything—a goal to work <u>toward</u>, a house to live <u>in</u>, and an income to live <u>on</u>.

7. **Avoid split infinitives.** Two words are required to express an infinitive: *to* plus a *verb*. The two words belong together. An infinitive is split when another word is placed between the two.

Incorrect	Correct
The superintendent used <u>to</u> occasionally <u>visit</u> the offices.	The superintendent used <u>to visit</u> the offices occasionally.
I plan <u>to</u> briefly <u>summarize</u> the report.	I plan <u>to summarize</u> the report briefly.

Exercise 1

Identify the weakness in each sentence and write an improved version.

1. It is essential that you learn to design spreadsheets that make financial information meaningful to users.

2. There are many online tools available that build relationships with customers.

3. I am submitting an employee testimonial to the company website, which I first posted to a presentation blog.

4. More companies are videoconferencing because of the need to significantly reduce travel costs.

5. To operate efficiently, you must perform periodic maintenance on your computer.

6. Planned store improvements include widening the aisles, improved lighting, and lower shelves for a sophisticated feel.

Pronoun Reference

1. **Make a pronoun agree in number with its antecedent (the specific noun for which a pronoun stands).**

   a. Use a plural pronoun when it represents two or more singular antecedents connected by *and*.

   The secretary <u>and</u> the treasurer will take <u>their</u> vacations.
   ["The" before "treasurer" indicates that the sentence is about two people.]

   The <u>secretary</u> and <u>treasurer</u> will take <u>his</u> vacation.
   [Omitting "the" before "treasurer" indicates that the sentence is about one person who has two sets of responsibilities.]

   b. Parenthetical remarks (remarks that can be omitted without destroying the basic meaning of the sentence) that appear between the pronoun and its antecedent have no effect on the form of the pronoun.

   President Ritter, <u>not the managers</u>, is responsible for his strategic goals.
   [Because "his" refers to President Ritter and not to "managers," "his" is used instead of "their."]

   c. Use a singular pronoun with *each*, *everyone*, *no*, and their variations.

   <u>Each</u> student and <u>each</u> team member will perform <u>his or her</u> own data collection.

   <u>Everyone</u> is responsible for <u>her or his</u> work.

   d. Use a singular pronoun when two or more singular antecedents are connected by *or* or *nor*.

   <u>Neither</u> Brandon <u>nor</u> Will can complete <u>his</u> work.

   Ask <u>either</u> Mallory <u>or</u> Suzanne about <u>her</u> in-service training.

   e. Use pronouns that agree in number with the intended meaning of collective nouns.

   The <u>team</u> has been asked for <u>its</u> contributions. ["Team" is thought of as a unit; the singular "its" is appropriate.]

   The <u>team</u> have been asked for <u>their</u> contributions. ["Team" is thought of as more than one individual; the plural "their" is appropriate.]

2. **Place relative pronouns as near their antecedents as possible for clear understanding.** A relative pronoun joins a dependent clause to its antecedent.

Ambiguous	**Clear**
The <u>members</u> were given receipts <u>who</u> have paid.	The <u>members</u> <u>who</u> have paid were given receipts.
The agreement will enable you to pay <u>whichever</u> is lower, <u>6 percent or $50</u>.	The agreement will enable you to pay <u>6 percent or $50</u>, <u>whichever</u> is lower.

Restate a noun instead of risking a *vague* pronoun reference.

Vague	**Clear**
The officer captured the suspect even though <u>he</u> was unarmed.	The officer captured the suspect even though <u>the officer</u> was unarmed.

3. **Do not use a pronoun by itself to refer to a phrase, clause, sentence, or paragraph.** A pronoun should stand for a noun, and that noun should appear in the writing.

Incorrect	**Correct**
He expects to take all available accounting courses and obtain a position in a public accounting firm. <u>This</u> appeals to him.	He expects to take all available accounting courses and obtain a position in a public accounting firm. <u>This plan</u> appeals to him.

Exercise 2

In each of the sentences below, choose the correct word in parentheses.

1. Conversation skills and good listening (affect, affects) a leader's effectiveness.

2. Each sales rep (was, were) trained to encourage customers to buy more than one size or color since shipping is free.

3. The production manager, not the controller, presented (her, their) strongly opposing views.

4. Neither Stephen nor Lydia (was, were) recognized for their contribution.

5. The company restructured (its, their) recreation event to avoid a frivolous perception.

6. The committee will present (its, their) recommendation at the next staff meeting.

7. Jenna forgot to retain her receipts; (this, this oversight) caused a delay in reimbursement.

Pronoun Case

1. **Use the correct case of pronouns.** *Case* tells whether a pronoun is used as the subject of a sentence or as an object in it.

   a. Use nominative-case pronouns (also known as subjective-case pronouns) (*I, he, she, they, we, you, it, who*) as subjects of a sentence or clause.

   <u>You</u> and <u>I</u> must collaborate. ["You" and "I" are subjects of the verb "collaborate."]

   Those <u>who</u> work will be paid. ["Who" is the subject of the dependent clause "who work."]

   b. Use objective-case pronouns (*me, him, her, them, us, you, it, whom*) as objects of verbs and prepositions.

   His mother texted <u>him</u> about the family emergency. ["Him" is the object of the verb "texted."]

   The customer feedback survey was sent to the project manager and <u>them</u>. ["Them" is the object of the preposition "to."]

   To <u>whom</u> should we send the analysis? ["Whom" is the object of the preposition "to."]

   TIP: Restate a subordinate clause introduced by *who* or *whom* to determine the appropriate pronoun.

   She is the type of manager <u>whom</u> we can promote. [Restating "whom we can promote" as "We can promote her (whom)" clarifies that "whom" is the object.]

   She is the type of manager <u>who</u> can be promoted. [Restating "who can be promoted" as "She (who) can be promoted" clarifies that "who" is the subject.]

   TIP: Change a question to a statement to determine the correct form of a pronoun.

   <u>Whom</u> did you call? [You did call *whom*.]

   <u>Whom</u> did you select for the position? [You did select *whom* for the position.]

   c. Use the nominative case when forms of the linking verb *be* require a pronoun to complete the meaning.

   It was <u>he</u> who received credit for the sale.

   It is <u>she</u> who deserves the award.

   ["It was he" may to some people sound just as distracting as the incorrect "It was him." Express the ideas in a different way to avoid the error and an expletive beginning.]

   He was the one who received credit for the sale.

   She deserves the award.

d. Use the possessive form of a pronoun before a gerund (a verb used as a noun).

We were delighted at his (not *him*) assuming a leadership role.
["Assuming a leadership role" is used here as a noun. "His" in this sentence serves the same purpose it serves in "We are delighted at his initiative."]

> **Exercise 3**
>
> In each of the sentences below, choose the correct pronoun in parentheses.
>
> 1. The professor agreed to award (we, us) partial credit for the confusing question.
>
> 2. Stacey requested that tasks be divided equally between Addison and (her, she).
>
> 3. It was (her, she) (who, whom) recommended revising the company's technology policy to include social networking sites.
>
> 4. The manager seemed unaware of (him, his) inability to relate to younger employees.
>
> 5. Emma is a leader in (who, whom) we have great confidence.

Verb Agreement

1. **Make subjects agree with verbs.**

   a. Ignore intervening phrases that have no effect on the verb used.

   Good material and fast delivery are (not *is*) essential.

   You, not the carrier, are (not *is*) responsible for the damage. [Intervening phrase, "not the carrier," does not affect the verb used.]

   The attitude of these investors is (not *are*) a deep concern. [The subject is "attitude"; "of these investors" is a phrase coming between the subject and the verb.]

   b. Use a verb that agrees with the noun closer to the verb when *or* or *nor* connects two subjects.

   Only one or two questions are (not *is*) necessary.

   Several paint brushes or one paint roller is (not *are*) necessary.

   c. Use singular verbs with plural nouns that have a singular meaning or are thought of as singular units.

The news is good.	Economics is a required course.
Twenty dollars is too much.	Ten minutes is sufficient time.

d. Use a singular verb for titles of articles, firm names, and slogans.

"Etiquette in the Age of Social Media" is an interesting article.

Forestieri and Chaudrue is the oldest firm in the city.

"Eat Smart for Hearts" is a campaign slogan directed at better nutrition for senior adults.

2. **Choose verbs that agree in person with their subjects.** *Person* indicates whether the subject is (1) speaking, (2) being spoken to, or (3) being spoken about.

First person: I am, we are.
[Writer or speaker]

Second person: You are.
[Receiver of message]

Third person: He is, she is, they are.
[Person being discussed]

She doesn't (not *don't*) eat well or exercise regularly.

They don't recognize the value of strong networking skills.

Verb Tense and Mood

1. **Use the appropriate verb tense.** *Tense* indicates time. Tense can be either simple or compound.

Simple tenses:

Present: I see you. [Tells what is happening now.]

Past: I saw you. [Tells what has already happened.]

Future: I will see you. [Tells what is yet to happen.]

Compound tenses:

Present perfect: I have seen you. [Tells of past action that extends to the present.]

Past perfect: I had seen you. [Tells of past action that was finished before another past action.]

Future perfect: I will have seen you. [Tells of action that will be finished before a future time.]

a. Use present tense when something was and still is true.

The speaker reminded us that Rhode Island is (not *was*) smaller than Wisconsin.

The consultant's name is (not *was*) Ryan Abrams.

b. Avoid unnecessary shifts in tense.

The carrier <u>brought</u> (not *brings*) my package but <u>left</u> without asking me to sign for it.

Verbs that appear in the same sentence are not required to be in the same tense.

The contract that <u>was prepared</u> yesterday <u>will be signed</u> tomorrow.

2. **Use subjunctive mood to express situations that are untrue or highly unlikely.** Be sure to use *were* for the present tense of to *be* to indicate the subjunctive mood. Use *was* when the statement could be true.

I wish the story <u>were</u> (not *was*) true.

If I <u>were</u> (not *was*) you, I would try again.

Exercise 4

In each of the sentences below, choose the correct verb in parentheses.

1. Only one of the free smartphone applications (has, have) value to me.

2. Taxpayers, not the government, (are, is) held accountable for paying the national debt.

3. Neither the manager nor the employees (was, were) aware of the policy change.

4. Both Josh and Krystal (was, were) notified of the impending layoffs.

5. The news from the rescue mission (is, are) encouraging.

6. *Good to Great* (has, have) been placed in the company library.

7. The sales manager announced that Portsmouth, South Carolina, (is, was) the site for the annual sales meeting.

8. Tylor (don't, doesn't) expect preferential treatment.

9. The client studied the financial analysis for a minute and (starts, started) asking questions.

10. If the applicant (was, were) experienced with databases, she would have been hired.

Adjectives and Adverbs

1. **Use an adjective to modify a noun or pronoun and an adverb to modify a verb, an adjective, or another adverb.**

   Adjective: Bryan gave an <u>impressive</u> sales pitch.

   Adverb: The new employee looked <u>enthusiastically</u> at the sales prospect. [The adverb "enthusiastically" modifies the verb "looked."]

   The team leader was <u>really</u> visionary. [The adverb "really" modifies the adjective "visionary."]

   Worker A progressed <u>relatively faster</u> than did Worker B. [The adverb "relatively" modifies the adverb "faster."]

2. **Use an adjective after a linking verb when the modifier refers to the subject instead of to the verb.** [A linking verb connects a subject to the rest of the sentence. "He is old." "She seems sincere."]

   The man entering the building looked <u>suspicious</u>. [The adjective "suspicious" refers to "man," not to "looked."]

3. **Use comparatives (to compare two) and superlatives (to compare three or more) carefully.**

   She is the <u>faster</u> (not *fastest*) of the two workers.

   Edwin is the <u>better</u> (not *best*) writer of the two team members.

   Exclude a person or thing from a group with which that person or thing is being compared.

   He is more observant than <u>anyone else</u> (not *anyone*) in his department. [As a member of his department, he cannot be more observant than himself.]

   "The X-60 is newer than <u>any other machine</u> (not *any machine*) in the plant." [The X-60 cannot be newer than itself.]

Exercise 5

Select the correct word in parentheses.

1. Despite the dangers, employees change their computer passwords (infrequent, infrequently).

2. Daniel looked (impatient, impatiently) at the new production assistant.

3. The server moved (quick, quickly) from table to table.

4. Of the several people I met during the recent speed networking event, Olivia made the (better, best) impression.

5. The Chicago plant has a higher safety record than (any, any other) plant.

Punctuation

Commas

1. **Use a comma**

   a. Between coordinate clauses joined by *and*, *but*, *for*, *or*, and *nor*.

      He wanted to pay his bills on time, <u>but</u> he did not have the money.

   b. To separate introductory clauses and certain phrases from independent clauses. Sentences that begin with dependent clauses (often with words such as *if*, *as*, *since*, *because*, *although*, and *when*) almost always need a comma. Prepositional phrases and verbal phrases with five or more words require commas.

Dependent clause:	<u>If you can postpone your departure</u>, the research team will be able to finalize its proposal submission. [The comma separates the introductory dependent clause from the independent clause.]
Infinitive:	<u>To get the full benefit of our insurance plan</u>, complete and return the enclosed card. [A verb preceded by "to" ("to get").]
Participial:	<u>Believing that her earnings would continue to increase</u>, she requested a higher credit card limit. [A verb form used as an adjective: "believing" modifies the dependent clause "she requested."]
Prepositional phrase:	<u>Within the next few days</u>, you will receive written confirmation of this transaction. [Comma needed because the phrase contains five words.]
	Under the circumstances we think you are justified. [Comma omitted because the phrase contains fewer than five words and the sentence is clear without the comma.]

   c. To separate three or more words in a series.

      You must choose between <u>gray</u>, <u>green</u>, <u>purple</u>, <u>and white</u>. [Without the comma after "purple," no one can tell for sure whether four choices are available, the last of which is "white," or whether three choices are available, the last of which is "purple and white."]

      You must choose between <u>purple</u> <u>and white</u>, <u>gray</u>, <u>and green</u>. [Choice is restricted to three, the first of which is "purple and white."]

   d. Between two or more independent adjectives that modify the same noun.

      New employees are given a <u>long</u>, <u>difficult</u> examination. [Both "long" and "difficult" modify "examination."]

      We want <u>quick</u>, <u>factual</u> news. [Both "quick" and "factual" modify "news."]

      Do not place a comma between two adjectives when the second adjective modifies the adjective and noun as a unit.

      The supervisor is an <u>excellent</u> <u>team</u> <u>player</u>. ["Excellent" modifies the noun phrase "team player."]

   e. To separate a nonrestrictive clause (a clause that is not essential to the basic meaning of the sentence) from the rest of the sentence.

      Kent Murray, <u>who is head of customer resource management</u>, has selected Century Consulting to oversee the product launch. [The parenthetical remark is not essential to the meaning of the sentence.]

      The man <u>who is head of customer resource management</u> has selected Century Consulting to oversee the product launch. [Commas are not needed because "who is head of customer resource management" is essential to the meaning of the sentence.]

   f. To set off or separate dates, addresses, geographical names, degrees, and long numbers:

      On <u>July 2, 2011</u>, Jason Kennedy made the final payment. [Before and after the year in month-day-year format]

      I saw him in <u>Tahoe City, California</u>, on the 12th of October. [Before and after the name of a state when the name of a city precedes it]

      <u>Jesse Marler</u>, President [Between the printed name and the title on the same line beneath a signature or in a letter address]

Tristan A. Highfield
President of Academic Affairs [No comma is used if the title is on a separate line.]

g. To separate parenthetical expressions or other elements interrupting the flow from the rest of the sentence.

Ms. Watson, <u>speaking on behalf of the entire department</u>, accepted the proposal. [Set off a parenthetical expression]

<u>Cole</u>, I believe you have earned a vacation. [After a direct address]

<u>Yes</u>, you can count on me. [After the words *No* and *Yes* when they introduce a statement]

Arun Ramage, <u>former president of the Jackson Institute</u>, spoke to the group. [Set off appositives when neutral emphasis is desired]

The job requires experience, <u>not formal education</u>. [Between contrasted elements]

Exercise 6

Insert needed commas. Write "correct" if you find no errors.

1. The employee who is featured in our latest television commercial is active in the community theatre.

2. Emoticons which are created by keying combinations of symbols to produce "sideway faces" communicate emotion in electronic messages.

3. Sean Cohen a new member of the board remained silent during the long bitter debate.

4. Top social networking sites include Facebook MySpace and Flickr.

5. The entire population was surveyed but three responses were unusable.

6. If you tag websites in a social bookmarking site you can locate them easily for later use.

7. To qualify for the position applicants must have technology certification.

8. We should be spending less money not more.

9. On May 9 2011 the company's Twitter site was launched.

10. Yes the president approved a team-building event to replace our annual golf outing.

Semicolons and Colons

1. **Use a semicolon**

   a. To join the independent clauses in a compound sentence when a conjunction is omitted.

   Your voice counts; email us with your ideas and concerns.

   b. To join the independent clauses in a compound-complex sentence.

   As indicated earlier, we prefer delivery on Saturday morning at four o'clock; but Friday night at ten o'clock will be satisfactory.

   We prefer delivery on Saturday morning at four o'clock; but, if the arrangement is more convenient for you, Friday night at ten o'clock will be satisfactory.

   c. Before an adverbial conjunction. Use a comma after the adverbial conjunction.

Adverbial conjunction:	The shipment arrived too late for our weekend sale; <u>therefore</u>, we are returning the shipment to you.

   Other frequently used adverbial conjunctions are *however*, *otherwise*, *consequently*, and *nevertheless*.

   d. Before words used to introduce enumerations or explanations that follow an independent clause.

Enumeration with commas:	Many factors affect the direction of the stock market; <u>namely</u>, interest rates, economic growth, and employment rates.
Explanation forming a complete thought:	We have plans for improvement; <u>for example</u>, we intend. . . .
	The engine has been "knocking"; <u>that is</u>, the gas in the cylinders explodes before the pistons complete their upward strokes.

   NOTE: The following exceptions require a comma to introduce the enumeration or explanation:

Enumeration without commas:	Several Web 2.0 tools are available, <u>for example</u>, blogs and wikis. [A comma, not a semicolon, is used because the enumeration contains no commas.]

| **Explanation forming an incomplete thought:** | A trend is to replace expensive employee networking events with purposeful recreation, for instance, community service events. [A comma, not a semicolon, is used because the explanation is not a complete thought.] |

e. In a series that contains commas.

Some of our workers have worked overtime this week: Smith, 6 hours; Hardin, 3; Cantrell, 10; and McGowan, 11.

2. Use a colon

a. After a complete thought that introduces a list of items. Use a colon following both direct and indirect introductions of lists.

| **Direct introduction:** | The following three factors influenced our decision: an expanded market, an inexpensive source of raw materials, and a ready source of labor. [The word "following" clearly introduces a list.] |
| **Indirect introduction:** | The carpet is available in three colors: green, burgundy, and blue. |

Do not use a colon after an introductory statement that ends with a preposition or a verb (*are*, *is*, *were*, *include*). The list that follows the preposition or verb finishes the sentence.

| **Incomplete sentence:** | We need to (1) expand our market, (2) locate an inexpensive source of materials, and (3) find a ready source of labor. [A colon does not follow "to" because the words preceding the list are not a complete sentence.] |

b. To stress an appositive (a noun that renames the preceding noun) at the end of a sentence.

A majority of white collar criminals report that a single factor led to their crimes: pressure to achieve revenue targets.

Our progress is due to the efforts of one person: Brooke Keating.

Exercise 7

Insert semicolons, colons, and commas where needed, and delete them where they are unnecessary. Write "correct" if you find no errors.

1. Some privacy concerns have become less important in recent years, however, most people feel extremely vulnerable to privacy invasion.

2. The following agents received bonuses Barnes, $750, Shelley, $800, and Jackson, $950.

3. Employees were notified today of the plant closing they received two weeks' severance pay.

4. This paint does have some disadvantages for example a lengthy drying time.

5. Soon after the applications are received, a team of judges will evaluate them, but the award recipients will not be announced until January 15.

6. The program has one shortcoming: flexibility.

7. The new bakery will offer: frozen yogurt, candies, and baked goods.

8. We are enthusiastic about the plan because: (1) it is least expensive, (2) its legality is unquestioned, and (3) it can be implemented quickly.

Apostrophes

1. Use an apostrophe to form possessives.

a. Add an apostrophe and *s* (*'s*) to form the posessive case of a singular noun or a plural noun that does not end with a pronounced *s*.

| **Singular noun:** | Jenna's position firm's assets employee's benefits |
| **Plural noun without a pronounced *s*:** | men's clothing children's games deer's antlers |

b. Add only an apostrophe to form the possessive of a singular or plural noun that ends with a pronounced *s*.

| **Singular noun with pronounced *s*:** | Niagara Falls' site Ms. Jenkins' interview |
| **Plural noun with pronounced *s*:** | two managers' decision six months' wages |

Exception: An apostrophe and *s* (*'s*) can be added to singular nouns ending in a pronounced *s* if an additional *s* sound is pronounced easily.

| **Singular noun with additional *s* sound:** | boss's decision class's party Jones's invitation |

c. Use an apostrophe with the possessives of nouns that refer to time (minutes, hours, days, weeks, months, and years) or distance in a possessive manner.

eight <u>hours'</u> pay   two <u>weeks'</u> notice

<u>today's</u> global economy   ten <u>years'</u> experience

a <u>stone's</u> throw   a <u>yard's</u> length

Exercise 8

Correct the possessives.

1. The new hires confidence was crushed by the managers harsh tone.

2. This companies mission statement has been revised since it's recent merger.

3. Employees who are retained may be asked to accept a reduction of one weeks pay.

4. Vendors' have submitted sealed bids for the construction contract that will be opened in two week's.

5. Younger workers must appreciate older employees extensive company knowledge.

Hyphens

1. Use a hyphen

a. Between the words in a compound adjective. (A *compound adjective* is a group of adjectives appearing together and used as a single word to describe a noun.)

An <u>eye-catching</u> device   A <u>two-thirds</u> interest

Do not hyphenate a compound adjective in the following cases:

(1) When the compound adjective follows a noun.

A design that is <u>eye catching</u>.

Today's consumers are <u>convenience driven</u>.

NOTE: Some compound adjectives that are familiar hyphenated words or phrases, remain hyphenated when they follow a noun.

The news release was <u>up-to-date</u>.

For jobs that are <u>part-time</u>, ...

(2) An expression made up of an adverb that ends in *ly* and an adjective is not a compound adjective and does not require a hyphen.

<u>commonly accepted</u> principle

<u>widely quoted</u> authority

(3) A simple fraction and a percentage.

Simple fraction:	<u>Two thirds</u> of the respondents
Percentage:	<u>15 percent</u> sales increase

b. To prevent misinterpretation.

<u>Recover</u> a chair [To obtain possession of a chair once more]

<u>Re-cover</u> a chair [To cover a chair again]

<u>Eight inch</u> blades [Eight blades, each of which is an inch long]

<u>Eight-inch</u> blades [Blades eight inches long]

Exercise 9

Add necessary hyphens and delete those that are unnecessary. Write "correct" if you find no errors.

1. The web based application was unavailable because of a denial of service attack.

2. State of the art computers provide quick access to timely-business information.

3. A large portion of holiday orders are time sensitive.

4. A two thirds majority is needed to pass the 5-percent increase in employee wages.

5. Nearly one-half of the respondents were highly-educated professionals.

Quotation Marks and Italics

1. Use quotation marks

a. To enclose direct quotations.

Single-sentence quotation:	The supervisor said, "We will make progress."
Interrupted quotation:	"We will make progress," the supervisor said, "even though we have to work overtime."
Multiple-sentence quotation:	The manager said, "Have a seat, Seth. Please wait a moment while I complete this email." [Place quotation marks before the first word and after the last word of a multiple-sentence quotation.]
Quotation within quotation:	The budget director said, "Believe me when I say 'A penny saved is a penny earned' is the best advice I ever had." [Use single quotation marks to enclose a quotation that appears within a quotation.]

b. To enclose titles of songs, magazine and newspaper articles, lecture titles, and themes within text.

"Candle in the Wind"   "Making an Impact"

The chapter, "Online Presence," . . . .

c. To enclose a definition of a defined term. Italicize the defined word.

The term *downsizing* is used to refer to "the planned reduction in the number of employees."

d. To enclose words used in humor, a word used when a different word would be more appropriate, slang expressions that need to be emphasized or clarified for the reader, or nicknames. These words can also be shown in italics.

Humor/ different word: Our "football" team. . . . [Hints that the team appears to be playing something other than football.]

Our football "team" . . . . [Hints that "collection of individual players" would be more descriptive than "team."]

. . . out for "lunch." [Hints that the reason for being out is something other than lunch.]

Slang: The "tipping point" in the planned reorganization is securing support of union management.

Nicknames: And now for some comments by Robert "Bob" Johnson.

2. Use italics

a. To mention words, letters, numbers, and phrases within a sentence.

He had difficulty learning to spell *recommendation*.

b. To emphasize a word that is not sufficiently emphasized by other means.

Our goal is to hire the *right* person, not necessarily the most experienced candidate.

c. To indicate the titles of books, magazines, and newspapers.

Creating a Culture of Excellence

The New York Times

Reader's Digest

Exercise 10

Add necessary quotation marks and italics.

1. Cynthia Cooper's Extraordinary Circumstances is required reading in some forensic accounting classes.

2. The article How to Persuade People to Say Yes appeared in the May 2009 issue of Training Journal.

3. The consultant's accomplishments are summarized on her opening blog page. [Indicate that a word other than *accomplishments* may be a more appropriate word.]

4. Connie said I want to participate in a volunteer program that serves such a worthy cause. [direct quotation]

5. The term flame is online jargon for a heated, sarcastic, sometimes abusive message or posting to a discussion group.

6. Limit random tweets but focus on ideas and issues that are interesting and relevant.

Dashes, Parentheses, and Periods

1. Use a dash

a. To place emphasis on appositives.

His answer—the correct answer—was based on years of experience.

Compare the price—$125—with the cost of a single repair job.

b. When appositives contain commas.

Their scores—Chloe, 21; Tairus, 20; and Drew, 19—were the highest in a group of 300.

c. When a parenthetical remark consists of an abrupt change in thought.

The committee decided—you may think it's a joke, but it isn't—that the resolution should be adopted.

NOTE: Use an em dash (not two hyphens) to form a dash in computer-generated copy.

2. Use parentheses for explanatory material that could be left out.

Three of our employees (Kristen Hubbard, Alex Russo, and Mark Coghlan) took their vacations in August.

All our employees (believe it or not) have perfect attendance records.

3. **Use a period after declarative and imperative sentences and courteous requests.**

We will attend. [Declarative sentence]

Complete this report. [Imperative sentence]

Will you please complete the report today. [Courteous request is a question but does not require a verbal answer with requested action]

Exercise 11

Add necessary dashes, parentheses, or periods.

1. Additional consultants, programmers and analysts, were hired to complete the computer conversion. [Emphasize the appositive.]

2. The dividend will be raised to 15 cents a share approved by the Board of Directors on December 1, 2011. [Deemphasize the approval.]

3. Would you link this YouTube video to my slide show?

Number Usage

1. **Use figures**

   a. In most business writing because figures provide deserved emphasis and are easy for readers to locate if they need to reread for critical points. Regardless of whether a number has one digit or many, use figures to express dates, sums of money, mixed numbers and decimals, distance, dimension, cubic capacity, percentage, weights, temperatures, and chapter and page numbers.

May 10, 2010	165 pounds
$9 million	Chapter 3, page 29
5 percent (use % in a table)	

   more than 200 applicants (or two hundred) [an approximation]

   b. With ordinals (*th, st, rd, nd*) only when the number precedes the month.

   The meeting is to be held on June 21.

   The meeting is to be held on the 21st of June.

   c. With ciphers but without decimals when presenting even-dollar figures, even if the figure appears in a sentence with another figure that includes dollars and cents.

   Miranda paid $70 for the cabinet.

   Miranda paid $99.95 for the table and $70 for the cabinet.

   d. Numbers that represent time when a.m. or p.m. is used. Words or figures may be used with o'clock.

   Please meet me at 10:15 p.m.

   Please be there at ten o'clock (or 10 o'clock).

   Omit the colon when expressing times of day that include hours but not minutes, even if the time appears in a sentence with another time that includes minutes.

   The award program began at 6:30 p.m. with a reception at 7 p.m.

2. **Spell out**

   a. Numbers if they are used as the first word of a sentence.

   Thirty-two people attended.

   b. Numbers one through nine if no larger number appears in the same sentence.

   Only three auditors worked at the client's office.

   Send 5 officers and 37 members.

   c. The first number in two consecutive numbers that act as adjectives modifying the same noun; write the second number in figures. If the first number cannot be expressed in one or two words, place it in figures also.

   The package required four 44-cent stamps. [A hyphen joins the second number with the word that follows it, thus forming a compound adjective that describes the noun "stamps."]

   We shipped 250 180-horsepower engines today. [Figures are used because neither number can be expressed in one or two words.]

Exercise 12

Correct the number usage in the following sentences taken from a letter or a report.

1. The question was answered by sixty-one percent of the respondents.

2. The meeting is scheduled for 10:00 a.m. on February 3rd.

3. These 3 figures appeared on the expense account: $21.95, $30.00, and $35.14.

4. The purchasing manager ordered 50 4-GB hard drives.

5. 21 members voted in favor of the $2,000,000 proposal.

6. Approximately one hundred respondents requested a copy of the results.

7. Mix two quarts of white with 13 quarts of brown.

8. Examine the cost projections on page eight.

Capitalization

Capitalize

1. **Proper nouns (words that name a particular person, place, or thing) and adjectives derived from proper nouns.** Capitalize the names of persons, places, geographic areas, days of the week, months of the year, holidays, deities, specific events, and other specific names.

Proper nouns	Common nouns
Jessica Moore	An applicant for the management position
Bonita Lakes	A land development
Centre Park Mall	A new shopping center
Veteran's Day	A federal holiday
Information Age	A period of time
Proper adjectives:	Irish potatoes, Roman shades, Swiss army knife, Chinese executives, British accent, Southern dialect

Do not capitalize the name of the seasons unless they are personified.

Old Man Winter

2. **The principal words in the titles of books, magazines, newspapers, articles, compact discs, movies, plays, television series, songs, and poems.**

   The Carrot Principle [Book]

   "Smart Moves for New Leaders" [Article]

   Time [Magazine]

   The White Album [Compact disc]

3. **The names of academic courses that are numbered, are specific course titles, or contain proper nouns.** Capitalize degrees used after a person's name and specific academic sessions.

   Addison Malone is enrolled in classes in <u>French</u>, <u>mathematics</u>, <u>science</u>, and <u>English</u>.

   Students entering the MBA program must complete <u>Accounting 6093</u> and <u>Finance 5133</u>.

   Allison Ward, <u>M.S.</u>, will teach <u>International Marketing</u> during <u>Spring Semester</u> 2011.

   Professor O'Donnell earned a <u>master's</u> degree in business from Harvard.

4. **Titles that precede a name.**

Mr. Ronald Moxley	Editor Deeden
Dr. Lauren Zolna	President Lopez
Uncle Ian	Professor Copley

Do not capitalize titles appearing alone or following a name unless they appear in addresses.

The <u>manager</u> approved the proposal submitted by the <u>editorial assistant</u>.

Jon Sharma, <u>executive vice president</u>, is responsible for that account.

Clint has taken the position formerly held by his <u>father</u>.

Address all correspondence to Colonel Michael Anderson, <u>Department Head</u>, 109 Crescent Avenue, Baltimore, MD 21208.

5. **The main words in a division or department name if the official or specific name is known or the name is used in a return address, a letter address, or a signature block.**

Official or specific name known:	Return the completed questionnaire to the <u>Public Relations Department</u> by March 15.
Official or specific name unknown:	Employees in your <u>information systems division</u> are invited . . . .
Return or letter address, signature block:	Mr. Blake Cain, <u>Manager, Public Relations Department</u>

6. **Most nouns followed by numbers (except in page, paragraph, line, size, and verse references).**

Policy No. 8746826	Exhibit A	Chapter 7
page 97, paragraph 2	Figure 3-5	Model L-379
Flight 340, Gate 22	size 8,	Style 319 jacket

7. **The first word of a direct quotation.**

   The placement officer warned, "Those with offensive email habits may be the first to lose their jobs during layoffs.

   Do not capitalize the first word in the last part of an interrupted quotation or the first word in an indirect quotation.

   "We will proceed," he said, "with the utmost caution." [Interrupted quotation]

   He said that the report must be submitted by the end of the week. [Indirect quotation]

8. **The first word following a colon when a formal statement or question follows.**

   Here is an important rule for report writers: Plan your work and work your plan.

   Each sales staff should ask this question: Do I really look like a representative of my firm?

Exercise 13

Copy each of the following sentences, making essential changes in capitalization.

1. The first question professor Burney asked me during interviewing 101 was "why do you want to work for us?"

2. The remodeling will give the store a more sophisticated feel according to the Public Relations Director.

3. As the Summer Season arrives, gas prices are expected to rise.

4. We recently purchased digital juice, an excellent source of copyright-free animated images.

5. Thomas Frieden, Director of the Center for Disease Control, is the agency's key communicator.

Words Frequently Misused

These words are frequently misused. If you're not certain of meaning or usage, check a dictionary or style guide.

1. Accept, except
2. Advice, advise
3. Affect, effect
4. Among, between
5. Amount, number
6. Capital, capitol
7. Cite, sight, site
8. Complement, compliment
9. Continual, continuous
10. Credible, creditable
11. Council, counsel
12. Different from, different than
13. Each other, one another
14. Eminent, imminent
15. Envelop, envelope
16. Farther, further
17. Fewer, less
18. Formally, formerly
19. Infer, imply
20. Its, it's
21. Lead, led
22. Lose, loose
23. Media, medium
24. Personal, personnel
25. Principal, principle
26. Reason is, because
27. Stationary, stationery
28. That, which
29. Their, there, they're
30. To, too, two

Exercise 14

Select the correct word or phrase in parentheses.

1. What (affect, effect) will the change have on us?

2. The consultant plans to (advice, advise) the company to eliminate the fourth shift for at least three months.

3. The (amount, number) of complaints from customers declined with the addition of online chat.

4. The (cite, sight, site) of the new 24/7 fitness center is being debated.

5. I consider your remark a (compliment, complement); I agree that the granite countertops (compliment, complement) the deep, earthy tones in the room.

6. The three panelists were constantly interrupting (each other, one another).

7. Generally staple merchandise is placed (farther, further) from the cashier than impulse items.

8. Limit your discussion to five or (fewer, less) points.

9. I (infer, imply) from Avanti's comments to the press that the merger will occur.

10. The hurricane seems to be (losing loosing) (its, it's) force, which is (different from, different than) predictions.

11. The chemical engineer (lead, led) the research team's investigation to eliminate (lead, led) from gas emissions.

12. Employees may handle (personal, personnel) business during e-breaks beginning next week.

13. Customer perception is the (principal, principle) reason for the change.

14. (Their, There, They're) planning to complete (their, there, they're) strategic plan this week.

15. The (to, too, two) external auditors expect us (to, too, two) complete (to, too, two) many unnecessary reports.

Solutions to Exercises

Exercise 1—Sentence Structure

1. You must learn to design spreadsheets that make financial information meaningful to users.

2. Many online tools are available that build relationships with customers.

3. I am submitting an employee testimonial, which I first posted to a presentations blog, to the company website.

4. More companies are videoconferencing because of the need to reduce travel costs significantly.

5. You must perform periodic maintenance on your computer to keep it operating efficiently. [The introductory phrase dangles.]

6. Planned store improvements include widening the aisles, improving lighting, and lowering shelves for a sophisticated feel.

   Planned store improvements include widened aisles, improved lighting, and lowered shelves for a sophisticated feel.

Exercise 2—Pronoun Reference

1.	affect	5.	its
2.	was	6.	its
3.	her	7.	this oversight
4.	was		

Exercise 3—Pronoun Case

1.	us	4.	his
2.	her	5.	whom
3.	she; who		

Exercise 4—Verb Agreement, Tense, and Mood

1.	has	6.	has
2.	are	7.	is
3.	were	8.	doesn't
4.	were	9.	started
5.	is	10.	were

Exercise 5—Adjectives and Adverbs

1.	infrequently	4.	best
2.	impatient	5.	any other
3.	quickly		

Exercise 6—Commas

1. Correct

2. Emoticons, which are created by keying combinations of symbols to produce "sideway faces," communicate emotion in electronic messages.

3. Sean Cohen, a new member of the board, remained silent during the long, bitter debate.

4. Top social networking sites include Facebook, MySpace, and Flickr.

5. The entire population was surveyed, but three responses were unusable.

6. If you tag websites in a social bookmarking site, you can locate them easily for later use.

7. To qualify for the position, applicants must have technology certification.

8. We should be spending less money, not more.

9. On May 9, 2011, the company's Twitter site was launched.

10. Yes, the president approved a team building event to replace our annual golf outing.

Exercise 7—Semicolons and Colons

1. Some privacy concerns have become less important in recent years; however, most people feel extremely vulnerable to privacy invasion.

2. The following agents received bonuses: Barnes, $750; Shelley, $800; and Jackson, $950.

3. Employees were notified today of the plant closing; they received two weeks' severance pay.

4. This paint does have some disadvantages, for example, a lengthy drying time.

5. Soon after the applications are received, a team of judges will evaluate them; but the award recipients will not be announced until January 15.

6. Correct

7. The new bakery will offer frozen yogurt, candies, and baked goods.

8. We are enthusiastic about the plan because (1) it is least expensive, (2) its legality is unquestioned, and (3) it can be implemented quickly.

Exercise 8—Apostrophes

1. hire's; manager's
2. company's; its
3. week's
4. Vendors; weeks
5. employees'

Exercise 9—Hyphens

1. web-based; denial-of-service attack
2. State-of-the-art; timely business
3. Correct
4. two-thirds; 5 percent
5. one half; highly educated

Exercise 10—Quotation Marks and Italics

1. Cynthia Cooper's *Extraordinary Circumstances* is required reading in some forensic accounting classes. [Italicizes a book title]

2. The article "How to Persuade People to Say Yes" appeared in the May 2009 issue of *Training Journal*. [Encloses the name of an article in quotation marks and italicizes the title of a journal]

3. The consultant's "accomplishments" are summarized on her opening blog page. [Uses quotation marks to introduce doubt about whether *accomplishments* is the right label; her undertakings may have been of little significance]

4. Connie said, "I want to participate in a volunteer program that serves such a worthy cause." [Uses quotations marks in a direct quotation]

5. The term *flame* is online jargon for "a heated, sarcastic, sometimes abusive message or posting to a discussion group." [Italicizes a defined term and encloses the definition in quotes]

6. Limit random "tweets" but focus on ideas and issues that are interesting and relevant. [Uses quotation marks to emphasize or clarify a word for the reader]

Exercise 11—Dashes, Parentheses, and Periods

1. Additional consultants—programmers and analysts—were hired to complete the computer conversion.

2. The dividend will be raised to 15 cents a share (approved by the Board of Directors on December 1, 2011).

3. Would you link this YouTube video to my slide show. [Uses a period to follow courteous request that requires no verbal response]

Exercise 12—Number Usage

1. The question was answered by 61 percent of the respondents.

2. The meeting is scheduled for 10 a.m. on February 3.

3. These three figures appeared on the expense account: $21.95, $30, and $35.14.

4. The purchasing manager ordered fifty 4-GB Flash drives.

5. Twenty-one members voted in favor of the $2 million proposal.

6. Approximately 100 respondents requested a copy of the results. [Approximations above nine that can be expressed in one or two words may be written in either figures or words, but figures are more emphatic.]

7. Mix 2 quarts of white with 13 quarts of brown.

8. Examine the diagram on page 8.

Exercise 13—Capitalization

1. The first question Professor Burney asked me during Interviewing 101 was "Why do you want to work for us?"

2. The remodeling will give the store a more sophisticated feel according to the public relations director.

3. As the summer season arrives, gas prices are expected to rise.

4. We recently purchased Digital Juice, an excellent source of copyright-free animated images.

5. Thomas Frieden, director of the Center for Disease Control, is the agency's key communicator.

Exercise 14—Words Frequently Misused

1. effect
2. advise
3. number
4. site
5. compliment; complement
6. one another
7. farther
8. fewer
9. infer
10. losing; its; different from
11. led; lead
12. personal
13. principal
14. They're; their
15. two; to; too

References

Chapter 1

1. Koncz, A. (2007, March 15). Employers cite communication skills, honesty/integrity as key for job candidates. National Association of Colleges and Employers. Retrieved from **www.naceweb.org/press/display.asp?year=2007&prid=254**.
2. http://money.cnn.com/magazines/fortune/bestcompanies/2011/snapshots/1.html.
3. Tapscott, D. (2008, December 8). Supervising Net Gen. *Business Week Online, 5*. Retrieved from Business Source Complete database.
4. Slayton, M. (1980). *Common sense & everyday ethics*. Washington, DC: Ethics Resource Center.
5. Slayton, M. (1991, May–June). Perspectives. *Ethics Journal*. Washington, DC: Ethics Resource Center.
6. When something is rotten. (2002, July 27). *Economist, 53+*.
7. A gift or a bribe? (2002, September). *State Legislatures, 2*(8), 9.
8. Mathison, D. L. (1988). Business ethics cases and decision models: A call for relevancy in the classroom. *Journal of Business Ethics, 10*, 781.
9. "Bernie Madoff Sentenced to 150 Years." Retrieved from http://abclocal.go.com/ktrk/story?section=news/national_world&id=6888994.
10. Jelly Belly Candy Company: Expanding internationally. (2007). *Talent Management*. Retrieved from **http://www.talentmgt.com/departments/application/54/**.
11. McGarry, M. J. (1994, June 9). Short cuts. *Newsday*, p. A50.
12. Mason, R. O. (1986). Four ethical issues of the information age. In Dejoie, R., Fowler, G., & Paradice, D. (1991). *Ethical issues in information systems* (pp. 46–55). Boston: Boyd & Fraser.
13. Felts, C. (1995). Taking the mystery out of self-directed work teams. *Industrial Management, 37*(2), 21–26.
14. Miller, B. K., & Butler, J. B. (1996, November/December). Teams in the workplace. *New Accountant*, 18–24.
15. Ray, D., & Bronstein, H. (1995). *Teaming up*. New York: McGraw Hill.
16. The trouble with teams. (1995, January 14). *Economist*, 61.
17. Frohman, M. A. (1995, April 3). Do teams . . . but do them right. *Industry Week*, 21–24.
18. Zuidema, K. R., & Kleiner, B. H. (1994). New developments in developing self-directed work groups. *Management Decision, 32*(8), 57–63.
19. Barry, D. (1991). Managing the baseless team: Lessons in distributed leadership. *Organizational Dynamics, 20*(1), 31–47.

Chapter 2

1. Interpersonal intelligence. (2009). My Personality. Retrieved from **www.mypersonality.info/multiple-intelligences/interpersonal/**.
2. Galpin, T. (1995, April). Pruning the grapevine. *Training & Development, 49*(4), 28+.
3. Hersey, P., & Blanchard, K. H. (1982). *Management of organizational behavior: Utilizing human resources* (4th ed.). Englewood Cliffs, NJ: Prentice-Hall.
4. Felts, C. (1995). Taking the mystery out of self-directed work teams. *Industrial Management, 37*(2), 21–26.
5. Mehrabian, A. (1971). *Silent messages*. Belmont, CA: Wadsworth.
6. Tapscott, D. (2008, December 8). Supervising Net Gen. *Business Week Online, 5*. Retrieved from Business Source Complete database.
7. Hillkirk, J. (1993, November 9). More companies reengineering: Challenging status quo now in vogue. *USA Today*, 1b.
8. Lehman, C., & DuFrene, D. Communication in Virtual Teams, Enrichment Module. Retrieved from http://www.cengagesites.com/academic/assets/sites/4004/bcomm/0538756055_Virtual%20Teams.pdf.
9. Zuidema, K. R., & Kleiner, B. H. (1994, October). Self-directed work groups gain popularity. *Business Credit*, 21–26.
10. Hunt, V. D. (1993). *Managing for quality: Integrating quality and business strategy* (p. 121). Homewood, IL: Business One Irwin.
11. Chaney, L. H., & Lyden, J. A. (1998, May). Managing meetings to manage your image. *Supervision, 59*(5), 13–15.
12. Munter, M. (1998, June). Meeting technology: From low-tech to high-tech. *Business Communication Quarterly, 61*(2), 80–87.
13. Ibid.
14. Gillette, B. (2006) Bad meetings can cost companies millions in money, time. *The Mississippi Business Journal*, September 6. Retrieved from http://www.allbusiness.com/north-america/united-states-mississippi/4089649-1.html.

Chapter 3

1. Canavor, N., & Meirowitz, C. (2005). Good corporate writing: Why it matters, and what to do; Poor corporate writing—in press releases, ads, brochures, web sites and more—is costing companies credibility and revenues. Here's how to put the focus back on clear communication. *Communication World, 22*(4), 30(4).
2. Dennett, J. T. (1988, September). Not to say is better than to say: How rhetorical structure reflects cultural context in Japanese-English technical writing. *IEEE Transactions on Professional Communication, 31*(3), 116–119. doi: 10.1109/47.7816.
3. Jury sent message with huge reward in Vioxx drug case. (2005, August 24). *Gainesville Times*. Retrieved from **www.gainesvilletimes.com**.
4. MacDonald, C. (2009, March 18). Madoff's accountant charged. *The Business Ethics Blog*. Retrieved from **http://open.salon.com/blog/chris_macdonald/2009/03/18/madoffs_accountant_charged**.
5. Goldberg, C., & Allen, S. (2005, March 18). Researcher admits fraud in grant data. Global Healing Center. Retrieved from **www.ghchealth.com**.
6. Another worker pays the price for fabricating resume. (2007, April 28). Retrieved from **www.physorg.com/news96987628.html**.
7. Telushkin, J. (1997). Avoid words that hurt. *USA Today*, 74.
8. Lutz, W. (n.d.). Life under the chief doublespeak officer. Retrieved from **www.dt.org/html/Doublespeak.html**.
9. Dolezalek, H. (2005). The clarity challenge: For too long, business writing has been a lifeless mass of jargon, obscurity, and unnecessary chatter. Can training help people to write more clearly? *Training, 42*(9), 28(5).
10. Obama has apologized for Special Olympics quip. (2009, May 20). *USA Today.com*. Retrieved from **http://news.yahoo.com/s/ap/20090320/ap_on_en_tv/obama_special_olympics**.
11. Horton, T. R. (1990, January). Eschew obfuscation. *Security Management, 34*(1), 22+.
12. Wentz, L. (2009, Oct. 6). McDonald's and Comcast Top Winners at ANA Multicultural Excellence Awards: 'McNugget Love' Picks Up Prize for Exceptional Results. Advertising Age. Retrieved from http://adage.com/article/news/mcdonald-s-comcast-top-winners-ana-multicultural-awards/139479/; and Cho, C., Holcombe, J., & Murphy, D. (2004). Multicultural marketing in contemporary U.S. Markets. Insights Marketing Group. Retrieved from http://www.insights-marketing.com/Documents/Multicultural+Marketing+in+Contemporary+US+Markets.pdf.

Chapter 4

1. Is email making bosses ruder? (2005). *European Business Forum, 21*, 72.
2. Rindegard, J. (1999). Use clear writing to show you mean business. *InfoWorld, 21*(47), 78.

3. Dyrud, M. A. (1996). Teaching by example: Suggestions for assignment design. *Business Communication Quarterly, 59*(3), 67–70.

4. Redish, J. C. (1993). Understanding readers. In C. M. Barnum & S. Carliner (Eds.), *Techniques for technical communicators.* New York: Prentice Hall.

5. Ibid.

6. Wrong number. (1995). *Central New Jersey Business, 8*(13), 3.

7. Neuwirth, R. (1998). Error message: To err is human, but darn expensive. *Editor & Publisher, 131*(29), 4.

8. UCSD sends acceptance email to wrong list. (2009, April 2). *Eschool News.* Retrieved from **http://www .eschoolnews.com/news/around-the-web/index.cfm?i=58045.**

9. Charlton, J. (Ed.) (1985). *The writer's quotation book.* Stamford, CT: Ray Freeman.

10. Charlie Sheen to ABC News: Apologizes for Radio Rants, Says He Will Sue; Details Past Drug Use (2011, Feb. 28). Retrieved from http://www.thefutoncritic.com/ video/2011/02/28/video-charlie-sheen-to-abc-news-apologizes-for-radio-rants-says-he-will-sue-details-past-drug-use-873504/20110228abc01/.

11. Moffit, L. (2010, April 10). Tiger Woods and Other Celebrities Apologize. *Los Angeles Times.* Retrieved from http:// www.latimes.com/entertainment/ news/celebrity/la-et-apologies10apr10-pg,0,1780197.photogallery.

Chapter 5

1. Hear no evil, see no evil: Business e-mail overtakes the telephone. (2007, August 20). *Network.* Retrieved from **www.networkworld.com/community/ node/18555.**

2. Silverman, D. (2009, April 14). Words at work: How to revise an email so that people will read it. Retrieved from **http://blogs.harvardbusiness.org/ silverman/2009/04/how-to-revise-an-email-so-that.html.**

3. Silverman, D. (2009, April 14). Words at work: Is your email businesslike—or brusque? Retrieved from **http://blogs .harvardbusiness.org/silverman/2009/ 05/is-your-email-businesslike-or.html.**

4. New technology makes work harder. (1999, June 1). *BBC News.* Retrieved from **http://news.bbc.co.uk/2/hi/ science/nature/357993.stm.**

5. Lacy, S. (2006, January 6). IM security one tough sell. *BusinessWeek Online*, 11.

6. Knapp, L. (2007, January 20). Switching to texting has pluses, minuses: Getting started. *The Seattle Times*, p. E6. Retrieved from General Business File database.

7. McGrath, C. (2006, January 22). The pleasures of the text. *The New York Times*, p. 15.

8. Knapp, L. (2007, January 20). Switching to texting has pluses, minuses: Getting started. *The Seattle*

Times, p. E6. Retrieved from General Business File database.

9. Electronic Privacy Information Center. (2008, September 15). Public opinion on privacy. Retrieved from **www.epic .org/privacy/survey.**

10. 9th circuit rules on text-message privacy. (2008, July 15). *Law.com.* Retrieved from **www.law.com/jsp/ legaltechnology/pubArticleLT .jsp?id=1202422970200.**

11. Brown, P. B. (2005, December 31). Resolved: I will take good advice. *The New York Times.* Retrieved from **http://www.nytimes.com/2005/12/31/ business/31offline.html.**

12. Mabrey, V., Scott, D. W., & Foster, M. (2008, March 24). Charges filed in Detroit mayor scandal. *ABC News.* Retrieved from **http://abcnews.go.com/ print?id=4355795.**

13. Varchaver, N. (2003). The perils of e-mail. *Fortune, 147*(3), 96+.

14. Ibid.

15. Downer, K. (2008). A great website in five steps. *Third Sector*, 9.

16. Tierney, J. (2007, April). Ignore universal web design at your own peril. *Multichannel Merchant*, 8.

17. Huettner, B. (2008, January 19). Web accessibility basics. *Professional Communication Society.* Retrieved from **http://ewh.ieee.org/soc/pcs/index .php?q=node/124.**

18. McAlpine, R. (2001). *Web word wizardry: A guide to writing for the Web and intranet.* Berkeley, CA: Ten Speed Press.

19. Fichter, D. (2001, November/December). Zooming in: Writing content for intranets. *Online, 25*(6), 80+.

20. How to write for the web. (2008, March 26). *The Online Journalism Review.* Retrieved from **www.ojr.org/ ojr/wiki/writing.**

21. Goodnoe, E. (2005, August 8). How to use wikis for business. *Information Week.* Retrieved from **www .informationweek.com/news/ management/showArticle.jhtml ?articleID=167600331&pgno= 3&queryText=&isPrev=.**

22. Weblog. (2005). *Loosely coupled.* Retrieved from **www.looselycoupled. com/glossary/weblog.**

23. Quible, Z. K. (2005). Blogs and written business communication courses: A perfect union. *Journal of Education for Business, 80*(6), 327–332.

24. Jones, D. (2005, May 10). CEOs refuse to get tangled up in messy blogs. *USA Today.* Retrieved from Academic Search Premier database.

25. DeBare, I. (2005, May 5). Tips for effective use of blogs in business. *San Francisco Chronicle*, p. C6.

26. Johnson, C. Y. (2008, July 7). Hurry up, the customer has a complaint: As blogs expand the reach of a single voice, firms monitor the Internet looking for the dissatisfied. *The Boston Globe.* Retrieved from **www.Boston.com.**

27. Hutchins, J. P. (2005, November 14). Beyond the water cooler. *Computerworld, 39*(46), 45–46.

28. How to get the most out of voice mail (2000, February). *The CPA Journal, 70*(2), 11.

29. Leland, K., & Bailey, K. (1999). *Customer service for dummies* (2nd ed.). New York: Wiley.

30. Berkley, S. (2003, July). Help stamp out bad voicemail! *The Voice Coach Newsletter.* Retrieved from **www.greatvoice.com/archive_vc/ archiveindex_vc.html.**

31. McCarthy, M. L. (1999, October). Email, voicemail and the Internet: How employers can avoid getting cut by the double-edged sword of technology. *Business Credit, 100*(9), 44+.

32. Krotz, J. L. (2008). Cell phone etiquette: 10 dos and don'ts. *Microsoft Business.* Retrieved from **www .microsoft.com/smallbusiness/resources/ technology/communications /cell-phone-etiquette-10-dos-and-donts .aspx#Cellphoneetiquettedosanddonts.**

33. Cell phone etiquette (2001, March). *Office Solutions, 18*(3), 13.

34. Coustan, D., & Strickland, J. (n.d.). How smartphones work: The future of smartphones. Retrieved from **http:// communication.howstuffworks.com/ smartphone5.htm.**

35. Cheng, R. (2011, April 25). So You Want to Use Your iPhone for Work? Uh-oh. How the smartest companies are letting employees use their personal gadgets to do their jobs. *The Wall Street Journal.* Retrieved from http://online.wsj.com/article/ SB10001424052748704641604576255223445021138.html?KEYWORDS= corporate+email.

Chapter 6

1. Williamson, M. (2008, June 11). Twittering the Internet. *TechnologyStory .com.* Retrieved from **http://www .technologystory.com/2008/06/11/ twittering-the-internet.**

Chapter 7

1. Swisher, K. (2007, October 15). AOL layoffs letter from CEO Randy Falco. *All Things Digital.* Retrieved from **http://kara.allthingsd.com/20071015/ aol-layoffs-letter-from-randy-falco/.**

2. Ethical workforce reflects honest management. (2008, June). *Internal Auditor*, 18–19.

3. Advice from the pros on the best way to deliver bad news. (2003, February). *IOMA's Report on Customer Relationship Management*, 5–6.

4. Purina on pet food recall 4-26-07. (2007). American Kennel Club. Retrieved from **http://clubs.akc.org/brit/NEWS/07 .PurinaPetFoodRecall.htm.**

5. Workers get better at bearing bad news. (2005, October 11). *Personnel Today*, 46.

6. Expert offers advice about how to lay off employees. (2008, October 9).

Immediate Care Business. Retrieved from **http://www.immediatecarebusiness.com/hotnews/laying-off-employees.html.**

Chapter 8

1. Cody, S. (1906). *Success in letter writing: Business and social* (pp. 122–126). Chicago: A. C. McClurg.
2. http://www.cannondale.com/bikes/road/performance-road/synapse.
3. http://www.apple.com/ipad/features/.
4. http://home.mcafee.com/Store/PackageDetail.aspx?pkgid=275.
5. Sinclair, B. (2003, July 20). Handle client complaints. *The Web design business kit.* Retrieved from **http://www.sitepoint.com/article/handle-client-complaints/.**
6. Steak and Ale. (1997). Signature style at Steak and Ale. Dallas, TX: Steak and Ale.

Chapter 9

1. Grimes, B. (2003, May 6). Fooling Google. *PC Magazine, 22*(8), 74.
2. Kinzer, S. (1994, August 22). Germany upholds tax on fast-food restaurants. *The New York Times,* p. 2.

Chapter 10

1. Gallo, C. (2008, December 10). Making YouTube work for your business. *Business Week Online.* Retrieved from **http://www.businessweek.com/smallbiz/content/dec2008/sb2008129_398437.htm?campaign_id=rss_tech.**
2. Martin, M. H. (1997, November 27). The man who makes sense of numbers. *Fortune,* 273–275.
3. Wright, P., & Jansen, C. (1998). How to limit clinical errors in interpretation of data. *Lancet, 352*(9139), 1539–1543.
4. Simons, T. (2004). The multimedia paradox. *Presentations, 18*(9), 24–25.

Chapter 11

No endnotes.

Chapter 12

1. Kalytiak, T. (2008, October). Overcoming speaking anxiety: Toastmasters sculpt shy speakers into outstanding orators. *Alaska Business Monthly.* Retrieved from **http://www.akbizmag.com.**
2. Axtell, R. E. (1992). *Do's and taboos of public speaking: How to get those butterflies flying in formation.* New York: John Wiley.
3. Britz, J. D. (1999, October). You can't catch a marlin with a meatball. *Presentations, 13*(10), A1–22.
4. Hughes, M. (1990). Tricks of the speechwriter's trade. *Management Review, 9*(11), 56–58.
5. Sommerville, J. (2003). Presentation tip: Stop the verbal spam. *About.com: Entrepreneurs.* Retrieved from **http://entrepreneurs.about.com/cs/marketing/a/infodumping.htm.**

6. Simmons, A. (2007). *Whoever tells the best story wins: How to use your own stories to communicate with power and impact.* New York: Amacon.
7. Gallo, Carmine. (2009, April 8). Making your presentations relevant. *Business Week Online,* 15.
8. Axtell, R. E. (1992). *Do's and taboos of public speaking: How to get those butterflies flying in formation.* New York: John Wiley.
9. Decker, B. (1992). *You've got to be believed to be heard.* New York: St. Martin's Press.
10. Hillary Campaign sends "docu-point" to House Dems. (2008, May 10). *Presentation Zen.* Retrieved from **http://www.presentationzen.com/presentationzen/2008/05/hillary-campaig.html.**
11. Earnest, W. (2007). *Save our slides: PowerPoint design that works.* Dubuque, IA: Kendall/Hunt.
12. Ibid.
13. Carson, E. (2009, April 19). DioGuardi on being idol judge: It's not easy. *ABC News.com.* Retrieved from **http://abcnews.go.com/Entertainment/wireStory?id=7374447.**
14. Axtell, R. E. (1992). *Do's and taboos of public speaking: How to get those butterflies flying in formation.* New York: John Wiley.
15. Decker, B. (1992). *You've got to be believed to be heard.* (p. 137). New York: St. Martin's Press.
16. Hanke, J. (1998, January). Presenting as a team. *Presentations, 12*(1), 74–82.
17. Ibid.
18. Ibid.
19. Ibid.
20. Davids, M. (1999). Smiling for the camera. *Journal of Business Strategy, 20*(3), 20–24.
21. Turner, C. (1998, February). Become a web presenter! (Really it's not that hard). *Presentations, 12*(2), 26–27.

Chapter 13

1. Jackson, T. (2003). Find a job you love and success will follow. Career Journal (*The Wall Street Journal*). Retrieved from **http://www.careerjournal.com/jobhunting/strategies/20030415-jackson.html.**
2. Riley, M. F. (2009). *The Riley guide: Employment opportunities and job resources on the Internet.* Retrieved from **http://www.rileyguide.com.**
3. Ireland. S. (2002, July–August). A résumé that works. *Searcher, 10*(7), 98(12).
4. Elefant, C. (2008, March 11). Do employers using Facebook for background checks face legal risks? *Legal Blog Watch.* Retrieved from **http://legalblogwatch.typepad.com/legal_blog_watch/2008/03/do-employers-us.html.**

5. Harshbarger, C. (2003). You're out! *Strategic Finance, 84*(11), 46(4).
6. Garone, E. (2009, March 18). Do references really matter? *WSJ.com: Careers Q&A.* Retrieved from **http://online.wsj.com/article/SB123672074032087901.html.**
7. Are you using the wrong résumé? (2009). *Careerbuilder.com.* Retrieved from **http://www.careerbuilder.com/Article/CB-998-Cover-Letters-and-Resumes-Are-You-Using-the-Wrong-R%C3%A9sum%C3%A9/.**
8. Résumés you don't see every day. (2006). Retrieved from **http://www.dummies.com/WileyCDA/DummiesArticle/id-1610.html.**
9. Young, J. (2002). "E-portfolios" could give students a new sense of their accomplishments. *Chronicle of Higher Education, 48*(26), 31–32.
10. Sipper, R. A. (2007, October 15). Tips for creating a YouTube video résumé. Retrieved from **http://www.associatedcontent.com/article/414702/tips_for_creating_a_youtube_video_resume.html?cat=3.**

Chapter 14

1. Vogt, P. (2006). Acing behavioral interviews. *CareerJournal.com.* Retrieved from **http://www.careerjournal.com/jobhunting/interviewing/19980129-vogt.html.**
2. Marion, L. C. (1997, January 11). Companies tap keyboards to interview applicants. *The News and Observer,* p. B5.
3. Thomson Learning announces name change to Cengage Learning. (2007, October). High Beam Research. Retrieved from **http://www.highbeam.com/doc/1G1-169755193.html.**
4. Burns, D. (2009). *The first 60 seconds: Win the job interview before it begins.* Naperville, IL: Sourcebooks.
5. Lai, P., & Wong, I. (2000). The clash of cultures in the job interview. *Journal of Language for International Business, 11*(1), 31–40.
6. Austin, N. K. (1996, March). The new job interview. *Working Woman,* 23–24.
7. Kennedy, J. L., & Morrow, T. J. (1994). *Electronic résumé revolution: Create a winning résumé for the new world of job seeking.* New York: John Wiley.
8. Kleiman, P. (2003, May). Armed for a multitude of tasks. *The Times Higher Education Supplement,* p. 4.
9. MIT Career Development Center (2008, September 16). STAR method: Behavioral interviewing. Retrieved from **http://web.mit.edu/career/www/guide/star.html.**
10. Stern, L. (2005, January 17). The tough new job hunt. *Newsweek,* 73–74.
11. Interviews: Handling illegal interview questions. *JobWeb.* Retrieved from **http://www.jobweb.org/interviews.aspx?id=1343.**

Index

Key terms are indicated in **bold**.

To help you succeed, we have designed a Review card for each chapter.

reviewcard/ CHAPTER 1
ESTABLISHING A FRAMEWORK FOR BUSINESS COMMUNICATION

Learning Objectives

LO¹: Define communication and describe the value of communication in business.

Communication is the process of exchanging information and meaning between or among individuals through a common system of symbols, signs, and behavior. Managers spend most of their time in communication activities.

LO²: Explain the communication process model and the ultimate objective of the communication process.

People engaged in communication encode and decode messages while simultaneously serving as both senders and receivers.

In this column you'll find summaries of each Learning Objective and key exhibits from the chapter.

effectiveness. Feedback and the opportunity to observe nonverbal signs are always present in face-to-face communication, the most complete of the three communication levels.

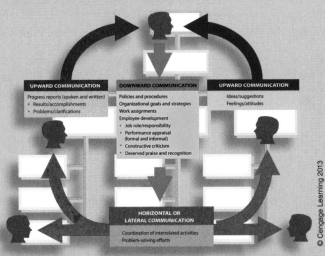

LO³: Discuss how information flows in an organization.

Both formal and informal communication systems exist in every organization; the formal system exists to accomplish tasks, and the informal system serves a personal maintenance purpose that results in people feeling better about themselves and others.

Communication flows upward, downward, and horizontally or laterally. These flows often defy formal graphic description, yet each is a necessary part of the overall communication activity of the organization. Communication takes place at five levels: intrapersonal (communication within one person), interpersonal (communication between two people), group (communication among more than two people), organizational (communication among combinations of groups), and public (communication from one entity to the greater public).

Key Terms

Each card has a list of its chapter's key terms and definitions.

Chronemics the study of how a culture

Diversity skills the ability to communicate effectively with both men and women of all ages, cultures, and minority groups

Downward communication a type of communication that flows from supervisor to employee, from policy makers to operating personnel, or from top to bottom on the organization chart

Encoding the process of selecting and organizing a message

Ethics the principles of right and wrong that guide one in making decisions that consider the impact of one's actions on others as well as on the decision maker

Ethnocentrism the assumption that one's own cultural norms are the right way to do things

External messages messages directed to recipients outside the organization

Feedback a receiver's response to a sender's message

Formal communication channel a channel of communication typified by the formal organization chart; dictated by the technical, political, and economic environment of the organization

Grapevine the best-known component of the informal communication system

Horizontal (or lateral) communication interactions between organizational units on the same hierarchical level

Informal communication channel a channel of communication that continuously develops as people interact within the formal system to accommodate their social and psychological needs

Interferences also called *barriers*; numerous factors that hinder the communication process

Internal messages messages intended for recipients within the organization

Kinesics the study of body language, which is not universal, but instead is learned from one's culture

Organizational communication the movement of information within the company structure

© 2013 Cengage Learning. All Rights Reserved. May not be scanned, copied or duplicated, or posted to a publicly accessible website, in whole or in part.

Proxemics the study of cultural space requirements

Stakeholders people inside and outside the organization who are affected by decisions

Stereotypes mental pictures that one group forms of the main characteristics of another group, creating preformed ideas of what people in this group are like

Synergy a situation in which the whole is greater than the sum of the parts

Team a ...
complem...
a commo...

Telecor...
working ...
and send...
company...

Upward...
municati...
requests ...

Polishing your language skills will help you prepare error-free documents that reflect positively on you and your company. To this end, each card presents a short quiz (and its solutions) to help you assess where your skills might need some additional work.

To refresh your understanding, check out the abbreviated review of grammar principles in the Style Card at the end of this book.

LO⁴: Explain how legal and ethical constraints, diversity challenges, changing technology, and team environment act as strategic forces that influence the process of business communication.

Communication occurs within an environment constrained by legal and ethical requirements, diversity challenges, changing technology, and team environment requirements.

- International, federal, state, and local laws impose legal boundaries for business activity, and ethical boundaries are determined by personal analysis that can be assisted by application of various frameworks for decision making.

- ...munication is ...ically impacted by diversity in nationality, culture, age, gender, ...unities to maximize talent, ideas, and ...erpretation of time, personal space ...slation.

- ...nent of tools for data collection and ...and more effective, and quick and easy ...ns. The use of technology, however, ...nership, access, and privacy.

- ...communication in teams differs from ...ctures. The result of effective teams is ...blems, and higher worker morale.

Grammar Quiz
Sentence Structure

Identify the weakness in each sentence and write an improved version.

1. It is essential that you learn to design spreadsheets that make financial information meaningful to users.
2. There are many online tools available that build relationships with customers.
3. I am submitting an employee testimonial to the company website, which I first posted to a presentation blog.
4. More companies are videoconferencing because of the need to significantly reduce travel costs.
5. To operate efficiently, you must perform periodic maintenance on your computer.
6. Planned store improvements include widening the aisles, improved lighting, and lower shelves for a sophisticated feel.

Grammar Quiz Solutions

6. Planned store improvements include widening the aisles, improving lighting, and lowering shelves for a sophisticated feel. *or* Planned store improvements include widened aisles, improved lighting, and lowered shelves for a sophisticated feel.
5. You must perform periodic maintenance on your computer to keep it operating efficiently.
4. More companies are videoconferencing because of the need to reduce travel costs significantly.
3. I am submitting an employee testimonial, which I first posted to a presentations blog, to the company website.
2. Many online tools available that build relationships with customers.
1. You must learn to design spreadsheets that make financial information meaningful to users.

Use the card before class to preview the new concepts you'll be introduced to in the chapter.

Use the card after class to make sure you've registered the key concepts.

When it's time to prepare for exams, tear out the card and study on the go.

Learning Objectives

LO¹: Define communication and describe the value of communication in business.

Communication is the process of exchanging information and meaning between or among individuals through a common system of symbols, signs, and behavior. Managers spend most of their time in communication activities.

LO²: Explain the communication process model and the ultimate objective of the communication process.

People engaged in communication encode and decode messages while simultaneously serving as both senders and receivers. In the communication process, feedback helps people resolve possible misunderstandings and thus improves communication effectiveness. Feedback and the opportunity to observe nonverbal signs are always present in face-to-face communication, the most complete of the three communication levels.

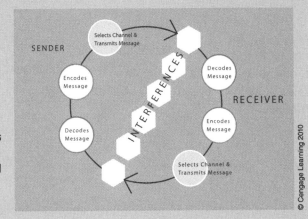

LO³: Discuss how information flows in an organization.

Both formal and informal communication systems exist in every organization; the formal system exists to accomplish tasks, and the informal system serves a personal maintenance purpose that results in people feeling better about themselves and others. Communication flows upward, downward, and horizontally or laterally. These flows often defy formal graphic description, yet each is a necessary part of the overall communication activity of the organization. Communication takes place at five levels: intrapersonal (communication within one person), interpersonal (communication between two people), group (communication among more than two people), organizational (communication among combinations of groups), and public (communication from one entity to the greater public).

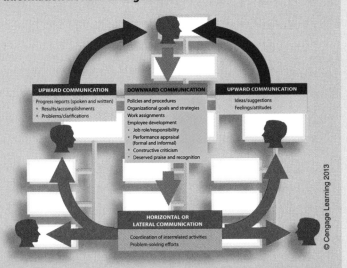

Key Terms

Chronemics the study of how a culture perceives time and its use

Decoding the process of interpreting a message

Diversity skills the ability to communicate effectively with both men and women of all ages, cultures, and minority groups

Downward communication a type of communication that flows from supervisor to employee, from policy makers to operating personnel, or from top to bottom on the organization chart

Encoding the process of selecting and organizing a message

Ethics the principles of right and wrong that guide one in making decisions that consider the impact of one's actions on others as well as on the decision maker

Ethnocentrism the assumption that one's own cultural norms are the right way to do things

External messages messages directed to recipients outside the organization

Feedback a receiver's response to a sender's message

Formal communication channel a channel of communication typified by the formal organization chart; dictated by the technical, political, and economic environment of the organization

Grapevine the best-known component of the informal communication system

Horizontal (or lateral) communication interactions between organizational units on the same hierarchical level

Informal communication channel a channel of communication that continuously develops as people interact within the formal system to accommodate their social and psychological needs

Interferences also called *barriers*; numerous factors that hinder the communication process

Internal messages messages intended for recipients within the organization

Kinesics the study of body language, which is not universal, but instead is learned from one's culture

Organizational communication the movement of information within the company structure

Proxemics the study of cultural space requirements

Stakeholders people inside and outside the organization who are affected by decisions

Stereotypes mental pictures that one group forms of the main characteristics of another group, creating preformed ideas of what people in this group are like

Synergy a situation in which the whole is greater than the sum of the parts

Team a small number of people with complementary skills who work together for a common purpose

Telecommuting also called *teleworking;* working at home or other remote locations and sending and receiving work from the company office electronically

Upward communication a type of communication that is generally a response to requests from supervisors

LO⁴: **Explain how legal and ethical constraints, diversity challenges, changing technology, and team environment act as strategic forces that influence the process of business communication.**

Communication occurs within an environment constrained by legal and ethical requirements, diversity challenges, changing technology, and team environment requirements.

- International, federal, state, and local laws impose legal boundaries for business activity, and ethical boundaries are determined by personal analysis that can be assisted by application of various frameworks for decision making.
- Communication is critically impacted by diversity in nationality, culture, age, gender, and other factors that offer tremendous opportunities to maximize talent, ideas, and productivity but pose significant challenges in interpretation of time, personal space requirements, body language, and language translation.
- Significant strides have occurred in the development of tools for data collection and analysis, creation of messages that are clearer and more effective, and quick and easy communication with audiences in remote locations. The use of technology, however, poses legal and ethical concerns in regard to ownership, access, and privacy.
- Team environment challenges arise because communication in teams differs from communication in traditional organizational structures. The result of effective teams is better decisions, more creative solutions to problems, and higher worker morale.

Grammar Quiz
Sentence Structure

Identify the weakness in each sentence and write an improved version.

1. It is essential that you learn to design spreadsheets that make financial information meaningful to users.
2. There are many online tools available that build relationships with customers.
3. I am submitting an employee testimonial to the company website, which I first posted to a presentation blog.
4. More companies are videoconferencing because of the need to significantly reduce travel costs.
5. To operate efficiently, you must perform periodic maintenance on your computer.
6. Planned store improvements include widening the aisles, improved lighting, and lower shelves for a sophisticated feel.

Grammar Quiz Solutions

6. Planned store improvements include widening the aisles, improving lighting, and lowering shelves for a sophisticated feel. *or* Planned store improvements include widened aisles, improved lighting, and lowered shelves for a sophisticated feel.
5. You must perform periodic maintenance on your computer to keep it operating efficiently.
4. More companies are videoconferencing because of the need to reduce travel costs significantly.
3. I am submitting an employee testimonial, which I first posted to a presentations blog, to the company website.
2. Many online tools are available that build relationships with customers.
1. You must learn to design spreadsheets that make financial information meaningful to users.

Learning Objectives

LO¹: Explain how behavioral theories about human needs, trust and disclosure, and motivation relate to business communication.

Behavioral theories that address human needs, trust and disclosure, and motivation are essential aspects of interpersonal communication. The needs of all individuals to be heard, appreciated, wanted, and reinforced significantly affect their interpersonal communications.

LO²: Describe the role of nonverbal messages in communication.

Nonverbal communication conveys a significant portion of meaning and includes metacommunications, which are wordless messages that accompany words, and kinesic communications, which are expressed through body language. The meanings of nonverbal messages are culturally derived.

	KNOWN TO SELF	NOT KNOWN TO SELF	
KNOWN TO OTHERS	I Free or Open Area	II Blind Area	
NOT KNOWN TO OTHERS	III Hidden Area	IV Unknown Area	

© iStockphoto.com/Stephen Strathdee

LO³: Identify aspects of effective listening.

Effective listening, which requires effort and discipline, is crucial to effective interpersonal communication and leads to career success. Various types of listening require different strategies.

LO⁴: Identify factors affecting group and team communication.

Organizations are increasingly using group structures to achieve goals. Effective group communication results from shared purpose, constructive activity and behaviors, and positive role fulfillment among members. A team is a special type of group that is typified by strong commitment among members; this commitment results in behaviors that produce synergy.

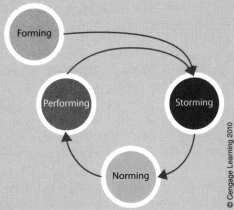

Forming → Storming → Norming → Performing

© Cengage Learning 2010

LO⁵: Discuss aspects of effective meeting management.

Face-to-face meetings and electronic meetings each offer certain advantages and disadvantages. Effective meeting management techniques and behaviors can enhance the success of meetings.

Key Terms

Agenda a meeting outline that includes important information (e.g., date, beginning and ending times, place, topics to be discussed, and responsibilities of those involved)

Brainstorming the generation of many ideas from among team members

Casual listening listening for pleasure, recreation, amusement, and relaxation

Consensus represents the collective opinion of the group, or the informal rule that all team members can live with at least 70 percent of what is agreed upon

Cross-functional team a team that brings together employees from various departments to solve a variety of problems

Directive behavior characterized by leaders who give detailed rules and instructions and monitor closely that they are followed

Empathetic listening listening to others in an attempt to share their feelings or emotions

Forming stage one of team development, in which team members become acquainted with each other and the assigned task

Intensive listening listening to obtain information, solve problems, or persuade or dissuade

Interpersonal intelligence the ability to read, empathize, and understand others

Listening for information listening that involves the search for data or material

Metacommunication a nonverbal message that, although not expressed in words, accompanies a message that is expressed in words

Norm a standard or average behavior

Norming stage three of team development, in which team members develop strategies and activities that promote goal achievement

Performing stage four of team development, in which team members reach the optimal performance level

Product development team usually cross-functional in nature; a group of employees who concentrate on innovation and the development cycle of new products

Quality assurance team a team that focuses on product or service quality; projects can be either short- or long-term

Role tasks employees assume that can involve power and authority that surpasses their formal position on the organization chart

Status one's formal position in the organizational chart

Storming stage two of team development, in which team members deal with conflicting personalities, goals, and ideas

Stroke emotional response one gets in a communication interaction that has either a positive or negative effect on feelings about oneself and others

Supportive behavior characterized by leaders who listen, communicate, recognize, and encourage their followers

Task force a team of workers that is generally given a single goal and a limited time to achieve it

Total Quality Management focuses on creating a more responsible role for the worker in an organization by distributing decision-making power to the people closest to the problem, empowering employees to initiate continuous improvements

Visual kinesic communication gestures, winks, smiles, frowns, sighs, attire, grooming, and all kinds of body movements

Vocal kinesic communication intonation, projection, and resonance of the voice

CHECK YOUR COMMUNICATION | Nonverbal Communication

Metacommunication

Metacommunication is a message that, although not expressed in words, accompanies a message that is expressed in words.

Grammar Quiz

Pronoun Reference and Verb Form

Correct the error in pronoun reference or verb form.

1. Conversation skills and good listening (affect, affects) a leader's effectiveness.
2. Each sales rep (was, were) trained to encourage customers to buy more than one size or color since shipping is free.
3. The production manager, not the controller, presented (her, their) strongly opposing views.
4. Neither Stephen nor Lydia (was, were) recognized for his or her contribution.
5. The company restructured (its, their) recreation event to avoid a frivolous perception.
6. The committee will present (its, their) recommendation at the next staff meeting.
7. Jenna forgot to retain her receipts; (this, this oversight) caused a delay in reimbursement.

Grammar Quiz Solutions

1. affect
2. was
3. her
4. was
5. its
6. its
7. this oversight

Kinesic Messages

Kinesic communication is an idea expressed through nonverbal behavior. In other words, receivers gain additional meaning from what they see and hear—the visual and the vocal:

- *Visual*—gestures, winks, smiles, frowns, sighs, attire, grooming, and all kinds of body movements.
- *Vocal*—intonation, projection, and resonance of the voice.

Understanding Nonverbal Messages

Metacommunications and kinesic communication have characteristics that all communicators should take into account. Nonverbal messages:

- Cannot be avoided.
- May have different meanings for different people.
- Vary between and within cultures.
- May be intentional or unintentional.
- Can contradict the accompanying verbal message and affect whether your message is understood or believed.
- May receive more attention than verbal messages.
- Provide clues about the sender's background and motives.
- Are influenced by the circumstances surrounding the communication.
- May be beneficial or harmful.
- May vary depending upon the person's gender.

© Stockbyte/Getty Images

Learning Objectives

© Cengage Learning 2010

STEP 1	STEP 2	STEP 3	STEP 4	STEP* 5	STEP* 6
Determine the purpose and select an appropriate channel	Envision the audience	Adapt the message to the audience's needs and concerns	Organize the message	Prepare the first draft	Revise and proofread for accuracy and desired impact

*You will focus on the planning process (Steps 1–4) in this chapter; you will learn to prepare the message in Chapter 4 (Steps 5–6).

LO¹: Identify the purpose of the message and the appropriate channel.

Writing is a systematic process that begins by determining the purpose of the message (central idea) and identifying how the central idea will affect the receiver. In view of its effect on the receiver, you can determine the appropriate channel for sending a particular message (e.g., face-to-face, phone call, text, letter, memo, email, instant message, blog, voice mail, or fax).

LO²: Develop clear perceptions of the audience to enhance the impact of the communication and human relations.

Before you compose the first draft, commit to overcoming perceptual barriers that will limit your ability to see an issue from multiple perspectives and thus plan an effective message. Then, consider all you know about the receiver, including age, economic level, educational or occupational background, culture, existing relationship, expectations, and needs.

LO³: Apply techniques for adapting messages to the audience, including strategies for communicating ethically and responsibly.

The insights you gain from seeking to understand your receiver will allow you to adapt the message to fit the receiver's needs. Developing concise, sensitive messages that focus on the receiver's point of view will build and protect goodwill and demand the attention of the receiver. Communicating ethically and responsibly involves stating information truthfully and tactfully, eliminating embellishments or exaggerations, supporting viewpoints with objective facts from credible sources, and designing honest graphics.

LO⁴: Recognize the importance of organizing a message before writing the first draft.

Outlining involves identifying the appropriate sequence of pertinent ideas. Outlining encourages brevity and accuracy, permits concentration on one phase at a time, saves writing time, increases confidence to complete the task, and facilitates appropriate emphasis of ideas. From a receiver's point of view, well-organized messages are easier to understand and promote a more positive attitude toward the sender.

LO⁵: Select the appropriate message pattern (deductive or inductive) for developing messages to achieve the desired response.

An essential part of the planning process is deciding whether the message should be deductive (main idea first) or inductive (explanations and details first). The main idea is presented first and details follow when the receiver is expected to be pleased by the message and the message is routine and not likely to produce a feeling of pleasure or displeasure. When the receiver can be expected to be displeased or not initially interested, explanations and details precede the main idea.

Key Terms

Clichés overused expressions that can cause their users to be perceived as unoriginal, unimaginative, lazy, and perhaps even disrespectful

Connotative meaning the literal meaning of a word plus an extra message that reveals the speaker's or writer's qualitative judgment

Deductive a message in which the major idea precedes the details

Denotative meaning the literal meaning of a word that most people assign to it

Doublespeak also called *doubletalk* or *corporate speak*; euphemisms that deliberately mislead, hide, or evade the truth

Euphemism a kind word substituted for one that may offend or suggest something unpleasant

Goodwill arises when a business is worth more than its tangible assets

Inductive a message in which the major idea follows the details

Jargon specialized terminology that professionals in some fields use when communicating with colleagues in the same field

Libel written defamatory remarks

Outlining the process of identifying central ideas and details and arranging them in the right sequence; should be completed prior to writing

Redundancy a phrase in which one word unnecessarily repeats an idea contained in an accompanying word (e.g., "exactly identical")

Slander spoken defamatory remarks

Subjunctive sentences sentences that speak of a wish, necessity, doubt, or conditions contrary to fact and employ such conditional expressions as *I wish, as if, could, would,* and *might*

Tone the way a statement sounds; it conveys the writer's or speaker's attitude toward the message and the receiver

Focus on the Receiver's Point of View

- Present ideas from the receiver's point of view, conveying the tone that the message is specifically for the receiver.
- Give sincere compliments.

Communicate Ethically and Responsibly

- Present information truthfully, honestly, and fairly.
- Include all information relevant to the receiver.
- Avoid exaggerating or embellishing facts.
- Use objective facts to support ideas.
- Design graphics that avoid distorting facts and relationships.
- Express ideas clearly and understandably.
- State ideas tactfully and positively to build future relationships.

Build and Protect Goodwill

- Use euphemisms to present unpleasant thoughts politely and positively. Use dysphemisms only when they will be viewed humorously. Avoid using euphemisms as well as dysphemisms when they will be taken as excessive, sarcastic, or cruel.
- Avoid doublespeak or corporate speak that confuses or misleads the receiver.
- Avoid using condescending or demeaning expressions.
- Rely mainly on denotative words. Use connotative words that will elicit a favorable reaction, are easily understood, and are appropriate for the setting.
- Choose vivid words that add clarity and interest to your message.
- Use bias-free language:
  - Do not use the pronoun *he* when referring to a group of people that may include women or *she* when a group may include men.

- Avoid referring to men and women in stereotyped roles and occupations, using gender-biased occupational titles, or differentiating genders in an occupation.
- Avoid referring to groups (based on gender, race and ethnicity, age, religion, and disability) in stereotypical and insensitive ways.
- Do not emphasize race and ethnicity, age, religion, or disability when these factors are not relevant.

Convey a Positive, Tactful Tone

- Rely mainly on positive words that speak of what can be done instead of what cannot be done, and of the pleasant instead of the unpleasant. Use negative words when the purpose is to sharpen contrast or when positive words have not evoked the desired reaction.
- Use second person and active voice to emphasize pleasant ideas. Avoid using second person for presenting negative ideas; instead, use third person and passive voice to de-emphasize the unpleasant.
- Consider stating an unpleasant thought in the subjunctive mood.

Use Simple, Contemporary Language

- Avoid clichés and outdated expressions that make your language seem unnatural and unoriginal.
- Use simple words for informal business messages instead of using more complicated words that have the same meaning.

Write Concisely

- Avoid redundancy—unnecessary repetition of an idea.
- Use active voice to shorten sentences.
- Avoid unnecessary details; omit ideas that can be implied.
- Shorten wordy sentences by using suffixes or prefixes, making changes in word form, or substituting precise words for phrases.

Grammar Quiz
Pronoun Case

Correct the error in pronoun case.

1. The professor agreed to award (we, us) partial credit for the confusing question.
2. Stacey requested that the tasks be divided equally between Addison and (her, she).
3. It was (her, she) (who, whom) recommended revising the company's technology policy to include social networking sites.
4. The manager seemed unaware of (him, his) inability to relate to younger employees.
5. Emma is a leader in (who, whom) we have great confidence.

Grammar Quiz Solutions

1. us
2. her
3. she, who
4. his
5. whom

© Stockbyte/Getty Images

review card/ CHAPTER 4
PREPARING SPOKEN AND WRITTEN MESSAGES

Learning Objectives

© Cengage Learning 2010

STEP 1	STEP 2	STEP 3	STEP 4	STEP* 5	STEP* 6
Determine the purpose and select an appropriate channel	Envision the audience	Adapt the message to the audience's needs and concerns	Organize the message	Prepare the first draft	Revise and proofread for accuracy and desired impact

*You focused on the planning process (Steps 1–4) in Chapter 3; you will learn to prepare the message (Steps 5–6) in this chapter.

LO¹: Apply techniques for developing effective sentences and unified and coherent paragraphs.

Well-written sentences and unified and coherent paragraphs will help the receiver understand the message clearly and respond favorably. To craft powerful sentences, rely on active voice and emphasize important points. To write effective paragraphs, develop deductive or inductive paragraphs consistently, link ideas to achieve coherence, keep paragraphs unified, and vary sentence and paragraph length.

LO²: Identify factors affecting readability, and revise sentences to improve readability.

The readability of a message is affected by the length of the sentences and the difficulty of the words. For quick, easy reading, use simple words and short sentences. A readability index (grade level at which the receiver must read in order to understand the material) in the eight- to eleventh-grade range is appropriate for most business writing. Writing a message with a readability index appropriate for an audience does not guarantee understanding but does provide feedback on the average length of the sentences and the difficulty of the words.

LO³: Prepare visually appealing documents that grab the receiver's attention and increase comprehension.

Visually appealing documents entice the reader to read the document, focus attention on important ideas, and move the reader smoothly through the organization of the document without adding clutter. Techniques for preparing appealing, easy-to-read documents include enumerations, enumerated or bulleted lists, headings, tables and graphs, lines and borders, and drawing tools and clip art.

LO⁴: Revise and proofread a message for content, organization, and style; mechanics; and format and layout.

Be willing to revise a document as many times as necessary to be certain that it conveys the message effectively and is error free. Use spell-check to locate keying errors, then follow systematic procedures for proofreading an onscreen and/or printed copy of the document. Proofread systematically for content, organization, and style; mechanics; and then for format and layout.

Key Terms

Active voice when the subject of a sentence is the doer of an action

Coherence cohesion, so that each sentence in some way is linked to the preceding sentences

Deductive paragraph a paragraph in which the topic sentence precedes the details

Inductive paragraph a paragraph in which the topic sentence follows the details

Passive voice when the subject of a sentence is the receiver of an action

Topic sentence a sentence that identifies the portion of the topic being discussed and presents the central idea of the paragraph

Powerful Sentences

- Use correct structure when writing simple, compound, complex, and compound-complex sentences. Avoid run-on sentences and comma splices.
- Use active voice to present important points or pleasant ideas. Use passive voice to present less significant points or unpleasant ideas.
- Emphasize important ideas:
  - Place an idea in a simple sentence.
  - Place an idea in an independent clause; for de-emphasis, place an idea in a dependent clause.
  - Use an important word more than once in a sentence.
  - Place an important idea first or last in a sentence, paragraph, or document.
  - Use words that label ideas as significant or insignificant.
  - Use headings, graphics, and additional space to emphasize important ideas.

Coherent Paragraphs

- Write deductively if the message will likely please or at least not displease. Write inductively if the message will likely displease or if understanding the major idea is dependent on prior explanations.
- Make sure the message forms a unit with an obvious beginning, middle, and ending and that the middle paragraphs are arranged in a systematic sequence, either deductively or inductively, as needed.
- Avoid abrupt changes in thought, and link each sentence to a preceding sentence. Place transition sentences before major headings.
- Vary sentence and paragraph length to emphasize important ideas.
- Limit paragraphs in letters, memos, email messages, and web pages to six lines and paragraphs in reports to eight to ten lines to maximize comprehension.

Readability

- Use simple words and short sentences for quick, easy reading (and listening).
- Strive for short paragraphs but vary their lengths.
- Create appealing, easy-to-read documents by:
  - Using enumeration or bulleted or enumerated lists for stronger emphasis.
  - Using headings, tables and graphs, lines and borders, and images to focus attention on important information.

Systematic Proofreading

- Use spell-check to locate simple keying errors.
- Proofread once concentrating on content, organization, and style; a second time on mechanics; and a third time on format and layout.

Grammar Quiz
Verb Agreement, Tense, and Mood

In each of the following sentences, select the correct word in parantheses.

1. Only one of the free smartphone applications (has, have) value to me.
2. Taxpayers, not the government, (are, is) held accountable for paying the national debt.
3. Neither the manager nor the employees (was, were) aware of the policy change.
4. Both Josh and Krystal (was, were) notified of the impending layoffs.
5. The news from the rescue mission (is, are) encouraging.
6. *Good to Great* (has, have) been placed in the company library.
7. The sales manager announced that Portsmouth, South Carolina, (is, was) the site for the annual sales meeting.
8. Taylor (don't, doesn't) expect preferential treatment.
9. The client studied the financial analysis for a minute and (starts, started) asking questions.
10. If the applicant (was, were) experienced with databases, she would have been hired.

© Stockbyte/Getty Images

Grammar Quiz Solutions

1. has	5. is	9. started
2. are	6. has	10. were
3. were	7. is	
4. were	8. doesn't	

Learning Objectives

LO¹: Discuss the effective use of email, instant messaging, and text messaging in business communication.

Email can be sent to receivers both inside and outside the organization. Email provides a fast, convenient way to communicate by reducing telephone tag and telephone interruptions, facilitating the transmission of a single message to multiple recipients, reducing telephone bills, eliminating time barriers, and fostering open communication among users in various locations. Although general writing principles apply, email formats are less formal than business letter formats. Real-time email, known as instant messaging, allows two or more people to converse online. Text messaging occurs primarily between users of portable devices. Abbreviations and online "shorthand" help to speed these means of rapid communication.

LO²: Explain principles for writing effectively for the Web.

Web pages facilitate an organization's continual communication with a wide audience. HTML and a Web browser turn ordinary text into a Web page. Writing for Web pages should be concise, jargon-free, and chunked to allow for scanning of content. Weblogs serve important needs in capturing information for further use but should be considered public and not confidential.

LO³: Discuss the effective use of voice and wireless technologies in business communication.

Voice recordings and messages should be clear and complete and considered as permanent records. Cell phones should be used with consideration for the receiver and the public. Cell phone communications should not be viewed as secure communications. Text messaging offers a limited avenue for exchanging quick, quiet messages. Applications and equipment to accommodate wireless communications continue to expand and offer flexibility for transmitting voice and data. Business decisions can be improved through the appropriate use of voice and wireless technologies.

LO⁴: Identify legal and ethical implications associated with the use of communication technology.

The following legal and ethical considerations should be taken into account when communicating through technology: (a) Be certain that information technology does not violate basic rights of individuals and that you abide by all laws related to the use of technology; (b) understand that email is not private and can be monitored by a company; (c) develop and use procedures that protect the security of information; and (d) develop a clear and fair privacy policy.

Key Terms

Extranet Web platform for distributing information to business partners such as vendors, suppliers, and customers; access limited to those with authorization

Instant messaging a real–time email technology that blends email with conversation; sender and receiver who are online at the same time can type messages that both see immediately

Intranet Web platform for distributing information to employees at numerous locations; access limited to those with authorization

Netiquette the buzzword for proper behavior on the Internet

Social networking sites websites that provide virtual communities in which people with shared interests can communicate

Text messaging messages that can be sent from one cell phone to another, a cell phone to a computer, or computer to computer; a refinement of computer instant messaging

Weblog (or blog) a type of online journal typically authored by an individual that does not allow visitors to change the original material posted, but to only add comments

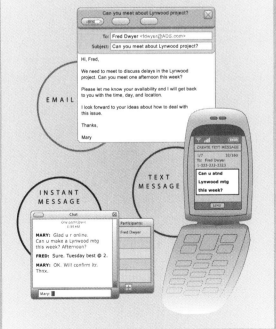

© Cengage Learning 2013

Email Messages

Organization, Content, Style, and Mechanics

- Provide a subject line that is meaningful to the recipient.
- Include only one main message idea related to the receiver's needs.
- Show empathy and logic to determine the idea sequence.
- Use jargon, technical words, and shortened terms carefully.
- Use bulleted lists, tables, graphs, or images as needed.
- Avoid flaming and use of overly emotional language.

Format

- Include an appropriate salutation, ending, and signature line (your name, address, phone, etc.)
- When possible, limit message width and length to one screen. Use attachments for longer messages.
- Single-space lines with a blank space between unindented paragraphs.
- Use mixed-case letters unless emphasis is needed with capital letters or quotation marks.
- Use emoticons and abbreviations in moderation only if the receiver understands them and content is informal.

Instant Messages

Organization, Content, Style, and Mechanics

- Consider previously listed email guidelines.
- Choose your message participants appropriately.
- Be aware of unwanted eavesdropping.

Format

- Use understandable shorthand and abbreviations for frequent words and phrases.
- Focus more on efficiency and less on spelling and grammar.

Text Messages

- Choose for exchanging quick, quiet messages.
- Avoid using text messaging as a substitute for richer communication mediums.

Web Communications

Writing for Websites

- Create brief, simple documents for easy reading. Break longer documents into smaller chunks.
- Use eye-catching headlines and techniques.
- Use jargon and technical terms cautiously.
- Avoid placing critical information only in graphic form that may be skipped by users of slow systems.

Writing for Wikis

- Avoid first-person language and conform to tone and flow of existing article.
- Present factual information in clear, concise, and neutral language.

Writing for Blogs

- Consider previously listed email guidelines.
- Communicate responsibly and ethically when writing anonymously.
- Develop a clear goal that leads to relevant content for the target audience. Revise and update regularly and promote actively to attract and retain readers.

Voice and Wireless Communications

Voice Recordings

- Leave your email address, fax number, or mailing address on your greeting if helpful to callers.
- Encourage callers to leave detailed messages.
- Instruct callers in how to review their messages or be transferred to an operator.
- Check voice mail regularly, and reply within 24 hours.

Voice Messages

- Speak slowly and clearly.
- Repeat your name and phone number at the beginning and end, spelling your name if helpful.
- Leave a detailed, specific message.
- Keep your message brief, typically 60 seconds or less.
- Ensure your message is understood; avoid calling from noisy environments and weak signal areas.

Voice and Wireless Etiquette

- Use judgment about silencing or turning off your phone.
- Respect others around you by speaking in low conversational tones and monitoring your content.
- Practice safety when using wireless communication devices while driving.

© Stockbyte/Getty Images

Grammar Quiz

Adjectives and Adverbs

In each of the following sentences, select the correct word in parentheses.

1. Despite the dangers, employees change their computer passwords (infrequent, infrequently).
2. Daniel looked (impatient, impatiently) at the new production assistant.
3. The server moved (quick, quickly) from table to table.
4. Of the several people I met during the speed networking event, Olivia made the (better, best) impression.
5. The Chicago plant has a higher safety record than (any, any other) plant.

Grammar Quiz Solutions

1. infrequently
2. impatiently
3. quickly
4. best
5. any other

Learning Objectives

LO¹: Describe the deductive outline for good and neutral news and its adaptations for specific situations and for international audiences.

When the receiver can be expected to be *pleased* by the message, the main idea is presented first and details follow. Likewise, when the message is *routine* and not likely to arouse a feeling of pleasure or displeasure, the main idea is presented first. The deductive approach is appropriate for positive news and thank-you and appreciation messages, routine claims, routine requests, responses to routine requests, routine messages, and responses about credit and orders. Cultural differences of international audiences may necessitate adjustments in writing style and to the typical deductive pattern for good- and neutral-news messages.

LO²: Prepare messages that convey good news, including thank-you and appreciation messages.

Use the deductive approach for letters, memos, and email messages that contain positive news as the central idea. Thank-you messages express appreciation for a kindness or special assistance and should reflect sincere feelings of gratitude. Appreciation messages highlight exceptional performance and should avoid exaggerations and strong, unsupported statements that the receiver may not believe.

LO³: Write messages presenting routine claims and requests and favorable responses to them.

A routine claim requests the adjustment in the first sentence because you assume the company will make the adjustment without persuasion. It continues with an explanation of the problem to support the request and an expression of appreciation for taking the action. An adjustment extends the adjustment in the first sentence and explains the circumstances related to correcting the problem. The closing may include sales promotional material or other future-oriented comments indicating your confidence that the customer will continue doing business with a company that has a reputation for fairness. A routine request begins with the major request, includes details that will clarify the request, and alludes to the receiver's response. A response to a routine request provides the information requested, provides necessary details, and closes with a personal, courteous ending.

LO⁴: Write messages acknowledging customer orders, providing credit information, and extending credit.

Form or computer-generated acknowledgment messages or email messages assure customers that orders will be filled quickly. With individualized acknowledgments that confirm shipment and include product resale, the company generates goodwill and future business.

When providing credit information, provide only verifiable facts to avoid possible litigation. A message extending credit begins with an approval of credit, indicates the basis for the decision, and explains credit terms. The closing may include sales promotional material or future-oriented comments. Credit extension messages must adhere to legal guidelines.

LO⁵: Prepare procedural messages that ensure clear and consistent application.

When preparing instructions, highlight the steps in a bulleted or numbered list or a flow chart and begin each step with an action statement. Check the accuracy and completeness of the document and incorporate changes identified by following the instructions to complete the task and asking another person to do likewise.

Key Terms

Acknowledgment message a document that indicates an order has been received and is being processed

Adjustment messages messages that are fair responses by businesses to legitimate requests in claim messages by customers

Claim a request for an adjustment

Deductive (or direct) sequence when the message begins with the main idea followed by supporting details

Good-news messages messages that convey pleasant information

Neutral-news messages messages that are of interest to the reader but are not likely to generate an emotional reaction

Persuasive claims messages that assume a claim will be granted only after explanations and persuasive arguments have been presented

Persuasive requests messages that assume that a requested action will be taken after persuasive arguments are presented

Resale a discussion of goods or services already bought

Routine claims messages that assume that a claim will be granted quickly and willingly, without persuasion

Routine requests messages that assume that a request will be granted quickly and willingly, without persuasion

Sales promotional material statements made about related merchandise or service

Content

- Clearly identify the principal idea (pleasant or routine idea).
- Present sufficient supporting details in logical sequence.
- Ensure the accuracy of facts or figures.
- Structure the message to meet legal requirements and ethical dimensions.

Organization

- Place the major idea in the first sentence.
- Present supporting details in logical sequence.
- Include a final idea that is courteous and indicates a continuing relationship with the receiver; it may include sales promotional material.

Style

- Ensure that the message is clear and concise (e.g., words will be readily understood).
- Use active voice predominantly and first person sparingly.
- Make ideas cohere by avoiding abrupt changes in thought.
- Use contemporary language; avoid doublespeak and clichés.
- Use relatively short sentences that vary in length and structure.
- Emphasize significant thoughts (e.g., position and sentence structure).
- Keep paragraphs relatively short.
- Adjust formality and writing style to the particular medium of delivery (letter, memo, email, text message, etc.).

Mechanics

- Ensure that keyboarding, spelling, grammar, and punctuation are perfect.

Format

- Use a correct message format.
- Ensure that the message is appropriately positioned.
- Include standard message parts in appropriate position and special parts as needed (subject line, enclosure, copy, etc.).

Cultural Adaptations

- Avoid abbreviations, slang, acronyms, technical jargon, sports and military analogies, and other devices particular to your own culture.
- Avoid words that trigger emotional responses.
- Use simple terms but attempt to be specific.
- Consider the communication style of the culture when selecting an organizational pattern.
- Use graphics, visual aids, and forms when possible to simplify the message.
- Use figures for expressing numbers to avoid confusion.
- Be aware of differences in the way numbers and dates are written, and write out the name of the month to avoid confusion.
- Adapt the document format for expectations of the recipient's country.

Grammar Quiz
Commas

Insert needed commas. Write "correct" if you find no errors.

1. The employee who is featured in our latest television commercial is active in the community theatre.
2. Emoticons which are created by keying combinations of symbols to produce "sideways faces" communicate emotion in electronic messages.
3. Sean Cohen a new member of the board remained silent during the long bitter debate.
4. Top social networking sites include Facebook MySpace and Flickr.
5. The entire population was surveyed but three responses were unusable.
6. If you tag websites in a social bookmarking site you can locate them easily for later use.
7. To qualify for the position applicants must have technology certification.
8. We should be spending less money not more.
9. On May 9 2011 the company's Twitter site was launched.
10. Yes the president approved a team-building event to replace our annual golf outing.

Grammar Quiz Solutions

1. Correct.
2. Emoticons, which are created by keying combinations of symbols to produce "sideways faces," communicate emotion in electronic messages.
3. Sean Cohen, a new member of the board, remained silent during the long, bitter debate.
4. Top social networking sites include Facebook, MySpace, and Flickr.
5. The entire population was surveyed, but three responses were unusable.
6. If you tag websites in a social bookmarking site, you can locate them easily for later use.
7. To qualify for the position, applicants must have technology certification.
8. We should be spending less money, not more.
9. On May 9, 2011, the company's Twitter site was launched.
10. Yes, the president approved a team-building event to replace our annual golf outing.

© Stockbyte/Getty Images

Learning Objectives

Key Terms

LO¹: Explain the steps in the inductive outline, and understand its use for specific situations.

Because the receiver can be expected to be displeased by the message, the inductive approach is appropriate for messages denying an adjustment, refusing an order for merchandise, refusing credit, sending constructive criticism, or conveying negative organizational messages. The steps in the inductive outline include (1) introducing the topic with a neutral idea that sets the stage for the explanation; (2) presenting a concise, logical explanation for the refusal; (3) implying or stating the refusal using positive language; (4) offering a counterproposal or silver lining statement that shifts focus toward the positive; and (5) closing with a positive, courteous ending that shifts the focus away from the bad news. While bad-news messages are typically expressed using paper documents or face-to-face means, electronic channels may be appropriate under certain circumstances.

The deductive approach can be used to communicate bad news when (a) the message is the second response to a repeated request; (b) a very small, insignificant matter is involved; (c) a request is obviously ridiculous, immoral, unethical, illegal, or dangerous; (d) a writer's intent is to "shake" the receiver; or (e) a writer–reader relationship is so close and long-standing that satisfactory human relations can be taken for granted.

LO²: Discuss strategies for developing the five components of a bad-news message.

The introductory paragraph should buffer the bad news and tactfully identify the subject. Following the introduction should be a logical discussion of the reasons for the refusal or bad news. The bad-news statement itself should be positioned strategically and (a) use the inductive approach, (b) not be set in a paragraph by itself, and (c) should sit in a dependent clause of a complex sentence. A counterproposal or silver lining should follow the bad-news statement, and the concluding paragraph of the message should demonstrate empathy.

LO³: Prepare messages refusing requests and claims.

A message refusing a request begins with a neutral idea and presents the reasons before the refusal. The close may offer a counterproposal—an alternative to the action requested.

A message denying a claim begins with a neutral or factual sentence that leads to the reason for the refusal. In the opening sentence, you might include resale to reaffirm the reader's confidence in the merchandise or services. Next, present the explanation for the refusal and then the refusal in a positive, nonemphatic manner. Close with a positive thought such as sales promotion that indicates you expect to do business with the customer again.

LO⁴: Prepare messages handling problems with customers' orders and denying credit.

A message refusing an order implies receipt of the order and uses resale to reaffirm the customer's confidence in the merchandise or service. Continue with reasons for your procedures or actions and benefits to the customer. Close with information needed for the customer to reorder or anticipate later delivery.

Credit refusal messages must comply with laws related to fair credit practices and should be reviewed carefully by legal counsel. Begin the message by implying receipt of an order and using resale that could convince the applicant to buy your merchandise on a cash basis when he or she learns later that credit has been denied. You must provide an explanation for the refusal (in writing or verbally) and may encourage the customer to apply for credit later or offer a discount on cash purchases. Your legal counsel may advise that you omit the explanation and invite the applicant to call or come in to discuss the reasons or to obtain more information from the credit reporting agency whose name, address, and telephone number you provide in the message.

LO⁵: Prepare messages providing constructive criticism, communicating negative organizational news, and responding to crises.

Because of the importance of maintaining goodwill with employees and outside parties, convey constructive criticism and negative organizational news in a sensitive, honest, and timely manner; use the inductive approach. The motive for delivering constructive criticism should be to help, not to get even. The message includes verifiable facts and omits evaluative words, allowing the recipient to make logical judgments based on facts. Negative information about an organization should be timely, honest, empathetic, and helpful. Crisis communication should be well planned and organized and should demonstrate concern, compassion, and control.

Counterproposal in a bad-news message, an alternative to the action requested that follows the negative news and can assist in preserving future relationships with the receiver

Fair Credit Reporting Act federal law that provides consumers the right to know the nature of the information in their credit file and gives them other protections when they apply for and are denied credit

CHECK YOUR COMMUNICATION | Bad-News Messages

Content

- Be sure the principal idea (the unpleasant idea or the refusal) is sufficiently clear.
- Use sufficient supporting details, and present them in a logical sequence.
- Verify accuracy of facts or figures.
- Structure the message to meet ethical and legal requirements.
- Make appropriate cultural adaptations (e.g., organizational pattern, format, language usage).

Organization

- Structure the first sentence to introduce the general subject
  - without stating the bad news.
  - without leading a receiver to expect good news.
  - without including obvious statements (e.g., "I am replying to your letter").
- Precede the main idea (bad news) with meaningful discussion.
- Follow up the bad news with a counterproposal or silver lining statement that moves discussion in a positive direction.
- Use a closing sentence that is positive (an alternative, resale, or sales promotion).

Style

- Write clearly and concisely (e.g., use words that are easily understood).

- Use techniques of subordination to keep the bad news from emerging with unnecessary vividness. For example, bad news may
  - appear in a dependent clause.
  - be stated in passive voice.
  - be revealed through indirect statement.
  - be revealed through the use of subjunctive mood.
- Use first person sparingly or not at all.
- Make ideas cohere by avoiding abrupt changes in thought.
- Keep sentences and paragraphs relatively short, and vary length and structure.
- Use original expression (sentences are not copied directly from the definition of the problem or from sample documents in the text); omit clichés.

Mechanics

- Ensure that keyboarding, spelling, grammar, and punctuation are perfect.

Format

- Use a correct document format.
- Include standard document parts in appropriate position.
- Include special parts if necessary (subject line, enclosure, copy, etc.).

Grammar Quiz
Semicolons and Colons

In each of the following sentences, insert or delete semicolons and colons where necessary. Write "correct" if you find no errors.

1. Some privacy concerns have become less important in recent years, however, most people feel extremely vulnerable to privacy invasion.
2. The following agents received bonuses Barnes, $750, Shelley, $800, and Jackson, $950.
3. Employees were notified today of the plant closing they received two weeks' severance pay.
4. This paint does have some disadvantages for example a lengthy drying time.
5. Soon after the applications are received, a team of judges will evaluate them, but the award recipients will not be announced until January 15.
6. The program has one shortcoming: flexibility.
7. The new bakery will offer: frozen yogurt, candies, and baked goods.
8. We are enthusiastic about the plan because: (1) it is least expensive, (2) its legality is unquestioned, and (3) it can be implemented quickly.

Grammar Quiz Solutions

1. Some privacy concerns have become less important in recent years; however, most people feel extremely vulnerable to invasion.
2. The following agents received bonuses: Barnes, $750; Shelley, $800; and Jackson, $950.
3. Employees were notified today of the plant closing; they received two weeks' severance pay.
4. This paint does have some disadvantages; for example, a lengthy drying time.
5. Soon after the applications are received, a team of judges will evaluate them; but the award recipients will not be announced until January 15.
6. Correct.
7. The new bakery will offer frozen yogurt, candies, and baked goods.
8. We are enthusiastic about the plan because (1) it is least expensive, (2) its legality is unquestioned, and (3) it can be implemented quickly.

© Stockbyte/Getty Images

Learning Objectives

LO¹: Develop effective outlines and appeals for messages that persuade.

The purpose of a persuasive message is to influence others to take a particular action or to accept your point of view. Effective persuasion involves understanding the product, service, or idea you are promoting; knowing your audience; presenting convincing evidence; and having a rational response to anticipated resistance to your arguments.

Effective persuasive communications build on a central selling point interwoven throughout the message. The receivers, rather than the product, serve as the subject of many of the sentences. Therefore, receivers can envision themselves using the product, contracting for the service, or complying with a request. Persuasive messages are written inductively.

LO²: Write effective sales messages.

A sales message is written inductively following the four AIDA steps for selling:

- **Gain attention.** Use an original approach that addresses one primary receiver's benefit (the central selling point) in the first paragraph.
- **Introduce the product, service, or idea.** Provide a logical transition to move the receiver from the attention-getter to information about the product, service, or idea. Hold the receiver's attention by using action-oriented sentences to stress the central selling point.
- **Create desire by providing convincing evidence.** Provide specific facts and interpretations that clarify features and quality. Include nonexaggerated, believable evidence and research and testimonials that provide independent support. De-emphasize price by presenting convincing evidence before the final paragraph, showing how money can be saved, stating price in small units, illustrating that the price is reasonable, or placing the price in a sentence that summarizes the benefits.
- **Motivate action.** State confidently the specific action to be taken and the benefits for complying. Present the action as easy to take, and provide a stimulus for acting quickly.

LO³: Write effective persuasive requests (claim, favor, and information requests, and persuasion within an organization).

A persuasive request is written inductively, is organized around a primary appeal, and is longer than a typical routine message because you must provide convincing evidence of receiver benefit.

- **Persuasive claim**—To convince an adjuster, gain the receiver's attention, develop a central appeal that emphasizes an incentive for making the adjustment, and end with the request for an adjustment you consider fair.
- **Request for a favor or information**—Gain the receiver's attention, build interest by emphasizing the reward for taking action, and encourage the receiver to grant the favor or send the information.
- **Persuasion within an organization**—When persuading an employee or supervisor to take specific actions, gain the receiver's attention, introduce and build interest and support for the proposed idea, address any major resistance, and encourage the receiver to take a specific action.

Key Terms

AIDA the four basic steps of the persuasive process, including gaining attention, generating interest, creating desire, and motivating action

Central selling point the primary appeal on which a persuasive message focuses

Persuasion the ability of a sender to influence others to accept his or her point of view

Grammar Quiz
Apostrophes

Correct the possessives.

1. The new hires confidence was crushed by the managers harsh tone.
2. This companies mission statement has been revised since it's recent merger.
3. Employees who are retained may be asked to accept a reduction of one weeks pay.
4. Vendors' have submitted sealed bids for the construction contract that will be opened in two week's.
5. Younger workers must appreciate older employees extensive company knowledge.

Grammar Quiz Solutions

1. hire's; manager's
2. company's; its
3. week's
4. Vendors; weeks
5. employees'

Sales Messages

Content

- Convince the reader that the product or service is worthy of consideration.
- Include sufficient evidence of usefulness to the purchaser.
- Reveal price (in the message or an enclosure).
- Make the central selling point apparent.
- Identify the desired specific action.
- Ensure that the message is ethical and abides by legal requirements.

Organization

- Use an inductive sequence of ideas.
- Ensure that the first sentence is a good attention-getter.
- Introduce the central selling point in the first few sentences and reinforce it throughout the message.
- Introduce price only after presenting receiver benefits.
- Associate price (what the receiver gives) directly with reward (what the receiver gets).
- End with a final paragraph that makes action easy and includes (a) the specific action desired, (b) the receiver's reward for taking action, and (c) incentive for quick action.

Style

- Use objective language.
- Ensure that active verbs and concrete nouns predominate.
- Keep sentences relatively short but varied in length and structure.
- Place significant words in emphatic positions.
- Make ideas cohere by avoiding abrupt changes in thought.
- Frequently call the central selling point to receiver's attention through repeated reference.
- Use original expression (sentences that are not copied directly from templates or sample documents). Omit clichés.
- Achieve unity by including in the final paragraph a key word or idea (central selling point) that was introduced in the first paragraph.

Mechanics

- Ensure that keyboarding, spelling, grammar, and punctuation are perfect.

Format

- Use correct document format.
- Include standard document parts in their appropriate positions.
- Include special parts if necessary (subject line, enclosure, copy, etc.).

Persuasive Requests

Content

- Convince the receiver that the idea is valid and that the proposal has merit.
- Point out ways in which the receiver will benefit.
- Incorporate the primary appeal (central selling feature).
- Identify the specific action desired.

Organization

- Use an inductive sequence of ideas.
- Use a first sentence that gets attention and reveals the message's subject.
- Introduce the major appeal in first few sentences and reinforce it throughout the message.
- Point out receiver benefits.
- Associate desired action with the receiver's reward for taking action.
- Include a final paragraph that makes reference to the specific action desired and the primary appeal. Emphasize easy, quick action.

Style

- Use objective and positive language.
- Ensure that active verbs and concrete nouns predominate.
- Keep sentences relatively short, but vary them in length and structure.
- Place significant words in emphatic positions.
- Make ideas cohere by ensuring that changes in thought are not abrupt.
- Call the primary appeal to the receiver's attention frequently through repeated reference.
- Use original expression (sentences that are not copied directly from templates or model documents). Omit clichés.
- Achieve unity by including the primary appeal in the final paragraph.

Mechanics

- Ensure that keyboarding, spelling, grammar, and punctuation are perfect.

© Stockbyte/Getty Images

Learning Objectives

LO¹: **Identify the characteristics of a report and the various classifications of business reports.**

The basis of a report is a problem that must be solved through data collection and analysis. Reports are usually requested by a higher authority, are logically organized and highly objective, and are prepared for a limited audience. Reports can be classified as formal or informal, short or long, informational or analytical, vertical or lateral, internal or external, or a proposal.

LO²: **Apply steps in the problem-solving process and methods for solving a problem.**

The four steps in the problem-solving process must be followed to arrive at a sound conclusion. The four steps are: (1) Recognize and define the problem; (2) select an appropriate secondary and/or primary method for solving the problem; (3) collect and organize data, using appropriate methods; and (4) interpret the data to arrive at an answer. Research methods in report preparation involve locating information from appropriate secondary sources to identify research that has already been done on the topic and then collecting the primary data needed to solve the problem. Primary data collection may include observational, experimental, or survey research processes.

LO³: **Use appropriate printed, electronic, and primary sources of information.**

Location of secondary sources of information involves appropriate use of printed indexes and application of electronic search techniques that can lead the researcher to books, periodicals, and other documents needed for topic exploration. Methods for collecting survey data include mailed questionnaires, email polling, telephone surveys, personal interviews, and participant observation. Collecting data through a survey involves selecting a sample that is representative of the entire population. Effective survey design and unbiased data collection are essential to assuring the validity and reliability of the data reported.

LO⁴: **Demonstrate appropriate methods of collecting, organizing, and referencing information.**

Information from published sources should be carefully read and interpreted. To avoid plagiarism, both direct quotes and paraphrases must be referenced using an acceptable method. Surveys are a common method for collecting data. Instruments should be carefully designed to solicit needed information, avoid ambiguity and confusion, and reflect accurate information. The researcher must work to avoid various data-gathering pitfalls including using small or unrepresentative samples, using biased sources or irrelevant information, and excluding relevant information.

LO⁵: **Explain techniques for the logical analysis and interpretation of data.**

Arriving at an answer in the research process involves proper analysis using appropriate statistical techniques. To maintain the integrity of the research, the interpretation of data should be objective and unbiased. Carefully presented findings give way to sound conclusions that lead to logical recommendations.

Statement of purpose the goal of the study; includes the aims or objectives the researcher hopes to accomplish

Validity the degree to which the data measure what the researcher intends to measure

Vertical report a report that can be upward- or downward–directed

Key Terms

Analytical report a report that presents suggested solutions to problems

Experimental research the study of two samples that have exactly the same components before a variable is added to one of the samples

External report a report prepared for distribution outside an organization

Formal report carefully structured report that is logically organized and objective, contains much detail, and is written in a style that tends to eliminate such elements as personal pronouns

Functional report a report that serves a specified purpose within a company

Hypothesis a statement to be proved or disproved through research

Informal report usually a short message written in natural or personal language

Informational report a report that carries objective information from one area of an organization to another

Internal report a report that travels within an organization, such as a production or sales report

Lateral report a report that travels between units on the same organizational level

Longitudinal studies reports that study the same factors in different time frames

Normative survey research research to determine the status of something at a specific time

Observational studies studies in which the researcher observes and statistically analyzes certain phenomena in order to assist in establishing new principles or discoveries

Periodic report a report that is issued on regularly scheduled dates

Plagiarism the presentation of someone else's ideas or words as your own

Primary research data collected for the first time, usually for a specific purpose

Problem statement the particular problem that is to be solved by the research

Procedures (or methodology) the steps a writer takes in preparing a report; often recorded as a part of the written report

Proposal a written description of how one organization can meet the needs of another

Reliability the level of consistency or stability over time or over independent samples

Sampling a survey technique that eliminates the need for questioning 100 percent of the population

Secondary research provides information that has already been reported by others

Problem Formation

- Decide what type of report is required.
- Formulate the problem statement.
- Determine boundaries for the research.
- Define specialized terms used in the report.

Research Methodology

- Select appropriate methods of solution, including relevant secondary and primary resources.
- Gather appropriate published and electronic sources.
- Plan appropriate primary research, using observational, experimental, or normative techniques.

Data Collection and Organization

- Document all quoted and paraphrased information using the appropriate referencing method.
- Develop effective data collection instruments; pilot test and refine prior to conducting research.
- Avoid data-collection errors that can minimize your research effort.

Data Interpretation

- Analyze data accurately and ethically.
- Interpret data to reach logical conclusions.
- Make recommendations that are well supported by the data presented.
- Avoid overgeneralizing results of research conducted in one setting to another group or setting.

Grammar Quiz
Hyphens

In each of the sentences below, add necessary hyphens and delete unnecessary hyphens. Write "correct" if you find no errors.

1. The web based application was unavailable because of a denial of service attack.
2. State of the art computers provide quick access to timely business information.
3. A large portion of holiday orders are time sensitive.
4. A two thirds majority is needed to pass the 5-percent increase in employee wages.
5. Nearly one-half of the respondents were highly-educated professionals.

Grammar Quiz Solutions

1. web-based; denial-of-service
2. State-of-the-art
3. Correct
4. two-thirds; 5 percent
5. one half; highly educated

© Stockbyte/Getty Images

Learning Objectives

LO¹: Communicate quantitative information effectively.

Graphics complement text by clarifying complex figures and helping readers visualize major points. Tabulating data and analyzing data using measures of central tendency aid in summarizing or classifying large volumes of data into manageable information you can interpret. You can then communicate this meaningful data using common language—fractions, ratios, and percentages—that the reader can easily understand.

LO²: Apply principles of effectiveness and ethical responsibilities in the construction of graphic aids.

A graphic aid should clarify, reinforce, or emphasize a particular idea and should contribute to the overall understanding of the idea under discussion. It should be uncluttered and easily understood and depict information honestly. Graphic aids used in spoken presentations should be large enough to be seen by the entire audience.

Graphic Type	Objective	Graphic Type	Objective
Table	To show exact figures	Gantt chart	To track progress toward completing a project
Bar chart	To compare one quantity with another	Map	To show geographic relationships
Line chart	To illustrate changes in quantities over time	Flowchart	To illustrate a process or procedure
Pie chart	To show how the parts of a whole are distributed	Photograph	To provide a realistic view of a specific item or place

© Cengage Learning 2010

© C Squared Studios/Photodisc/Getty Images

Key Terms

Area chart a graphic that shows how different factors contribute to a total; also referred to as a *cumulative line chart* or *surface chart*

Bar chart a graphic used to compare quantities

Common language reduces difficult figures to the common denominators of language and ideas

Flowchart a step–by–step diagram of a procedure or a graphic depiction of a system or organization

Gantt chart a specific type of bar chart that is useful for tracking progress toward completing a series of events over time

Graphics all types of illustrations used in written and spoken reports

Grouped bar chart a graphic used for comparing more than one quantity (set of data) at each point along the *y*–axis (vertical) or *x*–axis (horizontal); also called a *clustered bar chart*

Line chart a graphic that depicts changes in quantitative data over time and illustrates trends

Map a graphic that shows geographic relationships

Pictogram a graphic that uses pictures or symbols to illustrate objects, concepts, or numerical relationships

Pie chart a graphic that shows how the parts of a whole are distributed

Segmented bar chart a graphic used to show how different facts (components) contribute to a total figure; also called a *sub-divided, stacked bar,* or *100 percent bar chart*

Table a graphic that presents data in columns and rows, which aid in clarifying large quantities of data in a small space

LO³: Select and design appropriate and meaningful graphics.

The type of graphic used in a presentation should be chosen based on its ability to communicate the information most effectively. Tables present data in systematic rows and columns. Bar charts (simple, grouped, and stacked) compare quantities for a specific period. Line charts depict changes in quantities over time and illustrate trends. Pie charts, pictograms, and segmented and area charts show the proportion of components to a whole. Gantt charts track progress toward completing a series of events over time. Maps help readers visualize geographic relationships. Flow charts visually depict step-by-step procedures for completing a task; organization charts show the organizational structure of a company. Floor plans, photographs, cartoons, blueprints, and lists also enhance reports.

LO⁴: Integrate graphics within documents.

A graphic should always be introduced in text before it is presented. The graphic will then reinforce your conclusions and discourage readers from drawing their own conclusions before encountering your ideas. An effective introduction for a graphic tells something meaningful about what is depicted in the graphic and refers the reader to a specific figure number. The graphic should be placed immediately after its introduction if possible or positioned at the top of the next page after filling the previous page with text that ideally would have followed the graphic. Analysis or interpretation follows the graphic, avoiding a mere repetition of what the graphic clearly shows.

CHECK YOUR COMMUNICATION | Types of Graphic Aids

Tables

- Number tables and all other graphics consecutively throughout the report.

- Give each table a title that is complete enough to clarify what is included without forcing the reader to review the table.

- Label columns of data clearly enough to identify the items.

- Indent the second line of a label for the rows (horizontal items) two or three spaces.

- Place a superscript symbol beside an entry that requires additional explanation, and include the explanatory note beneath the visual.

- Document the source of the data presented in a visual by adding a source note beneath the visual.

Bar Charts

- Begin the quantitative axis at zero, divide the bars into equal increments, and use bars of equal width.

- Position chronologically or in some other logical order.

- Use variations in color to distinguish among the bars when the bars represent different data.

- Avoid using 3D-type formatting that makes values more difficult to distinguish.

- Include enough information in the scale labels and bar labels for clear understanding.

Line Charts

- Use the vertical axis for amount and the horizontal axis for time.

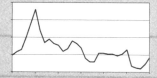

- Begin the vertical axis at zero.

- Divide the vertical and horizontal scales into equal increments.

Pie Charts

- Position the largest slice or the slice to be emphasized at the twelve o'clock position.

- Label each slice and include information about the quantitative size (percentage, dollars, acres, square feet, etc.) of each slice.

- Draw attention to one or more slices for desired emphasis.

- Avoid using 3D-type formatting that makes values more difficult to distinguish.

Maps

- Use to show geographic information visually.

Flowcharts

- Use to show step-by-step procedures or graphic depiction of a system or organization.

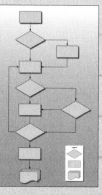

Grammar Quiz
Quotation Marks and Italics

Add necessary quotation marks and italics.

1. Cynthia Cooper's Extraordinary Circumstances is required reading in some forensic accounting classes.

2. The article How to Persuade People to Say Yes appeared in the May 2009 issue of Training Journal.

3. The consultant's accomplishments are summarized on her opening blog page. [Indicate that a word other than *accomplishments* may be a more appropriate word.]

4. Connie said I want to participate in a volunteer program that serves such a worthy cause. [direct quotation]

5. The term flame is online jargon for a heated, sarcastic, sometimes abusive message or posting to a discussion group.

Grammar Quiz Solutions

1. Cynthia Cooper's *Extraordinary Circumstances* is required reading in some forensic accounting classes. [Italicizes a book title.]

2. The article "How to Persuade People to Say Yes" appeared in the May 2009 issue of *Training Journal*. [Encloses the name of an article in quotation marks and italicizes the title of a journal.]

3. The consultant's "accomplishments" are summarized on her opening blog page. [Uses quotation marks to introduce doubt about whether "accomplishments" is the right label. His undertakings may have been of little significance.]

4. Connie said, "I want to participate in a volunteer program that serves such a worthy cause." [Uses quotation marks in a direct quotation.]

5. The term *flame* is online jargon for "a heated, sarcastic, sometimes abusive message or posting to a discussion group." [Italicizes a word used as a term and encloses its definition in quotation marks.]

Learning Objectives

LO¹: **Identify the parts of a formal report and the contribution each part makes to the report's overall effectiveness.**

As reports increase in length from one page to several pages, they also grow in formality with the addition of introductory and addenda items. As a result, reports at the formal end of the continuum tend to be repetitious. These report parts and their purposes are summarized in Figure 11-1 on page 174.

LO²: **Organize report findings.**

Organizing the content of a report involves seeing the report problem in its entirety and then breaking it into its parts. After the research or field work has been completed, the writer may begin with any of the report parts and then complete the rough draft by putting the parts in logical order. Writers determine the format and style best able to communicate the intended message.

LO³: **Prepare effective formal reports using an acceptable format and writing style.**

In preparing effective long reports, outlining assists the writer with logical sequencing. Appropriate headings lead the reader from one division to another. The writing style should present the findings and data interpretation clearly and fairly, convincing the reader to accept the writer's point of view, but in an unemotional manner. Opinions should be clearly identified as such.

LO⁴: **Prepare effective short reports in memorandum, email, and letter formats.**

Short reports are typically written in a personal writing style and in memorandum, email, or letter format. Form reports provide accuracy, save time, and simplify tabulation of data when a need exists for numerous, repetitive reports.

LO⁵: **Prepare effective proposals for a variety of purposes.**

Proposals can be written for both internal and external audiences. Proposals call for thorough organization and require writing methods that will be not only informative but convincing. Because they have discrete parts that can be prepared in any order and then assembled into whole reports, they are conducive to preparation by teams.

Key Terms

Addenda may include all materials used in the research but not appropriate to be included in the report itself

Analytical report a type of report designed to solve a specific problem or answer research questions

Executive summary short summary of the essential elements in an entire report; also called an *abstract*, *overview*, or *précis*

External proposal a proposal written to generate business; one organization describes how it can meet the needs of another by, for example, providing a product or service

Form reports reports that meet the demand for numerous, repetitive reports; include college registration forms, applications for credit, airline tickets, and bank checks

Internal proposals proposals used by managers to justify or recommend purchases or changes in the company

Justification report a report that outlines comparative information clearly to the reader; used commonly when comparing items for purchase

Preliminary parts report sections included to add formality to a report, emphasize report content, and aid the reader in locating information in the report quickly and in understanding the report more easily

Short reports reports that include only the minimum supporting materials to achieve effective communication

Solicited proposals proposals generated when a potential buyer submits exact specifications or needs in a bid request

Unsolicited proposal a proposal prepared by an individual or firm who sees a problem to be solved and submits a solution

Grammar Quiz

Dashes, Parentheses, and Periods

In each of the following sentences, add necessary dashes, parentheses, or periods.

1. Additional consultants, programmers and analysts, were hired to complete the computer conversion. [Emphasize the appositive.]
2. The dividend will be raised to 15 cents a share approved by the Board of Directors on December 1, 2011. [Deemphasize the approval.]
3. Would you link this YouTube video to my slide show?

Grammar Quiz Solutions

1. Additional consultants—programmers and analysts—were hired to complete the computer conversion.
2. The dividend will be raised to 15 cents a share (approved by the Board of Directors on December 1, 2011).
3. Would you link this YouTube video to my slide show. [Uses a period to follow courteous request that requires no verbal response.]

Transmittal Letter or Memorandum

Use a letter-style transmittal in reports going outside the organization. For internal reports, use a memorandum transmittal.

- Transmit a warm greeting to the reader.
- Open with a "Here is the report you requested" tone.
- Establish the subject in the first sentence.
- Follow the opening with a brief summary of the study. Expand the discussion if a separate summary is not included in the report.
- Acknowledge the assistance of those who helped with the study.
- Close the message with a thank-you and a forward look.

Title Page

- Include the title of the report, succinctly worded.
- Provide full identification of the authority for the report (the person or organization for whom the report was prepared and the preparer(s) of the report).
- Provide the date of the completion of the report.
- Use an attractive layout.

Table of Contents

- Use *Table of Contents* or *Contents* as the title.
- Use indentation to indicate the heading degrees used in the report.
- List numerous figures separately as a preliminary item called *Table of Figures* or *Figures*. (Otherwise, figures should not be listed because they are not separate sections of the outline but only supporting data within a section.)

Executive Summary

- Use a descriptive title, such as *Executive Summary*, *Synopsis*, or *Abstract*.
- Condense the major report sections.
- Use effective, generalized statements that avoid detail available in the report itself.

Report Text

- Avoid the personal *I* and *we* pronouns in formal writing. Minimize the use of *the writer*, *the investigator*, and *the author*.
- Use active construction to give emphasis to the *doer* of the action; use passive voice to give emphasis to the *results* of the action.
- Use proper tense.
- Avoid ambiguous pronoun references (they hinder clarity).
- Avoid expletive beginnings such as *There is* and *There are*.
- Use bulleted or enumerated lists for three or more items if listing will make reading easier.

- Incorporate transition sentences to ensure coherence.
- Use parallel construction in headings of equal degree in the same report section.
- Number consecutively figures (tables, graphics, and other illustrations) used in the report.
- Give each graph or table a descriptive title.
- Question each statement for its contribution to the solution of the problem.
- Use units of production, percentages, or ratios to express large numbers.
- Use objective reporting style that avoids emotional terms, assumptions and opinions, and unwarranted judgments and inferences.
- State the conclusions carefully and clearly, and be sure they grow out of the findings.

Citations

- Include a citation (in-text reference, footnote, or endnote) for material quoted or paraphrased from another source.
- Adhere to an acceptable, authoritative style or company policy.
- Present consistent citations, including adequate information for readers to locate the source in the reference list.

References

- Include an entry for every reference cited in the report.
- Adhere to an acceptable, authoritative style or company policy.
- When in doubt, include more information than might be necessary.
- Include separate sections (e.g., books, articles, and nonprint sources) if the references section is lengthy and your referencing style allows it.

Appendix

- Include cover messages and all other items that provide information but are not important enough to be included in the report body.
- Subdivide categories of information beginning with Appendix A, Appendix B, and so on.
- Identify each item with a title.

reviewcard/ CHAPTER 12
DESIGNING AND DELIVERING BUSINESS PRESENTATIONS

Learning Objectives

LO¹: Plan a business presentation that accomplishes the speaker's goals and meets the audience's needs.

Determine what you want to accomplish in your presentation and direct your presentation to the specific needs and interests of the audience. Identify the general characteristics (age, gender, experience, etc.), size, and receptiveness of the audience.

LO²: Organize and develop the three parts of an effective presentation.

An effective presentation has an introduction, body, and closing. The introduction should capture the audience's attention, involve the audience and the speaker, present the purpose statement, and preview major points. The body is limited to a few major points that are supported and clarified with relevant statistics, anecdotes, quotes from prominent people, appropriate humor, presentation visuals, and so forth. The closing should be a memorable idea that supports and strengthens the purpose statement.

LO³: Select, design, and use presentation visuals effectively.

Using visual aids reduces the time required to present a concept and increases audience retention. Available aids include handouts, models and physical objects, whiteboards, flip charts, overhead transparencies, electronic presentations, videotapes, and audiotapes. Each type provides specific advantages and should be selected carefully. An effective visual presents major ideas in a simple design large enough for the audience to read. Permissions should be obtained for the use of copyrighted multimedia content.

LO⁴: Deliver speeches with increasing confidence.

Business speakers use the impromptu and extemporaneous speech methods more frequently than the memorized or scripted methods. Professional vocal qualities include a medium or low voice pitch, adequate volume, varied tone and rate, and the absence of distracting verbal fillers. Articulate speakers enunciate words precisely and ensure proper pronunciation. Preparation, professional demeanor, and staying in tune with the audience are keys to a successful speech.

LO⁵: Discuss strategies for presenting in alternate delivery situations such as culturally diverse audiences, teams, and distance presentations.

When communicating with other cultures, use simple, clear speech. Consider differences in presentation approach, nonverbal communication, and social protocol that may require flexibility and adjustments to your presentation style. Effective team presentations result from the selection of an appropriate leader and team members with complementary strengths and styles who plan ahead and rehearse thoroughly. When delivering a videoconference or live Web presentation, determine whether a distance delivery method is appropriate for the presentation, attempt to establish rapport with the participants prior to the distance presentation, become proficient in delivering and using distance technology, and develop high-quality graphics appropriate for the distance format.

Key Terms

Articulation smooth, fluent, and pleasant speech

Extemporaneous presentation a presentation in which a speaker plans, prepares, and rehearses but does not write everything down; brief notes prompt the speaker, but the exact words are chosen spontaneously as the speaker interacts with the audience and identifies its specific needs

Impromptu presentation a presentation in which a speaker is called on without prior notice

Internet conferencing a method of real–time conferencing that allows a company to conduct a presentation in real time over the Internet simultaneously with a conference telephone call; also called *webcasting*

Manuscript presentation a presentation in which a speaker writes out the entire speech and reads it to the audience; also called a *scripted presentation*

Memorized presentation a presentation in which a speaker writes out a speech, commits it to memory, and recites it verbatim

Oral briefings informal presentations prepared and presented with little time for planning and developing

Phonation the production and variation of a speaker's vocal tone

Pronunciation using principles of phonetics to create accurate sounds, rhythm, stress, and intonation

Grammar Quiz
Number Usage

Correct the number usage in the following sentences taken from a letter or a report.

1. The question was answered by sixty-one percent of the respondents.
2. The meeting is scheduled for 10:00 a.m. on February 3rd.
3. These 3 figures appeared on the expense account: $21.95, $30.00, and $35.14.
4. The purchasing manager ordered 50 4-GB flash drives.
5. 21 members voted in favor of the $2,000,000 proposal.
6. Approximately 100 respondents requested a copy of the results.
7. Mix two quarts of white with 13 quarts of brown.
8. Examine the cost projections on page eight.

Grammar Quiz Solutions

1. The question was answered by 61 percent of the respondents.
2. The meeting is scheduled for 10 a.m. on February 3.
3. These three figures appeared on the expense account: $21.95, $30, and $35.14.
4. The purchasing manager ordered fifty 4-GB flash drives.
5. Twenty-one members voted in favor of the $2 million proposal.
6. Approximately 100 respondents requested a copy of the results. [Approximations above nine that can be expressed in one or two words may be written in either words or figures, but figures are more emphatic.]
7. Mix 2 quarts of white with 13 quarts of brown.
8. Examine the cost projections on page 8.

Planning and Organizing a Presentation

- **Identify your purpose.** Know what you hope to accomplish and choose supporting content.
- **Analyze your audience.** Identify common characteristics, number in audience, seating arrangements, and time of day.
- **Develop an effective opening.** Assure that the opening captures attention, initiates rapport with the audience, presents the purpose, and previews the main points.
- **Develop the body.** Select a few major and supporting points: statistics, anecdotes, quotes, and appropriate humor. Use simple, nontechnical language and understandable sentences.
- **Develop an effective closing.** Call for the audience to accept your idea or provide a strong conclusion with recommendations.

Selecting an Appropriate Presentation Visual

- Select a presentation visual appropriate for the audience and topic.
- Use whiteboards and flip charts for small audiences in an informal setting and when no special equipment is available. Prepare flip charts in advance when possible.
- Use overhead transparencies for small, informal audiences.
- Use slides for presentations requiring photography. Sequence the slides appropriately and show them in a darkened room.
- Use electronic presentations for large audiences and to enliven the topic with multimedia.
- Use models and physical objects to convey the idea presented.

Designing and Using Presentation Visuals

- Limit the number of visual aids to avoid overload.
- Clear all copyrights for multimedia content.
- Write descriptive titles and parallel bulleted lists.
- Create a standard design for each visual following these slide design principles:
  - Include only the major idea to be remembered.
  - Make the design concise, simple, and readable.
  - Avoid graphics that distort facts.
  - Proofread the visual carefully to eliminate errors.
- Paraphrase rather than reading, and step to one side for audience viewing.

Delivering a Presentation

Before the Presentation

- Prepare thoroughly to minimize natural nervousness.
- Prepare easy-to-read note cards or pages to prompt recall.
- Rehearse to identify organizational flaws or verbal potholes.
- Use a lectern for steadiness but not to hide behind.
- Request a proper, impressive introduction.
- Dress appropriately to convey a professional image.
- Arrive early to check out the room and last-minute details.

During the Presentation

- Use clear, articulate speech and proper pronunciation.
- Use vocal variety and adjust volume and rate to emphasize ideas.
- Avoid verbal fillers and annoying speech habits.
- Maintain steady eye contact with various audience members.
- Smile genuinely and use gestures naturally to communicate confidence and warmth.
- Watch your audience for important feedback and adjust your presentation accordingly.
- Handle questions from the audience politely.
- Keep within the time limit.

After the Presentation

- Be prepared for a question-and-answer period.
- Distribute handouts at the appropriate time.

Adapting to a Culturally Diverse Audience

- Use simple English and short sentences.
- Use a straightforward, direct approach.
- Adjust to differences in nonverbal communication and social protocol.

Delivering a Team Presentation

- Select a leader to lead in developing a cohesive presentation strategy and team members with complementary strengths and styles.
- Plan the presentation as a team.
- Rehearse thoroughly for cohesion and uniformity.

Delivering a Distance Presentation

- Determine whether a distance delivery method is appropriate for the presentation.
- Establish rapport with participants prior to the presentation.
- Become proficient in using distance technology.
- Develop high-quality, appropriate graphics.

© Stockbyte/Getty Images

Learning Objectives

LO¹: **Prepare for employment by considering relevant information about yourself as it relates to job requirements.**

As a job candidate, you should complete systematic self-, career, and job analyses. Gather information to make wise career decisions, asking questions about yourself, about a possible career, and about a specific job in your chosen field. Interview people already working. Recording and analyzing this information will aid in selecting a satisfying career and preparing an effective résumé and application message.

LO²: **Identify career opportunities using traditional and electronic methods.**

A job candidate can use traditional and electronic methods for the employment search. Names and addresses of possible employers may be obtained from networks, career services centers at schools, employers' offices, employment agencies and contractors, online databases and printed sources, professional organizations, electronic job fairs, news groups, and chat sessions.

LO³: **Prepare an organized, persuasive résumé that is adapted for print and electronic postings.**

A résumé typically includes identification, an objective, a career summary, qualifications, personal information, and references. The most effective résumé for a particular candidate could be a chronological, functional, or chrono-functional résumé.

- Chronological résumés have headings such as "Education" and "Experience" and list experiences in reverse chronological order; they are appropriate for applicants who have the apparent qualifications for the job.
- Functional résumés show applicant qualifications as headings; this format is especially effective for applicants who lack the appropriate education and experience.
- The chrono-functional résumé lists education and experience as headings and uses functional headings that emphasize qualifications.

Effective print (designed) résumés concisely highlight key qualifications and are formatted for quick, easy reading. Electronic résumé posting varies considerably, with popular options including a job bank posting, a website entry, a link to a personal Web page, an email attachment, and an inline résumé within the body of an email message. Scannable résumés are designed so that information can be scanned and processed by an applicant-tracking system. An effective keyword section summarizes qualifications and helps ensure that the résumé is identified during a search for matching requirements.

LO⁴: **Utilize employment tools other than the résumé that can enhance employability.**

The résumé may be supplemented with other employment tools that include a professional portfolio and a video recording of the applicant. Content for a portfolio or video should be carefully chosen to reflect the skills necessary for effective job performance and should complement information in the résumé.

LO⁵: **Write an application message that effectively introduces an accompanying print (designed) or electronic résumé.**

The purposes of the application message are to introduce the applicant and the résumé, create interest in the information given on the résumé, and assist an employer in seeing ways in which the applicant's services would be desirable. As such, it is a persuasive message—beginning with an attention-getter, including a central appeal and convincing evidence, and closing with an indirect reference to the enclosed résumé and desired action (invitation to an interview).

Key Terms

Application message a message placed on top of the résumé so it can be read first by the employer; also called a *cover message*

Beamer a quick version of a résumé designed in a format suitable for broadcasting on smartphones; also called a *beamable résumé*

Chrono-functional résumé a résumé that combines features of chronological and functional résumés

Chronological résumé the traditional organizational format for résumés with headings that spotlight an applicant's education and experience

Electronic applicant-tracking systems systems that increase the efficiency of processing résumés by storing scanned résumés in an electronic database where they can be sorted by keywords with a resulting ranking of applicants

Functional résumé the organizational format for résumés that highlights an applicant's transferable skills

Inline résumé a résumé included in the body of an email message

Multimedia résumé a résumé created with presentation software such as Camtasia Studio and sent to prospective employers on CD/DVD or posted on the applicant's personal website

Professional portfolio a portfolio presented in digital format and distributed to prospective employers via a website, CD/DVD, or other media; also called an *electronic portfolio* or *e-portfolio*

Résumé a vital communication tool that provides a basis for judgment about a person's capabilities on the job

Scannable résumé a résumé formatted to ensure a scanner can accurately read and convert it into a digital format

Targeted résumé a résumé that reflects the requirements of a specific job listing

Text résumé a plain text (unformatted) version of a résumé

Unsolicited application message an unrequested message sent to many prospective employers and containing the same basic message

Video résumé a résumé created as a video for posting on the Web, on sites such as YouTube.

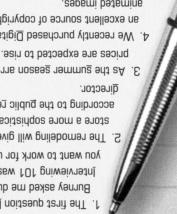
Résumés and
Application Messages

Print (Designed) Résumé

Content

- Include relevant qualifications compatible with the job requirements generated from analyses of self, career, and the job.
- Present qualifications truthfully and honestly.

Organization

- Choose an organizational pattern that highlights key qualifications: chronological, functional, or chrono-functional.
- Arrange headings in the appropriate sequence.
- Place significant ideas in an emphatic position.
- List experiences consistently, either in time sequence or in order of importance.

Style

- Omit personal pronouns.
- Use action verbs.
- Use past tense for previous jobs and present tense for present job.
- Place significant words in emphatic positions.

Mechanics

- Ensure there are *no* keying, grammar, spelling, or punctuation errors.
- Balance elements on the page.
- Use ample margins even if a second page is required.
- Include a page number on all pages except the first and "continued" at the bottom of the first page to indicate a multiple-page document.
- Position and format headings consistently throughout.
- Use an outline format or a bulleted list to emphasize multiple points.

Electronic Résumés

Content

- Adapt general guidelines for résumé preparation to fit the particular requirements of the submission.
- Place "Keyword Summary" on the first screen (first 24 lines of text) listing qualifications that match.
- Include a link or reference to your electronic portfolio.
- For scannable résumés, position your name as the first readable item on each page.

Professional Portfolio

Content

- Include items that showcase abilities and accomplishments.

Mechanics

- Choose an appropriate traditional or electronic format.
- For electronic formats, include links to your print résumé, plain text version of résumé, email address, and appropriate supplementary documents.

Application Message

Content

- Identify the message as an application for a certain job.
- Emphasize significant qualifications and exclude nonessential ideas.
- Make reference to the enclosed or attached résumé.
- End with an action closing that is neither apologetic nor pushy.

Mechanics

- Ensure that there are *no* keying, grammar, spelling, or punctuation errors.
- Include your address above the date or format as a letterhead since the letter is presented on plain paper that matches the résumé.
- Keep the first and last paragraphs relatively short; hold others to six or seven lines.

Grammar Quiz

Capitalization

Copy each of the following sentences, making essential changes in capitalization.

1. The first question professor Burney asked me during interviewing 101 was "why do you want to work for us?"
2. The remodeling will give the store a more sophisticated feel according to the Public Relations Director.
3. As the Summer Season arrives, gas prices are expected to rise.
4. We recently purchased digital juice, an excellent source of copyright-free animated images.
5. Thomas Frieden, Director of the Center for Disease Control, is the agency's key communicator.

Grammar Quiz Solutions

5. Thomas Frieden, director of the Center for Disease Control, is the agency's key communicator.

4. We recently purchased Digital Juice, an excellent source of copyright-free animated images.

3. As the summer season arrives, gas prices are expected to rise.

2. The remodeling will give the store a more sophisticated feel according to the public relations director.

1. The first question Professor Burney asked me during interviewing 101 was "Why do you want to work for us?"

© Stockbyte/Getty Images

Learning Objectives

LO¹: Explain the nature of structured, unstructured, stress, group, and virtual interviews.

Interviewers and interviewees can be considered as buyers and sellers: Interviewers want to know whether job candidates can meet the needs of their firms before making a "purchase"; interviewees want to sell themselves based on sound knowledge, good work skills, and desirable personal traits. Structured interviews follow a preset, specific, format; unstructured interviews follow no standard format but explore for information. Computer-assisted interviews provide standard, reliable information on applicants during the preliminary interview stages. Stress interviews are designed to reveal how the candidate behaves in high-anxiety situations. Group interviews involve various personnel within the organization in the candidate interview process.

LO²: Explain the steps in the interview process.

Successful job candidates plan appropriately for the interview so that they will know basic information about the company, arrive on time dressed appropriately for the interview, and present a polished first impression following appropriate protocol. During the interview, the candidate presents his or her qualifications favorably and obtains information about the company to aid in deciding whether to accept a possible job offer.

LO³: Prepare effective answers to questions often asked in job interviews, including illegal interview questions.

The successful job candidate effectively discusses key qualifications and skillfully asks questions that show initiative and genuine interest in the company. The candidate recognizes issues that fall outside the bounds of legal questioning. Refusing to answer an illegal question could be detrimental to your chances to secure a job, but answering the question may compromise your ethical values. An effective technique is to answer the legitimate concern behind the illegal question rather than to give a direct answer.

LO⁴: Compose effective messages related to employment (including application, follow-up, thank-you, job-acceptance, job-refusal, resignation, and recommendation request messages).

The job applicant should complete application forms accurately, neatly, and completely, and should only send a follow-up message after a few weeks of no response to an application. An applicant should send a prompt thank-you message following an interview as a professional courtesy. If a job offer is extended, an applicant should write a deductive job-acceptance message that includes the acceptance, details, and a closing that confirms the date the employee will begin work. If the applicant does not accept the job, he or she should write an inductive job-refusal message that includes a buffer beginning, reasons that lead to the refusal, a tactful decline to the offer, and a goodwill closing. Resignation notices should confirm that termination plans are definite and emphasizes positive aspects of the job. Requests for recommendations should include specific information about the job requirements and the applicant's qualifications.

Key Terms

Stress interview interview format designed to place the interviewee in an anxiety-producing situation so an evaluation of the interviewee's performance under stress may be made

Structured interview interview format generally used in the screening process, in which the interviewer follows a predetermined agenda, including a checklist of items or a series of questions and statements designed to elicit the necessary information or interviewee reaction

Unstructured interview a freewheeling exchange that may shift from one subject to another, depending on the interests of the participants

Virtual interview interview conducted using videoconferencing technology

Grammar Quiz

In each of the following sentences, select the correct word or phrase in parentheses.

1. What (affect, effect) will the change have on us?
2. The consultant plans to (advice, advise) the company to eliminate the fourth shift for at least three months.
3. The (amount, number) of complaints from customers declined with the addition of online chat.
4. The (cite, sight, site) of the new 24/7 fitness center is being debated.
5. I consider your remark a (compliment, complement); I agree that the granite countertops (compliment, complement) the deep, earthy tones in the room.
6. The three panelists were constantly interrupting (each other, one another).
7. Generally staple merchandise is placed (farther, further) from the cashier than impulse items.
8. Limit your discussion to five or (fewer, less) points.
9. The hurricane seems to be (losing, loosing) (its, it's) force, which is (different from, different than) predictions.
10. Customer perception is the (principal, principle) reason for the change.
11. (Their, There, They're) planning to complete (their, there, they're) strategic plan this week.
12. The (to, too, two) external auditors expect us (to, too, two) complete (to, too, two) many unnecessary reports.

Grammar Quiz Solutions

1. effect
2. advise
3. number
4. site
5. compliment, complement
6. one another
7. farther
8. fewer
9. losing, its
10. principal
11. They're, their
12. two, to, too

Interviewing for a Job and Preparing Employment Messages

Interviews

Planning Stage

- Learn as much as you can about the job requirements, range of salary and benefits, and the interviewer.
- Research the company with whom you are interviewing (e.g., its products/services, financial condition, growth potential, etc.).
- Identify the *specific* qualifications for the job and other pertinent information about the company.
- Plan your appearance: arrive clean, well groomed, and appropriately dressed.
- Arrive early with appropriate materials to communicate promptness and organization.
- Try to identify the type of interview you will have (structured, unstructured, virtual, stress, or group).

Opening Formalities

- Greet the interviewer by name with a smile, direct eye contact, and a firm handshake.
- Wait for the interviewer to ask you to be seated.
- Sit erect and lean forward slightly to convey interest.
- Avoid distractions such as looking at your cell phone.

Body of the Interview

- Adapt your responses to the type of interview situation.
- Explain how your qualifications relate to the job requirements using multiple specific examples.
- Identify illegal interview questions; address the concern behind an illegal question or tactfully avoid answering the question.
- Ask pertinent questions that communicate intelligence and genuine interest in the company. Introduce questions throughout the interview where appropriate.
- Allow the interviewer to initiate a discussion of salary and benefits. Be prepared to provide a general salary range for applicants with your qualifications.

Closing the Interview

- Watch for cues the interview is ending; rise, accept the interviewer's handshake, and communicate enthusiasm.
- Express appreciation for the interview and say you are eager to hear from the company.

Employment Messages

Application Forms

- Read the entire form before completing it and follow instructions precisely.
- Complete the form neatly and accurately.
- Respond to all questions; insert N/A for questions that do not apply.
- Retain a copy for your records.

Follow-Up Messages

- Remind the receiver that your application is on file and you are interested in the job.
- Present additional education or experience gained since previous correspondence; do not repeat information presented earlier.
- Close with a courteous request for an interview.

Thank-You Messages

- Express appreciation for the interview and mention the specific job for which you have applied.
- Refer to a specific point discussed in the interview.
- Close with a reference to an expected call or document conveying the interviewer's decision.

Job-Acceptance Messages

- Begin by accepting the job offer; specify position.
- Provide necessary details.
- Close with a courteous ending that confirms the date employment begins.

Job-Refusal Messages

- Begin with a neutral, related idea that leads to the explanation for the refusal.
- Present the reasons that lead to a diplomatic statement of the refusal.
- Close positively, anticipating future association with the company.

Resignation Messages

- Begin with a positive statement about the job to cushion the bad news.
- Present the explanation, state the resignation, and provide any details.
- Close with an appreciative statement about experience with the company.

Recommendation Requests

- Begin with the request for the recommendation.
- Provide necessary details including reference to an enclosed résumé to ensure a targeted message.
- End with an appreciative statement for the reference's willingness to aid in the job search.
- Send a follow-up letter explaining delays and extended job searches and expressing appreciation for continued help.

Thank-You for a Recommendation

- Begin with expression of thanks for the recommendation.
- Convey sincere tone by avoiding exaggerated comments and providing specific examples of the value of the recommendation.
- End courteously, indicating future association with the reference.

© Stockbyte/Getty Images

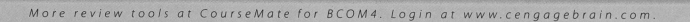

Decisions about page format impact the effectiveness of the message. Many companies have policies that dictate the page layout, letter and punctuation style, and other formatting issues. In the absence of company policy, make your format choices from among standard acceptable options illustrated on this style card.

Page Layout, Punctuation, and Letter Style

The default margins set by word processing software typically reflect the standard line length to increase the efficiency of producing business correspondence. Letters are balanced on the page with approximately equal margins on all sides of the letter, a placement often referred to as fitting the letter into a picture frame. Short letters (one or two paragraphs) are centered on the page; all other letters begin 2 inches from the top of the page. Side margins may be adjusted to improve the appearance of extremely short letters.

Current word processing software has increased the default line spacing and space between paragraphs for easier on-screen reading. If you prefer the tighter, traditional spacing, simply adjust the line spacing to 1.0. Also, to conserve space but keep the fresh, open look, try reducing the line spacing in the letter address but retaining the wider line and paragraph spacing in the body of the letter. Another new default is a crisp, open font such as Calibri (replacing the common Times New Roman) designed for easy reading on monitors.

New Document Look

July 24, 2011   **Tap Enter 2 times**

Mr. Bert A. Pittman
1938 South Welch Avenue
Northwood, NE 65432-1938   **Tap Enter 1 time**

Dear Mr. Pittman   **Tap Enter 1 time**

Your recent article, "Are Appraisers Talking to Themselves?" has drawn many favorable comments from local real estate appraisers.
            Tap Enter 1 time
The Southeast Chapter of the Society of Real Estate Appraisers . . .

Traditonal Spacing

July 24, 2011   **Tap Enter 4 times (QS)**

Mr. Bert A. Pittman
1938 South Welch Avenue
Northwood, NE 65432-1938   **Tap Enter 2 times (DS)**

Dear Mr. Pittman   **Tap Enter 2 times (DS)**

Your recent article, "Are Appraisers Talking to Themselves?" has drawn many favorable comments from local real estate appraisers.
            Tap Enter 2 times (DS)

The Southeast Chapter of the Society of Real Estate Appraisers . . .

Punctuation Styles. Two punctuation styles are customarily used in business letters: mixed and open. Letters using mixed punctuation style have a colon after the salutation and a comma after the complimentary close. Letters using open punctuation style omit a colon after the salutation and a comma after the complimentary close. Mixed punctuation is the traditional style; however, efficiency-conscious companies are increasingly adopting the open style (and other similar format changes), which is easier to remember.

Letter Styles. Business letters are typically formatted in either block or modified block letter styles. The Sample Letters card has examples of these two styles:

- **Block.** Companies striving to reduce the cost of producing business documents adopt the easy-to-learn, efficient block format. All lines (including paragraphs) begin at the left margin.
- **Modified Block.** Modified block is the traditional letter format still used in many companies. The dateline, complimentary close, and signature block begin at the horizontal center of the page. Paragraphs may be indented one-half inch if the writer prefers or the company policy requires it. However, the indention creates unnecessary keystrokes that increase the production cost. All other lines begin at the left margin.

Standard Letter Parts

Professional business letters include seven standard parts. Other parts are optional and may be included when necessary.

1

Dateline. When the letterhead shows the company name, address, telephone and/or fax number, and logo, the letter begins with the *dateline.* Use the month-day-year format (September 2, 2011) for most documents prepared for U.S. audiences. When preparing government documents or writing to an international audience, use the day-month-year format (2 September 2011). Company policy may require another format.

2

Letter Address. The *letter address* includes a personal or professional title (e.g., Mr., Ms., or Dr.), the name of the person and company receiving the letter, and the complete address.

3

Salutation. The *salutation* is the greeting that opens a letter. To show courtesy for the receiver, include a personal or professional title (for example, Mr., Ms., Dr., Senator). Refer to the *first line* of the letter address to determine an appropriate salutation. "Dear Ms. Henson" is an appropriate salutation for a letter addressed to Ms. Donna Henson (first line of letter address). "Ladies and Gentlemen" is an appropriate salutation for a letter addressed to "Wyatt Enterprises," where the company name is keyed as the first line of the letter address.

4

Body. The *body* contains the message of the letter. Because extra space separates the paragraphs, paragraph indention, which requires extra setup time, is not necessary. However, for organizations that require paragraph indention as company policy, the modified block format with indented paragraphs is the appropriate choice.

5

Complimentary Close. The *complimentary close* is a phrase used to close a letter in the same way that you say good-bye at the end of a conversation. To create goodwill, choose a complimentary close that reflects the formality of your relationship with the receiver. Typical examples are "Sincerely," "Cordially," and "Respectfully." Using "yours" in the close has fallen out of popularity (as in "Sincerely yours" and "Very truly yours"). "Sincerely" is considered neutral and is thus appropriate in a majority of business situations. "Cordially" can be used for friendly messages, and "Respectfully" is appropriate when you are submitting information for the approval of another.

6

Signature Block. The *signature block* consists of the writer's name keyed below the complimentary close, allowing space for the writer to sign legibly. A woman may include a courtesy title to indicate her preference (e.g., Miss, Ms., Mrs.), and a woman or man may use a title to distinguish a name used by both men and women (e.g., Shane, Leslie, or Stacy) or initials (E. M. Goodman). A business or professional title may be placed on the same line with the writer's name or directly below it as appropriate to achieve balance.

Title on the Same Line	Title on the Next Line
Ms. Leslie Tatum, President	Ms. E. M. Goodman
	Assistant Manager
Perry Watson, Manager	
Quality Control Division Head	Richard S. Templeton
	Human Resources Director

7

Reference Initials. The *reference initials* consist of the keyboard operator's initials keyed in lowercase below the signature block. The reference initials and the signature block identify the persons involved in preparing a letter in the event of later questions. Reference initials are frequently omitted when a letter is keyed by the writer. However, company policy may require that the initials of all people involved in preparing a letter be placed in the reference initials line to identify accountability in the case of litigation. For example, the following reference initials show the indicated level of responsibility. The reference line might also include department identification or other information as required by the organization.

SF:lm:cd

Person who signed document   **Person who wrote document**   **Person who keyed document**

Optional Letter Parts

Delivery and Addressee Notations. A *delivery notation* provides a record of how a letter was sent. Examples include *Air Mail*, *Certified Mail*, *Federal Express*, *Registered Mail*, and *Fax Transmission*. Addressee notations such as *Confidential* or *Personal* give instructions on how a letter should be handled.

Attention Line. An *attention line* is used for directing correspondence to an individual or department within an organization while still officially addressing the letter to the organization. The attention line directs a letter to a specific person (*Attention Ms. Laura Ritter*), position within a company (*Attention Human Resources Director*), or department (*Attention Purchasing Department*). Current practice is to place the attention line in the letter address on the line directly below the company name and use the same format for the envelope address. The appropriate salutation in a letter with an attention line is "Ladies and Gentlemen."

Reference Line. A *reference line* (*Re: Contract No. 983-9873*) directs the receiver to source documents or to files.

Subject Line. A *subject line* tells the receiver what a letter is about and sets the stage for the receiver to understand the message. For added emphasis, use initial capitals or all capitals, or center the subject line if modified block style is used. Omit the word *subject* because its position above the body clearly identifies its function.

Second-Page Heading. The second and succeeding pages of multiple-page letters and memorandums are keyed on plain paper of the same quality as the letterhead. Identify the second and succeeding pages with a *second-page heading* including the name of the addressee, page number, and the date. Place the heading one inch from the top edge of the paper using either a vertical or horizontal format as illusrated. The horizontal format is more time-consuming to format but looks attractive with the modified block format and may prevent the document from requiring additional pages.

Vertical Format

Communication Systems, Inc.

Page 2

January 19, 2011

Horizontal Format

Communication Systems, Inc.　　　2　　　　January 19, 2011

Company Name in Signature Block. Some companies prefer to include the *company name* in the signature block, but often it is excluded because it appears in the letterhead. The company name is beneficial when the letter is prepared on plain paper or is more than one page (the second page of the letter is printed on plain paper). Including the company name also may be useful to the writer wishing to emphasize that the document is written on behalf of the company (e.g., a letter establishing an initial customer contact).

Enclosure Notation. An *enclosure notation* indicates that additional items (brochure, price list, résumé) are included in the same envelope. Key the plural form (*Enclosures*) if more than one item is enclosed. You may identify the number of enclosures (*Enclosures: 3*) or the specific item enclosed (*Enclosure: Bid Proposal*). Avoid abbreviations (*Enc.*) that may give the impression that your work is hurried and careless and may show disrespect for the recipient. Some companies use the word *Attachment* on memorandums when the accompanying items may be stapled or clipped and not placed in an envelope.

Copy Notation. A *copy notation* indicates that a courtesy copy of the document was sent to the person(s) listed. Include the person's personal or professional title and full name after keying "c" for copy or "cc" for courtesy copy. Key the copy notation below the enclosure notation, reference initials, or signature block (depending on the optional letter parts used).

Postscript. A *postscript*, appearing as the last item in a letter, is commonly used to emphasize information. A postscript in a sales letter, for example, is often used to restate the central selling point; for added emphasis, it may be handwritten or printed in a different color. Often handwritten postscripts of a personal nature are added to personalize the printed document. Postscripts should not be used to add information inadvertently omitted from the letter. Because its position clearly labels this paragraph as a postscript, do not begin with "PS."

Computer File Notation. A *computer file notation* provides the path and file name of the letter. Some companies require this documentation on the file copy to facilitate revision. Place the computer file notation a single space below the last keyed line of the letter.

Block Letter Style with Open Punctuation

SOCIETY REAL ESTATE APPRAISERS
763 Collins Avenue ▪ Lansing, MI 48909-0763 ▪ (517) 555-9073 ▪ Fax (517) 555-9108

Begin 2" from top or 1/2" below letterhead

- **Dateline**

July 24, 2011   **Tap Enter 2 times**

- **Letter address**

Mr. Bert A. Pittman
1938 South Welch Avenue
Northwood, NE 65432-1938

- **Salutation**

Dear Mr. Pittman   **Tap Enter 1 time**

- **Body**

Your recent article, "Are Appraisers Talking to Themselves?" has drawn many favorable comments from local real estate appraisers.

Tap Enter 1 time

The Southeast Chapter of the Society of Real Estate Appraisers has felt a strong need for more information about appraisal report writing. About 200 members will attend our annual seminar. They would be glad to meet you and are interested in hearing you discuss "Appraisal Report Writing." The meeting will be at the Tilton Hotel on Thursday, August 23, at 7 p.m. We promise you a pleasant evening and an attentive audience.

Tap Enter 1 time

Along with your acceptance, we would appreciate a photograph by August 7 so that we can include your picture in the program.

Tap Enter 1 time

- **Complimentary close**

Sincerely

- **Signature block**
- **Reference initials**

Jennifer Malley **Tap Enter 2 times leaving space for signature**

Jennifer Malley
Program Chair
JM:tw

© Cengage Learning 2011

Right-side annotations:

- Begins all lines at left margin; uses easy-to-read jagged right margin and single-spaced, unindented paragraphs.

- Omits colon after salutation and comma after complimentary close in open punctuation style.

- Signs legibly in available space and identifies writer.

- Identifies person keying document.

The document illustrates contemporary spacing with 1.15 spaces between lines. If using traditional single spacing (1.0), tap Enter 2 times to double-space between paragraphs and 4 times to quadruple space after the dateline and the complimentary close.

Modified Block Letter Style with Mixed Punctuation

Begin 2" from top or 1/2" below letterhead

- **Dateline**

October 15, 2011   **Tap Enter 2 times**

- **Letter address**

Mr. Saunders Greyson, Manager
Tropical Importers, Inc.
1240 Coastal Lane
Miami, FL 33140-1000   **Tap Enter 1 time**

Dear Mr. Greyson: **Tap Enter 1 time**

- **Salutation**

It was a pleasure meeting you at the career fair this morning. The opportunities offered in logistics management identifies your company as being a leader in today's international marketplace.   **Tap Enter 1 time**

My experience and knowledge of logistics management enable me to be a valuable asset to your company:

- **Body**

- Realistic international experience with a delivery company.

- Demonstrated commitment to developing an appreciation for international cultures and business practices.

- Excellent performance evaluations, including special recognition for troubleshooting transportation problems to remote locations.
Tap Enter 1 time

Please message me so we can discuss my joining Tropical Importers.
Tap Enter 1 time

Sincerely,   **Tap Enter 2 times**
leaving space for signature

Brandon Shaw

Brandon Shaw

- **Complimentary close**

- **Signature block**

Begins dateline, complimentary close, and signature block at horizontal center.

Includes colon after salutation in mixed punctuation style.

Uses single-spaced, unindented paragraphs, but indentions are acceptable with modified block style.

Includes comma after complimentary close in mixed punctuation style.

Signs legibly in available space and identifies writer.

Omits reference initials since writer keyed document

© Cengage Learning 2011

Document illustrates contemporary spacing. If using traditional spacing (1.0) between lines, tap Enter 2 times to double space between paragraphs and 4 times to quadruple space after the dateline and the complimentary close.

Envelopes

An envelope should be printed on the same quality and color of paper as the letter and generated using the convenient envelope feature of your word processing program. Adjust defaults as needed to adhere to the recommendations of the United States Postal Service (USPS). To increase the efficiency of mail handling, use the two-letter abbreviations for states, territories, and Canadian provinces. USPS official state abbreviations are available at **www.USPS.gov**.

Most companies today do not follow the traditional USPS recommendation to key the letter address in all capital letters with no punctuation. The mixed case format matches the format used in the letter address, looks more professional, and allows the writer to generate the envelope automatically without rekeying text. No mail handling efficiency is lost as today's optical character readers that sort mail can read both upper- and lowercase letters easily. Proper placement of the address on a large and a small envelope generated using an envelope template available with word processing software is shown here:

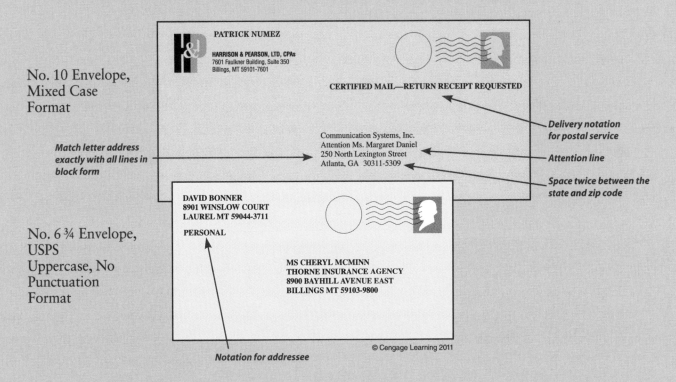

No. 10 Envelope, Mixed Case Format

Match letter address exactly with all lines in block form

Delivery notation for postal service

Attention line

Space twice between the state and zip code

PATRICK NUMEZ

HARRISON & PEARSON, LTD, CPAs
7601 Faulkner Building, Suite 350
Billings, MT 59101-7601

CERTIFIED MAIL—RETURN RECEIPT REQUESTED

Communication Systems, Inc.
Attention Ms. Margaret Daniel
250 North Lexington Street
Atlanta, GA 30311-5309

No. 6 ¾ Envelope, USPS Uppercase, No Punctuation Format

DAVID BONNER
8901 WINSLOW COURT
LAUREL MT 59044-3711

PERSONAL

MS CHERYL MCMINN
THORNE INSURANCE AGENCY
8900 BAYHILL AVENUE EAST
BILLINGS MT 59103-9800

© Cengage Learning 2011

Notation for addressee

Additionally, to create a highly professional image, business communicators should fold letters to produce the fewest number of creases. Here are the proper procedures for folding letters for large (No. 10) and small (6¾) envelopes:

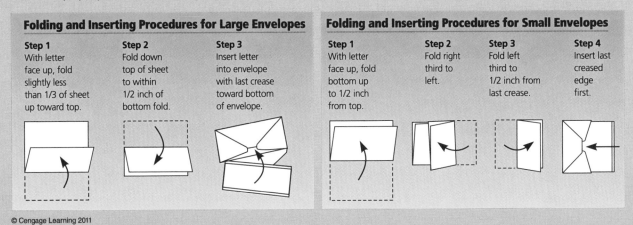

Folding and Inserting Procedures for Large Envelopes

Step 1
With letter face up, fold slightly less than 1/3 of sheet up toward top.

Step 2
Fold down top of sheet to within 1/2 inch of bottom fold.

Step 3
Insert letter into envelope with last crease toward bottom of envelope.

Folding and Inserting Procedures for Small Envelopes

Step 1
With letter face up, fold bottom up to 1/2 inch from top.

Step 2
Fold right third to left.

Step 3
Fold left third to 1/2 inch from last crease.

Step 4
Insert last creased edge first.

© Cengage Learning 2011

Memorandum Formats

To increase productivity of memorandums (memos), which are internal messages, companies use formats that are easy to input and that save time. Most companies use customized or standard memo templates found in most word processing software that include the basic headings (TO, FROM, DATE, SUBJECT) to guide the writer in providing the needed transmittal information. Memos may be printed on memo forms, plain paper, or letterhead depending on the preference of the company. Follow the guidelines for formatting a memo illustrated here.

Memo Format

Litton Best Foods, Inc.
6285 Northwest Blvd.   Laurel, MS 37450
(800)555-5291 Fax: (713)555-9214

Begin 2" from top of page or 1/2" below letterhead

- **Heading**

TO: Erin W. Lutzel, Vice President

FROM: Isako Kimura, Marketing Director *IK*

DATE: July 15, 2011

SUBJECT: Marketing Activity Report, June 2011

Tap Enter 1 time

The marketing division reports the following activities for June.

Tap Enter 1 time

Advertising

Three meetings were held with representatives at the Bart and Dome agency to complete plans for the fall campaign for Fluffy Buns. The campaign will concentrate on the use of discount coupons published in the Thursday food section of sixty daily newspapers in the Pacific states. Coupons will be released on the second and fourth Thursdays in June and July.

Estimated cost of the program is $645,000. That amount includes 2.2 million redeemed coupons at 20 cents each ($440,000).

- **Body**

A point-of-sale advertising display, shown on the attached sheet, was developed for retail grocery outlets. Sales reps are pushing these in their regular and new calls. The display may be used to feature a different product from our line on a weekly basis.

Sales Staff

We have dropped one sales rep from the northern California section and divided the area between the southern Oregon and Sacramento reps.

Call me should you wish to discuss the information presented.

Attachment

- **Enclosure notation**

- *Omits courtesy titles in informal document.*

- *Includes writer's written initials.*

- *Keys subject line in mixed case or all capitals for added emphasis.*

- *Uses headings to divide message into easy-to-read sections.*

- *Uses single spaced, unindented paragraphs and left-justified margins for easy reading.*

© Cengage Learning 2011

Formal Report Format

Page arrangement for reports varies somewhat, depending on the documentation style guide followed or individual company preferences. Take advantage of your software's automatic formatting features for efficient formatting and generating report parts. Portions of a sample report are shown below.

Margins. For formal reports, use one-inch side margins. If the report is to be bound, increase the left margin by one-half inch. Use a two-inch top margin for the first page of each report part (table of contents, executive summary) and a one-inch top margin for all other pages. Leave at least a one-inch bottom margin on all pages.

Spacing. While documentation style guides typically specify double spacing of text, company practice is often to single-space reports. Double spacing accommodates editorial comments and changes but results in a higher page count. Even if you choose to double-space the body of a report, you may opt to single-space some elements, such as the entries in your references page and information in tables or other graphic components.

Headings. Several levels of headings can be used throughout the report and are typed in different ways to indicate level of importance. Suggested formatting guidelines for a report divided into three levels are illustrated in the document on the next page. Develop fourth- and fifth-level headings simply by using boldface, underline, and varying fonts.

Formal Report Parts

Title page

Transmittal document

Table of contents

Executive summary

First page of report

Page with graphic

References in APA style

Appendix

© Cengage Learning 2011

- Capitalizes all letters in report title.

- Places first- and second-level headings at left margin and capitalizes initial letters. Larger font size makes the first level stand out.

- Includes intervening text between first- and second level headings.

- Uses default indentation and decreased spacing between enumerated and bulleted items.

- Places third-level subheadings at left margin and capitalizes first letter.

Format Pointers
This report document illustrates Word 2007 Style Set with style formats applied for the report title, the three heading levels, and the enumerated list. Creating a custom style set allows businesses to create a report style that is consistent with their company image and brand.

The increased spacing after each paragraph eliminates the need for indented paragraphs.

2″ top margin

REPORT TITLE Title style (26-point Cambria font)

Tap Enter 1 time

xxx xxxxxx xxxxxxx xxxxx xxxxxxxxx xxxx xxxxxx xxxxxx xxxxxxx xxxxx xx xxxxxx xxxx x xxxxx xxxxx xxxxxxxxxx xxx xxxx xxxxx xxxxx.

Tap Enter 1 time

First-Level Heading Heading 1 (14-point Cambria font)

Tap Enter 1 time

xxx xxxxxx xxxxxxx xxxxx xxxxxxxxx xxxx xxxxxx xxxxxx xxxxxxx xxxxx xx xxxxxx xxxx x xxxxx xxxxx xxxxxxxxxx xxx xxxx xxxxx xxxxx.

Tap Enter 1 time

Second-Level Subheading Heading 2 (13-point Cambria font)

Tap Enter 1 time

xxx xxxxxx xxxxxxx xxxxx xxxxxxxxx xxxx xxxxxx xxxxxx xxxxxxx xxxxx xx xxxxxx xxxx x xxxxx xxxxx xxxxxxxxxx xxx xxxx xxxxx xxxxx.

Tap Enter 1 time

1. xxxx x xxxxxx xx xxxxxx xxxx xxx xxxxxxxxx xx xxxxx xxxxx xx. xx xxxx xxx. Space automatically reduced between enumerated items.
2. xxxx x xxxxxx xx xxxxxx xxxx xxx xxxxxxxxx xx xxxxx xxxxx xx. xx xxxx xxx xxxxx xxxx xx x xxxxxxxxxx.

Tap Enter 1 time

Second-Level Subheading

Tap Enter 1 time

xxx xxxxxx xxxxxxx xxxxx xxxxxxxxx xxxx xxxxxx xxxxxx xxxxxxx xxxxx xx xxxxxx xxxx x xxxxx xxxxx xxxxxxxxxx xxx xxxx xxxxx xxxxx.

Tap Enter 1 time

Heading 3 (11-point Cambria font)
Third-Level Subheading. xxx xxxxxx xxxxxxx xxxxx xxxxxxxxx xxxx xxxxxx xxxxxx xxxxxxx xxxxx xx xxxxxx xxxx x xxxxx xxxxx xxxxxxxxxx xxx xxxx xxxxx xxxxx.

Tap Enter 1 time

Third-Level Subheading. xxx xxxxxx xxxxxxx xxxxx xxxxxxxxx xxxx xxxxxx xxxxxx xxxxxxx xxxxx xx xxxxxx xxxx x xxxxx xxxxx xxxxxxxxxx xxx xxxx xxxxx xxxxx.

A number of widely used reference styles are available for documenting the sources of information used in report writing. Two of the more popular style manuals for business writing are as follows:

Publication Manual of the American Psychological Association, 5th ed., Washington, DC: American Psychological Association, 2001.

Joseph Gibaldi, *MLA Handbook for Writers of Research Papers*, 6th ed., New York: Modern Languages Association of America, 2003. The *MLA Handbook* is designed for high school and undergraduate college students; the *MLA Style Manual and Guide to Scholarly Publishing*, 2nd ed. (1998) is designed for graduate students, scholars, and professional writers.

These sources, commonly referred to as the APA and MLA styles, provide general rules for referencing and give examples of the citation formats for various types of source materials. This style card reflects the rules along with examples for the MLA style. Whenever you are not required to use a particular documentation style, choose a recognized one and follow it consistently. Occasionally, you may need to reference something for which no general example applies. Choose the example that is most like your source and follow that format. When in doubt, provide more information, not less. Remember that a major purpose for listing references is to enable readers to retrieve and use the sources. This style card illustrates citation formats for some common types of information sources and refers you to various electronic sites that provide further detailed guidelines for preparing electronic citations.

In-Text Parenthetical Citations

The *MLA Handbook* supports the use of ***in-text citations***. Abbreviated information within parentheses in the text directs the reader to a list of sources at the end of a report. The list of sources at the end contains all bibliographic information on each source cited in a report. This list is arranged alphabetically by the author's last name or, if no author is provided, by the first word of the title.

The in-text citations contain minimal information needed to locate the source in the complete list. The *MLA* style includes the author's last name and the page number for both quotes and paraphrases, but not the date of publication. Note the format of the in-text parenthetical citations shown below.

One author not named in the text, direct quotation

"A recent survey . . . shows that more and more companies plan to publish their annual reports on the Internet" (Prinn 13).

Direct quotation, no page number on source

According to James, "traditional college students have a perspective that is quite different from adult consumers" (par. 2).

Use par. 2 *in place of missing page number only if paragraphs are numbered in original text.*

Multiple authors for sources not named in the text wording

Globalization is becoming a continuous challenge for managers . . . (Tang and Crofford 29).

"For all its difficulty, teamwork is still essential . . ." (Nunamaker et al. 163).

For sources by more than three authors, use et al. *after the last name of the first author or include all last names. Do not underline or italicize* et al.

More than one source documenting the same idea

. . . companies are turning to micromarketing (Heath 48; Roach 54).

More than one source by the same author documenting the same idea

Past research (Taylor, "Performance Appraisal" 6, "Frequent Absenteeism" 89) shows . . .

Reference to author(s) or date in the text wording

Kent Spalding and Brian Price documented the results . . .

In 2006, West concluded . . . (E2).

Omit a page number when citing a one-page article or nonprint source.

No author provided

. . . virtues of teamwork look obvious ("Teams Triumph in Creative Solutions" 61).

Include full title or shortened version of it.

Works Cited

The **works cited** page located at the end of your document contains an alphabetized list of the sources used in preparing a report, with each entry containing publication information necessary for locating the source. A researcher often uses sources that provide information but do not result in citations. If you want to acknowledge that you have consulted these works and provide the reader with a comprehensive reading list, include these sources in the list of works cited and refer to list as *Works Consulted*. Your company guidelines may specify whether to list works cited only or works consulted. If you receive no definitive guidelines, use your own judgment. If in doubt, include all literature cited and read, and label the page with the appropriate title so that the reader clearly understands the nature of the list.

To aid the reader in locating sources in lengthy bibliographies, you may include several subheadings denoting the types of publications documented, for example, books, articles, unpublished documents and papers, government publications, and nonprint media. Check your reference manual to determine if subheadings are allowed.

Formats for Print and Recorded References

Reference styles for a variety of print and recorded sources prepared using the MLA style are shown in Figure 3. Note that the following rules apply for MLA works cited.

Indention and spacing	Begin first line of each entry at at left margin and indent subsequent lines one-half inch. While the MLA style manual specifies double spacing within and between entries, common practice in preparing reports is to single space each entry and double space between entries.
Author names	List last name first for first author only. Use "and" before final author's name.
Date	Place date at end of citation for books and after periodical title and volume **for articles. Months are abbreviated.**
Capitalization	In titles of books, periodicals, and article titles, capitalize all main words.
Italicizing and quotation marks	Italicize titles of books, journals, and periodicals (or underline if directed). Place titles of articles within quotation marks.
Page notations	Omit the use of p. or pp. on all citations.

Figure 3 MLA (6th Edition Style)

Works Cited

"Best Business Attire." Executive Communications Group. 2003. 30 May 2006 <http://ecglink.com>.

Brody, Mary. "Dress codes: 'Business Conservative' is Making a Comeback." *HR Briefing* 1 Mar. 2003: 7.

Egodigwe, Laura, and Sonya Alleyne. "Here Come the Suits." *Black Enterprise* Mar. 2003: 59–60.

Hudson, Repps. "'Business Casual' on the Wane." *St. Louis Post Dispatch* 15 Apr. 2002. 30 May 2006 <http://seattlepi.nwsource.com>.

Jones, Clark. "Experts Discuss Ways to Dress in Business Attire for Summer." *Las Vegas Review* 8 June 2003.

Business and Company Resource Center. University of Houston Lib. 29 July 2006 <http:bcrc.college.com/>.

Koestner, Maury. "What Exactly is Business Casual?" *The News-Herald* 7 May 2005.

General Businessfile. Texas A & M lib. 31 May 2006 <http://www.epnet.com/>.

Molloy, John T. "Executives Find as Dress Gets Sloppier, Attitudes Slip." *The Houston Chronicle* 9 December 2005: D2.

White, Ronald. D. "Clashing Dress Styles." *Careerbuilder* 26 Aug. 2001. 12 June 2006 <http://www.latimes.com>.

Rough Draft of a Letter (excerpt)

- Adds mailing notation.
- Uses two-letter state abbreviation.
- Corrects spelling of name.
- Adds smooth transition to next paragraph.
- Divides into two sentences to enhance readability.
- Recasts from receiver's viewpoint.
- Corrects grammatical error.
- Includes specific action ending.
- Eliminates redundancy.
- Corrects grammatical error.

August 23, 2010
Fax Transmission

Tina Munoz, CEO
Hospital Technology Solutions
3405 Elm Street
Cedar Rapids, ~~Iowa~~ IA 68009

Dear Ms. ~~Numoz~~ Munoz:

With your years of experience training hospital staff in the use of XENOG software, our goal of using the latest technology to create more efficient and effective healthcare solutions will surely be accomplished. *We are excited to explore other ways our companies may benefit through shared expertise.*

One of the objectives of our new administrator Johna Fitzgerald ~~are~~ is to review all of the hospital's current technology and to create a plan to update it, if necessary, and to add capabilities where needed. As part of that process, Ms. Fitzgerald has asked me to form a planning committee ~~whose~~ *The committee's primary* ~~basic~~ functions ~~is~~ are to perform the review of our current systems and write a report containing its recommendations for improvement. The committee thus should consist of representatives from all areas of the hospital that ~~is~~ are currently involved in the use of technology.

Since you will be an important part of the implementation of some of ~~those~~ improvements, ~~we need~~ *your* ~~you're~~ input *is essential.* The time that you serve on the committee will be added to our current contract with your firm. Please ~~advise~~ *let* me ~~that~~ *know by September 15* whether or not you will serve on the Technology Steering Committee. A meeting will be scheduled as soon all ~~members~~ *members* have been selected.

© Cengage Learning 2011

Errors Undetectable by Spell-Check
Spelling of receiver's name, "Munoz."

Correct word substitutions: "you're" for "your."

Improving Readability through Cautious Use of a Grammar and Style Checker

Step 1:
Evaluate and respond to advice given for grammar and style errors detected.

Step 2:
Use counts, averages, and readability indexes as guides for adjusting writing level appropriately.

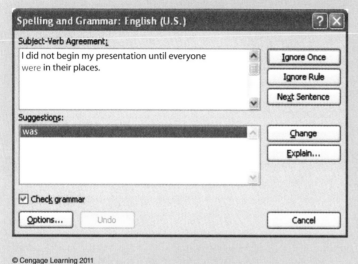

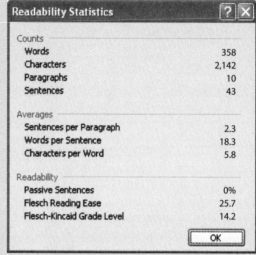

© Cengage Learning 2011

Improving Your Writing with the Computer

Hone your computer skills to spend more time writing and less time formatting.

- ☑ Draft in a font style and size easily read on-screen; postpone formatting until the revision is done.
- ☑ Use the *find* and *go to* commands to search and make changes.
- ☑ Learn time-saving keyboard shortcuts for frequently used commands such as *copy* and *cut*. Customize software so that you can access these commands easily.
- ☑ Use automatic numbering to arrange numerical or alphabetical lists and to ensure accuracy.
- ☑ Save time by using built-in styles such as cover pages, headers/footers, list and table formats, text boxes, and graphical effects.
- ☑ Save frequently used text such as a letterhead or your signature line so you can insert it with a single click.
- ☑ Use the *citations and bibliography* command to format references and the *document styles* feature to automatically generate a content page and index.

Use formatting features to create an organized and polished appearance.

- ☑ Add spacing between lines and paragraphs and use crisp, open fonts such as Calibri for a contemporary look that is easy to read on-screen.
- ☑ Apply color-infused document themes and built-in styles to reflect a consistent brand identity.

Use proofing features to locate errors.

- ☑ Use spell-check frequently as you draft and revise. Be aware that spell-check will not identify miskeyings (*than* for *then*), commonly misused words, homophones (*principle, principal*), omitted words, missing or out-of-order enumerations, and content errors.
- ☑ Use grammar check to provide feedback on usage, reading level, comprehension factors, and other errors and weaknesses that cannot be detected electronically.
- ☑ Use a thesaurus only when you can recognize the precise meaning needed.

Email Format

New Message

To:	All sales staff
CC:	
Subject:	Addition of Stephen Kerr to Our Staff

Everyone,

I'm pleased to announce the appointment of Stephen Kerr as communications specialist in the corporate communications department. He will fill the position vacated by Kenneth Shaw and will begin work on May 6.

FYI, Steve comes to us from Gynco Industries, where he was in charge of mass media relations. His duties with us will include long-range planning and acting as liaison with our ad agency. He has degrees in public relations and marketing.

Steve merits your full support. We wish him much success and extend a sincere welcome to our organization. :-)

Thanks,

Jenny

Jenny Veitch, Vice President of Operations
Franklin Corporation
875 Marshall Freeway, Suite 4500
Atlanta, GA 30304
(404) 555-3000, Extension 6139 Fax: (404) 555-9759

- *Includes descriptive subject line.*

- *Includes appropriate salutation for group of coworkers.*

- *Uses emoticon and email abbreviation in informal message to coworkers who understand and approve of this shorthand.*

- *Includes signature file that identifies writer.*

Format Pointers
Includes single spaced, unindented paragraphs and short lines for complete screen display.

Uses mixed case for easy reading.

Keeps format simple for quick download and compatibility.

© Cengage Learning 2011

Email Format

While certain email formats are standard, some degree of flexibility exists in formatting email messages. Primarily, be certain your message is easy to read and represents the standards of formality that your company has set. The following guidelines and the model email illustrated above will assist you in formatting professional email messages:

- ***Include an appropriate salutation and closing.*** You might write "Dear" and the person's name or simply the person's first name when messaging someone for the first time. Casual expressions such as "Hi" and "Later" are appropriate for personal messages but not serious business email. A closing of "Sincerely" is considered quite formal for email messages; instead, a simple closing such as "Best wishes" or "Thank you" provides a courteous end to your message.

- ***Include a signature file at the end of the message.*** The signature file (known as a .sig file) contains a few lines of text that include your full name and title, mailing address, telephone number, and any other information you want people to know about you. You might include a clever quote that you update frequently.

- ***Format for easy readability.*** Follow these suggestions:
  - Limit each message to one screen to minimize scrolling. If you need more space, consider a short email message with a lengthier message attached as a word processing file. Be certain the recipient can receive and read the attachment.

- Limit the line length to 60 characters so that the entire line is displayed on the monitor without scrolling.
- Use short, unindented paragraphs. Separate paragraphs with an extra space.
- Use mixed case for easy reading. Typing in all capital letters is perceived as shouting in email and considered rude online behavior.
- Emphasize a word or phrase by surrounding it with quotation marks or keying in uppercase letters.
- ***Use emoticons or email abbreviations in moderation when you believe the receiver will understand and approve.*** *Emoticons*, created by keying combinations of symbols to produce "sideways" faces, are a shorthand way of lightening the mood, adding emotion to email messages, and attempting to compensate for nonverbal cues lost in one-way communication:

:-)	smiling, indicates humor or sarcasm	%-(	confused
:-(	frowning, indicates sadness or anger	:-O	surprised

Alternately, you might put a "g" (for grin) or "smile" in parentheses after something that is obviously meant as tongue-in-cheek to help carry the intended message to the receiver. Abbreviations for commonly used phrases save space and avoid unnecessary keying. Popular ones include BCNU (be seeing you), BTW (by the way), FYI (for your information), FWIW (for what it's worth), HTH (hope this helps), IMHO (in my humble opinion), and LOL (laugh out loud).

Some email users feel strongly that emoticons and abbreviations are childish or inappropriate for serious email and decrease productivity when the receiver must take time for deciphering. Before using them, be certain the receiver will understand them and that the formality of the message and your relationship with the receiver justify this type of informal exchange. Then, use only in moderation to *punctuate* your message.

Good Example of an Email Message

To:	Rodney Spurlin, Software Compliance Officer
From:	Claire Henderson, Director of Legal Services
Subject:	Legal Liability for Downloaded Music

> *Provides subject line that is meaningful to reader and writer.*

Rodney,

Your immediate attention is needed to address the company's liability for employees' downloading copyrighted music.

The recording industry has announced its intent to prosecute organizations that allow their employees to download and store music files without proper authorization. This threat is real; one company has already agreed to a $1 million settlement.

The Recording Industry Association of America and the Motion Picture Association of America recently sent a six-page brochure to Fortune 1000 corporations. Please review the suggested corporate policies and sample communication to employees and determine whether you believe our corporation is at risk.

Please contact me when you are ready to discuss potential changes to our corporate code of conduct. I'll be online all week if you want to instant message once you've reviewed the brochure.

Later,

Claire

> *Includes salutation and closing to personalize message.*
>
> **Format Pointer**
> *Composes short, concise message limited to one idea and one screen.*

GOOD *Good Example of an Apology*

New Message

To: Allen Melton <amelton@meltonpr.com>

CC:

Subject: Yesterday's Advertising Presentation

Allen:

Please accept my apology for the inconvenience you experienced yesterday because of the unavailability of computer equipment. Fortunately, you saved the day with your backup transparencies and gave an effective presentation of the new advertising campaign.

The next time you make a presentation at our company, I'll be sure to schedule the LGI room. This room has the latest technology to support multimedia presentations. Just call and let me know the date.

Later,

Thomas Lee Raferty
Administrative Assistant

• *States the apology briefly without providing an overly specific description of the error.*

• *Reports measures taken to avoid repetition of such incidents, which strengthens the credibility of the apology.*

• *Closes with a positive statement.*

Format Pointers

Limits the message to a single idea—the apology.

Composes a short, concise message that fits on one screen.

Includes a salutation and closing to personalize the message.

GOOD

Good Example of an Appreciation Message

New Message

To:	Ellen Meyer <emeyer@techno.com>
From:	Martha Riggins <mriggins@techno.com>
Subject:	Appreciation for Outstanding Contribution

Ellen,

Thank you for spearheading the initiative to improve interpersonal communication within the office and for arranging for the training sessions to achieve that goal. It was a big commitment on your part in addition to your regular duties.

Your efforts are already paying off. I have observed the techniques we learned in the training sessions being used in the department on several occasions already. In times of uncertainty, anxiety can often spill over into people's professional lives, so the seminar was very timely in helping to ensure a collaborative and civil workplace where everyone is treated respectfully.

You have proven yourself a dedicated and insightful employee, a true asset to the continued success of our organization.

Best regards,
Martha

- Extends appreciation for employee's efforts to improve departmental communication.
- Provides specific evidence of worth of experience without exaggerating or using overly strong language or mechanical statements.
- Assures writer of tangible benefits to be gained from the training session.

Format Pointers
Uses short lines, mixed case; omits special formatting such as emoticons and email abbreviations for improved readability.

Developing the Components of a Bad-News Message

The current subprime mortgage situation and its subsequent effects on the economy have provided an opportunity to better educate loan seekers about the types of financial risk they might safely assume. For this reason, mortgage seekers may be restricted in the number of mortgage loans they might hold.

- Begins with statement with which both can agree. Sets stage for reasons for bad news.
- Reveals subject of message and transitions into reasons.

As part of the effort to help loan seekers reduce their financial risk, banks now limit the number of mortgages a person might judiciously hold to no more than four. Because of current sluggishness in the housing market, house sellers now have more difficulty selling homes in a timely manner, making such assets much less liquid. If a mortgage holder gets into trouble, he/she will have less ability to resell the property and recover the loan amount. This puts the mortgage holder and the lender at greater financial risk.

- Provides rule and clearly applies rule to situation.
- States refusal positively and clearly using complex sentence and positive language.

In order to secure an additional mortgage, you must first pay off one of your current mortgages. Alternately, our affiliated real estate brokers are available to help you sell one of your properties so that you might secure another. Please call me at 213-555-3400 to discuss these services.

- Includes counterproposal as alternative.
- Closes with sales promotion for other services, inferring a continuing business relationship.

© Cengage Learning 2011

Note the closing paragraph is a positive, forward-looking statement that includes sales promotion of other services the mortgage firm and its affiliated real estate brokers can offer.

GOOD *Good Example of a Claim Denial*

2937 Fox Cove Lane   Conway PA 76032-2937 (501) 555-1129   Fax (501) 555-3900

June 3, 2011

Ms. Dena Marcum
Accounting and Budget
SPL Industries
7821 South Third Street
Conway, AR 72032-7839

Dear Ms. Marcum:

PartyTime Limited was pleased to be part of your staff/alumni banquet and appreciated your staff's compliments on the quality of the food, service, and decorations.

You are correct that the amount of the invoice is more than the price specified by the contract. The contract price was based on the 250-guest estimate provided by your administrative assistant. The estimate considered the amount of food to be served and the number of servers required to serve 250 guests, as well as the cost of decorating the banquet hall.

Your invoice includes an additional $200 for the cost of food served to the 25 unexpected guests of your alumni. Although we typically prepare extra food for large, formal affairs such as yours, we did not anticipate the large number of additional guests that arrived that evening. I was relieved our staff was able to obtain additional food from our warehouse to serve these guests.

Had these 25 guests been included in the original estimate, we would have added $200 to the food cost estimate. We would also have included $80 for the cost of two additional servers. Although we were short-handed, our staff provided your guests with quality service. Your invoice does not include any additional charges for service.

Ms. Marcum, as you begin planning festivities for the upcoming holidays, keep our famous specialty desserts in mind for an extraordinary change from the traditional catered turkey lunch.

Sincerely,

Jared Harrelson

Jared Harrelson
Manager

- *Begins with a statement with which the reader can agree to get the message off to a good start.*

- *Presents a clear explanation for the additional charge.*

- *Continues the explanation.*

- *Uses the subjunctive mood to de-emphasize the refusal.*

- *Shifts emphasis away from the refusal by presenting sales promotion on other services.*

Format Pointer
Illustrates block format—all lines begin at the left margin.

GOOD Good Example of a Persuasive Claim

Palmdale Galleria
3109 Overlook Drive / Palmdale, CA 93550
P: (661) 555-2130 \ F: (661) 555-3129

October 27, 2010

Samantha Reynolds
Senior Architect
Primera Design
3400 Wilshire Boulevard
Los Angeles, CA 90052-3674

Dear Samantha:

When Palmdale Galleria selected your firm to redesign our retail space, we were impressed by the work that you had done in a number of hotels and mall properties in Las Vegas and other upscale developments throughout the country. We were most impressed with the fantasy world that you created for the Insight Hotel's shopping galleria, a space that attended to every aspect of the consumer's shopping experience, including sight, sound, smell, taste, and sensation, through the implementation of the latest technological and design advances.

In our meeting with your creative team, we asked for attention to the visual design, the entertainment elements, and the creation of an ambiance that addressed all aspects of the consumers' sensual experience. After reviewing the initial plan for our redesign, we find the degree of incorporation of entertainment and sensual experiences for consumers to be disappointing. The redesign incorporates the latest trends in architectural design but needs more attention to entertainment features, including spaces for "street" entertainers, mini-concerts, and amusement park rides, including bungee jumping, etc. We also expected a more complete integration of water features, such as fountains, waterfalls, and streams, with the associated opportunities for entertainment, such as a simulated river rafting experience. In the tropical forest region of the mall, we hoped to have a better integration of spaces for zoo animals and an apparatus to create the "smells" and "sounds" of the jungle. Consumers no longer go to malls to simply shop but to want to be transported to a world of leisure, pampering, and entertainment, one that appeals to all of their senses.

With Primera Design's reputation for creative productions, we are confident the redesign plan for the Palmdale Galleria will be revised to incorporate these elements. Please let us know if you would like to meet to discuss and clarify any of the design issues raised here. Because of the importance of this project, I am at your disposal. Please call me at 444-1920 to schedule a meeting.

Sincerely,

Martinique Cole

Martinique Cole
General Manager
Palmdale Galleria

- *Seeks attention by giving sincere compliment that reveals subject of message.*

- *Continues central appeal— commitment to creative redesign—while providing needed details.*

- *Presents reasoning that leads to request and subtle reminder of central appeal.*

- *Connects specific request with firm's commitment to develop a creative redesign.*

Legal and Ethical Consideration
Uses letter rather than less formal email format to emphasize importance of these differences regarding contractual agreement.

© Cengage Learning 2011

Down-Home Restaurants

83 South Pass Road • Chattanooga TN 37426-2723 • (423) 555-5320

March 15, 2011

Mrs. Joyce Smith
976 Thompson Road
Crossville, TN 38555-0976

Dear Mrs. Smith:

Meeting you and touring the building on your property last week was a pleasure. That little building provided me with a fascinating glimpse of the past. You must have found it convenient using the building as a big "attic," storing all your canned goods and old farm implements over the years.

As the manager of the Down-Home Barbeque in Mena, I am constantly looking for items to build and display in our restaurants. Our restaurants are constructed of weathered wood to create a genuine rustic atmosphere, which we think complements our "down-home" menu.

As I toured your building, I couldn't help but notice some of the unique items inside and the old weathered boards hanging outside. The wood from the building and its contents would enable us to build and furnish a new restaurant in Clarksville and refurbish our Jackson location. Marc Lane, owner of Down-Home Restaurants, has asked me to extend you the offer explained in the enclosed proposal.

Naturally, no amount of money can compensate you for a building that holds so many memories for you. However, we would be happy to purchase the entire contents of the building, excluding any special items of sentimental value that you may want to keep.

Although the thought of selling the building may sadden you, think of the "second life" that the old farm equipment, dishes, washboards, seed bags, and weathered boards would have in our restaurants. People who would otherwise never see such Americana will have the opportunity to learn a little about its rich past.

After you have reviewed the proposal, please call me at 555-3253 to discuss our offer to display your treasures in our restaurants.

Sincerely,

Karla Ash

Karla Ash, Manager
Chattanooga Store

Enclosure

• Opens with a compliment that introduces an appeal to the owner's pride in the old property.

• Introduces the writer's interest in acquiring property and continues the primary appeal (desire to preserve the past).

• Offsets reluctance to sell by acknowledging the sentimental value and suggesting options.

• Stresses benefits of selling property in terms of the primary appeal.

• Connects the specific request for action with the reward for saying "Yes."

Format Pointers
Illustrates modified block format—the date and closing lines (complimentary close and signature block) begin at the horizontal center.

Uses mixed punctuation—a colon follows the salutation, and a comma follows the complimentary close.

Uses an enclosure notation to alert the reader that something is included.

Example of an Effective Questionnaire

- *Uses variety of items to elicit different types of responses.*
- *Uses clear, concise language to minimize confusion.*
- *Provides clear instructions for answering each item.*
- *Provides additional lines to allow for individual opinions.*
- *Provides even number of rating choices to eliminate "fence" responses.*
- *Asks for easily recalled information.*
- *Provides non-overlapping categories of response and open-ended final category.*

Format Pointers
Provides adequate space for answering open-ended item.

Keeps length as short as possible while meeting survey objectives.

Includes instructions for submitting completed questionnaire.

1. Rank the following new vehicle purchase factors in order of their importance to you.

		1	2	3	4	5	6
a.	Price	○	○	○	○	○	○
b.	Overall performance	○	○	○	○	○	○
c.	Reliability	○	○	○	○	○	○
d.	Comfort	○	○	○	○	○	○
e.	Driving enjoyment	○	○	○	○	○	○
f.	Safety record	○	○	○	○	○	○
g.	Fuel economy	○	○	○	○	○	○
h.	Other (specify) ▼	○	○	○	○	○	○

2. Which of the following is the single most important purchase factor that you feel needs more attention by today's car makers? (Please select only one.)

- ○ Price
- ○ Overall performance
- ○ Reliability
- ○ Comfort
- ○ Safety record
- ○ Fuel economy
- ○ Other (specify) ▼

3. Would you purchase this vehicle again?

Definitely not	Probably not	I'm not sure	Only if improved	Probably would	Definitely yes
1	2	3	4	5	6
○	○	○	○	○	○

4. How would you rate your overall purchase satisfaction?

Very unsatisfied	Somewhat dissatisfied	Neutral	Somewhat satisfied	Satisfied	Very satisfied
1	2	3	4	5	6
○	○	○	○	○	○

5. Indicate your age group:

- ○ 20–29
- ○ 30–39
- ○ 40–49
- ○ 50–59
- ○ 60–69
- ○ 70 years and over

6. Indicate how many vehicles you have previously purchased.

- ○ None
- ○ 1–3
- ○ 4–6
- ○ 7–10
- ○ More than 10

7. What could the car maker do to enhance your satisfaction with your new car purchase?

Thanks for your participation. Click to submit your questionnaire.

[Submit]

© Cengage Learning 2011

Sample Report and References Pages in APA
(6th Edition) Style

Culturally diverse virtual teams do have a greater potential for conflict than do teams that are homogeneous and are able to meet face to face ("Collaborative Teams," 2008). While variations in beliefs, behaviors, and expectations occur within all cultural groups, certain generalities about one based on his or her cultural group can be useful for others seeking better understanding. "Given little or no other information about an individual's values and behaviours, culture provides a good first impression of that person" (Maznevski & Peterson, 1997, p. 37).

Neyer and Harzing (2008) found that experiences in cross-cultural interactions do serve to improve one's abilities to adapt in such situations. One advantage gained through experience is the overcoming of cultural stereotypes which often stand in the way of effective communication (Williams & O'Reilly, 1998). Cross-cultural experience also leads to the establishment of norms that support interaction among individuals and to the development of mutual consideration for others (Neyer & Harzing, 2008). Studies have established that individuals who learn a foreign language also gain appropriate culturally determined behavior and are thus better able to adapt to specific characteristics of the other culture (Harzing & Feely, 2008).

In addition to possessing strong technical skills, qualities that are important to successful membership on cross-cultural virtual teams include the following (Adler, 1991; Hurn & Jenkins, 2000):

▶ Flexibility and adaptability
▶ Strong interpersonal skills
▶ Ability to think both globally and locally
▶ Linguistic skills

References

Adler, N. J. (1991). *International dimensions of organizational behavior.* Boston: PWS Kent.

Collaborative teams. (2008, June). *Bulletpoint*, 152, 3–5.

Hurn, B. F., & Jenkins, M. (2000). International peer group development. *Industrial and Commercial Training*, 32(4), 128–131. doi: 10.1108/00197850010372205

Maznevski, M. L. & Peterson, M. F. (1997). Societal values, social interpretation, and multinational teams. In C. Granrose (Ed.), *Cross-cultural workgroups* (pp. 27–29). Thousand Oaks, CA: Sage.

Neyer, A., & Harzine, A. (2008). The impact of culture on interactions: Five lessons learned from the European Commission. *European Management Journal*, 26(5), 325–334. doi: 10.1016/j.emj .2008.05.005

Williams, K. Y., & O'Reilly, C. A. (1998). Demography and diversity in organizations. In B. M. Staw & R. M. Sutton (Eds.), *Research in organizational behavior* (pp. 77–140). Stamford, CT: JAI.

Choosing the Appropriate Graphic to Fit Your Objective

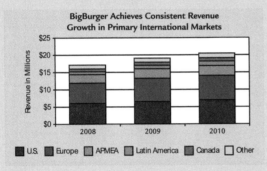

KoffeeKup Corporation
Market Price of Common Stock

	October 2, 2009		October 2, 2010	
Quarter	High	Low	High	Low
Fourth	$23.94	$21.29	$26.35	$23.08
Third	22.09	18.62	28.13	22.78
Second	19.48	16.15	30.80	24.79
First	16.50	14.40	31.94	23.53

Source: KoffeeKup Corporation, Annual Report, 2010

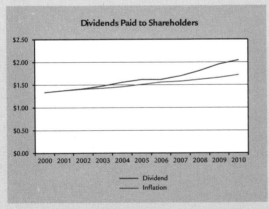

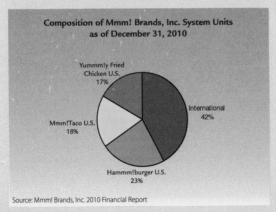

Source: Mmm! Brands, Inc. 2010 Financial Report

Graphic Type and Objective

Table—To show exact figures

Bar chart—To compare one quantity with another

Line Chart—To illustrate changes in quantities over time

Pie Chart—To show how the parts of a whole are distributed

Graphic Type and Objective

Gantt chart—To track progress toward completeing a project

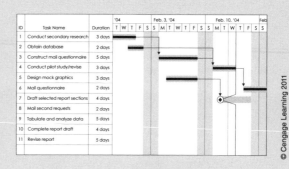

Map—To show geographic relationships

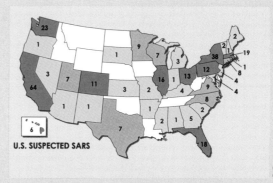

Flowchart—To illustrate a process or procedure

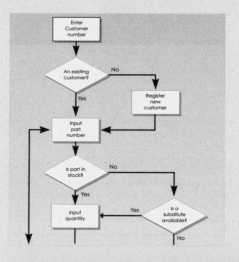

Photograph—To provide a realistic view of a specific item or place

Short, Periodic Report in Memorandum Format

ETO Industries

233 State Boulvard
Kansas City, MO 64123-7600

TO: Candice Russell, Director, Human Resources
FROM: Tim Johnson, Manager, In-House Exercise Program
DATE: January 1, 2010
SUBJECT: Annual Report on In-House Exercise Program, 2009

The in-house exercise center has made significant gains in the past year. Data related to participation in our programs and current staffing follow:

    Enrollment: 506 employees, up from 384 at end of 2008
    Staff: One full-time trainer/manager and two part-time trainers

Our goal for the coming year is to increase our enrollment in the in-house exercise programs another 10 percent. We also have plans to create a nutrition program that will be rolled out next month. If that program is successful initially, we may need to hire a certified nutritionist. This person might also be used part-time in the company cafeteria to improve the nutritional value of the lunches and snacks provided there.

Employees report overall satisfaction with the quality of the current program. At the end of 2009, we asked program participants to complete a questionnaire. Eighty-eight percent indicated that they were very satisfied or extremely satisfied with our program. The most frequently mentioned suggestion for improvement was the extension of hours until 7 p.m. This change would allow employees to work late and still take advantage of the exercise facility. A copy of the questionnaire is provided for your review.

Call me should you wish to discuss the nutritional program, extended service hours, or any other aspects of this report.

Attachment

- *Includes header to serve formal report functions of transmittal and title page.*

- *Includes horizontal line to add interest and separate transmittal from body of memo.*

- *Uses deductive approach to present this periodic report requested by management on an annual basis.*

- *Uses headings to highlight standard information; allows for easy update when preparing subsequent report.*

- *Includes primary data from survey completed by program participants.*

- *Attaches material to memorandum, which would be an appendix item in formal report.*

Format Pointer
Uses memorandum format for brief periodic report prepared for personnel within company.

Audit Report in Letter Format

- *Letterhead and letter address function as title page and transmittal.*

- *Introduces overall topic and leads into procedures and findings.*

- *Uses side heading to denote beginning of body.*

- *Closes with appreciation for business and offer to answer questions.*

Format Pointers
Uses letter format for short report prepared by outside consultant.

Includes reference initials of typist, who did not write message.

 Paragon Accounting Group

767 RIVER ROAD, SUITE 216
BOSTON, MA 10812-0767
800-555-3000

January 30, 2011

Melinda Forrester, CEO
Randall and Associates
366 State Street
Boston, MA 10810-1796

Dear Ms. Forrester:

We have audited the accompanying balance sheet of Randall and Associates as of December 31, 2010, and the related statement of income, retained earnings, and cash flow for the year ended on that date. These financial statements are the responsibility of the company. Our responsibility is to express an opinion about these statements based on our audit.

PROCEDURES

We conducted our audit using generally accepted auditing standards. Those standards require that we plan and perform the audit to obtain reasonable assurance that the financial statements are free of material mistakes. An audit includes assessing whether generally accepted accounting principles are used and whether the significant estimates made by management and overall financial statement presentation are accurate. We believe that our audit provides a reasonable basis for our opinion on these matters.

FINDINGS

In our opinion, the financial statements referred to above present fairly, in all material aspects, the financial position of Randall and Associates as of December 31, 2010. The results of its operations and its cash flows for the year ended December 31, 2010, are in conformity with generally accepted accounting principles.

Thank you for the opportunity to serve your organization in this manner. Should you wish to discuss any aspects of this report, please call me.

Sincerely,

Karla Schmidt

Karla Schmidt
Senior Auditor

tsr

Selecting an Appropriate Presentation Visual

VISUAL	ADVANTAGES	LIMITATIONS
HANDOUTS 	• Provide detailed information that audience can examine closely • Extend a presentation by providing resources for later use • Reduce the need for note taking and aid in audience retention	• Can divert audience's attention from the speaker • Can be expensive
BOARDS AND FLIPCHARTS	• Facilitate interaction • Are easy to use • Are inexpensive if traditional units are used	• Require turning speaker's back to audience • Are cumbersome to transport, can be messy and not professional looking • Provide no hard copy and must be developed on-site if traditional units are used
OVERHEAD TRANSPARENCIES	• Are simple to prepare and use • Allow versatile use; prepare beforehand or while speaking • Are inexpensive and readily available	• Are not easily updated and are awkward to use • Must have special acetate sheets and markers unless using a document camera • Pose potential for equipment failure
ELECTRONIC PRESENTATIONS 	• Meet audience expectations of visual standards • Enhance professionalism and credibility of the speaker • Provide special effects to enhance retention, appeal, flexibility, and reuse	• Can lead to poor delivery if misused • Can be expensive, require highly developed skills, and are time-consuming • Pose technology failure and transportability challenges
35MM SLIDES 	• Are highly professional • Depict real people and places	• Require a darkened room • Creates a formal environment not conducive to group interaction • Lacks flexibility in presentation sequence
MODELS OR PHYSICAL OBJECTS 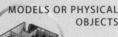	• Are useful to demonstrate an idea	• Can compete with the speaker for attention

Writing Effective Slide Content: Poor (left) and Good (right) Examples

Humor

- Important element in any presentation
- Easy connection with the audience
- Gets attention
- Alleviates boredom
- Reduction of mental tension
- Discourages conflict
- Enhances comprehension
- Shouldn't embarrass people
  - Ethnic jokes are inappropriate
  - Profane language is definitely not recommended

Value of Humor in a Presentation

- Establishes a connection with the audience
- Increases audience's willingness to listen
- Makes message more understandable and memorable
- Alleviates negativity associated with sensitive subjects

© Cengage Learning 2011

The revised slide

- Includes a descriptive title that captures major idea of slide, in this case, the value of humor.
- Omits items unrelated to value of humor. Specifically, "important element in any presentation" is a verbal transition, not needed on slide; "shouldn't embarrass people" and related subpoints will appear on a separate slide focusing on tips for using humor.
- Collapses remaining content into a few memorable points that use parallel structure for clarity and grammatical accuracy (singular action verbs).
- Proofreads carefully to avoid misspellings that damage credibility, such as "conflect" in original slide.

Engaging Conceptual Slide Design: Poor (left) and Good (right) Examples

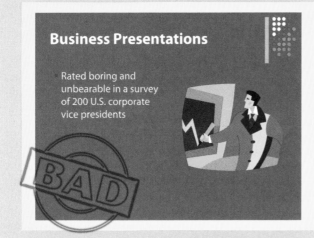

Business Presentations

- Rated boring and unbearable in a survey of 200 U.S. corporate vice presidents

How Well Do Business Presentations Measure Up?

Boring. Unbearable.

© Justin Horrocks/iStockphoto.com

Survey of 200 corporate vice presidents, 2005

© Cengage Learning 2011

The revised slide

- Uses descriptive title that captures central idea of dissatisfaction with typical business presentation.
- Selects images that imply intended message—ineffectiveness of business presenters; enlarges images for slide appeal and balance.
- Trims text to emphasize central idea and eliminates bullet, as bulleted list should have at least two items.
- Moves source to less prominent slide position to add credibility to research data while keeping focus on central idea.

GOOD Chronological Résumé

Cassandra Jensen
783 Ash Street
Palmdale, CA 83307
(204) 555-6789
cjensen@hotmail.com

- *Includes email address that reflects professional image.*

- *Reveals type of work sought.*

- *Positions education as top qualification for recent graduate. Includes high GPA (B or better).*

- *Edges out competition reflecting related experience and work achievements.*

- *Uses separate section to emphasize language proficiencies listed in job requirements.*

- *Emphasizes activities that reflect service attitude, high level of responsibility, and people-oriented experiences.*

CAREER OBJECTIVE
Challenging position in finance or investment banking with international promotion opportunities.

EDUCATION
California State University *August 2006–May 2010*
Bachelor of Science in Business Administration
Corporate Finance and International Business
GPA 3.6 on a 4.0 scale

RELATED EXPERIENCE
Intern, **Citicorp,** Los Angeles, CA *June 2009–Present*
- Assisted in the management of guided portfolio management accounts for high net-worth clients
- Interpreted statements and conducted money wire transfers
- Developed an understanding of secured financial transactions

Intern, **Financial Solutions**, *May 2008–October 2008*
Century City, CA
- Conducted research to create stock portfolios, including an organic food portfolio that grew 10% in 8 months.
- Assisted in the management of accounts for high net-worth clients

LANGUAGES
- English: Native fluency
- Spanish: Fluent (speaking, reading, writing, comprehension)

LEADERSHIP & HONORS
Order of Omega Honor Society, *August 2009–Present*
Co-Vice President of Conference
Organized a leadership conference for members of the CSU Greek System

CSU Panhellenic Council, *January 2008–December 2008*
Vice President of Communications
- Developed and produced content for a new Panhellenic website
- Representative at the Western Regional Greek Leadership Conference

Kappa Kappa Gamma, Sorority *August 2006–Present*
Representative at Kappa Kappa Gamma
Province Leadership Convention

Matthew and Teresa S. Arnold *2008/2009 and 2009/2010*
Endowed Scholarship Recipient

Format Pointers
Places name at top center, where it can be easily seen when employers place it in file drawer (top right is also acceptable).

Uses bold sans serif font to distinguish identification section and headings from remaining text in serif font.

Creates visual appeal through custom format rather than commonly used template, short readable sections focusing on targeted qualifications, and streamlined bulleted lists.

GOOD

Functional Résumé

- *Includes clear objective statement to grab attention and invite close reading.*

- *Uses headings that show applicant knows what skills are needed to succeed in sales.*

- *Arranges qualifications into sections that emphasize applicant's relevant skills and accomplishments.*

- *Uses employers' names and dates to match skills with work history.*

- *Lists references for employer convenience and to strengthen résumé.*

Format Pointers
Creates visual appeal with easy-to-read columnar format and balanced page arrangement.

Places name at top center, where it can be easily seen.

Uses bold font to distinguish identification section and headings from remaining text.

Lists education and work history as quick overview of basic qualifications and to accommodate employers' preference for chronological format.

Clarence Foster
715 Armadillo Circle
San Antonio, TX 78710-0715
(512) 555-1396
cfoster@hotmail.com

OBJECTIVE   Position in retail clothing sales with advancement to sales management.

CUSTOMER SERVICE
- Processed customer financial transactions within assigned limits and established guidelines.
- Provided excellent customer service in completing transactions efficiently and in a friendly, professional manner.
- Met sales and referral goals by identifying and selling financial products and services beneficial to the customer needs.
- Identified fraudulent activity to prevent potential losses to the bank.

SALES
- Provided quality customer service to store patrons.
- Handled cash transactions and daily receipt balances.
- Usually surpassed weekly goal of opening new credit accounts.
- Employee of the month.

COMMUNICATION SKILLS AND WORK ETHIC
- Ability to communicate effectively over the phone and in person.
- Ability to work well unsupervised.
- Experience working on team projects both at work and in courses.
- Report consistently and promptly when scheduled for work.

COMPUTER SKILLS
Proficient in spreadsheet and word processing software.

EMPLOYMENT HISTORY   Sales Associate, Claremont Department Store, 2006–Present

Customer Service Associate, Union Bank, 2005–2006

EDUCATION   B.S., Marketing, Claremont State College, Expected graduation, May 2010

REFERENCES   Clare Randall, Sales Manager, Claremont Department Store, 435 Main Street, Claremont, TX 78009, (818) 555-2345

Daniel Shore, Professor, Marketing Department, Claremont State College, 890 Alamo Street, San Antonio, TX 87003, (803) 555-8907

Lisa Cox, Senior Teller, Union Bank, 900 Main Street, Claremont, TX 87303, (818) 555-1234

 *Example of a Follow-Up Letter*

Dear Mr. Nguyen:

Recently, I applied for an information specialist position at TechPro and now have additional qualifications to report.

The enclosed, updated résumé shows that I have successfully passed the certification exam for Linux operating systems. In addition, I have learned a great deal about troubleshooting corporate computer systems in my recently completed internship with Crandon & Crandon Technology Systems, which I can immediately apply in a position with TechPro.

Mr. Nguyen, I would welcome the opportunity to visit your office and talk more about the contributions I could make as an information specialist at your firm. Please write or call me at (303) 555-8237.

© Cengage Learning 2011

- States main idea and clearly identifies position being sought.

- Refers to enclosed résumé; summarizes additional qualifications.

- Assures employer that applicant is still interested in job.

Format Pointers

Formats as formal business letter but could have sent message electronically if previous communication with employer had been by email.

Prints letter and envelope with laser printer on paper that matches résumé and application letter.

 *Example of a Thank-You Message to a Reference*

Thank you so much for the letter of recommendation you prepared for my application to law school. I learned today that I have been accepted by Cleveland University for the fall semester.

Because of the rigor of that law program, I believe your comments about my work ethic, dedication to high-quality work, and willingness to seek out feedback for improvement carried a great deal of weight. The dean commented that she was impressed with the detailed evidence and examples you provided to support your statements, unlike the general recommendations she often receives.

Dr. Kenney, I appreciate your helping me secure a seat in a highly competitive academic discipline with such a well-regarded law program. Thanks for the recommendation and your outstanding instruction. I will keep you informed about my law school experience and hope to stop by your office next time I am in town to catch up.

- States main idea of appreciation for recommendation. Informs reference of success in acceptance to academic program.

- Communicates sincere appreciation for assistance; uses specific examples and avoids exaggeration.

- Restates main idea and anticipates continued relationship; is original and sincere.

© Cengage Learning 2011

Example of a Thank-You Message

New Message

To:	wrfann@viking.com
From:	mperkins@hotmail.com
Subject:	Appreciation for Plant Interview

Dear Mr. Fann:

Thank you for the opportunity to visit Viking Range for a plant interview yesterday. I enjoyed meeting you and appreciated the complete tour of the operation and the opportunity to learn about the exciting research efforts underway at Viking.

Viking's success in developing higher quality products than its competitors after such a short time in the refrigeration market is impressive. Additionally, I was impressed with the many friendly, enthusiastic employees who were willing to share with me their knowledge and commitment to Viking.

After visiting your plant on Thursday, I am confident that my interest and previous experience in research and development at the DIAL labs in Starkville would allow me to contribute to Viking's important research efforts in the refrigeration area. I would also gain valuable real-world experience needed to enhance the mechanical engineering degree I'm pursuing at Mississippi State.

Mr. Fann, I am eager to receive an offer from Viking for the co-op position. If you need additional information in the meantime, please contact me.

Thanks,

Matt Perkins

- *States main idea of appreciation for interview and information gained.*

- *Includes specific points discussed during interview, increasing sincerity and recall of applicant.*

- *Assures employer of continued interest in position.*

- *Politely reminds employer that applicant is awaiting reply.*

Format Pointer
Prepared as email message because previous communication with the company has been by email.

© Cengage Learning 2011

Example of a Job-Refusal Message

I appreciate your spending time with me discussing the sales associate position.

Your feedback regarding my fit for your organization and the opportunities available to me were particularly valuable. Having received offers in both sales and marketing, I feel that a career in the latter field better suits my personality and long-term career goals. Today, I am accepting an entry-level marketing position with Fashion Trends, Inc.

Thank you for your confidence demonstrated by the job offer. When I hear about Marasol's continued success, I will think of the dedicated people who work for the company.

- *Begins with neutral but related idea to buffer bad news.*

- *Presents reasons diplomatically that lead to refusal.*

- *Ends message on positive note that anticipates future association with company.*

© Cengage Learning 2011